Law and Development

The International Library of Essays in Law and Legal Theory
Series Editor: Tom D. Campbell

Schools

Natural Law, Vols I & II *John Finnis*
Justice *Thomas Morawetz*
Law and Economics, Vols I & II *Jules Coleman and Jeffrey Lange*
Critical Legal Studies *James Boyle*
Marxian Legal Theory *Csaba Varga*
Legal Reasoning, Vols I & II *Aulis Aarnio and Neil MacCormick*
Legal Positivism *Mario Jori*
American Legal Theory *Robert Summers*
Law and Language *Fred Schauer*
Sociological Theories of Law *Kahei Rokumoto*
Rights *Carlos Nino*
Law and Psychology *Martin Levine*
Feminist Legal Theory *Frances Olsen*
Law and Society *Werner Krawietz*

Areas

Criminal Law *Thomas Morawetz*
Tort Law *Ernest Weinrib*
Contract Law, Vols I & II *Larry Alexander*
Anti-Discrimination Law *Christopher McCrudden*
Consumer Law *Iain Ramsay*
International Law *Martti Koskenniemi*
Property Law, Vols I & II *Elizabeth Mensch and Alan Freeman*
Constitutional Law *Mark Tushnet*
Procedure *Denis Galligan*
Evidence and Proof *William Twining and Alex Stein*
Administrative Law *Denis Galligan*
Child Law *Harry Krause*
Family Law, Vols I & II *Harry Krause*
Welfare Law *Peter Robson*
Medicine and the Law *Bernard Dickens*
Commercial Law *Ross Cranston*
Communications Law *David Goldberg*
Environmental Law *Michael Blumm*
Conflict of Laws *Richard Fentiman*
Law and Religion *Wojciech Sadurski*
Human Rights Law *Philip Alston*
European Community Law, Vols I & II *Francis Snyder*

Legal Cultures

Comparative Legal Cultures *Csaba Varga*
Law and Anthropology *Peter Sack*
Hindu Law and Legal Theory *Ved Nanda*
Islamic Law and Legal Theory *Ian Edge*
Chinese Law and Legal Theory *Michael Palmer*
Socialist Law and Legal Theory *W. Butler*
Japanese Law and Legal Theory *Koichiro Fujikura*
Law and Development *Anthony Carty*
Jewish Law and Legal Theory *Martin Golding*
Legal Education *Martin Levine*

Future Volumes

Labour Law, Common Law and Legal Theory, Civil Law and Legal Theory, African Law and Legal Theory, Legal Ethics and Cumulative index.

Law and Development

Edited by

Anthony Carty

Senior Lecturer in International Law
University of Glasgow

NEW YORK UNIVERSITY PRESS
REFERENCE COLLECTION

Manufactured in Great Britain

First published in the U.S.A. in 1992 by
NEW YORK UNIVERSITY PRESS
Washington Square
New York NY 10003

Library of Congress Cataloging-in-Publication Data
Law and development / edited [by] Anthony Carty.
p. cm. – (The International library of essays in law and legal theory. Legal cultures)
Includes bibliographical references and index.
ISBN 0-8147-1473-0
1. Law and economic development. 2. International law.
I. Carty, Anthony. II. Series.
K3820.L37 1992
341.7'59–dc20 92-1173
CIP

Contents

PART III INTERNATIONAL LAW AND DEVELOPMENT

Acknowledgements

The editor and publishers wish to thank the following for permission to use copyright material.

The American Journal of International Law for essay: Philip Alston (1984), 'Conjuring Up New Human Rights: A Proposal for Quality Control', *The American Journal of International Law*, **78**, pp. 607–21.

California Western International Law Journal for essays: Jack Donnelly (1985), 'In Search of the Unicorn: The Jurisprudence and Politics of the Right to Development', *California Western International Law Journal*, **15**, pp. 473–509, and Ndiva Kofele–Kale (1988), 'The Principle of Preferential Treatment in the Law of GATT: Toward Achieving the Objective of an Equitable World Trading System', *California Western International Law Journal*, **18**, pp. 291–333. Copyright © California Western International Law Journal.

The Georgia Journal for essay: Edward Kwakwa (1987), 'Emerging International Development Law and Traditional International Law – Congruence or Cleavage?', *Georgia Journal of International and Comparative Law*, **17**, pp. 431–55. Copyright © The Georgia Journal.

Hamburger Gesellschaft für Völkerrecht und Auswärtige Politik for essay: Anthony Carty (1986), 'The Third World Debt Crisis: Towards New International Standards for Contraction of Public Debt', *Verfassung Und Recht in Übersee* (Law and Politics in Africa, Asia and Latin America), **19**, pp. 401–19.

Harvard Law School for essay: Daniel K. Tarullo (1985), 'Logic, Myth and the International Economic Order', *Harvard International Law Journal*, **26**, pp. 533–52. Permission granted by Harvard International Law Journal. Copyright © 1985 by the President and Fellows of Harvard College.

JAI Press Inc for essay: David F. Greenberg (1980), 'Law and Development in Light of Dependency Theory', *Research in Law and Sociology*, **3**, pp. 129–59. Copyright © JAI Press, Inc.

Journal of World Trade for essay: Phedon Nicolaides (1987), 'How Fair is Fair Trade?', *Journal of World Trade Law*, pp. 147–62. Copyright © Journal of World Trade Law.

Temple University for essays: Anthony Carty (1984), 'From the Right to Economic Self-determination to the Right to Development: A Crisis in Legal Theory', *Third World Legal Studies*, pp. 73–86, and James C.N. Paul and Clarence J. Dias (1982), 'State–Managed Development: A Legal Critique, *and* Alternative Development: A Legal Prospectus', *Third World Legal Studies*, pp. 35–58 and 284–311.

The University of Chicago Press for essay: Anthony Carty (1988), 'Liberal Economic Rhetoric as an Obstacle to the Democratization of the World Economy', *Ethics*, pp. 742–56. Copyright © The University of Chicago Press.

The University of Texas at Austin for essay: Joseph J. Jova, Clint E. Smith and T. Frank Crigler (1984), 'Private Investment in Latin America: Renegotiating the Bargain', *Texas International Law Journal*, **19**, pp. 3–32.

University of Miami Inter-American Law Review for essay: Bruce Zagaris (1988), 'Law and Development or Comparative Law and Social Change – The Application of Old Concepts in the Commonwealth Caribbean', *University of Miami Inter–American Law Review*, **19**, pp. 549–93. Copyright © University of Miami Inter–American Law Review.

The Wisconsin Law Review for essay: Thomas M. Franck (1972), 'The New Development: Can American Law and Legal Institutions help Developing Countries?', *Wisconsin Law Review*, pp. 767–801. Copyright © The Wisconsin Law Review.

The Yale Law Journal Company and Fred B. Rothman & Co. for essay: David M. Trubek (1972), 'Toward a Social Theory of Law: An Essay on the Study of Law and Development', *The Yale Law Journal*, **82**, No. 1, pp. 1–50. Reprinted by permission of The Yale Law Journal Company and Fred B. Rothman & Co. from *The Yale Law Journal*, Vol. **82**, pp. 1–50.

Every effort has been made to trace all the copyright holders, but if any have been inadvertently overlooked the publishers will be pleased to make the necessary arrangement at the first opportunity.

Series Preface

The International Library of Law and Legal Theory is designed to provide important research materials in an accessible form. Each volume contains essays of central theoretical importance in its subject area. The series as a whole makes available an extensive range of valuable material which will be of considerable interest to those involved in the research, teaching and study of law.

The series has been divided into three sections. The Schools section is intended to represent the main distinctive approaches and topics of special concern to groups of scholars. The Areas section takes in the main branches of law with an emphasis on essays which present analytical and theoretical insights of broad application. The section on Legal Cultures makes available the distinctive legal theories of different legal traditions and takes up topics of general comparative and developmental concern.

I have been delighted and impressed by the way in which the editors of the individual volumes have set about the difficult task of selecting, ordering and presenting essays from the immense quantity of academic legal writing published in journals throughout the world. Editors were asked to pick out those essays from law, philosophy and social science journals which they consider to be fundamental for the understanding of law, as seen from the perspective of a particular approach or sphere of legal interest. This is not an easy task and many difficult decisions have had to be made in order to ensure that a representative sample of the best journal essays available takes account of the scope of each topic or school.

I should like to express my thanks to all the volume editors for their willing participation and scholarly judgement. The interest and enthusiasm which the project has generated is well illustrated by the fact that an original projection of 12 volumes drawn up in 1989 has now become a list of some 60 volumes. I must also acknowledge the vision, persistence and constant cheerfulness of John Irwin and the marvellous work done by Mrs Margaret O'Reilly and Mrs Sonia Bridgman.

TOM D. CAMPBELL
Series Editor
The Faculty of Law
The Australian National University

Introduction

This introduction is intended to orientate the reader to the selection of essays which follows. It is above all an attempt at a *tour d'horizon* of the literature, much of which has appeared in books rather than in journals, and much of which is in French. It accepts that ideological, and not simply jurisprudential, controversy surrounds the field. However, it assumes that the problem of radical economic inequality between Western and Third World countries remains, that the economic affairs of the latter, whether domestic or international, are enmeshed in law, and that law will continue to play a role in the drama of these economic relations.

Part I Law and Modernization: The Legal Imperialism Debate

The theory of law and development has been so marked by controversy in the United States that it can be said to be almost stillborn, at least as a credible field of academic interest (that is, which can gain funding and support careers in American law schools). However, the controversy concerning the American 'liberal endeavour' to transport American values through American law to so-called Third World countries, debated in Trubek and Galanter's 'Scholars in Self-Estrangement',[1] can be regarded as an internal American disagreement which should not be allowed to dominate the problematic of law and development as such. The controversy in this form is not confined to the United States. It has also marked the French university discipline *le droit du développement* which grew quite openly out of colonial law and the law of cooperation in the period preceding the independence of the French colonies. The most extensive statement of similar French criticism not merely of the liberal but also of the social democratic theory of development is M. Benchikh's *Droit international du sous-développement*, extended further to include the whole attempt to elaborate rules of international law suitable for development.[2]

The roots of this juridical or even jurisprudential controversy are ideological. They are to be seen as an aspect of Marxist dependency theory critique of the liberal model of capitalist development. As such they have been overtaken by the post-ideological (in my view post-modernist) critique of dependency theory itself. At the level of methodology it might be said that the intellectual background for present development studies is both radically pluralist and thus democratic, and yet so sceptical of Western liberal values as to be receptive to non-Western values, even if they appear pre-modern. The work of David Apter on post-modern theory and development is helpful in this regard.[3]

The language of post-modernity and post-structuralism is intended to convey the conviction or, more exactly, the consciousness that the problems of underdevelopment are interwoven with the West and are not be solved except through a global inter-cultural mixing. Such theories as structural dependency suppose that the process of influence and dominance is exclusively north-south and never south-north. The aim of the essays selected here is to show that the movement towards development in the south has affected the whole global process. The one world which is emerging is not catastrophic in the sense that it appears to dissipate Western values, although several contributions do suggest that. Indeed, it is equally the case that the study of law and development only appears, in some quarters, to be fading out, precisely because it has decisively penetrated legal studies at a global level and has not left Western liberal legal values their cherished autonomy. I would argue that the movement which is sweeping the world at the moment – a radical wave of democracy – is a triumph of ideals of development over hierarchical freedoms.

This problematic leads the present editor to a deliberately eclectic approach to the selection of materials. A lawyer engaged in development issues in a post-modern environment is not committed to Trubek and Galanter's charge that he thinks himself to have 'an explicit body of knowledge that could chart the relationship between legal systems and social, political and economic change in the Third World'.[4] Indeed underlying this critique of the role of law in development there may well be an ethnocentric impatience. Instead of social and political pluralism, Trubek and Galanter find that 'in much of the Third World the grip of tribe, clan and local community is far stronger than that of the nation-state'.[5] What is needed is a more nuanced and less engaged picture.

T.M. Franck's essay examines the extent to which American law and legal institutions have helped developing countries. He outlines the scope of 'New Development', keeping in mind the limitations of American-style representative political institutions and the combative style of American confrontational politics.[6] Hierarchical structures of development, however representative, should in his view give way to horizontal ones which recognize the importance of 'a functional process of structural dialogue between the people'.[7] Franck stresses the role of the lawyer as a social negotiator, as one adept at promoting reciprocity – 'the fundamental facilitator of social behaviour', the assumption being that such lawyers will be drawn from that part of American society (Franck is writing in the early 1970s) which is sympathetic to the social dimensions of development.[8]

Apart from this, the essay affords a nuanced understanding of the quite different roles assigned to lawyers in American and various Third World societies. While sensitive to the criticisms of 'interference' by American lawyers in development, the author is nonetheless firmly committed to modernization in the development process, defined as a search for unity, industrialization and social welfare. The essay is in fact a defence of the framework for democratic development outlined in US Congressional Foreign Assistance legislation in 1966. It is firmly within the framework of social engineering, albeit so widely conceived as to be compatible with the philosophy of People's law versus State law, which is one subject of the second selection of readings.

The essay by Trubek has been chosen as a lucid critical exposition of the liberal, democratic 'law and development' school, particularly as exemplified in the US. It is less concerned to engage in polemics with individual American scholars, but rather sets out in full what a *modernizing* theory of law would require, in terms of the social theory of modernity through rationalization as expounded by Max Weber. Trubek argues for the limited success that can be expected from the introduction of Western legal institutions and practices in ensuring a democratic industrialization of developing countries. He stresses that Weber's argument is not that modern law produces economic development, but merely that it helps to structure the free market system. Even more importantly, modern law does not promote political development, but merely supports centralized bureaucratic states, depending for their legitimacy on a belief that their decisions are rational.[9]

These arguments set the scene for a case study of the functioning of a regulatory system of law in an authoritarian political system such as Brazil. Trubek undertakes a case study of the 'law' relating to capital markets, demonstrating that it is superfluous in a system which functions not on the basis of a pluralistic free market governed by an autonomous legal order protecting private rights, but on the basis of an authoritarian political order more concerned with direct administrative control over economic activity. This activity centres on a very few powerful groups which are actively supported by the government and on whose success the government depends.[10]

This case study highlights the actual function of law in developing countries: it is public and administrative. Trubek has outlined the framework within which developing countries usually engage in such activities as control of foreign investment and trade (see Part III). This perception of the function of law is quite different from that held in the US, *except within the context of a siege or war economy*. However, in the view of the elites in developing countries during the 1970s and 1980s, law in this sense had a modernizing function. This has nevertheless come to be questioned both by the liberal, pluralist ideologues who inhabit the higher echelons of the international economic and development agencies (see Part III), and by the proponents of People's law against State law (see Part II). For different reasons, each of these would prefer decentralized, horizontal legal structures, of which more later.

Greenberg's essay is intended to deepen the perspective on law by introducing an historical perspective on colonialism. While he refers to recent analyses of the modern world system, through Wallerstein, his work is easily read as a study of the completely instrumental employment of law as one of the tools of conquest and plunder, upon which England and France in particular built their industrial revolutions.[11] Greenberg's work is closely integrated with the first two essays: he objects to each. Franck may well claim that developing countries' governing elites have proved receptive to the idea of transplanting American legal ideals, of wide participation in public affairs and the promotion of social welfare. Yet this can hardly be taken as a serious representation of the human rights condition in most such countries.[12] Trubek and Gallanter are correct in identifying a growing self-questioning of American lawyers who realize that Third World realities are incompatible with their programme for development. However, as I have already remarked, their analysis of these 'realities' extends no further than generalities about 'haves' and 'have-nots'.[13]

If one is even to begin to understand the enormity of the task of development, one must unreservedly accept the extent to which the West, in particular England and France,[14] have torn apart the political and economic structures of Third World societies and *used their legal systems* to do so. In other words, not only has law not had an automatically positive function in ensuring political and economic development, it has also had an ambiguous and even negative significance as the instrument used to subject these countries to exploitative trading relations, to land seizures, to discriminatory and even enslaving personal laws and to concepts of public order and administration which were intended to be incapacitating.[15] Greenberg gives a very pertinent warning that the colonial era is not necessarily over. Those he calls legal 'diffusionists' – Trubek's legal modernists – are, knowingly or unknowingly, the same legal 'merchants' who pursued profit for trading companies from the 17th century onwards.[16] This argument is much more forceful than those of Trubek and Gallanter because the latter could, and probably do, encourage their colleagues to withdraw from matters which are somehow not their concern because 'beyond their understanding'. This leaves the field wide open for their co-nationals in state agencies, multinational corporations and international economic institutions, controlled by Western state interests through the system of weighted voting (see Part III), to continue to insist upon a type of legal regulation of north-south relations reminiscent of colonial experience. For instance, to require open-door conditions for Western investment and trade (as the IMF and the World Bank usually do) as a prerequisite for giving financial support is very similar to the forceful opening up of China, Japan and Ottoman Turkey in the 19th century (see Part III).

It was felt appropriate to conclude this section with a paper which reports upon a 'law and development' project with which I was involved – the Caribbean Justice Improvement Project. Zagaris' essay, published as late as 1988, rehearses, albeit quite summarily, all the usual objections to the idea of law and development.[17] He gives a very lucid definition of the field: a desire to share legal modernity and technical skills with developing countries, stressing action rather than an interest in theory. Zagaris states,[18] the Project assumed that the law attorney is a social engineer and that law can lead to social change.

From the University of Glasgow, I undertook full academic charge of a course on teaching young private and public sector lawyers the rudiments of negotiating international contracts.[19] From Zagaris' point of view, the biggest potential deficit of the Project was that its funds and its approval were derived from a foreign policy goal emphasizing US national security.[20] The merit of his paper is that it sets out in detail what precisely was involved in the Project as a whole, a level of detail that inevitably has a rather pedestrian quality. The aspect of the Project in which I was engaged was funded by the EEC (my own expenses) and the US AID, (those of the participants). The course material was based primarily on accessible standard-form contract clauses in areas of activity such as mining, technology transfer, hotel management, loans from public development agencies and private banks. Course preparation included consultation with the Government law offices of the Commonwealth Caribbean, but did not include model contracts from the area which I felt would have been a prerequisite for a fully effective course. Participation in the course was virtually ensured through identification with the Law Faculty of the University of the West Indies.

The judgement of the participants was that such a course was informative. However, the level of competence of the English–speaking Caribbean lawyers, whether public or private, was already very high. They, in turn, identified a problem concerning these contracts and what served their national interests. Most politicians in the region were lawyers. When contracts came up for negotiation, they were usually handled by the Prime Minister or Attorney-General privately through their own legal offices – that is, through private firms. Thus the Crown law officers did not have the opportunity to ensure that contracts met with 'state of the art' developments in terms of standard clauses. What served 'the national interest' was regarded as a political matter. There could easily be a quid pro quo beyond the contract which ensured acceptance of antiquated contract clauses (such as giving special 'freedom' to the foreign commercial partner). This would not necessarily imply corruption. A politician might judge a traditional-style concession agreement for a sugar processing plant to be worth the prospect of immediate employment. On the other hand, an unreasonable public transport management contract might be concluded for very superficial prestige reasons with a suspicion of 'financial kickbacks'. A further criticism was voiced that some Caribbean lawyers began their career in government service and then 'graduated' to private practice, taking with them the experience they had gathered. The course had been designed for public service lawyers, with only a few private practitioners included. Inevitably its impact could only be modest.

Part II State Law versus People's Law and the Development Process

The main scope of Part II is to explain issues which concern law and development in the domestic context. The practical dimension of the subject is illustrated by two texts by Paul and Dias taken from Third World Legal Studies, an association which meets approximately every two years and publishes reflections on the practice of law in the context of developing countries. The basic assumptions of their approach are twofold, set out extensively in *Lawyers in the Third World: Comparative and Developmental Perspectives*.[21] Firstly, the political administrative framework left by colonial powers is not suited to the evolution of Third World societies towards democracy, because such frameworks were put in place precisely to administer local populations so as to fulfil the needs of the former cosmopolitan powers. Secondly, legal services are normally adapted to the needs of the small Westernized middle classes instead of to those of the general population. If this approach is regarded as too politically naive, one can look further to the reader prepared by Luckham, Ghai and Snyder, *The Political Economy of Law*.[22] In addition to extensive texts from Marx, Gramsci and Poulantzas, this compilation also considers the problems of the legal profession and the class structure, the administration of justice, and law as an instrument of social change. Their consideration of international aspects of development is welcome, but this subject will be postponed to Part III.

The question is how to allow development to happen without falling into the trap of a mere laissez faire liberalism, given that it is the presence of existing state structures which is holding people back.[23] In fact Paul and Dias move towards a radically new concept of law which should be universally applicable. By law they presumably mean lawyers – that is, the profession. Law's function is 'to discover through dialogue, the potentialities of law as a resource to deal with shared but often inchoate grievances;...in the mobilization process in galvanizing determination to deal with problems through collective action'.[24] For instance, administrative law rules have traditionally given government officials virtually unlimited discretion, thereby encouraging them to expect to be obeyed.[25] Paul and Dias stress that work is still to be done to ensure recognition of the rights of peoples, groups and villages affected by economic changes initiated by the government officials.[26]

This is the kind of work which Trubek and Galanter savage in their presumably theoretic rather than empirical statement: 'Law and development studies never succeeded in securing institutional status within the universities. Few if any scholars made their basic career commitments to the area'.[27] Although not annotated, these remarks may be taken to mean that domestic development law is not *à la mode*. Whether it can succeed can hardly be gauged by the ten-year span which they appear to allow for its development. In any case the work of Dias, Paul, Luckham, Ghai and Snyder has aimed to ensure that law should evolve in response to the conditions and needs of Third World countries.

It would be wrong to think that their work was completely marginal, since the fierce controversy surrounding the alleged right to development indicates that there is plenty of heat in this area, even if not much light. The return of jurisprudential, indeed ideological, controversy in the middle of the 1980s indicates that the role which law *might be allowed to play* in the development of Third World countries is one which people are anxious to control. For instance, the leading international law journal published Alston's call for 'quality control' of new human rights, which I include in this volume. The essay is not exclusively concerned with the right to development. However, four years later, Alston stated that of all the various new rights which have been proposed, this had attracted the greatest scholarly attention. Yet much work remains to be done 'before the concept can attain the degree of specificity or concreteness which would enable it to be operationally significant at either the national or international levels'.[28] His main thesis is probably that the prospects for significant governmental acceptance of the right are weak, at least until such time as the philosophical, economic, political and legal ramifications of the concept are better understood. He says that this is a task that only scholars can accomplish but that they have barely begun.[29]

The essay on quality control identifies the important function of the language both of the right to development and the related right to popular participation in the battle of political rhetoric, especially in international organizations such as the United Nations. It surveys the possibility of 'quality control' particularly through the introduction of procedural requirements to ensure that there is enough deliberation prior to the adoption of a right.[30] However the main interest of the paper is how it illustrates international community attempts to conceptualize such issues as development and the difficulty entailed in trying to elaborate a new philosophy through legal debate in political fora.

The essays by Donnelly, Rich and myself offer some reflections on the theoretical dimensions of the right to development. Donnelly functions as devil's advocate, showing why countries such as the US oppose a right to development. Anxious to reject what he regards as collectivist thought, he repudiates the possibility that Western countries might have to accept legal responsibility for maintaining the social fabric of developing countries. Although development may be necessary for the enjoyment of numerous individual human rights, he contends that this necessity does not generate a right to development any more than the need for a healthy liver implies a right to a liver transplant.[31] Even more fundamentally, Donnelly objects that notions of solidarity and interdependence concern the quality of relationships between human persons. As such they cannot generate rights attaching to persons *qua* persons.[32] In any case law enters the picture where interdependence reaches the point of a willingness to enter into a cooperative relationship, a joint venture, partnership or contract.[33]

Rich provides an alternative 'group' perspective. Recognition of group rights is essential for protecting the rights of individuals who comprise minorities or indigenous populations and in preventing racial discrimination.[34] The right to development recognizes that unless a state can achieve effective development, it cannot guarantee any basic rights to its citizens.[35] Rich's perspective is thus diametrically opposed to that of Donnelly. Equally, he insists on a duty of international legal solidarity: 'It is the emergence of the concept of global community... that may eventually... allow more general application of the principle of equity as a balancing element in their [nations'] relationships'[36] Rich accepts that the major 'compensation' to the West is supremely innovative in terms of concepts of public law. The developing country is not just a creditor receiving development assistance; 'it becomes a debtor because it then owes a duty to its people to allow and encourage the full development of individuals'.[37]

The debate about the right to development thus represents a fundamental challenge to basic concepts of both private and public law in respect of the Third World. Since this constitutes five-sixths of the planet, it can justifiably be taken to have general implications for legal theory. My own essay, on the crisis in legal theory accompanying the debate about the right to development, attempts to trace the legal controversy back to the triumph of secular liberalism in the West in the course of the 17th century. Natural law doctrines of equity and proportionality were an integral part of pre-modern European civilization, and the question is posed whether a return to them, or an optimistically cyclical view of history, could provide a bridge to the predominantly non-Western Third World. In other words, it is the process of technical (and eventually industrial) progress in the West which is unsympathetic to the idea of international development law as such. The belief that the individual can separate himself from both his common human kind and the natural world, only to return to them entirely on his own terms through some kind of original contract or through reference to a transcendental principle of personal autonomy is the foundation point to which one is forced to return in this theoretical legal controversy. The explosion of purported legal rights not merely to development, but to peace, to a clean environment and to popular participation (as referred to by Alston) represent an unsettling of Western categories of legal thought which merits the word 'crisis' because it threatens what has already been acquired.

Part III International Law and Development

International law and development is firmly established both in France and within the international legal profession as a distinct branch of international law. The International Law Association has a Committee on the New International Economic Order, which has provided the framework for the book *International Law and Development*, edited by de Waart and published in 1988.[38] The Free University in Amsterdam devotes professional expertise to the committee, with support from the Dutch government. A second book has been published in anticipation of the 1992 meeting of the ILA in Cairo, P. de Waart and E. Denters (eds) (1992), *The Right to Development in International Law*, Nijhoff. In England a book with a similar title, edited by Snyder and Slinn in 1987,[39] constituted the Proceedings of an Anglo-French Symposium on the subject. This demonstrates that international law and development has found a firm, if controversial, place in French international law discourse, although English common law jurisdictions are much less sympathetic. A court-based system fails to provide the expertise for a discipline which, in France, has started from an interdisciplinary theory of the state and its place in international economic relations. Traditionally, English 'international economic law' has confined itself to 'hard' case law, above all, commercial arbitration. However, there were contributions to the Proceedings from the London School of Oriental and African Studies and the Universities of Edinburgh, Glasgow and Warwick, where full-time academics devote a major part of their careers to the subject. In the US, Garcia Amador has written *The Emerging International Law of Development*, published first in Spanish in 1987 and then in English in 1990. Unfortunately this work is largely rhetorical and considers various issues – the language of Third World state sovereignty over natural resources, the right to development assistance and to non-reciprocal tariff preferences and the duty to cooperate for development – almost exclusively in the context of United Nations practice. In Britain this is theoretically unacceptable, given its distrust of the UN as a source of international law. In practice the book also leaves out too many substantive topics (see below).

The most recent French contribution, in the form of a student text and reference book, is *Droit et politiques du développement* by J. Bouveresse, also published in 1990.[40] This is the most comprehensive theoretical *and* technical introduction to the problems of international law and development yet produced. It introduces the dimension of cultural difference, as well as the obvious one of economic disparity, into the field. At the same time it gives extensive technical detail regarding problems of multinational corporations, technology transfer, commodity agreements, public international finance and the vital area of international trade law. As such, the subject is not entirely distinct from the French *droit international économique*[41] which recognizes that the impact of the Third World on the international economic system is reflected, to some degree, in positive legal institutions. A more extensive description of the institutions of this branch of law is given in G. Feuer and H. Cassan, *Droit international du développement*, also published in a student edition in 1985.[42] Flory and Pellet were authors of pathbreaking works at a much earlier stage.[43] The latter has subsequently edited a large collection on culture, development and international law, published in Paris in 1992. The international law of development grew out of the law of French colonial administration and was, for a time, the law of international economic cooperation.

What is remarkable in England is that, with the exception of the work of Slinn at the School of Oriental and African Studies, the legal experience of the British Commonwealth has not given direct rise to a university discipline of international law and development. There is no adequate manual or reference book in English on the subject. English international law has considered the Third World primarily under the rubric of state responsibility for damage to property of aliens. Apart from this it has resisted 'reformist' attempts by the UN system to modify traditional international customary and treaty law. Insofar as Americans have directed their minds to this subject, they have adopted a similar course. The selection of papers which follows will attempt to cover both the interdisciplinary and practical aspects of the subject in the light of this situation.

The essay by Jova and others examines the context and means of national control over the activities of multinational corporations in Latin America in the 1970s. It is written from the point of view of US diplomats and corporate lawyers who had contact with Mexico. The study gives a clear exposition of the development of the so-called law of state responsibility since the 19th century, the attempts of Third World countries to modify this through UN diplomatic-legal pressure in the 1970s and, finally, an exposition of Latin American, Andean and particularly Mexican legislation to control the activities of foreign corporations in Latin America. The essay explains how dependency theory – a neo-Marxist theory of the international economy – has shaped national laws. For instance, since foreign business was regarded as a cause of balance of payments problems, legislation usually tried to regulate specifically for each new company's impact.[44] This brought development law directly into the field or discipline of law and regulation.[45] The dismantling of foreign investment legislation in Canada since 1984 was influenced by the 'deregulation' wave of the 1980s.[46] In the Latin American context, however, relaxation of controls has been much more a function of the weakening international bargaining power of countries hit by world recession and escalating debt burdens.[47] The paper explains how the drafting of national legislation has to be seen in the wider context of continuing negotiations at an interstate level.[48]

The 'heart' of international development law has been the attempt to change the 'rules of the game' in international trade law. Four of the essays selected are concerned with this matter. These indicate a considerable development of normative theory in international economic relations, well beyond the traditional parameters of international law. Kwakwa points to the formulation of the principle of preferential treatment in the Charter of Economic Rights and Duties of States (1974). Non-reciprocal and non-discriminatory treatment should be accorded with a view to accelerating economic growth and bridging the gap between rich and poor (Article 19).[49] His own paper is intended to illustrate how international lawyers conduct arguments about whether such a principle is legally binding upon states. The primary question is whether UN resolutions and declarations, such as the aforementioned Charter, together with the actual practice following therefrom (that is, the preferences which have been accorded), can be assimilated into general customary law as practice which states recognize as binding upon them. This involves a classic case of having to decipher such evidence as state rhetoric, propaganda and diplomatic pressure to determine what statesmen really regard as matters of serious engagement.[50] Kwakwa himself moves away from what he concludes is an elusive search for serious legal intention on the part of states towards a concept of equity. This represents a typical and necessary attempt to overcome the *is-ought* dichotomy which, as noted earlier, bedevils any attempt to draw principles of development law from Western-based liberal notions of personal autonomy; that is, from an essentially will-based consent theory of law. He contends that if international law is to remain effective, it must change so as to conform to the sociological structure of the international community, supposing somehow (which is precisely the theoretical problem) a dialectic relationship between an economic infrastructure and a legal superstructure.[51]

Kofele-Kale takes up the same issue from this point. He systematically opposes what he calls an 'equitable' internationalist to a 'liberal' internationalist perspective on the key question of trade preferences for developing countries. Kofele-Kale discusses frankly the economic merits of various types of trade liberalization. For instance, it might be said that world welfare increases to the extent that duty-free imports from preferred DCs displace less efficient domestic production in the preference-granting countries. However world welfare decreases to the extent that imports from preference-beneficiaries displace more efficiently produced imports from other non-preferred industrialized countries.[52] Kofele-Kale does not break completely with traditional arguments about the sources of international law; in effect, he sidesteps these issues by focusing on the specificity of GATT as the framework for international trade. He points out that GATT rests upon an abstracted notion of an international division of labour based on a principle of comparative advantage which is seen, artificially, as an abstracted, static quality attaching to states. In fact these elements are historically constructed and work very unequally against states at present.[53] As an alternative perspective, he recommends that GATT be seen as a unique mixture of law, economics and politics. The challenge of *law in development* may thus be, *inter alia*, to reconcile two opposed trade policies: temporary protection for infant industries in DCs on the one hand and complete free trade, with no state restrictions supportive of national industries on the other. Kofele-Kale concludes firmly: 'The debate over legal rules merely camouflages this basic and historical tension between two competing perspectives on how international trade should be conducted'.[54]

Nicolaides and Tarullo carry the argument further. Their essays are not intended simply to demonstrate more support for an international law of development, but to show how the style of normative reasoning just described has become *mainstream* in the construction of arguments about the international economic system. The challenge of 80 per cent of the world's population transforms legal categories into contested concepts. Writing for the interdisciplinary *Journal of World Trade Law*, for instance, the economist Nicolaides claims that to require some allocation of trade to satisfy ethical preconceptions regarding 'proper' international exchange is a subjective matter about which nothing more can be said. The problem is that in order to define 'proper' shares, one must determine whether existing shares are acceptable or not.[55] These difficulties have put an end to the international regulation of commodities: the world market is regarded as too volatile. Nicolaides goes so far as to contend that equity is incompatible with economics. He does this by broaching a binary opposition crucial to international trade relations: similarity and difference. International exchange is beneficial exactly because economic conditions, knowledge, resources, skills and preferences are different in different countries. 'Complete equality defeats the purpose of trade.'[56]

Indeed a paradox of the Third World drive for equity through difference lies in the question of whether, once accepted, differences are in fact discriminations. Why grant trade advantages to some developing countries rather than to others? For instance, the Lomé Convention favours former African colonies at the expense of Asia and Latin America.[57] The question of difference goes to the foundations of modernism. If it is given that there are no natural qualities in 'things' which, of themselves, have compelling normative force, then difference can be of only *conventional* significance. The modernist 'insight' is that there 'are no *natural* categories or divisions lying out there waiting to be discovered'.[58] For instance, disputes over 'unfair practices' in international trade arise because there is no 'normal' conception of the state's economic rule in 'post–industrial' society.[59] The dilemma is well stated. Conscious efforts to resolve disagreements, whether through legal principles or otherwise, revolve around the production of images of sameness where they do not already exist. At the same time, the logic of normalcy and sameness appears inexorable in an increasingly integrated world economy.[60]

The purpose of the two concluding essays by myself is to try to 'complete' Tarullo's argument. If it is true that there are no 'natural' laws of international economic relations, then arguments usually advanced by liberals – concerning respect for the nature of the international economy, the development of capitalism, technological progress and efficiency – have to be treated as spurious in an advanced liberal-capitalist world economy. It has to be recognized, instead, that democratic values must be paramount in a pluralist world society. It is not acceptable that the world economy still be given direction by a small number of individuals whose legitimacy rests on the alleged *weight* which they enjoy in that economy. Western societies treat domestic economic questions as political rather than 'natural'. Yet the conduct of an institution such as the IMF is still premised upon the belief that decisions to give financial assistance have to be 'conditioned' upon the imposition of 'sound' financial practices arrived at by a system of weighted voting.[61] I suggest that international economic institutions should correspond to the recommendation of the Group of Experts who completed a report on 'A New United Nations Structure for Global Cooperation'. They called for a revision of the system of weighted voting 'to reflect the new balance of economic power and the legitimate interest of developing countries in having a greater voice in the operation of that institution'.[62] At present it is controlled by the US, Japan and Western Europe.

The IMF plays only a part in the direction of international financial affairs, although it does have a crucial coordinating role in Third World questions, linking up public and private international banks with both Western and Third World governments in arranging 'financial packages'. Obviously the Group of Ten, which decides financial questions within the general framework of the IMF (but from the standpoint of Western interests), is not subject to any global democratic control. Nor are private international banks accountable to anyone, even their own national governments. The virtue and vice of the Euro-dollar market is that it escapes all individual national jurisdictions. I try to argue that this situation should be recognized for what it is – an international legal vacuum.[63] Private international financial matters have been particularly impervious to demands that loan agreements be adapted to the needs of developing countries. I suggest that there are, in fact, no principles of international *ordre publique* governing private international loan agreements. I recommend that no loan agreement should be concluded with the government of a developing country unless it can be attested that the agreement itself has received genuine democratic approval from the people of the country concerned.

Notes

1 D. Trubek and M. Galanter (1974), 'Scholars in Self-Estrangement: Some Reflections on the Crisis in Law and Development Studies in the United States', *Wisconsin Law Review*, Vol. **14**, p. 1062.
2 Its subtitle is *Nouvel Ordre dans la dépendance* (1983), Paris/Algers: Publisud Office Press Universitaire d'Alger. See also articles by M. Chemillier-Gendreau, such as 'Droit du Développement et Effectivité de la Norme' in M. Flory and others (eds) (1984), *La Formation des Normes en Droit International du Développement*, Paris: Alger, p. 273; also 'Relations between the Ideology of Development and Development Law', in F. Snyder and P. Slinn (1987), *International Law and Development*, London: p. 57; also A. Carty, 'Vers une sociologie du droit international du développement' in Flory *supra*, p. 95.
3 D.E. Apter (1987), *Rethinking Development: Modernization, Dependency and Postmodern Politics*, Beverly Hills: Sage Publications.
4 Trubek and Galanter, p. 1066.
5 ibid., p. 1080.
6 Franck in this volume, pp. 11–12.
7 ibid., pp. 10, 12.
8 ibid., pp. 14–15.
9 Trubek in this volume, p. 53.
10 ibid., p. 86.
11 Greenberg in this volume, p. 101.
12 ibid., pp. 95–6.
13 ibid., p. 97.
14 D. Senghaas denies that other European countries, particularly Germany and Scandinavia, owe anything to colonial exploitation. See (1982), *Von Europa Lernen*, Frankfurt: Suhrkamp.
15 Greenberg in this volume, pp. 99–105.
16 ibid., pp. 109–12.
17 Zagaris in this volume, pp. 123–6.
18 ibid., p. 159.
19 ibid., p. 154.
20 ibid., p. 161.
21 (1981), Uppsala: International Center for Law and Development.
22 (1987), New Delhi.
23 Paul and Dias in this volume, pp. 305–7.
24 ibid., p. 322.
25 ibid., p. 282.

26 ibid., pp. 283–4.
27 Trubek and Galanter, *supra*, p. 1089.
28 P. Alston, 'Making Space for New Human Rights: The Case of the Right to Development', *Human Rights Yearbook*, **1**, pp. 3–39.
29 ibid., p. 15.
30 Alston, p. 220, in this volume.
31 Donnelly in this volume, p. 181.
32 ibid., p. 187.
33 ibid., pp. 189–90.
34 See R. Rich (1988), 'The Right to Development, A Right of Peoples', in J. Crawford (ed.), *The Rights of Peoples*, p. 39 at p. 44.
35 See Rich in this volume, p. 257.
36 ibid., pp. 230–1.
37 ibid., p. 262.
38 (1988), Nijhoff.
39 Snyder and Slinn, *supra*.
40 (1990), Paris: Press Universitaire de France.
41 D. Carreau, T. Flory, P. Juillard (1980), *Droit International Économique*, 2nd edition, Paris: Librairie General de Droit et Jurisprudence.
42 (1985), Paris: Dalloz.
43 M. Flory (1977), *Droit International du Développement*, Paris: Press Universitaire de France. A. Pellet (1987), *Le Droit International du Développement*, Paris: Librairie General de Droit et Jurisprudence.
44 Jova and others in this volume, pp. 346–7.
45 See, for instance, S. Breyer (1982), *Regulation and its Reform*, Cambridge: Harvard University Press.
46 See, for instance, R.B. Leckow and I. Mallory (1991), 'The Relaxation of Foreign Investment Restrictions in Canada', *ICID Foreign Investment Law Journal*, **6** (1), pp. 1–41.
47 For a focus on the context of a developing country's external economic relations and the importance of its political culture as a bargaining factor, see A. Carty (1988), 'The Theory and Sociology of Economic Self-Determination' in P. de Waart et al., *International Law and Development*, Nijhoff, pp. 45–58.
48 Jova in this volume, pp. 359–61. The assumption of the essay is that bargains can be reached in the context of the overall across–the–board relations between 'northern' and 'southern' countries. Clearly this is controversial. There are a series of essays on US-Mexican economic relations and the question of a North American Free Trade Area in *Comercio exterior* (Mexico City), **41** (7), July 1991.
49 Kwakwa in this volume, p. 415.
50 ibid., p. 417 et seq.
51 ibid., pp. 426, 431. This is to expose a fundamental tension which is of general application in modern international law; see, for instance, A. Carty (1991), 'Liberalism's Dangerous Supplements: Medieval Ghosts of International Law', *Michigan Journal of International Law*, **13** (1), pp. 601–11.
52 Kofele-Kale in this volume, p. 383.
53 ibid., especially pp. 388–91. For a general treatment of how GATT is failing, across-the-board, to promote and safeguard the interests of developing countries in the present multilateral trading negotiations, see C. Raghavan (1990), *Recolonization, GATT, the Uruguay Round and the Third World*, New Delhi/London: Oxford University Press.
54 ibid., p. 405; see also, in the same vein, A. Carty, 'Legal Dimensions of Contemporary Protectionism', in Snyder and Slinn, *supra*, at pp. 203–14.
55 Nicolaides in this volume, pp. 493–4.
56 ibid., p. 498.
57 See Tarullo in this volume, especially pp. 474, 476.
58 ibid., p. 477.

59 ibid., p. 484.
60 ibid., p. 486.
61 Carty (1988), in this volume.
62 See R.F. Meagher (1979), *An International Redistribution of Wealth and Power: A Study of the Charter of Economic Rights and Duties of States*, New York: Preuger, p. 71.
63 Carty (1986), in this volume.

Part I
Law and Modernisation: The Legal Imperialism Debate

[1]

THE NEW DEVELOPMENT: CAN AMERICAN LAW AND LEGAL INSTITUTIONS HELP DEVELOPING COUNTRIES?†

THOMAS M. FRANCK*

American lawyers and legal institutions have not always been appropriate for developing countries. Today, however, the United States and the new nations of Africa and Asia share many common values, largely as a result of recent American emphasis on domestic social welfare as a developmental goal. In an attempt to redefine the role of law in development not only abroad, but in our own society as well, Professor Franck explores the possibilities for cooperative ventures in the development of new legal institutions and roles for lawyers as social engineers in order that potentials for development may be realized.

In title IX of the Foreign Assistance Act of 1966,[1] Congress authorized the Agency for International Development (AID) to emphasize the assurance of "maximum participation in the task of economic development on the part of the people of the developing countries, through the encouragement of democratic private and local governmental institutions."[2] The purpose underlying this new directive is both obvious and commendable. Despite their evident benefits, economic development programs, like military assistance programs, have distortive effects on aspects of the recipient society. In some instances, such programs have tended to entrench the power elite; also, the "trickle down" economic benefits, at times, have been less than expected. Moreover, rapid economic development, if not accompanied by planned social development, can subvert desirable facets of traditional structures, culture, and environment. In sum, development is a value-laden concept; Congress, in title IX, opted in favor of human and social values.

AID has moved cautiously toward implementation of its new

† This is a revised version of a paper presented for discussion at the 1971 Annual Meeting of the Association of American Law Schools. It does not purport to present the findings, views, or conclusions of AID or the Government. The author is indebted to Professor Robert Stevens, Yale Law School; Jonathan Silverstone, Chief, Civic Participation Division, Bureau for Program and Policy Coordination, New State, Agency for International Development; and Members of the Colloquia of the Center for International Studies, for useful comments and assistance.

* Professor of Law and Director of the Center for International Studies, New York University. B.A., 1952; LL.B., 1953, University of British Columbia; LL.M., 1954; S.J.D., 1959, Harvard University.

1. 22 U.S.C. § 2218 (1970).
2. *Id.*

mandate. Although realizing that this policy decision is well intentioned, AID understands the process of assisting social and political development in a sovereign state to be a sensitive task—even more so than the giving of direct economic or military assistance.

The Center for International Studies of New York University was asked to assume responsibility for a series of country studies examining the feasibility of implementing title IX in the area of law.[3] Our objectives were threefold. First, we examined the relationship of legal institutions and processes to development in a range of countries. Second, we investigated whether the technology and experience of American legal institutions, lawyers, and law-oriented private and public bodies could be transferred and adapted to assist new nations in improving the quality of their development. Finally, we attempted to test the water to determine whether developing countries were in fact interested in such assistance. From January 1 to September 31, 1971, teams of researchers were sent to Botswana, Zambia, Kenya, Uganda, Turkey, Malaysia, Singapore, and South Korea. Team members included lawyers, a federal circuit judge, law and political science professors, former advisers to African governments, and a Turkish and a Korean professor.[4]

Team reports, embodying over 400 pages of data and recommendations, were compiled and submitted to AID. Some recommendations suggest things to do; however, many more suggest things to avoid doing. For a time, we felt somewhat guilty about using scarce State Department funds to investigate and to recommend things not to do. Nevertheless, given the experience of the past seven years, the Government may well be grateful for abstemious advice, and to the extent that teams recommended against expenditures which would not likely have brought dividends, the money was well spent. On the other hand, we did find a number of circumstances which seemed propitious for assistance.

I. The Feasibility Study: Basic Considerations and Lessons

A. *The "Cultural Imperialism" Specter*

We knew, of course, that even the mere study of the legal institutions of a foreign country involved sensitivities. These sensitivities were undoubtedly compounded by the very focus of our study, which was not purely descriptive. Rather, we wished to

3. It should be emphasized that although our study was limited to law and legal institutions, title IX is not so limited. Feasibility studies are therefore under way in other areas as well.

4. The project was quite aware of country sensitivity. In fact, during our visit to Turkey, the Turkish professor was named to the cabinet of his country.

examine the potential for making legal institutions better serve the ends of popular participation in the development process and of distributive justice.

No useful purpose would be served by obscuring the fact that we were interested not in legal institutions and lawyers per se, but rather in a certain kind, or texture, of legal development. The questions we asked were therefore, of necessity, culture-bound and value-loaded. We started from the assumption that the United States and a number of other countries have developed institutions, techniques, and concepts which, although imperfect, serve to make law relevant to social and political change. With this in mind, our teams asked two general questions: (1) Whether Ugandans and Kenyans, Turks and Malaysians, thought it profitable and functional to attempt to borrow from this experience, adapting it freely to their own needs; and (2) whether indigenous experiments were already underway to achieve comparable, or better, results.

On numerous occasions, we were warned by American Africanists, Asianists, diplomats, and friends that use of an American model, however freely adaptable, as the basis for anything in Africa or Asia was political dynamite and would be viewed as neocolonialism. Some went so far as to suggest that anything American and, indeed, all Americans were now unwelcome in the touchy, newly independent nations. Thus, although persons in the teams had long been leaders in the battle against neocolonialism and paternalism—both at home and in Africa, Asia, and Latin America—we nevertheless undertook our project with some misgivings and considerable caution.

We were impressed, however, by the eagerness of most African and Asian leaders to discuss methods of structuring and strengthening institutions to make law more relevant to development. The occasional suspicion and rejection encountered often came from British expatriates who felt their own roles threatened by new, unfamiliar ideas, or from American foreign service officers who suspected all intellectuals, and "title IX intellectuals" more than most. From Africans or Asians, on the other hand, we encountered only friendly cooperation and a sense of professional solidarity.

Any anxiety felt was thus rapidly dispelled; we found persons in the African and Asian countries visited sensitive to, not about, new ideas. Particularly in the professions, they have the self-confidence and identity to consider innovations willingly—in some cases even eagerly—and to accept both technical and financial assistance to help them modernize their programs of legal training and their institutions of lawmaking and law reform.

Two or three years ago, we might not have reached this conclusion. But if such receptivity is indeed now typical, reassessment of American involvement in development abroad is certainly in order. Having only recently begun to learn the lessons Africans and Asians have been attempting to teach us regarding officious intervention, cultural imperialism, and neocolonialism, some Americans may now be in danger of overlearning these lessons. But one may as well fall flat on one's face as lean over too far backwards. Or as one African government official put it: "Nowadays, if you are drowning in the sea and a Ford Foundation officer passes by and you shout to him for help, he'll insist you find him a 'counterpart' African through whom help can be channeled." Misapplication of the lessons of decolonization and anti-imperialism, or use of them as an excuse for withholding American assistance which Africans are willing and able to apply to their own circumstances would, therefore, be a serious mistake. Oversensitivity and overfastidiousness in this respect may be no more helpful to Africa and Asia than was the earlier phase of insensitivity and condescending paternalism. What is needed is help given and taken, with mutual respect, and without strings, to promising projects, backed by responsible individuals and institutions in recipient states.

Thus, we interpreted our terms of reference as a license not to go project shopping, but rather to determine general receptivity, to identify pressure points, and to suggest key prototypical individuals, role players, and institutions whose participation in the negotiation and execution of an actual project would be essential to its success. When we became aware of a need for the conceptualization and development of new law and legal institutions, but found no individual or institutional base upon which to build, we tried at least to identify signposts which might, in the future, presage the emergence of such a base. We also suggested minor ways in which an emergent tendency towards base formation might be encouraged without officious stagemanaging.

We did, however, observe the anti-imperialism stricture in one important respect: We tended to treat project requests which depended for their development and execution primarily on American personnel as not feasible, not only because of political sensitivity but also because American law experts should not be expected to assume primary responsibility for adapting an American concept or institution to African or Asian needs. The outsider cannot ordinarily be expected to understand these local needs fully, nor to be seen to understand them. The United States could, however, expand the experience of established African legal experts by allowing them to observe American practices—at worst to help others avoid our mistakes; at best to permit cross-cultural borrowing. But for the most part, the projects treated as feasible were ones in which Africans or Asians could assume key roles from project inception and all roles within a reasonable time.

It should also be noted that the Africanization or Asianization of project personnel can usually be expected to occur more rapidly than could Africanization or Asianization of funding. We did not regard our terms of reference as restricting us to projects that could be bought cheaply, nor did we find that meaningful innovations can be expected without considerable expenditure. On the other hand, we did attempt to limit our definition of feasibility to projects which were both of such priority and of such manageable dimensions as to stand a good chance of being absorbed, over time, into the recurrent budgets of recipients.

B. *Title IX and the New Development*

Few team members were country or area specialists, and only two or three had had previous experience with international development projects. They were not part of the "aid culture" which has developed over the past two decades, and this had both negative and positive implications. Instead, teams were deliberately composed of lawyers with primarily domestic experience in community legal services, civil rights organizations, legal aid societies, criminal law reform, and court administration. Also, in view of the role taxation has played in implementing American social policies, we included lawyers with experience in tax administration and reform. Thus, team members were well acquainted with the current stage into which our law and legal institutions have entered: concern for social justice and popular participation in decisionmaking. A few years ago, such a team would not likely have been sent to Africa or Asia, and certainly not on behalf of the American government. Was it appropriate even now?

Social scientists have generally noted that nations go through three stages of development: (1) Unification, (2) industrialization, and (3) social welfare.[5] It is also commonly recognized that legislatures, courts, and lawyers adapt their roles in society to accord with, and to facilitate, each successive stage of development.[6] In the past decade the United States has moved rapidly from its industrialization era, which spanned more than a century, to its era of social welfare. In this third phase, as in the other two stages of our national development, law, lawyers, and legal institutions are playing an important part in the changeover to, and synthesis of, a new national system of norms and values.[7] This new ethos does not, of course, eradicate earlier concern with national unity and industrialization, but instead attempts to integrate that concern with new social priorities. Each stage in the

5. A. ORGANSKI, THE STAGES OF POLITICAL DEVELOPMENT 7-221 (1965).

6. Mendelson, *Law and the Development of Nations*, 32 J. POL. 223 (1970).

7. For an analysis of legal/development phases in the United States see Auerbach, *Legal Development in Developing Countries: The American Experience*, 63 PROC. AM. SOC'Y INT'L L. 81 (1969).

American experience has not only built on the preceding one, but has also, to some extent, radically altered and repealed that stage and its underlying values. Our legal culture has served the central function of legitimizing change, thereby making these potentially divisive and revolutionary transitions seem orderly, peaceful, and to some extent, less perceptible.

This ability to promote orderly yet radical transition—a skill well represented on the teams—is relevant to Africa and Asia. Nevertheless, there is an important difference between our social universe and that in which Afro-Asian lawyers and legal institutions operate today. The United States underwent the three stages of development consecutively. Without exception, the new nations perceive all three stages—unification, industrialization, and social welfare—as necessary and equal objectives and, therefore, are pursuing all three concurrently.

This "accordioning" of the developmental stages is disorienting to many American students and theorists. Conventional wisdom teaches that national unification, the creation of stable and viable communities and markets, is the prerequisite to establishment of an industrial infrastructure, and that industrial growth, in turn, is the prerequisite to dealing successfully with such social concerns as poverty, illiteracy, and disease. Rejecting these assumptions, the new nations assert, instead, that unity is as much a *product* as a *prerequisite* of industrialization and social welfare, and that industrialization without concern for social welfare merely postpones for future generations the unpaid accounts of angry people, blighted cities, and despoiled countrysides.

Historically, men may have been unable to imagine a factory until they had created a secure community or to invent unemployment benefits until they had built a factory. The new nations of Africa and Asia, however, are taking their political, industrial, and social revolutions all in one, and the consciousness of their people encompasses all three phases simultaneously. Hence, despite what economists may teach regarding stability, infrastructure, and capital accumulation, politicians in these countries are not free to follow the historic step-by-step approach to development. Africans and Asians intend to move from drums to the full range of communications technology; they do not intend to begin from the bottom by reinventing the wireless.

Two recent attitudinal shifts have also led developers to ask whether a stage-by-stage approach might not in fact be the least desirable path to development. First, people in the developed world are themselves beginning to question the wisdom of having undergone a period of industrialization relatively free of social welfare concerns.[8] We ask whether a purely GNP oriented defi-

8. The achievements of 19th-century American capitalism were great. But its social costs were very high. The law did little to

nition of growth does not, ultimately, defeat the purpose of economic development by failing to bring about social unity, stability, and happiness. We fear that, in the developed nations, quality may have been deemphasized in the interests of quantity, and that our self-styled "affluent" societies have excessively squandered scarce resources. Thus, a model derived from the developed nations may be less than ideal, if not actually inappropriate for developing countries.

This concern in developed states with their own unsatisfactory quality of life has not been overlooked by the more imaginative developing nations. Several have deliberately decided to incur reduction in their GNP growth rate by decentralizing hydroelectric and industrial development, discouraging the growth of megalopolises, and providing relatively costly social services.[9] Thus, they are prepaying charges which our own grandfathers chose to pass along to us for collection.

The second relevant shift in attitude is the recent realization that popular participation makes for better development than does elitist autocracy—better qualitatively and, ultimately, better quantitatively. According to Goulet, a leading exponent of this new school of development, "Optimum consultation stands as a valid goal [of development] both because it is anti-elitist and because the masses' knowledge, sensitivity, and dreams are indispensable inputs to the development equation which planners cannot ignore."[10] Thus, "development is the combination of mental and social changes of a population which render it apt to cause its real global product to increase, in a cumulative and durable fashion."[11]

A first step towards these mental and social changes is the transformation of "they" to "we" in popular thinking about the state, its policies, activities, and potentials. Here participation itself becomes an ingredient in development. "People 'participate' in the public life of their country mainly by having opinions about many matters which, in the isolation of traditional society, did not concern them."[12] And people have opinions about matters with which they feel a certain familiarity and regarding which they be-

> curb the extravagant exploitation of our natural resources. Forests were despoiled. Soil was permitted to erode. Game was exterminated. Air and water supplies were polluted and fish life destroyed. Natural gas was burned to get oil, which was squandered. Unplanned railroad development left a heritage of problems with which we are still struggling today.
>
> Human resources were also cruelly used. The public health was nobody's concern. The work day and work week were very long and earnings very low . . . .

Id. at 87.

9. *See* D. GOULET, THE CRUEL CHOICE 147-48 (1971).
10. *Id.* at 164-65.
11. F. PERROUX, L'ECONOMIE DU XXe SIÈCLE 155 (1964).
12. D. LERNER, THE PASSING OF TRADITIONAL SOCIETY 412 (1958).

lieve their opinions are wanted and carry weight—matters in which they are encouraged to participate.

This approach to development seconds the assertion that development is better, although more complex, in a society which pursues the goals of unity, industrialization, and welfare concurrently, rather than consecutively.[13] It also suggests adoption of a new index to measure development, replacing GNP with a set of progress indicators that include social and cultural, as well as economic, factors.[14] Moreover, this interpretation rejects the previously popular notion that nation building is essentially a job for powerful, charismatic, authoritarian, modernizing elites. Instead, borrowing from the structural anthropology of Levi-Strauss and the phenomenologists, the exponents of the New Development define as fundamental to all real national growth the building of a functional process of structural dialogue between the people—involvement groups—and emphasize the importance of popular elites possessing limited power under strict mandate to consult with those most likely to be affected by any proposed decisions.[15]

This new direction in development thinking confirms the desire of new nations to pursue development in a fashion different from that of older countries. Equally, it operationalizes the intent of title IX. The question then becomes not whether the new nations can achieve development without passing consecutively through the stages the developed nations endured, but rather whether, given our own history of unbalanced development, we can help other nations attain the balanced development toward which we, ourselves, are only now aspiring.

So posed, the question does not invite rash optimism. The past century's literature on social structure, for example, has focused

---

13. "If, as I maintain, the goals of development are optimum life-sustenance, esteem, and freedom . . . [development] strategies ought to obey the principles of subordinating quantitative gains to qualitative progress, create expanded webs of solidarity, and optimize participation . . . ." GOULET, *supra* note 9, at 168.

14. A former Assistant Secretary of State for Economic Affairs put it thusly:

> But the economic growth rate is not the only index to look at. Employment, rural improvement, redistribution of income, social welfare, family planning, educational and regional development, decent and competent government on the local as well as the national level, freedom of speech, a functioning system of law, and national self-support all have their importance. Any addition to the list of objectives beyond simple economic productivity greatly expands the number of considerations and variety of actions which enter into the policy choices involved in the development process.

W. Thorp, THE REALITY OF FOREIGN AID 305 (1971). Thorp also adds such objectives as change in the social attitudes towards change itself, as well as in attitudes towards work, time, women, children, mobility, crime, poverty, disability, and old age.

15. *See generally* D. APTER, THE POLITICS OF MODERNIZATION (1965).

almost wholly on: (1) *authority* (Austin and Marx); and (2) *socialization* (Durkheim, Weber, Parsons, and Skinner). Both approaches are fundamentally inappropriate to the stage into which developed and developing nations are currently trying to enter. They deal preponderantly with the study of power in quantity: "big" government and "big" society, each hierarchically enforcing norms of legitimate authority to establish systems and to reinforce behavior among groups of persons under such rubrics as law, order, morality, progress, and legitimacy. There is a surprising dearth of contemporary American literature on either the horizontal, as distinct from the vertical, flow of power or the horizontal formation of authority by equals in small communities jointly sharing tasks and responsibilities.[16] The difference is not merely one between dictatorship and democracy, but also between two kinds of democracy: the vertical and the horizontal or, more conventionally, the *representative* and the *participatory*. During the past hundred years the United States has loaded almost all its democracy onto a representational grid: The Presidency, Congress, state legislatures, and municipal councils. However, most less developed countries (LDC's) are not developing in this manner. Representative democracy, in most although not all instances, is being replaced by other systems which, in some of the more interesting experiments, utilize, rather than combat, the sociocultural facts of decentralization in rural, tribal societies.

Today, there is serious concern in the United States with the efficacy of our own authority system, and new methods of legitimization are being sought. We are experimenting with ways to involve more citizens individually or in small subgroups directly, rather than through remote representatives, in decisionmaking, at least on those levels that affect them most intimately. Thus, the social welfare phase of American development involves not merely a substantive reordering of priorities, values, and laws, but an even more fundamental reorganization of the procedures by which priorities are set and laws made. To this extent, we are beginning to think more like the LDC's and our experiments should become increasingly relevant to their own aspirations. At the same time, while our more radical experiments in social welfare and in popular participation may often be those with which the LDC's can most readily empathize, many of the radicals promoting and implementing those innovations are, paradoxically, alien to the style and circumstances of the new nations. Since these countries have not undergone a capitalist-industrial age, their leaders do not share with our radicals the need for revolutionary style or rhetoric. It puts them off, or rather, they react adversely to the flamboyant tactics of some of our innovators, especially those who seek to export not only the

16. Bettelheim is an important exception.

reforms, but also the combative tactics of their American movements.[17]

It is, in any event, inappropriate for American AID programs to foist off new development theories on poor nations. Certainly "it is a bit presumptuous for theorists from the richest nations in the world to tell the poor nations that what they need is not more economic resources, but better political institutions."[18] On the other hand, it is also somewhat absurd to tell American taxpayers to spend money in other countries to enable these countries to make the very errors in development for which the taxpayer is also spending money to correct at home.

Nevertheless, we found that concepts of the New Development are under active consideration by planners and leaders in most of the LDC's visited. These concepts tend to be compatible with the political constraints within which the leaders are operating. Naturally, the applications of new concepts will vary as between the United States and the LDC's. If the new nations are less concerned with ecology than with industrialization, that judgment merely reflects their efforts to balance both factors at a time when Americans are trying to emphasize one to redress the excessive prior emphasis on the other. To the extent that we have not yet achieved balanced growth, our emphasis will necessarily be somewhat different. However, the United States does now recognize itself as a developing country, with a development problem. Despite its history, it now understands that concern for national unity, industrialization, and social welfare must somehow be reconciled, balanced, and synthesized. And finally, it is beginning to recognize that this essentially political balancing process cannot be left wholly to hierarchical structures, however representative, but must seek, through essentially horizontal structures, to involve those most directly affected by decisions in the processes of making them. Now, at least in comparison to even a decade ago, seems a propitious time for the LDC's and the United States to embark on the kind of mutual learning experience envisaged by title IX.

C. *The Lawyer and the New Development*

We have noted that in the United States the role of lawyers and judges, and the contents of law itself, have changed to accommodate

17. Any transplantation to foreign states under the guise of aid of the American professional "agitprop-as-social-reform ethic," which tackles every specific social condition, whether inadequate schools or uncollected garbage, as if the logical first step were to bring down the government, would be particularly dangerous. *See also* D. MOYNIHAN, MAXIMUM FEASIBLE MISUNDERSTANDING 164 (1969): "'[P]articipatory democracy' [in the wrong hands] can mean the end of both participation and democracy."

18. Lyman, Building a Political-Economic Approach to Development, at 5, Sept. 9, 1970 (paper presented at the 66th Annual Meeting of the American Political Science Association).

the three successive phases in our national development. If, as in the new developing states, these three phases are to be pursued concurrently, the legal culture must concurrently accommodate all three types of law, lawyers, and legal institutions: those adept at achieving national unification and integration, those expert in promoting industrial and commercial growth, and those functioning to foster social justice, human welfare, and the equitable distribution of rights and privileges, duties and burdens. Moreover, to achieve optimum results in the pursuit of each set of values represented by the three kinds of development, all three kinds of law, lawyers, and legal institutions will need to be sensitized to each other.

Furthermore, since three phases of development are to be pursued concurrently, rather than consecutively, there will be an even greater need to reconcile three potentially competing sets of values—unity, economic growth, and social welfare—in decision-making.[19] Although many have attempted such a reconciliation, no planners or theorists have yet offered an adequate framework in which to resolve these value conflicts: Certainly there are no formulas for conflict resolution involving only the routine application of unambiguous administrative rules.

Conflict is, nevertheless, inevitable, and a stable society must find answers. For example, the most direct method of suppressing a regional separatist movement may be by use of military force. But effective suppression cannot be the sole concern; the effects of such a response on investor confidence, on regional economic infrastructure, and on the people, their well being, and their willingness to participate in the process of social mobilization, cannot be discounted. Similarly, social welfare can perhaps best be promoted by giving to each citizen according to his needs. But this course of action would likely cripple both national unity, which must normally make concessions to the autonomy of disparate regional economies, and economic development, which seems to require financial incentives.

In the LDC's these balancing problems arise almost every time the society faces a choice. Other, older societies, which developed along a linear three-step progression from unity to social welfare, encountered lesser difficulties by ignoring certain values while exalting others. Conflict there always was—between feudal, nationalist, and mercantilist values—particularly in periods of transition, and even when a set of values predominated, countervailing popular values were never wholly excluded. Nev-

19. It has been suggested that in view of the social cost of single mindedly pursuing any particular social goal, system of values, or framework of norms, better social consequences may ensue when the society allows "several incompatible goals . . . to live in compromise, even though logically they are mutually exclusive." J. SHKLAR, LEGALISM 122 (1964).

ertheless, western nations, at each stage of their development, could usually measure the efficacy of a policy according to the progress it enabled the society to make toward a preponderant goal. Newer nations are pursuing a complex of goals simultaneously; therefore, they must pursue each in ways least likely to hinder the pursuit of them all.

This delicate balancing requires predictive foresight, a shrewd awareness of potential trade-offs, and an ability to devise new incentives for compromise. Yet such balancing, if creatively done, may maximize conditions for unity, economic growth, *and* social welfare more effectively than could the pursuit of any one goal to the exclusion of the other two. The very process of balancing provides opportunities for experimentation and social involvement, at least when that process is sensitive to the entire population, when it draws the demos into the actual balancing process. By involving people in the process of limiting their own preferences and harmonizing them with the preferred values of others, the government may create a new, more widely shared, and more popular set of tasks and objectives, as well as a greater dedication to their realization.

To achieve such results, new kinds of laws, lawyers, and legal institutions may be needed, ones which specialize in maximizing the participation of affected publics in the making and eventual execution of development decisions. "Trade-offs" and "incentives" —words generations removed from the old legal maxims—speak to the lawyer in his role as social negotiator rather than as barrister, as social planner rather than as private litigator. This role may be assumed by lawyers and nonlawyers alike;[20] however when nonlawyers are involved, they may need to acquire quasi-legal skills.

We know less about the "don'ts" than the "do's" of this new role. Obviously, a rigid adversary process, structured to provide either-or answers, is not the best way to decide social policy issues or to reconcile, balance, integrate, and synthesize distinct, even contradictory, social goals. Nor is the adversary process conducive to fostering that measure of accommodation and cooperation among the interested parties ultimately needed to promote social unity and to ensure success in implementing the decision once made.

Yet lawyers in the United States, at least the better ones, have learned to be not merely adversary advocates, but conciliators as well. They have been persuaded, and have themselves persuaded their clients, that it is often more advantageous to settle than to fight. They have, moreover, helped devise both ad hoc and institutional systems which promote negotiated settlement in place of litigation. Indeed, disputes are now more frequently resolved to

20. *See generally* section II. A. *infra*.

maximize benefits and minimize costs to all concerned, rather than to determine who is right. And the purpose of dispute settlement is increasingly understood to be not primarily to redress a wrong, but instead, to establish a continuing basis for "cooperation among individuals with common or reciprocal goals . . . ."[21] Disputes are also, increasingly, structured as trilateral, rather than bilateral relations, with the public interest forming the apex of the triangle.

American lawyers are also becoming adept at facilitating and maximizing the reciprocal exchange of costs and benefits, and at factoring seemingly unrelated or nonconvertible charges and benefits into mutual media of reciprocal exchange that permit bargaining and settlement. In most developing, industrializing societies, for example, bureaucratic red tape per se has become a commodity. Its cost in time, money, and citizens' peace of mind can actually be calculated. A government may, therefore, choose to bargain with this new "commodity." It can, for example, offer to absorb part of a manufacturer's cost to comply with new pollution controls by radically simplifying reporting in more conventional areas, such as taxation, or by substituting random sampling for universal inspection of facilities by sanitation and quality controllers.

Lawyers can do much to promote reciprocity, the fundamental facilitator of social behavior. If human beings are to live and work together, to share and allocate responsibility, they must have a basic reconciling belief in the fairness of the social system, both as it operates in general and as it affects them in particular. When that belief fails, illegal and antisocial conduct increases. This proposition is not limited to robbery and violence by poor believing themselves aggrieved. The respectable businessman who suspects the tax authorities are unfairly harassing him may similarly become perniciously diligent in claiming every exemption, no matter how small, on the ground that the authorities are requiring that he pay more than his fair share under the regulations as reasonably applied.

It is within the lawyer's professional province to reconcile society's disaffected, in part by seeing that the process of law enforcement is public and equal. Further, wherever possible, the creative legal mind should seek to substitute self-regulatory systems of fair law enforcement for hit-or-miss post hoc adjustment procedures. Thus, one answer to unfair tax harassment is to require authorities to pay the costs of the citizen's accountant at tax hearings if no substantial errors in his returns are proven, while charging stiff penalties if deliberate or negligent underpayment is found. Similarly, the innocent party in a criminal proceeding can-

21. Karst, *Law in Developing Countries*, 60 LAW LIB. J. 13, 18 (1967).

not really be reconciled to his society if he has been forced to bear the costs of his own defense. In sum: By becoming specialists in the free convertibility and the balanced flow of rights and duties, lawyers can thus play a part "[b]oth in minimizing the confrontation between a social reform and the old legal order, and in the building of post-reform institutions . . . ."[22]

Such creative lawyers, however, are in the minority, even in the United States, and in many developing countries our observations confirmed that of Kenneth Karst: "[T]here is no general shortage of lawyers, but only of lawyers who perceive that the law is more than a body of rules, and that law has a positive, creative role to play in the development process."[23]

Supplementing these thoughts with four months in the field, we are now able to formulate several tentative operational hypotheses. First, the sensitivity of lawyers, judges, and legislators to the competing values of national unity, economic growth, and social justice must be heightened. If all three goals are to be pursued concurrently, there must be lawyers who are experts at each, and lawyers who are experts at only one must also be reasonably at home in the concepts and data of the other two. This hypothesis suggests the need for three priorities in specialized legal training, and also for a broad, common, interdisciplinary base. Unfortunately, such training did not yet exist in any law school in any LDC visited.

Second, both the judicial or quasi-judicial decisionmaking processes and the legal and quasi-legal processes of regulating and reconciling will inevitably be central to the LDC's concurrent pursuit of unity, economic growth, and social justice, as well as to the task of reconciling these diverse kinds of development and of discovering the appropriate mix of the three in specific decisions. New nonadversary instruments for legitimizing authority, balancing social values, and mobilizing popular participation will become valuable instruments for making and carrying out successful policy. Few LDC's have begun to innovate along these lines, but many are interested. However, the suggestion that tribal institutions might be renovated for this purpose was not favorably received by any LDC's visited.

Third, the availability of relevant data frequently is, or ought to be, crucial. Data serves several important reconciliatory functions for the planner. Whereas a clash of values tends to widen a conflict, "hard" data tends to narrow it; moreover, if it involves participation by the community studied, the process of data gathering can itself be an important step towards a reconciling and mobilizing decision. For effective decisionmaking, such empirical data-

22. *Id.*
23. *Id.* at 19-20.

gathering must involve not only lawyers, but also social scientists and economists. Yet in no country visited was anything like this underway. Therefore, neither judges nor legislators had access to adequate data derived directly from the society. And society too often offered no input into decisions purporting to affect it.

Fourth, lawyers operating in a society concurrently pursuing the goals of unity, industrialization, and social welfare will respond to market forces by gravitating towards serving the first two, rather than the third.[24] Thus, if the third goal is to remain effective, the legal profession, government, and interested publics must deliberately set about to redress the balance through legal education and imaginative institutional innovations. In the United States, this redress is being attempted through use of public interest law firms, public defender or legal aid bureaus, paraprofessional and clinical law programs, and storefront legal services. Also significant in this country is the assumption of increasing social responsibility by bar associations.

Finally, a lack of institutional or procedural alternatives to formalistic structures of vertical representation generally limits the extent to which the society can promote meaningful public participation in development planning. Yet such participation is probably essential to, although not a guarantee of successful execution; particularly if "success" is measured by a more meaningful scale than a purely short-run materialistic one. It is also essential that the public be able to protest effectively against, and get relief from bureaucratic obduracy and the pernicious or capricious exercise of administrative discretion, and that it be able to do so without recourse to the formal legal process. In response, lawyers in the United States and other Western states have played a significant role in diversifying the modes of direct participation through such devices as petition, litigation, lobbying, and hearings, and in devising new institutions such as the ombudsman. In virtually every instance, however, lawyers in the LDC's have not yet become instigators and expediters of dialogue between planners and publics, decisionmakers and those affected. However, governments and the legal professions are watching the American experience with a view to finding better ways to regularize the processes of participation and redress, especially in local planning and administration.

---

24. The fact that in revolutionary and other radically progressive societies—which include many of the newly sovereign emergent or under-developed countries outside Europe—the function and status of the lawyer tend to be modest underlines the traditionally conservative function of the lawyer as a defender of established interests rather than an innovator.

Friedmann, *The Role of Law and the Function of the Lawyer in the Developing Countries,* 17 VAND. L. REV. 181 (1963).

D. *Limitations on the Relevance of the American Model*

We have observed that the United States today is beginning to view itself as an LDC, albeit one with very special problems, not of poverty, but of imbalance. We may, therefore, have more in common with the new states than was perceived even a decade ago. Lawyers, legal institutions, and law in the United States are all being challenged by a process of profound social change. At least some in this country are addressing themselves to the very same questions being asked by Asians and Africans.

But this coincidence of predicaments can be misleading. The cultures, particularly the *legal* cultures, of our respective societies are profoundly different, and these differences block all facile attempts at interchange. First, to our knowledge no other country uses lawyers and legal institutions so extensively and expansively. For countless social and political reasons, courts and lawyers occupy a vital and powerful role in the United States.[25] This omnipresence, however, is not characteristic of other countries; unlike the United States, most prefer that change come through legislation, rather than litigation. Most new nations also fear poverty and ignorance more than government arbitrariness. Thus, they are hesitant to create the checks and balances by which lawyers and judges "weigh in" against dynamic political action. Mass exportation of American legal paraphernalia, therefore, would be quite inappropriate.

Many, indeed most, developing nations, even those with an Anglo-Saxon common law tradition, do not look to conventional American legal institutions as models, not least because they have heard disturbing reports about how they do not work. Nor do their cultures prescribe the training or use of lawyers as social engineers, policy makers, initiators, synthesizers, or expediters. This negative observation is equally applicable to both the public and the private sectors of the economy, and to the bureaucracy as well. To be sure, there are a few countries, Kenya for one, to which this generalization does not quite apply. Also, in all countries, Diogenean individuals are trying to alter the education, the professional self-definition, and the social role of lawyers. But they are the exception, not the rule.

Why do lawyers in most foreign countries seem but lowly technicians to visiting Americans? The answer stems, at least in part, from the perceptive set of the observer. Americans expect to find foreign lawyers radically affecting the totality of law in their countries through litigation; hence they are almost invariably

25. *Cf.* 1 A. DE TOCQUEVILLE, DEMOCRACY IN AMERICA, 321-31 (1st Schocken ed. 1961): "In America there are no nobles or literary men, and the people is apt to mistrust the wealthy; lawyers consequently form the highest political class, and the most cultivated circle of society." *Id.* at 328.

disappointed. Virtually nowhere is litigation the weapon of social transformation that it has become in the United States during the past 25 years.

The United States is almost unique in the extent to which it entrusts the general lawmaking process, in addition to that of dispute settlement, to its courts. While this tendency was particularly notable during the Warren Court years, American courts have, almost from the Revolution, been central to our legal development, alternately as a transformative and conservative force. Although this phenomenon may be traced to the Lockean influences on the drafters of our Constitution, American judicial supremacy seems even more closely related to two other factors.

One is the coalition-oriented quality of American society which makes majoritarian political rule untenable under certain circumstances. The courts in the United States perform the task of protecting minorities against political majorities. And since almost everyone in the United States belongs to some minority, whether ethnic, racial, regional, or professional, the American social compact rigorously restricts government by political majority. That restriction, although undemocratic in the majoritarian, populist sense, has been incorporated not only into the first 10 amendments to the Constitution but also into the mystique of American democratic pluralism. It has, indeed, become the cherished guarantee of freedom and liberty. The federal judiciary, being to some extent insulated from the majoritarian-populist politics that dominate so many aspects of American representative government, has developed into the instrument for enforcing this guarantee against any excesses a majority might perpetrate against a minority.

Of more recent origin is the other relevant factor supporting the predominance of the American judiciary: the inability of much of the American social machinery to induce rapid change and the relative reluctance of American politicians to make decisions that cost votes. Thus, desegregation, reapportionment, and the reform of criminal procedure have all been undertaken by the federal courts because the political branch could not, or would not, effect desperately needed change.

Moreover, since constitutional amendment is relatively difficult in our federal system, the courts themselves have been forced to tinker with the Constitution to keep it running *au courant* over 200 years of enormous social and economic change.

In all, the courts in the American legal culture have played a key role in the game, as umpires perhaps, but as umpires in games replete with crucial plays, the outcomes of which were often uncertain and sometimes of vast public interest. In some instances the courts have protected minorities from populist movements that threatened established rights of liberty, expression, and property. On other occasions they have permitted the majority to achieve important social changes that had been blocked by minorities with disproportionate power in the political arena. Incongruously, the courts have thus appeared, at various times and in various ways, to be the champions not only of minorities endangered by encroaching majorities, but also of reforming majorities reduced to impotence by recalcitrant minorities. And, overall, the courts have established a reputation for the peaceful resolution of large and small disputes in a way that has provided an orderly alternative to both politics and violence.

The factors underlying judicial power in the United States are obviously not internally consistent nor systemically rational; they are not *necessary* but *actual* responses to the historic challenges of a given time, place, and culture. As such they generally cannot be replicated elsewhere, and this is a central factor controlling the conclusions of our study.

The governments of most developing states are not afraid to rule. We found no developing nations where the political arm of the government preferred to pass the buck to the courts as our Congress did for so long in, for example, civil rights matters. Nor is there any reluctance to make big, difficult decisions affecting the entire society.

This attitude might simply reflect the fact that most developing countries are willing to sacrifice political responsiveness, at least to minority wishes, or procedural due process in the interests of more rapid decisionmaking. However, it might also reflect an historic distrust of courts, which during the anticolonial struggle often represented colonial law-and-order, by those political leaders, now constituting the executive, who represented the populist forces. Much like our own founding fathers, African and Asian politicians as a class may have emerged from independence looking better than judges; thus, at this early stage of independence, courts continue to be wary of engaging in power and popularity contests against political leaders.

This attitude, however, may be changing. As the political fathers of independence are replaced, in one way or another, by their political or military lieutenants, the new leaders usually do not inherit their predecessors' special cachet. The balance between political leaders and judges may consequently be expected to shift at least somewhat in the judges' favor.

Nevertheless, in the developing countries visited, certain areas traditionally patrolled by judges in the United States are, and will continue to be, out of bounds to the judiciary. The protection of minority rights is not, by and large, considered a judicial function and, indeed, may deliberately be no one's function. The reasons for this vary. In a very few countries, there simply is not much of a minorities problem.[26] In other countries, for example Turkey, a minorities problem does exist, but is officially buried by the political arm of government under the weight of political edicts and political enforcement of national unity and conformity. In still others, such as Malaysia, conformity through edict is being pursued—less successfully, but no less energetically—despite the acknowledged existence of important minorities. These countries have embarked on a forced march towards national unity, cutting across diversity, and it is difficult to castigate political leaders in this regard when the alternative so often appears to be national disintegration and civil war.

Finally, some countries, such as Kenya and Singapore, are trying to achieve unity through coalition-subgroup bargaining processes, sometimes with one subgroup clearly dominant but concerned with keeping smaller subgroups from exercising their negative power, which is usually stronger than their positive power, by acts that sabotage the stability essential to development. This interest-aggregation type of bargaining, however, takes place exclusively in the political arena, and the resulting protections and benefits are themselves political. Courts, obviously, cannot sit at this bargaining table.

Nowhere, then, did we find courts playing an established role as the protector of minority rights.[27] These rights were either protected by political bargaining or deliberately left unprotected.

Thus, in each country visited, the balance of power between courts and the political arms of government was found to be quite different from that in the United States. Indeed, we noted a general absence of the Lockean belief that "the rule of law," enforced by courts, was a desirable barrier against infringement of individual rights by government. In one sense, individual rights, like minority rights, have been deliberately rendered vulnerable; but mainly, the rule of law, to the extent that it exists at all, is everywhere embedded in the political or administrative, not the judicial, process.

This does not imply that many citizens are not disaffected by government policies or by the political process in various developing countries, or that civil rights are not sometimes felt to be violated unnecessarily. The disaffected, however, generally do not blame their constitutional system for such inadequacies, but rather attribute them to the individuals or party currently in

26. Tanzania, not one of the countries visited, is the best example.

27. India, which we did not visit, is largely sui generis to this entire discussion, although the activist role of the Indian courts has been criticized for reasons similar to those expressed to us in Turkey—that the courts' favorite minorities were the privileged and the propertied. *See generally* H. MERILLAT, LAND AND THE CONSTITUTION IN INDIA (1970).

power. Consequently, they see reform not in terms of less concentrated government power, but, instead, in terms of *changing governing persons.* Reform, like protection of basic rights, is thus perceived to be a political task, not a judicial function.

The sole exception to this pattern of power allocation is Turkey which, during the Menderes regime in the 1950's, experienced a period of particularly authoritarian political rule, albeit backed by a parliamentary majority. When the 1960 coup ousted Menderes, instead of merely substituting a different group of political leaders operating within the same system, the Turks, led by young officers, decided to transform the system fundamentally. Borrowing from the American and French experiences, they moved vigorously in the direction of judicial supremacy.

Significantly, this experiment is now generally agreed to have failed. The resultant complex of regular courts, administrative courts, and the constitutional court was perceived by politicians and bureaucrats, fairly or not, to have become so powerful as to stultify political initiatives toward national development. The next Turkish coup, in 1971, is frequently defined by both the new leaders and many interested bystanders as a coup against, among other things, judicial supremacy.

The Turkish experience highlights the fact that regardless of the theoretical merits of judicial supremacy over, or judicial equality with, the political arm of government, such a balance of power is not likely to be tolerated by the LDC's of the 20th century, particularly if the role of the judiciary is perceived to be primarily conservative-negative. Judicial activism is only justified by the socially desirable results the courts achieve or, more accurately, by a widespread popular belief that judicial activism fills an important need. We detected little such feeling.

In summary then, the United States has a system of lawmaking which assigns a key role to the judiciary, but which is historically and culturally specific. This is not to say that the role is nontransferable, but only that its transferability is neither self-evident, nor indicated by actual instances of successful transfer.

However, this negative assessment might be viewed as the right answer to the wrong question. Perhaps the centrality of litigation and courts in the American legal culture is the product, primarily, of the industrial phase of national and legal development. If so, then perhaps the belated entry of the United States into its postindustrial, social welfare stage will give rise to new legal institutions and new roles for lawyers, as well as to new functions for law. These new institutions and new legal roles and functions may be more relevant to the LDC's, less historically idiosyncratic, than the older American legal culture.

The American legal culture of the future will probably be rooted in social factors which are more likely to be shared by the United States and the new nations. For instance, we are witnessing a common tendency to regard litigation as costly and wasteful, not merely to the litigants but to society. Thus, laws may so alter the causal relationship between social events and legal rights as to do away with the need for much litigation. Among the laws in this category would be those abolishing many categories of "social" crime (abortion, homosexuality, adultery, and even usury), those creating "no fault" liability relationships (in motor vehicle cases, for example), and those creating a broader scope for private arrangements (as in divorce by consent, or in the abolition of distinctions between legitimacy and illegitimacy).

Both in the United States and in the LDC's the growth of regulatory bureaucracy has created a demand for more self-regulation. Laws creating the necessary incentives may help to preserve some of the benefits of individual autonomy in an era of burgeoning socialization. Incentive legislation in place of criminal mandate is cheaper to administer, and can be more effective, as well as less oppressive.

Similarly, legal institutions may be restructured to respond to commonly felt needs of the social welfare stage of development. Quasi-judicial tribunals might strive to facilitate compromise and negotiation between parties, as well as the more conventional, adversary, win-lose relationships, fostered by courts. Also, legal processes less technical than mandamus may be invented to perform the essentially "lyrical" function of compelling those in power routinely to hear those most directly affected *before*, and separate from, the process of deciding; thus a new, administrative forum of "*oyer sans terminer*" might develop. Borrowing from the past, magisterial tribunals could be introduced, in which lesser social crimes would be handled informally by social scientists and peers, rather than by judges and juries. These tribunals would utilize nonretributive, nonpunitive remedies of social restitution.

Finally, autonomous, but publicly funded, commissions for legal research and law reform, composed of ad hoc teams of lawyers, social scientists, and members of the affected public could respond to the growing awareness of a social data gap. A commission's function might be to review the operation of a particular area of law to determine: (1) What the law as written, interpreted, and applied really is; (2) what, if anything, it was designed to accomplish; (3) what it is accomplishing in practice; (4) what it ought to accomplish; and (5) how it could best be reformed to accomplish it.

Lawyers themselves might also assume new roles. There may be need for legal, or paralegal, practitioners who specialize in alerting the citizens—particularly the poor—to their basic rights against bureaucrats, creditors, parents, landlords, and defaulting spouses; who have the practical expertise necessary to pursue such rights or to defend against claimed rights; and who will provide services for modest fees from readily accessible offices, through readily accessible tribunals.

If such a transformation of the legal culture is indeed occurring in the United States, our experiences may prove more transferable than have those of more familiar, older American models. This possibility will be enhanced if the development of our new legal culture has, from inception, proceeded as a joint cooperative venture of Americans and leaders of the legal cultures in other countries.

II. THE LAWYER AND DEVELOPMENT

A. *Does Law Promote Development? Do Lawyers?*

Unfortunately, because the law-and-development fraternity sometimes does not ask the hard questions, the hard conceptual tasks may not get done. Nevertheless, we believe it essential to confront the pervasive notion that whatever the idiosyncracies of national legal cultures and national development modes, somehow law and lawyers cannot help but be a good thing when it comes to development. As lawyers, we incline to this old shibboleth, often without examining it seriously; moreover laymen confirm our illusion by their deference to law-as-medicine, or even as magic. But deeper in our minds, if not our hearts, we know that law, as such, is neither good nor bad, either for development or for anything else. We also know that the socially desirable tasks we theorists have been assigning to new legal institutions or to a new breed of lawyers in the development process need not necessarily be performed by legal institutions, nor by lawyers.

Of course, we have recognized the role played by law and lawyers in facilitating development in the United States. We would also accept the assertion that law is everywhere an essential instrument of government. But good law aids development; archaic law hinders it. Good lawyers help, bad lawyers do not. Thus, in itself, law is only an implement,[28] and lawyers are but servants. Law is not imbued with qualities of its own.[29] Nor has the legal

28. As one observer stated: "[L]aw is a tool, a technique. Thus viewed, it does not involve any particular value assumptions or any particular set of functions within the broad scope of arranging, channeling and directnig forces within the social group." W. HARVEY, LAW AND SOCIAL CHANGE IN GHANA 343 (1966). Nevertheless, we believe this statement may unintentionally overstate the "colorlessness" of law. Law, as an instrument, does have its own inherent tendencies. So do most tools. *See* note 29 *infra*.

29. This statement is not strictly true, but we have let it stand in order to emphasize our principal point: Law is an implement, rather than something which is, in itself, pro- or anti-development. However, as a particular kind of implement it nevertheless is frequently said to have qualities which, in themselves, are neither pro- nor anti-development. Surpris-

profession any divine right to a central role in development, not even in legal development.

Lawyers and judicial processes have played an important part in unifying, modernizing, and egalitarianizing America. But this hardly proves that lawyers or judicial processes are, somehow, inherently developmental. Clearly, good lawyers, properly trained in international concession agreements, or good legislative draftsmen, can service the wheels of progress, just as narrow, pedantic, unimaginative, and ill-trained lawyers can hinder development. Nevertheless, lawyers and judges have no monopoly on, nor inherent qualifications for either function. In many societies, laws are conceived, enacted, and administered by nonlawyers, without necessarily better or worse consequences than if the same work had been done by lawyers.

Unlike lawyers, law is indispensable to all societies. But law is neutral about development and about kinds or directions of development.[30] To forget this essential neutrality of law can lead the well-intentioned developer to focus on law when he should be addressing political, economic, or social factors. Peider Könz, for

---

ingly, we have found no comprehensive theoretical attempt to analyze the qualities inherent in law. Most authorities recognize that "law" has the quality of "consistency," that it is "the stationary pole in the flux of phenomena." M. HAMBURGER, THE AWAKENING OF WESTERN LEGAL THOUGHT 125 (1942). But even this generalization is false if one considers the ease with which statutes and regulations are amendable by most governments, particularly those in developing countries. Perhaps the place to begin is by making a distinction between judicial and legislative law. Judicial law, allegedly, does have a quality of consistency, although many authorities, particularly contemporaries in the United States, regard this quality as more apparent than real. Lawyers trained to work with courts tend to be advocates of consistency even when they are not arguing a case. Judicial law also has a quality of intellectual refinement, since the court in which such law is made removes the public market of ideas to the courthouse, where lawmaking is conducted by dispassionate appeals to reason, while decently confined within established boundaries of relevance and precedence. Perhaps lawyers, even when out of court, have a structural sense of relevance. Finally, it is alleged that judicial law is accompanied by detailed explanation and reasoning which has a pacifying, educating, and reconciling effect on the parties and on the society at large.

Legislative law in a democracy, by contrast, has the quality of representing "popular will" which is conscious and deliberately achieved by "coalition parties" representing "interest aggregation" and "trade-offs." Such law is publicly debated, publicly decided, and subject to public amendment or repeal. It thus has behind it the sanction not merely of the sovereign, but of the society and its "social fabric." It need not be consistent for legislatures do not bind themselves as do courts. But legislative law does have the quality of generality, of universal and of socially unifying fairness which is absent from ad hoc fiat or bills of attainder. This is, of course, more an idealization than a description of the qualities of both kinds of law per se.

30. "It is a value-neutral tool." Seidman, *Law and Economic Development in Independent, English-Speaking, Sub-Saharan Africa*, in AFRICA AND LAW 3 (T. Hutchison ed. 1968).

example, has noted that "even in . . . India, law has not been particularly responsive to environmental needs. Nor has it, to any appreciable extent, retarded processes of national disintegration or degradation of authority where they occurred . . . ."[31] What Könz means is that *people*—legislators and judges—have failed the environment or have degraded authority; to say, "the *law* has failed," adds little or nothing to our understanding of what has gone wrong in India. There are certainly bad persons; but bad institutions and bad laws are an effect, not a discrete cause of social ills or ideological myopia.

This distinction is of practical significance to anyone interested in the strategy of change. A "bad" law can rarely be changed merely by pointing out that a different law would produce better results. And changing a bad law is usually a task involving far more than well-intentioned lawyers.

Why then should lawyers insist on assigning priority in the development field to themselves, to law, and to legal institutions, when mere parity will do? Is it not sufficient simply to justify our concern with lawyers because we happen to be lawyers, and because our experience in the American legal culture leads us to believe that as long as a country has a legal profession, that profession, like any other, ought to be sensitive to national goals? The precise role of lawyers in a given country emerges from the interaction of a variety of forces affecting that country, and, therefore, the kinds of roles lawyers play in national development ought to be viewed as a sociopolitical choice which each nation must make for itself. We should try to understand that choice and take it as a given; then, if help is requested, assistance must work within the parameters the request establishes.

Justice Holmes once observed that "inasmuch as the real justification of a rule of law, if there be one, is that it helps to bring about a social end which we desire, it is no less necessary that those who make and develop the law should have these ends articulately in their minds."[32] We might add that the means towards those ends employed by lawyers, laws, and legal institutions must be constantly updated to accord with the specific society, in all its multivarious complexity, and with each intricate, delicately balanced system of national goals and values.

B. *The Self-Definition of the Role of Law and Lawyers in Social Development*

The role of law and of lawyers in a nation's development is determined largely by its social culture and its ideology. Both factors, and the clusters of dependent variables associated with each,

31. Könz, *Legal Development in Developing Countries*, 63 PROC. AM. SOC'Y INT'L L. 91, 92 (1969).

32. O.W. HOLMES, *Law in Science and Science in Law*, in COLLECTED LEGAL PAPERS 210, 238-39 (1920).

can be changed by evolutionary, as well as by revolutionary means. However, for the foreign specialist concerned with aid to a developing nation's legal system and profession, social culture and ideology must be givens not amenable to manipulation. This inevitably circumscribes the advice he can give or the help he can recommend.

In Turkey, for example, we observed that lawyers define their role primarily as experts in code searching, law and contract drafting, and securing compliance with the vast network of subsidiary regulations. Legal education at the two law schools, Ankara and Istanbul, is structured to perpetuate this definition. Since lawyers neither see themselves as social engineers, nor are trained to engage in social engineering, it is hardly surprising that they do not occupy policymaking positions in government or business, and that they are not, in general, highly regarded by those who do play the policymaking and initiatory roles. The manner in which lawyers are trained and perceived and the manner in which they perceive themselves, are part of a closed system of role definition which is both mutually reenforcing and close to the core of the whole social culture and ideology of Turkey. Most senior government officials are not lawyers, although many have received enough legal training at Syasal Bilgiler Fakultesi, the political science faculty of Ankara University, to feel themselves able to dispense with legal services in all but the most technical matters. In general, senior bureaucrats and cabinet officers perceive their departmental legal advisers as essentially instrument drafters and gainsaying experts who are well versed in explaining why a proposed initiative, obviously desirable in itself, is impossible.

While Turkey may be an extreme case in this respect, to a considerable extent, the same was found true of each of the other countries visited: Botswana, Zambia, Kenya, Uganda, Singapore, Korea, and Malaysia. Each of the six Commonwealth countries, for example, came out of a period of British rule during which an unreconstructed British solicitors' view held sway over professional self-definition. Lawyers were not perceived by the consumers of their services, or trained by their teachers, to be policy scientists; naturally they did not perceive themselves as such, either. Instead the lawyers, although more highly regarded than those in Turkey, became specialists in drafting legislation and contracts and in persuasive court rhetoric based on the citation of available higher court decisions. However, in none of these countries do lawyers play any significant role in the policymaking echelons of the civil service, except in the attorney general's office, nor are many lawyers found in the higher policymaking ranks of corporate management.

One reason for this self-definition is that the legal culture of each country encompasses an imposed British ethic, as well as imported British laws. Lawyers generally practice alone, rather than in firms, and this both retards specialization and creates a need to hustle, particularly among what is usually the first generation of young indigenous, as distinguished from British or Indian lawyers. A hustling practitioner, however, is unlikely to become involved in social questions. Furthermore, the tradition of legal education, although currently under revision, has been that of the British Inns of Court—a method scarcely designed to produce social engineers. Finally, the laws of each country ensure the legal profession almost boundless opportunities to expand atop a broadening economy, without having to imagine more economical or more socially beneficial services to render the community. With almost half the litigation in most courts of the new nations devoted to motor vehicle cases, and more to land title disputes, these socially useless aspects of the profession, unless curbed by deliberate changes in the law, will probably drain off for years the legal talent trained at high cost by the society.

When the legal culture deliberately sets about to cut off important outlets for such entrepreneurial lawyers' services, then the resultant surplus of lawyers may force the profession to seek out more useful functions in government or in public interest practice. But this is unlikely to happen without deliberate changes both in law and in legal training. Whether such changes will in fact occur depends, however, on currents far deeper in the society than are contained in the concept of legal culture. A society embarked on Marxian or other radical socialist-statist growth, such as Tanzania, is likely to cause private entrepreneurial legal services to dry up. But, at the same time, Tanzania does not encourage lawyers to enter into public interest law firms, legal services for the poor, or legal services for redress of public grievances. The Tanzanian law graduate tends to be absorbed into the state bureaucracy, fulfilling fairly conventional roles. When these are filled, the training of lawyers will probably be cut back at the University, in favor of other professional training priorities. For the American model of the development lawyer to be exportable, then, the recipient state must not only be embarked on a deliberate strategy of social reform, but must have determined to make lawyers and legal institutions a part of that strategy. It must, moreover, have resolved to encourage lawyers to enter private practice for the pursuit of public causes—not a very commonly understood or desired policy among the LDC's we visited.

Nevertheless, none of this discussion should obscure the important fact that the role, particularly in government, so commonly played by lawyers in the United States, does not stand vacant in any developing country—not even in the more radical nations. Whereas in the United States one *expects* to find lawyers occupying most positions in government departments at the assistant secretary level, in several of the countries visited, we found primarily engineers (why after all should not *they* be the "social engineers"?), architects, professional administrators, and economists all more numerous in these roles than were lawyers. In corporations, welfare organizations, and private interest groups, nonlawyers engaged in many of the expediting functions we assign to lawyers, and handled informal complaint and grievance procedures at both the citizen's and government's ends. Most important, it was far from clear, at least on the basis of our rather superficial examination, that these incumbents of the social engineering role did their job significantly better, or worse, than might most lawyers.

C. *The Minimal Social Engineering Role for Lawyers: Government Roles in Search of a Profession*

The fact that other professionals seem capable of serving adequately as social engineers in government and in the private and quasi-public sectors suggests that lawyers are not indispensable to development, the United States experience notwithstanding. Nevertheless, several reasons may be offered to support the argument that at least some lawyers should develop the capacity for social engineering for use by a developing society.

One reason is paramount: All developing societies, including the United States, exist in a condition of tension between the demands for rapid, radical change and the seemingly contradictory need to achieve stability and confidence. In the United States, more so than in any other country, the lawyer has successfully reconciled these contradictory social demands. He has become an expert at designing both profound social transformation and pragmatic incremental initiatives, while maintaining intact those guidelines of consistent, reciprocal, orderly social interaction essential to stability and mutual confidence, features which distinguish change from chaos, evolution from revolution. The American lawyer has learned that it is easier to persuade most people to accept change or to compromise if they can be convinced that its pace and direction is not arbitrary, that it is linked to both the past and the future, and that it is based on a principle of reciprocity which gives today's loser a chance to be tomorrow's winner.

For example, within the policymaking echelon of government, the demand for rapid social transformation generally calls for wide discretionary powers. Thus, the governor of the central bank of a developing country will undoubtedly have broad powers to deny or grant applications for foreign exchange. Politicians in government often attempt to influence the governor to use his power to reward allies and punish enemies. Economic advisers will urge that discretion be used in each individual case to reflect the current state of such fluctuating economic factors as liquidity and exchange balances. In such circumstances a departmental lawyer might be a valuable advocate for consistency, advising that each individual application be measured against certain flexible but consistent standards of meritoriousness which may take into account a complex of political, economic, commercial, and social indicators. Undoubtedly, some such legal input into the decision-making process of the governor of the bank would promote commercial confidence, fiscal stability, and the long-range cooperation of the business community, all aspects of development.

Thus, lawyers, if properly trained, can be effective exponents of flexible consistency and of techniques for convincing people—even staunch adversaries—to participate in the search for a principled, rational solution. However, most lawyers in most of the countries studied were not adequately trained to play this role—a difficult part, quite unlike that of judicial advocate. But no other profession played it at all, and thus it remained, almost invariably among LDC's, a role in search of a profession.

A second reason to encourage the training of lawyers as social engineers may also be advanced. Lawyers, as trained in the better law schools in the United States, have become experts at broadening the range of options available to policymakers. In the countries studied, most bureaucrats conventionally implement policies by mandating or prohibiting. However, lawyers trained in law and sociology know that having led a horse to water, there are many ways to make it drink. A finely variegated pattern of incentives and disincentives, devised primarily by lawyers, runs through much American legislation. Properly executed, this is an exercise in formulating systems of self-regulation, not only for professions and industries, but also for other interest groups and individual citizens. New ways to achieve compliance with law or national goals, other than by mandating or prohibiting, are being devised in the United States. The creative synthesis of law with sociology, and of law with economics, is producing a wider range of options for persuading, inducing, and delegating. In most developing countries this range of alternative options has not yet been developed. Momentum in this direction awaits reform in legal education that would expose law students to the social and behavioral sciences in the context of law reform.

Both these roles could be filled by other professionals. Principled advocacy, for example, is well within the intellectual range of a competent philosopher. Practically, however, our studies made it apparent that if lawyers did not undertake these tasks, they would remain undone.

D. *Non-Law for Lawyers or Law for Nonlawyers?*

Most law schools in the LDC's visited have not yet begun the process of training some lawyers to play quasi-legal modernizing roles, nor have they begun to design, let alone train, staff for new kinds of quasi-legal institutions. In rare instances legal education was being broadened to include exposure to the social and behavioral sciences, toward the end of redefining the lawyer's role under the auspices of a benevolent government willing to co-opt such lawyers into roles appropriate to their training. In other countries, probably still a majority, the trend against using lawyers creatively, both in the public and private sectors, was strong and the narrow conceptualization of legal education firmly established. Prejudice against lawyers and lawyers' pedestrian performance in public and private sectors seemed locked into mutually reinforcing social fixations.

When this is so, the United States cannot be the unlocking agent; any useful attempt to help a country make its legal culture more relevant to its development goals must work within the parameters of that country. Thus, the United States must begin by accepting the status quo, and then look for ways to help LDC's fill certain modernizing roles with nonlawyers trained in at least those aspects of law essential to those roles. By so approaching this issue we may find opportunities to help willing law schools train engineers, architects, economists, and sociologists for work in public administration, nongovernmental public service, and in business.

Having had little experience in the United States with this type of legal education for nonlawyers, we cannot be specific about design. Clearly, the needs of the United States and the LDC's in this respect differ. It is noteworthy, however, that a recent report by the Association of American Law Schools recommended starting similar programs in this country.[33] Here may be an opportunity to establish a partnership with LDC's in a mutual learning experience.

In many countries, the engineers in government will continue to design legislation for slum clearance, land consolidation, and pollution control. In most such instances, they will not only design, but will actually write the laws, with lawyers entering only in the final stages to provide the cosmetic "whereas's." Certainly an engineer faced with the task of designing socially significant and legally complex legislation ought to have the training necessary to draw on the comparable regulatory experience of others—for example, an exposure to comparative law bibliography and methodology; similarly, he ought to be aware of the wide range of options for regulating, say, pollution through the tactical deployment of such other diverse branches of law as taxation, patents, and copyrights. He also ought to be given some sense of the functional importance of clear, concise, and consistent rules and their application. Finally he ought to develop an understanding of the principles and utility of procedural due process, particularly

33. CURRICULUM PROJECT STUDY COMMITTEE, ASS'N OF AM. L. SCHOOLS, *Training for The Public Profession of the Law: 1971,* in ASS'N OF AM. L. SCHOOLS 1971 ANNUAL MEETING PROCEEDINGS, pt. 1, § 2 (1971).

the uses of *audi alteram partem* in legitimizing bureaucratic decisions.

In this connection, it is again important to keep in mind that we are not talking about transferring old, established American legal institutions into new states. Rather, we are asking whether it may be possible to create conditions in which some new nations may wish, and may be able, to participate as partners in the evolution of a new phase of the legal culture in their countries and in our own.

III. HELPING LESS DEVELOPED COUNTRIES TO UPDATE THEIR LEGAL CULTURE WHILE TRYING TO UPDATE OUR OWN: PRACTICAL STEPS IN MUTUAL ASSISTANCE

Having said something about the inhibitors of legal assistance to developing countries, we turn now to positive conclusions. There are some things that could be done but the inspiration for them will not be found in those safe, conventional aspects of our legal culture which have in the past defined the role of law in American development. These are generally irrelevant to the needs of the LDC's. Instead, we must look to aspects of the legal culture only beginning to emerge in the United States.

There are obvious dangers in this approach. Should we invite passengers along on a largely uncharted voyage to ports unknown on vessels that may not stay afloat? There are two good reasons for a qualified "yes" to that question. First, these projects are still flexible and could probably better accommodate an international or comparative perspective at a lower cost than could older, better established ones. Second, the new American legal culture, insofar as it is beginning to emphasize the significance of balancing the society's commitments to unity, economic growth, and social welfare, is unquestionably more *au fait* with the emerging social ideology and legal cultures of the LDC's than was its predecessor. There are risks in this approach, but a more conventional one eliminates risk only by guaranteeing failure.

Thus, new developments at law schools in the United States—the discovery of America's poor, the development of clinical programs, the training of nonlawyers, the emphasis on quasi-legal, nonadversary processes, and the discovery or rediscovery of social and behavioral science and social policy as lawyers' tools—could bring a few of our most progressive law schools closer to the needs of the most promising law faculties in the LDC's. In some instances, these needs are hardly perceived in the LDC's. In others, the need is felt, but strong cultural and ideological commitments militate against the use of lawyers to advance social reform. Nevertheless, there exists at least the possibility of some meaningful experiments in mutual cooperation and real partnership in learning. "Participation," after all, might begin with joint efforts to clarify the goals and techniques of inter-institutional cooperation among a few American and Third World law schools impelled by similar visions of their role in the New Development.

We have observed that important problem areas in the legal and social culture of the United States relate us to states still in the underdeveloped category. The search for solutions will inevitably, and rightly, proceed separately, as each country responds in its own way, at its own pace, to its own variations on related themes. Even so, we can probably learn from each other if we choose. Efforts to upgrade magistrates' courts are a promising instance.

No country can function without these local courts, and in every society the quality of justice, as perceived by the common man, is most directly shaped by the instrument of law most likely to touch him directly. Usually this is the magistracy or its equivalent. Yet at this lowest court level, the caseload is commonly immense, the pay frequently poor, and the legal training of the judges often inferior. At this level incompetence and pettiness tend to subdue justice. Yet it is precisely here that the citizens most frequently judge their rulers. It is at this level, too, that most citizens form their opinion of the law and decide whether the state is "we" or "they."

Obviously, any government has a vested interest in guaranteeing that this level of adjudication works—and is seen to work—speedily, openly, fairly, and economically. Since only a tiny fraction of the cases decided by magistrates involves government interests, or are in any respect political, there is rarely any point in permitting less than the highest standards to prevail. Yet high standards are rarely attained, either in the United States or in the LDC's. However, in the United States a number of experiments have begun—some administered by judges—to upgrade the training and efficiency of the lower judiciary and the administration of their courts. These efforts should be reviewed to determine whether they show promise for, and interest in developing an "AID capability."

Similarly, no government anywhere can have a deliberate interest in bad, authoritarian, corrupt, facile, or arbitrary conduct by its bureaucracy or police. Much popular disaffection is caused not so much by the policies of political leaders as by the manner in which those policies are implemented, particularly at the lowest village and rural levels. The issue, here, is not democracy, but fairness. Indeed, it may in fact be true that the *more* authoritarian the country's political leadership, the greater should be the leaders' interest in ensuring fair administration. Such fairness is always desirable; in authoritarian systems it can supply an element of mitigating legitimization for laws enacted with limited democratic participation.

Corruption, a particularly acute form of unfairness and of popular alienation, according to many authorities, "has become the central enemy of development . . . ."[34] Moreover, as the most obvious aspect of the common disregard for legality by officials, corruption undermines the citizen's sense of fairness and his willingness to participate in national development, a process which he sees as merely a game fixed to his disadvantage by the dealers.

But it is all too easy to generalize that "corruption . . . permeates the fabric of most African states,"[35] or Asian nations. It is a problem we all have in common. There are leaders, both in Africa and in Asia, who are notably incorruptible and who are anxious to make their ministers and their bureaucracies adhere to equally incorruptible standards. These leaders tend to be the pace setters for both continents, and it would be a sound investment to help them experiment with corruption detection and control systems that enlist the confidence and aid of the citizenry and the business community. There must be mayors, police chiefs, and budget officers at various levels of government in the United States who would find these experiments relevant to their own problems and their own search for remedies. Singapore and Malaysia are, in fact, currently experimenting with resident neighborhood police and complaint bureaus in an effort which somewhat parallels New York City's rather tentative ventures into community control and localization. It is too early, as yet, to know whether local control increases or decreases the propensity to corruption, but it is a question being answered in practice by more than one society. Kenya is studying the ombudsmanship in its Scandinavian, British, and Tanzanian adaptations. In the United States, variations on this institution are being tried in cities, schools, even in prisons. We share these problems with the LDC's; perhaps we can also share aspects of the search for ways to solve them.

Every country visited also shared with us a concern for lack of congruity between the social purposes of specific laws and the actual social consequences of their enactment and enforcement. In virtually every instance, we found an interest in establishing a standing law commission, along the lines of the Law Reform Commission of New York State or the Law Commission of Britain.

In Uganda, for example, the government cannot move ahead with a broad program of social and economic development in the rural areas until a comprehensive system of tenure has been enacted. And, so long as farmers, because of complex tribal, familial, or other institutions, do not have legal title, they cannot generate credit from lending institutions for agricultural modernization. Therefore, although a Ugandan land tenure law ranks

34. Seidman, *supra* note 30, at 27.
35. *Id.*

high on Kampala's agenda, it would be useless for politicians and draftsmen to sit down and write a new land title act; without popular acquiescence, such a law would be unenforceable, since land is the central fact of life for 90 percent of the population. Ugandan leaders recognize that the first step toward law reform is a thorough survey of actual customary practice and the effects of that practice on economic and sociocultural behavior throughout the country. However, since practice varies considerably from region to region, this is a major task. Even this first step requires customary law experts, a range of social scientists, and an organized research program, backed by an institutional staff with at least two or three years of committed funding.[36]

Similarly, the states of Africa and Asia have experimented with various forms of public participation in the means of production. Independent statutory corporations, state enterprises of varying degrees of dependence, joint public-private ventures employing various mixes of control as well as apportionment of rights and duties, and franchise and licensing operations—all have been tried. However, no systematic effort has been made in any single country, much less among states of a region, to compare the social, economic, and political costs and benefits of the various participation schemes.

As these examples suggest, a continuing research forum is needed in which law and the social sciences, government, and university, could each add their special cachet to the endeavor. Such law reform commissions or, as they are sometimes called, law development centers, are expensive. Regionalization, providing one commission or center to serve a contiguous area, would have the benefit of spreading the cost and, perhaps, to some extent, of insulating the institution from national political pressures. Unfortunately, regional animosity seems at the moment more common than regional friendship. It may be that links can sometimes more readily be established between nations whose friendship is unencumbered by proximity. Law and society research-and-reform programs developing in the United States, Britain, and Canada, should be considered with a view to their potential for a mutual aid-and-learning experience.

Another problem shared by almost all countries, including our own, is that of providing adequate legal services for the poor. In none of the countries visited did indigent criminal defendants have the right to free legal counsel, except in capital offenses. National leaders themselves consider this scandalous; thousands of persons are imprisoned without even understanding the nature of

36. Similarly, although many of the countries visited employed corporal punishment rather freely for various offenses, none has ever attempted a followup study to determine whether the desired deterrent effects were being achieved.

the labyrinthine legal proceedings in which they find themselves helplessly lost. Plainly, criminal rehabilitation gets off to a disastrous start when the accused is convicted and sentenced by a process incomprehensible to him.

Fortunately, enlightened attempts to deal with this problem have emerged. Zambia has an extensive legal aid system, based on cooperation between government and the law school. A typical daily notice for the High Courts of Lusaka shows that a substantial majority of criminal defendants are represented by legal aid attorneys. In Kenya, there is evident interest in starting a public defender system in the attorney general's chambers which would borrow partly from the experience of some American states and partly from that of Zambia. In Singapore, a ten-year-old model government funded legal aid program is operating, but it handles only civil cases—assistance to mothers in nonsupport cases is apparently more politically palatable than is assistance to criminals. In each case, however, the question is whether nations can, and are willing to acquire the capability for transnationalizing their experiments. If so, there appears to be a positive interest on the part of other countries in participating.

IV. MULTILATERALIZATION

Programs of assistance such as those described above operate within the limits of the current interests of most countries, even those whose culture has traditionally confined the lawyer's role rather narrowly. A strong case can therefore be made for multilateralizing any such assistance. First, it reduces the political risks to donors in what is obviously a relatively high risk enterprise. Second, multilateralization makes it harder for political foes to accuse the government of being lackeys of imperialism, for the "imperialist" is a consortium; the political risks to the recipient are thus reduced. Third, multilateralization, involving a number of developed as well as developing states, shares predictably high costs. Fourth, it permits utilization of the skills and experiences of a range of developed countries, such as Canada, as well as those of more advanced developing states like Singapore. Moreover, most of the feasible proposals are not in areas particularly or exclusively within the American experience.

V. CONCLUSION

Development in the LDC's has tended to encompass the concurrent pursuit of at least three goals—unification, industrialization, and social welfare—which more developed countries pursued, essentially, consecutively. There is evidence that this concurrent pursuit of all three goals is both feasible and even desirable. However, the planning, reconciling, adjusting, and balancing required to pursue the three goals concurrently requires special skills of the society's leaders; the lawyer's role in this process is essentially new and little developed. In the United States, contemporary developments potentially link us as a "developing nation" to the other LDC's. New laws, legal institutions, and legal roles are emerging in the United States in response to needs and values shared with LDC's. This apparent congruence is not necessarily manifest in similar development of the legal culture.

We are nevertheless at a stage where modest cooperative experimentation in the development of at least some new legal institutions and roles is possible. The best prospects for such ventures are in the fields of legal education for nonlawyers; the use of social and behavioral science resources to achieve reliable mapping of a problem prior to legal reform; legal and paralegal services for the masses; and the development of simple, decentralized procedures for bureaucratic grievance redress and corruption control.

[2]

The Yale Law Journal

Volume 82, Number 1, November 1972

Toward a Social Theory of Law: An Essay on the Study of Law and Development*

David M. Trubek†

Law is a practical science. It does not ordinarily dwell on fundamental questions about the social, political, and economic functions of the legal order. Satisfied with implicit working assumptions about these matters, legal thought moves rapidly to more tractable questions. But when law's solutions to social problems fail to satisfy, it becomes necessary to examine the basic theory from which they derive.[1] This is such an era. In a time when men speak casually of a crisis of law, and ask "is law dead?"[2] it is clear that law's role in society has become problematic. Such an age demands a social theory of law.

It is now necessary to frame explicit and concise questions on the relationship between law and social life, and to answer these questions by disciplined inquiry. Since the implicit, a priori conclusions about the role of law are no longer valid, we must turn to systematic efforts to understand the relationships among the legal, social, economic, and political orders. In any such effort, comparative research and cross-cultural generalization will play a major role. This essay examines one area in which such research has begun, the field of "law and develop-

* I wish to thank Jan Deutsch, Lawrence Friedman, Duncan Kennedy, Bolivar Lamounier, Leon Lipson, Robert Seidman, and Henry Steiner for their valuable assistance in the preparation of this article. I must acknowledge a special debt to Roberto Mangabeira Unger. In addition to his advice on this essay, his extraordinary unpublished study "The Place of Law in 'Modern' Society" (undated, on file in Yale Law Library) clarified ideas that had been merely vague musings. Yet I, not my colleagues, must assume responsibility for any errors or ambiguities in what follows. I first addressed these issues in an essay published in Portuguese as Part I of a volume of studies on the Brazilian capital market: D. Trubek, J. Gouvea Vieira & P. Sa, O Mercado de Capitais e os Incentivos Fiscais 23-92 (1971). As the reader will note, I have modified a number of the views set forth in that piece.

This study was supported in part by a grant from the Agency for International Development to the Yale Law School's Program in Law and Modernization. The information and conclusions in this study do not necessarily reflect the position of A.I.D. or the United States Government. Finally, I wish to thank Robert Peck for helping me with the research.

† Associate Professor of Law, Yale Law School, B.A. 1957 University of Wisconsin, LL.B. 1961 Yale University.

1. *Cf.* T. Kuhn, The Structure of Scientific Revolutions (1962).

2. For a discussion of recent literature on these themes see, *e.g.*, Mazor, *The Crisis of Liberal Legalism* 81 Yale L.J. 1032 (1972).

ment"; there, lawyers and some social scientists have attempted to understand the function of law in the Third World—those nations which have not yet achieved, but generally aspire to, self-sustaining economic growth. Despite its commitment to comparative analysis and the formulation of universal principles, however, this research on law and development has not fulfilled its promise; it has produced few original conceptions or insights, and seems incapable of formulating a satisfactory research program.

While the field has reached something of an impasse, this was not an inevitable result. Rather, it stems from the easy acceptance of certain underlying assumptions which have hampered fruitful inquiry.[3] This essay attempts to analyze these assumptions and their effects, and it suggests that their baneful influence can be avoided if more promising intellectual perspectives are adopted. In so doing, the essay is concerned primarily with clarifying those questions which should be asked, and suggesting methods by which they can be answered. Its primary goals, therefore, are to develop a few concepts and correct some major errors, in order to clear the decks for further inquiry.

As the argument is somewhat complex, I shall briefly summarize its dominant themes. We begin with an attempt to identify the basic features of contemporary thought on law and development, setting forth a synthetic restatement of such thought, termed the "core conception of modern law." The essay then argues that this conception has misdirected the study of law and development by asserting that one type of law—that found in the West—is essential for economic, political, and social development in the Third World. This conclusion, I contend, stems from the core conception's ethnocentric and evolutionist generalization from Western history. The article concludes by developing a preliminary typology which may permit more discriminating study, and suggests its application to some recent developments in the legal life of a major Third World nation.

I. Contemporary "Law and Development" Thought: The Core Conception

Modern social thought arose to explain the causes and impact of industrialization, nationalism, and urbanization in the West.[4] Con-

3. On the effect of fundamental assumptions in limiting fields of social inquiry, see A. Gouldner, The Coming Crisis of Western Sociology 29-35 (1970).

4. *See generally* R. Nisbet, The Sociological Tradition (1966).

temporary studies of economic, political and social development carry on this tradition in an effort to understand the Third World. But since development research has not viewed law as a major aspect of society,[5] it has left the study of law and development primarily to the lawyers. Perhaps because legal thought is generally pragmatic and professional,[6] writings on law are, when compared to other development studies, relatively fragmentary and unsystematic. Many are merely offshoots of "law reform" activities, not the result of organized academic endeavors. Accordingly, a significant amount of law and development "theory" is either implicit or unwritten.

This does not mean, however, that such theory is elusive or insignificant. There are a fiercely held set of ideas and beliefs which underlie the major studies on law and development and the legal reform projects carried out by lawyers from the United States and Europe.[7]

5. For example, development economists generally concede that development requires some legal framework, which usually means a minimal provision of law and order. Having said this, they usually drop the issue. *See, e.g.*, H. BURTON, PRINCIPLES OF DEVELOPMENT ECONOMICS 359-62 (1965); E. HAGEN, THE ECONOMICS OF DEVELOPMENT 480-84 (1968); S. KUZNETS, MODERN ECONOMIC GROWTH 451-53 (1966); W.A. LEWIS, THE THEORY OF ECONOMIC GROWTH 408-15 (1955).

Development economics normally deals only with two polar situations in analyzing "law." Either a society is completely lacking in the "essential" legal institutions, or those institutions are present in sufficient "amounts" so that there is always "enough" law to meet the current needs of the economy. In the former case, all that theory can say is that "adequate legal institutions" should be created. In the latter, law is simply defined away as a non-problem, and it is assumed that adequate supplies of this factor will always emerge as needed. To paraphrase Sir Arthur Lewis, in the typical economic development model, development proceeds with "unlimited supplies of law." Lewis, *Economic Development With Unlimited Supplies of Labour*, 22 MANHATTEN SCHOOL 13a (1954).

Contemporary economic development theorists seem to have forgotten or rejected the 19th century belief in the importance of law. For example, when European colonialists encountered the civilizations of Africa, Latin America, and Asia, they frequently concluded that these societies lacked the "rule of law," which, they held, was a cardinal feature of the West. J. FURNIVALL, COLONIAL POLICY AND PRACTICE *passim* (1956); L. PYE, ASPECTS OF POLITICAL DEVELOPMENT 113-25 (1966). Much colonial "economic-development" policy assumed that if the "rule of law" were instituted in traditional societies, economic progress would follow. *See* L. PYE, *supra* at 114-16. Finally, no one has stressed the importance of law in economic progress more than Jeremy Bentham, the founder of utilitarianism, and thus the grandfather of modern economics. J. BENTHAM, *Principles of the Civil Code*, chs. II-V, XVII, in THEORY OF LEGISLATION 96-102, 148-57 (R. Hildreth transl. 1871). *See generally* E. STOKES, THE ENGLISH UTILITARIANS AND INDIA (1959).

6. Two studies have appraised the resistance of law schools and the legal profession to the introduction of social science techniques and theories. Riesman, *Law and Sociology: Recruitment, Training, and Colleagueship*, in LAW AND SOCIOLOGY: EXPLORATORY ESSAYS 12, 24-40 (W.M. Evan ed. 1962); Stevens, *Two Cheers for 1870: The American Law School*, in 5 PERSPECTIVES IN AMER. HISTORY 405, 470-548 (D. Fleming & B. Bailyn eds. 1971).

7. *See, e.g.*, Rheinstein, *Problems of Law in the New Nations of Africa*, in OLD SOCIETIES AND NEW STATES: THE QUEST FOR MODERNITY IN ASIA AND AFRICA 220 (C. Geertz ed. 1963) [hereinafter cited as Rheinstein]; David, *A Civil Code for Ethiopia: Considerations on the Codification of the Civil Law in African Countries*, 37 TUL. L. REV. 187 (1963) [hereinafter cited as David]; Allott, *Legal Development and Economic Growth in Africa*, in CHANGING LAWS IN DEVELOPING COUNTRIES (J.N.D. Anderson ed. 1963); Merillat, *Law and Developing Countries*, 60 AM. J. INT'L L. 71 (1966) (report of a July, 1965 conference) [hereinafter cited as Merillat]; Galanter, *The Modernization of Law*, in MODERNIZATION: THE DYNAMICS OF GROWTH 153 (M. Weiner ed. 1966) [hereinafter cited

The Yale Law Journal Vol. 82: 1, 1972

These ideas are not less influential for their unsystematic nature. But it would be impossible to study or criticize them without a more complete articulation of their teachings—a synthesis of their views here called "the core conception of modern law."[8]

A. *The Nature of Modern Law*

The core conception views modern law as a specific social process emerging from the overall process of development. Modern law has three principal characteristics: It is primarily a system of rules; it is a form of purposive human action; and it is simultaneously part of, yet autonomous from, the nation-state.[9]

All societies, if they are to endure, must contain some system or

as Galanter]; Karst, *Law in Developing Countries*, 60 L. LIBRARY J. 13 (1967) [hereinafter cited as Karst]; Friedman, *Legal Culture and Social Development*, 4 L. & SOC'Y REV. 29 (1969); Friedman, *On Legal Development*, 24 RUTGERS L. REV. 11 (1969) [hereinafter cited as Friedman]; Könz, *Legal Development in Developing Countries*, 1969 PROCEEDINGS OF THE AM. SOC'Y INT'L L. 91 [hereinafter cited as Könz]; Rosenn, *The Reform of Legal Education in Brazil*, 21 J. LEGAL ED. 251 (1969) [hereinafter cited as Rosenn]; Mendelson, *Law and the Development of Nations*, 32 J. of POL. 223 (1970) [hereinafter cited as Mendelson]; Steinberg, *Law, Development and Korean Society*, 3 J. COMP. AD. 215 (1971) [hereinafter cited as Steinberg]; Steiner, *Legal Education and Socio-Economic Change: Brazilian Perspectives*, 19 AM. J. COMP. L. 39 (1971) [hereinafter cited as Steiner]; D. TRUBEK, LAW, PLANNING, AND THE DEVELOPMENT OF THE BRAZILIAN CAPITAL MARKET (Yale Law School Studies in Law and Modernization No. 3) [reprinted from BULL., Nos. 72 & 73 (N.Y. Univ. Grad. School of Business Admin., April, 1971)] [hereinafter cited as Trubek]; D. TRUBEK, J. GOUVEA VIEIRA & P. SA, O MERCADO DE CAPITAIS E OS INCENTIVOS FISCAIS 23-92 (1971) [hereinafter cited as D. TRUBEK, J. GOUVEA VIEIRA, & P. SA]; Kozolchyk, *Toward a Theory of Law in Economic Development: The Costa Rican USAID—ROCAP Project*, 1971 L. & SOCIAL ORDER 681 [hereinafter cited as Kozolchyk]; Seidman, *Law and Development: A General Model*, 6 L. & SOC'Y REV. 311 (1972) [hereinafter cited as Seidman].

8. In constructing and documenting the core conception, I have relied on my own research and experience, studies by others, and private discussions with my colleagues in law and development. Although I may have omitted some of the subtleties of my colleagues' work, my purpose in constructing the core conception is not to condemn anyone (including myself), but rather to illuminate the dominant and implicit assumptions which have misdirected the study of law and development.

The explication of the core conception is intended to show the need for a basic intellectual shift in law and development study. Gouldner has noted that when the background or domain assumptions of a social theory come to operate in new conditions for which they are inapposite, an uncomfortable dissonance is created for the theorist, and a basic intellectual shift impends. A. GOULDNER, *supra* note 3, at 34.

One can see such dissonance in Steiner. While his piece, *supra* note 7, articulates the "core conception" for regulated market economies, it also includes a perceptive critique of it. The article, as a result, appears at times inconsistent. This comes, I believe, from Steiner's awareness that his ideas on law and development were not fully capable of grasping what he perceived in Brazilian legal life. As a result, the piece manifests a dissonance between the received ideas and perceived reality.

Growing awareness of the gap between conventional notions and Third World legal phenomena has generated dissonance in writers like Steiner; at the same time critical analysis of domain assumptions has heightened the dissatisfaction with core conception ideas. A major critique has been articulated by Duncan Kennedy and Roberto Mangabeira Unger; Unger's unpublished essay "The Place of Law in 'Modern' Society" (undated, on file in the Yale Law Library) [hereinafter cited as Unger] sets forth this critique systematically.

9. The most concise, systematic statement of the elements of "modern" law, one which conforms exactly to this tripartite outline, is in Galanter, *supra* note 7, at 154-56.

process which contains the egoistic tendencies of individuals and controls the conflict of groups. The core conception believes that modern societies achieve order primarily through law, that is, through a system of rules. Since it posits that modern society cannot exist without such rules, the core conception argues that modernization or development necessarily entails the institutionalization of such social control.[10]

The nature of modern law can be seen most clearly when contrasted with the processes of social ordering in traditional societies.[11] There, patterns of conduct are defined and maintained by primary social groups, such as the village, lineage, or tribe. As a result, normative prescription varies with geographic place and social situation: There is a separate "law" for each village or tribe, and the "law" that binds the lord is not the law that binds the serf or burgher. Modern law, on the other hand, consists of general rules applied by specialized agencies universally and uniformly through all regions and to all social strata. Modern law is also relatively autonomous from other sources of normative order. Thus, one unitary and superior social entity—the modern legal system—replaces the village or tribe in social control.

The concept of purposiveness is a third contrast between modern law and traditional social ordering. It is assumed that the prescriptions of traditional society are shaped from history and custom. Modern law, by contrast, is conscious and rational; and since it has been consciously constructed, modern law must necessarily have some self-conscious purpose. But the core conception of purposiveness is broader than that implied by mere conscious design. Modern law is also viewed as an instrument through which a variety of possible social goals may be achieved.[12] Thus, it not only releases man from the grasp of traditional norms and values, it also gives him the means to shape the world in which he lives. The core conception of legal purposiveness is, therefore, highly instrumental: It assumes that social life can be shaped by some social will, for example a modernizing elite, which brings about development through legal enactment and enforcement.

10. *See* Karst, *supra* note 7, at 16-19; Rosenn, *supra* note 7, at 253; Seidman, *supra* note 7, at 311-16.

11. *See* Galanter, *supra* note 7, at 154-56; Rheinstein, *supra* note 7, at 225-28, 242-44; Steinberg, *supra* note 7, at 223-27. *See also* David, *supra* note 7, at 194, 203.

12. Galanter stresses that "the system is rational . . . . Rules are valued for their instrumental utility in producing consciously chosen ends . . . ." Galanter, *supra* note 7, at 155. Friedman observes that legal systems become "modern" only when men perceive law to be an instrument employed "to advance in a rational way toward some knowable goal." Friedman, *supra* note 7, at 30. *See also* David, *supra* note 7, at 194, 203-04; Kozolchyk, *supra* note 7, at 746, 751; Merillat, *supra* note 7, at 73; Seidman, *supra* note 7, *passim;* Steinberg, *supra* note 7, at 216; Trubek, *supra* note 7, at 10.

Purposiveness and rules, though necessary, are not sufficient conditions for a viable system of modern law: Such law can affect social order only if it also has behind it the organized force of the state. The core conception believes that without a strong, relatively centralized state, the rules of law will not shape and determine social life.[13] They will be mere paper artifacts, incapable of restraining conflict or bringing about purposive goals. Just as law needs a strong state to be "effective," so the existence of law enhances the state's power. The state creates the system of rules and the courts and other institutions which make, apply, and enforce the law; the rise of modern law supplants local, "particularistic," and traditional forces, and is thus the vehicle through which the state replaces communal or traditional authority. As national law grants men rights and immunities, they escape from the hold of village and tribe.[14] Similarly, modern law's rationality and universality strengthens the state: By professing to be the manifestation of reason, and treating all men as equals, modern law legitimates the state, and thus enhances its ability to impose specific substantive norms, rules, or purposes.[15]

B. *The Relationship Between Modern Law and Economic Development*

Like a power grid or transportation network, modern law is viewed in the core conception as a functional prerequisite of an industrial economy.[16] While all modern law thinkers share this view, few articulate the relationship between law and economic growth with real clarity. To the extent that such articulation occurs, one can identify different and potentially conflicting tendencies within the core conception.

One explanation stresses the role of law in market economies. This perspective assumes that market institutions are necessary for economic growth, and sees modern law as essential to the creation and

13. *See* p. 7 *infra*.

14. Cohn, *Some Notes on Law and Change in North India*, in LAW & WARFARE 139, 155-59 (P. Bohannan ed. 1967); Friedman, *supra* note 7, at 47-48; Galanter, *supra* note 7, at 162; Rheinstein, *supra* note 7, at 225, 235. *See also* David, *supra* note 7, at 202.

15. C. BLACK, THE DYNAMICS OF MODERNIZATION 14-15 (1966); Braibanti, *The Role of Law In Political Development*, in INTERNATIONAL AND COMPARATIVE LAW OF THE COMMONWEALTH 3 (Wilson ed. 1968); Könz, *supra* note 7, at 91; Mendelson, *supra* note 7, at 224, 229-32; Rheinstein, *supra* note 7, at 225; Seidman, *supra* note 7, at 328-30; Steinberg, *supra* note 7, at 217-18. *See also* Friedman, *supra* note 7, at 48-49, 52-53.

16. David, *supra* note 7, at 188-89; Könz, *supra* note 7, at 98; Mendelson, *supra* note 7, at 232; Merillat, *supra* note 7, at 74; Parsons, *Evolutionary Universals in Society*, 29 AM. SOCIOLOGICAL REV. 339, 350-53 (1964); Rheinstein, *supra* note 7, at 226; Rosenn, *supra* note 7, at 253.

Toward a Social Theory of Law

maintenance of markets.[17] The emphasis here is on modern law's predictability as a set of universal rules uniformly applied. As a result of such predictability, modern law encourages men to engage in new forms of economic activity and guarantees that the fruits of this activity will be protected. Law thus frees the individual from "the prescriptive usage of the particularistic group"[18] and assures the individual that his decisions will be enforced by state authority, his acquisitions protected from the depredations of others.[19] Through institutions such as contract and private property rights, modern law promotes the development of markets and hence economic growth.

The second, and perhaps conflicting, explanation of the relationship between law and growth stresses law's purposiveness and power. In this perspective, development is viewed as a consciously willed transformation of economic activity. The state is seen as the chief vehicle through which this conscious design is articulated and imposed upon the population; modern law is the instrument through which such development goals are translated into specific, enforceable norms.[20] The more effectively these norms define and channel behavior, the more likely economic growth will occur.

Because the core conception holds this view of law, it is concerned with maximizing the "effectiveness" and social "penetration" of modern rules. Penetration and effectiveness are the measure of the state's capacity to exert its power. And legal development is often equated with an increase in the state's power to use law for the realization of its economic goals.[21]

Consequently, some writers argue that research on law and economic development should be directed toward questions which identify those variables in legal culture and organization which increase legal "effectiveness."[22] For some these questions have been answered: What is

17. Karst, *supra* note 7, at 15; Kozolchyk, *supra* note 7, at 737, 739, 741-42; Mendelson, *supra* note 7, at 226-27, 230-31, 232; Rheinstein, *supra* note 7, at 229-30, 232, 238-40, 243, Steiner, *supra* note 7, at 47-48; Trubek, *supra* note 7, at 10.

18. Galanter, *supra* note 7, at 162. *See also* note 14 *supra*.

19. David, *supra* note 7, at 188-89; Karst, *supra* note 7, at 13-16; Rheinstein, *supra* note 7, at 232; Trubek, *supra* note 7, at 54-55. *See also* Mendelson, *supra* note 7, at 226-27, 230-32.

20. David, *supra* note 7, at 203-04; Friedman, *supra* note 7, at 30; Kozolchyk, *supra* note 7, at 746; Rheinstein, *supra* note 7, at 221; Seidman, *supra* note 7, *passim*; Steinberg, *supra* note 7, at 232-33, 245; Trubek, *supra* note 7, at 10.

21. *See* Friedman, *supra* note 7, at 30; Könz, *supra* note 7, at 94-95; *cf.* Kozolchyk, *supra* note 7, at 738, 740-41; Trubek, *supra* note 7, at 54-55. Elsewhere, Friedman also stresses the importance of "penetration" and "effectiveness." He notes that both may be linked as much to "participation" as to increased power. Friedman, *Legal Culture and Social Development*, 4 L. & Soc'y Rev. 29, 44 (1969).

22. Friedman, *supra* note 7, at 58-61; Könz, *supra* note 7, at 95-96; Kozolchyk, *supra* note 7, at 744-45; Seidman, *supra* note 7, *passim*. *See also* Rheinstein, *supra* note 7, *passim*; Trubek, *supra* note 7, at 54-56.

needed is an increase in the instrumental capability of the legal system. The more law becomes a mechanism or an instrument to advance rationally toward specified goals, the more effective it will become. This will be achieved, it is argued, only if the legal culture embraces an instrumental conception of law which fosters the clarification of economic goals and their relationship to the legal system.[23] For those who accept this belief, the problem of legal development is solved: One must merely discover which local changes lead to greater instrumentalism.[24] But as we shall see, this may at times and in certain places prove to be a dangerous formula.

C. *The Relationship Between Modern Law and Political Development*

Modern law is also viewed as an essential element in political development. In the core conception, such development means not only the creation of a strong, central state, but also the construction of a pluralist, liberal-democratic government.[25] Thus, the core conception also sees law as the primary restraint on arbitrary state action. Care is taken to distinguish law from power: One writer equates law with "principled adjudication";[26] others find it essential to political development because it eliminates arbitrary exercises of state power.[27] In this sense, law is not merely a technique of state control to be applied for any purpose; rather, it is seen as *necessarily* committed to specific values, such as even-handedness and fairness.[28] Some writers even identify law with the liberal society and democracy; for them, development of modern law necessarily means the attainment of such liberal goals as wider participation in the formation of social norms and the guarantee of specific individual rights.[29]

23. Kozolchyk, *supra* note 7, at 751; Merillat, *supra* note 7, at 73; Rheinstein, *supra* note 7, at 227-28, 235; Seidman, *supra* note 7, *passim*; Trubek, *supra* note 7, at 9-10, 24-28, 52-53.

24. Freidman, *supra* note 7, *passim*; Kozolchyk, *supra* note 7, at 736, 741-42; Rheinstein, *supra* note 7, at 244; Rosenn, *supra* note 7, at 251-55; Seidman, *supra* note 7, at 331-32.

25. Karst, *supra* note 7, at 16-19; Steinberg, *supra* note 7, at 246-47; Trubek, *supra* note 7, at 9, 53 Könz notes that the adoption of foreign legal models "has introduced democratic concepts which are as valid in Africa and Asia as they are in Western countries." Könz, *supra* note 7, at 95.

26. Karst, *supra* note 7, at 18.

27. *See, e.g.*, A. Rivkin, Nation-Building in Africa; Problems and Prospects 112-30 (1969); Braibanti, *Public Bureaucracy and Judiciary in Pakistan*, in Bureaucracy and Political Development 360-440 (J. LaPalombara ed. 1963); Karst, *supra* note 7, at 18-19; Steinberg, *supra* note 7, at 230-31, 237, 247-49.

28. Kozolchyk, *supra* note 7, at 741-42; Steiner, *supra* note 7, at 48-50, 58.

29. Friedman, *supra* note 7, at 30; Karst, *supra* note 7, at 16-19; Kozolchyk, *supra* note 7, at 746; Rheinstein, *supra* note 7, at 245-46; Steinberg, *supra* note 7, at 236-37, 246-48; Trubek, *supra* note 7, at 9, 53.

Toward a Social Theory of Law

It is apparent that if "law" or "the legal system" is to constrain the state, it must be in some way autonomous.[30] For this reason, the core conception assumes—often implicitly—that an independent judiciary, techniques to curb administrative discretion, constitutionalism, and even judicial review are necessary elements in the development of modern law.[31]

D. *The Program of Legal Development*

There is considerable consensus on the program of "legal development" that follows from the core conception. Since modern law is a process by which rules governing social life are consciously formulated and consistently applied, the basic goal is to ensure that social life is effectively governed by universal and purposive rules. As the core conception views reality, this goal entails many changes in the legal system of Third World nations. First, law already on the books must be perfected. "Modern" substantive rules, such as those guaranteeing freedom of contract and protecting political association must be adopted,[32] if necessary, by importing foreign codes.[33] These rules must be truly universal; residual particularisms must be suppressed; customary and special law must yield to "rationally" enacted modern law.[34] Rules on paper must become rules in fact; impartial application must become a reality.[35] Legislators in more or less representative bodies must learn to formulate rules that are impartial, yet simultaneously achieve priority developmental goals. Lawyers must learn to argue and judges to reason in terms of these rules and the goals which underlie them.

The centrality of legal purposiveness in the core conception's legal development program emphasizes the importance of legal education reform.[36] The core conception finds that the legal systems of the Third

30. A. Rivkin, *supra* note 27, at 112-30; Galanter, *supra* note 7, at 156; Karst, *supra* note 7, at 18-19; Steinberg, *supra* note 7, at 247-49.

31. *See generally* pp. 8-9 *supra* and notes.

32. A. Rivkin, *supra* note 27, at 112-30; Karst, *supra* note 7, at 18-19; Kozolchyk, *supra* note 7, at 739; Mendelson, *supra* note 7, at 227-31; Rheinstein, *supra* note 7, at 226, 232, 236-38 (emancipation of women), 240 (law of inheritance); Steinberg, *supra* note 7, at 246-48; Trubek, *supra* note 7, at 54-55.

33. David, *supra* note 7, *passim*; Könz, *supra* note 7, at 95.

34. David, *supra* note 7, at 194, 203; Friedman, *supra* note 7, at 52-53; Galanter, *supra* note 7, at 158-61; Rheinstein, *supra* note 7, at 226-28, 235; Steinberg, *supra* note 7, at 219-20.

35. Friedman, *supra* note 21, at 29, 43; Trubek, *supra* note 7, at 54.

36. J. Murphy, Legal Education in a Developing Nation: The Korea Experience 54-60 (Korea Law Study Series No. 1, 1967); Allott, *supra* note 7, at 207; Karst, *supra* note 7, at 19-20; Könz, *supra* note 7, at 99-100; Kozolchyk, *supra* note 7, at 751-55; Merillat, *supra* note 7, at 76; Rosenn, *supra* note 7, *passim*; Steinberg, *supra* note 7, at 222, 232-33; Steiner, *supra* note 7, *passim*; Trubek *supra* note 7, at 53; von Mehren, *Law and Legal Education in India: Some Observations*, 78 Harv. L. Rev. 1180 (1965).

World are formalistic and traditional.[37] Lawyers who work in such traditions, it is argued, see law as a body of relatively sacred and immutable principles which are applied to social life through highly formal or ritualistic techniques. The core conception argues that legal development must begin by forcing Third World lawyers to redefine their concepts of law and its social function; once this is accomplished, the correct program of legal development will hopefully become apparent. Thus legal education reform is the wedge leading to reform of the entire legal system. And, given the basic assumptions about the economic and political functions of modern law,[38] the core conception promises that this education-spurred reform will stimulate economic development and political democracy.[39]

II. An Appraisal of the Core Conception

A. *Introduction*

The core conception is able to prescribe positive programs for the legal development of the Third World because it believes it has discovered a key to understanding the relationship between law and development. Since economic and political development are thought to require "modern law," efforts to create a modern legal system will necessarily foster development.

There are two elements to this credo. First, there is the implicit concept of development which equates it with gradual evolution in the direction of the advanced, industrial nations of the West.[40] Second, given its definition of development, the core conception quite predictably equates modern law with the legal structures and cultures of the West.[41] The Third World is thus assumed to be doomed to

37. *E.g.*, Kozolchyk, *supra* note 7, at 746; Merillat, *supra* note 7, at 73; Rosenn, *supra* note 7, at 254-57; Steinberg, *supra* note 7, at 240, 244-45, 249; Steiner, *supra* note 7, at 52-55; von Mehren, *supra* note 36, at 1181-82, 1186-87.

38. *See* pp. 6-9 *supra*.

39. *See, e.g.*, Rosenn, *supra* note 7, at 283; Steiner, *supra* note 7, at 70-82. But Steiner hedges considerably on the promise. Steiner, *supra* note 7, at 86-90.

40. This approach is apparent in Mendelson's statement of a universalistic, three-stage model of development which sees every nation evolving from primitive unification to industrialism to welfare statism. Mendelson, *supra* note 7, at 223. A similar monistic theory permeates the literature: Men abandon the traditional social order, and regroup into centralized nation states. *See* pp. 5-6 and notes 11, 14, 15 *supra*. Economic growth is viewed as based exclusively on the market system, p. 7 and note 17 *supra*. *See* C. Black, *supra* note 15, for an excursion along the path of modernization—and Westernization—in five areas of human existence.

41. The concepts of pluralism, and individual rights against the state, legal autonomy, and the rule of law are Western in origin. Pp. 8-9 and notes 25-31 *supra*. Thus, deviations from Western traditions are viewed skeptically at best: Galanter sees indigenous legal revivalist movements doomed to failure, *supra* note 7, at 163. Steinberg worries about the encroachment of Japanese legal concepts in Korea, *supra* note 7, at 250-52, and Könz about the institution of informal conciliation boards in Ceylon, *supra* note 7, at 97-98.

underdevelopment until it adopts a modern Western legal system.

Because these beliefs are held to be self-evident, the core conception is not timid about prescribing desired legal reform for nations with a diversity of legal and cultural traditions, economic organizations, or political structures. For example, Western European observers will prescribe rigorous codification of civil law for nations as disparate as Ethiopia[42] and Turkey,[43] while Americans will prescribe a more instrumental form of legal education as the true path to development in Brazil,[44] Korea,[45] and India.[46]

Moreover, since the relationships between law and development are thought to be invariable, the core conception is more concerned with the exportation of Western systems than with efforts to understand the legal life of the Third World. Having answered in cursory fashion the major questions about the relationship between law and development, the core conception concerns itself with implementation.

The conception's ideas about the relationship between law and development derive from its interpretation of the fact that the modern legal system, the centralized state, and the industrial economy arose in the West in the same historical period. From this historical observation, the core conception concludes that in some measure legal development caused this associated political and economic transformation. Finally, it believes that this asserted causal relationship will repeat itself in the experience of the Third World.

In this section, these concepts will be analyzed. It will be argued that by fleshing out the core conception's loose imputations of the role for modern law in Western history, its assertion that Western experience is necessarily a guide for the Third World can be refuted.

B. *The Role of Law in the Development of the West: The Work of Max Weber*[47]

The key to this argument is the work of the German sociologist, Max Weber, who attempted to identify and explain systematically the

42. David, *supra* note 7.

43. Lipstein, *Conclusions, Reception of Foreign Law in Turkey*, 9 INT'L SOC. SCI. BULL. 70, 72, 81 (1957). Lipstein concludes that "a Western system of law can be effectively introduced in a country of a different cultural background if the law is codified . . . ." Similarly, Rheinstein suggests that application of the Civil Code requires less of a law library and less time to learn, and is, therefore, more easily extended to Africa than the common law system. He notes that English law was introduced into India and British East Africa in codified form. Rheinstein, *supra* note 7, at 244-45.

44. *See* Rosenn, *supra* note 7; Steiner, *supra* note 7.

45. MURPHY, *supra* note 36, at 54-60; Steinberg, *supra* note 7, at 222.

46. Von Mehren, *supra* note 36. At least one American prescribed the same reform elixir for legal "hypertension" in as developed and Westernized a country as Israel. Laufer, *Legal Education in Israel: A Visitor's View*, 14 BUFF. L. REV. 232 (1964).

47. *See* Trubek, *Max Weber on Law and the Rise of Capitalism*, 1972 WIS. L. REV. 720. *See also* R. BENDIX, MAX WEBER: AN INTELLECTUAL PORTRAIT 385-457 (1962).

role of the modern legal system in the emergence of Western civilization.[48] Weber's explanation went beyond the observation that legal "development" occurred simultaneously with the political and economic transformations that led to the industrial system and the centralized nation-state. Rather, he showed with precision that these changes were mutually causative, supporting his historical conclusions with an analytic explanation of the kind lacking in the core conception.

Weber's major intellectual concern was explaining the rise of capitalism and industrial civilization: Why, he asked, had they first developed in Europe? European law offered a partial explanation. As he believed European law had special characteristics which were conducive to capitalism, Weber had to demonstrate the uniqueness of the legal order of the West.

His research led him to three basic conclusions. First, that the more "rational" a legal system was, the more conducive it would be to the emergence of a capitalist, industrial system. Second, that European legal systems were more rational than those which had emerged in other civilizations. Finally, that this legal rationalism existed in large measure in Europe *before* the full development of the industrial economic system. From these observations Weber concluded that Europe's legal system was one of the factors responsible for the rise of capitalism.

Weber's concept of legal rationality is composed of three sub-variables: autonomy, conscious design, and universality. In Weber's schema, a legal system is said to be rational to the extent that: (i) it is autonomous from other spheres of society; (ii) the norms it formulates and enforces are consciously wrought; and (iii) those norms are consistently applied to all similar cases. Weber noted that in some systems norms are not consciously wrought but rather originate from immutable tradition or the commands of an extraordinary, charismatic leader. Similarly, he found that norms may not be applied by specialized professionals, but rather enforced by religious, political or other elites. Finally, in some systems decisions are not subsumed under general rules or related to prior precedents, but rather are made on an ad-hoc basis.

Weber argued that the European system, on the other hand, combined the three essential elements of legal rationality. As a result, it,

48. Weber's most significant attempt to deal with the interrelationships between law and what we call today "development" or "modernization" is contained in his outline of interpretative sociology, WIRTSCHAFT UND GESELLSCHAFT. GRUNDRISS DER VERSTEHENDEN SOZIOLOGIE (4th ed. J. Winckelmann ed. 1956). In this discussion I have relied primarily on the recent English edition of the complete work, M. WEBER, ECONOMY AND SOCIETY (Roth and Wittich eds. 1968) [hereinafter cited as ECONOMY AND SOCIETY].

Toward a Social Theory of Law

and it alone, developed a type of legal thought termed "logically formal rationality"—the decisive indication, for Weber, of a modern system. A "rational" system, therefore, relies on pre-existing rules to resolve social conflict and guarantees that these rules will be (i) elaborated by a specialized profession, using distinctive modes of thought, (ii) consistent with one another, (iii) universal, and (iv) precise. Although the source of these rules is total social life, the system that elaborates and applies them is differentiated from other forms of normative ordering or social control. Its rules are formulated independently of religious or narrowly political considerations. Thus, Weber's model of a "rational" system is, in large measure, the same one set forth by the core conception as "modern law."[49]

But while he employed a concept of modern law similar to that of the core conception, Weber carried his analysis of the developmental significance of law much further. In contrast to contemporary analysts, he explained why a rational legal system fostered economic development and a centralized state. In so doing, he made precise the conditions under which "modern law" causes economic and political change.

In his economic sociology, Weber stressed two important relationships between "rational" law and economic development. He found that this type of normative system had formal and substantive characteristics which were essential in the industrial system which emerged in the West. A rational legal system was highly predictable; only such a normative order could generate certain substantive provisions necessary to the industrialized system. These characteristics were essential to the operation of a free market economy. Such markets could not operate if men were subject to traditional prescription; yet they required some normative structure to constrain egoistic tendencies. The system had to be authoritative, that is, capable of effectively constraining behavior which conflicts with its prescriptions. Yet given the nature of economic decision-making in a market system, it also had to be predictable: When one must make rapid decisions based on forecasts of another's behavior, it is essential that he know which norms constrain others and that those norms will be enforced.

Although his explanation stressed formal characteristics—particu-

49. I believe that most American readers of Weber have been misled by his stress on "legal thought" as an index of legal modernity, and his interpretation of continental legal science as the acme of rational legal thought. They are naturally unwilling to accept his judgment that the common law tradition is an inferior form of "modern law"; indeed, they consider the common law legal process more rational. By focusing on the difference between these ideological pictures of the two legal worlds, they have failed to see that *functionally* the Weberian model and the American or modern law model are similar in many respects.

larly formal predictability—Weber was also concerned with the generation of substantive rules and principles. Chief among these was the complex of rules that allowed freedom of contract and guaranteed the enforcement of individually bargained agreements.

The only system of normative ordering that could meet these formal and substantive requirements was rational law. Only an autonomous, consciously designed set of universal rules could be (i) precise enough to be integrated into economic decision-making, (ii) applied with sufficient consistency to be predictable, and (iii) legitimate enough to be authoritative. Furthermore, in his political sociology Weber explained the political conditions under which such a normative system could emerge: a centralized, bureaucratic state which secured men's loyalties through a claim that its decisions were rational.

Weber identified three "ideal types"[50] of political systems (forms of domination). He classified them according to their basic claim to legitimacy: traditional, charismatic, and legal. According to this trichotomy, members of a social organization will view societal commands as legitimate because they are issued in accordance with immutable custom, are decreed by an individual with extraordinary or exemplary characteristics, or rest on rational, legal enactment. Since legal decisions are part of the total structure of domination, they, like all actions of the rulers, must be legitimized by making some basic claim to men's loyalties.

As a result, the structure of domination and the legal system are mutually determinative: Traditional regimes apply norms thought to be immutable and sacred; charismatic systems claim that their norms are derived from the inspired, exemplary leader. Such ties make it impossible to develop legal structures that meet Weber's criteria of rationality. The very concepts of tradition and charisma are inconsistent with the idea of consciously wrought norms. Moreover, traditional and charismatic regimes have an inherent need to make ad hoc, particularistic decisions and promote specific programs; as a result, they cannot tolerate legal autonomy and are hostile to any insistence on universality.

This is not, however, the case with rational or legal domination. This type of regime finds its legitimacy in its capacity to create and

50. The term "ideal-type" is an intellectual construct employed in the social sciences. It does not denote a normatively desirable situation. Rather, such a concept is "ideal" because it represents an abstraction of certain salient features of social life the scientist wishes to explore. In Weber's work, ideal type was meant to denote a value-neutral scientific instrument. *See* R. ARON, 2 MAIN CURRENTS IN SOCIOLOGICAL THOUGHT 201-04, 205 (1967).

Toward a Social Theory of Law

maintain universal rules governing social life. Legal domination leads to the modern bureaucratic state which, far from being hostile to formal rationality, actively requires and encourages it. For these reasons, Weber concluded that the truly bureaucratic state could emerge only in Europe where all the prerequisites for rational law existed. Similarly, he argued that only under such a bureaucratic state could these elements develop into the final model of European law. Thus, Weber answered his original question about the causal relationship between law and capitalism. Rational law fostered the competitive market system; the rise of the market in turn encouraged further rationalization of the law, a rationalization which made possible the development of the centralized nation-state.

Weber's analysis cannot, of course, be accepted as established historical fact. While he adduced substantial evidence to support his thesis, he himself qualified his conclusions and admitted that there was at least one case which it did not explain.[51] Nevertheless, until refuted, his explanation stands as the most convincing and coherent analysis of the causal relationship between law and development in the West.

The nature of Weber's explanation helps to identify a major flaw in the core conception's reasoning—its contention that legal development will in some way cause political and economic development. Modern law thinkers frequently invoke Weber, arguing that his analysis supports their conclusions.[52] Yet in fact just the opposite is true; rather than supporting the core conception, the Weberian thesis suggests that it is, at best, without rationai foundation, and, at worst, simply wrong.

Weber's analysis shows that law's relation to development is actually determined by two intervening variables: Modern law does not *produce* economic development; it merely helps structure the free market system. Moreover, modern law does not bring about political development; it merely supports the centralized bureaucratic state which depends for its legitimacy on a belief that its decisions are rational. To the extent, therefore, that economic development in the Third World is not based on free markets Weber's work cannot support any inference that modern law as defined by the core conception

51. That case was England, which was the first nation to develop capitalism, yet which never achieved what Weber would consider true "logically formal rationality." For more complete discussions of Weber's "England Problem" see Trubek, *supra* note 47, at 746-48, and J. Guben, "The England Problem" and the Theory of Economic Development (unpublished Yale Law School Program in Law and Modernization Working Paper No. 9, 1972).

52. *See, e.g.*, Friedman, *supra* note 7, at 29, 50, 51; Kozolchyk, *supra* note 7, at 742-43 n.204; Steinberg, *supra* note 7, at 216.

will cause or contribute to economic development.[53] And to the extent that Third World nations do not seek legitimacy through adherence to the rule of law, there is no assurance that strengthening the legal system will enhance the efficacy of the regime.

Thus, if we accept Weber's explanation of the relationship between formal rationality and European industrialization, we must conclude that the core conception is on very weak grounds. We know that few Third World nations have developed competitive markets, and none have primarily market-oriented or laissez-faire economic policies. If modern law contributes to economic growth only under these conditions, as Weber suggests, the core conception's assumption that Western history will repeat itself is probably wrong. Similarly, we know that Third World regimes are legitimated by many things, but that their adherence to the rule of law is not first among them. Thus, a conclusion that enhancing the effectiveness of the legal system as a restraint on the state will enhance the effective power of Third World leaders (as Weber argued it strengthened the European nation-state) is also rather dubious.

C. *Ethnocentricity and Evolutionism: Dangers and Dilemmas of the Core Conception*

The core conception is clearly ethnocentric in interpreting diverse cultures in terms of Western history. It is evolutionist in viewing history as a series of identical stages repeated in all societies. As a result of these implicit assumptions, the conception cannot deal effectively with the realities of legal life in the Third World. This section identifies some of its errors and inconsistencies, and in so doing, casts further light on both the origins and limitations of the core conception.

1. *The Conflict Between Evolutionism and Reformism*

There is a clear conflict between the core conception's evolutionism and its commitment to legal reform, a conflict which reveals a great deal about the motivations behind the core conception.

History, in the core conception, tends toward a knowable result in uniform stages. Societies are classified as traditional or modern, under-

53. Some writers have defined "modern law" in such sweeping terms that this analysis is inapposite. For example, though he seems at times aware that law is separate and distinct from the state, Friedman defines law as any public process within society. Friedman, *supra* note 7, at 15. Thus if state action can contribute to economic growth, so will "modern law."

developed or developed, static or dynamic,[54] and are viewed as integrated systems in which sub-systems have related characteristics. A "traditional society" will have a "traditional" legal system; "modern" societies have modern law.[55] Change is seen as an organic process: Like the life cycle of the butterfly, "development" proceeds through highly distinct stages to a defined end.[56]

This type of determinism assumes that law merely results from and reflects social and economic phenomena.[57] The core conception cannot accept such a view of the origins of legal development. Rather, it must see legal change as possible without, and as potentially capable of causing, social change. Modern law thought goes to great lengths to make legal development a very problematic matter: Nascent legalism in the Third World is perceived as a very fragile flower requiring hothouse care.

Thus, a paradox is created. While modern law thinking argues that the rest of the world *will* repeat the Western experience of simultaneous legal and socioeconomic development, it also presupposes that legal development is *not* guaranteed and that strenuous efforts must therefore be made to ensure that modern law is adopted.

If one's primary commitment were to the view that economic, social and political change does not necessarily lead to modern law and that conscious legal development is needed if the Third World is to follow the West, one might quite logically abandon the whole structure of evolutionary thought.[58] In such a conception, "modern law" would be seen not as a necessary prerequisite to change in other spheres, nor even as the inevitable result of such change, but as merely something that is *possible* under certain historical conditions.[59] But while the

54. *See* C. Black, *supra* note 15; Friedman, *supra* note 7, at 30; Mendelson, *supra* note 7, *passim*; *cf*. p. 10 and note 40.

55. *See* Galanter, *supra* note 7, *passim*; Rheinstein, *supra* note 7, at 222-26. Steinberg seems to accept this view, but notes that colonial administrations may have led to a law "out of phase" with the indigenous culture. Steinberg, *supra* note 7, at 216-19.

56. On the use of organic metaphors in social theory, see R. Nisbet, Social Change and History (1969).

57. Thus it resembles a model of development with unlimited supplies of law. *See* note 5 *supra*.

58. That is, one might see society as made up of relatively distinct spheres which are only related to one another in a very loose fashion. This would mean abandoning the idea that there are parallel stages of development of all aspects of society, and the assumption that there are strong forces of social integration that tend to bind separate spheres together.

59. This approach to law-society relationships would entail a number of intellectual shifts and solve certain problems of the core conception. For example, it would better explain how societies can—as they clearly do—go through periods of rapid economic development without a corresponding spurt of "legal development." Moreover, this approach and the abandonment of evolutionary determinism would bring to the surface the fact that the commitment to "modern law," and its export to the Third World, involves a distinct set of value choices. This, in turn, might focus scholarly attention on the nature and implications of these values.

determinism of the evolutionary scheme conflicts with the strongly-held faith in reformist intervention, the core conception adheres to both. It attempts to solve this inherent conflict by positing the possibility of "lags" or "barriers" to "legal development" which, it is asserted, can retard evolutionary change yet be overcome by vigorous reformism.[60] Thus, the modern law thinker can observe that the legal code of country X has "failed to keep up" with economic and social changes, that its lawyers employ "outmoded" ideas about the law, or that its legal education is "antiquated."[61] The idea of lags and barriers maintains the need for conscious efforts to identify and "overcome" them. Yet at the same time these concepts assume that there is some "normal" process of change that is being frustrated.

One reason that modern law thinking clings to both evolutionism and reformism is the utility these perceptions have in justifying the role of the foreigner prescribing law reform measures. Such a reformer, writing a code for a developing nation or advising it on how to reform its legal education, must argue that legal development is problematic—otherwise he has no role. Yet he must also retain evolutionism, as it serves two key functions. First, it tends to remove any suggestion that there are normative questions at stake: Modern law is merely the unfolding of history. Second, the evolutionary concept means that the foreigner from a "developed," "modern" nation has a special expertise to offer the "traditional," "underdeveloped" one: He has seen the future and he knows how it works. Thus, he is indispensable to legal development.

From this perspective, it is possible to understand why modern law thought contains apparently contradictory strands. To legitimize foreign involvement in the legal life of the Third World, it must be simultaneously reformist and evolutionary, voluntaristic and deterministic.

2. *An Instance of Ethnocentricity: Legal Instrumentalism versus the Democratic State*

Evolutionism obscures the normative choices necessarily involved in legal development programs. Yet ethnocentricity may increase the difficulty of designing projects which foster consciously held values. Because the modern law thinker's vision is clouded with concepts from

60. *See, e.g.*, David, *supra* note 7, at 194, 203-04; Kozolchyk, *supra* note 7, at 751; Steinberg, *supra* note 7, at 25-52; Könz, *supra* note 7, at 97, 98; Trubek, *supra* note 7, at 24-28, 52-53.

61. David, *supra* note 7, at 203; Karst, *supra* note 7, at 19-20; Könz, *supra* note 7, at 99; Kozolchyk, *supra* note 7, at 746; Rheinstein, *supra* note 7, at 226; Rosenn, *supra* note 7, at 254-55; Steinberg, *supra* note 7, at 245; Steiner, *supra* note 7, at 70-72.

his own society on the nature of law and its functions, he may actually propose measures counterproductive in the societies of others.

Consider the case of education projects designed to foster purposeful legal thought. American scholars, government agencies, and private foundations promoting such efforts assume that they will strengthen the "rule of Law" and foster democratic values.[62] The core conception refuses to recognize any other possibility and assumes that the resulting shift from a traditional concept of law to an instrumental one will simultaneously increase the state's capacity to guide social behavior and the legal system's capacity to restrain arbitrary executive action.[63] Thus, the core conception argues that measures to increase legal purposiveness will both foster legal autonomy and strengthen liberal and democratic tendencies.[64]

Increasing instrumentalism may, in fact, have quite the opposite effect. Efforts to render legal thinking more instrumental may make the legal order increasingly dependent on state apparatus,[65] and when authoritarian groups seize control of that apparatus, such dependence will strengthen their position.[66] This will occur when instrumentalism erodes the legitimacy of autonomous legal thought, and thus denies judges and lawyers any valid premise for decision-making other than that of implementing state policy. Instrumental thought is a technique of selecting appropriate means for given ends.[67] Thus it is a tool, a means by which specific goals are achieved. But under authoritarian conditions it may be a tool which is dependent in the final analysis on the goals supplied by the state. Since it cannot supply its own goals, increasing instrumentalism in legal thought decreases legal autonomy. As the core conception makes clear, it is the very nature of "modern society" that non-state sources of norms and values are weakened. This tendency can become especially acute in developing nations, where pressures for rapid growth enhance the dominance of the state.

62. This core concept is often hidden from public and published view. *But see* D. TRUBEK, J. GOUVEA VIEIRA & P. SA, *supra* note 7, at 80; Murphy, *supra* note 36, at 57-58; Rosenn, *supra* note 7, at 283; Steiner, *supra* note 7, at 70-82.

63. *See* A. RIVKIN, *supra* note 27; Karst, *supra* note 7, at 18-19; Steinberg, *supra* note 7, at 247-48.

64. *See* Karst, *supra* note 7, at 15-19; Steinberg, *supra* note 7, at 247-48.

65. *See* Unger, *supra* note 8, at sec. 3.51.

66. *See* F. NEUMANN, *The Change in the Function of Law in Modern Society*, in THE DEMOCRATIC AND THE AUTHORITARIAN STATE 22 (1957). Critics of legal positivism have long stressed the debilitating effects which this school's view of law has on the lawyer's ability to resist the inroads of authoritarian and undemocratic forces which have gained control of the instruments of the state. *See* L. FULLER, THE LAW IN QUEST OF ITSELF 120-25 (1940); *see also* Auerbach, *Legal Tasks for the Sociologist*, in LAW AND THE BEHAVIORAL SCIENCES 18, 19-20 (L. Friedman & S. Macaulay eds. 1969).

67. *See* 1 ECONOMY AND SOCIETY, at 24, 26, 30.

The Yale Law Journal Vol. 82: 1, 1972

Consequently, purposeful legal thought must confront a dilemma which may ultimately destroy its claim to autonomy: If the state is the only valid source of essential goals, legal thought can find no basis for resistance to the state. Shorn of any transcendent premises on which to base its reasoning, the legal system becomes a mere instrument of state power.

Although some European scholars were acutely aware of this problem,[68] contemporary modern law literature has only begun to recognize the possible conflict between legal autonomy and instrumentalism.[69] The core conception's failure to realize fully this potential conflict is further proof of its ethnocentricity. The assumption that instrumentalism is necessary for the effective operation of an autonomous legal system is simply a generalization from American conditions, resting on the fact that American legal thought assumes the existence of a pluralist political system.[70] In American pluralist theory, "the state" is not viewed as an entity distinct, and hierarchically superior to, social life, but rather as a system or process which organizes and guides an ongoing struggle between competing and conflicting groups. "Government," in this view, is both the structure that maintains pluralist competition and the policy output that results from it.[71]

In a pluralist society, "law" can be seen in large measure as the result of this competitive process.[72] The political process resolves (or avoids) potential group conflict, and law is its final and authoritative settlement. It is, in this sense, a contractual manifestation of the compromise of competing forces. Furthermore, in a pluralist society, law is also the set of rules, primarily constitutional, which structure this process of group formation and competition. But pluralism will work only if all legitimate groups have an opportunity to be heard; indeed,

68. Commenting on the decline of natural law and the rise of a view of law as a technical instrument, Weber observed:

> This extinction of the metajuristic implications of the law is one of those ideological developments which, while they have increased scepticism towards the dignity of the particular rules of a concrete legal order, have also effectively promoted the actual obedience to the power, now viewed solely from an instrumentalist standpoint, of the authorities who claim legitimacy at the moment. Among the practitioners of the law this attitude has been particularly pronounced.

2 ECONOMY & SOCIETY, *supra* note 48, at 875. *See also* F. NEUMANN, *supra* note 66.

69. *See* Unger, *supra* note 65. *See also* Steiner, *supra* note 7, at 50.

70. This point was suggested to me by Lawrence Friedman.

71. *See* Deutsch, *Neutrality, Legitimacy and the Supreme Court: Some Intersections between Law and Political Science*, 20 STAN. L. REV. 169, 250-57 (1968).

72. I have in mind here primarily statutory law. The relationship between judge-made law and pluralism is somewhat more complex. A substantial amount of our constitutional law theory, for example, recognizes that our commitment to pluralism and our commitment to a creative role for the judiciary may be in conflict. *See, e.g.*, Clark & Trubek, *The Creative Role of the Judge: Restraint and Freedom in the Common Law Tradition*, 71 YALE L.J. 255 (1961); Deutsch, *supra* note 71.

much of constitutional law is aimed at guaranteeing that groups can be organized, that their views will be recognized and occasionally adopted, and that the compromises reached will be accepted as legitimate.

To the extent that law is viewed as the result of this competitive process of pluralistic interaction, instrumental legal thought becomes not an enemy of democratic values and individual liberty, but rather a necessary way to maintain them. Under the conditions posited by pluralist theory, instrumental legal thought does not expand the power of the "state"; to the contrary, it serves to keep government from exceeding the bounds established by pluralism. To the extent that the only valid goals are those which arise out of, or preserve the pluralist process, instrumentalism limits the government to those measures which further the compromises struck in the legislative arena. Since there is no other value to override such goals, lawyers are properly trained to identify them clearly and to relate them to specific measures. In so doing, they serve to preserve the pluralist system. There is thus no conflict between instrumentalism and democracy.

However, where political pluralism is not institutionalized, the effect of instrumentalism is very different. Indeed, in the absence of pluralism, legal thought relying on formalistic or traditional arguments may be a more effective way to resist authoritarian measures. The core conception with its implicit pluralism is unable to deal with non-pluralist situations—situations which are, of course, the norm, not the exception, in the Third World.

III. Towards a New Intellectual Perspective: The Challenge and Future of Research on Law and Modernization

A. *The Challenge: Learning from the Core Conception*

While the core conception has failed to yield a satisfactory social theory of law, we can learn from it. After all, "law and development" might have been defined merely as the exportation of legal systems or as country-specific social engineering: The core conception at least attempts to formulate valid generalizations about the relationships between law and the major economic, social, and political transformations associated with industrialization. Moreover, it has approached this task through an attempt to delineate key variables and define their relationships. Accordingly, when it posits a distinction between "modern" and "traditional" legal systems, and explains these variations in terms of the level or stage of social development, the core conception articulates a crude social theory. Although we may question the ethnocentric model employed, and the objectivity of its observation of alleged differences, some form of general classification and some type of explanation of observed differences are essential to any genuine social theory of law.

Moreover, the core conception does articulate certain theoretical generalizations that are beyond question. Most Third World nations are committed to some form of industrialization; and there are undoubtedly universals which will lead to some convergence with industrialized Western societies. Similarly, when modern law thinkers assert that in the transition from traditional to industrial society governmental processes become more purposive and rational, few would take issue.

Unfortunately, these conclusions are so broad that they have little analytic or practical utility. If we wish to develop more precise and concrete ideas about law and development, we must go beyond the core conception. Since its evolutionism contains no coherent idea about the causal relationships between legal and social phenomena, modern law thought is never clear which factor causes the other. The core conception circumvents analysis of the co-variation between legal and other variables and discourages causal enquiry.

B. *Beyond the Core Conception: Learning from Weber*

What is needed, then, is an intellectual perspective which will transcend these limits, a paradigm for future work. This must be a social theory capable of formulating and verifying propositions about the relationship between legal and social variables. It should start from the assumption that there are systematic and universal relations between such variables and address itself to the task of uncovering them. So the question becomes: How may law and development be studied in a more systematic way? To answer, we must examine several possible criteria and suggest strategies for movement to a more scientific approach.

First, it is rather clear that the phenomena with which we are concerned cannot be studied experimentally. We obviously cannot manipulate the behavior of nations in order to determine the interaction of social change and law. We can, however, employ a methodology of comparative research to isolate the underlying relationships between

Toward a Social Theory of Law

legal and social variables.[73] This is, of course, the method Weber employed. His ideal types both define key variables and indicate relationships among them. His typology of law permitted him to differentiate among different legal systems in terms of relative rationality. The ideal types of legal domination and the market economy simultaneously identify important political and economic variables and posit causal relationships between them and the legal order.[74]

Having hypothesized these relationships, Weber conducted comparative studies to prove, for example, that only societies with rational law had bureaucratic staffs, that no society with a traditional or patrimonial form of domination developed rational law, or that no society lacking rational law developed an industrial economy. Such historical evidence that certain variables always occurred together, or never appeared simultaneously, supported his conclusions on causation.[75]

While many of Weber's conceptions and propositions are questionable in light of current knowledge, his approach can be a guide for our own efforts.[76] At its most ambitious, our program should be guided by the following criteria. First, in order to analyze the relationships between law and other variables, we must separate "legal" phenomena from key social variables which interact with them. With these key variables in mind, we must construct ideal types. Further, if comparative study is to determine the relationship between variables, they must be so defined to be both comparable and operational. Thus, legal and social variables should be set forth in terms which guarantee that similar things are observed in all societies and that discrete states or quantities of the variables can be observed and measured. Finally, it must be possible to go beyond the establishment of mere correlations to true causal analysis. That is, it must be possible to posit the dependent and independent variables in our theory of law and development.

The remainder of the essay is primarily concerned with the first of these criteria, developing a set of ideal types which identify relation-

73. *See, e.g.*, COMPARATIVE METHODS IN SOCIOLOGY: ESSAYS ON TRENDS AND APPLICATIONS (I. Vallier ed. 1971). This volume includes a comprehensive bibliography on comparative studies.

74. Weber's typology of domination, for example, identifies as key variables the degree of legal rationality, the nature of the regime's claim to legitimacy, and the type of administrative staff associated with the ruler. *See* Trubek, *supra* note 47.

75. While sociologists may recognize that this is a controversial interpretation of Weber's methodology, the text follows substantially the interpretation of Weber in R. Warner, The Methodology of Max Weber's Comparative Studies (unpublished 1972 Ph.D. dissertation on file with the *Yale Law Journal*). *But see* W. RUNCIMAN, A CRITIQUE OF MAX WEBER'S PHILOSOPHY OF THE SOCIAL SCIENCES (1972).

76. Unlike modern law thought, Weber dissected society into component spheres, positing mutual interactions among the spheres of law, polity, social structure, and economy. This scheme enabled him to identify causal relationships with greater specificity than the core conception's two-variable system allows.

ships between legal and other variables in contemporary modernization. In this analysis, I have attempted to provide a preliminary typology of two key sub-systems of any modernizing state, the economy and polity. Their variables are then related to differences in legal structures. Such analysis and concept formulation is a necessary precursor to, but not a substitute for, the future formulation and verification of precise propositions through comparative and empirical research.

The study of law and development is far from producing any systematic theory. The necessary comparative studies must await the accumulation of much more data about legal life in the Third World. The ideal types set forth in the remainder of this essay are meant to help shape such efforts.

IV. Economic Organization and Legal Structure: Market vs. Command

What is the relationship between law and the economy in the Third World? To answer, we need a broader perspective than has been heretofore offered. Most analysis of law and development, from Weber to the core conception, stresses the contrast between traditional and industrial economies, but obscures the fact that the traditional economy is largely a thing of the past. All nations now aspire to increase their level of economic well-being through industrialization. What is more crucial today is that there are many roads to such development, and a society can adopt very different means for its industrial drive. This choice, in turn, will significantly affect the structure and function of the nation's legal system.

Thus, the social theory of law must differentiate between economic structures. To do so, we begin with a crude typology which identifies two radically different approaches to the relationships between state and economic activity. These types are called "market" and "command."[77] To the extent that production priorities are set by autonomous entities based on prices established through exchange, the economic organization is termed "market." To the extent that such decisions are made by the state, it is called "command."[78]

77. The following discussion is based on a number of sources. I found COMPARATIVE ECONOMIC SYSTEMS (M. Bornstein ed. rev. ed. 1969) and F. KNIGHT, THE ECONOMIC ORGANIZATION (1934) especially useful.

78. The theoretical distinction between "command" and "market" and their related legal phenomena are ideal types used to analyze empirical reality, rather than depict it. In the capitalist world, while markets play a major role, the pure "market" structure of

Toward a Social Theory of Law

In the pure market system, the economy is clearly separated from the polity. The economic system is perceived as a self-contained sub-system capable of functioning with only the most minimal state intervention. Economic activity is managed by independent units responding to the signals of impersonal markets. The market is theoretically capable of deciding all questions about production and allocation; since consumer decisions determine ultimate production, the system functions to give people "what they want." While the state may provide some services like defense and education which the market either cannot provide or provides inefficiently, all other economic decisions are left to autonomous, presumably private, bodies.[79]

In the command economy, there is no such division between state and economy. In the extreme, the economy completely merges with the state; in other command systems, the market is retained but merely as an instrument of economic policy or measuring rod of desirable state action. What really distinguishes command from market is that in the command economy state decisions are the ultimate arbiters of economic activity, *i.e.*, all matters of production, allocation and distribution.

A. *"Law" in a Pure Market System: Voluntary Commitment*

Since the pure market system eschews any role for the state in economic life, it is not immediately apparent why law should have any economic function at all. Of course, public law is necessary to define the limits of state action. But the economic role of private law, that is, the rules which govern relations between individual market actors, is far from clear. Yet the rules of contract, tort, and property do constrain (at least in part) the decisions of economic actors. How is this

competitive, laissez-faire capitalism has been replaced by economies wherein large, often oligopolistic industries predominate, and government regulation of industry is the rule and not the exception. *See, e.g.*, P. SAMUELSON, ECONOMICS 487-89, 500-07, 140-41 (8th ed. 1970). In the socialist world, the model of a command economy has had a strong impact. *See generally* COMPARATIVE ECONOMIC SYSTEMS, *supra* note 77. Yet some socialist systems consciously use market structures to achieve certain economic results. *See* Bicanic, *Economics of Socialism in a Developed Country*, *id.* at 222-35; Dirlam, *Problems of Market Power and Public Policy in Yugoslavia*, *id.* at 236-51; Lange, *On the Economic Theory of Socialism*, *id.* at 68-76; Montias, *East European Economic Reforms*, *id.* at 324-36. In the Third World, the idea of economic planning and regulation has spread to even the most market-oriented governments. *See, e.g.*, G. MYRDAL, AN APPROACH TO THE ASIAN DRAMA (1970) especially ch. 15. While a more sophisticated typology than the market-command is clearly desirable, the dualistic typology is better than none at all. Yet we must always be cautious in employing such primitive tools; one of the greatest dangers is the tendency to think that our two types encompass all possible relations being charted here, state and economy. No such claim is being made for the two types employed.

79. In the pure market system, state economic activity, such as anti-trust law, may affect the market, but only to maintain its structure and smooth functioning.

consistent with a market theory which stresses the necessary autonomy of such decisions?

The answer lies in an inherent conflict within the market, a conflict which law alone can resolve. In the pure market system economic actors or units strive to increase *their own resources* under the principle of profit maximization. While increasing profit may result from a net increase in *total resources*, competition also involves a struggle in which each unit seeks to gain at the expense of others. Yet the competing units are simultaneously dependent on one another: Given the division of labor and other complexities of modern economies, the greatest possibilities for economic gain lie in each unit's ability to secure the cooperation of others. For example, unless the unit that controls steel producing equipment can secure the cooperation of those who control iron ore and coal (not to mention those who "control" labor power), no amount of self-seeking activity will avail them in their search for profits.

The instrument that initially resolves this conflict is exchange through markets.[80] But while the initial act of exchange may resolve primary conflict, the matter does not end there. Exchange, rarely instantaneous, often involves promises of future transfers. Thus, each unit's control of resources depends in large measure on the *future behavior of other actors.* The unit's effective control derives from its ability to predict that in specific situations others will act, or refrain from acting, in certain ways.[81]

A fundamental tension thus emerges between the dynamic of profit maximization and the connection of control with predictability. To the extent that each actor seeks to maximize his own position, it makes no sense to honor yesterday's commitment if more is to be gained by repudiating it and assuming another.[82] Yet each autonomous actor needs the assurance of others that *they* will not break *their* commitments, for if past promises yield to present possibilities, the system will be destroyed.

In the pure market model, legal coercion is the only form of social control that can resolve this conflict. Market actors are presumed to

80. "Rationally-oriented exchange is the resolution of a previously open or latent conflict of interests by means of a compromise." 1 ECONOMY AND SOCIETY, *supra* note 48, at 72.

81. *See id.* at 67-68. "Economic action," as Weber defines it, requires that actors have the power of control and disposal over economic resources. In a "modern private enterprise economy" this is achieved through "legal protection of such powers held by autonomous and autocephalous economic units." *Id.* at 67.

82. As Lon Fuller has put it, "Before the principle of marginal utility nothing is sacred; all existing arrangements are subject to being reordered in the interest of increased economic return." L. FULLER, THE MORALITY OF LAW 28 (1964).

be self-interested maximizers, indifferent to either traditional or ethical constraints. Some system which can exercise coercion is essential to them to keep from furthering their self-interest at the cost of others.[83] The argument that this coercion must be applied by the state is based on historical observation. While it may be possible to structure coercion in other ways, this has, by and large, not occurred. In part, this is due to the success of the market itself, which erodes many of the traditional foci of authority which might have substituted for the state.[84] It is also related to the development of the state, which has, for obvious reasons, attempted to monopolize the use of force. As a result, market societies tend to lack sources of coercion outside the state, and the pure market model must, accordingly, rely on state coercion through private law as its chief instrument of social control.

A second justification for legal coercion results from the pace of economic activity and the rational calculations characteristic of a market economy. It is not enough for the capitalist to have a general idea that someone will probably deliver more or less the amount of a good purchased on or about the time stipulated. He must know that specific performance will be forthcoming. But given the potential conflict between self-interest and obligation, this means that the businessman must know that coercion will be applied to the recalcitrant, and that potential contract violators, trespassers, or tort-feasors are similarly aware that such behavior will be held liable.

But it is not enough for the state to provide a coercive framework for economic activity. Given the need for predictability, the state itself must act in a calculable way. State coercion must be "legal," that is, based on general *rules* uniformly applied. For this reason the legal system of a pure market system must be autonomous from the state. To the extent that the legal system is kept free of intermittant political influences, its results will be highly predictable; but when it is

83. This sociological analysis of market behavior in terms of the inevitability of conflicts between self-seeking individuals in market societies, and the need for coercion in market relations, is drawn from Weber and Parsons. *See* 1 ECONOMY AND SOCIETY, *supra* note 48, at 3-62; T. PARSONS, THE STRUCTURE OF SOCIAL ACTION 89 (1968); Parsons, *et al.*, *Some Fundamental Categories of The Theory of Action: A General Statement*, in TOWARD A GENERAL THEORY OF ACTION (T. Parsons & E. Shils eds. 1967); Trubek, *supra* note 47. Some contemporary lawyers and economists have assumed that there are no necessary conflicts in market relationships, except those caused by "transaction costs." *See* Calabresi, *Transaction Costs; Resource Allocation and Liability Rules*, J. LAW & ECON. 67 (1968); Coase, *The Problem of Social Cost*, 3 J. LAW & ECON. 1 (1960). While it would be ideal to merge these sociological and economic perspectives into one systematic view on the law's role in economic behavior, it seems advisable at this stage for each approach to develop along its own lines, bearing in mind the contributions of complementary fields. *Cf.* N. SMELSER, ESSAYS IN SOCIOLOGICAL EXPLANATION 3-44 (1968).

84. 2 ECONOMY AND SOCIETY, *supra* note 48, at 635-40.

subject to interference by those who seek to apply coercion for purposes inconsistent with the rules, it loses its predictability.[85]

This autonomous legal system will have characteristic structures, such as general rules applied to all economic actors similarly situated. It will become highly differentiated from social life and the other aspects of the state apparatus. It will also be associated with characteristic ideas about the nature of law—ideas which seek to legitimate legal coercion. As Weber made clear, no system of order effectively constrains behavior solely by applying force. While coercive systems must be prepared to penalize transgressors, they must also appeal to men to obey their dictates without actual physical force. In a market system, a coercive order must seek legitimacy through an appeal to enlightened self-interest. Thus, law will be presented as mandated by the selfish proclivities of market man, yet it will apply no more constraint than is necessary to allow individuals to maximize their preferences through interdependent economic activity.[86] In such a system, law will not be viewed as coercion applied by external agencies, but rather as immanent in, and arising from, society itself. The constraints of law are accepted by all economic actors in the enlightened pursuit of self-interest; in the market conception, man's commitment to law is voluntary.[87]

B. *Law in a Pure Command System: Involuntary Commitment*

While law in the market model can be identified as organized coercion through general rules, one must employ a different concept in a command economy. There, all economic decisions are made at the center by one omnipotence; all economic institutions are part of a single, hierarchical structure. The central organ does not pass *laws* in the sense of general rules; rather, it issues more or less specific

85. The model of law and economics in the text is radically simplified, and must be qualified. First, while it assumes that industrial societies lack any non-legal forms of social control which can restrain egoistical conflicts in market situations, market societies do develop sets of normative ideas which constrain self-interested economic behavior without resort to formal, legal action. *See, e.g.*, Macauley, *Non-Contractual Relations in Business: A Preliminary Study*, 28 Am. Soc. Rev. 55 (1963). Second, the "enlightened self-interest" of the rational maximizing economic actor may make conventional or legal coercion unnecessary. *Id.* at 61-65. Finally, as Weber pointed out, a truly "legalistic" system will not always produce results favorable to business interests, which may prefer substantive benefits to formal predictability. 2 Economy and Society, *supra* note 48, at 885.

86. This perspective is set forth clearly by Bentham, the quintessential thinker of the market tradition. *See* J. Bentham, Principles of the Civil Code 93-113. For a more contemporary statement of this perspective, *see, e.g.*, Michelman, *Property, Utility and Fairness: Comments on The Ethical Foundations of "Just Compensation" Law*, 80 Harv. L. Rev. 1165 (1967).

87. For a definition of law as a constraint that men "impose upon themselves," *see* L. Fallers, Law Without Precedent 2 (1969).

directives to enterprises telling them how to carry out their economic functicns. These are often reflected in a plan, which is typically expressed in terms of the output of physical rather than monetary quantities. In a number of ways, these directives resemble military orders: The issuer is presumed to have authority over the recipient, who is obligated to comply with the directives. The plan is binding on all economic actors, and may be enforced by criminal sanctions, dismissal, or demotion. In the pure command economy, the only thing equivalent to "law" is this system of directives.

In a completely nationalized system, there would be, in theory, none of the conflicts that are hypothesized to be the very nature of the market economy. There would be, therefore, no need for legal coercion as a conflict-resolving mechanism.[88] Moreover, as the very essence of the system is the implementation of state decisions about economic activity, there is absolutely no need to shield economic actors from state intervention. Such action is *ex hypothesi* the most rational form of economic decision, and the problem for "law" is merely guaranteeing that these decisions are faithfully followed.

Since law in a command economy does involve coercion, it too must seek some legitimization. However, the concepts of law associated with command differ markedly from those prevalent in a market system. The command system will have a teleological, instrumental concept of law, viewing it as a means of achieving specific goals set forth in the plan. The ultimate goal which legitimizes all legal coercion is the plan itself. The plan, in turn, may be justified on scientific-technical, or political-historical grounds.

Thus, law in a command system is viewed as something imposed from without. It is expressly recognized to be the exercise of coercion to achieve stated and highly-valued goals. It is not an expression of something natural in society, but rather an instrument by which behavior is to be molded in conformity with new, consciously designed standards. In the command system, one's commitment to law is involuntary.

C. *Law in the Mixed Economy*

While the ideal types of market and command assist us in analyzing the economic role of law in industrial or industrializing nations, no

88. Of course, in practice, conflicts do arise between the separate economic enterprises of even the most highly centralized economies. Nations like China and the Soviet Union do have contract law, and institutions for resolution of contractual disputes. *See generally* Loeber, *Plan and Contract Performance in Soviet Law*, 1964 U. OF ILL. LAW FORUM 128; Pfeffer, *The Institution of Contracts in the Chinese People's Republic*, THE CHINA QUARTERLY 153, Apr.-June 1963 (Part I); and 115, July-Sept. 1963 (Part II).

economy is either pure market or pure command. A more sophisticated typology would thus probably specify several "mixed-economy" types, and would accordingly permit a more discriminating comparative analysis of law and development. Moreover it may be possible to imagine systems that involve totally different relations than those suggested in these two types.

Without waiting, however, for the construction of more sophisticated schemes, we may suggest some of the phenomena characteristic of systems involving a mix of command and market. We should begin with an examination of *regulatory law,* a typical form of state economic involvement.

Regulatory law is a hybrid of the universal rules of pure market and the specific directives of pure command: It is more specific than the general rules that establish contract, tort and property rights; yet more general than the specific directives of the command economy. It is thus characteristic of economies where the state is not willing to allow economic priorities to be set exclusively by the market, yet is either unable or unwilling to assume complete control of economic decisions.

Regulatory law consciously attempts to influence the decisions of economic actors who are simultaneously subject to market constraints. In such cases, economic decisions will be basically influenced by price considerations, but such signals will be supplemented by law. A simple example of a regulatory law is the tax credit. The rules that establish credits for certain types of investments do not command that economic units build low-income housing, invest in underdeveloped regions, etc. But the benefits offered through such credits may, when included in a cost-benefit analysis based on market and production data, influence output decisions.[89] Of course, most law in a market system has some such effect.[90] For example, nineteenth-century tort law affected the allocation of resources, even though the judges who established liability rules might not have consciously planned to favor certain industries or activities. The laws of contract and property, even if not consciously designed to influence economic activity, have a similar effect.

Thus, in distinguishing regulatory from all economically relevant

89. For a discussion of this type of law in the context of an economic development program, see D. TRUBEK, J. GOUVEA VIEIRA, & P. SA, *supra* note 7, at 23-92.

90. Weber distinguished law as a "formal order" structuring economic activity and as substantive regulation affecting resource allocation. *See* Trubek, *supra* note 47, at n.47. He recognized, however, that even purely formal rules will have some accidental or unintended effects on resource allocation.

law, we must stress two dimensions. The first is explicitness of intent: While general law will affect the allocation and distribution of resources, regulatory law is consciously shaped to achieve relatively precise goals. The second dimension is the specificity of the provisions enacted: Laws enacting tax credits or prescribing detailed rules for the conduct of certain activities (for example, zoning law) will tend to be more detailed and specific in defining acceptable and unacceptable behavior than more general bodies of law, and to entail a more elaborate administrative machinery.

The rise of regulatory law in market systems can generate tensions within the legal profession, since much regulatory law seems inconsistent with the market concept of law. Lawyers wedded to the pure market model of law will see the rise of regulatory law as a threat to law itself. In civil law countries, for example, as vast bodies of administrative regulations come and go, bereft of the coherence and precision of traditional civil codes, scholars contend that regulatory legislation lacks two elements essential to "law"—generality and permanence.[91] One Brazilian observer, reflecting his alarm, has characterized this type of state decree as "legislation that is not yet law."[92] In the United States the tension between regulation and "law" has focused on the New Deal regulatory agencies. While the regulations issued by these agencies were frequently given a quasi-judicial cast, and appeared to represent a merger between traditional law and government economic control, several scholars expressed concern over the threat this control posed for "law."[93] Indeed for some, regulatory "law" was a contradiction in terms; the purpose and process of government economic control, they felt, was totally inconsistent with any commitment to a system of universal rules.[94]

This legal discomfort can be viewed as a reflection of the emergence in capitalist societies of the welfare state, with its broad commitment to control and direction of economic activity. Seen in the context of the polarity of market and command law, such fears reflect the underlying transition from a market to mixed system and the tensions engendered thereby.

91. *See, e.g.*, G. RIPERT, ASPECTS JURIDIQUES DU CAPITALISME MODERNE 209-58 (1946).
92. *See, e.g.*, Lamy Filho, *Crise no ensino juridico*, SINTESE POLITICA, ECONOMICA, SOCIAL, nos. 37-38 (1968).
93. *See* Reich, *The Law of The Planned Society*, 75 YALE L.J. 1227 (1966), wherein the author observes that by casting government regulation and planning in a legalistic form, the New Deal hid the degree to which planning was actually being conducted. Similarly, Lon Fuller observes that it is wasteful and unwise to adapt the model of legalism to the task of governmental economic allocation. L. FULLER, *supra* note 82, at 170-77.
94. *See, e.g.*, F. HAYEK, THE ROAD TO SERFDOM 72-87 (1944).

D. *The Legal Structure of Contract Under Market and Command: Private Right versus Public Policy*

In order to see more precisely the utility of this typology, let us examine the implications of market and command in one specific area. The differences between the two legal systems are rather clear in the economically significant institution of contract. In the pure market system, contract is an institutional device fostering individual goals and decisions. In the pure command system, it is just one more part of the structure implementing state decisions.[95]

A key feature of a market economy is its encouragement and protection of the freedom of contract. The contract system operates to guarantee individual freedom to make production and consumption decisions in response to prices and to ensure that these decisions will be implemented. Underlying contract in market economies is a legal system of private rights. The essence of this system is that the individual is free to invoke (or not to invoke) the coercive power of the state to enforce duties created by legal rules.

The system of private rights reflects a belief that such freedom is essential for optimal economic performance.[96] Initial contracting decisions must be left to the parties, as a contract will foster efficient resource allocation only if it represents voluntary choice. Similarly, individuals must be free to invoke or not to invoke legal sanctions. For example, assume A and B enter into a contract, and B fails to perform. The system of private rights leaves A the option of suing. If the value to A of the damages, discounted by the costs of suit (including the loss of good will in continuing relations with B), is lower than the value of forgetting the whole matter, A must be free to drop the suit.

Thus, the freedoms *not* to contract and *not* to sue are equally essential to a market system. "Private rights," incorporating these "negative" freedoms, function to guarantee that a system of free-market exchange will determine the utility of alternative economic possibili-

95. One of the major shifts in Western legal organization which Weber observed was the movement from the "status contract" to that of the "purposive contract." A status contract, typical of traditional societies, affects the total legal position or social status of the person involved, for example the contract between a serf and his lord. Purposive contracts, as exemplified by the money contract in exchange economics, are "specific, quantitatively delimited, qualityless, abstract and usually economically conditioned." 2 ECONOMY AND SOCIETY, *supra* note 48, at 674. While Weber's typology may explain the role of contract in the rise of capitalism, it is not very helpful in an analysis of the economics of contemporary industrializing nations where the distinctions among contracts are more a function of the economic role of the state than the duties imposed on the individual contractors.

96. *See* Calabresi, *supra* note 83.

ties and the most efficient method of producing the "most desired" package of goods and services.

By contrast, the command contract is a tool of public policy, a device which ensures that the goals of the plan are realized. The original decision that A and B are to contract with one another is made by some state planning agency which determines that an input or output must be transferred from one economic unit to another. Similarly, the state may modify command contracts: Since the agreement between A and B is merely a tool to attain overall plan objectives, a change in economic conditions dictating new ways to achieve those objectives justifies state modifications.

Similarly, while the parties to a command contract may invoke official remedies in the event of a breach, they are not free to decline such intervention if they find it not to be in their best interest. In a command system the state must be able to invoke sanctions for non-performance even if the parties would prefer to forgive and forget.[97]

Finally, while in the market system courts look to a set of general rules to resolve contractual disputes, in the pure command system the dispute is viewed primarily in terms of its relationship to the plan.[98] The correct resolution is that which will most effectively further the plan. This method of resolving contractual disputes about command contracts must be solved according to detailed knowledge about the plan and the relationship between it and the disputed transactions; accordingly the agency that resolves contractual disputes must have access to—or be part of—the planning agency or ministry.

While all systems reflect a mix of command and market,[99] the recent expansion of market principles in one socialist nation demonstrates that major changes in the structure of economic organization will lead to

97. Pfeffer, *The Institution of Contracts in the Chinese People's Republic, Part II*, THE CHINA QUARTERLY, *supra* note 88, at 130.

98. Pfeffer, *Contracts in China Revisited, With a Focus on Agriculture, 1947-1963*, THE CHINA QUARTERLY 106, 114-17, Oct.-Dec. 1966.

99. Pure systems of command or market contracts probably do not exist. Obviously, in centralized economies like China and the Soviet Union, the system more closely approximates the command model. State enterprises are obligated to enter into closely approximates the common model. State enterprises are obligated to enter into contracts which are frequently determined by plan instructions. Contract disputes are resolved by "arbitration boards" which resolve conflicts in terms set by the plan. *See* Loeber, *supra* note 88, at 131-34; Pfeffer, *supra* note 98, at 115-16. On the other hand, Western capitalist economies employ market contracts as a rule. Economic relations between private firms are governed by a system of private rights adjudicated in courts, not arbitration boards. But public policy considerations may enter into the decisions of courts resolving contract disputes, and some transactions, like government contracts, or arrangements in regulated industries may also approximate the plan contract system.

shifts in the contract system,[100] and that the ideal types of command and market contract are thus useful in explaining historical phenomena. The nation, Hungary, instituted a broad set of economic reforms designed to reduce the amount of centralized planning and increase the role of the market as an allocative device. Under the previous system of central planning, Hungarian enterprises were under a legal obligation to enter into contracts specified by the plan. Under the reform, the state enterprises are free to enter into any contract they find in their economic interest. While the state arbitration board formerly could order any contract modified, this power has now been substantially reduced. Perhaps most significantly, the entire structure of contract enforcement has changed. Under the prior system, enforcement was handled by the state arbitration board, a de facto arm of the planning ministry. It resolved disputes not by applying general rules of contract law, but rather by determining the best solution in light of the overall plan. Under the new system, independent and autonomous economic courts will resolve contract disputes by applying a general body of civil law. The dispute settlement agency will be freed of its former dependence on the planning ministry and will be part of the career judiciary. Reflecting the shift in the economic functions of dispute settlement, the system is becoming "legalized," relying on general rules articulated and enforced by autonomous legal entities. Such reform, to the extent that it is realized, would reflect movement from command toward market contract.

V. Law, Politics, and Development: Authoritarian Modernization

Just as legal structure will vary with the form of economic organization, so it will differ with the form of political system. Research on law and development must be sensitive to the varieties of political systems that emerge in the Third World and their characteristic effects on the legal order. Once we abandon the core conception belief that "modern law" encourages democracy, it becomes necessary to reassess our theories of law and politics and construct a more sophisticated perspective for further research.

Such a complete theory is beyond the scope of this essay: While a full treatment would require an appraisal of the entire range of politi-

100. The following discussion is based on a study by Gyula Eorsi, member of the Hungarian Academy of Sciences, Eorsi, *Law and Economic Reform in Hungary*, in LAW AND ECONOMIC REFORM IN SOCIALIST COUNTRIES (G. Eorsi & Harmathy eds. 1971), and on an interview with Dr. Eorsi in New Haven on May 4, 1972.

cal varieties from democratic pluralism to full totalitarianism, authoritarianism is selected for present analysis as it is a theoretically distinct form of political system pervasive in the Third World.[101]

A. *Authoritarian Regimes*

Authoritarian regimes like Franco's Spain, Vargas' Brazil, Nasser's Egypt, and Salazar's Portugal[102] are not covered by classical concepts of democracy and totalitarianism. Authoritarianism is not merely an arbitrary point in the continuum from democracy to totalitarianism; rather, it is *sui generis*.[103] Unlike totalitarian systems, such regimes permit some line between state and society; but unlike democracy, they tolerate only a very limited degree of pluralism. In contrast to democratic and totalitarian systems, both of which encourage and require high degrees of political participation, authoritarian systems lack the articulated ideology and administrative capacity necessary to mobilize a populace.

Authoritarian regimes seek control of the legal order. One development that may facilitate such effort is the spread of instrumental legal thought. The core conception supports efforts to make legal thought more instrumental partly because it assumes that democracy and increased instrumentalism go hand in hand.[104] But under authoritarian conditions, the spread of legal purposiveness may in fact strengthen, not weaken, authoritarian tendencies.

B. *The Problem of Legitimacy in Authoritarian Systems*

Many of the political problems of modernization[105] center on the crisis of legitimacy which rapid social and economic change create. Industrialization, urbanization, and rapid communication erode the myths by which traditional authority is legitimated and unleash forces

101. *See generally* S. HUNTINGTON, POLITICAL ORDER IN CHANGING SOCIETIES (1968).

102. The classic discussion of this type of regime is Linz, *An Authoritarian Regime: Spain*, in CLEAVAGES, IDEOLOGIES AND PARTY SYSTEMS 291 (E. Allardt and Y. Littunen eds. 1964) [hereinafter cited as Linz].

103. For Linz, authoritarian regimes are:

> political systems with limited, not responsible, political pluralism: without elaborate and guiding ideology (but with distinctive mentalities); without intensive or extensive political mobilization (except at some points in their development); and in which a leader (or occasionally a small group) exercise power within formally ill-defined limits but actually quite predictable ones.

Linz, *supra* note 102, at 297.

104. *See* pp. 19-20 *supra*. Some have also felt that authoritarian politics can hamper economic development by weakening the legal structures needed to provide a framework for market relations and thus for economic growth. *See* Steiner, *supra* note 7, at 56; and pp. 43-45 *infra*.

105. *See* D. APTER, THE POLITICS OF MODERNIZATION (1965), and S. HUNTINGTON, POLITICAL ORDER IN CHANGING SOCIETIES (1968) for useful commentary on the politics of modernization.

which it cannot contain.[106] Modernizing nations in the Third World are unable to employ a strategy available to nineteenth-century European states in offering the market as a justification for legal domination.[107] Unlike those older states, contemporary developing societies confront existing models of mature, industrialized nations and are painfully aware that they are "underdeveloped" or "backward." This perception affects political life, creating expectations of instant economic development. The private sectors of such nations are typically backward, disorganized, and inefficient, and governments simply cannot leave economic development to the invisible hand of the private market. As late modernizers, they are inevitably influenced by modern models of economic organization. Today, when laissez-faire has been abandoned in the West, and developed command economies exist in the Socialist bloc, contemporary developing nations almost inevitably lean toward a degree of government economic involvement.

As a result, economy and polity must merge to some degree in the contemporary "development state." The state is viewed as the main instrument in overcoming "underdevelopment" and political struggle focuses on reaching the hypothesized state of "development." The developmental state must offer its own positive program of action as one of its legitimating principles. It must convert vague yearnings for change into a coherent set of aspirations for "development," and offer itself as the best method of achieving them.[108]

At some point the developmental state must produce economic progress or lose the support of the population. Consequently, it must not only create a developmental "mentality," but must also assume re-

106. Urbanization and the rapid expansion of mass communications are profoundly secularizing forces which erode traditional bases of legitimacy, and create demands for new forms of government "output" which traditional ruling groups are not equipped to provide. *See* Huntington, *supra* note 105, at 35. *See also* J. Habermas, Toward a Rational Society 94-96 (1970).

107. In the 19th century, European states may to some degree have been able to profer the market system itself as a factor legitimating domination. As Weber indicated, nascent market forces pre-existed and helped develop the European nation state, and a "market ideology" emerged that claimed that free market relations will lead to a just and equitable apportionment of social rewards. This market ideology—which eventually led to the *laissez-faire* ideals which took shape in the 19th century—served to legitimate the nation-state, which in turn helped create and then preserve the market system. Since, it was argued, market relations fostered freedom and achieved social justice, and the state nurtured and protected the market, then the state's actions, albeit coercive, led to a free and just society. By thus explaining why state commands should be obeyed, the political market ideology did not so much constrain the state as explain to men why they should accept the constraints imposed by it. *See* Habermas, *supra* note 106, at 97.

108. In a recent speech, Brazilian President Garrastazu Medici argued that the state's ability to foster "development" justified the extraordinary powers which the government had granted itself. Jornal do Brasil, July 4, 1972, at 1, col. 1. These powers included the right to close congress, deny political rights to public officials, and try political prisoners in military courts. For a commentary on these powers, see Carl, *Erosion of Constitutional Rights of Political Offenders in Brazil*, 12 Va. J. Int'l L. 157 (1972).

sponsibility for major allocative and production decisions. At the same time, it must encourage the social and cultural transformations essential for the creation of a rationalized industrial system which alone can satisfy the demand for an increased standard of living. Yet in Third World nations, where traditional cultural ideas and social structures remain strong, such transformations may generate conflict intense enough to threaten the very stability necessary for an industrial economy.

This tension between social transformation and industrialization may begin to explain the prevalence of authoritarianism in the Third World, where nations typically lack the ideological and organizational development necessary to sustain full totalitarianism, yet are too riven by class, racial, and cultural cleavages to tolerate democratic pluralism.

Whatever the reasons for the emergence of authoritarianism, such regimes typically reduce and limit political participation, fragment opposition, and coopt powerful groups whenever possible. While they may resort to violence, they normally attempt to discourage political action by making it appear unnecessary. They stifle political mobilization by converting political issues into technical problems and then asserting the regime's monopoly on technical skills. This tactic not only defuses independent political activity, but also increases the legitimacy of state action by cloaking it in the mystique of technology.

C. *Purposive Legal Thought and the Legitimization of Authoritarianism*

Law is one form of technical discipline employed for legitimizing purposes. Identifying anything as a legal problem denies to a significant extent that it involves any political questions, since an issue is generally termed "legal" if there is some pre-existing norm or standard which will determine the controversy.[109] Once political issues have been "legalized" in this fashion, they can be resolved only by the specialized elite who know the existing rules and the techniques of their application.[110]

109. In his study of authoritarianism in Germany, Ralf Dahrendorf has noted that legalism, through its search for authorities above the conflicts of parties, discourages democratic forms. Observing that a misplaced faith in the "rule of law" was one of the underpinnings of the authoritarian political system of imperial Germany, he concludes that "the exaggerated faith in the rule of law as an institution beyond all conflicts of interest betrays the same aversion to discord, and thus the same evasion of the uncomfortable diversity of uncertainty, that is inherent in the German idea of the state." R. DAHRENDORF, SOCIETY AND DEMOCRACY IN GERMANY 197 (1969). *See also* J. SHKLAR, LEGALISM (1964).

110. Linz observes: "The persistence of the previous social order that goes with limited pluralism and co-optation means that the legal profession so important in democratic politics and even under traditional rulers, will play a much greater role in au-

But this strategy of legalizing politics can be a two-edged sword: If the legal specialists are hostile to the regime, or if existing law contains rules or principles inconsistent with its goals, legalization will merely produce a new set of conflicts. Thus, it is not enough for the regime to legalize political issues; it must also politicize the legal system by coopting the profession and neutralizing those aspects of the legal tradition antagonistic to authoritarian ends.[111] In this task instrumentalism plays a major role.

The core conception contends that lawyers trained as problem solvers will be likely to ask searching questions about underlying social maladies and thus to formulate solutions which will be more "developmental" and more responsive to popular desires. This may occur. But under conditions of authoritarian modernization, increased legal instrumentalism may also have precisely the opposite effect. Instrumentalism may dampen basic conflicts emerging between the authoritarian regime and the legal profession and thus help the regime to legalize fundamental social and political issues.

There are a number of potential causes of conflict between legal professions and authoritarian states. First, friction may result when a regime suppresses aspects of the legislative process, such as a responsive legislature or interest group formation, which the legal profession may believe are vital. Second, the system of regulation needed for economic growth may be incompatible with the profession's belief in a system of universal rules.[112] Third, regulation often attempts to create new institutions through laws of a utopian character which are impossible to enforce, and which confuse and demoralize the legal

thoritarian regimes than in totalitarian systems. The same is true of civil servants. Their presence may contribute to the strange combination of *Rechtsstaat* and arbitrary power, of slow legalistic procedure and military command style, that characterizes some of these regimes. This preoccupation with procedure ultimately becomes an important factor in the constant expansion of a state of law, with an increase in predictability and opportunities for legal redress of grievances. At the same time it may prevent political problems from being perceived as such, irreducible to administrative problems and not soluble by legislation. Legal procedures are often seen particularly in the continental legal tradition, as an adequate equivalent of more collective, political expressions of interest conflicts." Linz, *supra* note 102, at 327.

111. Certain types of legal thought have long been recognized as especially conducive to the maintenance of authoritarian rule and hostile to democratice pluralism. For example, German lawyers in the 1920's and 1930's had a legalistic or rule-bounded notion of politics: Influenced by Hegelian notions of the state as an entity standing above the individualist struggles of "civil society," they preferred the authoritative invocation of pre-existing rules to pluralistic, competitive conflict as methods of determining social issues. Since they held this orientation, the German lawyers were tied to the status quo—to existing law and to whatever group, including the Nazi regime, which exercised power in the name of the state. Moreover, the lawyers' conceptions of state and society led them to be actively hostile to democratic rule, which challenged their notions of how social life should be governed. This hostility led the German legal class to invoke "natural law" to restrict the actions of the more pluralistic government of the Weimar Republic. R. DAHRENDORF, *supra* note 109, at 232-48.

112. *See* p. 31.

profession.[113] Negative reactions of the judiciary and the profession may range from overt hostility to feigned indifference,[114] further encouraging the government to by-pass the organized bench and bar in achieving its regulatory goals and thus widening the breach between the regime and the profession.

But once the legal profession adopts a purposive view of law it is far easier for the state to legitimize its system of regulations.[115] Since instrumentalism places a higher value on ends than on legal form or tradition, it is less sensitive to deviations from the model of rules; since it accepts the state as the source of goals, it is less critical of a non-pluralist process of goal formulation. When combined with the belief that all problems can be solved by the state's technocratic apparatus, instrumentalism thus provides the regime with a justification for the demobilization of professional associations and groups. Moreover, as lawyers find that they can define their role and reform their professional activity only by accepting this technical view of social problems, they will find themselves gradually coopted by the technocratic apparatus of the developmental state. Thus, the spread of instrumentalism will erode professional autonomy and forge close links between state structure and the profession.[116]

Finally, the concept of law as a purposive instrument can aid the authoritarian leader who supplants a more democratic regime in defeating challenges based on liberal ideals. The secular, instrumental view of law destroys any sacred quality of the traditional legal restraints that might have been a part of a nation's constitutional law or lore. Since "law" is an instrument to achieve specific goals articulated by the government, any values or principles of an older legal tradition inconsistent with the regime's purposes can easily be discarded.[117]

D. *Towards a New Typology for the Comparative Study of Law in the Politics of Development*

As the foregoing demonstrates, the core conception's assumption that instrumentalism has an "elective affinity" with liberal democracy

113. *See* Steiner, *supra* note 7, at 54-55.

114. For a vivid description of one such reaction by a Brazilian jurist, see M. Seabra Fagundes, A Legalidade Democratica (1970).

115. To the extent that the legal profession can shift to purposive thought, it will no longer sense a conflict between its skills and the regulatory output of the state. The legal thinker who looks at law purely as a purposive instrument is satisfied with exploring the policy goals set forth in positive legislation and determining the "effectiveness" of concrete measures taken to reach these goals.

116. Unger, *supra* note 8, at sec. 3.8.

117. *See* note 68 *supra*.

The Yale Law Journal Vol. 82: 1, 1972

is facile. Nevertheless, instrumentalism and authoritarianism may exist without each other. Obviously, in any comparative study of legal culture our own would rank very high in its commitment to an instrumental view of law. But one would hardly be correct in asserting that we therefore have an authoritarian political system. Although the transition to increased legal purposiveness is in some sense a universal feature of modernization, it is not sufficient by itself to explain the relationship between law and politics in every modernizing nation.

Thus, in constructing a useful typology for further study it is necessary to identify the varying types of purposive legal thought. For example, as the previous discussion suggests, there appears to be a distinction between pluralist and statist forms of legal instrumentalism. While both accept the view that law is an instrument to achieve specific goals, they differ as to how those goals are determined. While statist instrumentalism looks exclusively to the bureaucratic-administrative entities of the state, a pluralist concept would insist that policy goals be determined by a more open, representative, and competitive process. Though this is a somewhat crude distinction, such constant refinement of our concepts will be necessary to develop a truly comparative social theory of law.[118]

VI. Brazil: A Case Study of Legal, Economic and Political Development in the Third World

Theoretical analysis, conceptual refinement, and the construction of ideal types are not ends in themselves. Rather, such efforts must demonstrate that they enable the observer to order and comprehend empirical and historical data. This section examines recent legal, economic, and political trends in Brazil, and demonstrates the problems of modern law thought and the utility of the broader perspective this essay advocates.

A. *The Advantages of the "Brazilian Case"*

Brazil, with a population of over one hundred million, is the largest nation in Latin America and one of the most important countries

118. Of course, these ideas must be rendered more concrete and operational if they are to orient comparative study. One criterion that might be employed to distinguish between the types of instrumentalism would be the extent to which that basic legal doctrine incorporates notions of pluralistic process. Such notions as "institutional capacity," deference to legislative decisions, and similar ideas which mark American legal doctrine would, in this view, indicate that our system approximates the pluralist model.

in the Third World. It contains Latin America's most advanced industry and its worst poverty. In recent years, it has experienced one of the higher rates of economic growth in the world, and now aspires to full industrialization.[119] Since in addition to this size and economic progress, Brazil has a rich legal tradition and sizeable profession,[120] it is not surprising that it has been one of the primary targets of "law and development" scholars and activists.[121] Thus, the "Brazil Case" allows us to examine emerging relationships among law, economy, and policy—along with the "law and development" analysis of them.

First, however, some background. The studies to be examined, and the events in Brazilian legal life they analyzed, occurred in the late 1960's and early 1970's, a period marked by four major phenomena: increased and more efficient state economic direction, rapid growth, increased authoritarianism, and tensions between the government and legal profession.[122]

The Brazilian polity prior to 1964 could be characterized as a semi-pluralist, semi-authoritarian system. A liberal democratic constitution, in force since the 1946 overthrow of the truly authoritarian *Estado Novo,* allowed substantial political competition. There were strong residues of the prior authoritarian pattern, but these were counter-balanced by other, more democratic factors. For example, an independent judiciary and liberal constitutional provisions offered guarantees for freedom of association and speech; a multi-party system and direct popular elections led to substantial political mobilization.

This system collapsed in 1964 when, after a series of crises, the armed forces seized power.[123] While promising to "restore democracy," the military regime has since moved toward full authoritarian

119. On Brazilian socio-economic and political history in general, see W. BAER, INDUSTRIALIZATION AND ECONOMIC DEVELOPMENT IN BRAZIL (1965); THE ECONOMY OF BRAZIL (H. Ellis ed. 1969); C. FURTADO, THE ECONOMIC GROWTH OF BRAZIL (1968); N. LEFF, ECONOMIC POLICY MAKING AND DEVELOPMENT IN BRAZIL 1947-1964 (1968); P. SCHMITTER, INTEREST CONFLICT AND POLITICAL CHANGE IN BRAZIL (1971); R. SCHNEIDER, THE POLITICAL SYSTEM OF BRAZIL: EMERGENCE OF A "MODERNIZING" AUTHORITARIAN REGIME, 1964-1970 (1971); T. SKIDMORE, POLITICS IN BRAZIL, 1930-1964 (1967); A. STEPAN, THE MILITARY IN POLITICS: CHANGING PATTERNS IN BRAZIL (1971); J. WIRTH, THE POLITICS OF BRAZILIAN DEVELOPMENT: 1930-1954 (1970).

120. *See* Steiner, *supra* note 7, at 44-46, 62-63.

121. The studies included Rosenn, *supra* note 7; Steiner, *supra* note 7; and Trubek, *supra* note 7. In addition, a lengthy report on Brazilian legal education and its role in development was prepared by Peter Hornbostel for the International Legal Center of New York. P. Hornbostel, Legal Education in Brazil, Oct. 1971 (unpublished study for the International Legal Center, 866 United Nations Plaza, N.Y., N.Y.).

122. *See generally* sources cited in note 120 *supra.*

123. Schmitter, *supra* note 20, sees the 1964 military takeover as a "restorationist" movement. He argues that, since the 1930's of the Vargas *Estado Novo,* the basic political structure of Brazil has been authoritarian. The liberalism and semi-competitive politics introduced by the 1946 constitution partially constituted, in his view, a facade behind which substantial elements of authoritarianism survived.

rule by purging the Brazilian polity of most of its democratic elements. Simultaneously, the regime has assumed more direct control over economic activity. While professing to believe in the free market, it has increased the economic role of the state and has subjected the private sector to a pervasive system of regulatory law. From 1964 to 1970, over ten thousand new laws and decrees were passed, many of major significance.[124] The codification of tax law, for example, transformed a hodge-podge of revenue measures into a conscious instrument of economic development. Similarly, complete new systems of housing finance, banking, and capital markets were enacted. Most of these laws, drafted by planners and technocrats, were issued as executive decrees.

Initially, this "blitzkrieg" of regulatory law caused dismay in the legal profession. Brazil's lawyers found themselves totally incapable of dealing intellectually with the new bodies of regulatory law. Accustomed to thinking of "law" as general rules applied through deductive techniques, they could not grasp the inherent logic of the new legal order which contained few general rules, was not highly systematized, and could be applied only through unfamiliar logical forms.[125]

But while this regulatory blitzkrieg dismayed Brazil's lawyers, it delighted the foreign law and development activists and researchers. In the government's output, we saw the raw material for research, a vast corpus of legal "stuff" designed to bring about "development." In the legal profession's inability to deal with this new law, we saw an outlet for our reformism. These impulses merged in two studies which will provide the focus for the remainder of this analysis. One (which I conducted) examined the role of law in the development of the Brazilian capital market;[126] the other attempted to determine which changes would and should occur in Brazilian legal education as a result of the economic transformations occurring in the nation.[127]

B. *Law and Development Research in Brazil: The Basic Assumptions*

In the design of these studies and the interpretation of our "data," we shared many of the core conception's assumptions about law and society. We saw Brazil primarily as a market economy.[128] The state's

124. *The Law Will Rule*, BRAZIL, 1969, at 144 (Center for Inter-American Relations, 1970).

125. Steiner, *supra* note 7, at 70-72.

126. Trubek, *supra* note 7. That article is a condensation of my contribution to the Portuguese language study of the Brazilian capital market, D. TRUBEK, J. GOUVEA VIEIRA, AND P. SA, *supra* note 7, at 23-92.

127. Steiner, *supra* note 7.

128. *Id.* at 43.

role in economic life was analogized to that of the Welfare State in developed capitalist nations: The market was the primary source of economic allocation; government intervention merely maintained and protected market structures, while supplementing market decisions in a limited sphere.[129] We assumed further that this market economy required an autonomous legal system creating and guaranteeing private rights, through the promulgation of general rules. We therefore reasoned that market growth was impossible without the development of such a legal system.[130] We predicted the emergence of adequate substantive rules of contract and property law, an efficient and autonomous judicial system, and an independent and technically competent legal profession able to advise economic actors on the significance of substantive legal rules.[131] To ensure that these rules would be certain and calculable, we reasoned that the action of the state would have to be constrained by the "rule of law."[132]

While this concept of the "rule of law" was largely implicit, it was extremely broad. Law was a commitment not only to orderly and regular governmental procedure, but also to more specific processes and values (for example, the dignity of the individual or fairness in state action).[133] The rule of law was assumed to involve a social philosophy which accepted diversity and the maintenance of a normative structure that harmonized or compromised conflict.[134]

At the same time, we recognized that the market must be regulated to guarantee that development priorities would be obeyed. It was thus clear that Brazilian economic development would require an effective system of regulation in addition to one of purely private rights.[135] This would require the inculcation of instrumental legal skills.[136] We saw no potential conflict between an autonomous system of rules guaranteeing private rights and increased instrumentalism in legal thought. Accordingly, it was assumed that a legal system combining both could be institutionalized and that the resulting system would be simultaneously liberal, instrumental, and pluralist. We therefore worked

129. *Id.* at 43, 49.
130. *Id.* at 48; Trubek, *supra* note 7, at 54-56: D. TRUBEK, J. GOUVEA VIEIRA, & P. SA, *supra* note 7, at 55-59.
131. Steiner, *supra* note 7, at 48; Trubek, *supra* note 7, at 54-56; D. TRUBEK, J. GOUVEA VIEIRA, & P. SA, *supra* note 7, at 55-59.
132. Steiner, *supra* note 7, at 48-49, 56.
133. Steiner, *supra* note 7, at 49, 55, 89. D. TRUBEK, J. GOUVEA VIEIRA, AND P. SA, *supra* note 7, at 80.
134. Steiner, *supra* note 7, at 48-49; Trubek, *supra* note 7, at 53, 55.
135. Steiner, *supra* note 7, at 51-52; D. TRUBEK, J. GOUVEA VIEIRA, & P. SA, *supra* note 7, at 64-68; Trubek, *supra* note 7, at 10, 52-53.
136. Steiner, *supra* note 7, at 70-72, 86-87; Trubek, *supra* note 7, at 53.

and argued for this form of legal development, selecting legal educational reform as our primary vehicle.

But legal development, defined in these broad and liberal terms, seemed inherently in conflict with authoritarianism. We saw a dilemma emerging, with Brazil's political organization and economic policy on a collision course and "law" the point of impact.

On the one hand, the nation had experienced rapid economic development by adopting a private sector, market-oriented policy with limited government regulation. Our premises about the necessary relationship between market growth and law led us to assume that this course would necessitate an autonomous legal system, enforcing private rights through general rules. Since we believed that the Brazilian legal system was, in these terms, quite "underdeveloped," we reasoned that future market expansion would require the institution of both private rights and regulatory systems. We assumed that in time Brazilian planners would see this need to add "legal development" to their list of priority sectors.

On the other hand, we recognized that the regime's commitment to authoritarianism made it hostile to certain features of Brazilian legal life which we felt were essential to the rule of law. Rather than fostering legal development, the regime was systematically destroying the legal order. The military had abandoned all but the barest pretext of abiding by constitutional norms (or any other check on executive discretion). It had abolished substantive protections of individual rights, including freedom of speech and habeas corpus. It had packed the Supreme Court and purged the lower levels of the judiciary. The Congress had been closed; legislation was promulgated increasingly by executive decree. Military courts had been given jurisdiction over vaguely defined political crimes, and defense counsel who dared take political cases were subjected to increasing harassment, imprisonment, and torture.[137]

Given the premises from which we started, there was thus an inherent conflict between Brazil's model of authoritarian politics and its commitment to market development. Eventually, one would have to succumb to the other. Thus, we speculated that either rapid market growth would strengthen the system of autonomous private rights and thus help restore liberal pluralism,[138] or continued authoritarianism would defeat the attempt to develop a market by undermining

137. See Carl, note 108 *supra*.

138. Trubek, *supra* note 7, at 71; D. TRUBEK, J. GOUVEA VIEIRA, & P. SA, *supra* note 7, at 80.

the essential framework which only a private rights system could create.[139] If the former occurred, Brazil would have both economic development *and* democracy; if, however, the latter came to pass, *it could have neither.*

C. *The Studies*

1. *Law, Planning and the Development of the Capital Market*

The impact of these assumptions and "dilemmas" on thought and action is apparent in several specific studies. The first—my own analysis of the relationship between law and the development of the capital market—included speculation about legal development and financial growth which represented a detailed application of our assumptions about law-market relationships. In this study of the military government's ambitious capital markets development program, I set forth two related ideas. First, having observed that Brazil's capital markets had not grown as rapidly as its planners had expected, I speculated that this might be attributed to legal underdevelopment.[140] The planners had provided substantial incentives designed to foster the growth of a new issues market, by encouraging savers to hold stock and debentures in lieu of real estate investments, foreign currency, etc. When these measures failed to elicit the desired behavior, I reasoned that investor reluctance could be explained by the fact that the Brazilian private rights system was underdeveloped.[141] I observed that rules governing creditor and shareholder rights were imperfect, that courts were neither accessible nor efficient, and that sanctions were ineffective. Moreover, investors were unaware of their rights, and the bar was not organized to inform or defend them.[142] Consequently, the system failed to give potential stockholders and creditors sufficient guarantees. In short, the system failed to supply predictability to the economic actors.[143]

Second, I suggested that if those legal barriers were bypassed and market development began, this growth would in turn bring about further legal development.[144] Having observed that after some initial disappointments the capital market program had adopted new forms

139. Steiner, *supra* note 7, at 56.
140. Trubek, *supra* note 7, at 52-56.
141. *Id.* at 55-56.
142. *Id.*
143. *Id.* at 10, 54-56.
144. *Id.* at 71.

of incentives and had succeeded in evoking some desired investor behavior, I reasoned that as the markets boomed they would generate pressure for improvement of the private rights system. The financial sector would demand "modern" substantive codes, a more stable and coherent body of laws, a reduction in government ad hoc decision-making, judicial reform, rationality in legal thought, and a restructuring of professional organization. Accordingly, I praised the new program as a brilliant maneuver which circumvented legal underdevelopment, initiated market growth, and left any remaining legal barriers for a "mopping up" operation by inexorable market pressures.[145] These developments led me to predict that the hypothesized legal development would follow closely on market growth.[146]

Finally, I argued that this legal development—which to my mind implied the full program of liberal, pluralist, instrumental legalism—could be seen as one of the "external benefits" of a development policy that emphasized the private capital market rather than government coercion or inflation as techniques for mobilizing economic surplus.[147] This analysis allowed me to associate the capital market program with liberal political ideals and to suggest that this program would strengthen liberal tendencies in Brazilian political life and thus combat distasteful authoritarian trends.[148]

2. *Reform in Legal Education*

The study of legal education reform in Brazil paralleled and complemented my research on the capital market. It hypothesized that while the Brazilian private rights system was relatively developed in a formal sense, it was functionally inefficient. Courts, codes, lawyers, and regulatory agencies existed, indeed abounded; the problem, however, was that they were incapable of effectively performing their tasks.[149] Given the basic core conception assumptions, these inefficiencies jeopardized economic growth. The study examined trends in legal education and concluded that a significant part of this legal "underdevelopment" could be explained by flaws in the nation's method of training its lawyers.[150] It then argued for major reforms in legal education, including the inculcation of more instrumental

145. *Id.*
146. *Id.*
147. Trubek, *supra* note 7, at 69-71; D. TRUBEK, J. GOUVEA VIEIRA, & P. SA, *supra* note 7, at 80.
148. D. TRUBEK, J. GOUVEA VIEIRA, & P. SA, *supra* note 7, at 80.
149. Steiner, *supra* note 7, at 51, 55, 56-62.
150. *Id.* at 62-72.

modes of legal thought.[151] It was thought that these reforms would strengthen market institutions, and at the same time it was hoped that they would preserve liberal values which were explicitly identified with the "basic traditions of Brazilian law."[152] This program for improvement of legal education meshed with my concepts of the need for the improvement of the private rights system: The newly trained lawyers and judges would man the new institutions demanded by the growing private market system. Both studies contained the hope that economic planners would grasp the argument and lend active support for this new system, thus, perhaps unwittingly, undermining their own political system.[153]

But for all their lofty ambitions, these hopes, assumptions, and efforts were soon dashed. Contrary to our predictions (or more accurately our hopes), market growth has not engendered an autonomous, pluralist legal system. Market growth seems to have had little effect on legal life; moreover, those legal changes which have occurred have not hindered the government's efforts to dismantle the liberal aspects of Brazil's legal order. The capital market has expanded vastly; yet, while there has been significant improvement in the government's regulatory capacity, there is little evidence that any substantial pressure is being exerted by market operators for the development of full private rights or an autonomous legal system. Nor is there any sign that the lack of such development is impeding market growth.

Recent developments in legal education similarly mock our predictions. It is possible to detect a growing emphasis on instrumental thought in Brazil. But there is some reason to believe that this has taken the form of authoritarian instrumentalism, and has functioned more to resolve previous tensions between the legal profession and the state than to generate new ones.[154] Thus, in the final analysis, liberally motivated efforts to assist educational reform may have actually aided in the consolidation of the authoritarian regime.

151. *Id.* at 77-79.

152. *Id.* at 79.

153. This was another rarely articulated premise. This hope was perhaps more evident in an article on which we collaborated. Steiner and Trubek, *Brazil—All Power to the Generals*, 49 FOREIGN AFFAIRS 464 (1971).

154. Brazilian lawyers and law students are learning the ropes of "legal engineering" and thus are making themselves more valuable to the government in the process of statutory drafting and promulgation. They are cutting out for themselves at least that part of the niche we envisioned them occupying in modern society. But these attitudes may undermine commitment to the traditional values of legal formalism, deference to procedural requisites or to a pluralist view of law making, that is, to those elements of the "rule of law" which had made the legal profession unpopular with the state apparatus but upon which we had placed our hopes for democratizing the modernization program. *See* p. 39.

D. *Towards a New Perspective*

In Brazil we see the tragic implications of reliance on the core conception, and the darker side of law and development research. For, as is often the case in planned social change, the very ideas that prompted reform efforts became obstacles to the realization of the reformers' goals. The concepts failed both as guides to action and as a structure for scholarly investigation.

Where then do we go from here? Perhaps the first step would be a reappraisal of the Brazilian experience. Any such attempt would have to view as problematic many of the relationships the core conception finds invariable. The following are some of the conclusions of such a reappraisal.

First, the structure of economic organization in Brazil, while relying on market forms, is much closer to the paradigm of command than initial studies suggested. The Brazilian regime is more concerned with securing direct administrative control over economic activity than in encouraging the type of autonomous market development we posited. Even the capital market program, which envisioned a market form of organization, is implemented within a highly regulated and controlled environment in which state policy plays a central role.

Second, although many Brazilian economic decisions are in private hands, this system has relatively little need for an autonomous legal order guaranteeing private rights through general rules. The economic functions posited for law in the market paradigm are not particularly appropriate for the actual structure of Brazilian markets. This is certainly true in the financial arena. A private rights system and the rule of law, assumed by Weber and classical political economists to be essential for market development, do guarantee a relative degree of predictability where the actors lack economic power over each other and where government decisions are economically neutral. But the emerging structure of the Brazilian financial market seems to be one in which a very few powerful groups are actively supported by government policy, and where the government, in turn, is just as dependent on the success of these groups. In other words, state intervention in the economy is not pure command, but favors certain economic actors over others, so that predictability for the state and the powerful groups is a consequence of their mutual dependence.

Recently, the government has encouraged consolidation in commercial banking, and in a short time only a few large units may remain. Informal relations of mutual dependence with the government guarantee that policies will be sufficiently "predictable" and substantively attractive to these units regardless of how incoherent they may appear to the rest of the nation. In this context, real power over the source of rule-making is more important than any formal, universal quality of predictability. And where these groups exert substantial economic power over other market actors, a private rights system is probably of secondary importance. In this structure, efforts to develop such a system of rights may not have a central role in economic development policy. Thus, an authoritarian regime which fears the political implications of market law may, at no cost, avoid "legal development" measures suggested by modern law thought.

Conversely, we should consider as problematic the relationship between such measures, even if taken, and liberal pluralist political structures. While we originally associated one with the other, it is certainly possible to imagine a form of legal system relating to the market that has little or no pluralist implications. Substantial expansion and improvement of the judiciary, and changes in legal organization could provide an improved legal framework for the Brazilian economy without affecting the political situation. Once we realize that even a highly developed *market legal structure* need not be liberal and pluralist, we leave open for empirical research the relationships that the core conception assumes invariable. In such research, the scholar will be forced to consider the full complexity of legal relationships in development.

Much more careful research must be done on legal life in Brazil and comparable Third World nations before the Brazilians or anyone else can understand the true nature of the complex processes that are at work there today.[155] While no definite conclusions about Brazil can be drawn from this impressionistic reappraisal of earlier studies, one point is clear: To the extent that scholars in the developed world can have any genuine understanding of legal life in Brazil and throughout the Third World, they will attain it only through more careful study, oriented by clear concepts, and an awareness of the preconceptions and normative values affecting the researcher. Only by casting off the ideological baggage of the core conception can they contribute

155. The situation in Brazil today is extremely complex. The government has made some effort both to improve the private rights system and upgrade its regulatory capacity. There has been a tentative commitment to a new civil code, and to new corporation laws. Yet the civil code has not been passed, perhaps partly because such a major, quasi-constitutional event would serve as a dramatic reminder of the unrepresentative quality of law-making in today's Brazil. The regime has moved to curb the independence of the judiciary, and has limited severely the powers of the civilian courts in political crimes. Yet it has not waged full scale war on the courts, and has obviously felt the political importance of maintaining a commitment to the legal order.

to a study of law and development which will be more than the facile export of outworn ideas.

VII. Conclusion

Legal scholars thus must avoid two major failings of previous efforts. They must keep their value preferences and intellectual preconceptions from blinding them to the actual phenomena of legal life in the Third World. At the same time, they must attempt to construct more precise and universal conceptual categories conducive to realistic generalizations.

Naturally, there is a profound tension between these two goals. We have seen how universal propositions have obscured rather than clarified empirical perception in the past, and we may justifiably fear that a mere search for empirical details will lead to nothing more than the accumulation of unrelated and unrelatable bits of data. Yet if we can maintain this tension, we can make some progress toward a genuine social theory of law.

[3]

LAW AND DEVELOPMENT IN LIGHT OF DEPENDENCY THEORY

David F. Greenberg

The recent revival of macrosociological interest in law has stimulated a renewed interest in the treatment of the relationship between law and the rise of capitalism in classical social theory; e.g., in the writings of Marx, Weber and Durkheim (see, for example, Unger, 1976). Though much can be learned from these sources, it is necessary to transcend their conceptual limitations if we are to advance our understanding of how law and capitalism are related.

One important limitation of the classical sources involves their implicit assumption that the relationship between law and capitalism in the non-industrial, less-developed countries (LDCs) as they develop will be similar to what it has been in the Western industrialized world.[1] However plausible that view may once have seemed, it is no longer tenable in the light of Asian, African, and Latin American history. Yet an alternative understanding, more faithful to the experience of the Third World, has yet to emerge. Recent analyses of the "modern world system" (Wallerstein,

Research in Law and Sociology, Volume 3, pages 129–159.

ISBN: 0-89232-186-5

1974) provide conceptual resources for a more dialectical understanding of the relationship between law and economic development, an understanding that is not predicated on a now discredited unilineal evolutionary view of world history.

LEGAL DIFFUSIONISM

The study of law and development was revived during the 1960s when the US government, the Ford and Rockefeller Foundations, and international agencies sought non-communist strategies for "modernizing" the newly independent nations of Africa and Asia, as well as the older independent states of Latin America. Legal scholars who shared this practical concern discussed the contribution that law and lawyers might make to the process of modernization (David, 1963; Tunc, 1966; Rosenn, 1969; Mendelson, 1970; Steinberg, 1971; Steiner, 1971; Seidman, 1972a; Trubek, 1972a; Hager, 1972; Franck, 1972).

Recent critics of the work of these scholars (Trubek, 1972a, Trubek and Galanter, 1974) note that, despite differences in emphasis and perspective, they share a consensus that legal reform has a major role to play in the economic and political development of the LDCs, and that the direction of this reform should be such as to bestow on the LDCs legal systems that are fundamentally similar to those found in the Western world. As this conception of reform entails the transfer to the Third World of ideas and institutions developed in the West in the hope of producing convergent economic, social, and political development, it makes sense to refer to this perspective as "legal diffusionism."[2]

Legal diffusionist doctrine sees modern law as a functional prerequisite of industrialization (implicitly assumed to occur within the framework of a capitalist economy) much like electricity and literacy. By providing a set of stable expectations, it is thought that modern law can shift domestic investment from short-term speculation to long-term productive investment, stimulate the economy by providing private entrepreneurs with greater certainty than exists in traditional legal systems, and limit state interference with the private economy. By providing guarantees against nationalization, confiscatory taxation, import restrictions and limits on the repatriation of profits, it can also encourage foreign investment, thus stimulating the importation of capital and technology. Conceived instrumentally, law can also direct or evoke economic activity regarded as desirable for the development of the national economy by regulating credit, land tenure, foreign currency transactions, import and export activities, wages and, through tax policy, social welfare measures, etc. (Njenga, 1966; Nwabueze, 1966; Seidman, 1966; Steinberg, 1971; Trubek, 1972a). In this literature, customary law is regarded as too unpredictable to reassure investors, yet not flexible enough to develop the new law needed for an industrial economy—because it lacks an instrumental orientation to law—and because it remains too responsive to traditional values. Legal diffusionism is thus much like subcultural explanations of poverty within an industrialized society. It attributes the lack of modern industry and the low standard of living to cultural deficiencies of the non-industrialized society, just as "subculture of poverty" theories explain poverty in terms of the cultural deficits of those who are poor.

Legal diffusionists argue further that the replacement of traditional pluralistic legal institutions by a centralized, monolithic legal system can help to unify a nation (David, 1963; Trubek, 1972a) and weaken traditional elites who preserve their privileged positions by obstructing secularization and industrialization. Legal diffusionists also argue that modern law can foster political democracy by facilitating public participation in political institutions, and by protecting citizens against arbitrariness and the deprivation of civil liberties (Seidman, 1966; Trubek and Galanter, 1974). Possible contradictions between the centralization of power and the weakening of traditional elites on the one hand, and the preservation of democracy and individual rights on the other hand, received little attention (Trubek, 1972a).

It is implicit in this view that legal change can be introduced exogenously into a society with major impact on its economic structure and political culture. This view of legal change led legal diffusionists to propose an agenda for legal reform that entailed bringing the legal systems of Third World nations into congruence with those of Europe, England, and the US by importing Western legal codes (bringing "law on the books" up to date) with only minor modifications to take local circumstances into account (David, 1963), and as a concession to customs that are regarded as likely to be intractable to legal pressure (e.g., marriage customs); teaching indigenous lawyers and judges to use the new law;[3] and reforming legal education in the LDCs so that new lawyers in these countries will take a less formalistic, more instrumental conception of law[4] (Paul, 1962; von Mehren, 1965; Rosenn, 1969; Steiner, 1971). These newly trained lawyers would then be able to shape law and legal institutions in directions that would help to promote development (Trubek, 1972a). Implementation was to be under the leadership of existing national political elites, with assistance from Europe and the U.S.

On the basis of these premises, Harvard and Yale established law programs in Brazil; Stanford brought Chileans to the US for specialized legal training; New York University Law School established a special program for foreign law students; and funding was provided for legal education programs in Africa, Brazil, Chile, Colombia, and Costa Rica by the Ford Foundation, Rockefeller Foundation, Agency for International Development, and the Peace Corps. The Algerian government has recently sent students to study corporate law at Georgetown University; and the People's Republic of China has recently indicated (Klement, 1979) that it is preparing a set of commercial laws in connection with its decision to open the country to foreign investment.

Legal diffusionists found support for their conception of the contribution law could make to economic development in the writings of Weber and Parsons, who both argued that a rational, universalistic, and partially autonomous legal system had been critical to the genesis of capitalism in Europe and England (Trubek, 1972a), and that a legal system with these qualities had developed there for reasons largely unrelated to the economy.[5] If so, it would not be unreasonable to suppose that modern law could be introduced into other countries with much the same effect.

American and Japanese history lent superficial plausibility to these ideas. Following American independence, the US government fostered capital accumulation through land grants, tax law, protective tariffs, direct subsidy to industry, and repeal of feudal land law, while preserving and extending a pluralistic political democracy (Auerbach, 1969; Horwitz, 1977). At the time of the Meiji restoration in 1869, Japan imported European legal codes as part of its effort to create an indigenous capitalism, and in the space of 50 years became a major industrial power.

At the same time, a number of features of the legal systems of LDCs that seem to stand in the way of capitalist industrialization could readily be identified. In parts of Africa where communal land tenure prevails, lending institutions have been unwilling to grant farmers the credits needed for agricultural investment, ostensibly on the grounds that the land cannot be used as collateral for loans and farmers have no incentive to plant cash crops if the harvest will occur only after periodic land redistribution has given possession to someone else. An individual's motivation to increase earnings can be reduced when traditional family law upholds obligations to support a large extended family (Dunning, 1968). In Islamic states, the Shari'a law does not recognize executory contracts, as it considers speculative business transactions to be a form of gambling, which the Koran prohibits (Seidman, 1966). In Tunisia, commercial transactions involving land have been blocked because the religious courts have jurisdiction.

At independence, many of the former West African colonies had no bankruptcy law (Seidman, 1966), and the lack of codification poses obstacles to the discovery of just what current law is (Dunning, 1968). According to Schiller (1965), "It is generally recognized that the indigenous systems of law in Africa are deficient in the areas of commerce, finance, labor, and social welfare. Further, the indigenous law is considered inadequate in the field of obligations and property. . . ." Seidman (1966) adds that "If customary law is deficient in the area of commercial and business law, it is completely empty in the area of modern public law. There simply is not even the germ of such institutions as planning, state enterprises, import control, central banking, exchange control, limitations on the repatriation of profits, income taxation, trade unions and labor law, and a host of others."

Although it may be true that specific forms of economic activity require certain legal frameworks, a moment's reflection raises serious questions about the extent to which legal reform can stimulate economic activity. For example, European law at one time contained provisions that were inimical to the expansion of capitalism (e.g., the prohibition of usury), but ultimately these provisions were swept away. If that hasn't happened in the LDCs, one must consider the possibility that no important social group favors such change, or that powerful social groups stand in the way. In either case, the prospects for carrying through a major program of legal reform would appear slight.

Although a number of 19th century Latin American constitutions were modeled on the US Constitution,[6] and civil codes derived from the Napoleonic Code were adopted in most Latin American countries during the 19th century,[7] the political and economic development of Latin America has diverged sharply from that of the US and Europe; thus, it is implausible that legal change is the critical variable in development. If legal reform did so little for Latin America a century ago, why should it do so much more now? According to Karst and Rosenn (1975:51), Latin American commercial law, widely criticized as outdated and an obstacle to economic development, is "changing rapidly as a result of pressures generated by rapid industrialization and economic growth." If this is so, then law should not be regarded as primarily exogenous to the economy, and the need for an externally sponsored program of legal reform may be limited.

THE CONSEQUENCES OF LEGAL REFORM

The observed economic and political trends in the non-industrialized world tend to reinforce these doubts about the capacity of law to bring about economic development. In Turkey, Shari'a law was abolished, and modified versions of the German Commercial Code, Italian Penal Code, and Swiss Civil Code were adopted shortly after the Republic was proclaimed in 1924. Since 1933, the state has played an active role in economic development, using legal tools to foster industrialization. Although Turkey has managed to achieve some degree of industrial development, its economic growth has slowed in recent years, (Herschlag, 1968). Today, with an unemployment rate of 20 percent and an annual inflation rate of 70 percent, Turkey is reluctant to adopt the austerity measures demanded by the International Monetary Fund (IMF) in return for loans, because to do so would exacerbate economic discontent and risk the overthrow of the government (New York Times, 1979).

In Brazil, where the military junta which came to power in the 1964 coup was applauded by legal diffusionists because it took an instrumental approach to law and enacted a host of measures to stimulate the economy (Trubek, 1972a), the annual growth in the GNP has fallen from the 8 percent sustained during the 1960s to 4 percent in 1975 (Vandervort, 1978). The "economic miracle" has sharpened economic inequality: while the share of income going to the upper 10 percent increased from 39 percent in 1960 to 47 percent in 1970, real wages fell, and price controls on rent and utilities were eliminated, along with subsidies on gasoline and basic food items. Because the changed distribution of income has shifted the structure of economic demand, per capita production of food, textiles and clothing fell slightly between 1964 and 1970, while production of luxury goods such as automobiles increased (Hewlett, 1975). Following the coup, a shift in medical spending from public health to curative medicine (a shift favoring the rich) has been accompanied by epidemics of meningitis, encephalitis, and polio (Erickson, 1977).

Following the 1973 coup in Chile (another participant in the program to reform legal education), much of the population has suffered a sharp decline in the standard of living, while small and medium-sized businesses are being wiped out by the economic policies the junta has adopted on the recommendation of its US economic advisors. In 1975 alone, the Chilean GNP fell by 12 percent, with declines of 27 percent in manufacturing, 35 percent in construction, and 8 percent in mining; the annual rate of inflation has soared to 341 percent; real wages had fallen by 8 percent, while unemployment grew to approximately 20 percent (compared to 3.1 percent before the coup). Between 1972 and 1975, the share of national income going to the propertied classes had increased from 37.1 percent to 61.8 percent, a massive shift away from the working classes (Stallings and Zimbalist, 1975; Letelier, 1976; Chossudovsky, 1977).

In Mexico, which has had a modern legal code for decades, income and regional disparities have grown, and the growth of a landless rural population that cannot be absorbed by industry has led to massive migration to the US[8]—a development all the more significant in that Mexico is the only Latin American nation apart from Cuba to have undergone a social revolution—following which, the state, in conformity with the prescriptions of legal diffusionists, used legal tools as an instrument of economic transformation (Muller, 1973; Hamilton, 1975).

Amin (1974), surveying economic conditions in West Africa, finds few bright spots; despite a variety of legal strategies to promote economic development, growth has slowed or stopped, the standard of living has declined for major sectors of the population, and dependence on the industrial nations has increased. On the basis of his in-depth study of the Ghanaian economy, Pozen (1976:170) concludes that almost all legal reforms proposed to improve the performance of the state sector—which in much of the Third World has been made the linchpin of strategies for planned economic development—"are of doubtful feasibility because of the serious non-legal constraints . . . which cannot be overcome by lawyers who would formulate and enforce these legal reforms. . . ."

Several recent quantitative studies of economic growth have found that while foreign aid and investment can stimulate short-run spurts of growth, their long-run effect is to reduce economic growth and exacerbate economic inequality[9] (Beckford, 1971; Chase-Dunn, 1973; Bornschier et al., 1978). This is a finding that has important implications for legal diffusionists, who have argued for legal reform partly on the grounds that it is needed to encourage foreign investment and utilize aid effectively. In a general survey of economic conditions in the Third World, Barraclough (1978) notes a projection that the number of people in the world living in "absolute poverty" will rise from 800 million at present to between 1.3 and 1.7 billion in the year 2000.

These failures cannot be attributed to lack of implementation. Although the recipes of the legal diffusionists have not been followed everywhere—a fact that testifies to the inefficacy of the recommendations themselves—where they have been tried they have failed to produce the promised economic benefits.

The political results of legal reform have been no more promising. In Ethiopia, where a French-drafted legal code was promulgated in the 1950s, a revolutionary junta has killed an estimated 30,000 people and suppressed all political opposition (An Observer, 1977). Following the military coup in Brazil in 1964, the instrumentally-minded junta empowered the president to suspend Congress, quash election results, rule by decree, deprive citizens of political rights, and suspend habeus corpus (Karst and Rosenn, 1975:214–215.). The democratically elected Popular Unity government in Chile was overthrown in 1973, and the political opposition killed, or driven into exile or the underground. Seidman's (1966) survey of politics in anglophone Africa noted the prevalence of military or one-party dictatorships, rubberstamp legislatures, and the absence of an independent judiciary and an independent press.[10]

Not many years ago, New York University sent teams of lawyers to Botswana, Kenya, Malaysia, Singapore, South Korea, Turkey, Uganda, and Zambia at State Department expense to determine whether there was sympathy for the transplantation of American legal institutions that would encourage wide participation in public affairs and protect democratic private and local government institutions and social welfare. Franck

(1972) reports that elites in the countries visited expressed their receptivity to this transplantation. Yet some of these nations are notorious for their gross violations of human rights.

Although some legal diffusionists have been aware that repression is carried out by Third World governments, few have considered what this might mean for their program. Rosenn (1969), for example, noted that the mass arrest of students was interfering with the implementation of the reform of Brazilian legal education, but without reflecting on the implications this had for the transformation of Brazilian society through legal reforms. Steinberg (1971) notes in the South Korean context that while it would be naive to think that law alone could disperse the political power of the dictatorship, hope lay in economic expansion and international economic contacts. Yet Western-based multinational corporations have been implicated in the overthrow of democratically elected goverments and have given (and received) strong support from politically repressive regimes. Insofar as popular sentiment in Third World countries is more likely to run against foreign corporations than to favor them, the multinationals may have little reason to undermine a dictatorship.

That the United States goverment is itself a major obstacle to the realization of human rights in many parts of the world (Chomsky and Herman, 1977) seems to lie entirely outside the consciousness of legal diffusionists. Their conception of political development consists of little more than evolution toward the American model through the diffusion of political culture and the adoption of Western institutions, with friendly assistance and technical advice from Western governments and social scientists.

RECENT CRITICISM OF LEGAL DIFFUSIONISM

Several scholars have commented on the failures of legal reform programs in recent years. Steinberg (1971) notes that in Korea, modern law had been imposed by Japanese and American occupations, and had been used to expropriate the best farm land and to support a hated secret police system. As a result, it is perceived as alien by much of the population, which prefers traditional conciliatory mechanisms for processing disputes over modern, "rational," legal institutions. Seidman (1972b) has noted that communication of legal reforms to the target population may be ineffective except where a revolutionary party has mobilized the population; and Beckstrom (1974) has observed that where the level of education is low, judges may not be able to understand modern law.

Trubek (1972a) has pointed to a number of contradictions and questionable assumptions in the conceptualization of the relationship between law and economic development in the legal diffusionist literature, while Trubek and Galanter (1974), extending this critique, go so far as to describe law and development specialists as "self-estranged' because of their growing realization that Third World realities are incompatible with their program for development. Trubek and Galanter note, for example, that universalistic law will be universalistic in practice only if the relevant officials have largely abandoned loyalty to family, clan or tribe—an assumption that is false in much of the Third World (and judging from the extent of nepotism and political corruption in the West, it may well be false there as well). The formalization of decision-making that is implied by the introduction of modern law may reduce rather than enhance popular participation in public affairs; after all, the tribal moot may have been unpredictable and lacking in formal rationality, but it was a popular institution. Trubek and Galanter add that in an economically and politically stratified society, the "haves" will enjoy preferential access to lawyers, and may use this access to resist social change that would undermine their advantaged positions.

When legal decision-makers are drawn from elite social backgrounds, they may themselves use modern law to legitimate their own resistance to change. Thus, during the administration of Indira Gandhi, the Supreme Court of India, an institution whose members are almost entirely drawn from well-to-do families and that is generally regarded as a protector of one minority only—the rich—overturned the government's attempts to deprive the ex-rulers of their privileges and purses (Roberts, 1972). Similarly, the 1971 coup in Turkey has been attributed to the role of the judiciary in blocking economic development (Franck, 1972). In this connection, Trubek (1972a) and Trubek and Galanter (1974) call attention to the possible tension between law as a protector of individual rights and a technocratic-instrumental approach to law. In an authoritarian state, an emphasis on law as an instrument of planned social change may erode respect for civil liberties.

For Trubek and Galanter, second thoughts about these matters have been magnified by loss of faith that rule through rational, universalistic and democratically formulated law has enhanced social well-being and protected minority interests even in the United States, that the US can or should serve as a model for the rest of the world, and by skepticism concerning the motives of the US goverment[11] and the governments of host countries in promoting legal change in the Third World.[12] Perhaps it is not an incremental approach to development through legal reform that should be given priority, they suggest, but political change.

There is unquestionably much insight in these criticisms. Nevertheless, they are somewhat scattershot, and fail to build an alternative analysis of the relationship between law and economic development on the foundation of fully justified reservations. Such an analysis must rest on a more clearly articulated conceptualization of the social structures of the LDCs than the distinction Trubek and Galanter (1974) make between "haves" and "have-nots" and of the relationship between the economics of the industrial nations and those of the LDCs. Such an approach must implicitly abandon the view of Parsons and Weber—and held by legal diffusionists—that explains the economic development of a nation entirely in terms of the characteristics of that nation alone.

Dependency theory (Frank, 1967, 1969, 1973; Dos Santos, 1970; Cardoso, 1972; Furtado, 1973a; Leys, 1975; Oxaal, 1975; Amin, 1976; Palmer and Parsons, 1977) or "world systems theory" (Wallerstein, 1974), though not yet fully developed conceptually, and perhaps not free from theoretical difficulties, seems to avoid some of the more obvious pitfalls of legal diffusionism, and thus provides a promising alternative framework for investigating the relationship between law and economic development.

Dependency theorists characterize capitalism as having been an international system almost from its birth. The incorporation of non-capitalist societies into a capitalist world system occurred in such a manner as to differentiate "core" states (England, Western Europe, and the U.S.) from a periphery (colonies of core states, as well as their politically independent satellites). Military intervention on the part of the core states, as well as the structure of international trade and investment, has had divergent effects on the core and the periphery. In the core, capitalism led to autonomous, self-sustaining growth, and raised the general standard of living. In the periphery, it did not have this effect. Contrary to the theory of comparative advantage in neo-classical economics (according to which international economic specialization and trade benefit both parties and ultimately lead to convergent economic development), dependency theory sees international economic relations in a world capitalist system as contributing to the underdevelopment or distorted (dependent) development of states in the periphery.

Dependency theorists have not specifically addressed the role of law in peripheral capitalism. However, the general framework of dependency theory would lead us to suspect that the relationship between law and economic development might be quite different in peripheral societies than it has been in the core. Even if Weber was correct in arguing that the introduction of formally rational legal systems in Western Europe contributed to economic growth by providing a stable framework for market transactions and investment, we cannot necessarily assume that the same social processes that gave rise to formally rational law in the West were, or will be, repeated in other parts of the world.[13]

Although my investigation of the introduction of Western law into Third World societies is still in its earliest, exploratory stages, some highly suggestive patterns have emerged—though at this point, my interpretations must be regarded as highly tentative.

THE ROLE OF LAW IN IMPERIAL DOMINATION

Ireland—England's First Colony

Ireland makes a convenient starting point for our discussion because it became a colony prior to the appearance of capitalism in England, when the 12th-century feudal army of the Earl of Pembroke, acting on behalf of Henry II, defeated the Irish clan armies. Unable to hold the countryside, the English established a Pale of protected settlement surrounding Dublin. English law promulgated to regulate life within the Pale was not concerned with the economic exploitation of the colony, but with preventing the settlers from assimilating, protecting their estates, and with keeping them dependent on England. Thus, according to Hallinan (1977), the Statutes of Kilkenny, written in 1376:

> forbade English intermarriage, . . . adoption of Irish national dress, language names or customs; violations could result in forfeiture of both land and tenants. Toleration of, or submitting to Irish law was high treason, and anyone found permitting Irish tenures or Septs (a subdivision of the Irish clan) to graze on crown-granted land or estates forfeited all land; anyone found harboring Irish minstrels, rhymers or story tellers would suffer heavy fines, and Irish priests were forbidden to enter monasteries or churches. . . . The Irish were not barred from entering the Pale, but they could live in it provided they agreed to adopt English customs and manners.

During the mercantile era, the changing character of English interests in Ireland was reflected in changes in the substantive content of law. The establishment of vast plantations settled by English Protestants in the early 17th century as a way of relieving England of the problem of a surplus population generated by the enclosures entailed the dispossession of the Irish from their land.[14] Heavy taxes were imposed on settlers who hired Irish labor or permitted Irish tenants to remain on the land, regardless of whether the Irish adopted English language and customs—and thus they went farther than the Statutes of Kilkenny (Hallinan, 1977). Whereas secular law in Europe and England had moved substantially during the late feudal period in the direction of universalism by substituting territorial law for the law of personality (i.e., national origin), a tendency that was reinforced by the continuing centralization of political authority in the mercantile era, English law in Ireland reintroduced national distinctions.

Under the Stuarts, mercantile restrictions forbade the export of woolen cloth and other manufactured products such as glass, china, and woven silk from Ireland, while the export of raw wool to the English textile industry was subsidized. Under Henry VII, English merchants succeeded in having Irish fairs banned, forcing Irish trade to be channeled through the Pale where the English merchants could control it. A penal code promulgated at the end of the 17th century prohibited the Irish from entering the professions (except medicine), precluded Catholic involvement in trade on any substantial scale, and, by abolishing primogeniture, forced the division of land among all male heirs—measures that interfered with the accumulation of capital and the development of an Irish landed, commercial or professional middle class that could challenge English domination. The Irish were being turned into landless tenants by law—law backed up not by any of the forms of legitimation discussed by Weber, but by military conquest (Hechter, 1975; Hallinan, 1977).

Apart from the intensification of particularistic distinctions between settlers and natives, we see the English using law in Ireland during the mercantile period to separate the native population from access to the means of production (at this point, land), to structure trade to the advantage of the colonial power, and to shape the class structure of the colony in a direction consistent with colonial domination.

Plunder, Commerce and Law in the Mercantile Colonies

Where early contacts between Europe and non-Western civilizations occurred in the context of trade without conquest, the encounters had few direct legal ramifications for native peoples. Thus, although the West African slave trade had major social consequences in Africa (Amin, 1974: 320–322), indigenous customary legal systems remained intact. Dutch and English settlers in North America created legal institutions derived from those they knew in Europe (with modifications reflecting dissenting religious doctrine and changed economic and political conditions), leaving the Indians whose land they purchased to continue governing themselves.

Yet trade without conquest was the exception rather than the rule. Contact with a number of non-Western societies was structured by competition between the various mercantile states of Europe, and by Europe's comparative poverty and military superiority. Trade with the prosperous and wealthy civilizations of China, Indonesia, India, the Aztecs, and Incas was difficult because Europe had so little that these people wanted.[15] Military conquest gave the mercantile states the exclusive right to plunder and to force natives to trade on unfavorable terms (Griffin, 1969).

In some colonies, this transfer of wealth was accomplished through legal devices, such as the quasi-feudal *encomienda*, through which conquistadores in New Spain were consigned Indians from whom they were entitled to demand tribute and labor (used for the mining of precious metals and for agriculture). Elsewhere, the trade monopoly itself was the critical factor. In any event, the legal dimensions of colonialism at this stage were quite limited.

Predation carried out under the aegis of the colonial powers was frequently devastating in its impact on the native populations. The peoples of the South Pacific and the Caribbean were decimated in a matter of decades, and the population of Mexico and Peru fell by an estimated 75 percent in the 16th century (Griffin, 1969; Borah, 1951: 11). In India, "Thirty millions of human beings were reduced to the extremity of wretchedness" (Adams, 1896) by English plunder. The European economies, on the other hand, prospered as a result of this "primitive accumulation." Thus, English officials in India, according to Adams (1896: 294ff):

> were absolute, irresponsible, and rapacious, and they emptied the private hoards. Their only thought was to wring some hundreds of thousands of pounds out of the natives as quickly as possible, and hurry home to display their wealth. Enormous fortunes were thus rapidly accumulated at Calcutta. . . . Very soon after . . . the Bengal plunder began to arrive in London, and the effect appears to have been instantaneous, for all authorities agree that the "industrial revolution," the event which has divided the nineteenth century from all antecedent time, began with the year 1760. Prior to 1760 . . . the machinery used for spinning cotton in Lancashire was almost as simple as in India; while in 1750 the English iron industry was in full decline.

Similarly, in France

> The growth in colonial establishments, the progress in trade and transport, and rise in power, wealth and reputation of the metropolitan country, all these resulted from the slave trade. France's external trade in the eighteenth century enjoyed a favourable balance of several million *livres*, and this was due to the export of colonial products which were the fruit of slave labor (Father Rinchon, 1929: 18).

While it would be simplistic to attribute the "take-off" of the European economies to this factor alone, the stimulus provided by this infusion of wealth may well have been considerable. In the words of Marx (1967: 751, 753–4):

> The discovery of gold and silver in America, the extirpation, enslavement and entombment in mines of the aboriginal population, the beginning of the conquest and looting of the East Indies, the turning of Africa into a warren for the commercial hunting of black-skins, signalised the rosy dawn of the era of capitalist production. . . . The treasures captured outside Europe by undisguised looting, enslavement, and murder, floated back to the mother-country and were there turned into capital."

Curiously, no legal diffusionist has proposed that the Third World enlarge its capital at the expense of the West through methods similar to those Europe once employed.

The industrial revolution in Europe led to a more extensive articulation of mercantile economic relations with colonies, usually involving colonial production and export of food crops and mining, and importation of manufactured goods from Europe.

Where extensive white settlement took place, the colonizing powers refused to recognize native land tenure systems, and legitimized the larger-scale confiscation of land. In Southern Rhodesia, whites, who make up roughly 10 percent of the population, took 49 million acres of land, leaving 28.5 million acres for native Africans. In the Union of South Africa, 89 percent of the land was reserved for Europeans; in Swaziland, 49 percent (Woddis, 1960: 1–51). During the 1930s, the British Colonial Office in Kenya validated white seizure of land by setting aside almost 17,000 square miles of the best land for exclusive white settlement (Weeks, 1975). Similarly in Peru, a small number of settlers were granted vast latifundia formed from land confiscated from the Indians, who were forced to farm on small plots on mountainous slopes (Griffin, 1969). During the 19th century, the French confiscated large quantities of Algerian land for French settlers, and relocated the dispossessed communities on poorer land (Lazreg, 1976: 41–45).

To prevent African farmers from competing with English settlers, the former were forbidden by law from growing export crops (e.g., coffee in Rhodesia), and railroads were located far from native reserves. The high population density in native reserves, where land was often malarial, swampy, or of generally poor quality, impoverished the native population. This, together with the imposition of a cash head tax, forced Africans to work on European plantations. The preservation of the reserves by such measures as the prohibition of land transfers between Africans and Europeans and regulations preventing Africans from living in Salisbury and other East African cities[16] (Seidman, 1966), allowed African workers to receive partial support from a "traditional" economy, thus permitting plantation owners to pay them less than their marginal product. Somewhat analogous arrangements characterized the plantation economies of Latin America.

In West Africa, where few whites settled, separate European and native areas were not established, and the head tax was minimal. Instead of working on plantations or in mines, native peasants cultivated such crops as cocoa, rubber, groundnuts and oil-palm products on their own small-holdings and sold them for export to large European corporations like Unilever, with the collection and transportation of crops managed by an African middle class (Woddis, 1960; Seidman, 1966; Fitch and Oppenheimer, 1968).

In either case, the British established a dual legal system in Africa,[17] one for disputes growing out of precapitalist social relations,[18] and the other for disputes growing out of capitalist social relations. The former sector consisted of customary law, often codified by the English, and enforced as long as it was not considered by the English appeals courts to be inconsistent with "natural justice, equity, or good conscience." The "modern" legal system, applicable to Europeans and to Africans, involved in the capitalist sector of the economy, consisted of English common law, doctrines of equity, and statutes in effect at the time of the reception.[19] Wage employment of African laborers on European-owned plantations and in mines, and the sale of crops to export firms, were governed by English law. However, 20th-century developments in English law, such as welfare law and labor law, were not imported. Nor was English constitutional law. Arbitrary imprisonment without trial was permitted. Colonialism could not have been maintained without these restrictions to the reception of English law.

The partial legal intrusion typically allowed the cooptation of native elites. The powers of native chiefs in carrying out dispute resolution were often enhanced by the colonial rulers. In Bengal at the end of the 18th century, the East India Company made native tribute collectors owners of the land on which they collected taxes, while peasants were transformed into serfs (Griffin, 1969; Amin, 1976: 298).

Even prior to the age of colonial conquest, Europeans had commented on the unequal benefits of trade with the non-Western world;[20] the mercantile restrictions imposed on the colonies greatly exacerbated this inequality. To prevent native manufacturing from competing with goods manufactured in the dominant country, the export of goods made in the colonies was discouraged or prohibited, and measures to protect infant colonial industries were disallowed. Consequently, machine-produced English goods made by an industry that had itself grown up sheltered from foreign competition flooded colonial markets. Domestic crafts and manufacturing were ruined in Africa, India (Amin, 1976: 299), the Middle East (Farsoun and Carroll, 1976), and Indonesia (Griffin, 1969); mercantile restrictions imposed by Spain and Portugal had a comparable effect in destroying Latin American industry.[21] During the 1840s, the Indonesians faced mass starvation because the Dutch forced them to grow crops for export rather than for their own consumption (Caldwell, 1968: 39).

As with British rule in Ireland, we see colonial legal systems that are particularistic, making distinctions between Europeans and native populations substantively and procedurally. These legal systems structured economic relations between colonizer and colonized to the advantage of the former and the detriment of the latter. As in Ireland, colonization transformed the indigenous class structure of African, Asian, and Latin American colonies, usually by the creation of a small, privileged native elite or a somewhat larger settler elite that occupied an advantaged position in the colonial economy. Although these legal systems may have limited the disorganized, individual plunder which characterized the first stages of colonial rule, they permitted the more systematic, organized transfer of wealth from native populations to settlers and to capitalists in the dominant nation.[22]

Free Trade Imperialism

That national independence did not necessarily remedy this situation is well illustrated by 19th-century Latin American history. Because the Napoleonic Wars weakened Spanish and Portuguese control of their colonies (in some cases the parent country was directly occupied), the creole bourgeoisie was able to gain national independence and thus to be free from Spanish or Portuguese taxes, restrictions on imports, and high prices on imported goods. The end of foreign expropriation of surplus generated a temporary stimulus to the economy. In the ensuing civil wars of the 1830s and 1840s between an industrializing bourgeoisie favoring protection for infant industries and an export-oriented bourgeoisie based in agriculture, mining and commerce, and favoring free trade, British intervention on behalf of free trade was decisive (Frank, 1967, 1972).

Following this victory, civil and commercial codes derived from the Napeoleonic Code were adopted in much of Latin America (see footnote 7). These codes provided for contractual freedom; their formally rational and universalistic qualities, which made no distinction between domestic and foreign economic actors, meshed perfectly with a *laisser-faire* policy—a policy now favored by England because English manufacturing had become so efficient that it could undersell goods produced elsewhere, making mercantile restrictions unnecessary. The result was the destruction of existing Latin American industry. For example, the Chilean metallurgical industry which had grown up in the nineteenth century

> manufactured plows, threshing machines, locomotives, railroad freight cars, large bells, etc.; they also constructed four steam locomotives. The initiative developed in the metallurgical industry showed its efficiency by being able to provide the necessary arms and equipment for the Chilean army and navy during the War of the Pacific. Nevertheless, this effort, so promisingly begun, was later nullified for the most part by competition from imported products (Nolff, cited in Frank, 1967: 60).

As a result, Latin American economies remained dependent on imports for most consumer goods and equipment. On the other hand, the agro-extractive sector, based on export, grew substantially, stimulating by rising demand in Europe, and facilitated by road and railway construction financed by British loans. Britain also came to dominate trade and banking; and toward the end of the 19th century, many local firms passed into foreign ownership. The domination of agriculture by large estates and the political power of the large landowners combined to depress wages to farm laborers, maintaining a highly unequal distribution of income.

Under British pressure in the early 19th century, the Ottoman bureaucracy underwent a series of reforms involving (Sunar, 1974: 52–53):

> the establishment of formal equality for all citizens, the recognition of the right to private property, the transfer of state lands to private individuals, the codification of

> penal and commercial laws, the regulation of economic relations through a European system of codes and courts, and the enforcement of a liberal economic policy of *laisser faire*.

The economic consequences included the displacement of Turkish artisans in the face of British industrial imports, a shift toward agricultural production for export (Britain had pressured Turkey in this direction because it wanted to lower the cost of imported raw materials by increasing production in other countries), and in many cases the ruin of peasants connected with the transformation of land tenures (Sunar, 1974: 49). Similar developments occurred throughout the Middle East.

Irish industry, which had begun to develop behind tarriff barriers toward the end of the 18th century, was destroyed after union with England in 1801 ended the ability of the Irish parliament to protect Irish industry (Leys, 1975: 7; Hechter, 1975: 91–93). Crafts and manufacturing were similarly ruined in western Sicily in the early 19th century as a result of legal reforms adopted during the brief British occupation following the Napoleonic Wars (Schneider and Schneider, 1976).

Comparable developments can be traced in Africa and in the West Indies, where former colonies pursued an export-based economy following independence. Although such a strategy can bring short-term spurts of growth to an economy when unemployed labor or resources are called into production, the long-run consequences of this approach have been the destruction of tendencies toward diversification and autonomous economic development, producing economic dependence on the core economies, stagnation when demand from the industrial nations has slackened or competition on the part of the producer nations has led to overproduction, and in many cases, deteriorating terms of trade. The domination of international trade by the core has further disadvantaged the periphery; thus, in West Africa, the monopsonistic power of the export firms enabled them to purchase crops from Africans at extremely low prices (Seidman, 1966). It thus seems fully justified to speak, as Frank (1967) does, of the "development of underdevelopment" in the Third World.

Development Based on Import Substitution

Economic relations between Latin America and the industrial nations were partly disrupted during the First World War and again during the Depression and Second World War. For example, the collapse of the demand for coffee during the Depression ruined the Brazilian coffee industry and brought a halt to the importation of manufactured goods that had previously been purchased with foreign exchange earned in the export sector. This period saw a substantial growth in manufacturing based on import substitution (*desarrollo hacia adentro*) (Frank, 1967: 1975). Other nations (e.g., Turkey in the period following 1933) have attempted to stimulate domestic manufacturing by restricting the importation of consumer goods.

Although import substitution has stimulated the growth of national industry, as a strategy for development it is inherently constrained by the skewed distribution of income in the LDCs to produce luxury consumer goods that were previously imported by the wealthy; no one else has enough money to constitute an economically effective demand. The limited size of the upper income stratum poses limits to the growth of the production of goods for domestic consumption in the absence of a major redistribution of income.

To a limited extent, the populist movements that came to power in several of the Latin American countries (Brazil in 1930, Argentina in 1945) did redistribute income by raising wages and providing benefits to the urban working class, thus expanding demand for consumer goods; and financed the importation of capital goods with foreign exchange earnings and foreign loans. But the failure to enact land reform has kept agricultural wages down, and the introduction of high technology machinery imported from the industrial nations where labor is scarce restricted the expansion of wage employment in the industrial sector. Moreover, the need to import capital goods and inputs for manufacturing and to repay foreign loans has meant that import substitution has done little to solve balance of payments problems (Frank, 1972: 85; Dos Santos, 1970; Furtado, 1972). Similar difficulties have plagued other nations that have adopted import substitution strategies (Amin, 1974: 18).

Following the Second World War, the international capitalist system was reorganized under US leadership. In the post-war years, US direct private investment in the Third World has grown through the purchase of existing firms and the opening of branches for production or assembly of parts where tariff barriers stand in the way of selling finished products; the consequence has been the progressive denationalization of the formerly national manufacturing sector in those countries where manufacturing had developed. So, for example, by 1970 more than 80 percent of Peruvian industry was foreign-owned; by 1972, 70 percent of Brazilian manufacturing was foreign-owned; and by 1969, 90 percent of Chilean mining was American-owned. A similar dominatiom of the industrial sector has developed in newly independent colonies that encouraged foreign investment in the hope (usually misplaced) that benefits would result from the importation of capital and technology.

This growth in American investment in the Third World has been actively promoted by American political and military intervention, through strings attached to foreign "aid," and in some cases by bribery of

Law and Development 147

local politicians and businessmen. But much of this growth has been due not to corruption or Machiavellian manipulation on the part of the industrialized capitalist nations, but to the severe structural constraints on Third World development, such as the industrial world's monopoly on advanced technology. There now exists a substantial literature documenting the deleterious effects of this foreign investment: the export of capital from periphery to core through repatriated profits and transfer payments; destruction of domestic industry through inability to compete with large multinational corporations; the channeling of local investment funds to foreign owned enterprises; the creation of a well-paid salariat in the foreign sector (as well as in the state administration) with consumer tastes oriented to the importation of foreign made consumer goods; the weakening of political and economic independence.[23]

Some authors have argued that these effects are so severe that industrialization cannot occur at all in the Third World. Although this conclusion is unwarranted, and is in fact empirically false (Warren, 1973; Szymanski, 1974, 1976), the effects just noted do inhibit industrialization; and where industrialization does take place, expansion is limited and development remains shaped by external direction.

State Interventionist Strategies and Development

In a number of politically independent LDCs, the state, headed by military figures or by a revolutionary but non-socialist elite, has begun to play an active role in economic development. In the case of an export-based strategy, this may entail such measures as the establishment of marketing boards, the provision of agricultural credits and the introduction of new seeds, new crops, and new technology ("the Green Revolution"); in the case of development based on import substitution, it may entail the establishment of tariffs, import and export controls, a tax policy favorable to foreign and/or domestic investment in manufacturing, subsidies, wage controls, and the creation of publicly owned or jointly owned enterprises.[24] On occasion, it has involved the nationalization of foreign-owned enterprises, particularly in the extractive sectors. The state is especially likely to assume this role when existing classes are too weak to carry through a program of industrial development by themselves.[25]

A nationalistically oriented intervention strategy may bring the state into conflict with already industrialized nations whose economic interests are threatened, as happened not long ago when Brazil's decision to develop its own nuclear power posed a challenge to the US nuclear industry. Similarly, US-Peruvian relations were strained when the military regime in Peru nationalized a subsidiary of Standard Oil without compensation, but since other foreign investment was not taken (in fact, Peru continued to welcome foreign investment[26]), the conflict was contained. Earlier conflict between Mexico and the United States connected with the nationalization of Standard Oil was similarly kept within limits because, among other things, Mexican President Cardenas believed that Mexico needed foreign investment.

Where the challenge to foreign capital has been greater, so has the response,[27]—witness the overthrow of the Mossadegh government in Iran in 1953, the Arbenz Guzman government in Guatemala in 1954, the Allende government in Chile in 1973 (to name only a few), the economic blockade of Cuba and attempts to assassinate Fidel Castro—though changed foreign and domestic circumstances make this response much more difficult for the U.S. now than it was in the past.[28]

Active intervention in Third World economies on the part of their own governments has had several sources. In Latin America, social welfare measures to benefit an urban working class were adopted by populist governments (Vargas in Brazil, Peron in Argentina) to gain political support. Steps to foster economic growth have originated wtih local bourgeoisie, state managers, or even foreign capital and reflect their own immediate economic goals as well as the desire to forestall working class and peasant unrest. A nationalist program to reduce foreign domination of the economy can bring about support for economic growth from all classes.

One would anticipate that the abandonment of free trade doctrines would be reflected in a shift away from legal formalism toward a more instrumental conception of law. There is evidence that this is happening. Thus, the post-revolutionary Mexican Civil Code of 1928 contrasts with the Latin American codes of the late 19th century in the extent to which it reflects social concerns. Statutory law in other Latin American countries, where a significant amount of urbanization and industrialization has occurred, have likewise provided for social security, minimum wages, and similar measures.

Many have argued that active state intervention to stimulate economic growth requires legal tools extending far beyond those available to the state in a *laisser faire* free trade economy, and this line of reasoning has been influential in much of the Third World. For example, the Kenyan decision to seek rapid growth by encouraging foreign investment led the Kenyan government to seek legal methods for regulating, taxing, and controlling foreign exchange (Leys, 1975). A program to shift domestic investment can also require legal tools, such as taxation policy. This is, of course, exactly the direction that legal diffusionists have advocated for the Third World.

Yet, in at least some parts of the Third World, the possible effectiveness of legal tools in achieving these goals is doubtful. The smaller Third World countries are economically weak by comparison with the large multinational corporations; indeed, the assets of some multinationals exceed the budgets of some LDCs. When Kaiser contracts with African governments, it employs its own form contracts and includes a provision that in case of disputes, California law is applicable (Seidman, 1966). Given the limited administrative apparatus in newly independent nations, we should expect tax laws and business regulations to be easily evaded. It thus comes as no surprise to learn that one recent student of development (Rosen, 1978) has concluded that:

> Despite the importation of elaborate Western commercial codes in Ghana, public corporations controlling utilities and state factories remain beyond government regulation. Similarly, the reliance on formal systems of taxation as the panacea for channelling consumption, redirecting investment, and altering agrarian patterns has proved illusory.

It is, of course, worth keeping in mind that Ghana should not be confused with the entire Third World. Where the state bureaucracy is better developed, and where national economic and political power is relatively greater, relations with foreign corporations may be less one-sided.[29] In these cases, legal methods may have limited usefulness in structuring these relationships. For example, the Algerian code for foreign investments does limit foreign ownership of Algerian resources and industry. But its ability to do this is predicated on Algeria's possession of non-legal sources of power. And it is the limits of this power that limit the ability of law to secure an independent economic development. These limits are severe, even if not totally constraining.

Although it is conceivable that legal diffusionists have placed so much stress on the importance of developing a more instrumental conception of law because they thought it important to protect foreign populations from unregulated foreign giant corporations, it seems more likely that their goal was rather to further the interests of the muti-nationals themselves. It has become apparent long ago in the United States that state regulatory measures could be circumvented by large corporations, or utilized to reduce competition and increase profits, while at the same time reassuring the public that business was operating under government scrutiny. In the context of an administratively handicapped, economically weak Third World nation, regulation would be expected to be even more ineffective.

Whether intended or not, the instrumental conception of law prompted by legal diffusionists was one especially suited to American corporate penetration of the economies of the LDCs in the context of state-directed capitalistic economic development. With the economic power to dominate the state (and with backing from the US State Department), the large corporation does not need the legal protection against state intervention in the economy that a small business does—a need which is expressed in legal formalism and *laisser faire* policy. In fact, jointly owned enterprises benefit the foreign corporation by coopting the state and local bourgeoisie and shielding the corporation from nationalist populism, thus reducing the risks of nationalization (Rose, 1970).

Legal education programs established by American law schools to train Third World lawyers make sense in this light, for in American discussions concerning ways that lawyers could contribute to development, the need for indigenous lawyers who could handle the legal problems of foreign investors loomed large (Merillat, 1966). In this concern for the interests of the foreign corporation, legal diffusionists need not have seen themselves as representing business interests *against* those of the Third World. More plausibly, they did not regard those interests as being in conflict. After all, eminent sociologists and economists assured them that Western law and business investment would foster economic growth and democracy. Many of those in the Third World believed this too (see, for example, Nwabueze, 1966). Alternative models of development (e.g., Chinese, Russian, Cuban), in which legal development would have played a rather different role,[30] and in which quite different nonlegal strategies would have been contemplated, were given little consideration for political reasons and because they did not provide opportunities for foreign investment.

Where programs for legal development were undertaken on the part of core governments, rather than at the initiative of academics or Third World scholars and politicians, there may be grounds for being less charitable with regard to motives. For example, at present, the United States goverment is involved in an attempt to create a system of patent law in Ghana (private communication from Beverly Houghton). Since few patents for inventions developed in Ghana come on the world market, the effort can hardly be explained by fear that Ghanaian inventors will fail to earn royalties on their inventions. It is more plausible to assume that the U.S. goverment wants to ensure that American corporations receive royalties on products built or sold in Ghana. This is hardly in the interests of Ghana.

Third World Development and Human Rights

Additional light on the relationship between law and an interventionist approach to economic development is shed by considering that a number of these "activist" governments came to power through coups that toppled populist governments (e.g., Argentina, Brazil, Chile). With the slowing of economic growth based on import substitution and the deterioration of balance of payments deficits created by the need to repay the loans that financed the purchase of capital goods and by the repatriation of profits in the foreign-owned sector, military coups occurred, generally with the support of both the American government and the domestic bourgeoisie, as well as the middle class employed by or otherwise dependent on foreign-owned business.

The new governments have been committed to renewing the accumulation of capital on behalf of the bourgeoisie (both foreign and domestic) by dismantling popular redistributive programs. Wages in the industrial sector have been kept low in much of the Third World by the underdevelopment of agriculture (a consequence of the failure of land reform, or, where the Green Revolution has taken place, by the effect of economies of scale and of inadequate provision of credit to small farmers). The consequence has been migration to the cities in numbers larger than the industrial sector can absorb, especially when industrialization is based on advanced technology that requires few workers. This has helped generate high profits, though it has also hampered the realization process by limiting the domestic market. The populist governments had interfered with market forces by establishing minimum wages in the urban sector. This expanded the domestic market and made growth based on import substitution more feasible. But by increasing the costs of business, the increased wages ultimately contributed to stagnation and slowed growth. Now the military governments have reduced the wage bill by repealing minimum wage laws, restoring profits.[31]

The deterioration in the standard of living of the masses, and sharpened inequality noted earlier with regard to Brazil and Chile, necessitate the repression of political opposition (Furtado, 1973b), while the reduction of wages contracts the domestic market for consumer goods, necessitating production for export. However, when multinational corporations license local firms to use their technology, they often prohibit production for export to avoid creating competition for themselves (Muller, 1973). Moreover, the industrial powers, who could provide a large market for manufactured goods, are increasingly adopting protectionist measures to defend their own stagnating industries. Consequently, the more industrialized of the LDCs (e.g., Brazil) are exporting to the less industrialized, a process that is likely to interfere with the process of industrialization in the latter countries.[32] Revenues from the export of oil and other primary products may be large enough, at least for a time, to permit some few non-industrial nations to purchase enough from those that are industrializing to permit the development of a diversified export sector. However, the need to keep wages down to make inefficient industry competitive on the world market will preclude the restoration of political democracy. As a result, rapid economic growth in the context of a capitalist world system is likely to be incompatible with "rule by law" in the political sense,[33] at least in those countries where populist or socialist mobilization has taken place[34] (Brazil, Chile). If this is so, the legal diffusionist program can only be described as a capitalist pipe dream—a pipe dream that is innocent of contradiction.

But not innocent! Jimmy Carter would hardly have made so much of a "human rights" campaign when his own administration and preceding administrations have done so much to undermine human rights in so many parts of the world, if the concept of human rights did not have ideological value in generating support for US foreign policy in the aftermath of Vietnam.

ACKNOWLEDGMENTS

An earlier version of this paper was first presented to the 1979 meeting of the British Sociological Association. I am grateful to David Muchnick for first turning my attention to this problem and for many stimulating ideas. Marnia Lazreg and June Nash provided helpful comments on an earlier draft.

NOTES

1. Weber is a partial exception, as he did draw on Chinese, Hindu, Islamic, and ancient Hebrew law. However, as he did not study law in societies that had been colonized by capitalist nations, his view of the relationship between law and capitalist economic development remained stunted and Eurocentric.

2. Trubek and Galanter (1974) characterize these writings with the phrase "legal liberalism," an expression I find less than satisfying because of its lack of specificity. I have adopted this expression from Hechter's (1975) "diffusion model of national development."

3. Where this was not done, legal reform has had virtually no impact. Thus, the legal code prepared for Ethiopia by French legal scholars had little impact after it was adopted because the poorly educated Ethiopian judges were not able to understand it (Bookstrom, 1974).

4. Latin American legal education has been criticized for its emphasis on rote learning and its treatment of law as a closed, deductive system. Prior to the 1964 coup, administrative law was not taught in Brazil because it was considered "unaesthetic" (Steiner, 1971). Similar complaints about legal education in Asia and Africa have been voiced by Merillat (1966).

5. As Trubek (1972b) notes, the richness of Weber's conceptualization of this process was lost in much of the law and development literature, which overlooks Weber's argument that modern law stimulated the development of capitalism only in the presence of a number of other factors, many of which are not present in the LDCs.

6. The 19th century constitutions of Argentina, Brazil, Mexico and Venezuela were all based on the American model, and included such features (some of them later dropped) as federalism, the separation of powers (including judicial review), and protection of individual liberties and private property (Karst and Rosenn, 1975: 43).

7. French-derived civil codes were adopted in Haiti, the Dominican Republic, Bolivia, Chile, Ecuador, Colombia, El Salvador, Nicaragua, Panama, Argentina, Brazil, Uruguay, and Cuba (Karst and Rosenn, 1975: 47).

8. Estimates of the fraction of the Mexican labor force now in the United States range from one-sixth to one-third.

9. A number of case studies indicate that where economic growth has occurred it has been accompanied by increased unemployment and sharper income disparities, as well as a deterioration in the standard of living of the lower strata in absolute terms in a number of the LDCs (Seers, 1969; ul Haq, 1971; Furtado, 1972). This obviously raises questions about the meaningfulness of the very concept of "development."

10. There are, however, many Third World countries for which such a statement could not be made. The independence of the judiciary in India has received a good deal of publicity during the past few years, to cite only one example.

11. It is, I think, remarkable that it took law and development specialists so long to entertain these doubts; the cards concerning the nature of American imperialist involvement in the rest of the world have been on the table for a very long time. This naiveté suggests that legal diffusionists were remarkably ignorant of the United States and its involvement in the Third World.

12. Here, too, the views of the legal diffusionists can only be described as breathtaking. For example, Sedler (1968) asserts with regard to legal reform in post-colonial Africa, that "the value assumptions on which the new law will be based involve a change from the values (and interests) of a foreign elite, i.e., the colonial power, to those of an indigenous elite who (*it can be assumed*) wish to change the society for the betterment of *all* people" (emphasis added).

13. For two somewhat different accounts of the relationship between the development of capitalism of rational law in Europe, see Weber (1968) and Tigar and Levy (1976). At this point, it is appropriate to indicate that I am appropriating from dependency theory only selected insights. Some of its more controversial elements (e.g., its tendency to define capitalism in terms of circulation rather production) are irrelevant for my purposes and will be ignored.

14. For example, in 1609, 20,000 English and Scottish settlers were given 500,000 acres of arable land confiscated from Irish clans in Ulster, laying the seeds for the current conflict in Northern Ireland (Hallinan, 1977).

15. Thus, Helen Lamb notes (cited in Mandel, 1968: 442): "By the eighteenth century India had attained a high degree of development in pre-industrial terms. Agriculture was sufficiently developed to support a relatively large number of non-agricultural workers; there were highly skilled craftsmen in iron, steel, textiles, shipbuilding and metalwork. India produced manufactured goods not only for home consumption but for export." According to Vlekke (1946: 178), "when the first Dutch merchants and sailors had come to the island world of the Indies, they had been amazed by the variety of its nature and civilization, and the more observant among them had recognized that southern and eastern Asia were far ahead of western Europe in riches as in commercial ability and mercantile skill." During the period of Islamic expansion, "the Christian West had little or nothing to offer, but rather flattered Islamic pride with the spectacle of a culture that was visibly and palpably inferior" (Cipolla, 1965). The Opium Wars were fought to force China to accept opium grown in India so that England could earn the foreign exchange with which to pay for tea and other imports from China.

16. The "pass system" in South Africa has served a similar function. To curb the destruction of the Indonesian economy in the early 19th century, the Dutch imposed legal restrictions on the transfer of land to Europeans. Fitzpatrick (1980) has underscored the role that colonial law has played in strengthening "traditional" sectors of indigenous societies. Because Africans were excluded from the East African cities, Indians often dominated commerce. Similarly in Thailand, where native Thai peasants were not permitted to reside in Bangkok to prevent the loss of rural labor on plantations, Chinese merchants came to control trade and small business sectors of the Thai economy (Elliot, 1978).

17. In India, the British maintained their own courts for British residents in three cities and Hindu and Islamic courts for Indians—staffed for the most part by British judges until

1861, when the courts were unified—and enforced a Penal Code and Codes of Civil and Criminal Procedure based on a synthesis of British and Hindu law.

18. It is common to refer to this as the "traditional" sector of the economy,and to the capitalist sector as "modern," but this language can be misleading, as neither the cultivation of single crops for export nor the intensive farming (which precluded traditional crop rotation) in the East African reserves was in fact traditional. Indian villages in Mexico and Peru are likewise not traditional, but represent an adaptation to the destruction of Aztec and Inca civilizations. In short, the "traditional" economy is often a modern creation, and consists of a synthesis of elements of traditional culture with elements introduced from outside as a result of incorporation into a world capitalist system.

19. Ghana was the first British colony to receive English law; as this occurred in 1876, English statutory law up to 1874 was valid in Ghana.

20. Thus, at the beginning of the 17th century, William Wisselinx, the Dutch merchant, wrote (quoted in Mandel, 1968: 109): "the trade on the Guinea coast was indeed profitable to the country in two ways: first, commodities of great value were obtained there from people who are as yet ignorant of their true value: secondly, these commodities were obtained in exchange for European goods of much smaller value." After describing the extensive French trade with the Middle East in the late 18th century, the traveller Volney (1966) commented "and all this at the expense of the Orientals." Emmanuel (1972) has recently treated the subject of unequal exchange analytically.

21. During the European depression of the 17th century, Latin American industry had reached a level of considerable proportions; for example, Brazilian iron output exceeded that of England (Frank, 1967: 60).

22. These mercantile features persisted surprisingly long in some parts of the world. For example, during and after the Second World War, the Labor Government in Britain established marketing boards in Malaya and Africa with a monopoly in the purchase and sale of most commodities. Although the purpose of the boards was ostensibly to stabilize prices paid to peasants, prices of export crops were forced down far below the world market price, and the substantial balance used to finance Britain's foreign exchange deficit (Fitch and Oppenheimer, 1968). Similarly, in Mozambique, according to *Le Monde*, "prices have always been fixed advantageously for Portugal and profits have rarely been plowed back into Mozambique" (cited in Baumgartner and Burns, 1974).

23. Many of these effects also exist when it is the agro-extractive sector that is heavily foreign-dominated.

24. Some colonial governments (e.g., England) had created public corporations to serve their own mercantile goals. In those parts of Africa where such had been the case, the post-independence governments left them intact and also created new ones, but staffed by Africans and oriented to domestic goals. Ostensibly, these public corporations were to foster economic growth, but in practice they were often used to provide patronage jobs to political supporters and to serve other political ends (Pozen, 1976).

25. Lazreg (1976) has noted this phenomenon in her study of post-independence Algeria. Japan provides another case in point. Threatened with foreign intervention at a time when none of the existing classes was strong enough to dominate the state, state bureaucrats of the late Tokugawa and early Meiji periods took steps to create an industrial capitalist class and a proletariat (Trimberger, 1977). Japan westernized its legal system at this time to provide the legal framework for a new economic system (Takayanagi, 1963). In many instances, the weakness of existing classes is the consequence of under-development which exists because of earlier foreign domination. Thus, Vargas came to power in Brazil in 1930 with support from the industrialists of Rio Grande do Sul in the south, where the economy was less linked to export, but foreign domination of the economy as a whole limited the strength of this class, so that it was not able to displace the old dominant groups of agrarian and commercial

interests, but was forced to share power with them. This circumstance precluded land reform (Frank, 1967: 170).

26. The regime has, however, attempted to steer investment out of the agro-extractive sector into manufacturing. Until the 1950s, foreign investment was almost entirely in the former sectors (Quijano, 1971).

27. In the case of Japan, accommodation with the other industrial nations occurred only with a high level of conflict because of the more advanced level of Japanese industrialization. Japan had industrialized without significant foreign investment and thus had never been actively "underdeveloped" by the west. As the size of the domestic market in Japan was limited by the low wage-level, production of consumer goods was largely for foreign markets. Competition with the west for foreign markets ultimately led to Japan's military defeat and subsequent acceptance of American hegemony (Trimberger, 1977), with economic competition now occurring at a lower level.

28. It is significant that the relative moderation of the US response to Peru and to Mexico during the 1930s was displayed during a period of comparative US weakness.

29. In this connection, Warren (1973) has argued that competition among the multinationals and among industrial nations, together with agreements among Third World nations (such as OPEC for the oil exporters) has strengthened the hands of the LDCs, giving them greater bargaining power.

30. For example, the People's Republic of China has no tax law or commercial code, and is taking steps to develop the latter only now that it is inviting foreign investment.

31. Countries that have never had populist governments but that are now attempting to attract "runaway industries" (e.g., South Korea, Taiwan, Hong Kong, Singapore, Mexico) are similarly trying to keep wages down (Amin, 1974).

32. It is noteworthy in this connection that the Andean Pact, which was to have provided an economic common market for the seven Andean nations, fell apart because the less developed members felt that the more developed were benefitting disproportionately.

33. This incompatibility has placed the Carter administration on the horns of a dilemma. Thus, a recent New York Times article (Miller, 1978) reports that the administration supports a transition from military to democratic civilian rule in Peru. At the same time, it supports drastic austerity measures demanded by the International Monetary Fund in return for credit. The announcement of the austerity measures evoked "rioting, strikes and bloodshed. . . . That in turn forced the military government to declare martial law, suspend constitutional guarantees of assembly and free speech and postpone the Peruvian elections, the first in 15 years. . . . Many US Government and independent analysts now fear that the unpopular austerity measures may prevent a successful return to civilian rule. . . . Some analysts see the Peruvian crisis as typical of the economic, political and social problems of developing nations . . . some analysts fear that only the most repressive, undemocratic regimes will be able to enforce stabilization policies adequate to 'solve' debt problems."

34. This conclusion is predicated on the assumption that the potential for mass mobilization has not been destroyed by terror. Where that premise is false, there may be a return to limited formal democracy where the regime seeks wider public support, or where the US fears that its own interests may be jeopardized by its support for a weak and unpopular dictatorial regime. Withdrawal of US support for the Somoza dictatorship in Nicaragua at a point when it was collapsing is a case in point.

REFERENCES

Adams, Brooks, *The Law of Civilization and Decay*. New York, 1896.

Amin, Samir, *Neocolonialism in West Africa*. New York: Monthly Review Press, 1974.

————, *Unequal Development: An Essay on the Social Formations of Peripheral Capitalism*. New York: Monthly Review Press, 1976.

An Observer, "Revolution in Ethiopia," *Monthly Review* 29 (1977): 46–60.

Auerbach, Carl, "Legal Development in Developing Countries: The American Experience." *American Society of International Law, Proceedings* 63 (1969): 81.

Barraclough, Geoffrey, "The Struggle for the Third World," *New York Review of Books* (November 9, 1978): 47.

Baumgartner, T., and Burns, T., "A Structural Theory of Exchange." Paper presented to the Eastern Economic Association (1974).

Beckford, George L., *Persistent Poverty: Underdeveloped in Plantation Regions of the World.* New York: Oxford University Press, 1972.

Beckstrom, John H., "Transplantation of Legal Systems: An Early Report on the Reception of Western Laws in Ethiopia," *American Journal of Comparative Law* 2 (Fall, 1974): 697–712.

Borah, Woodrow, *New Spain's Century of Depression*. Berkeley, CA.: Ibero-Americana, 1951.

Bornschier, Volker, Chase-Dunn, Christopher, and Rubinson, Richard, "Cross-National Evidence of the Effects of Foreign Investment and Aid on Economic Growth and Inequality: A Survey of Findings and a Reanalysis." *American Journal of Sociology* 84 (1978): 651–683.

Caldwell, M., *Indonesia*. Oxford: Oxford University Press, 1968.

Cardoso, F., "Dependency and Development in Latin America." *New Left Review* 74 (July–August, 1972): 83–95.

Chase-Dunn, Christopher, "The Effects of International Economic Dependence on Development and Inequality: A Cross-National Study." *American Sociological Review* 40 (December, 1975): 720–738.

Chomsky, Noam, and Herman, Edward S., "The United States versus Human Rights in the Third World." *Monthly Review* 19 (July–August, 1977): 22–45.

Chossudovsky, Michael, "Capital Accumulation in Chile and Latin America." Unpublished reprint, University of Ottawa Economics Department (1977).

Cipolla, C.M., *Guns and Sails in the Early Phase of European Expansion, 1400–1700*. New York: Collins, 1965.

David, René, "A Civil Code for Ethiopia." *Tulane Law Review* 37 (1963): 187.

Dos Santos, T., "The Structure of Dependence." *American Economic Review* 60 (May, 1970): 231–236.

Dunning, Harrison C., "Law and Economic Development in Africa: The Law of Eminent Domain." *Columbia Law Review* 68 (November, 1968): 1286.

Elliot, David, *Thailand: Origins of Military Rule*. London: Zed Press, 1968.

Emmanuel, Arghiri, *Unequal Exchange: A Study of the Imperialism of Trade*. New York: Monthly Review Press, 1972.

Erickson, Kenneth Paul, *The Brazilian Corporative State and Working Class Politics*. Berkeley: University of California Press, 1977.

Farsoun, Samih and Carroll, Walter, "The Civil War in Lebanon." *Monthly Review* (June, 1976): 12–38.

Fitch, Bob, and Oppenheimer, Mary, *Ghana: End of an Illusion*. New York: Monthly Review Press, 1966.

Fitzpatrick, Peter, "Law, Modernization and Mystification," in Steven Spitzer (ed.), *Research in Law and Sociology*, vol. III. Greenwich, Conn.: JAI Press, Inc., 1980.

Franck, Thomas M., "New Development: Can American Legal Institutions Help Developing Countries?" *Wisconsin Law Review* 1972 (1972): 767.

Frank, Andre Gunder, *Capitalism and Underdevelopment in Latin America*. New York: Monthly Review Press, 1967.

———, Latin America: *Underdevelopment or Revolution: Essays on the Development of Underdevelopment and the Immediate Enemy*. New York: Monthly Press, 1969.

———, *Lumpen-Bourgeoisie and Lumpen-Development: Dependence, Class and Politics in Latin America*. New York: Monthly Review Press, 1973.

Furtado, Celso, "The Concept of External Dependence in the Study of Underdevelopment," in Charles K. Wilber (ed.), *The Political Economy of Development and Underdevelopment*, pp. 118–123. New York: Random House, 1973a.

———, "The Brazilian 'Model' of Development," in Charles K. Wilber (ed.) *The Political Economy of Development and Underdevelopment*, pp. 297–306. New York: Random House, 1973b.

Griffin, Keith, *Underdevelopment in Spanish America*. London: George Allen & Unwin, 1969.

Hager, L.M., "Role of Lawyers in Developing Countries." *American Bar Association Journal* 38 (1972): 33

Hallinan, Conn Malachi, "The Subjugation and Division of Ireland: Testing Ground for Colonial Policy." *Crime and Social Justice* 8 (Fall-Winter, 1977):53–57.

Hamilton, Nora Louise, "Mexico: The Limits of State Autonomy." *Latin American Perspectives* 2 (Summer, 1975): 81.

Haq, ul Mahbub, "Employment in the 1970's: A New Perspective," *International Development Review* 13 (1971): 9–13.

Hechter, Michael, *International Colonialism: The Celtic Fringe in British National Development, 1536–1966*. Berkeley: University of California Press, 1975.

Herschlag, Z.Y., *Turkey: The Challenge of Growth*. E.J. Brill, 1968.

Horwitz, Morton J., *The Transformation of American Law, 1780–1860*. Cambridge: Harvard University Press, 1977.

Karst, Kenneth L., and Rosenn, Keith S., *Law and Development in Latin America: A Case Book*. Berkeley: University of California Press, 1975.

Klement, Alice, "Any Room for Lawyers on the Orient Express?" *The National Law Journal* (January 1, 1979): 4.

Lazreg, Marnia, *The Emergence of Classes in Algeria: A Study of Colonialism and Socio-Political Change*. Boulder: Westview Press, 1976.

Letelier, Orlando, "Economic 'Freedom's' Awful Toll: The 'Chicago Boys' in Chile." *Review of Radical Political Economics* 8 (Fall, 1976): 44–52.

Lewis, B., *The Emergence of Modern Turkey*. Oxford: Oxford University Press, 1961.

Leys, Colin, *Underdevelopment in Kenya: The Political Economy of Neo-Colonialism*. Berkeley: University of California Press, 1975.

Mandel, Ernest, *Marxist Economic Theory*. New York: Monthly Review Press, 1968.

Marx, Karl, *Capital: A Critique of Political Economy*, vol. 1, New York: International Publishers, 1967.

Mendelson, Wallace, "Law and the Development of Nations." *Journal of Politics* 32 (1970): 112.

Merillat, H.C.L., "Law and the Developing Countries." *American Journal of International Law* 60 (1966): 71.

Miller, Judith, "Peru Crisis: A Dilemma." *New York Times* (May 24, 1978), p. D7.

Müller, Ronald, "The Multinational Corporation and the Underdevelopment of the Third World," in Charles K. Wilber (ed.), *The Political Economy of Development and Underdevelopment*. New York: Random House, 1973.

New York Times, "Talking Turkey with Aid in Mind." (January 21, 1979), p. E2.

Njenga, F.X., "Investment Guarantees." in G.F.A. Sawyerr (ed.), *East African Law and Social Change*. Nairobi: East African Publishing House, 1966.

Nwabueze, B.O., "Legal Aspects of Economic Development," in Andre Tunc (ed.), *Les Aspects Juridiques du Développment Économique*. Paris: Librairie Dalloz, 1966.

Oxaal, Ivar, Barnett, Tony, and Booth, David, *Beyond the Sociology of Development*. Boston: Routledge and Kegan Paul, 1975.

Palmer, Robin, and Parsons, Neil (eds.), *The Roots of Rural Poverty in Central and Southern Africa*. Berkeley: University of California Press, 1977.

Pozen, Robert C., *Legal Choices for State Enterprises in the Third World*. New York: New York University Press, 1976.

Quijano, Anibal, *Nationalism and Capitalism in Peru: A Study in Neo-Imperialism*. New York: Monthly Review Press, 1971.

Rinchon, R.P., *La Traité et l'Esclavage des Congolais par les Européens*. Wetteren: Meester and Sons, 1929.

Roberts, Neal A., "The Supreme Court in a Developing Society: Progressive or Reactionary Force: A Study of the Privy Purse Case in India." *American Journal of Comparative Law* 20 (1972): 79–110.

Rose, Sanford, "The Poor Countries Turn from Buy Less to Sell More." *Fortune* (April, 1970), pp. 90–91.

Rosenn, Keith, "The Reform of Legal Education in Brazil." *Journal of Legal Education* 21 (1969): 251.

Schiller, "Law" in Lystad (ed.), *The African World: A Survey of Social Research*, p. 178 (1965).

Schneider, Jane and Schneider, Peter, *Culture and Political Economy in Western Sicily*. New York: Academic Press, 1976.

Sedler, Robert Alan, "Law Reform in the Emerging Nations of Sub-Saharan Africa: Social Change and the Development of the Modern Legal System." *St. Louis University Law Journal* 13 (1968): 195.

Seers, Dudley, "The Meaning of Development." *International Development Review* 11 (December, 1969): 2–6.

Seidman, Robert M., "Law and Economic Development in Independent, English-Speaking, Sub-Saharan Africa." *Wisconsin Law Review* (1966) 999–1070.

————, "Law and Development: A General Model." *Law and Society Review* 6 (1972a): 211.

————, "The Communication of Law and the Process of Development." *Wisconsin Law Review* (1972b): 686.

Stallings, Barbara and Zimbalist, Andy, "The Political Economy of the Unidad Popular." *Latin American Perspectives* 2 (Spring, 1975): 68.

Steinberg, David, "Law, Development, and Korean Society," *Journal of Comparative Administration* 3 (1971): 215.

Steiner, Henry, "Legal Education and Socio-Economic Change: Brazilian Perspectives." *American Journal of Comparative Law* 19 (1971): 39.

Sunar, Ilkay, *State and Society in the Politics of Turkey's Development*. Ankara: Ankara University Faculty of Political Science, 1974.

Szymanski, Al, "Marxist Theory and International Capital Flows." *Review of Radical Political Economics* 6 (Fall, 1974): 20–40.

————, A Response to Andre Gunder Frank and Martin Murray." *Review of Radical Political Economics* 8 (Summer, 1976): 77–83.

Takayanagi, Kenzo, "A Century of Innovation: The Development of Japanese Law, 1868–1961," in A. von Mehren (ed.), *Law in Japan*. Cambridge: Harvard University Press, 1963.

Tigar, Michael E. and Levy, Madeleine R., *Law and the Rise of Capitalism*. New York: Monthly Review Press, 1977.

Trimberger, Ellen Kay, "State Power and Modes of Production: Implications of the Japanese Transition to Capitalism." *The Insurgent Sociologist* 7 (Spring, 1977): 85.

Trubek, David, "Toward a Social Theory of Law: An Essay on the Study of Law and Development." *Yale Law Journal* 83 (1972a): 50.

________, "Max Weber on Law and the Rise of Capitalism." *Wisconsin Law Review* (1972b): 710.

________ and Galanter, Marc. "Scholars in Self-Estrangement: Some Reflections on the Crisis in Law and Development Studies in the United States." *Wisconsin Law Review* (1974): 1062.

Tunc, André (ed.), *Les Aspects Juridiques du Développement Économiques*. Paris: Librairie Dalloz, 1966.

Unger, Roberto M., *Law in Modern Society: Toward a Criticism of Social Theory*. New York: Free Press, 1976.

Vandervort, Bruce, "The Brazilian Model becomes Unglued." *In These Times* (March 22–28, 1978): 9.

Vlekke, B.H.M., *The Story of the Dutch East Indies*. Cambridge: Harvard University Press, 1946.

Volney, C.F., "État du Commerce du Levant en 1784, d'apres les Registres de la Chambre de Commerce de Marseille," in C. Issawi (ed.), *The Economic History of the Middle East, 1800–1914: A Book of Readings*. Chicago: University of Chicago Press, 1966.

Von Mehren, A., "Law and Legal Education in India: Some Observations." *Harvard Law Review* 78 (1965): 1180.

Wallerstein, Immanuel, *The Modern World-System: Capitalist Agriculture and the Origins of the European World-Economy in the Sixteenth Century*. New York: Academic Press, 1974.

Warren, Bill, "Imperialism and Capitalist Industrialization." *New Left Review* 81 (September-October, 1973): 3–45.

Weber, Max, *Economy and Society*. New York: Bedminster Press, 1968.

Weeks, John, "Imbalance between the Centre and the Periphery and the 'Unemployment Crisis' in Kenya," in Ivan Oxaal et al. (eds.), *Economy and Society in Latin America and Africa*, pp. 86–104. Boston: Routledge and Kegan Paul, 1975.

Woddis, Jack, *Africa: The Roots of Revolt*. New York: Citadel, 1960.

LAW AND DEVELOPMENT OR COMPARATIVE LAW AND SOCIAL CHANGE—THE APPLICATION OF OLD CONCEPTS IN THE COMMONWEALTH CARIBBEAN

BRUCE ZAGARIS*

---

* Partner, Berliner & Maloney, Washington, D.C., Chairperson, Committee on Caribbean Law, Section of International Law & Practice, American Bar Association, 1982-87; Lecturer, Faculty of Law, University of the West Indies, 1977-78; Consultant, A.I.D., Justice Improvement Project for Commonwealth Caribbean, 1986; Chairperson, Committee on Criminal Law and Procedure, Inter-American Bar Association; representative Association Internationale de Droit Penal (A.I.D.P.) to the Organization of American States; and editor, International Enforcement Law Reporter. The author is grateful for the assistance of the Project Director in preparing this paper and for comments on an earlier draft by Jay A. Rosenthal, the author's colleague.

I. INTRODUCTION

Nearly twenty years after the foundation and decline of United States law and development programs, such a program, known as the Administration of Justice program, is flourishing in the Commonwealth Caribbean.[1] This article traces the origin, oper-

1. For background generally on the Commonwealth Caribbean legal system, see V.

ation, and classification of this recent program and its application to a new project in the Commonwealth Caribbean. To set the stage for this analysis, the evolution of the law and development movement in the 1960s, its evolution and the reaction against it in the 1970s, and its revival in 1985 in Central America and in 1986 in the Commonwealth Caribbean, are traced. The discussion considers the foreign policy background of the new program and how that background is reflected in the program. Next the article discusses the goals and components of the Commonwealth Caribbean project. The article also is designed to classify and analyze the new trends in light of current scholarly discussions. Significantly, although some of the prior patterns of the law and development movement are followed, new ground has been broken. In particular, the conception and implementation of the project shows progress in using local resources as well as in multilateralizing the activities. Because the Commonwealth Caribbean project is only in its stage of infancy, the discussion of its components and classification are necessarily tentative and incomplete.

II. Concepts

Law and development has been referred to as the specialized area of academic study in the United States concerned with the relationship between the legal systems and development — that is, the social, economic and political changes — taking place in developing countries.[2] Indeed the definition of the field of law and development has always been relatively flexible and not rigidly limited by accepted theory.[3] An abundance of literature about the United States law and development programs exists.[4] The motivations and rationale for the law and development movement have been catalogued chronologically.[5] Initially legal assistance was used

---

Newton, Commonwealth Caribbean Legal Systems: A Case Study of Small Jurisdiction (Council Legal Education, East Indies and Commonwealth Legal Education Association 1985).

2. Trubek & Galanter, *Scholars in Self-Estrangement: Some Reflections on the Crisis in Law and Development Studies in the United States*, 1974 Wis. L. Rev. 1062, 1064.

3. Merryman, *Comparative Law and Social Change: On the Origins, Style, Decline & Revival of the Law and Development Movement*, 25 Am. J. Compar. L. 457, 459 n.8 (1977) (quoting from the statement of purposes of the $3 million grant to establish the International Legal Center, as set forth in the 1966 Ford Foundation Annual Report 23).

4. For a discussion of the chronological origins and evolution of the law and development movement, see Burg, *Law and Development: A Self-Estrangement*, 25 Am. J. Compar. L. 492, 495-98 (1977).

5. J. Gardner, Legal Imperialism 7 (1980).

as an administrative mechanism for nation building and as a means of bringing stable and predictable commercial transactions within an implicit liberal capitalist economy.[6] This concept of national development was based on industrialization and economic growth.[7] Later legal assistance was provided to promote political development, rule of law, participatory democracy, and in general more humanistic notions of development.[8] Throughout, a missionary and humanitarian desire to share legal modernity and technical skill with developing countries motivated the law and development movement.[9] However, professional self-interest, namely the service-oriented self-image of the American legal profession and an interest in expanding one's sphere of professional activity and perhaps opening a specialization as a development lawyer, also motivated participants in the law and development movement.[10]

This article analyzes three models for classifying the law and development movement. The three models then will serve as a basis for classifying and analyzing the Administration of Justice project for the Commonwealth Caribbean. The first model, law and development or comparative law and social change, comes from Professor John Henry Merryman, an academic who has examined, written, and taught law and development as well as the law of Latin America and the Caribbean. The second model, the role of law in social change, comes from Abelardo Valdez, who has been a policy-maker and practitioner, specializing in the Caribbean and Latin America. The third model is a process of transference of the models postulated by James A. Gardner. Although the three models are well known among law and development scholars, there is by no means unanimity among scholars concerning the validity of the primary models.

---

6. For a discussion of the relationship between modern law and economic development, see Trubek, *Toward a Social Theory of Law: An Essay on the Study of Law and Development*, 82 YALE L.J. 1, 6-8 (1972)[hereinafter Trubek I]; Trubek, *Max Weber on Law and the Rise of Capitalism*, 1972 WIS. L. REV. 720 [hereinafter Trubek II].

7. J. GARDNER, *supra* note 5, at 7.

8. *Id.*; Burg, *supra* note 4, at 504. For an early discussion of a broad view of law and development, see Friedman, *On Legal Development*, 24 RUTGERS L. REV. 11, 57 (1969).

9. J. GARDNER, *supra* note 5, at 7.

10. *Id.*

A. Law and Development or Comparative Law and Social Change — The Merryman Thesis

Recently scholars such as John Henry Merryman have dissected and analyzed the emergence in the 1960s of the "law and development movement" as a potential new field of scholarship. As Professor Merryman and others have explained, the movement received generous support from the Ford Foundation, the United States Agency for International Development (USAID), and from its own foundation, the International Legal Center, established in 1966 as a spin-off of the Ford Foundation.[11] According to Professor Merryman, the dominant intellectual style of the movement contributed to its decline.[12] Merryman also postulates that a sub-field — comparative law and social change — is responsive to the interest of the persons who performed the most significant law and development work and offers a useful paradigm for its continuation, albeit under another name.[13]

1. The Intellectual Origins of the Law and Development Movement

According to Merryman, the idea of progress, the movement toward law reform, the emergence of an interest in law and society and its various components (sociology of law and politics), the notion of social engineering through law, and the post-World War II commitment by the United States to foreign assistance were the intellectual origins which led to the law and development movement.[14] One of the analogues of law and development to which Professor Merryman refers is especially relevant to the Commonwealth Caribbean: colonial administration. The experience in colonial administration is important to the law and development movement for several reasons.[15] The principal objective of much of the colonial administration was exploitation, although in later times

11. Merryman, *supra* note 3. For a discussion of the sponsorship of law and development by USAID and the Ford Foundation, see Burg, *supra* note 4, at 496-97.

12. Merryman, *supra* note 3, at 460.

13. *Id.*

14. *Id.* at 461. For a useful and critical discussion of the post World War II missionary zeal behind the law and development movement, see GARDNER, *supra* note 5, at 35-38.

15. For a useful discussion of the colonial administration's effect on the legal system in the Commonwealth Caribbean, see NEWTON, *supra* note 1, at 42-51. *See also* Patchett, *Reception of Law in the West Indies* 1973 JAMAICA L.J. 17; Morrison, *The Reception of English Law in Jamaica*, 1979 W. INDIAN L.J. 43.

increasing emphasis was placed on colonial development.[16] Since the colonial government was legalistic in its approach to colonial governance and used law as an instrument of colonial progress, law became an important component of colonial administration.[17] Professor Merryman points out, however, that despite the substantial existence of law and development literature, relatively little study has been made of the experience or theory of related disciplines.[18]

2. The Intellectual Style of the Law and Development Movement

Professor Merryman classifies the law and development movement into three categories: (1) whether their principal thrust is in the direction of action or inquiry; (2) whether they express theoretical interests; and (3) whether they employ a quantitative approach to the description and discussion of reality.[19] The intellectual style in the law and development movement of the United States has emphasized action. American participation in law and development has been motivated by a desire to accomplish development. Rather than trying to learn from the study of some aspect of law in one or more developing societies, the U.S. lawyer has been more interested in accomplishing development and in engineering social progress through law reform.[20]

This preoccupation with action causes Americans to proceed on law and development work without trying to build or test a theory or to examine its implications. Rather, the attempt is to proceed on more or less implicit working assumptions, without the need for or any real interest in theory. Since American lawyers are accustomed to *stare decisis*, the practical, professional bias of

16. For a discussion of the view that the British colonial administration emphasized exploitation, see Lindsay, *The Myth of Civilizing Mission: British Colonialism and the Politics of Symbolic Manipulation* (Kingston: I.S.E.R., U.W.I., Working Paper No. 31, 1981).

17. Merryman, *supra* note 3, at 467-68. For additional discussion of the imposition of formal legal systems by colonial rule, see Metzger, *Legal Services to the Poor and National Development Objectives*, in LEGAL AID AND WORLD POVERTY: A SURVEY OF ASIA, AFRICA, AND LATIN AMERICA 3 (1974).

18. Merryman, *supra* note 3, at 472. For instance, references are often made to colonial administration, the post-World War II occupation, the administration of internal colonies, regional development, law and social change, and leading law reform, etc. However, Professor Merryman explains that the fact that no meaningful attempts to examine these related disciplines have been made is not unusual.

19. *Id.* at 473.

20. *Id.* at 474.

American legal education is impatient with theory.[21] The concept of the lawyer as a social engineer is not prominent in Britain or in British colonial history. Hence, British legal scholarship has a distinct intellectual style — more modest and more philosophical — and is addressed to a differently-constituted legal order.[22]

According to some critics, including Professor Merryman, the problem with the law and development movement is that Americans have not had time to propose and test a theory and to become well acquainted with the foreign culture.[23] Instead, Americans have used the access of the law and development project and the project funds to become experts on local law. They have taken with them an implied superiority of their own domestic "development" over foreign "underdevelopment" expertise — that is to say, the notion that their work in so-called developed or modernized legal systems automatically has given them a superior status over attorneys from less developed or less modern legal systems. The recommendation of foreign law and development attorneys would determine whether money would be forthcoming for legal projects, providing additional leverage. As a result, the American lawyers working in law and development have had a privileged status and have had an opportunity for lateral entry at the very top without the usual requirement of slow advancement through the local legal culture either in the United States or in the target country.[24] As a result, Professor Merryman diagnoses that the law and development movement has suffered from an unfamiliarity with the target culture and society (including its legal system), lack of theory, artificially privileged access to power, and relative immunity to consequences. In other words, the U.S. attorneys have failed at proposing or executing third world law and development action. Hence, the movement was largely misdirected and the decrease of interest in law and development, within USAID, the foundation, and among the law and development scholars, is the result of recognition that American law and development work was ineffectual or harmful as technical assistance, and peripheral as scholarship.[25]

---

21. *Id.* at 475.

22. *Id.* at 479.

23. *Id.* at 479. *See also* J. Gardner, *supra* note 5, at 8 (discussion of the difficulties of American legal assistance due to its cultural unawareness, ethnocentricity, and its sociological vacuum).

24. Merryman, *supra* note 3, at 481.

25. *Id.* For similar criticisms of ethnocentricity of the law and development movement and its cause of the demise of the movement, see Trubek I, *supra* note 6, at 16-21.

According to Professor Merryman, third world law and development action is premature until the U.S. legal community has tested a reliable theory (vis-a-vis the target society).[26] After the theory is reliably tested, the U.S. law and development effort will be more responsible and productive if it limits itself to third world law and development.[27] In that way, the United States can begin to build theory of the sort that eventually may provide a more adequate basis for third world action. Hence, Professor Merryman and others believe that the future of the third world law and development movement lies in inquiry and the pursuit of theory.[28] It would be properly named "comparative law and social change." The name would draw the readers' attention to the core field of study: law and social change (which includes development). According to Merryman, "comparative" reminds us that we are working with other societies and other legal systems, including those in developing countries. The new designation also provides a greater dimension which allows the scholar interested in studying law and social change in developing countries two disciplinary homes, two groups of interested colleagues, and two bodies of relevant literature.[29] Most importantly, Merryman and others have concluded that the law and development movement has declined because it was, for the most part, a flawed attempt by persons without cultural awareness or a proper theory of the third world.[30]

B. The Role of Law in Social Change — The Valdez Thesis

Another major analyst of the trends in law and development movement in the Caribbean has been Abelardo Valdez, a policy-maker in the Carter Administration and an activist in the development of the Caribbean for many years prior to his policy-making

26. Some scholars believe that not only is the law and development premature without a theory, but also that it is questionable because it has not been shown that law even matters in development. *See* Burg, *supra* note 4, at 529.

27. Indeed even in the late 1960s and early 1970s the law and development movement already was turning towards law and development inquiry. *See* J. GARDNER, *supra* note 5, at 12, 44. Gardner notes that in the 1960s some inquiry tried to understand the role of Western law in Asia and Africa. For discussion of the need for a better intellectual perspective based on a social theory to formulate the relationship between legal and social variables, see Trubek I, *supra* note 6, at 21-40.

28. Merryman, *supra* note 3, at 483. *See also* J. GARDNER, *supra* note 5, at 211-30. For similar criticism, see also Trubek I, *supra* note 6, at 16-21.

29. Merryman, *supra* note 3, at 483.

30. *Id.* J. GARDNER, *supra* note 5, at 28-29. *See also* Trubek & Galanter, *supra* note 2, at 1080-82 (discussion of misassumptions of social developments in the Third World).

role. His 1975 law review article provided an insight into the issues of past failures or inadequacies of U.S. foreign assistance to law reform projects in developing countries, and provided a more rational justification for such assistance.[31]

Valdez provides two principal rationales for assisting in the development of the role of law in social change in the Caribbean.[32] The first is that there exists a lack of knowledge about the role of law in social change and such knowledge is required in order to develop the law as a positive force in social change.[33] According to Valdez, law or legal institutions are involved in the social change or development process. Hence, it is necessary to better comprehend the important relationship between law and development, and law and social change. In order to do so, Valdez believes that research is needed to determine the extent to which the law affects social change and how it can be developed to achieve positive, just, and humane progress.[34] Valdez wonders whether the types of legal systems and institutions in the Caribbean help or hinder these societies in their developmental process; whether these countries can successfully import laws from more developed countries; and whether they can accomplish "social engineering" through regulatory laws which effect social change.[35] Valdez complains that for the most part, U.S. development assistance organizations, both private and governmental, have not supported research and study of these important questions, but have instead focused almost exclusively on the reform of legal education. The emphasis, according to Valdez, has been unsuccessful.[36]

---

31. Valdez, *Developing the Role of Law in Social Change: Past Endeavors and Future Opportunities in Latin America and the Caribbean*, 7 Law. Am. 1 (1975) (all references to Valdez' article refer to the Lawyer of the Americas article). *See also* Valdez, *Law and Socio-Economic Change in Latin America and the Caribbean*, 10 J. Int'l L. & Econ. 553 (1975).

32. For an additional discussion of the turn towards research on law and social change by the law and development movement in the 1970s, see J. Gardner, *supra* note 5, at 12.

33. Valdez, *supra* note 31, at 2. For a discussion of the tendency towards the instrumentalist conception of law and development, that is, the tendency to regard law as an instrument of change, see Burg, *supra* note 4, at 505-11.

34. Valdez, *supra* note 31, at 2-3. *See also*, Friedman & Macaulay, *Preface* to Law and the Behavioral Sciences (1969). Interestingly, some critics of the law and development movement point out the law is as much a reflection of social conditions as their cause. *See* Burg, *supra* note 4, at 517.

35. Valdez, *supra* note 31, at 3-4. For a discussion of the influence of law on development and development on law and its application to pragmatic problem-solving in the Third World, see Trubek & Galanter, *supra* note 2, at 517.

36. Valdez, *supra* note 31, at 4. For a similar criticism of misguided emphasis by U.S. development assistance organizations on reform of legal education and the need to develop the role of law in social change in a positive manner, see Trubek I, *supra* note 6, at 1-20.

The second rationale is that resolution of the problem of unequal access to representation within the legal system is necessary to achieve equal justice in Latin America and the Caribbean. Valdez explains that in the late 1960s, assistance to law and development projects in Latin America was focused almost exclusively on legal education reform.[37] The goal of these projects was for lawyers in less developed countries to alter their formalistic and traditional concepts of law since development requires institutionalization of social control. By achieving legal education reform, it was thought that reform of the entire legal system would occur. The U.S. organizations believed that attorneys who were trained as rigorous problem-solvers would ask penetrating questions about underlying social problems and find solutions which would be more developmental and more responsive to the needs of their societies.[38] Technical assistance was primarily in the form of visiting U.S. professors, training in U.S. schools, use of U.S. teaching materials, and fellowship experience.[39] Valdez points out that, rather than focusing on the legal problems of the poor, the law schools receiving U.S. assistance made no effort to restructure their curriculum to offer courses relating to these problems.[40] Furthermore, Valdez criticizes the U.S. law and development program for not offering substantive courses on law reform (e.g., credit, housing, land reform, civil liberties, access to courts, and the legislative process or employment rights). Rather, they introduced the Socratic method of teaching, improved library facilities, developed teaching materials, and provided scholarships for law studies in the United States.[41] In the end, Valdez explains, the programs were discontinued because, rather than achieving social reform, they only solidified existing power structures and worked against the poor.[42] Valdez comments that one problem was the misguided at-

37. Valdez, *supra* note 31, at 6. *See also* J. GARDNER, *supra* note 5, at 40-44 (discussion of the emphasis of American legal assistance to legal education).

38. Valdez, *supra* note 31, at 7. For the view that the Latin American lawyer could not participate actively in social change and development due to his inferior education which focused on the traditional, formalistic idea of law, see Trubek I, *supra* note 6, at 48-50. *See also* Brown, *Recent Significant Trends in Legal Education in the Americas*, 3 U. MIAMI INTER-AM. L. REV. 55 (1961).

39. J. GARDNER, *supra* note 5, at 10; Valdez, *supra* note 31, at 8.

40. Valdez, *supra* note 31, at 8. Other commentators have also criticized the law and development models as lacking in ethical and value content or informed social theory, being too closely identified with policy and power, and vulnerable to executive or authoritarian ordering and abuse; *See, e.g.*, J. GARDNER, *supra* note 5, at 11.

41. Valdez, *supra* note 31, at 8.

42. *Id.* at 9. For similar criticism that law and development projects actually increased

tempt to reform teaching methodology without reforming the content. Another difficulty was that those providing technical assistance did not understand the significance of the socio-economic background, values, and goals of the law students, nor did they believe in the teachings underlying this reformed legal education.[43]

An interesting feature of Valdez' article is his discussion of how the assistance had been redirected in the 1970s. Curriculum reform, rather than being value-neutral, emphasized substantive reform in the content of the curricula.[44] Emphasis was also placed on adequate and effective delivery of legal services to the poor in order to ensure the operation and integrity of the legal system.[45] Legal service programs, Valdez explained, attempt to improve access to legal services by the poor. Such programs can also assist in achieving social change or development: they educate the poor and make them aware of their legal rights and potential services by a legal aid program; they stimulate participation by members of the poor community in community organization; and they facilitate implementation of legal and non-legal solutions to social problems.[46] In particular, one of the initiatives of the law and development program in the 1970s was the establishment of the Kingston Legal Aid Clinic in 1972.

An additional reason for law-reform-oriented law and development projects is the absolute need to achieve effective enforcement of existing legislation which was intended to benefit lower-income and other disadvantaged groups. Although developing countries have impressive bodies of social welfare, antidiscrimination, and regulatory legislation, much of it is not effective because of fatal defects within the legislation itself, ineffective enforcement, or unrealistic assumptions about the resources available to private parties to facilitate effective enforcement.[47] For instance, the unavailability of class action, limited interpretations of standing to sue, and the lack of the concept of precedent can make wholesale national

---

social inequality and diminished participation in decision-making by increasing the formalization of legal decision-making, see J. GARDNER, *supra* note 5, at 11; Trubek & Galanter, *supra* note 2, at 1076.

43. J. GARDNER, *supra* note 5, at 11; Valdez, *supra* note 31, at 10.

44. J. GARDNER, *supra* note 5, at 12, 216-20; Valdez, *supra* note 31, at 12-13.

45. For a discussion of law reform in the context of law and development, see Friedman, *supra* note 8, at 41-49.

46. Valdez, *supra* note 31, at 12-13. For a discussion of the role of lawyers in assisting the effective penetration of national law to the indigenous population, see Metzger, *supra* note 17, at 10-11.

47. Metzger, *supra* note 17, at 12.

enforcement of previously ineffective social welfare and regulatory legislation difficult to achieve through litigation.[48]

Valdez criticizes the use of grants primarily for research by U.S. attorneys because attorneys from the region are more knowledgeable about local conditions, have more influence in their communities, and hence are more deserving of the grants.[49] Valdez cautions that the Caribbean had been an area dominated by a foreign sovereign which imposed its own laws, but now has entered an era of potentially dramatic change.[50] By considering the values, customs, and needs of society in producing that change and law reform, an important contribution can be made.[51] Hence, Valdez reiterates Professor Merryman's concern about the need for inquiry and theory. Nevertheless, Valdez emphasizes action, and brings with him the tools of a crusading legal aid attorney of the 1970s intent on using his social engineering skills to produce social change.

C. The Process of Transferring Law and Development Models — The Gardner Thesis

According to John A. Gardner, a process for the transference of law and development can be used to provide a typology of transfer. The forms include: (1) direct transfer of legal institutions and instruments (e.g., constitution, code, statute, court); (2) indirect transfer of legal concepts and models (e.g., legal values or ideas, jurisprudential or professional models); (3) invited legal transfer process which comes from the recipient legal culture (e.g., the requested importation of specific legal instruments or legal models); and (4) imposed or uninvited legal transfer at the initiative of the exporting legal culture. An additional category is suggested, namely, one which distinguishes infused (premeditated or planned) processes of legal transfer, direct or indirect, where the initiative is from the exporting legal culture; from more occasional *ad hoc* borrowing, which is less systematic and culture or time specific, and

48. Valdez, *supra* note 31, at 5.

49. For a discussion of the lack of any effort for expansion of legal services to the poor to take cognizance of the distinctive conditions in which such programs function in the developing countries, see Metzger, *supra* note 17, at 5-7.

50. *See generally* F. ALEXIS, CHANGING CARIBBEAN CONSTITUTIONS 248-69 (1984) (discussion of the dramatic changes on the legal system in the Caribbean); F. PHILLIPS, WEST INDIAN CONSTITUTIONS: POST-INDEPENDENCE REFORM (1985).

51. Valdez, *supra* note 31, at 33-34.

more of an ongoing process of cultural and intellectual interchange generally.[52]

According to Gardner, the American legal assistance experience generally can be categorized as indirect, infused, or planned legal export. Within the context of legal transfer generally the law and development movement encountered the difficult task of transferring abstract models and concepts that were neither invited nor imposed in the usual sense, but rather, infused through a particular transfer process. Gardner states that preconditions for the direct transfer of American legal institutions and instruments did not exist. Much of the legal infrastructure-building was achieved by the time the American law and development movement started and developing countries had neither strong interest in direct American financial and program strength, nor the mandate, to undertake direct legal export on a major scale. The real initiative and interest in law and development originated within the American legal culture. The movement did not involve an *ad hoc* nor an ongoing international legal transfer process. Hence, in the end the movement evolved into an attempt to indirectly transfer abstract American legal models and concepts that were neither invited nor imposed, but rather infused, through American legal assistance.[53]

D. The Current U.S. Administration of Justice Improvement Projects

1. The Kissinger Report

The U.S. Agency for International Development (USAID)/ University of the West Indies Justice Improvement Project for the Commonwealth Caribbean, like most of the foreign policy initiatives of the Reagan Administration, emanates from the preoccupation of the Administration with the national security of the United States in the region.[54] In particular, the Report of the National Bi-

52. J. GARDNER, *supra* note 5, at 21-22. The deviation of the basic structural elements of the legal systems of the developing countries from the West and the education of the legal profession within the Western legal tradition had contributed to a tendency to look toward the former colonial power for leadership in legal reform. Metzger, *supra* note 17, at 14.

53. J. GARDNER, *supra* note 5, at 33-34.

54. For the best concise presentation of the Reagan Administration's goals in the Caribbean and Central America, see Kirkpatrick, *U.S. Security and Latin America*, COMMENTARY 71 (1) 29-41 (Jan. 1981). *See also* Erisman, *Colossus Challenged: U.S. Caribbean Policy in*

partisan Commission on Central America, known as the Kissinger Report, comments that there was agreement among the region's leaders, both in government and in the private sector, that there must be greater equity in the distribution of economic benefits and greater justice in social relations.[55] The Report also recommends that the United States government should encourage the Central American countries to develop and nurture democratic cultures, institutions, and practices, including "strong judicial systems to enhance the capacity to redress grievances concerning personal security, property rights, and free speech."[56] The Report also recommends the use of U.S. economic assistance to:

a. enhance the training and resources of judges, judicial staff, and public prosecutors' offices;

b. support modern and professional means of criminal investigation; and

c. promote availability of legal materials, assistance to law faculties, and support for local bar associations.[57]

2. Legislative Framework

Congressional support of the Administration of Justice initiative is found in U.S. legislation. Section 534 of the Foreign Assistance Act of 1961, (FAA) as amended, authorized the use of up to $20 million in Economic Support Funds in both fiscal year 1986 and 1987 for Administration of Justice activities in countries in Latin America and the Caribbean.[58] The activities authorized under Section 534 included: specialized professional training, scholarships and exchanges for continuing legal education; programs to enhance judicial and prosecutorial capabilities; programs to enhance investigative capabilities, conducted under judicial or prosecutorial control; strengthening organizations in order to promote both services to members and the role of the bar in judicial selection, enforcement of ethical standards, and legal reform; increasing the availability of legal materials and publications; semi-

---

the 1980s, in COLOSSUS CHALLENGED: THE STRUGGLE FOR CARIBBEAN INFLUENCE 1-46 (Erisman & Martz, eds. 1982).

55. Report of the National Bipartisan Commission on Central America 38 (Jan. 1984).

56. *Id.* at 51.

57. *Id.* at 74.

58. Pub. L. No. 87-195, pt. II, Ch. 4, § 534, as added Pub. L. No. 99-83, Title VII, § 712, 99 Stat. 244 (1985) (codified as 22 U.S.C. § 2346c (1985)).

nars, conferences, and training and educational programs to improve the administration of justice and strengthen the respect for the rule of law and internationally recognized human rights; and revision and modernization of codes and procedures.

In addition to the specific authorization which was provided by Section 534 of the FAA, Congress has enacted legislation that eases the restrictions barring USAID support for police activities.[59] Since the mid-1970s Section 660 of the FAA has barred USAID from providing training, advice or financial support to police. However, section 660(c) of the FAA makes a general exemption to the prohibitions contained in Sections 660(a) and (b) for any country with a longstanding democratic tradition, which does not have a standing army, and does not engage in a consistent pattern of gross human rights violations. A further exception to Section 660 was provided in Section 534 of the FAA for programs to enhance police investigative capabilities conducted under judicial or prosecutorial control. The authority of Section 534 expired on September 30, 1987.

3. Overview of Goals and Activities

To put the Justice Improvement Project for the Commonwealth Caribbean into proper perspective requires an understanding of the Reagan Administration's direction of the program for the Western Hemisphere. The Administration's own description of the program, as well as the background from which the program arose, emphasizes its political character.[60] The focus of the Justice Improvement Project is to enable the rule of law to build a cornerstone of democracy and be a positive force for just economic and social development.[61] The program combines public and private resources. The Department of State, USAID, the United States Information Agency (USIA), the Department of Justice, and private

59. For a discussion of the enactment of the administration of justice provisions enacted in 1985, see *Administration of Justice Provisions Pass*, 1 INT'L ENFORCEMENT L. REP. 19 (1985).

60. *See, e.g.*, U.S. DEP'T OF STATE, U.S. AND CENTRAL AMERICA: IMPLEMENTING THE NATIONAL BIPARTISAN COMMISSION REPORT 6-8 (Spec. Rep. No. 148, Aug., 1986). The political emphasis of the administration of justice project in Central America is indicated by the inclusion of electoral assistance and legislative training and support, USAID, Congressional Presentation Fiscal Year 434 (1986).

61. BUREAU OF PUBLIC AFFAIRS, U.S. DEP'T OF STATE, HEMISPHERIC COOPERATION IN THE ADMINISTRATION OF JUSTICE (Spec. Rep. No. 145, Apr. 1986) [hereinafter U.S. DEP'T OF STATE].

U.S. educational and professional organizations participate in activities with hemispheric counterparts. The cooperation involves international organizations, such as the United Nations Institute for the Prevention of Crime and Treatment of Offenders in Latin America (ILANUD), the Inter-American Institute for Human Rights (IIHR), and the Organization of American States (OAS).[62] The program encourages the formation of national commissions representing various legal community sectors to determine the status of the administration of justice and develop a national plan for improving it. The United States is providing financial and technical assistance to such commissions. Regional organizations, such as ILANUD or the IIHR, have conducted courses to improve practical legal and functional skills and knowledge. These courses upgrade the quality of legal training and stimulate increased cooperation among legal professionals.[63] The program supports nonpartisan recruitment and the selection of judges on the basis of merit. Similarly, the program assists governments wanting to design and implement performance-based career structures for their magistrates, with appropriate training and evaluation of the judicial cadre. The program also supports the recruitment, training, and development of prosecutors and public defenders. To assure humane law enforcement, conviction of the guilty, and protection of the rights of the accused and the public, and thereby promote confidence in the judicial system, the program assists through specialized training that promotes effective coordination among investigative, prosecutorial and judicial authorities.[64] Court administrators and associated support personnel, normally not legal professionals, also are eligible for assistance. The program also provides for the diagnosis of the needs of the court system, particularly services such as docket management, financial planning, record keeping, and building maintenance.[65] This is a supplemental activity of the Commonwealth Caribbean Project as a result of a recent agreement with the National Center for State Courts in Williamsburg, Virginia. The program also supports information

---

62. *Id.*

63. *Id.* For a discussion of the potential for dynamic cooperation among international non-governmental organizations in international criminal law in the region, see Zagaris & Papavizas, *Using the Organization of American States to Control International Narcotics Trafficking and Money Laundering*, 57 REV. INT'L DROIT PENAL 119, 128-33 (1986).

64. For background on the criminal investigative training program, see Zagaris, *Justice Starts Program on Criminal Investigative Training in Americas*, 2 INT'L ENFORCEMENT L. REP. 79 (1986).

65. U.S. DEP'T OF STATE, *supra* note 61.

system and record management. The goals are to help codify and disseminate new statutes and other legal materials, so that judges can determine applicable law in particular cases, increase court efficiency, and assure fair application of law. In particular, ensuring up-to-date records management, safeguarding of evidence, and classification of court documents are activities eligible for program assistance as a result of the same agreement.[66]

The program encourages professional associations. It seeks to encourage professionalism and commitment to the principles of justice within the legal profession through exchanges among fraternal institutions, specialized orientation visits and training in the United States and other countries, invitational travel to professional conferences and association meetings, and assistance for professional groups such as bar associations.[67] For instance, USIA and USAID have given grants to the Inter-American Bar Foundation to host conferences, some in conjunction with the meetings of the Inter-American Bar Association. Similarly, the Inter-American Law Committee has held conferences in Central America funded by USAID.[68] USIA and USAID provided grants to the American Bar Association (ABA) to invite Latin Americans to the ABA annual convention and to organize a workshop for the visitors.[69] The Inter-American Bar Association received funds from the program to hold the First Inter-American Judicial Conference at the Association's November 1985 meeting in Mexico. The Conference included a series of workshops on practical problems of judicial structure and function. The participants discussed ways in which their bar associations had worked and could work to improve the administration of justice.[70]

Finally, the program has a public information and education component. The rationale for this component is: equal protection under the law and equal justice within a social order which vigi-

66. *Id.*

67. For a discussion of technical assistance provided by the Inter-American Law Committee to certain Central American Bar Associations, see *Administration of Justice Programs Progress*, 1 INT'L ENFORCEMENT L. REP. 39 (1985); Memorandum, The Administration of Justice in Latin America and the Caribbean, presented by Faye Armstrong, Office of Legal Advisor, U.S. Dep't of State, at a mid-winter meeting of the A.B.A. Sec. of Int'l L. & Prac., *reprinted in* 3 INT'L ENFORCEMENT L. REP. 43 app. (1985). *See also USAID Regional Administration of Justice Grant to ILANUD*, 3 INT'L ENFORCEMENT L. REP. 12, 14 (1985) (discussion of grant agreements between USAID and U.S. institutions).

68. U.S. DEP'T OF STATE, *supra* note 61.

69. *Id.*

70. *Id.*

lantly safeguards the individual's basic human rights requires public knowledge of the operation of the judicial system and of the resolution of disputes and legitimate grievances through peaceful legal means. The program assists such efforts to inform and educate the public of their basic human rights.[71]

These professional exchanges and public information and education efforts combined with the bicentennial of the U.S. constitution to produce a number of programs. The USIA has supported exchanges to enable U.S. and Latin American jurists to come together to discuss issues on constitutional law and related legal issues. For instance, USIA funded the American Bar Association and its Brazilian counterpart to organize a seminar in Rio de Janeiro on the American constitutional experience and enabled a senior U.S. court administrator to spend a month working with the University of the Andes and with the Colombian Government. USIA and USAID also supported the American Enterprise Institute's Second International Conference on Constitutionalism.[72] During January and February of 1986, USIA sponsored a month-long program in Spanish on the U.S. legal system. Latin American judges and practitioners traveled together and studied the administration of justice in the United States. Supreme Court Justice Sandra Day O'Connor traveled to Mexico in 1986 as the Lincoln Lecturer, delivering an address entitled, "Shield of Freedom: The United States Constitution and Its Courts."[73] Other programs in 1987 included a USIA-sponsored seminar on the U.S. constitution in Brasilia and a lecture at the State Department by Carlos Del Rio Rodriguez on the bicentennial of the U.S. constitution.

4. Central American Projects

At present, two major administration of justice projects under way in Central America are the Regional Administration of Justice Project ($10 million) and the El Salvador Judicial Reform Project (over $9 million).[74] The major component of the Regional Administration of Justice Project is a five-year grant to the United Nations-affiliated Latin American Institute for the Prevention of

---

71. *Id.*

72. *Id.*

73. *Id.*

74. For a more comprehensive summary of the Central American Administration of Justice projects, see *Office of Administration of Justice Created*, 1 INT'L ENFORCEMENT L. REP. 20 (1985).

Crime and Treatment of Offenders (ILANUD) to enhance its training and technical assistance capabilities with respect to El Salvador, Costa Rica, Honduras, Panama, the Dominican Republic and Guatemala. As a result of the grant, ILANUD has substantially expanded its operations and has responded to specific requests for assistance. Some background on the purpose and programs of the ILANUD project will provide insight into the purposes of the USAID program.

In February 1985, USAID proposed and implemented the ILANUD project for Central America. The project's short-term purpose is to strengthen regional and national institutions in order to provide services necessary for the improvement of administrative, technical, and legal performance of national justice systems, with major emphasis on criminal justice system improvement. The project is directed at supporting national initiatives underway as well as assisting the stimulation and development of new initiatives. The project has four components: training; advisory services; support services for ILANUD; and an extension facility to meet country-specific needs. Additionally, a grant fund is included to finance expected grant agreements with other regional, international, and U.S. public and private institutions.[75]

The training component of the ILANUD project involves an expanding number of seminars and workshops, short courses, study tours, and longer-term training, as well as support for popular education efforts in human rights and legal rights and guarantees. Training in regional level is occurring in Costa Rica and in other host countries. Training efforts have focused on the practical aspects of the administration of justice and on bringing together key judges, administrators, bar representatives, and prosecutors to exchange views of technical, administrative and legal issues.[76]

The advisory services component is providing technical expertise to national institutions, ILANUD and other projects of USAID, as well as to other donor groups. ILANUD is developing an in-house capacity to offer such assistance after the project ends. Major elements of the advisory services elements include justice sector assessments for each participating country, pilot projects to improve criminal justice statistics, bibliographic assistance, and as-

---

75. U.S. Int'l Dev. Cooperation Agency, U.S. Agency for Int'l Dev. (USAID), ROCAP Project Paper Regional Administration of Justice 15 (AID/LAC/P-219 Project No. 596-0133) [hereinafter USAID, Project Paper].

76. *Id.*

sistance to reform cataloging and reporting of legislation and jurisprudence.[77]

The institutional development and support for ILANUD and other regional institutional components will provide support services consisting largely of facilities that will be added by ILANUD to support training and advisory services.[78] This is to strengthen ILANUD as an indigenous regional institution committed to project goals. Inputs include: design of project management to facilitate harmonious introduction into the ILANUD structure; advisors contracted by USAID to provide technical assistance; and material and equipment provided to ILANUD. In addition, some assistance will be provided to strengthen the Inter-American Institute for Human Rights.[79]

Compared with the Administration of Justice Project for the Commonwealth Caribbean, the Central American and Salvadoran projects were conceived more hastily to deal with perceived security-related emergencies. As a result, the approval and implementation of the projects afforded less opportunity for theoretical discussions. The continuing violence and deterioration of law and order in Central America were also primary factors motivating those projects which did not exist in the proposal of the Commonwealth Caribbean Project. A detailed analysis of the Central American Project is beyond the scope of this article.

5. The Commonwealth Caribbean Project

On August 28, 1986, an agreement was signed by Mr. James S. Haltaway, Director, on behalf of the United States Agency for International Development, and Dr. F. R. Augier, the Acting Vice Chancellor, on behalf of the University of the West Indies,[80] establishing the Commonwealth Caribbean Project, known as the Caribbean Justice Improvement Project (CJIP). Ten million dollars, to be distributed over the next five years, has been appropriated for the Project. The Regional Development Office/Caribbean of

77. *Id.*

78. Because ILANUD at the beginning of the project did not have a large budget or substantial accounting or other related technical capabilities, USAID provided funds to Florida International University to assist ILANUD in developing such capabilities.

79. USAID, Project Paper, *supra* note 75.

80. Caribbean Justice Improvement Project (CJIP), University of the West Indies (UWI) Quarterly Activity Schedule (Sept.-Dec. 1986). For details on the project, see USAID, Project Paper, Caribbean Justice Improvement (AID/LAC/P-318 Project No. 598-0645).

USAID will receive $7.8 million, with an additional $2.2 million earmarked specifically for Jamaica. A grant agreement has been negotiated with the University of the West Indies (UWI) acting through the Faculty of Law situated at the Cave Hill Campus in Barbados. A project agreement between the Government of Jamaica and USAID/Jamaica obligates the $2.2 million Jamaica component. Although the Project is designed to benefit the rule of law throughout the entire English-speaking Caribbean, the primary areas of focus are Belize and the six independent states in the Eastern Caribbean: Antigua and Barbuda; Dominica; Grenada; St. Christopher Nevis; St. Lucia; and St. Vincent and the Grenadines. Under the $7.8 million grant, UWI will make subgrants to, and execute contracts with, regional, subregional and national institutions and entities. The Project contemplates that the more developed countries in the region, namely Trinidad and Tobago, Barbados, and Jamaica, will participate as donors, providing technical assistance by hosting training programs and making their existing activities and institutions available to professionals from the seven participating countries. By design, Guyana is not part of the Project.[81]

According to the project paper, the purpose of the effort is to use local and regional institutions in implementing the Project.[82] The paper recognizes the important structural differences between the United States and the Commonwealth approaches to the common law and hence, the limitation on U.S. influence in the region. The Project's rationale is that if the United States government allows the legal system of the Commonwealth Caribbean to continue to deteriorate, the rule of law and democratic tradition in the Commonwealth Caribbean will be undermined. In this regard, the project report recalls that the Grenadian 1979 revolution was the only coup d'etat in modern times in the English-speaking Caribbean.[83] Coincidentally, President Reagan announced the Project for the first time in public in an address in Grenada on February

81. The omission of Guyana from the Project is partly technical, due to Guyana's default on prior U.S. and International Monetary Fund loans; it is, however, political as well. *See* Zarr, The Rule of Law in the Commonwealth Caribbean: How Long Can the Machinery of Justice Run on Empty? 75 (Bureau of Latin America and the Caribbean, USAID, Nov. 1, 1985) ("in practically every state except possibly Guyana judicial independence exists"); USAID, Project Paper, *supra* note 75, at 12 ("[A]ll but Guyana are functioning democracies and inheritors of an abiding democratic tradition.").

82. USAID, Project Paper, *supra* note 75, at 7-8.

83. Zarr, *supra* note 81, at 78-79. For a discussion of the importance of the Granada revolution of 1979 and military intervention of 1983, see F. PHILLIPS, *supra* note 50, at 3-51.

20, 1986.[84] The Project views as the solution to the problem of deteriorating legal systems due to lack of maintenance, the transference of successful, reproducible innovations from some of the region's larger, better endowed states to poorer territories.[85] Therefore, the Project plans to rely almost solely on Caribbean institutions as resources. Although U.S. bar groups, universities and other entities may be involved in specific project components as a particular need or opportunity arises for which a U.S. entity is an appropriate contractor or supplier, no U.S. entity will be involved in the full range of project activities.[86] In many substantive areas the UWI goal simply will be to raise the poorer states up to the regional standard. In other cases the regional standard itself may need improvement (such as in court registries, where even the wealthier states have antiquated systems). To classify the proper conceptual framework into which the Commonwealth Caribbean Project fits, the Project and its initial implementation must be reviewed in more detail.

III. The Components of the Commonwealth Caribbean Project

The major Project components include: law revision and reform; case reports/textbook revolving fund; law library enhancement; country-specific activities; UWI operational support; and regional technical assistance/training.[87] The major components were selected as a pragmatic compromise. Already the Project is seeking to expand the components as well as the scope of existing components.

---

84. Remarks by President Reagan to the Citizens of Grenada, Queen's Park, St. George's Grenada (The White House, Office of the Press Secretary, Feb. 20, 1986). The text states as follows: "Finally, I would like to announce that the United States will be undertaking, in conjunction with Caribbean governments, a 5-year, $5.5 million program to help support the free and independent judicial systems of the Caribbean islands — recognized around the world as a pillar of your democratic traditions."

85. USAID, Project Paper, *supra* note 75, at 8. For a discussion of the need to solve the problem of deteriorating legal systems generally, see Patchett, Legal Resource Needs in Small States: Report on Bermuda and the Caribbean 71 (Lond: Commonwealth Secretariat) [hereinafter Legal Resource Needs]; Patchett, Assistance to Small States to Meet Their Legal Needs, Papers of the Meeting of Commonwealth Law Ministers 23-28 (Feb. 1983) [hereinafter Assistance to Small States].

86. *Id.* For a discussion of the need for local or regional initiative for an administration of justice program and a discussion of the ineffectiveness of "made-in-the-U.S.A." solutions, see U.S. Dep't of State, *supra* note 61.

87. USAID, Project Paper, *supra* note 75, at 15-19.

A. *UWI Operational Support*

This component, for which $900,000 is allocated, provides UWI with the operational support required to implement and manage the Project. The Project funds the UWI project director and staff for the life of the Project. Considering the Faculty of Law members' substantial experience, UWI can manage the multi-faceted regional project with a relatively small operational staff. One reason that the UWI was selected as the Project's grantee was its existing expertise in similar projects and existing professional and support staff.[88] During the first year, the Project employed a stenographer clerk and an administrative assistant.[89]

B. *Law Library Development*

This component, for which $600,000 is allocated, enables the UWI to provide technical assistance and training to participating countries to develop and maintain a law library. The goal is to develop a single adequate library serving the courts, government, and the practicing bar in a country, rather than the haphazard system of books scattered around both Government and private offices.[90] The absence of a centralized law library or collection of legal materials has precluded preparation of soundly-researched opinions or of forensic arguments. In addition, relevant precedents in case or statutory law or even commentaries on law are unavailable in the smaller participating countries of the Project.[91] Existing government collections will be consolidated, except for essential items needed by prosecutors, legal draftsmen and others for immediate reference.

Prior to participation in a law library development activity for a country, UWI concludes a Memorandum of Understanding (MOU) with the government relating to the activity. The specific elements which the MOU addresses are:

1. Within thirty days of MOU signing, the government designates a suitable candidate for training as a paraprofessional in

---

88. CJIP, UWI Quarterly Activity Report 2 (Apr. - June 1987) (on file with the Project Administrator and the author).

89. *Id.* at 15.

90. For a useful survey of existing legal material in the Commonwealth Caribbean, see V. Newton, Commonwealth Caribbean Legal Literature (1987) (a bibliography of all primary sources to date and secondary sources for 1971-85).

91. Assistance to Small States, *supra* note 85, at 37.

law librarianship, giving the assurance of a reasonably remunerated career.

2. The government provides adequate physical accommodations for the library in proximity to major users.

3. A user fee system for the practicing bar is established, with profits allocated for library purposes. Revenue derived from use of photocopy machinery likewise will be used for library purposes.

4. Suitable budgetary provision for library upkeep and maintenance is established.[92]

C. *Case Reports/Textbook Revolving Fund*

Since the Commonwealth Caribbean legal system is a common law system, which relies heavily on court-made law,[93] a significant problem in the smaller territories of the Commonwealth Caribbean is the absence of adequate law reporting. No court reports have ever been published for Belize or any of the Leeward Islands (Anguilla, Antigua and Barbuda, British Virgin Islands, Montserrat, St. Christopher Nevis) and only one volume, covering cases between 1866 and 1907, has ever been published for the Windward Islands (Dominica, Grenada, St. Lucia, and St. Vincent and the Grenadines). The West Indies Reports, published commercially in Britain, covers cases from the most developed states, whose lawyers account for the bulk of the book sales (i.e., Jamaica, Trinidad, Barbados, and Guyana). Hence, the West Indies Reports does not meet the needs of the micro-states for reported judicial decisions.[94] In order to bridge this gap, to assist in providing teaching materials for the Faculty of Law, and to offer an incentive for much-needed legal scholarship, the Project will have a revolving fund in the amount of $250,000. A committee will administer the fund under the chairmanship of the dean of the Faculty of Law, and the UWI finance officer, law librarian, and project director. The Project budgets funds to produce case reports and textbooks on topics of importance and interest to the participating countries.[95]

---

92. *Id.* at 16.

93. *Id.* at 16-17. For a useful discussion of the problem caused by lack of sufficient case reports and information generally about judicial decisions, see F. Alexis & H. Fraser, Eminent Caribbean Jurist 173-74 (1985).

94. USAID Project Paper, *supra* note 75, at 15-16; Zarr, *supra* note 81, at 36-37. For a useful summary of existing law reports, current informal law reporting, and series no longer published, see V. Newton, *supra* note 1, at 319-39.

95. USAID Project Paper, *supra* note 75, at 15-16.

The goal is to select legal topics for publications with enough interest that sales will be sufficient to restore the fund. A compilation of regional constitutional and administrative law reports, which is now in preparation, should be successful commercially. As the Faculty of Law gains in reputation, it is anticipated that this will lead to additional sales in currently less-marketable areas.[96]

The grant agreement does not provide formal maintenance of value undertakings. According to the plan, however, book sales will generate sufficient revenue to enable the fund to maintain principal. As an incentive for legal scholarship, income from proceeds of book sales will be restored to the fund with any excess divided between the author or compiler of the text and the fund. Additionally, the Project allows the negotiation of royalties from the sale of books, although USAID has the right under a royalty-free license to use such published material. The committee chairman will produce annual reports on the funds with a financial statement of account prepared by the UWI finance officer.[97]

D. *Law Revision and Reform*

The $1,750,000 allocated to this component will enable attorneys and lay persons to locate statutes. Although seven countries currently participate, only Belize has revised its laws in the past twenty years and those revisions did not extend to subsidiary legislation. Although law revision should occur every ten to fifteen years, the last revision for St. Vincent, St. Lucia and the Grenadines, and Grenada, occurred in 1926, 1957, and 1958, respectively.[98]

The lack of publication of revised laws has been exacerbated by many substantive constitutional and post-independent changes which have occurred since the last revisions. The existing legislation, quite apart from antiquated language and formulation, reflects constitutional forms which have been replaced, sometimes several times.[99] Consequently, several shortcomings are obvious: some laws have been repealed more than once; others have been

96. *Id.*

97. *Id.*

98. *Id.* at 17-18. For a discussion of the problems caused by lack of law revision, see Legal Resource Needs, *supra* note 85; Assistance to Small States, *supra* note 85, at 36.

99. Legal Resource Needs, *supra* note 85. For a discussion of the changes occasioned by constitutional changes in the post-independence period, see F. ALEXIS, *supra* note 50; F. PHILLIPS, *supra* note 50.

amended after repeal; and officials designated in the statutes have been altered, with later amendments referring to the officer by the original designation. Thus, any legal professional has extreme difficulty understanding the applicable law.[100]

The United Kingdom, the Commonwealth Fund for Technical Cooperation and the United Nations Development Program have financed technical experts in law revision in the past and will continue doing so under the Project. Therefore, USAID financing is projected only for the cost of preparation of materials, printing, and publishing. Since all seven states require law revision, and $270,000 is an average printing cost per state, a total of $1.75 million is estimated for this component.

Since the laws have not been updated in such a long period and are often the creature of a colonial master, a dire need exists for law reform. Law revision normally takes three years per state, while law reform is a longer process. However, without the deadline imposed by law revision, law reform may never occur.

Another ongoing project is legal harmonization of the Organization of Eastern Caribbean States (OECS) through the OECS Secretariat in St. Lucia. An important step preparatory to law revision undertaken by the Secretariat is to standardize format, title, chapter headings and content for statute books of the OECS states.[101]

E. Country-Specific Activities

This component, allocated $2 million, provides funds for activities which the individual countries have determined to be priority items. To ensure coordination, avoid duplication and effectively target activities, the UWI Faculty of Law has to be aware of the projects of the United Nations Development Program, the Commonwealth Fund for Technical Development, the Canadian International Development Agency, and the British Development Division in the Caribbean within the legal environment of the target countries. In dollar amount, court management activities and renovation/adaptation of existing structures are likely to be among the largest users of these funds. Pilot computer applications in records management, technical assistance in establishing a public defender

100. Legal Resource Needs, *supra* note 85.
101. USAID, Project Paper, *supra* note 75, at 17-18.

system, and essential commodity procurement (i.e., typewriters, file cabinets, disks, photocopiers) are other likely candidates for funding.[102]

F. Regional Technical Assistance/Training

This project area, budgeted $700,000, covers a variety of national and regional training and technical assistance activities not included in other project components. Essentially, this category covers other worthwhile activities in support of the rule of law and legal systems in the region whose financing under the USAID Grant might otherwise have been doubtful. The component may fund the following types of activities:

1. Regional training for police prosecutors conducted by the Regional Police Training Center in Barbados.[103]

2. Regional training for paralegals offered, for example, by the Kingston Legal Aid Clinic and the Barbados Community College.[104]

3. Teleconferencing under the University of the West Indies Distance Teaching Experiment (UWIDITE) Project as a training vehicle for prosecutors, magistrates, court registries, etc.[105]

4. A UWI subgrant to the Organization of Commonwealth Caribbean Bar Association (OCCBA) to help local bar associations establish legal aid offices in participating states.[106]

IV. Initial Activities of the Commonwealth Caribbean Project

During the first nine months, the Project's activities have produced tangible results. The Project has shown a surprising capacity to expand into related areas. By the end of December, 1986, the Project Director had visited all the main beneficiary countries under the agreement: Antigua, Belize, Dominica, Grenada, St.

102. *Id.* at 18.

103. Zarr, *supra* note 81, at 16-17.

104. *Id.* at 53-54.

105. Zarr, *supra* note 81, at 83. The UWIDITE Project enables transmission of programs among the UWI main campuses (in Cave Hill, St. Augustine, and Mona) and the Extramural Departments in the six OECS countries and Belize. Currently used for teaching courses, its additional potential uses are infinite.

106. USAID, Project Paper, *supra* note 75, at 18.

Christopher-Nevis, St. Lucia, St. Vincent and the Grenadines. Project officials also visited the OECS Secretariat and the Bahamas.[107]

Moreover, the Project concluded a Memorandum of Understanding for Quick Impact Activities, permitting each country to receive a $50,000 disbursement for project activities. In response, five countries have already submitted illustrative lists for funding.

The Project has an office adjacent to the University of the West Indies campus at Cave Hill. In addition to the Project Director, the Project has employed two senior staff persons experienced at the University and the Law Faculty. The Project has approval to purchase four computers — one each for the project office, Law Faculty, OECS Secretariat, and Law Library.[108]

The Implementation Unit has the additional temporary role of acting as a clearing house between the Organization of Commonwealth Caribbean Bar Associations (OCCBA) and its constituent members in the territories.[109] Because the OCCBA has no Secretariat nor facility to house its operations, its activities are very limited. However, with ABA assistance in the structure and organization of management staff, financing, and services, eventually the OCCBA can be self-supporting.

A. *Organizational Activities in the Member Territories*

Carl Joseph, formerly acting Attorney General in St. Vincent, received an appointment to the post of Deputy Director for three years from May 1, 1987, and will operate from the Legal Secretariat of the Organization of Western Caribbean States in St. Lucia.[110]

Except for Belize, all of the territories opted initially for the appointment of part-time country coordinators. Generally those chosen are persons who hold office in the judicial and legal service of their respective countries. In Grenada, for example, it is the Acting Chief Justice; in Dominica and St. Vincent and the Grenadines the Solicitor General; in St. Lucia the Director of Public Prosecu-

---

107. CJIP, *supra* note 80, at 1.

108. Minutes of Meeting of Project Committee 2 (Mar. 5, 1987) (on file with the Project Administrator and the author).

109. CJIP, UWI Quarterly Activity Report 1 (Jan. - Mar. 1987) (on file with the Project Administrator and the author).

110. Minutes of Meeting of Project Committee 4 (Mar. 5, 1987) (on file with the Project Administrator and the author).

tions; and in Antigua and St. Christopher-Nevis a Crown Counsel performs those duties.[111]

B. International Organizational Activities

From the outset the Project was conceived as multilateral, able to involve as many donor organizations and governments as possible.[112] Hence, the Project established a Donors' Committee. At the second meeting representatives from the Organization of American States and the Commonwealth Fund for Technical Cooperation (CFTC) attended for the first time. At this gathering the Caribbean Development Bank (CDB) agreed to participate. This development is heartening because the CDB plays an important technical and leadership role in development projects and had initially declined to participate.

The current membership of the Committee includes: Principal of UWI, K. D. Hunte, Chairman; Pro-Vice Chancellor R. V. Goodridge; the Campus Registrar; the Finance Officer, the Dean of the Faculty of Law; the Senior Assistant Registrar (Planning); the Project Director; and representatives of the British Development Division; the Caribbean Development Bank; the Canadian International Development Agency; the Commonwealth Technical Development Fund; Organization of American States (OAS); Organization of East Caribbean States (OECS); and the USAID.[113]

The Project has been successful in multiplying the quality and the amount of its programs by inducing other governments and organizations to participate in the Project or related activities. For instance, the American Bar Association has participated in several of the Project's activities. Multilateral participation by non-U.S. organizations assists in insulating the Project from the anthropomorphism usually inherent in a law and development project.

The American Bar Association (ABA) has cooperated with the Project in proposing that the United States Information Agency (USIA) provide necessary funding to bring a group of approximately fifteen chief executive officers from selected bar associations in the Commonwealth Caribbean countries to the United

111. CJIP, *supra* note 109, at 1.

112. USAID, Project Paper, *supra* note 75, at 23-24. For a discussion of the urgent need for coordination of aid activities in the administration of justice in the Commonwealth Caribbean, see Assistance to Small States, *supra* note 85, at 37-38.

113. CJIP, *supra* note 109, at 1.

States in August 1988 to participate in a three week seminar on the United States constitutional system and to attend the ABA Annual Meeting in Toronto. The program has been developed to further Goal VIII of the ABA: "To Advance the Rule of Law in the World," as well as Summary Objective III under Goal VIII: "To maintain relations and further cooperation with other professional organizations, including foreign and international bar associations concerned with multinational and international legal matters." A major objective of the proposed program is development of a framework which will create the necessary links for inter-bar exchanges in the future. The primary theme of the program will be the "U.S. Constitutional System at work."[114]

A principal issue for the Donors' Committee since its inception has been a request by St. Kitts for a new Court House. This request has been approved, and the OAS has offered to provide the services of an expert on Archives, to advise the other territories on ways to solve space problems in their respective registries.[115]

Another proposed activity for the Donors' Committee is registry reorganization. As a result of a visit to the United States late in 1986, the Project invited two experts from the National Center for State Courts to join a former Chief Registrar of the OECS Supreme Court in an examination of the present operations of the court registries and to make recommendations for improvement where necessary. A recent meeting of the Attorneys General of the OECS lent enthusiastic support to this proposal.[116]

The University of the West Indies convened a meeting on UWIDITE in Mona, Jamaica on April 1-2, 1987. The Project Director outlined the nature of the contributions the Project could expect for the territories of St. Kitts, St. Vincent and Belize. According to reports received by the Project Office, Grenada will receive the UWIDITE system from another source.[117]

C. *Law Library Development*

The Project has identified central libraries in each territory. However, in each case the physical facilities were found to be

114. Draft Project Paper, ABA Annual Meeting Foreign Bar Executives Program, Concept Paper, 1-2 (undated) (on file with the author).

115. CJIP, *supra* note 109, at 1.

116. *Id.* at 5.

117. *Id.*

clearly inadequate. A need exists in all the territories to provide physical space in order to plan for and realize the full benefits of law library development. The Project has prepared and approved a training program for librarians which contemplates training one individual as law librarian. However, since insufficient work exists for one individual's time to be directed exclusively to the work of a law librarian, the Project's librarian consultants have recommended the consideration of the training of two persons in law librarianship as well as in other registrarial functions. The training for the OECS librarians will take place at the Cave Hill Faculty of Law Library while the trainees from Belize will attend the Supreme Court Library in Jamaica.[118] The preliminary meeting of the regional law librarians selected to visit the territories and conduct on-the-spot needs assessments, occurred in Trinidad in January 1987.[119] They visited the seven territories concerned, and met in Barbados in the middle of April 1986 to present their reports and make firm recommendations regarding the training of staff, the ordering of books and equipment, and the adequacy of existing or proposed physical space in those countries.[120] The Professional Law Librarians held their second meeting in Barbados on April 16, 1987. A training course for potential law librarians took place at the UWI Law Library in Barbados from September 15 to October 30, 1987.[121] The Project has prepared written reports on the status and needs of law libraries for all of the territories. Velma Newton, UWI Law Library at Cave Hill, is coordinating the lists of books and equipment and is preparing a master list for use in responding to publishers of law books when the Project makes a procurement request.

D. *Case Reports/Textbook Revolving Fund*

At its meeting held on October 10, 1986, the Board of the Faculty of Law established a Committee to advise the Project Director on the operation of this fund. The Committee's initial meeting occurred on November 4, 1986, at which time it established certain guidelines. The Advisory Committee recommended that the fund help produce tests and reports likely to bring quick mon-

118. CJIP, *supra* note 80, at 2.

119. *Id.*

120. CJIP, *supra* note 109, at 2.

121. CJIP, UWI Quarterly Activity Report 3 (Apr.-June, 1987) (on file with the Project Administrator and the author).

etary returns to replenish the fund. Another priority goal was that the fund should add an impetus to the Faculty's outreach program by making the first year law course available to students in smaller territories who cannot afford to do the first year outside of their home territory. The Committee deemed the production of texts and other materials in the first year subjects a priority. Since a casebook on constitutional law and a collection of Grenada Law Reports were in their advance stages of preparation, they will be the first publications to be financed from the fund.[122] A third text, hoped to comprise the first volume of the OECS Law Reports, has been compiled by retired Justice Cecil Hewlett of Antigua, and is being edited by the Project Director.[123] The Faculty of Law is planning to complement the activities of the fund by appointing a Research Fellow whose responsibility will be the coordination of research work necessary for these publications. Where additional assistance is required from law students, the fund will employ them. Concentration will be on the first year subjects Constitutional Law, Criminal Law, and Law and Legal Systems of the Caribbean.[124] The Project has employed students at the UWI law faculties in Barbados and Trinidad to classify unreported cases stored in both institutions under subject-matter headings. The classification work will assist future author of Case Reports and/or Textbooks in locating the relevant materials more easily than before.[125]

E. Law Revision and Reform

The OECS Secretariat has submitted a proposal for Anguilla, Antigua, the British Virgin Islands, Montserrat and St. Kitts for joint revision of the laws including the prior harmonization of chapter headings.[126]

Belize has succeeded in arranging for the Commonwealth Fund for Technical Cooperation (CFTC) to approve an application from its Government for the appointment of a suitable person to revise the subsidiary legislation of that country.[127] The Belize Government requested the Faculty of Law to submit proposals for the

122. CJIP, *supra* note 80, at 2; CJIP, *supra* note 109, at 2.
123. CJIP, *supra* note 109, at 2.
124. CJIP, *supra* note 80, at 3.
125. CJIP, *supra* note 121.
126. Minutes of Meeting of Project Committee 2 (Mar. 5, 1987) (on file with the Project Administrator and the author).
127. *Id.* at 3.

revision of its subsidiary legislation.[128] The CFTC representative indicated that due to a shortage of funds, it informed the Government of Belize that for the next two years it could fund only one of the projects for which that Government had applied.[129] The choice was between a compilation of a revised edition of the subsidiary laws of Belize or an expert review of the constitutionality of the statute laws of Belize. The Government of Belize chose the former.[130]

Grenada approached the United Nations Development Program (UNDP) to obtain the services of a Law Revision Commissioner.[131] Dominica's law revision project, which is being done with the assistance of the UNDP, is quite advanced and the Government of Dominica is expected to approach the Project soon for the printing costs.[132] St. Vincent plans to appoint John Havers as its Law Revision Commissioner.[133]

The Project Director noted the similarity of the Civil Code of St. Lucia to that of Quebec and suggested that the Canadian International Development Agency (CIDA) could undertake to revise the laws of St. Lucia.[134] The CIDA representative promised to look into the matter. St. Lucia is discussing obtaining assistance in its law revision from the Canadian Government with the participation of the Civil Law Section of the University of Ottawa, which will be the Canadian Institutional link.[135] The Deputy Project Director reported that the standardization of the headings of the laws of the OECS states is proceeding well.[136]

F. Regional Technical Assistance/Training

At the Donors' meetings the priority for training needs of the

---

128. CJIP, *supra* note 80, at 3.

129. CJIP, *supra* note 109, at 3.

130. Minutes of Meeting of Project Committee 3 (Mar. 5, 1987) (on file with the Project Administrator and the author).

131. *Id.*

132. *Id.* at 2.

133. *Id.* at 3.

134. CJIP, *supra* note 80, at 3. For background on the St. Lucia legal system and its Quebec roots, see WHITE, SOME PROBLEMS OF A HYBRID LEGAL SYSTEM: A CASE STUDY OF SAINT LUCIA (1975); ANTHONY, VIABILITY OF THE CIVILEST TRADITION IN SAINT LUCIA: A TENTATIVE APPRAISAL (1984).

135. Minutes of Meeting of Project Committee 4 (Mar. 5, 1987) (on file with the Project Administrator and the author).

136. CJIP, *supra* note 121, at 3.

various territories focused largely on the provision of legal draftsmen personnel in the Registry Offices, police prosecutors and other court personnel.[137] A workshop for magistrates is proposed.[138] The Project Director wrote to the CFTC requesting to conduct a workshop similar to the workshop for Magistrates organized by the CFTC funded by the Commonwealth Foundation and the Nuffield Foundation, held in Zambia in August of 1986. The Project Director circulated the report to the Chief Justices, Attorneys General and Chairmen of the National Advisory Committees in order to discover any interest in such a workshop in the Caribbean.[139]

Two training workshops were planned for 1987. The first was planned for the Regional Police Training Center and brought together magistrates and police prosecutors from the region to discuss methods of shortening the time devoted in the preliminary investigation stage of serious crimes. A second workshop utilized the resources of the European Community and the Project, the expertise of UWI, the University of Glasgow, and the International Development Law Institute (Rome) to teach young private and public sector lawyers the rudiments of negotiating international contracts.[140]

The Project organized a Regional Workshop on Committals by Statement for the magistrates and police prosecutors in the region. Every territory in the region except Guyana participated. The workshop was extremely successful and the Project plans to conduct supplemental workshops in the territories. The Government of Antigua is already actively considering the introduction of similar legislation (for committals by statements) in that country.[141]

The seminar on the negotiation of International Contracts conducted by the Faculties of Law of UWI and the University of Glasgow occurred from September 21 to October 3, 1987. The European Community agreed to provide partial funding.[142]

---

137. Minutes of Meeting of Project Committee 3 (Dec. 15, 1986) (on file with the Project Administrator and the author).

138. For a discussion of the problems with lack of training of magistrates, see Zarr, *supra* note 81, at 51.

139. Minutes of Meeting of Project Committee 4 (Mar. 5, 1987) (on file with the Project Administrator and the author).

140. CJIP, *supra* note 80, at 4.

141. CJIP, *supra* note 109, at 5; DeMerieux, Report on Workshop Committals by Written Statement, 5 (CJIP-USAID/UWI-Faculty of Law, Mar. 5, 1987) (on file with the Project Administrator and the author).

142. CJIP, *supra* note 109, at 5.

The Project's members have discussed the need for an annual meeting of OECS judges. The Attorneys General of the OECS pledged support for that meeting and for a meeting of the Court Registries.[143]

The newly unified Lawyers Association of Trinidad and Tobago, and OCCBA have requested technical assistance to improve their structure and ability to deliver services.[144] Similarly, OCCBA, a regional bar organization which consists of the national bar associations in the Commonwealth Caribbean, has requested that the American Bar Association provide technical assistance on structure and organization so that it can improve its management staff services, financing, and other services.[145]

On March 13, 1986 the OCCBA Subcommittee on Legal Aid met in Barbados. Discussion concerned a proposed seminar on legal aid which was scheduled to be held in Trinidad in September 1986. The subcommittee concluded that the funds (US $48,000) for the proposed seminar should be conserved and used to render technical assistance to the territories for establishing viable legal aid programs. Hence, the subcommittee abandoned the seminar idea[146] and is concentrating on preparing a proposal to design a regional legal aid program for the Eastern Caribbean.[147] The subcommittee has sought the assistance of Michael Millemann, a legal expert, and the American Bar Association in preparing the proposal.[148]

Technical assistance for court registries in the territories has begun. In November 1986, the Project Officer and the Project Director visited the offices of the National Center for State Courts in

143. *Id.* at 6.

144. *Id.*; Letter from Keith S. Sobion, Secretary, The Law Association of Trinidad and Tobago, to Dr. N.J.O. Liverpool (Apr. 27, 1987).

145. Memorandum, "Contribution of the ABA to the Caribbean Justice Improvement Project in 1987" (the Project Director, Apr. 26, 1987)[hereinafter Memorandum]; Draft Memorandum from the author, "Proposed Assistance from American Bar Association."

146. CJIP, *supra* note 121, at 6.

147. The background to the proposal is contained in a memorandum, by Nancy M. Anderson, Attorney-at-Law, Kingston Legal Aid Clinic in consultation with Lloyd Barnett, President, OCCBA, "OCCBA Memorandum on Legal Aid Services in the Commonwealth Caribbean" (Feb. 1987).

148. *See* Memorandum, *supra* note 145. For a discussion by a distinguished Caribbean jurist on the need for legal aid, see F. ALEXIS, *supra* note 93, at 160-61. A draft proposal has now been prepared and circulated. See letter from Millemann to Barnett, dated Nov. 24, 1987, and Appendix 1, Draft Proposal for a Civil Legal Aid Proposal (14 pp.)(on file with author).

Williamsburg, Virginia. As a result of the visit, an agreement will be concluded between UWI and the Center. Under the agreement the Center will provide court registry and management experts' visits to Barbados and the territories which are within the jurisdiction of the OECS Supreme Court, in order to make recommendations to improve the efficiency of the registries. Ernest Wilkinson, a former Chief Registrar of the OECS Supreme Court and a member of the team, visited the Washington office of the Center with the Project Director to assist in formulating questionnaires which are currently under preparation by the registrars and chief magistrates concerned.[149]

Another technical assistance activity is para-legal training. The Barbados Community College has agreed to act as coordinator and external examiner for a para-legal course for the OECS territories. The Project has requested that the Kingston Legal Aid Clinic in Jamaica conduct similar training for Belize. The Institute of Accounting and Business Studies, Ltd. is planning to operate the course in Trinidad and Tobago.[150]

G. *Country Specific Activities*

As required by the Project Agreement, national advisory committees have been established in six of the seven participating states: Antigua, Belize, Dominica, Grenada, St. Christopher Nevis, St. Vincent and the Grenadines. The committees will remain in existence during the life of the Project; all are functioning. At the end of December 1986, Quick Impact Activity funds had been approved for five territories and two had signed and returned their MOU's.[151]

H. *Collateral Activities*

Activities collateral to the actual USAID grant have contributed to the overall administration of justice for the Commonwealth Caribbean Project.

The International Criminal Investigative Training Assistance Program (ICITAP) of the United States Department of Justice cosponsored a five-month course on "Instruction Development and

149. *Id.*
150. *Id.*
151. CJIP, *supra* note 80, at 4.

Basic Criminal Investigation" in the last half of 1986 at the Regional Police Training Center in Barbados.[152] The course attracted students from Barbados and from six other Caribbean countries, including Dominica, Grenada, St. Lucia, and Antigua. Paul Russo, the U.S. Ambassador to Barbados, presented equipment during the course to Hewitt Rose, the Commandant of the Regional Police Training Center (RPTC). The equipment, which was valued at $18,000, included a video cassette recorder and television, a photostat machine, and an overhead projector. The course is significant because it affords more sophisticated training for policemen in the Eastern Caribbean. It also promotes regional cooperation within the RPTC, which has existed since 1871, to ensure its continuation. Organizations outside of the Commonwealth Caribbean Project have supplemented the RPTC's activities.[153] The exclusion of ICITAP's activities from the Project will insulate USAID and UWI from potential human rights and political problems involved in training police.[154] To the extent the region can persuade international organizations, such as the United Nations, Interpol, and the Commonwealth, to provide such training, the more value-neutral and professional the training is likely to be and the less likely its adverse political consequences.[155]

A program on the bicentennial of the United States constitution took place on September 26, 1987. The program included a presentation on the protection of human rights in the Caribbean as viewed from the judiciary, by Sir William Douglas, former Chief Justice of the Barbados Supreme Court and currently Barbados Ambassador to the United States and the O.A.S., and a presenta-

152. For more discussion of the course, see Zagaris, *U.S. Government Assists Caribbean Regional Police Training*, 3 INT'L ENFORCEMENT L. REP. 23 (1987).

153. For background on the history of the Regional Police Training Center and suggestions on improving regional cooperation, see Zagaris & Kamta, *Regionalism and Criminal Justice in the West Indies: The Regional Police Training Center Development*, 7 ABSTRACTS POLICE SCI. 283-96 (Netherlands, 1979); Zagaris, *The West Indies Regional Police Training Center: A Model of Intergovernmental Cooperation in Criminal Justice*, 8 J. POLICE SCI. & ADMIN. 460-63 (1980).

154. For a discussion of the role of external factors and regional and interregional cooperation in criminal justice planning and police training in the Commonwealth Caribbean, see Zagaris, *The Beginning of Criminal Justice Planning in the British West Indies*, 10 POLICE SCI. ABSTRACTS ii, xii, xv (No. 4 July/Aug. 1982).

155. For a discussion of the controversy surrounding assistance to police in El Salvador, see Zagaris, *U.S. Police Aid to El Salvador Opposed by Americas Watch on Human Rights Grounds*, 3 INT'L ENFORCEMENT L. REP. 311 (1987) and Cohen, *U.S. Aid to Security Forces of El Salvador Reduced Because of Human Rights Violations*, 3 INT'L ENFORCEMENT L. REP. 358 (1978).

tion on making a new constitution, a viewpoint from Belize by Edward A. Laing, former lecturer of law and comparative law and development scholar, currently Belize Ambassador to the United States and the O.A.S.[156]

V. Classification and Analysis of the Project

The USAID Administration of Justice Project for the Commonwealth Caribbean derives its intellectual origins from certain components of the law and development movement. The Project arises from law and politics, the notion of social engineering through law, and the residue of the post-World War II commitment by the United States to foreign assistance. Indeed, some of the architects of the Commonwealth Caribbean Project were active participants in the 1960s law and development movement and, hence, that movement itself influenced the existing Project. The intellectual style of the Commonwealth Caribbean Project is easy to discern: it is directed towards action rather than inquiry. The Project expresses the idea that the legal systems of the smaller and poorer countries in the Commonwealth Caribbean can be raised to those of the more developed countries, with funds to maintain the quality of the legal system in the Commonwealth Caribbean and technical assistance from the principal regional law school and most developed countries of the Commonwealth. In some cases the idea is to raise the regional goal. To that extent, the project administrators may look to extra-regional models. The chief models come from legal systems in the Commonwealth (i.e., Canada, Australia, the United Kingdom) and the United States. Although many differences exist between the legal systems of the Commonwealth Caribbean and the United States, even before the Project, important interactions between the two legal systems were evident. Judges and attorneys in the Commonwealth Caribbean referred to United States cases and statutes for models. The frequent meetings between members of the legal profession due to travel, commerce, education, and cultural contacts have influenced legal developments in the Commonwealth Caribbean significantly. To the extent UWI and OCCBA seek assistance in providing services and organizing bar association activities, U.S. models will inevitably

---

156. For a summary of the program, see Zagaris, "Comparative Constitutional Law Development—Bicentiennial Constitutional Program," The Washington Foreign Law Society News Letter 6-7 (Winter, 1987).

appear as a major alternative.

One of the major, albeit subtle, theoretical models is the cultural model of the U.S. attorney as a social engineer. Such a model is becoming increasingly popular, especially with younger, idealistic attorneys in the Caribbean. However, many of the attorneys in the Commonwealth Caribbean have studied and worked in the United States and are friendly with individuals such as the late Averill Harriman, who had a home in Barbados. The lawyer who moves between careers and works for government, practices, teaches, participates actively in politics, and consults for governments is not unusual in the Caribbean. Without question the Justice Improvement Project for the Commonwealth Caribbean is not designed for inquiry. Almost necessarily, the USAID sponsorship and mandate towards action means that the emphasis in style is on action rather than inquiry.

The Project is based fundamentally on the idea of the attorney as a social engineer and the idea that law can lead social change. Although the initial architect of the project, Gerald Zarr, visited each of the countries in the region and carefully listened for more than one year to a multitude of lawyers, sociologists, policymakers, economists, and others, the Project's goals nevertheless reflect many of the United States development goals in the Commonwealth Caribbean. Indeed, Professor Merryman would probably want more comparative law and social change. Hopefully, the fact that an academic institution is the recipient and distributor of funds and since its Donor's Committee encourages other personal organizations to participate, scholars such as Professor Merryman may want to undertake inquiry. Undoubtedly, such proposals would be welcome by the Faculty of Law and USAID. The initiation a few years ago of an LL.M. program at the Cave Hill Campus, the establishment of a summer law school program in cooperation with Florida State University, and the excellent law library at Cave Hill facilitate inquiry. At present, however, the Project is focusing more on development and less on inquiry.

The Project does have several activities, however, which are designed to facilitate inquiry. The law library development activities will accomplish this in the participating countries. The case reports/textbook revolving fund will enable practitioners, scholars, and policy-makers to review case decisions and textbooks written by persons in the region. Presently a shortage of both case reports and textbooks makes inquiry, especially by local professionals as opposed to external experts, difficult.

Valdez and Ronny Thwaites, a pioneer of legal services in Jamaica and the region, would probably urge that the Project emphasize more social change and assistance to the poor and indigent. For instance, Valdez would probably lament that too much emphasis is placed on improving non-reform mechanisms such as law libraries, case reports, and textbooks, and implementing law revision as opposed to law reform — all activities which do not specifically focus on access to law by the poor. Unfortunately, due to lack of funding, initially the Project provided for law revision but not law reform. Similarly, the Project paper discussed the need for legal aid, but did not fund such activities. However, in response to a request of OCCBA and the Project for a review of the potential for starting legal aid in the Eastern Caribbean, the American Bar Association and other U.S. groups (i.e., Inter-American Foundation) have expressed interest. Clearly the Commonwealth Caribbean Project is not focused on the method of legal teaching. Rather, the Project addresses social soundness. It is designed to "help the poor and vulnerable groups in the Commonwealth Caribbean gain better access to the legal systems in the region."[157] The Project is premised on the fact that the laws inherited from the British colonial system based on a plantation society are no longer relevant and the funding shortages, which have prevented participating countries from collecting and publishing the changes in law, hit hardest at the poor and vulnerable groups in society. The Project also discusses how its activities may result in the establishment of legal services if leaders of donee countries are provided bare-bone funding and an office. Trinidad and Jamaica are mentioned as the obvious sources of technical assistance in legal aid.[158] One of the open questions with respect to the social soundness and the ability of the Project to accomplish social change is the extent to which the Project and national committees have the foresight and ability to design and implement legal services programs, especially ones which have a developmental, as distinguished from a traditional orientation.

As a result of the Valdez thesis, the Commonwealth Caribbean Project has persons within the region perform and even design the work rather than use Americans, persons unfamiliar with the sys-

157. USAID, Project Paper, *supra* note 75, at Annex C (Social Soundness), at 1.
158. *Id.*

tem and culture of the Caribbean. The architects of the Project, heeding the writings of persons such as Valdez and sensing dissatisfaction with the diversion of project funds to Americans in the Central American administration of justice project, provided project funds exclusively to the University of the West Indies and persons it selects to perform the work.[159] Even the USAID attorney representative, Dennis Darby, is a Jamaican attorney who worked with the agency in Jamaica immediately before assuming his present position. The use solely of persons from the region should eliminate the problems of unfamiliarity with the local legal culture, artificial privileged access to power, and relative immunity to the consequences of the Project.

The Commonwealth Caribbean Project derives its intellectual origins and style from the law and development movement, but also learns from the mistakes and analyses of Professor Merryman and Mr. Valdez. History repeats itself. The architects are a product primarily of the U.S. legal system, social engineers of the 1960s law and development movement. The biggest potential deficit of the Project is that its funds and its approval were derived from a foreign policy goal emphasizing U.S. national security. Many experts believe that if the real motives behind United States government assistance are military security or preservation of economic interests, then government supported legal development assistance will be at best a tainted peripheral activity, and at worst, a program masquerading as humanitarian operation concealing the imposition of American foreign policy. In this context, to the extent that legal development assistance, whether supported by the government or privately funded, contributes to foreign policy goals, it becomes suspect.[160] The deficit, if not offset, may be fatal to the Project's success.

The extent to which the Project accomplishes the goals of multilateralization and value-neutrality will largely govern the success of the Project. A valid criticism of prior initiatives of the Reagan Administration in the Caribbean has been lack of multilateralism.[161] The control of money and programs by UWI and the active

159. Actually John Dyrud is a U.S. attorney who, after teaching at the University of Maryland, has since the mid-1970's been head law librarian and law professor at Cave Hill.

160. Trubek & Galanter, *supra* note 2, at 1092; J. GARDNER, *supra* note 5, at 38.

161. *See, e.g.*, Feinberg & Newfarmer, *The Caribbean Basin Initiative: Bold Plan or Empty Promise*?, in FROM GUNBOATS TO DIPLOMACY 210, 212-13 (Newfarmer ed. 1984) (criticism of the absence of multilateralism in the Caribbean Basin Initiative); Review of the Impact and Effectiveness of the Caribbean Basin Initiative: Hearings Before the Sub Comm.

participation of multilateral organizations and other governments, such as the British and Canadian, have the potential to provide dynamics of their own and to counterbalance the foreign policy/ national security genesis of the Project. Active donors helping legal institutions in the Commonwealth Caribbean include the United Nations Development Program which has financed a law revision in Dominica, legal draftsmen for St. Kitts and Antigua, a legal advisor for Grenada, and grant for narcotics control in Jamaica.[162] The Commonwealth Fund for Technical Cooperation has assisted in revising the laws of Belize, provided parliamentary draftsmen, stenotype training for Caribbean court reporters at the Jamaica Secretarial College, and acquired law books for various Supreme Court libraries and Attorney Generals' chambers.[163] The United Kingdom has provided salary supplements for expatriate judges and government lawyers through the Overseas Services Aid Scheme. The West Indies Legislation Indexing Project, financed by the British Development Division in Barbados, has assisted making statutory law accessible to the smaller states.[164] The Canadian International Development Agency has provided small legal aid grants in Belize and Jamaica and has supported archives and registration of documents activities.[165] Prior to the commencement of the Project, UWI and U.S. officials requested their active collaboration. Indeed, the project is still so new that the reader of this article may want to take the Florida State University (FSU) summer school course next summer at UWI[166] or arrange to undertake study and review at the law library of UWI on a study tour.[167] An-

on Oversight of the House of Representatives Comm. on Ways and Means, 99th Cong., 2d Sess., 474, 486-87 (1986) (testimony by Bruse Zagaris). The absence of multilateralism in the Caribbean was a reflection of the global unilateralist policy generally at the outset of the Reagan Administration. The U.S. pursued policies unilaterally, outside of policies of other governments and international organizations. *See* Keohane & Nye, *Two Cheers for Multilateralism*, 60 FOREIGN POL'Y 148 (1985).

162. USAID, Project Paper, *supra* note 75, at 23.

163. *Id.* at 24.

164. *Id.*

165. *Id.*

166. For background on the FSU-UWI summer law program on comparative law, see *University of the West Indies, Cave Hill Campus Summer Program*, 3 CARIBBEAN L. NEWSL. 10 (1987) (published by the Committee on Caribbean Law, ABA Section of International Law, on file with the author).

167. For background on the use of study tours as a means for U.S. persons to visit the Caribbean and as a trend in Caribbean tourism, and one worth technical assistance, see Zagaris & Emery, *Tourism: The Orphan of Caribbean Programs*, 27 J. TRAVEL RES. 24-28 (1988); Zagaris, "Tourism as an Export," Written Statement to Hearing, Foreign Commerce & Tourism Subcommitte, Senate Commerce, Science and Transportation Committee, May

other advantage is that private institutions from the United States and elsewhere are participating in the Project. For instance, FSU Law School has concluded an agreement with the UWI Law Faculty at Cave Hill to establish a Caribbean Law Institute to assist the Caribbean countries in unification of law and other comparative and international law projects. The Institute would concentrate first on a Caribbean commercial code in order to facilitate trade between the countries of the West Indies and the United States. Talbot "Sandy" D'Alemberte, Dean of the FSU Law Faculty, has worked with members of Congress for a $1.5 million dollar appropriation in each of five years to support the Institute.[168] A key figure in the Institute proposal, Elwin Griffith, a Barbadian and member of the FSU Law Faculty, has close ties with and recently took his sabbatical teaching at UWI Law Faculty in Barbados. In the summer of 1987, UWI and FSU operated a Caribbean Legal Studies Program. Four courses on Caribbean legal institutions were taught during a five week period at Cave Hill.[169]

An important application of the Gardner typology is whether the Project was the initiative of the Caribbean or the United States. On the one hand, several studies emanating from the Commonwealth Caribbean had called for the refurbishment of its legal institutions.[170] On the other hand, the actual initiation of the Administration of Justice program and of the Commonwealth Caribbean Project arose from the Reagan Administration's interest in the region's security and particularly from the Kissinger Report. The Gardner typology for transferring American legal models in a large sense does not apply at all because the Project is based on the proposition that the existing models, although largely sufficient, merely suffer from lack of management.[171] The Project calls

---

21, 1988.

168. Memorandum, from Talbot D'Alemberte to Working Group List, Caribbean Law Institute, Inc. (Sept. 2, 1987). *See also* House Bill introduced by Congressman Obey, Committee on Appropriations, "making appropriations for foreign operations, export financing, and related programs for the fiscal year ending September 30, 1988, and for other purposes." The proposed Institute raises a series of the same issues about how it should be classified within the law and development movement. For instance, some Caribbean officials have questioned whether the establishment of an organization on Caribbean legal system should be in the U.S. rather than the Caribbean and whether U.S. officials will exercise control over it.

169. *See infra* note 166.

170. For a discussion on the need to refurbish the legal institutions in the Commonwealth Caribbean, see the two studies by Patchett, *supra* note 85.

171. Critics of the law and development movement predicted that the movement's ties to developments in American foreign policy and to the historical needs of law and develop-

for upkeep of the current legal infrastructure, and, to the extent the University or other Project participants can obtain more assistance, the extension of the Project into new areas, such as law reform, may encourage use of foreign models, including but certainly not limited to American models. To the extent U.S. concepts and models become involved, it will be largely a decision of the University or participants to adopt programs, for instance, of certain bar associations. An important question on which Gardner focuses and on which past movements have failed, is the lack of sufficient financial and program strength and/or mandate to undertake the project to its successful completion. Since the project originated under the Reagan Administration and was preoccupied with security concerns, the political and financial impetus, especially in a time when Congress is slashing the foreign assistance budget, is certainly a question.[172] The issue of the desirability of the program and the commitment of U.S. legal institutions and the U.S. Government requires more inquiry. Hence, the project for the Commonwealth Caribbean fits well into the title of comparative law and social change.

To be successful, the Project must avoid close interaction with security assistance and counterterrorism programs.[173] These programs, which have been prominent in U.S. assistance to Central America, will doubly taint the Project. They will deprive the substance of the Project of value-neutrality and impose ethnocentric, *real politik* of the United States and will undermine the political credibility of donees in many parts of the Commonwealth Caribbean. Similarly, to the extent other organizations, such as governments, international governmental organizations and non-governmental organizations participate and complement the Project's activities, they will enhance the Project's substantive and political diversity and its prospects for diminishing ideological and foreign policy implications behind the Project. For instance, activities of

---

ment scholars for funding caused a naive, often fatal weakness. *See* Burg, *supra* note 4, at 515; Trubek & Galanter, *supra* note 2, at 1087.

172. For a discussion of the criticism of counterterrorism assistance in Central America, see Zagaris, *Crime and Social Justice Publication Examines Contragate for Counterterrorism Implications*, 3 INT'L ENFORCEMENT L. REP. 225 (1987). For background on the Central American Counterterrorism Act of 1985, see Weidinger, *Central American Counterterrorism Legislation*, 1.3 INT'L ENFORCEMENT L. REP. 25 (1985) and *Central American Counterterrorism Act of 1985*, 1.4 INT'L ENFORCEMENT L. REP. 4 (1985).

173. The realization by USAID and other law and development organizations of the need to multilateralize law and development projects can be traced at least to the 1970s. *See* J. GARDNER, *supra* note 5, at 221.

Interpol and the Inter-American Drug Abuse Commission (CICAD) can complement the Project, especially in the sensitive area of criminal justice and international criminal cooperation.[174] The inclusion of countries such as Guyana in the Project on the basis of non-political criteria is vital to the Project's credibility.[175] Most importantly, of course, the legal professionals in the Commonwealth Caribbean must rise to the challenge of active participation in the design and implementation of all activities. Otherwise, the Project, as it continues to unfold, will not achieve the maximum opportunity to reflect the goals and culture of the people of the Commonwealth Caribbean.

174. For a discussion of the programs of legal development of the Inter-American Drug Abuse Comm'n, see Zagaris, *Inter-American Drug Abuse Commission Holds First Session*, 3 INT'L ENFORCEMENT L. REP. 123 (1987). For a discussion of Interpol programs in the Caribbean, see Zagaris & Simmons, *Interpol Makes Progress on Economic Crime and Other Fronts*, 3 INT'L ENFORCEMENT L. REP. 273, 276 (1987).

175. Guyana is also one of the most unique and rich of the Commonwealth Caribbean's legal systems, partly due to its unusual Dutch-English legal background, and more recently due to experimentation with so-called cooperative and socialist models. *See e.g.*, SHAHABUDDEEN, THE LEGAL SYSTEM OF GUYANA (1973). *See also*, F. ALEXIS, *supra* note 50, at 75-116; F. PHILLIPS, *supra* note 50, at 53-72; Hazard, *Guyana's Alternative to Socialist and Capitalist Legal Models*, 16 AM. J. COMPAR. L. 507, 507-23 (1968).

Part II
The Debate about the Right to Development as a Human Right or State Law versus People's Law and the Development Process

[5]

ARTICLES

IN SEARCH OF THE UNICORN: THE JURISPRUDENCE AND POLITICS OF THE RIGHT TO DEVELOPMENT*

JACK DONNELLY**

A philosopher is a person who goes into a dark room on a moonless night to look for a nonexistent black cat. A theologian comes out claiming to have found the cat. A human rights lawyer, after such an on-site visit, sends a communication to the Commission on Human Rights; and a member of the Commission leaves the room drafting a resolution on the treatment of black cats. This, in a nutshell, is uncomfortably close to the history of the so-called human right to development.

In the early seventies, the first intrepid investigators began to claim success in their searches. The initial sighter, the eminent jurist Keba M'Baye, was a distinguished member of the Commission on Human Rights which, not surprisingly, was soon discussing the right to development. Both the Commission and the General Assembly quickly passed resolutions proclaiming its existence. Today, there is near unanimity in both diplomatic and scholarly discussions that the human right to development not only exists but is of great importance.

Possessed of something of a philosophical temperament, I readily joined the quest but came up empty handed. I did, however, come upon the idea of turning on the light. The room, alas, proved empty. This article is a chronicle of my search for the right to development.

---

* I am grateful to Rhoda Howard, Bob Rupen, Joe Grieco and Claude Welch for their comments on various earlier drafts.

** Professor of Political Science, University of North Carolina; B.S.F.S., M.A., Georgetown University; Ph.D., University of California, Berkeley.

I. THE BRIEF HISTORY OF THE RIGHT TO DEVELOPMENT

Fifteen years ago, a human right to development was completely unknown. Ten years ago, it had never been discussed in the UN. But in less than three years after its initial mention in the Commission on Human Rights in 1977, it had been proclaimed as a human right by the Commission, United Nations Educational, Scientific and Cultural Organization (UNESCO) and the General Assembly. Today, the Commission is at work on drafting a declaration on the right to development.

Keba M'Baye first broached the concept in his 1972 Inaugural Lecture to the International Institute of Human Rights in Strasbourg.[1] At the time, M'Baye admitted that introducing the idea involved considerable "temerity."[2] As late as 1978, in a revised version of his original paper, he still referred to the idea as "somewhat venturesome."[3] Nonetheless, as Chairman of the Commission on Human Rights in 1977, he was instrumental in securing the first formal recognition of a human right to development with only the most cursory discussion.[4] The Commission adopted Resolution 4 (XXXIII),[5] which contains the first explicit mention of a right to development in a UN resolution. Paragraph 4 of Resolution 5 provides:

> 4. *Recommends* to the Economic and Social Council to invite the Secretary-General, in cooperation with UNESCO and the other competent specialized agencies, to undertake a study on the subject "The international dimensions of the right to development as a human right in relation with other human rights based on international cooperation, including the right to peace, taking into account the requirements of the New International Economic Or-

1. M'Baye, *Le droit au developpement comme un droit de l'homme*, 5 REVUE DES DROITS DE L'HOMME [REV. DR. L'HOMME] 505 (1972). *Cf.* Salcedo, *El derecho al desarollo como un derecho humano*, 25 REVISTA ESPANOLA DE DERECHO INTERNATIONAL [REV. ESP. D. INT.] 119 (1972). The only earlier reference I have been able to find in English or French is in an obscure document, *Les droits des peuples sous-developpe au developpement* issued by the Commission "Justice et Paix" d'Algerie. *See* Sanson, *Droits des peuples sous-developpes au developpement au droits des hommes et des communautes a etre soi, non seulement par soi, mais aussi par autres* in ACADEMIE DE DROIT INTERNATIONAL DE LA HAYE, COLLOQUE 1979, LE DROIT AU DEVELOPPEMENT AU PLAN INTERNATIONAL 204 ff. (R-J. Dupuy ed. 1980) [hereinafter cited as Dupuy].

2. M'Baye, *supra* note 1, at 505.

3. M'Baye, (paper delivered at the UNESCO Meeting of Experts on Human Rights, Human Needs and the Establishment of a New International Economic Order, in Paris, (June 19-23, 1978)), *reprinted in* UNESCO Doc. SS-78/CONF.630/8 at 1.

4. *See* U.N. Doc. E/CN.4/SR.1389, 1392-1398 (1977).

5. Commission on Human Rights, Report on the Thirty-Third Session, 62 U.N. ESCOR Supp. (No. 6), U.N. Doc. E/5927 (1978).

der and the fundamental human needs," and to make this study available for consideration by the Commission on Human Rights at its thirty-fifth session.

I quote this paragraph in full to underscore the peculiarly brusque yet oblique entry of the right to development into the UN human rights arena.

Prior to this resolution, such a right had never even been discussed in the UN system. The scholarly literature was similarly silent; other than M'Baye's article, I have been able to find no substantial scholarly discussion of the right to development in either English or French before 1979. The Commission, nonetheless, after almost no discussion, not only called for a study of the right (rather than simply an investigation of the possibility that it did exist or ought to be established), but felt itself competent to specify the appropriate conceptual context for such a study.

Except for suggestions that it required a somewhat more precise definition, virtually no one questioned the idea, and it moved through the usually labyrinthine UN system with incredible speed. In 1978 a right to development was proclaimed in two solemn declarations, the Declaration on the Preparation of Societies for Life in Peace, adopted as General Assembly Resolution 33/73, and the UNESCO Declaration on Race and Racial Prejudice.[6] But it was in 1979 that the human right to development exploded into international prominence.

In early January, 1979, the Secretary-General's Report[7] asked for in Resolution 4 (XXXIII) was issued. Even today, this remains the most thorough discussion of the sources and content of the human right to development.[8] The Commission, in part on the basis of this Report, passed Resolution 5 (XXXV) in which it "*reiterated*" the existence of a human right to development, in effect taking its backhanded introduction of the concept two years earlier as a definitive proclamation.[9] Also in 1979, the Hague Academy of Interna-

6. Adopted by the General Conference of UNESCO on Nov. 27, 1978.

7. The International Dimensions of the Right to Development as a Human Right in relation with other Human Rights based on International Cooperation, including the Right to Peace, taking into account the Requirements of the New International Economic Order and the Fundamental Human Needs, Report of the Secretary-General, U.N. Doc. E/CN.4/1334 (1979) [hereinafter cited as Secretary-General's Report].

8. This is less a compliment to the Secretary-General's Report, which is superficial and poorly reasoned, than a comment on the dismal lack of progress in the discussion and conceptualization of the right to development over the last half dozen years.

9. This oblique introduction of the concept is usually overlooked, or actively obscured. *See, e.g.*, Hassan, *Solidarity Rights: Progressive Evolution of International Human Rights Law?*, N.Y.L. SCH. HUM. RTS. ANN. 51, 54 (1984), where it is argued, without the slightest basis,

tional Law held a Workshop on The Right to Development at the International Level.[10] The General Assembly followed suit and recognized the right to development in Resolution 34/46 on November 23, 1979, again after only the most cursory discussion.[11]

Since then, reiteration of the right to development has been an annual ritual in the Assembly.[12] The Commission has received follow-up studies on the regional and national dimensions of the right,[13] and has also regularly reaffirmed its existence.[14] In 1981, work began on a declaration in a special Working Group of Governmental Experts on the Right to Development.[15] A small scholarly literature has begun to develop.[16] The right to development has figured prominently in international seminars sponsored by UNESCO,[17] the Division of Human Rights,[18] and the International Commission of Jurists.[19] It has been a subject of discussion at regular scholarly meetings.[20] It has even been included in one regional human rights instrument, the African (Banjul) Charter on Human and Peoples'

that the 1977 resolution recognized the right to development "as a major goal of the world community."

10. Dupuy, *supra* note 1.

11. See U.N. Doc. A/C.3/34/SR.24-30, 33-38, 41.

12. G.A. Res. 174, 35 U.N. GAOR (1980); G.A. Res. 133, 36 U.N. GAOR (1981); G.A. Res. 199, 37 U.N. GAOR (1982); G.A. Res. 124, 38 U.N. GAOR (1983); and the draft resolution adopted by the Third Committee on Nov. 30, 1984, U.N. Doc. A/C3/39/L36.

13. U.N. Doc. E/CN.4/1421 and U.N. Doc. E/CN.4/1488.

14. *See, e.g.*, Res. 6 (XXXVI) and Res. 1983/15.

15. The Reports of the Working Group are available as U.N. Doc. E/CN.4/1489, U.N. Doc. E/CN.4/1983/11, and U.N. Doc. E/CN.4/1984/14. The report of the 1984 session will be officially issued later this year.

16. *See, e.g.*, Dupuy, *supra* note 1; Development, Human Rights and the Rule of Law, Report of the Conference held in The Hague by the International Commission of Jurists (Apr. 27-May 1, 1981) [hereinafter cited as Int'l Comm'n of Jurists]; Espiell, *The Right to Development as a Human Right*, 16 TEX. INT'L L.J. 189 (1981); Mestdagh, *The Right to Development*, 28 NETH. INT'L L. REV. 30 (1981); Paul, *Introduction: Law, Socialism, and the Human Right to Development in Third World Countries*, 7 REV. OF SOCIALIST L. 235 (1981); Marks, *Emerging Human Rights: A New Generation for the 1980s?*, 33 RUTGERS L. REV. 435 (1981); Hassan, *supra* note 9; Donnelly, *The "Right to Development": How Not to Link Human Rights and Development*, in HUMAN RIGHTS AND DEVELOPMENT IN AFRICA (C. Welch & R. Meltzer ed. 1984).

17. UNESCO, Colloquium on the New Human Rights: The "Rights of Solidarity," in Mexico City (Aug. 12-15, 1980); *see* Final Report, UNESCO Doc. SS-80/CONF.806/4.

18. Seminar on the Effects of the Existing Unjust International Economic Order on the Economies of the Developing Countries and the Obstacle that this represents for the Implementation of Human Rights and Fundamental Freedoms, Geneva, Switzerland (June 30-July 11, 1980), *reprinted in* U.N. Doc. ST/HR/SER.A/8 (1980); Seminar on the Relations that Exist between Human Rights, Peace and Development, United Nations Headquarters, New York, N.Y. (Aug. 3-14, 1987), *reprinted in* U.N. Doc. ST/HR/SER.A/10 (1981).

19. Int'l Comm'n of Jurists, *supra* note 16.

20. For example, a panel was devoted to the right to development at the 23rd Annual

Rights.[21]

In virtually all of these contexts, a human right to development has been taken to be largely self-evident; at best, the superficial arguments of the Secretary-General's 1979 Report have been briefly rehashed. Even as careful a lawyer as Philip Alston was writing as early as 1981 that "as a general proposition in terms of international human rights law, the existence of a right to development is a *fait accompli*."[22] While this assessment is widely shared in scholarly and diplomatic discussions,[23] I shall argue that it is completely unjustified. Careful examination of the alleged sources of the right to development reveals that it is almost entirely without basis: there are no solid grounds for claiming that there is a legal right to development, and even the moral arguments are largely baseless.

There are indeed vital relationships between human rights and development, which were overlooked in the fifties and sixties and even in the seventies; for example, "human rights" is never mentioned in the strategy adopted for the Third Development Decade.[24] The quite proper, even essential, desire to link human rights and development[25] clearly lies at the heart of the appeal of the idea of a human right to development.[26] It also helps to explain the lack of

Convention of the International Studies Association (USA), Cincinnati, Ohio, March 24-27, 1982.

21. June 27, 1981, O.A.U. Doc. CAB/LEG/67/3/Rev.5, *reprinted in* 21 INT'L LEGAL MATERIALS 59 (1982).

22. Alston, *Development and the Rule of Law: Prevention versus Cure as a Human Rights Strategy*, in Int'l Comm'n of Jurists, *supra* note 16, at 106. *But cf.* Alston, *A Third Generation of Solidarity Rights: Progressive Development or Obfuscation of International Human Rights Law?* 29 NETH. INT'L L. REV. 307 (1982) [hereinafter *Third Generation*]; Alston, *Conjuring up New Human Rights: A Proposal for Quality Control*, 78 AM. J. INT'L L. 607, 612 (1984) [hereinafter *Conjuring up New Human Rights*].

23. *See, e.g.*, U.N. Doc. E/CN.4/1489 at para. 10; U.N. Doc. A/C.3/38/SR.41 at para. 53 (Poland); U.N. Doc. A/C.3/37/SR.40 at para. 21 (India); U.N. Doc. E/CN.4/SR.1639 at para. 86 (Algeria); Zacklin, *The Right to Development at the International Level: Some Reflections on Its Sources, Content and Formulation*, in Dupuy, *supra* note 1, at 116; SS-80/CONF.806/4 at para. 22. The only major exceptions are Eide, *Maldevelopment and the "Right to Development": A Critical Note with a Constructive Intent*, in Dupuy, *supra* note 1, at 397. *See generally* Donnelly, *supra* note 16.

24. G.A. Res. 56, 35 U.N. GAOR (1980). *Cf.* Alston, *Human Rights and the New International Development Strategy*, 10 BULL. PEACE PROP. 281 (1979).

25. *See* Howard, *The "Full-Belly Thesis": Should Economic Rights Take Priority over Civil and Political Rights? Evidence from Sub-Saharan Africa*, 5 HUM. RTS. Q. 467 (1983); Donnelly, *Human Rights and Development: Complementary or Competing Concerns?*, 36 WORLD POL. 255 (1984); Goodin, *The Development-Rights Tradeoff: Some Unwarranted Economic Assumptions*, 1 UNIVERSAL HUM. RTS. 39 (1979); *see also supra* note 22.

26. *See, e.g.*, Alston, *The Right to Development at the International Level*, in Dupuy, *supra* note 1, at 111; Abi-Saab, *The Legal Formulation of a Right to Development*, *id.* at 159; U.N. Doc. E/CN.4/SR.1483 at para. 57 (Theo. Van Boven); U.N. Doc. E/CN.4/SR.1614 at para.

criticism of the concept; who, after all, would object to linking human rights and development?

I will argue, however, that right to development is neither philosophically or legally justified nor a productive means to forge such a linkage. To return to my initial metaphor, the right to development is not merely a delusion of well-meaning optimists, but a dangerous delusion that feeds off of, distorts, and is likely to detract from the urgent need to bring together the struggles for human rights and development.

II. THE RIGHT TO DEVELOPMENT: AN OVERVIEW

Rights establish a special type of relationship between right-holders and duty-bearers with respect to rights-objects: A is entitled to x with respect to B, who stands under correlative obligation y. Analysis of a right thus requires, at minimum, specification of the *source* of the right, its *content* (or object), the *right-holder* (or active subject), the *duty-bearer* (or passive subject), and the right's *correlative obligations*.[27] Proponents of a human right to development have advanced a variety of accounts of all of these aspects of the alleged right.

The Secretary-General's Report argues that "there are a variety of ethical arguments which may be considered to support the existence, in ethical terms, of a right to development."[28] These include the fact that "development is the condition of all social life," the international duty of solidarity, the duty of reparation for colonial and neo-colonial exploitation, increasing moral interdependence, economic interdependence, and the cause of world peace, which is threatened by underdevelopment.[29]

M'Baye advances a similar list of moral grounds for a right to development. He argues that development is demanded by justice and that its denial is not only an injustice but a provocation that

---

12 (Netherlands); U.N. Doc. E/CN.4/1983/SR.17 at para. 64 (Brazil); U.N. Doc. A/C.3/38/SR. 39 at para. 2 (Australia); U.N. Doc. E/CN.4/1984/SR.16 at para. 3 (India) and para. 49 (Canada).

27. For further development of such an analysis of rights, with special reference to human rights, see J. DONNELLY, THE CONCEPT OF HUMAN RIGHTS chs. 1-3 (1985). *Cf.* Shue, *Rights in the Light of Duties*, in HUMAN RIGHTS AND U.S. FOREIGN POLICY (P. Brown & D. MacLean ed. 1978); H. SHUE, BASIC RIGHTS: SUBSISTENCE, AFFLUENCE AND U.S. FOREIGN POLICY (1980) [hereinafter cited as BASIC RIGHTS]; A. GEWIRTH, REASON AND MORALITY 63-68 (1978).

28. Secretary-General's Report, *supra* note 7, para. 54.

29. *Id.* paras. 40, 42, 54, 47, 48, 50-51.

threatens confrontation and violence.[30] Trade and investment give rise to reciprocal duties, as do ideological subjugation and the use of Third World strategic bases. Such obligations are strongly reinforced by the West's historical responsibility for colonialism, neocolonialism and coercive underdevelopment.[31] But "it is above all solidarity that should be invoked to justify the right to development."[32]

The Secretary-General's Report also argues that "there is a very substantial body of principles . . . which demonstrate the existence of a human right to development in international law."[33] Among the more prominent international legal sources cited are: Articles 55 and 56 of the UN Charter; the Universal Declaration of Human Rights, especially Article 22 (the right to social security and to the realization "of the economic, social and cultural rights indispenable to [human] dignity and the free development of [the human] person") and Article 26(2) ("Education shall be directed to the full development of the human personality . . ."); Article 1 of both International Covenants on Human Rights (the right to self-determination); and the International Covenant on Economic, Social and Cultural Rights, especially Article 2(1) (the obligation to implement progressively the enumerated rights) and Article 11 ("the right of everyone to an adequate standard of living"). Reference is also made to specialized human rights conventions, such as those on *apartheid* and discrimination in education; regional instruments such as the European Social Charter and the American Declaration of the Rights of Man; the charters of specialized agencies, especially the Declaration of Philadelphia (1944), which was incorporated into the Constitution of the International Labor Organization; and resolutions of the General Assembly and other UN bodies, especially on such topics as development, self-determination, and the New International Economic Order. To these we can add the UNESCO Declaration on Race and Racial Prejudice, the Banjul Charter, and the resolutions of the Commission on Human Rights and the General Assembly since 1979 referred to above. Other authorities provide a very similar list of legal sources.[34]

30. M'Baye, *supra* note 3, at 1, 5, 8.

31. *Id.* at 5-8.

32. *Id.* at 9, 13, 12.

33. Secretary-Generals Report, *supra* note 7, para. 78ff.

34. *See, e.g.*, Haquani, *Le droit au developpement: fondements et sources*, in Dupuy, *supra* note 1, at 29-40; Mestdagh, *supra* note 16, at 34-46; Zacklin, *supra* note 23, at 117-118; U.N. Doc. E/CN.4/1489 at para. 21.

The preceding is by no means the full list. Others alleged sources include the right to life in peace, the progress of science and technology, the "dialectical correlation between sovereignty and equality," "present practical necessities," "the economic crisis," the law of nations, the League of Nations' Minorities System, international social justice, human unity, the responsibility to help one's fellow man, the need for development, the need for justice, and the principles of sovereignty, equality and nonintervention, not to mention the claim that it derives "spontaneously from present-day reality".[35]

There is somewhat less volume and variety in accounts of the content of the right to development. Article 1(1) of the "technical consolidated text" of the draft Declaration on the Right to Development notes that "equality [of] opportunity [for development] is a prerogative of nations and of individuals within nations,"[36] a formulation that has been standard since General Assembly resolution 34/46 in 1979. Whatever the ambiguity of "equal opportunity," this does provide a fairly clear substantive core to the right to development. Working out from this core, the technical consolidated text stresses that the right to development implies "the full realization of the right of peoples to self-determination" and a new international economic order.[37] Given the conventional UN readings of the character of the current and new international economic orders, such changes clearly are implied by equality of opportunity for development.

In contrast to this relatively narrow reading, however, the right to development is at least as often presented as a comprehensive synthesis of many or even all previously recognized human rights. This tendency is very strong even in the technical consolidated text.

> By virtue of the right to development, every human person, individually or collectively, has the right to participate in, contrib-

35. U.N. Doc. E/CN.4/1983/SR.19 at para. 21, 23 (Poland); U.N. Doc. E/CN.4/1982/SR.32 (Togo); U.N. Doc. E/CN.4/1982/SR.33 (Iraq); Haquani, *supra* note 34, at 27, 28, 31; U.N. Doc. E/CN.4/1984/SR.18 at para. 62 (Togo); Umbricht, *Right to Development*, in DUPUY, *supra* note 1, at 97-98; Alston, *supra* note 22, at 104; E/CN.4/SR.1488 at para. 19 (Senegal); U.N. Doc. E/CN.4/SR.1489 at para. 4 (Canada); E/CN.4/AC.34/WP.11 at 5; MacDermot, *Opening of Plenary Discussion*, in Int'l Comm'n of Jurists, *supra* note 16, at 27; Zacklin, *supra* note 23, at 117; UNESCO Doc. SS-80/CONF.806/4 at 26.

36. U.N. Doc. E/CN.4/1984/13 (Annex II) at 2. This document is only a basis for discussion within the Working Group and does not have the consensus of the Experts. However, it reflects what seems to be the majority view and is the closest thing to an authoritative draft text that has yet been publicly aired.

37. *Id.* arts. 1(3), 8.

> ute to, and enjoy a peaceful international and national political, social and economic order, in which all universally recognized human rights and fundamental freedoms can be fully realized.
>
> In a spirit of solidarity and regardless of the differences which exist between political, economic and social systems, States and the international community as a whole should focus on the creation of local, national and international conditions favorable to the promotion and protection of the rights set forth in the Universal Declaration of Human Rights and the International Covenants on Human Rights.
>
> All States should co-operate with a view to promoting, encouraging and strengthening the universal respect for and observance of all human rights and fundamental freedoms for all without any distinction as to race, sex, language and religion.[38]

In diplomatic and scholarly discussions, the conception of the right to development as a synthesis of more traditional human rights clearly predominates.

> For most speakers, the right to development embodied all rights.[39]
>
> The view was expressed by many participants, that the right to development was a synthesis of already defined human rights.[40]
>
> The approach by which the right to development is viewed as a synthesis of a large number of human rights has found favor with a number of commentators.[41]
>
> In the view of most experts, this right is a combination of existing rights recognized by the international community and contributing to the development of peoples and states.[42]
>
> Le droit au developpement integre les droits et libertes publiques.[43]
>
> The right to development comprises the full range of rights ensuring the satisfaction of the human being's many and varied needs.[44]

---

38. *Id.* arts. 1(2), 5(1), 7(1). *Cf.* arts. 5(3), 9(1).

39. U.N. Doc. E/1981/25 at para. 117.

40. U.N. Doc. ST/HR/SER.A/8 at para. 72.

41. Secretary-General's Report, *supra* note 7, para. 65.

42. U.N. Doc. E/CN.4/1489 at para. 22. *Cf.* para. 30, 31.

43. M'Baye, *Le droit au developpement*, in Dupuy, *supra* note 1, at 73. *Compare* Abi-Saab, *supra* note 26, at 164; and Alston, *supra* note 22, at 104.

44. U.N. Doc. E/CN.4/1984/SR.18 at para. 105 (Byelorussian SSR). *Compare* U.N. Docs. E/CN.4/1984/SR.18 at para. 46 (Bangladesh), with E/CN.4/1983/SR.18 (Yugoslavia) and para. 74 (Italy); U.N. Doc. E/CN.4/1983/SR.19 at para. 21 (Poland); U.N. Doc. E/CN.4/1983/SR.20 at para. 43 (Algeria); U.N. Doc. E/CN.4/1982/SR.31 at para. 37 (Senegal); U.N. Doc. E/CN.4/1982/SR.32 at para. 47 (France); U.N. Doc. E/CN.4/SR.1486 at para. 5 (K. Vasak); U.N. Doc. E/CN.4/SR.1612 at para. 13 (France) and para. 63 (Brazil); U.N. Doc. E/CN.4/AC.34/WP.11 at 37. One commentator who rejects the synthesis interpretation argues that it "correlates to all other rights." U.N. Doc. E/CN.4/AC.34/WP.12 at paras. 4, 12.

This interpretation fits nicely with the tendency to trace the right to development back to virtually every major document on human rights or development from the last forty years.

Three major right-holders have been identified: individuals, peoples and States. It is also occasionally suggested that minorities have a right to development.[45] As we shall see below, however, there are considerable disagreements over whether the right is held by all three (or four) of these right-holders, or just one or two.

Developed countries (individually or collectively) and the international community as a whole usually are specified as the principal duty-bearers of the right to development. Many proponents of the right also see it as imposing duties on national governments in the developing countries, and a few see it as binding individuals as well.[46] Again, we shall see below that there is great controversy over the exact nature of the primary duty-bearers.

Discussion of the duties correlative to the right to development rarely moves beyond fairly general demands for the NIEO, although it is sometimes also argued that (unspecified but fundamental) structual change is also required at the national level. But in light of the lack of agreement or clarity as to the content, sources, right-holders and duty-bearers of the right to development, it is not surprising that correlative duties are only vaguely specified.

Given this almost bewildering diversity of views, the 1983 Report of the Commission on Human Rights presents a classic case of diplomatic understatement when it notes that "with respect to the nature of the right to development, a variety of views was expressed."[47] In what follows, I will argue that this "variety of views" arises not from any special difficulties in specifying the human right to development, but from the fact that no such right exists. As with any other nonexistent object, the reports of those who claim to have seen it cannot but be expected to show great diversity.

III. LEGAL SOURCES OF THE RIGHT TO DEVELOPMENT

The principal legal sources of the standards of the international human rights regime are the United Nations Charter, the Universal Declaration of Human Rights,[48] and the International Covenants on

45. Secretary-General's Report, *supra* note 7, para. 87-93. U.N. Doc. E/CN.4/AC.34/WP.11 at 28ff.

46. *Id.* at paras. 94-114.

47. U.N. Doc. E/1983/13 at para. 97.

48. G.A. Res. 217, U.N. Doc. A/810 (1948) at 71.

Human Rights,[49] often referred to collectively as the International Bill of Human Rights. If a right to development were enshrined in these documents, as is often claimed, it would indeed be firmly established as a human right in international law. In fact, however, it is not.

Occasional claims are made that the right to development is explicitly recognized in the International Bill of Human Rights. " 'The right to development' . . . is already enscribed in filigree in the Charter of the United Nations."[50] "The relationship between the right to development and the other human rights had already been stated in the Preamble of the United Nations Charter."[51] "Several of the individual rights in [the International Covenant on Economic, Social and Cultural Rights] appear, implicitly or explicitly, to be components of the human right to development."[52] In fact, a right to development is nowhere mentioned explicitly in the International Bill of Human Rights; the Charter lists no specific human rights, let alone a right to development, while the Universal Declaration[53] and the Covenants, like the Charter, treat development as a goal rather than a right.

Individual development is an object or consequence of respect for, and exercise of all human rights. For example, economic, social and cultural rights are recognized as "indispensable for [human] dignity and the free development of [human] personality," while the aim of education — and by implication, the aim of all human rights — is "the full development of the human personality and the sense of its dignity."[54] But not everything that is good or desirable, nor even everything that is the goal of the enjoyment of a right, is itself a right.

49. International Covenant on Economic, Social & Cultural Rights, G.A. Res. 2200, 21 U.N. GAOR Supp. (No. 16) at 49, U.N. Doc A/6316 (1966); International Covenant on Civil and Political Rights, G.A. Res. 2200, 21 U.N. GAOR Supp. (No. 16) at 52, U.N. Doc. A/6316 (1966).

50. M'Baye, *Chairman's Opening Remarks*, in Int'l Comm'n of Jurists, *supra* note 16, at 7. *Cf.* U.N. Doc. E/CN.4/SR.1492 at para. 21 (Argentina), U.N. Doc. E/CN.4/SR.1612 at para. 15 (Brazil).

51. U.N. Doc. E/CN.4/1982/SR.32 at para. 2 (China). *Compare* U.N. Doc. E/CN.4/1982/SR.33 at para. 27 (Iraq), *with* U.N. Doc. E/CN.4/1982/SR.31 at para. 16 (Algeria).

52. Secretary General's Report, *supra* note 7, para. 60. *Compare* Haquani, *supra* note 34, at 32, *with* U.N. Doc. E/CN.4/1984/SR.16 at para. 55 (China) and U.N. Doc. E/CN.4/1982/SR.31 at para. 16 (Algeria). Since the right to development is never mentioned in the Covenant, it is simply impossible that any of the enumerated rights could be advanced explicitly as parts of the right to development. Such examples of blatant misrepresentation and wild exaggeration are unfortunately all too common in discussions of the right to development.

53. Two efforts to include something very much like a right to development in the Universal Declaration were unsuccessful. *See* Alston, *supra* note 22, at 100.

54. Universal Declaration, *supra* note 48, art. 22. International Covenant on Economic,

Therefore, these passages do not in themselves establish the right to development that some have claimed.[55] Suppose for example, that A establishes a trust fund for B, the purpose of which is to assure B's future financial security. B's right to the proceeds of the trust will in fact contribute to his financial security. B does not, however, *ipso facto* have a right to financial security.

Individual development *is* a likely (although not a necessary) consequence of respect for economic and social rights. In fact, *all* human rights, civil and political as well as economic, social and cultural, aim at the development of individual personality and the protection of inherent human dignity. For example, the Covenants present "inherent human dignity" as the source of the rights they enumerate, and the realization of this dignity clearly implies personal development. But this would seem to be precisely the reason that a right to development is *not* recognized: development is one of the primary objectives of all human rights, not a right in itself.

There are, however, two promising implicit sources of a right to development in the International Bill of Human Rights. Both Covenants include, as Article 1(1), a right to self-determination. "All peoples have a right to self-determination. By virtue of the right they freely determine their political status and freely pursue their economic, social and cultural development." If the right to development means the right of peoples freely to pursue their development, then it can be plausibly argued to be implied by the Covenants' right to self-determination. However, such a right to development is without interest; it is already firmly established as the right to self-determination.

A substantially broader right to development, however, cannot be extracted from this right to self-determination. The right to self-determination recognized in the Covenants does not imply a right to live in a developing society;[56] it is explicitly only a right to *pursue* development. Neither does it imply an *individual* right to development; self-determination, again explicitly, is a right of peoples only. In no sense does it imply a right to be developed. Thus the claim that the right to development is simply the realization of the right to self-determination[57] is not based on the Covenants' understanding of self-

Social and Cultural Rights, *supra* note 49, art. 13(1). *Cf.* Universal Declaration of Human Rights, *supra* note 48, art. 26(2).

55. See, e.g., U.N. Doc. E/CN.4/1984/SR.18 at para. 47 (Bangladesh).

56. U.N. Doc. ST/HR/SER.A/10 at para. 91.

57. U.N. Doc. ST/HR/SER.A/8 at paras. 74, 131. *Cf.* U.N. Doc. E/CN.4/AC.34/WP.25 at para. 3.

determination.

It might also be argued that because development is necessary for self-determination, development is itself a human right. Such an argument, however, is fallacious. Since we will come across this form of argument again, let us look briefly at this "instrumental fallacy." Suppose that A holds mineral rights in certain oil-bearing properties. Suppose further that in order to enjoy these rights fully, she requires $500,000 to begin pumping the oil. Clearly A does not have a right to $500,000 just because she needs it to enjoy her rights. Suppose that B is in sure danger of imminent death unless he receives a liver transplant. Although B cannot enjoy his right to life without a liver transplant, that does not entail that he has a right to a liver transplant, let alone a right to have a suitable liver implanted should one become available. The same reasoning applies to the link between development and the right to self-determination. Even assuming that development is necessary for, rather than a consequence of, full enjoyment of the right to self-determination, it simply does not follow that peoples have a right to development.

Allowing such an argument to prevail would result in a proliferation of bizarre or misguided rights. Since the realization of human dignity is the objective of all human rights, it would imply a human right to dignity. While such a right has occasionally been advanced,[58] human dignity clearly is treated as the goal of all human rights rather than a right in itself. All human rights aim to prevent particular denials of human dignity. This does not, however, imply that there is a human right to dignity. Likewise, although the Universal Declaration holds that education "shall be directed to the full development of the human personality . . . [and] shall promote understanding, tolerance and friendship among all nations,"[59] a human right to understanding or to friendship among nations is of course silly, while a right to the full development of one's personality is absurdly overambitious.

Simply because A requires *x* to enjoy right *r* does not entail that A has a right to *x*. It may be desirable that A have a right to *x*. Justice or morality may even demand that A ought to have a right to *x*. Nonetheless, the instrumental necessity of *x* for the enjoyment of A's right *r* simply does not establish that A has a right to *x*.

The second promising implicit source of a right to development is Article 28 of the Universal Declaration: "Everyone is entitled to a

58. *E.g.*, U.N. Doc. E/CN.4/1982/SR.32 at para. 25 (Pakistan).

59. Universal Declaration, *supra* note 48, art. 26(2).

social and International order in which the rights and freedoms set forth in this declaration can be fully realized." If development is essential to such an order, then it might be argued that a right to development is implied by Article 28.[60] One might even argue that this is precisely the sort of elaboration anticipated by this elastic clause.

The Universal Declaration, although initially passed as a resolution of the General Assembly, and thus a recommendation only, has over the last thirty years been almost universally accepted by States. While practice often falls far short of the Declaration's standards, virtually all States accept those standards as legally binding (although not enforceable by international action). Therefore, let us accept that the Universal Declaration does have the force of customary international law.

Unlike most other provisions of the Declaration, however, Article 28 was not confirmed by a parallel provision in the Covenants, which were drafted precisely to give the force of treaty law to the standards of the Universal Declaration. This absence of a passage equivalent to Article 28 is most plausibly interpreted as representing its tacit renunciation. Such an interpretation is particularly powerful in light of the fact that the absence of a provision parallel to the Declaration's Article 17—"Everyone has the right to own property alone as well as in association with others"—often *is* taken as implying the international renunciation of a human right to private property. If this is so, then the argument ought to hold for Article 28 as well. This is a particularly troublesome argument because many of the strongest proponents of the right to development reject a right to private property.[61]

More substantively, one might question whether "development" falls under the notion of a social and international order referred to in Article 28. "Development" suggest a process or result; the process of development or the condition of being developed. "Order," by contrast, implies a set of principles, rules, practices or institutions; neither a process nor a result but a structure. Article 28, therefore, is most plausibly interpreted as prohibiting *structures* that deny oppor-

60. Technical Consolidated Text, Draft Declaration on the Right to Development, *supra* note 36; the Text includes a reference to Article 28 of the Universal Declaration as its second preambulatory paragraph, immediately following the more or less obligatory reference to the general provisions of the UN Charter, and prior to the reference to the Covenants.

61. Conversely, critics of the right to development who also are strong defenders of a human right to private property cannot avail themselves of this argument against the right to development.

tunities or resources for the realization of civil, political, economic, social or cultural human rights. To get a right to development out of this would require showing that development is impossible or positively denied by current national or international structures. Clearly such an argument, while often made, is most contentious. Fortunately, we need not address its substance here in order to determine whether there is (rather than ought to be) a legal (rather than moral) right to development.

There must be a broad, nearly universal consensus on a derived right to development before it can be accepted as a part of (customary) international law. Such consensus clearly does not exist. While it is widely accepted that the current international economic order presents impediments to development, it is by no means agreed that it precludes or denies development—and a few States even deny the existence of serious structural impediments of any sort. Furthermore, even if there were such a consensus, Article 28 would seem to imply only a right to the removal of such impediments to development—at most a right to a new international economic order—not a right to *development*.

Suppose, though, that Article 28 *were* to be taken to imply a human right to development. What would that right look like? It would be an *individual* right, and only an individual right; a right of persons, not peoples, and certainly not States. It would be a right to the enjoyment of traditional human rights, not a substantively new right. It would be as much a civil and political as an economic and social right—Article 28 refers to *all* human rights—and would be held equally against one's national government and the international community. In other words, if Article 28 of the Universal Declaration is the source of the right to development, it rules out most standard contemporary interpretations of that right, as we shall see in greater detail below.

Continuing our review of alleged legal sources, we find that other provisions of the International Bill of Human Rights are unquestionably inadequate as a source of a legal right to development. For example, Article 22 of the Universal Declaration provides for the "realization, through national effort and international cooperation and in accordance with the organization and resources of each [S]tate" of basic economic, social and cultural rights. This implies at most a right to a fair share of available resources, not a right to development.[62] Any attempt to derive a right to development from such passages would involve recourse to the instrumental fallacy. Likewise, the right to an adequate standard of living either results in a right to development that is of no interest (because it adds nothing to the right to an adequate standard of living) or yields a right to development only through the instrumental fallacy.

Sources of a legal right to development outside of the International Bill of Human Rights reveal a variety of inadequacies. None have the near universal acceptance of the Universal Declaration and the Covenants. Many, such as General Assembly resolutions and UNESCO declarations, have no clear law-creating force. Others, such as the Banjul Charter and the American Declaration of the Rights of Man, are only of regional significance. In any case, a right to development is rarely mentioned explicitly, while the suggested derivations of an implicit right are tortured. For example, the claim that the prohibition of calculated denial of the full development of racial groups found in the International Convention on the Suppression and Punishment of the Crime of *Apartheid*[63] implies a general human right to development[64] is ludicrous; *apartheid* involves the systematic and conscious denial of human rights and development for nonwhites, but rejection of the practice of *apartheid* in no way implies a universal human right to development.

I do not want to suggest that there are not occasional passages that might be very loosely read to point towards something that might look vaguely like a human right to development. The strongest such passage is from the 1944 Declaration of Philadelphia, incorporated into the constitution of the International Labor Organization as an Annex: "all human beings, irrespective of race, creed or sex, have the right to pursue their material well-being and their spiritual development in conditions of freedom and dignity, of economic security and equal opportunity."[65] This principle, however, is a very tenuous source for a legal right to development, even within the context of the ILO. The ILO Constitution is not ordinarily thought of as creating human rights, and nothing even vaguely resembling such a "right" has been recognized in the organization's *explicit* human rights standard-setting through conventions and recommendations.

62. *Cf.* International Covenant on Economic and Social Rights, *supra* note 48, art. 2.

63. G.A. Res. 3608, 28 U.N. GAOR Supp. (No. 30) at 75, U.N. Doc. A/9030 (1973).

64. Secretary-General's Report, *supra* note 7, para. 64. *Cf.* paras. 67, 70, 71 for similar arguments based on documents prohibiting discrimination against children, women and the mentally retarded.

65. Annex to the Constitution of the International Labor Organization, Principle II(a).

Furthermore, it simply is implausible to argue that a right which is not recognized in the central international texts explicitly directed to human rights is somehow recognized in international law by virtue of such an ambiguous reference in the ILO Constitution.

Development certainly is, and should be, an important topic in international law. But a *law of* development is a far cry from a *right to* development.[66] It simply is not the case that all forms of legal regulation bestow substantive rights—let alone *human* rights. For example, there are international laws of nationality, recognition and fisheries, but they do not imply (human) rights to nationality, recognition or fisheries. Some topics receive legal regulation that involves parallel rights, and others do not.

Therefore, arguments that a right to development has emerged or is emerging out of a law of development must show that the major conceptual gap between "There is a law of *x*" and "There is a right *x*" has been or is being bridged. This would require showing that the form taken by the law of development includes legal recognition of a human right to development. Arguments of this sort, however, simply have not provided the necessary evidence.[67] Of course, none of this implies that a (new) human right to development *should not* be created through the ordinary processes of law creation, an argument that rests largely on the moral case for a right to development. But if arguments for a *moral* right to development fail, then the case for creating a new legal right would seem to be fatally weakened.

IV. MORAL SOURCES OF A RIGHT TO DEVELOPMENT

While a sizeable number of commentators do allow that its current legal status is debateable, and even that the right to development is more incohate than established,[68] virtually everyone seems to believe that the moral arguments for a human right to development are compelling. I shall argue, however, that even the moral case is largely baseless.

The most common moral argument infers a right to development from a moral concern for, or obligation to contribute to, development.[69] Such arguments, however, confuse one particular sphere

66. *Cf.* M'Baye, *supra* note 43, at 73; Mestdagh, *supra* note 16, at 35; Espiell, *supra* note 16, at 190, 192; Marks, *supra* note 16, at 442.

67. *See, e.g.*, Marks, *supra* note 16, at 442ff.

68. *See, e.g.*, Alston, *supra* note 22, at 99, 104-106.

69. *See, e.g.*, Secretary-General's Report, *supra* note 7, paras. 40-42 and the passages cited therein.

of morality—rights, special entitlements—with moral righteousness in general. Not all moral "oughts" are grounded in or give rise to rights: one does not *have a right* to everything that it is or would *be right* for one to do or possess; we do not *have* rights, in the strict and strong sense of titles and claims, to everything that is right.[70]

In a just world, underdevelopment would not be permitted; morality and justice do demand development. But this alone does not establish, or even strongly suggest, a moral *right* to development, any more than a law of development suggests a legal right to development. Demonstrating a moral or legal obigation will not establish a parallel right; many obligations, including many very important obligations, simply are not connected with rights.[71]

This distinction—between rights and righteousness, having a right and being right, entitlement and obligation—is of great conceptual importance. *Having* a right to *x* means not merely that it is or would be good, right, just or desireable to enjoy *x*, but that one is specially entitled to *x*, is owed *x*, has *x* as one's due.[72] Furthermore, this entitlement justifies right-holders in making claims with the special force of rights, a force that in ordinary circumstances "trumps" other considerations.[73] A right-holder is not merely a passive beneficiary of someone else's obligation, but an active participant in a relationship that he in large measure controls.[74]

This special force and control is why it is so important to establish a right to development: its advocates want to be able to press stronger claims for development assistance and new forms of international cooperation, and they want to be able to play a more active, even controlling role in such cooperation. But grounding the right to development on the general moral righteousness of development

70. This conceptual error — namely, confusing rights and obligations — is widespread in contemporary discussions of human rights. For an examination, in greater detail and in quite different contexts, see Donnelly, *Natural Law and Right in Aquinas' Political Thought*, 33 W. POL. Q. 520 (1980); Donnelly, *Human Rights and Human Dignity: An Analytic Critique of Non-Western Conceptions of Human Rights*, 76 Am. Pol. Sci. Rev. 303 (1982); DONNELLY, *supra* note 27. *Compare also* Golding, *The Concept of Rights: An Historical Sketch*, in BIOETHICS AND HUMAN RIGHTS (E. Bandman & B. Bandman ed. 1978); Melden, *Are There Welfare Rights*? in INCOME SUPPORT: CONCEPTUAL AND POLICY ISSUES (P. Brown, C. Johnson, & P. Vernier ed. 1981).

71. On the correlation of rights and duties, see Donnelly, *How Are Rights and Duties Correlative*?, 16 J. VALUE INQ. 287 (1982); for a more direct application to human rights, see DONNELLY, *supra* note 27, at 309-310.

72. *See* DONNELLY, *supra* note 27, at ch. 1.

73. *See* R. DWORKIN, TAKING RIGHTS SERIOUSLY xi, 90 (1977). *Cf.* DONNELLY, *supra* note 27, at 5, 12, 20-22, 56, 81.

74. *See* DONNELLY, *supra* note 27, at 11-12, 51-55.

strips it of its special force as a right. Collapsing rights, in the sense in which one *has* a right, with mere righteousness (morality, what *is* right), is a self-defeating strategy which emasculates the alleged "right" and provides no additional force to claims for development.

This confusion between rights and righteousness is surprisingly widespread in the discussion of the right to development. It is perhaps understandable that a semi-popular book entitled "*The Right to Development*" in fact never discusses such a right, but instead mounts an argument for development assistance on general moral and religious grounds.[75] More surprising, however, and entirely without justification, is the repetition of the same conceptual error in scholarly legal literature, most blatantly in articles that include the right to development in their title but never once mention such a right in the text.[76] The logical gap between obligations (or morality) and rights (a special type of moral practice) is a major one, which far too many arguments for a right to development do not even attempt to bridge.

The argument from solidarity, which is often advanced as the single most important moral argument for a right to development,[77] is merely a variant on this basic conceptual error of confusing rights and duties. "Solidarity, the fundamental principles of sharing and helping those who are unable to help themselves,"[78] reflects the special bonds between members of a community, which establish reciprocal obligations of assistance owed by each member to any other member in special need. At the international level, "solidarity" refers to the obligations arising from membership in the cosmopolitan moral community; "the brotherhood of man," in another idiom. While solidarity may establish strong moral obligations to assist the underdeveloped, it does not establish a *right to* assistance, let alone a right to *development*. "The innate responsibility to help one's fellow men"[79] establishes at most a moral obligation to act to promote development, not a right to development.

The attempt to base a right to development on the principle of solidarity is part of a major new approach to human rights questions. Along with other alleged new rights, such as human rights to peace, to a healthy environment, and to share in the fruits of the exploita-

75. G. DUNNE, THE RIGHT TO DEVELOPMENT (1974).

76. *See, e.g.*, Yusuf, *Differential Treatment as a Dimension of the Right to Development*, in Dupuy, *supra* note 1; Trivedi, *Human Rights, Right to Development and the New International Economic Order — Perspectives and Proposals*, in Int'l Comm'n of Jurists, *supra* note 16.

77. *See, e.g.*, M'Baye, *supra* note 3, at 9.

78. Secretary-General's Report, *supra* note 7, para. 42.

79. U.N. Doc. E/CN.4/SR.1489 at para. 4 (Canada).

tion of the common natural heritage of mankind, the right to development is often presented as one of the "third generation" of human rights, a conceptualization initially developed by Karel Vasak.[80] Just as the "first generation" of civil and political rights (based on the idea of "liberty" and providing protection against State violations of the person) was supplemented by a "second generation" of economic and social rights (based on "equality" and guaranteeing positive access to essential social and economic goods, services and opportunities), so now a "third generation" of solidarity rights, (based on "fraternity" and requiring new forms of international cooperation) is argued to be required in order to overcome the international inequality that has frustrated the realization of the first two generations of rights, particularly in the Third World.

The metaphor of generations, however, is a most troubling one. Biological generations beget, and therefore, must precede, one another. Such a reading of the metaphor would suggest that first generation civil and political rights must be established before economic and social rights, which themselves must precede solidarity rights. This reading flys in the face of the widely accepted notion of the interdependence and synergistic interaction of all human rights. The other standard use of "generations" is a technological one: a new generation of technology replaces, and renders obsolete, the preceding generation. Again, the metaphor denies the interdependence of all human rights. It also suggests that solidarity rights ought to *replace* already established civil, political, economic and social rights, the preceding "generations" that will be rendered obsolete by these new rights. This reading is even more dangerous to human rights.

Furthermore, however we read the metaphor of generations, solidarity cannot logically serve as a source of *human* rights, as they have ordinarily been understood. Human rights, as the Covenants put it, "derive from the inherent dignity of the human person." Civil, political, economic, social and cultural rights all clearly arise from the idea of innate personal dignity.[81] Solidarity, however, is a

80. *See, e.g.*, Vasak, *A 30 Year Struggle*, UNESCO COURIER 29 (Nov. 1977); M'Baye, *supra* note 43, at 88; U.N. Doc. ST/HR/SER.A/8 at para. 91; U.N. Doc. E/CN.4/1982/SR.31 at para. 18 (Algeria); U.N. Doc. E/CN.4/SR.1483 at para. 55 (Theo. Van Boven); U.N. Doc. E/CN.4/Sub.2/1983/24 at para. 125. The claim that solidarity rights have been referred to since 1776 and 1789 (UNESCO Doc. SS-80/CONF.806/6 para. 36) is completely without basis, and a striking example of the rhetorical overexuberance (or outright misrepresentation) unfortunately characteristic of so many recent discussions.

81. For more detail on this argument, see Donnelly, *Human Rights as Natural Rights*, 4 HUM. RTS. Q. 391 (1982).

relation among persons or groups. Any rights that might arise would be quite different kinds of rights; even if we were to allow that solidarity gave rise to rights, they would not be *human* rights.

To have a human right, one need be nothing other than a human being, nor do anything other than be born human. In the human rights tradition, the very fact that one is a human person entails the possession of basic rights; to be human is to have human rights.[82] Solidarity, however, is based on membership in a particular community. At the international level, that community happens to have roughly the same membership as the group of human beings who have human rights. This, however, is only a contingent fact; it is logically and phenomenologically quite possible to be a human being, and thus possessed of human rights, without perceiving oneself or being considered by others to be a member of the international community, and thus a beneficiary of rights or duties of solidarity. Even if we allow that the same people hold both kinds of rights, the rights remain quite different in source and standing.

The third generation of solidarity rights simply are not, and logically cannot be, *human* rights—unless "human rights" is now to be taken to mean something other than it has always meant. If they are a "third generation," they cannot rest on the principle of solidarity, while if they are "solidarity rights," they cannot be human rights. In other words, we have in these alleged new rights not merely a difference in substance, analogous to the difference in substance between civil and political and economic and social rights, but a radical qualitative difference in types of rights. (A similar qualitative difference would exist if we were to allow that mere righteousness gave rise to parallel rights; such rights, whatever else they might be, would not be *human* rights.)

Other moral arguments are no more successful. Interdependence, both economic and moral, is often advanced as a source of the right to development. [83] Interdependence, which implies a cooperative joint undertaking, is likely to involve contractual or quasi-contractual rights (particularly rights establishing and assuring an equitable distribution of mutual gains). Such undertakings, however, do not give rise to broad, general moral rights—let alone human rights. Even if the current international economic order distributes the mutual benefits of international economic interdependence un-

82. *Compare* DONNELLY, *supra* note 27, at ch. 3.

83. *See, e.g.*, Secretary-General's Report, *supra* note 7, paras. 47, 48; U.N. Doc. E/CN.4/1489 at para. 47.

fairly, this suggests only a (moral) right to a fair share of the proceeds, not a right to development, and certainly not a human right of any sort.

Another set of arguments rests on the instrumental value of development, particularly the threat to international peace and security posed by underdevelopment. "The desire to safeguard peace is another justification of the right to development." "The interests of world stability and the pursuit of a lasting peace require universal respect for the right to development."[84] Here we have further instances of the instrumental fallacy.

That development would be conducive to peace is a fortunate fact—assuming that it is a fact, and that development would not simply increase the destructiveness of war. It says nothing, however, about the existence of a (human) right to development; at best, it merely suggests that development has additional instrumental value. Much the same can be said of the argument that "because of its multitudinous effects and its central character, the question of development could jeopardize human rights as a whole."[85] Again we have a fortunate fact, and an additional reason to seek development, but no further argument for a right to development.

As was the case with legal sources, the alleged moral sources establish not that there is, or even should be, a moral right to development, but only that development has considerable moral significance—a point that has never been in question. Just as development is an important subject in international law, it is a most important topic in international morality. But reemphasizing the moral importance of development in no way implies that there is, or ought to be, a (human) right to development.

V. SUBJECTS OF THE RIGHT TO DEVELOPMENT

In examining other dimensions of the alleged right to development, we again find a diversity of interpretations that borders on confusion. In the case of the subjects of the right to development—that is, the right-holders and duty-bearers—we find that major interpretations actually threaten human rights.

If human rights arise from the inherent dignity of the human

84. M'Baye, *supra* note 3, at 8; Secretary-General's Report, *supra* note 7, para. 51.

85. U.N. Doc. E/CN.4/SR.1612 at para. 71 (Yugoslavia). *Compare* Secretary-General's Report, *supra* note 7, para. 43 *with* U.N. Doc. E/CN.4/1982/SR.30 at para. 67 (Ethiopia). For a similar argument attempting to establish rights to peace and to a healthy environment, see UNESCO Doc. SS-80/CONF.806/4 at para. 14.

person—are the rights one has simply as a human being—then it would seem undeniable that the human right to development, assuming that it exists, is an individual right. This, however, has been denied by several commentators. For example, Abi-Saab argues that it is "very difficult, impossible," to conceive of a general individual right to development. Therefore, it must be viewed as a collective right.[86] Sanson, even more explicitly, refers to the right to development as "the analog, for peoples, of human rights, for individuals."[87] Such an argument is a frequent feature of diplomatic discussions: "the main thrust of the right to development is collective and dynamic, emphasizing the struggles of peoples, nations and States for the elimination of obstacles which impede development;" it is "a collective right of sovereign States or of peoples fighting for their independence;" "a profoundly human right which goes beyond mere individual rights."[88] This interpretation is even left open by the consolidated technical text of the Draft Declaration, which in Article 1 proclaims that "the right to development is an inalienable human right of every person, individually *or* in entities established pursuant to the right of association, and of other groups, including peoples."[89]

More commonly, the right to development is argued to be both, and more or less equally, an individual and a collective right.[90] An intermediate position of sorts holds that is *primarily* a collective right.[91] In contrast to this apparent consensus that the right to development is (at least partially) a collective right,[92] I want to challenge the very idea of collective human rights and argue that the human right to development, assuming it to exist, must be primarily, if not exclusively, an individual right.

It is occasionally argued that all individual rights are derived

86. Abi-Saab, *supra* note 26, at 163-164.

87. Sanson, *supra* note 1, at 1985 (translation provided).

88. U.N. Doc. E/CN.4/1983/SR.17 at para. 60, 65 (Brazil); U.N. Doc. E/CN.4/1982/SR.31 at para. 1 (Byelorussian SSR); U.N. Doc. E/CN.4/1983/SR.17 at para. 14 (Mozambique). *Compare* U.N. Doc. E/CN.4/1984/SR.17 at para. 70 (USSR).

89. U.N. Doc. E/CN.4/1984/13 (Annex II) (emphasis added).

90. *See, e.g.*, M'Baye, *supra* note 43, at 74-75; Alston, *supra* note 22, at 108; Tardu, *supra* note 1, at 269; U.N. Doc. A/37/PV.111 at 21 (Singapore) and 47-48 (Morocco); U.N. Doc. E/CN.4/1984/SR.16 at para. 58 (China); U.N. Doc. E/CN.4/1982/SR.17 at para. 30 (France); U.N. Doc. E/CN.4/1983/SR.18 at para. 6 (Australia); U.N. Doc. E/CN.4/1984/SR.18 at para. 47 (Bangladesh); U.N. Doc. E/CN.4/1983/SR.18 at para. 46 (Yugoslavia).

91. *See, e.g.*, U.N. Doc. E/CN.4/1983/SR.19 at para. 14 (Finland); U.N. Doc. E/CN.4/1489 at para. 16; U.N. Doc. E/CN.4/AC.34/WP.25 at para. 10; U.N. Doc. E/CN.4/SR.1486 at para. 5 (K. Vasak).

92. Dupuy, *supra* note 1, at 267.

from collective rights.[93] The more common view among advocates of collective rights, however, is that some human rights are primarily individual, while others, including the right to development, are primarily, or at least equally, collective. For example, Ambassador Koh clearly struck a chord in the General Assembly when he argued that "human rights have both a collective and an individual aspect," and that while some countries give "greater emphasis to civil and political rights and the individual aspect," and others give "greater emphasis to social and economic rights and to the collective aspect," what was needed was balanced emphasis and strong international support for both.[94] In fact, however, all the rights of the International Bill of Human Rights, with one exception, are entirely individual rights.

Realization of the right to development certainly would require substantial collective action. Likewise, the full realization of economic and social rights requires collective action. The same, however, is true of most civil and political rights. For example, rights to popular participation in government and to a nationality include society and the state in their very formulation, while freedoms of speech, press, religion and assembly can no more be fully realized in the absence of collective social action than can rights to education or social security.

All human rights require collective action if they are to be fully realized for all. This understanding is explicit as far back as the social contract theorists who first formulated the modern idea of human rights, and who saw society and the state largely as instruments for the full realization of the natural rights of man.[95] The fact that collective action is required to realize a right in no way suggests that the right is a collective right.

Even the economic and social rights recognized in the International Bill of Human Rights are individual rights—entirely individual rights. Social security, work, rest and leisure, an adequate standard of living, education and the like are rights of individuals, individual claims against social resources; they are no more held collectively than are civil and political rights. Economic and social human rights (which must be clearly distinguished from economic

93. *See, e.g.*, U.N. Doc. A/C.3/38/SR.41 at para. 57 (Cuba).

94. U.N. Doc. A/37/PV.111 at 21.

95. *See, e.g.*, Locke, *Second Treatise*, in TWO TREATISES OF GOVERNMENT para. 95; (P. Laslett ed. 1967); T. PAINE, THE COLLECTED WRITINGS OF THOMAS PAINE 1, 5, 276-277 (P. Foner ed. 1945); DONNELLY, *supra* note 27, at 69-73.

and social goods and services) regulate the pattern of distribution of certain collective resources and opportunities by assuring to all individuals a minimum share of selected goods, services and opportunities.

If these rights are to be realized, there must be social resources available to distribute. The same is true, however, for most civil and political rights. No human rights are secure—not even civil rights are likely to be securely maintained—in the absence of collective action and social and political exertion, which will always involve at least opportunity costs, and usually substantial direct costs as well.[96]

The sole exception to the rule of individual human rights is the right to self-determination, recognized in Article 1 of both Covenants as a right of *peoples*. Clearly this is the model relied on by advocates of a collective human right to development. But while a plausible defense of such a collective human right can be mounted, I want to suggest that the notion is at best dubious.

If human rights derive from the inherent dignity of the human person, collective human rights are logically possible only if we see social membership as an inherent part of human personality, *and* if we argue that as part of a nation or people, persons hold human rights substantively different from, and in no way reducible to, individual human rights. This last proposition is extremely controversial. While I cannot here attempt to refute it decisively, let me suggest that conceptually, morally, and politically as well, it is fraught with difficulties.

The very concept of human rights, as it has heretofore been understood, rests on a view of the individual person as separate from, and endowed with inalienable rights held primarily in relation to, society, and especially the state. Furthermore, within the area defined by these rights, the individual is superior to society in the sense that ordinarily, in cases of conflict between individual human rights and social goals or interests, individual rights must prevail.[97] The idea of collective *human* rights represents a major, and at best confusing, conceptual deviation.

I do not want to challenge the idea of collective rights *per se* or

96. *Compare* Shue, *supra* note 27, *with* BASIC RIGHTS, *supra* note 27, at ch. 2. To argue that the social aspect of human rights made all human rights collective rights would be still another variant on the instrumental fallacy.

97. For a more detailed exposition of this understanding of human rights, *see* DONNELLY, *supra* note 27, at chs. 2, 5; Howard & Donnelly, *Human Rights, Human Dignity and Political Regimes: Liberal and Illiberal Societies and the Standard of Human Rights* (paper presented to the 26th Annual Convention of the International Studies Association (Mar. 1985)).

even the notion of peoples' rights; groups, including nations, can and do hold a variety of rights. But these are not *human* rights as that term is ordinarily understood. If for no other reason than clarity and precision, in order to help to preserve the conceptual integrity of the much abused idea of human rights, I would suggest that we ought to follow the conceptualization of the Banjul Charter, which is explicitly a declaration of human *and peoples'* rights.[98] Whatever their relative importance, (individual) human rights and (collective) peoples' rights, as well as other group rights, are very different kinds of rights, and therefore should be kept distinct.[99]

It is rarely denied that there are legitimate social limits on the exercise of all individual rights. Society does have certain rights, or at least responsibilities, that legitimately constrain the exercise of many human rights; a properly ordered society must balance individual rights (against society) with individual duties (to society) and social responsibilities to the community at large. Thus the Universal Declaration, after concluding its enumeration of rights, explicitly notes (in Article 29) the existence and importance of individual duties.

Human rights, however, refer to but one side of this balance between individual rights and social duties. While human rights may have to be weighed against social needs, they should not be confused or conflated with them. It makes no more sense to try to conceive of individual duties as collective human rights than it does to try to reduce all social duties to obligations correlative to individual human rights. While both rights and duties are important, they cannot be reduced to one another; rights are rights and duties are duties, and while they are often correlated, they are quite different. In any case, the real danger today is not an overemphasis on individual human rights, which in most countries are only tenuously protected, but rather conceptual obfuscation resulting in an overemphasis on social duties, which can only ease the task of repressive regimes.

A further problem with collective human rights is determining who is to exercise the right; the right-holder is not a physical person, and thus an institutional "person" must exercise it. In the case of a right held by a people, or by society as a whole, the most plausible

98. *Compare* A. ROBERTSON, HUMAN RIGHTS IN THE WORLD 196 (2d ed. 1982). I would also argue that the right to self-determination ought to be placed in this category of peoples' rights.

99. *Compare* U.N. Doc. A/C.3/36/SR.49 at para. 50 (Finland) *with* U.N. Doc. A/C.3/37/SR.39 at para. 28 (Sweden).

"person" to exercise the right is, unfortunately, the state. Again this represents a radical reconceptualization of human rights—and an especially dangerous one. All traditional human rights, both civil and political and economic, social and cultural, are rights held primarily *against* the state; whether the duties correlative to these rights require forebearance, protection or positive assistance, the state is the principal duty-bearer. Human rights are essentially instruments to protect the individual against the state or to assure that the state guarantees to each individual certain minimum goods, services and opportunities. Other legal, moral and social principles or practices aim to protect the legitimate interests of society in instances of conflict between the individual and the community. To confuse the two seriously risks undermining the protections provided by human rights.

Indeed, the very idea of a human right held by the state is incoherent. Even if we allow that it is plausible to view individuals as possessed of special human rights in their capacity as members of a nation/people, there is no such parallel membership of (all) persons in the state that would justify a human right of states. The very term "human rights of states" involves a logical contradiction.

In the case of the human right to development, however, it is regularly argued that the state is a holder of the right, a view advanced not only by the Soviet bloc States,[100] who tend to see all human rights as contingent grants to individuals by the state,[101] but also by a variety of Third World States,[102] the Director of the Division of Human Rights,[103] and academic commentators as well.[104] The danger here is that the state is thereby placed in a position to use *its* "human rights" to deny the human rights of individuals, while still plausibly claiming to be pursuing human rights. "Human

100. *See, e.g.*, U.N. Doc. E/CN.4/1984/SR.16 at para. 83 (Ukranian SSR); U.N. Doc. E/CN.4/1983/SR.20 at para. 52 (Byelorussian SSR); U.N. Doc. E/CN.4/AC.39/5. *Cf.* Graefrath, *The Right to Development in a World-Wide Debate*, 1 GDR COMM. HUMAN RIGHTS BULL. 11-13 (1982); U.N. Doc. E/CN.4/1489 at para. 17; U.N. Doc. ST/HR/SER.A/8 at para. 64. One delegate has even referred to the right to development as a "natural right of all States." U.N. Doc. E/CN.4/1984/SR.18 at para. 103 (Poland) (emphasis added).

101. *See* DONNELLY, *supra* note 27, at 309-311.

102. *See, e.g.*, U.N. Doc. E/CN.4/1984/SR.18 at para. 64 (Togo); U.N. Doc. E/CN.4/1983/SR.17 at para. 65 (Brazil); U.N. Doc. E/CN.4/1983/SR.19 at para. 76 (Colombia). *Cf.* U.N. Doc. E/CN.4/1983/SR.18 at para. 46 (Yugoslavia).

103. U.N. Doc. E/CN.4/SR.1483 at para. 58 (Theo. Van Boven).

104. *See, e.g.*, Haquani, *supra* note 34, at 31; Sanson, *supra* note 1, at 195; de Waart, *An Outlook for the Future: Embedding Development in a Right Under International Law*, E/CN.4/AC.34/WP.12 para. 5, 21, 24.

rights" are thus transformed into but another mechanism of political tyranny and social oppression.

Most proponents of the state as a holder of the right to development also argue that it is held by peoples as well (and usually individuals too); for example, Sanson argues that internally the right to development is primarily "a right of the people against the state."[105] It might be suggested that this at least reduces the danger, if not the incoherence, of recognizing a State's right to development. Unfortunately, however, besides the difficulty of imagining what such a right would imply (a right to the growth of bureaucracy or the development of the state's coercive powers, perhaps?) or conceiving how and by whom such a right could be exercised (in contrast to pursuing development nationally through the exercise of traditional human rights), our experience with the right to self-determination, the only internationally recognized collective human right, suggests otherwise.

The right to self-determination usually is interpreted as a right to be free from alien political domination (roughly, a right to decolonization), and a right of States (and peoples under colonial domination) against foreign economic control or coercion. In no standard interpretation is it viewed as a right of peoples or subnational groups against "their own" sovereign States. This is the way any collective right is likely to be interpreted today; given the current state of international law and politics, it is hard to imagine a collective right to development obtaining a meaningful national dimension in practice.

It might also be suggested that the dangers of a right to development of States could be greatly reduced if the right were restricted to a right of States in international relations, "a right of the State . . . against other States and the international community."[106] As such, however, it is clearly no longer a human right (even if we were to allow that States are potential holders of human rights). Even if it is desirable to establish a right of States to development in international law, this says nothing about a human right to development.

Who are left, then, as possible holders of the right to development, assuming that such a right exists? Individuals. Certainly there is no conceptual problem in recognizing individuals as holders of a new human right to development. There are, however, difficulties in

105. Sanson, *supra* note 1, at 195 (translation provided).

106. *Id.* at 195 (translation provided).

specifying the substance of an individual right to development.[107]

VI. THE SUBSTANCE OF THE RIGHT TO DEVELOPMENT

In its broadest, and most defensible understanding, the right to development is a right to pursue full personal development along all major dimensions of human life. If all human rights aim at the further development of the human person, then a right to full personal development can stand as a summary of traditional rights. It also might be argued that it stresses the organic interconnections between separate human rights—both civil and political and economic, social and cultural—which are but pieces of the broader struggle for full, autonomous personal development, the ultimate aim of all human rights. For example, Alston presents the right to development as "a synthesis of existing rights, informed and given an extra dimension by the emergence of a growing international consensus on a variety of development objectives" and "a means by which to reinforce the importance of existing rights and to emphasize the interdependence and indivisibility" of civil, political, economic, social and cultural rights.[108]

As noted above, however, we must carefully distinguish between a human right to *pursue* development, to strive for self-actualization in conditions of dignity, and a human right to *be* developed. The latter is extravagant and even dangerous; one does not have a right to be a fully developed person simply because one is a human being. A right to pursue personal development is on its face at least substantively plausible. But does it serve any real purpose?

Alston, addressing the charge that a synthetic right to development is superfluous, argues that it has at least psychological significance. "In addition it serves to highlight the need to create a new international order, in social and cultural as much as in economic terms, to accompany the achievement of a new national order through improved respect for human rights." Furthermore, he ar-

107. As noted above, discussions of duty-bearers of the right to development are particularly underdeveloped. This is largely a function of lack of clarity in specifying the holders and substance of the right, which implicitly provide a large part of the specification of the right's passive subjects. For example, if the right of development is primarily a right of States, it would be held primarily in relation to other States, while as a right of peoples it would be held against States (one's own or others), and perhaps even individuals as well. If we accept the arguments above against interpreting the human right to development as a right of States or peoples, the right to development, as an individual human right, creates obligations primarily for one's own government.

108. Alston, *supra* note 22, at 102, 107.

gues, it puts established rights in a new light; for example, revealing the right to food to be not just a right to escape starvation or malnourishment, but a right to enough food to permit the pursuit of full personal development.[109] These sorts of conceptual changes lie behind the claim that the synthesis represented by the right to development is greater than the sum of its parts.[110]

Even granting that this is true, however, we cannot ignore the danger that a stress on the whole will divert attention from the parts; that is from internationally recognized civil, political, economic, social and cultural human rights. Discussion of the right to development as "the synthesis of all human rights"[111] shifts the focus from particular rights to the package as a whole. This is most likely to lead not to a broader and more comprehensive view but rather an increasing detachment from the realities of implementation in particular cases; that is, it is likely to obscure the central fact that progress in realizing the whole must be achieved by hard work in implementing the "parts," the separate civil, political, economic, social and cultural rights already recognized internationally. Similarly, the shift in focus from national to international questions—most discussions stress the international dimensions of the right to development in contrast to the primarily national focus of traditional human rights[112]—is likely to be used to divert attention from systematic national violations of human rights, and even to absolve Third World governments of their responsibility for human rights violations.[113]

Such attempts to shift attention from particular rights to general issues, and from the primary role of the state as a violator of human rights to external forces that also contribute to human rights violations, are regular strategies of repressive regimes seeking to justify

109. *Id.* at 107-108.

110. *See, e.g.*, U.N. Doc. ST/HR/SER.A/8 at para. 72; U.N. Doc. E/CN.4/Sub.2/477 at para. 95; Espiell, *supra* note 16, at 205; U.N. Doc. E/CN.4/1421 at para. 15(b).

111. Espiell, *supra* note 16, at 205. *Compare* Mestdagh, *supra* note 16, at 47, 49, 53; U.N. Doc. E/CN.4/SR.1612 at para. 77 (Algeria); U.N. Doc. E/CN.4/SR.1486 at para. 5 (K. Vasak).

112. *Compare* M'Baye, *supra* note 43, at 77; Dupuy, *supra* note 1; Int'l Comm'n of Jurists, *supra* note 16; U.N. Doc. E/CN.4/1489 at para. 39. The only significant exceptions are U.N. Doc. E/CN.4/1421 and U.N. Doc. E/CN.4/1488, the (largely neglected) followups to the Secretary-General's original study.

113. For example, M'Baye explicitly argues that rapacious Third World elites, which are a major source of human rights violations, are simply an effect of international induced underdevelopment. M'Baye, *supra* note 43, at 85. *Compare* U.N. Doc. E/CN.4/SR.1393 (Yugoslavia). Thus I would argue that Alston is simply mistaken in claiming that the right to development represents a break with the tendency to attribute human rights problems to external factors. *See* Alston, *supra* note 22, at 110.

their behavior in human rights terms. We can see this, for example, in the priority in the UN's human rights work mandated by the General Assembly for massive and flagrant violations arising from *apartheid*, racial discrimination, colonialism and neo-colonialism,[114] and the vociferous, although ultimately unsuccessful attacks on a recent resolution which provided a more balanced place for individual rights and the national dimensions of human rights violations, while still emphasizing international impediments and collective rights.[115]

The context of international law lies not only in changes in the world and the character of States, but also in the way in which international law (and related moral arguments) will be used by States to pursue their own purposes—and it is here that the greatest dangers of a right to development lie. If we could be sure that the right would be interpreted as at least primarily a right of the individual to pursue full personal development, there would be little reason for concern; at worst it would be a vague but relatively innocuous right. But we have already seen the strong tendency to interpret it as a collective right, with the attendant conceptual and political dangers. Furthermore, there are similar dangers in several standard interpretations of its substance. As a result, while the right to development "should enhance the commitment of Governments to the promotion and protection of human rights,"[116] in practice the reverse is more likely to be the case.

For example, one standard interpretation presents the right to development as primarily or exclusively an economic right, a right "parallel, on the economic level, to self-determination on the political plane."[117] It is regularly referred to as "the right to economic and social development;" "the right of the individual to an equal share in the benefits of economic and social development;" "the right to an adequate standard of living;" or simply "economic and social rights,

---

114. G.A. Res. 130, 32 U.N. GAOR (1977).

115. G.A. Res. 200, 37 U.N. GAOR (1982). The debate on the resolution can be found in U.N. Doc. A/C.3/37/SR.49, 60 and U.N. Doc. A/37/PV.111. Opponents of this resolution went so far as to introduce amendments in plenary session and to provoke a vigorous debate in plenary, an extremely rare occurence in a body that, especially in the area of human rights, usually functions as nothing more than a rubber stamp for committee decisions.

116. U.N. Doc. E/CN.4/SR.1614 at para. 61 (Australia).

117. Progressive Development of the Principles and Norms of International Law Relating to the New International Economic Order. Report of the Secretary-General. Addendum: ANALYTICAL STUDY PREPARED BY UNITAR, U.N. Doc. A/39/504/Add.1 (Oct. 23, 1984) at para. 212. *Compare* U.N. Doc. E/CN.4/Sub.2/1983/24 at para. 128; M'Baye, *supra* note 43, at 75; Sanson, *supra* note 1, at 195.

or the right to development."[118] Even within the Commission on Human Rights, the right to development is discussed under an agenda item devoted entirely to economic and social rights: "Question of the realization in all countries of the economic, social and cultural rights contained in the [International Bill of Human Rights] and study of the special problems which the developing countries face in their efforts to achieve these rights, including (a) problems relating to the right to enjoy an adequate standard of living, the right to development; (b) the effects of the existing unjust international economic order on the economies of the developing countries, and the obstacles that this represents for the implementation of human rights and fundamental freedoms."

This reading, particularly when the right to development is presented as a synthesis of all human rights, is part of a distressing tendency to subordinate civil and political rights to economic and social rights and national dimensions of human rights violations to international dimensions.[119] (Reduced to a right to an adequate standard of living, it encompasses not even the full range of economic and social rights.) This can easily transform human rights concerns related to development into little more than an additional device to obtain economic concessions from the North, as is clear in the types of links drawn between the right to development and the New International Economic Order. While it cannot be denied that the structure of international economic relations presents serious impediments to the realization of human rights, especially economic and social rights, it is a gross, one-sided distortion to argue that the NIEO represents the "blueprint of the right to development."[120]

Even more troubling is the tendency to reduce the right to development to a mere tool in the struggle for a new international economic order, turning the end (human rights) into a means (to achieve the NIEO), and vice versa.

> The right to development [is] a composite right which, in encompassing a number of already recognized rights, enhance[s] their value and [makes] them a true force for the establishment of the

118. U.N. Doc. A/C.3/37/SR.39 at para. 15 (Brazil) and para. 27 (Sweden); U.N. Doc. E/CN.4/1982/SR.33 at para. 6, 10 (Nigeria); U.N. Doc. E/CN.4/1984/SR.16 at para. 7 (India). *Compare* U.N. Doc. E/CN.4/SR.1612 at para. 14 (France); U.N. Doc. E/CN.4/SR.1488 at para. 14 (Senegal).

119. For an extreme and explicitly polemical version of this interpretation of UN human rights doctrine, see Donnelly, *Recent Trends in UN Human Rights Activity: Description and Polemic*, 35 INT'L ORG. 633 (1981). *But compare* Alston, *The Alleged Demise of Political Human Rights at the UN: A Reply to Donnelly*, 37 INT'L ORG. 537 (1983).

120. Abi-Saab, *supra* note 25, at 167.

> new international economic order.[121]
>
> The question of the right to development has been raised by the developing countries in order to challenge the existing unjust international economic order.[122]
>
> The reason for subscribing to the concept of the right to development is . . . to mobilize international solidarity within the context of the new international economic and social order.[123]
>
> Any consideration of solidarity rights must . . . give priority to the study and promotion of a new international economic order.[124]
>
> The explicit consecration of this right is linked to the very future of the "new international economic order."[125]

Even when the NIEO is presented as a means to realize human rights, discussion usually overlooks the fact that success in achieving a new international economic order would not necessarily assure progress in implementing human rights. Simply increasing the goods and services available to Third World countries or within Southern economies—which is all that the NIEO seeks to do—will increase the enjoyment of human rights only if these resources are equitably distributed, which is largely a matter of domestic politics. There is a huge gap between providing economic and social *goods* in the aggregate and assuring the enjoyment of economic and social *rights*, which requires guaranteeing the entitlement of all to certain shares of available social resources. Unless the gains of the NIEO are passed on to the masses—and figures on income distribution in the Third World clearly indicate that they are not likely to be passed on—even the enjoyment of economic and social rights will not improve. We should also note that the connection between development, the NIEO and civil and political rights is even more tenuous.

National governments are the major violators of human rights, and thus must be the main target of human rights action. Even in the more limited area of human rights and development, national governments must substantially alter, even radically rethink, their development strategies if human rights concerns are to be adequately addressed. There is much that can and needs to be done about human rights at the national level, regardless of the success or failure

121. U.N. Doc. E/CN.4/SR.1486 at para. 5 (K. Vasak). *Compare* U.N. Doc. E/CN.4/SR.1492 at para. 21 (Argentina); U.N. Doc. E/CN.4/1983/SR.17 at para. 13 (Mozambique); U.N. Doc. E/CN.4/Sub.2/459 at para. 69.

122. U.N. Doc. E/CN.4/1983/SR.19 at para. 45 (China).

123. UNESCO Doc. SS-80/CONF.806/6 at para. 33.

124. *Id.* para. 14.

125. UNESCO Doc. SS-80/CONF.806/4 at para. 22.

of efforts to establish the NIEO. It is at this level that Third World States that are sincere about improving the enjoyment of human rights have the greatest power and opportunity for positive action. We must not lose sight of the fact that most human rights violations are directly perpetrated on people by the governments of their own countries. Discussions of the right to development, however, seem to have the effect, and perhaps even the intent, of obscuring this central point.

The political dangers of subordinating human rights are especially great when development or the NIEO appear as *preconditions* for the realization of human rights, or when the right to development itself is presented as a precondition to the enjoyment of traditional human rights.[126] Since satisfaction of these preconditions is a long way off, such arguments readily lend themselves to claims that Third World regimes ought not be held to international human rights standards. As preconditions multiply,[127] we reach a situation where it appears as if the world would need to be "transformed into an earthly paradise"[128] before human rights could be realized.

The right to development and its preconditions thus lend themselves to use as an excuse not to act on human rights now. This, I would argue, is the central contemporary political fact about the right to development. Logically, the right to development need not be interpreted in this way. Unfortunately, it is almost certainly utopian to expect that it won't. The readily defensible argument that international structures and external forces share a part of the responsibility for failures to implement human rights in the Third World is too easily transformed into an argument that removes the responsibility for human rights violations from repressive regimes.

The right to development, therefore, in its substance as in other aspects, is subject to both relatively defensible and entirely undefensible interpretations. The problem is that the defensible interpretation, as an individual right to full personal development in all areas of human life, is rather innocuous, while the indefensible interpreta-

126. For such arguments see U.N. Doc. E/CN.4/1984/SR.18 at para. 68 (Togo); U.N. Doc. E/CN.4/SR.1491 at para. 40 (Brazil); Abi-Saab, *supra* note 26, at 171, 172. *Compare also* U.N. Doc. A/C.3/37/SR.39 at para. 28 (Sweden).

127. For example, the right to peace is often advanced as a precondition to the right to development or to human rights generally. *See, e.g.*, U.N. Doc. E/CN.4/AC.34/WP.25 at para. 2; U.N. Doc. A/C.3/37/SR.39 at para. 29 (GDR); and U.N. Doc. E/CN.4/SR.1490 at para. 43 (USSR).

128. U.N. Doc. E/CN.4/1984/SR.17 at para. 81 (Italy).

tions are quite dangerous. In other words, the dangers posed by the right to development far outweigh its benefits.

It is easy to exaggerate the practical importance of international doctrine. Nonetheless, the codification of the right to development that is emerging in the UN probably will at least marginally hinder the pursuit of human rights and certainly will provide still one more excuse for States to fail to implement human rights in their development plans and in other aspects of national politics—but this time, in the very name of human rights. This is at least perverse, and if we take doctrine seriously, a genuine tragedy.

One final rescue effort should be considered; namely, the claim that I have merely shown existing arguments for the right to development to be inadequate and standard interpretations to be dangerous. The implication of such an argument, of course, is that sound justifications and defensible interpretation are possible and will be formulated. Therefore, we should not abandon the idea of a human right to development. Such an argument, however, is both implausible and disingenuous.

In this article, I have reviewed virtually the entire scholarly literature and the whole of the diplomatic discussion of the right to development. I find it incomprehensible that scholars and jurists, or even serious diplomats, would resort to the sort of weak and obviously flawed arguments that are the staple of these discussions if better arguments were available. My only conclusion is that misguided optimists and cynical opportunists alike have been caught up in the pleasing rhetoric of the right to development.

It is time to step back and see what's really there — or isn't. It's time to stop repeating that there *might* be a right to development (and then take this as proof that there is such a right), and confront the failure to establish even a vaguely plausible case that there is such a right. In five years, the discussion has not advanced in any significant way. I would suggest that it is time to admit that it is not going to advance. The problem is not human fallibility, our inability to muster the possible arguments needed to justify this right, but rather the fact that a human right to development is incapable of justification.

The burden of proof lies firmly on those who claim that such a right exists. Proponents of the right to development have utterly failed to discharge this burden. It is a well-known fact of logic that a universal negative existential proposition cannot be conclusively proved; it is no more possible to demonstrate beyond *all* doubt that there is no right to development than it is to show that no purple polka-dotted elephants exist. (It's always possible that we've failed to look some place or consider a particular argument.) But just as we can show, through the accepted cannons of science and common sense, that there is not a purple polka-dotted elephant here and now, we can show—and in this article I believe that I have shown—through the established procedures of legal and moral argument, that there is not, here and now, a moral or legal right to development.

To anyone who would argue otherwise, my response is simple. Show me. Only one good argument is needed to refute my case, which thus ought to stand as an attractive challenge to proponents of the right to development. Nonetheless, I do make the claim: there is no right to development.

VII. CONCLUSION: A MYTHICAL POSTSCRIPT

We can conclude, as we started, with a metaphor—but this time with the metaphor of the title of this paper, the unicorn. The right to development often appears, like the unicorn, as the embodiment of goodness and purity. As one diplomat rather sarcastically remarked last year, realization of the right to development is often presented as if it would involve "peace, domestic and international, and . . . the realization of all the purposes and principles of the United Nations."[129] But when we look at what advocates of the right to development have brought forward, we find little more than a run-down horse with a plastic horn glued to its head—or rather, a series of pretenders, one more ludicrous and mishappen than the next.

If this were a children's book, or if we could leave things at the level of myth, we could perhaps just not look too carefully, and agree that yes, what we have here is that rarest and most precious of beasts. But we are dealing with charlatans, who would use their hoax to defraud innocent and well-meaning people. The right to development is not just a charming delusion, but a threat to human rights, and a particularly insidious threat because it plays upon our fondest hopes and best desires, and diverts attention from more productive ways of linking human rights and development.

The search—for black cats, unicorns, whatever the creature—perhaps began as a noble one. In the end, however, we found not merely nothing, but worse. Mythic beasts—and equally unreal

129. U.N. Doc. E/CN.4/1984/SR.17 at para. 81 (Italy). *Compare* U.N. Doc. E/CN.4/AC.34/WP.11 at 10 ("The right to development has inherent the guarantee of the fundamental human values in society.").

rights—are perhaps best left alone, for when they are conjured into existence, the results may, as in the case of the right to development, be frightening, and nothing like what we naively imagined when we set out on the quest.

[6]

CONJURING UP NEW HUMAN RIGHTS: A PROPOSAL FOR QUALITY CONTROL

*By Philip Alston**

Writing in 1968, the year of the 20th anniversary of the adoption of the Universal Declaration of Human Rights,[1] Richard Bilder concluded that "in practice, a claim is an international human right if the United Nations General Assembly says it is."[2] Fifteen years later, as the 35th anniversary is celebrated, the authoritative role that Bilder correctly attributed to the General Assembly is in serious danger of being undermined.

The problem has manifested itself in three ways. First, the General Assembly has, on several occasions in recent years, proclaimed new rights (i.e., rights which do not find explicit recognition in the Universal Declaration of Human Rights or the two International Human Rights Covenants[3]) without explicitly acknowledging its intention of doing so and without insisting that the claims in question should satisfy any particular criteria before qualifying as human rights. Second, there has been a growing tendency on the part of a range of United Nations and other international bodies, including in particular the UN Commission on Human Rights, to proceed to the proclamation of new human rights without reference to the Assembly. Third, the ease with which such innovation has been accomplished in these bodies has in turn encouraged or provoked the nomination of additional candidates, ranging from the right to tourism to the right to disarmament, at such a rate that the integrity of the entire process of recognizing human rights is threatened.

In principle, both the validity and the necessity of a dynamic approach to human rights, as well as the expansion, where appropriate, of the list of recognized human rights, cannot reasonably be disputed. However, reason for serious concern with respect to current trends arises not so much from the proliferation of new rights but rather from the haphazard, almost anarchic manner in which this expansion is being achieved. Indeed, some such rights seem to have been literally conjured up, in the dictionary sense of being "brought into existence as if by magic."[4]

* Lecturer on Law, Harvard Law School, 1984–1985; on leave from the UN Centre for Human Rights. The views expressed are not necessarily those of the United Nations. The author gratefully acknowledges comments on an earlier draft from Georges Abi-Saab and Oscar Schachter.

[1] GA Res. 217A, UN Doc. A/810, at 71 (1948).

[2] Bilder, *Rethinking International Human Rights: Some Basic Questions,* 1969 WIS. L. REV. 171, 173. In this respect, there may be an uncomfortably close parallel between the authority of the Assembly and that asserted in Lewis Carroll's *Alice in Wonderland* by the Red Queen who majestically proclaimed that "words mean what I say they mean."

[3] International Covenant on Economic, Social and Cultural Rights, *adopted* Dec. 16, 1966, *entered into force* Jan. 3, 1976, Annex to GA Res. 2200, 21 UN GAOR Supp. (No. 16) at 49, UN Doc. A/6316 (1966); International Covenant on Civil and Political Rights, *adopted* Dec. 16, 1966, *entered into force* Mar. 23, 1976, Annex to GA Res. 2200, *id.* at 52.

[4] THE CONCISE OXFORD DICTIONARY 214 (1976 ed.).

The absence of any established procedure by which candidates for new rights are scrutinized has resulted in an unfortunate situation: bodies at a lower level in the international organizational hierarchy than the General Assembly have tended to proclaim the existence of new rights without adequate consideration of the basis for, let alone the advisability or implications of, such action and without leaving the Assembly with an adequate opportunity to determine whether or not the giving of its imprimatur is warranted.

The purpose of this comment is to trace the manner in which several new human rights have emerged in recent years and, in the light of the shortcomings identified in those instances, to propose the adoption by the United Nations General Assembly and the Commission on Human Rights of procedural reforms designed to ensure more adequate reflection and coordination.

I. The General Assembly as Arbiter in Transforming Rhetoric into Right

Proclamation of the existence of human, natural or other forms of inalienable rights as a means by which to mobilize public support through the invocation of high moral principles in a given cause or struggle is a time-honored and proven technique. From the Magna Carta, through the British Bill of Rights of 1688 and the great American and French texts of the 18th century, to the Communist Manifesto of 1848 and the Atlantic Charter of 1941, manifestos, charters, and declarations of various kinds have succeeded both as catalysts to reform or revolution and as a means of confirming and perhaps even entrenching concessions on matters of basic principle already made by the established forces in society. In a number of obvious respects, the international law of human rights, particularly as it has evolved within the United Nations framework, is one of the main heirs to this tradition.

By the same token, however, the adoption of the Universal Declaration in 1948 constituted a qualitatively different undertaking in at least two respects. First, the fact that the international community had reached agreement on a comprehensive package of human rights which was said to represent a "common standard of achievement for all nations and all peoples" was, in itself, a unique and remarkable achievement. Second, this breakthrough was only made possible by the fact that most member states of the United Nations implicitly recognized the authority of the General Assembly to determine which claims should be deemed rights and which should not. For the first time in history, at the international level, a final arbiter had emerged in an area where conflicting ideologies, cultures and interests had previously made the prospect of general agreement seem far beyond reach and even utopian. Even when the drafting of the Universal Declaration was well under way, many distinguished commentators doubted the feasibility of reaching any meaningful consensus and urged that far more modest goals should be set.[5]

The authority that was nevertheless vested in the General Assembly was reinforced in the period from 1949 to 1966 when the two International Human

[5] *See, e.g.*, Croce, *The Rights of Man and the Present Historical Situation*, in UNESCO, Human Rights: Comments and Interpretations 93–95 (1949).

Rights Covenants, as well as a number of other instruments of more limited scope, were being drafted. During the whole of this time, the role of the Assembly as the final arbiter was never seriously called into question even by those states that were unhappy with the direction in which the majority was moving (with regard, for example, to the adoption of two separate Covenants, the inclusion of the right to self-determination and the exclusion of the right to petition and the right to property).

In one sense, the authority vested in the Assembly to proclaim human rights is based on firm legal foundations. It is a logical and direct outcome of the Assembly's mandate, contained in Article 13 of the United Nations Charter, to "initiate studies and make recommendations for the purpose of . . . assisting in the realization of human rights and fundamental freedoms for all without distinction as to race, sex, language, or religion." The exercise of this mandate with a view to proclaiming an "International Bill of Rights" had clearly been foreseen at the San Francisco Conference of 1945, which adopted the UN Charter.[6]

However, in another sense, which is in many respects more profound, the continuing validity in practice of the declaratory authority of the Assembly in this domain is dependent on its capacity to maintain its credibility as a responsible and discerning arbiter and as a weather vane of the state of world public and governmental opinion.[7] It is in this intangible sense, rather than in formal legal terms, that the General Assembly's authority is somewhat precarious.

II. Pressures to Proclaim More New Rights

Recognition of the essential dynamism of the notion of human rights inevitably requires a willingness to consider the need to proclaim additional human rights. The challenge is to achieve an appropriate balance between, on the one hand, the need to maintain the integrity and credibility of the human rights tradition, and on the other hand, the need to adopt a dynamic approach that fully reflects changing needs and perspectives and responds to the emergence of new threats to human dignity and well-being. Those who have attached greater importance to the first rather than to the second of these goals have long voiced fears that the endorsement of new human rights would be the equivalent of trying to rewrite the Koran or the Bible.

Such fears, however, have proven largely groundless, and the success of a considerable range of new instruments adopted over the past three decades has served to encourage demands for the recognition of additional rights.

[6] Thus, in his closing address to the San Francisco Conference, President Truman said in reference to the Charter that "[u]nder this document we have good reason to expect the framing of an international bill of rights acceptable to all the nations involved." 13 DEP'T ST. BULL. 3, 5 (1945).

[7] This issue is but one limited aspect of a much broader question on which Oscar Schachter has recently shed considerable light: whether General Assembly resolutions which purport to be declaratory of the law and "which have been used to legitimize action by international institutions as well as by states in their international—and sometimes even domestic—affairs" are legitimate, and to what extent they should be regarded as authoritative by the states to which they are addressed. Schachter, *The Crisis of Legitimation in the United Nations,* 50 NORDISK TIDSSKRIFT INT'L RET: ACTA SCANDINAVICA JURIS GENTIUM 3, 4 (1981).

Probably the longest list is that proposed by Galtung and Wirak of needs "that might be considered as important candidates on the world waiting list for processing into rights":

—the right to sleep;

—the right not to be killed in a war;

—the right not to be exposed to excessively and unnecessarily heavy, degrading, dirty and boring work;

—the right to identity with one's own work product, individually or collectively (as opposed to anonymity);

—the right to access to challenging work requiring creativity;

—the right to control the surplus resulting from the work product;

—the right to self-education and education with others (as opposed to schooling);

—the right to social transparency;

—the right to co-existence with nature;

—the right to be a member of *some* primary group (not necessarily the family);

—the right to be a member of *some* secondary group (not necessarily the nation);

—the right to be free to seek impressions from others (not only from media); and

—the right to be free to experiment with alternative ways of life.[8]

Other academic commentators have emphasized the need not only to proclaim new human rights but also to adopt whole new declarations of such rights.[9]

Additional proposals have come from nongovernmental organizations. In the framework of the "Armand Hammer Conference," proposals for a third international human rights covenant featuring a range of "third generation solidarity rights" have been strongly advocated. This group of rights has been said to include: the right to development, the right to peace, the right to a healthy environment, the right to communicate, the right to be different, the right to benefit from the common heritage of mankind, and the right to humanitarian assistance.[10] It is significant that the first three of these rights have

[8] Galtung & Wirak, On the Relationship between Human Rights and Human Needs, UNESCO Doc. SS-78/CONF.630/4, at 48 (1978); also Galtung & Wirak, *Human Needs and Human Rights: A Theoretical Approach*, 8 BULL. PEACE PROPOSALS 251 (1977).

[9] E.g., Mallman, Human Rights and Responsibilities: Their Relation to Human Needs, Human Values and the New International Economic Order, UNESCO Doc. SS-78/CONF.630/9 (1978).

[10] *See* Marks, *Emerging Human Rights: A New Generation for the 1980's?*, 33 RUTGERS L. REV. 435 (1981). For a critique of the concept, see Alston, *A Third Generation of Solidarity Rights: Progressive Development or Obfuscation of International Human Rights Law?*, 29 NETH. INT'L L. REV. 307 (1982).

already been recognized in the African Charter on Human and Peoples' Rights of 1981.[11]

Similar new rights were proposed by the International Association of Democratic Lawyers in 1982 in the context of a Draft Declaration of Human Rights and the Rights of Peoples to Peace and Disarmament.[12] On the grounds that there currently exists "a grave omission in international law which requires repairing," the draft proposed immediate recognition by the General Assembly of:

> —the right of every individual and people to permanent peace;
>
> —the right of every individual to enjoy the highest attainable standard of physical and mental health, and in particular, the right to freedom from genetic mutation or damage;
>
> —the right of all individuals and peoples to an environment of such quality as to enable them to live with dignity and enjoy a state of well-being;
>
> —the right of all individuals and peoples to live in a peaceful region which is to become neither the theater of an armed conflict nor the subject of that conflict;
>
> —the right of every individual and all peoples to live in freedom from threats;
>
> —the right of all individuals and peoples to disarmament; and
>
> —the right of all individuals and peoples to progress and development.

A thorough search of the relevant literature would certainly yield a significant number of other, still unrecognized "human rights" ranging from those dealing with fundamental ethical issues[13] through frivolous claims such as that put forward by the World Tourism Organization (an intergovernmental body) that "tourism has become increasingly a basic need, a social necessity, a human right."[14]

III. The Proclamation by UN Organs of New Human Rights Since 1972

These diverse pressures to proclaim new rights have in fact borne fruit in a variety of United Nations organs over the past decade or so. The considerable shortcomings of the process by which some of these rights have achieved formal recognition is best illustrated by taking several specific examples.

[11] Text approved by OAU Ministerial Conference in January 1981 *reprinted in* 21 ILM 59 (1982).

[12] Brussels, May 8, 1982.

[13] Givanovitch, *Le Suicide est-il l'un des droits de l'homme?*, 23 Rev. Int'le Droit Pénal 407 (1952).

[14] UN Doc. E/1978/98. *See also* UN Office at Geneva Press Release ECOSOC/1977, July 18, 1978.

The Right to a Clean Environment

The right to a clean environment was recognized for the first time in the framework of the United Nations in 1972. In June of that year, the United Nations Conference on the Human Environment proclaimed the principle that "[m]an has the fundamental right to freedom, equality and adequate conditions of life, in an environment of a quality that permits a life of dignity and well-being. . . ."[15] Although the General Assembly endorsed that declaration in general terms,[16] it has never specifically proclaimed the existence of a right to a clean environment, despite proposals that it do so.[17]

The Right to Development

Unlike the right to a clean environment, the right to development has been recognized by the General Assembly on several occasions.[18] However, its existence was first proclaimed in 1977, not by the Assembly, but by the Commission on Human Rights on the basis of no prior examination of the matter and without the assistance of any relevant documentation.[19] In fact, neither the Commission nor the Assembly has ever formally held a debate on whether or not the right to development should be considered a human right and neither body has specifically acknowledged that an entirely new right or at least a new formulation of existing rights was being proclaimed.

The Right to Peace

The status of the right to peace is similar to that of the right to development. It has been proclaimed in varying formulations by both the Commission[20] and the Assembly, but neither its status as a human right nor its precise formulation, let alone its content, has ever been studied or formally debated. This did not, however, deter the General Assembly from adopting in 1978, on the recommendation of its First Committee, but without any reference either to the Commission or to the Third Committee (which is responsible for human rights matters), a declaration proclaiming the principle that "every nation and every human being . . . has the inherent right to life in peace."[21]

[15] REPORT OF THE UNITED NATIONS CONFERENCE ON THE HUMAN ENVIRONMENT, STOCKHOLM, 5–16 JUNE 1972, at 4 (UN Pub. Sales No. E.73.II.A.14).

[16] GA Res. 2994 (XXVII) (1972).

[17] E.g., P.-M. Dupuy, *Le Droit à la santé et la protection de l'environnement*, in THE RIGHT TO HEALTH AS A HUMAN RIGHT 340, 413 (R.-J. Dupuy ed. 1979).

[18] GA Res. 34/46 (1979), 35/174 (1980), 36/133 (1981), and 37/199 and 37/200 (1982).

[19] At that time, the Commission called for a study on "the international dimensions of the right to development as a human right," but the starting point for that study was the presumption that the right already existed. Comm'n on Human Rights Res. 4 (XXXIII) (1977). The resulting study is contained in UN Doc. E/CN.4/1334 (1979).

[20] Comm'n on Human Rights Res. 5 (XXXII) (1976), para. 1, "recalls that everyone has the right to live in conditions of international peace and security."

[21] Declaration on the Preparation of Societies for Life in Peace, GA Res. 33/73, pt. I, para. 1 (1978).

The Right to Popular Participation

In 1983 the Commission on Human Rights proclaimed that popular participation is a human right.[22] In the course of the Commission's four discussions of the item dealing with popular participation, no reference had been made to the desirability or otherwise of proclaiming a new human right.[23] It was not until a draft resolution was proposed by Yugoslavia, calling for "a comprehensive analytical study on 'the right to popular participation . . . ,'" that attention was drawn to the matter by several delegations opposed to the proclamation of a new right. Thus, the United Kingdom, Ireland and Australia opposed the use of the term "right" on the grounds that "the Commission could not . . . reiterate what it had not yet discussed or reaffirm a right which had not been declared as such by the United Nations."[24] In the event, the Commission adopted the language proclaiming the new right by 27 votes in favor to 3 against, with 13 states abstaining.[25]

In summary, then, the process by which new rights have recently been proclaimed has generally suffered from the following shortcomings: there has been no prior discussion, not to mention analysis, of the major implications of the proposed innovation; there has been no attempt to seek comments from governments, specialized agencies or nongovernmental organizations; there has been no request to the Secretariat or to any other expert group for advice on technical matters relating either to the general principles involved or to the specific formulations proposed; there has been no explicit recognition of the fact that a new human right was being proclaimed; and there has been insufficient debate on the basis of which to ascertain, with some degree of precision, the real intentions underlying the affirmative votes of states.[26] One result is that many of the new rights are characterized by inordinate vagueness. Indeed, to a considerable extent, it is their chameleon-like quality that has facilitated the degree of consensus support they have received. Thus, states have been able to vote in favor of the relevant resolutions without thereby committing themselves to any precise normative formulation or to any specific measures for the effective realization of the norm.

This approach is all the more extraordinary when it is contrasted with the painstaking and time-consuming negotiations that have been required to complete

[22] Comm'n on Human Rights Res. 1983/14; *see also* ECOSOC Res. 1983/31.

[23] UN Doc. E/CN.4/1983/SR.17–20.

[24] UN Doc. E/CN.4/1983/SR.31, para. 44 (Australia).

[25] *Id.*, para. 47.

[26] *See generally* Schachter, *supra* note 7. It is reasonable to assume that the more frequently states are asked to endorse new rights, the more blasé they become about the significance of their affirmative votes. Such "endorsements" may easily come to be seen as little more than a gesture of goodwill to a political ally or a powerful bloc. In 1967 Schwebel criticized the fact that

> resolutions may be voted for in the U.N. blithely, one might say, irresponsibly, because key decision-makers, normally not lawyers, having it fixed in their skulls that the General Assembly has no decision-making, no law-making authority, will vote for almost anything of transient political advantage, unaware that such votes may have a law-forming character.

THE EFFECTIVENESS OF INTERNATIONAL DECISIONS 494 (S. Schwebel ed. 1971). Today, it would be difficult to exempt lawyers from such criticism.

the drafting of instruments designed merely to spell out in greater detail the specific rights and obligations that flow from an already accepted right.

Before means of remedying some of these deficiencies are considered, it is appropriate to note the difference between the situation existing today and that which prevailed when the Universal Declaration and the Covenants were being drafted. The major difference derives from the fact that the initial or "incubation" phase of any given human right in the domain of international law is now taking place within the UN system at a much earlier stage than was previously the case. Thus, the rights in the Universal Declaration were, for the most part, if not entirely, claims which had long been made at the national level and which, in many instances, had been formally recognized as rights in national constitutions or other legislation. By the time they reached the General Assembly, such claims were reasonably mature in terms of their transformation into law, having already passed through a relatively demanding, although in some respects informal, filter system. By contrast, many of the claims now being asserted as rights were conceived directly in international forums and have not had the benefit of careful prior scrutiny at the national level. As a consequence, they are being presented to the international community for endorsement as rights when they are much closer, in terms of what Abi-Saab has referred to as "the life cycle of a legal rule," to general social values than to legal principles.[27]

IV. The Usefulness of Substantive Requirements

As the perceived usefulness of attaching the label "human right" to a given goal or value increases, it can be expected that a determined effort will be made by a wide range of special interest groups to locate their cause under the banner of human rights. Thus, in the course of the next few years, UN organs will be under considerable pressure to proclaim new human rights without first having given adequate consideration to their desirability, viability, scope or form.

Such a proliferation of new rights would be much more likely to contribute to a serious devaluation of the human rights currency than to enrich significantly the overall coverage provided by existing rights. It is thoroughly unnecessary to impugn or even question the motivation of the proponents of these recently proclaimed or proposed rights in order to conclude that a more orderly and considered procedure should be followed before the United Nations accords the highly prized status of a human right to any additional claims.

If we were to seek to establish a list of criteria a given claim must satisfy in order to qualify as a human right in terms of international law,[28] it might look something like this. The proposed new human right should:

[27] Abi-Saab, *The Legal Formulation of a Right to Development*, in THE RIGHT TO DEVELOPMENT AT THE INTERNATIONAL LEVEL 159, 161 (R.-J. Dupuy ed. 1980).

[28] Many other criteria could of course be proposed. Thus, for example, Ramcharan has argued that

> human rights are legal rights which possess one or more of certain qualitative characteristics, such as: appurtenance to the human person or group; universality; essentiality to human

—reflect a fundamentally important social value;

—be relevant, inevitably to varying degrees, throughout a world of diverse value systems;

—be eligible for recognition on the grounds that it is an interpretation of UN Charter obligations, a reflection of customary law rules or a formulation that is declaratory of general principles of law;

—be consistent with, but not merely repetitive of, the existing body of international human rights law;

—be capable of achieving a very high degree of international consensus;

—be compatible or at least not clearly incompatible with the general practice of states; and

—be sufficiently precise as to give rise to identifiable rights and obligations.

The question to be answered then is how to apply these or comparable criteria in practice. The possible options are to establish substantive or procedural requirements, either or both of which would have to be satisfied before a given claim could be recognized as a new right.

At first glance, the laying down of specific substantive requirements such as those listed above is appealing, and it has in fact been advocated (without always being thus identified) by a number of commentators.

Thus, for example, a UNESCO Committee on the Theoretical Bases of Human Rights, established in 1947 with a view to contributing to reflection on the approach to be adopted in the proposed Universal Declaration of Human Rights, defined a "right" as "a condition of living, without which, in any given historical stage of a society, men cannot give the best of themselves as active members of the community because they are deprived of the means to fulfil themselves as human beings." "Liberty" was defined to mean not only the absence of restraint but "also the positive organization of the social and economic conditions within which men can participate to a maximum as active members of the community and contribute to the welfare of the community at the highest level permitted by the material development of the society."[29]

Another, oft-quoted example of such a list of criteria is that proposed by Maurice Cranston, according to which "a human right by definition is a universal moral right, something which all men everywhere, at all times ought to have, something of which no one may be deprived without a grave affront to justice, something which is owing to every human being simply because he is human."[30]

> life, security, survival, dignity, liberty, equality; essentiality for international order; essentiality in the conscience of mankind; essentiality for the protection of vulnerable groups.

Ramcharan, *The Concept of Human Rights in Contemporary International Law*, 1983 CAN. HUMAN RIGHTS Y.B. 267, 280.

[29] The Grounds of an International Declaration of Human Rights, in UNESCO, HUMAN RIGHTS, *supra* note 5, App. II, at 263.

[30] M. CRANSTON, WHAT ARE HUMAN RIGHTS? 36 (1973).

But while philosophers can always have a field day debating the elements to be included in such a list of substantive criteria for determining whether a given claim qualifies as a human right, when intergovernmental organizations undertake the same exercise, it becomes infinitely more difficult. The reasons are, first, that the establishment of criteria of enduring relevance is almost impossible in a field that is constantly undergoing evolutionary flux, and second, even if such criteria could be agreed upon, the process of transforming a claim into an international human right is far from being scientifically pure. The point is well illustrated by the lengthy debates during the 1950s over whether or not self-determination could or should be considered a human right. Those states (essentially Western) which were opposed to the idea sought implicitly to establish a list of substantive criteria against which self-determination could be shown not to be a right. They included, for example, the criteria that: human rights must by definition embrace only the rights of individuals; the formulation of a right must be precise; and its implications must be clearly understood. In response, some of the proponents of the right simply rejected the proposed criteria, while others argued that the criteria were in fact satisfied in the case of self-determination.[31]

As that example well shows, it would at best be an artificial and unrewarding task to seek to distill from the broad range of human rights already proclaimed by the General Assembly any scientifically valid criteria that would be capable of practical application in respect of new claims. Thus, for example, by applying his own criteria, Cranston arrived at the conclusion that the rights proclaimed in the International Covenant on Economic, Social and Cultural Rights were simply not valid since they did not satisfy the requirements of practicability or paramount importance. By contrast, other philosophers have applied the same criteria and arrived at the opposite conclusion.[32]

Similar difficulties have been encountered in considering which basic economic, social and cultural rights might be suitable for inclusion in an expanded European Convention on Human Rights. In a study on the subject prepared for the Council of Europe, Professor F. G. Jacobs suggested three "general criteria which seem relevant."[33] They were: (1) the right must be fundamental; (2) the right must be universal in the sense both that it is universally or very widely recognized and that it is guaranteed to everyone; and (3) the right must be capable of sufficiently precise formulation to give rise to legal obligations on the part of the state rather than merely setting a standard. Yet it is clear that the application of these three criteria will inevitably be largely a political, rather than a technical/scientific, exercise. For example, in rejecting environmental rights, Jacobs opines that "as a matter of priorities it may seem that the movement for protection of the environment has not yet reached the advanced stage of the movement for the recognition and enforcement of social and economic

[31] *See* Annotations on the text of the draft International Covenants on Human Rights: Prepared by the Secretary-General, UN Doc. A/2929, ch. IV (1955).

[32] Raphael, *The Liberal Western Tradition of Human Rights,* 18 INT'L SOC. SCI. J. 22 (1966).

[33] Jacobs, The *Extension of the European Convention on Human Rights to Include Economic, Social and Cultural Rights,* 3 HUMAN RIGHTS REV. 166 (1978).

rights."[34] On that score he may or may not be right, but it is clear that the issue of whether to proclaim some form of environmental rights cannot realistically be resolved through the application of standardized criteria; it is, after all, a quintessentially political issue.

The application of a formal list of substantive requirements is thus an unworkable approach. To be useful, it would imply a degree of rationality and objectivity in the selection of rights that simply does not and could not characterize the approach of a body such as the United Nations. In other words, the normative validity of rights recognized by the General Assembly cannot be made dependent upon their validity in terms of philosophical or any other supposedly "objective" criteria. Hence the appropriateness of Bilder's pragmatic conclusion that a claim is an international human right if the General Assembly says it is.[35]

V. The Usefulness of Procedural Requirements

The difficulty of devising and applying universally acceptable substantive criteria must not be permitted to obscure the fact that procedural requirements may be used as an indirect means to achieve many of the same objectives. Indeed, "conformity with minimum procedural standards relating to the decision process" is, as Professor Schachter has recently written, "an essential requirement for legitimizing international decisions."[36] It is significant that most of the shortcomings identified above with respect to the present approach to new human rights concern the procedure followed rather than the outcome sought to be achieved.

In the present context, it is instructive to consider briefly the procedures used in other international contexts to legitimize the declaration of new norms. Probably the most elaborate of these is the approach followed by the International Labour Organisation (ILO), which generally involves the following steps:[37]

(1) the ILO Secretariat prepares a preliminary survey of national legislation and other materials relevant to a proposed standard-setting exercise;

(2) the ILO Governing Body (of tripartite composition, with representatives of governments, employers and workers) decides whether or not to place the item on the agenda of the annual ILO Conference;

(3) on the basis of a survey, and of replies by governments to a detailed questionnaire, the ILO Secretariat prepares a report indicating the principal questions requiring consideration by the Conference;

(4) the Conference refers the matter to a special tripartite technical committee;

(5) on the basis of those discussions, the Secretariat prepares a first draft of an instrument;

[34] *Id.* at 177.

[35] *See* note 2 *supra* and accompanying text.

[36] Schachter, *supra* note 7, at 18.

[37] *See generally* N. Valticos, Droit international du travail 215–19 (1983).

(6) the draft is sent to governments for comments and a revised draft is subsequently drawn up, which is again sent to governments at least 3 months before the next Conference;

(7) at the Conference, the draft is considered by a technical committee, then in plenary and then by a drafting committee prior to the vote on its adoption; and

(8) the Conference votes on adoption of the instrument, which requires a two-thirds majority of the delegates.

An equally elaborate, but rather more drawn-out, procedure is followed by the International Law Commission in its work on the progressive development of international law.[38] While both the ILO and the ILC procedures are concerned more with the drafting of detailed instruments than with the straightforward declaration of new norms, the principles and assumptions underlying them would seem equally applicable to both cases. This view is supported by the approach adopted in the drafting of the Universal Declaration[39] and in the elaboration of subsequent human rights instruments.[40]

The major difference between the existing approach of the General Assembly to proclaiming new rights and that of the ILO to adopting new instruments is that the relevant procedural safeguards are mandatory in the case of the ILO but entirely ad hoc (and thus dispensable) in the case of the Assembly. The challenge therefore is to devise, and in some way entrench, procedural safeguards to govern the proclamation of new human rights within the UN system.

VI. TOWARDS AN *APPELLATION CONTRÔLÉE:* A SPECIFIC PROPOSAL

In essence, what is required is the human rights equivalent of the French system of *appellations contrôlées* applied to wines from the best wine-growing regions. The *appellation* is not in itself a guarantee of quality, but it does affirm that the wine was made in the prescribed manner, taking account of the conditions

[38] In its work both on codification and on progressive development, the Commission adopts basically the following approach: a special rapporteur is appointed and an appropriate work plan is formulated for each topic; governments are invited to submit relevant laws, etc.; the special rapporteur submits a report on whose basis a provisional draft is approved by the Commission; the draft is submitted to the General Assembly and governments for comments; and a revised report is drawn up on whose basis a final report is submitted by the Commission to the Assembly. *See* UNITED NATIONS, THE WORK OF THE INTERNATIONAL LAW COMMISSION 11–13 (3d ed. 1980).

[39] At the preliminary ("nuclear") session of the Commission on Human Rights in 1946, it was agreed that "the fullest possible documentation and information . . . was of the utmost importance" in drafting the Universal Declaration (UN Doc. E/38/Rev.1, at 3 (1946)). On the basis of that information, which included several comprehensive drafts, the Secretariat was asked to prepare an "Outline," which then became the starting point for the drafting undertaken by the Commission and its working groups. The text was further refined by the General Assembly before its adoption in December 1948. *See* J. HUMPHREY, THE GREAT ADVENTURE: HUMAN RIGHTS AND THE UNITED NATIONS (1983).

[40] *See generally* UNITED NATIONS ACTION IN THE FIELD OF HUMAN RIGHTS (UN Pub. Sales No. E.83.XIV.2).

and traditions prevailing in the relevant region. It also attests that the proper ingredients were used and that quality was not sacrificed to quantity.

In the human rights field, responsibility for ensuring compliance with some form of procedural standards clearly belongs (for historical as well as hierarchical reasons) to the General Assembly. In the past, the Assembly has acquiesced in the partial erosion of its authority by permitting other bodies to take it upon themselves to proclaim the existence of new rights without at any stage seeking the Assembly's imprimatur. But although the Assembly must be the final arbiter in such matters, the views of the Commission should also be taken into account. The extension of the latter's terms of reference in 1979 to include responsibility for assisting the Economic and Social Council "in the co-ordination of activities concerning human rights in the United Nations system"[41] provides a strong basis for such an advisory role. Moreover, experience in recent years points to the need for greater coordination in order to avoid the duplication of effort involved when different organs deliberate on the same, or at least similar, issues, and to ensure that incompatible, or even contradictory, standards are not adopted.[42]

On this basis, the General Assembly could consider mandating a precise modus operandi to be followed when the proclamation of a new human right has been proposed. In doing so, account should be taken of the following considerations: (1) the desirability of obtaining inputs from a wide variety of sources; (2) the need for these inputs to be addressed to as many as possible of the qualitative or substantive issues listed above;[43] (3) the need to establish several phases in the process of considering the proposal so as to allow adequate time for analysis, consultation, reflection and revision prior to the proclamation

[41] ECOSOC Res. 1979/36.

[42] For example, a "Draft Declaration on the Rights and Responsibilities of Youth," submitted by the Governments of Costa Rica, Guinea, Indonesia, Lebanon, Romania and Rwanda, was presented to the General Assembly in 1982 (UN Doc. A/37/348, Appendix). The draft contains a very large number of "youth rights" that have no exact counterpart in the existing range of human rights. Thus, for example, the draft proclaims the right "to participate in the preparation and implementation of national development plans and in the execution of international co-operation programmes in the field of development" (pt. II(b)); as well as the rights "to perform useful work" (pt. IV, para. 2); "to fight illiteracy" (pt. VI(a)); "to be associated in appropriate forms, with the efficient management of a healthy educational climate" (pt. VI(c)); and "to take a suitable part in efforts to modernize teaching" (pt. VI(d)). The draft also proclaims a range of responsibilities and duties such as "the social duty, in accordance with their individual abilities and training, to perform useful work and to choose their jobs and the type of work they are to perform, taking into account national objectives" (pt. IV, para. 2).

In addition to the problem of the compatibility of the draft with existing standards, there is a problem of coordination flowing from a request by the Commission on Human Rights to the Sub-Commission on Prevention of Discrimination and Protection of Minorities to draw up "draft principles on the right and responsibility of individuals, groups and organs of society to promote and protect universally recognized human rights and fundamental freedoms" (Comm'n on Human Rights Res. 1982/30 and 1983/31). Nevertheless, on the basis of existing practice, the draft declaration concerning youth is unlikely to be referred to the Commission on Human Rights for its comments or proposals.

[43] *See* text accompanying note 28 *supra*.

of any new right; and (4) the desirability of providing for "expert" input, first, from the UN Secretariat, and second, from an expert group constituted either on an ad hoc basis or within the framework of the Commission or its Sub-Commission or of the General Assembly itself.

In general terms, a procedure designed to reflect these considerations might take something like the following form:

> *Step 1:* the process would be activated by a decision by a UN organ that consideration should be given to the desirability of recognizing a particular claim as a new human right;
>
> *Step 2:* the Secretary-General would prepare a preliminary study identifying the major qualitative issues raised by the proposal such as: the content and definition of the proposed norm, the basis on which it may be considered to be a part of international law, its relationship to the existing range of human rights norms, and the extent to which it reflects existing (or proposed) state practice;
>
> *Step 3:* comments on, inter alia, the issues identified in the preliminary study would be solicited by the Secretary-General from governments, relevant international and regional organizations and nongovernmental organizations;
>
> *Step 4:* the Secretary-General would then prepare a comprehensive study reflecting the comments received under step 3 and dealing with all relevant aspects of the proposal;
>
> *Step 5:* an ad hoc committee designated by the Commission on Human Rights would report, within 3 months of being appointed, to the Commission on the proposal;
>
> *Step 6:* the Commission would adopt a recommendation on the matter addressed to the General Assembly; and
>
> *Step 7:* the matter would be considered by the General Assembly, and the process would culminate in the proclamation of a new human right or in a decision to defer action on the proposal (either indefinitely or for a given period of time).

VII. Conclusion

While the proposed procedure may appear rather cumbersome, it is in fact no more complicated than those regularly used by other international organs in comparable undertakings.[44] In any event, the importance of ensuring, first,

[44] It is considerably less complicated than a procedure proposed in 1973 by Sir Gerald Fitzmaurice by which legislative effect could be given to relevant General Assembly resolutions. His procedure would be embodied in a treaty and would provide for the examination of appropriate resolutions by a "Consortium of jurists" nominated by an authority independent of the General Assembly. The Consortium's recommendation ("project") would then be submitted to a standing "College of the United Nations" and, if adopted by a large majority of the states that had originally supported the resolution, would become binding on all of them (but not on states that had never participated in the scheme). *See* Fitzmaurice, *The Future of Public International Law and the International Legal System in the Circumstances of Today*, in INSTITUT DE DROIT INTERNATIONAL, LIVRE DU CENTENAIRE 1873–1973: EVOLUTION ET PERSPECTIVES DU DROIT INTERNATIONAL 196, 271–75 (1973). *See also* comments on the proposal by, inter alia, Virally (*id.* at 376), Bindschedler (*id.* at 377), Seidl-Hohenveldern (*id.* at 381) and Waldock (*id.* at 384).

that the recognition of a new human right is generally accepted as being authoritative (in the sense of giving rise to realistic expectations of compliance by states), and second, that the integrity and standing of the existing body of rights is maintained, easily justifies the adoption of such a procedure. Moreover, the introduction of the proposed safeguards would eliminate the existing possibility that new rights could be proclaimed without any prior reflection or scrutiny, ensure that organs subordinate to the General Assembly could not undermine the Assembly's authority by unilaterally proclaiming new human rights, and ensure that states' endorsement of a particular norm would be based on an understanding both of the broad content of the norm and of the legal significance of their support for it.

It must be emphasized, however, that just as the *appellations contrôlées* system neither provides an ironclad guarantee of high-quality wine nor eliminates the possibility of fraudulent practices, so too would the procedure proposed above not be immune to manipulation or even circumvention by a determined political majority in the General Assembly. Nevertheless, such practices would be rendered considerably more difficult than at present.

[7]

COMMENTARY

The Right to Development as an Emerging Human Right

ROLAND Y. RICH*

The right to development is at the threshold of general acceptance as positive international law. It has been the subject of detailed assessment by academicians and practitioners.[1] It figures in one of the major works on the International Law of Development,[2] and has been accepted as a fundamental human right by two current judges of the International Court of Justice (I.C.J.).[3] Both the United Nations General Assembly[4] and the Commission on Human

---

* Australian Department of Foreign Affairs, Canberra. B.A., LL.B., University of Sydney; Master of International Law, Australian National University.

The views expressed herein are those of the author and do not necessarily represent those of the Department of Foreign Affairs.

1. See Hague Academy of International Law and United Nations University Workshop, The Right to Development at the International Level (R.-J. Dupuy, ed. 1980) [hereinafter cited as Hague Academy/UNU Workshop].

2. See M. Flory, Droit international du développement 29 (1977).

3. See K. M'Baye, Le droit au développement comme un droit de l'homme, 5 Revue des droits de l'homme 503 (1972); M. Bedjaoui, Towards a New International Economic Order 72 (1979).

4. See, e.g., Alternative Approaches and Ways and Means Within the United Nations System for Improving the Effective Enjoyment of Human Rights and Fundamental Freedoms, G.A. Res. 34/46, U.N. GAOR Supp. (No. 46), U.N. Doc A/34/704 (1979). "[The General Assembly] *[e]mphasizes* that the right to development is a human right and that equality of opportunity for development is as much a prerogative of nations as of individuals within nations . . . ." Id. para. 8.

Rights[5] have included the idea in various resolutions. Most recently, a resolution passed by the Commission on Human Rights requested a working group of governmental experts to continue work on a draft Declaration on the Right to Development.[6] The adoption of such a Declaration promises to focus the existing debate on the nature and content of this right.

Any analysis of the right to development requires an examination of the very nature of human rights and must therefore evaluate a number of intrinsically complex areas. Ultimately, recognition of the right to development would require international acceptance of a significant expansion of international law. International law has long recognized the individual as the beneficiary of human rights and has relatively recently recognized that peoples may exercise certain human rights. But the right to development would require international acceptance of a human right designed to benefit individuals, peoples, and nations in a holistic and interconnected manner.

An analysis of the right to development must also address broader questions concerning the process of development of international law. It must address the status of General Assembly resolutions and the more challenging issue of the interpretation of state practice. Because state practice is often unaccompanied by articulation of underlying obligations and reasons for actions taken, the *opinio juris* of the actors is difficult to discern. In addition, this practice inevitably does not fully match the expectations of the General Assembly resolutions.

Perhaps the most fundamental question in an analysis of this unique right is the very role of international law. Has it evolved into a discipline that can influence the course of events and lead even reluctant nations towards a common goal? Or is it merely a code that assists States to interrelate?

Discussion of these issues will necessarily recur throughout this

---

5. See, e.g., C.H.R. Res. 4/33, 62 U.N. ESCOR Supp. (No. 6) at 74-75, U.N. Doc. E/CN.4/1257 (1977); C.H.R. Res. 10/34, 63 U.N. ESCOR Supp. (No. 4) at 114-15, U.N. Doc. E/CN.4/1292 (1978); C.H.R. Res. 4/35, 64 U.N. ESCOR Supp. (No. 6) at 106-07, U.N. Doc. E/CN.4/1347 (1979); C.H.R. Res. 5/35, 64 U.N. ESCOR Supp. (No. 6) at 108-09, U.N. Doc. E/CN.4/1347 (1979); C.H.R. Res. 6/36, 65 U.N. ESCOR Supp. (No. 3) at 162-64, U.N. Doc. E/CN.4/1408 (1980); C.H.R. Res. 7/36, 65 U.N. ESCOR Supp. (No. 3) at 164-66, U.N. Doc. E/CN.4/1408 (1980); C.H.R. Res. 36/37, 66 U.N. ESCOR Supp. (No. 5) at 237-40, U.N. Doc. E/CN.4/1475 (1981).

6. C.H.R. Res. 17/38, 67 U.N. ESCOR Supp. (No. 2) at 130, U.N. Doc. E/CN.4/1982/L.24/Rev.1 (1982).

Commentary. Nonetheless, the major task remains an examination of the right to development itself. This Commentary will first identify some of the possible bases on which the right to development may be founded, recognizing that as with all human rights the bases are not restricted to legal principles, but include broader moral and ethical concerns. It will then weigh the evidence pointing towards the existence of this human right. Next, the nature of the right to development will be analyzed and set in context with other human rights. This Commentary will then discuss whether it is necessary or useful to have such a right. Finally, the inescapable question will be examined: is the right to development part of international law?

I. THE SOURCES OF THE RIGHT TO DEVELOPMENT

It has been argued that the right to development springs from a moral duty owed by the industrialized nations to the developing world.[7] While moral imperatives by themselves do not create international law, a process that still requires legal articulation and widespread practice, they are today the driving force behind the emergence of new principles of international law.[8] It is therefore useful to examine some authoritative expressions of this moral duty before turning to the issue of its translation into legal doctrine.

The clearest exposition of this duty can be found in several papal pronouncements dating back to 1941. In that year, Pope Pius XII emphasized the "imprescriptible requirement that the material goods created by God for all men be equitably divided amongst all, according to the principles of justice and of charity."[9] Twenty years later Pope John XXIII stated that the "solidarity that unites all men into one family" imposes a duty on more developed nations to help alleviate the poverty of developing countries and to

7. M'Baye, supra note 3, at 522.

8. Fifty years ago, the argument that moral imperatives have no place in international law could have been sustained. Such an argument, however, is no longer tenable in a discipline that outlaws the threat or use of force, see U.N. Charter art. 2, para. 4 ("[a]ll members shall refrain in their international dealings from the threat or use of force"), and that sets aside treaties as contrary to *jus cogens*. E.g., Vienna Convention on the Law of Treaties, May 23, 1969, art. 53, U.N. Doc. A/CONF.39/27, reprinted in 8 I.L.M. 679 ("[a] treaty is void if, at the time of its conclusion, it conflicts with a peremptory norm of general international law").

9. Haquari, Le droit au développement: fondements et sources, in Hague Academy/UNU Workshop, supra note 1, at 22, 25.

assist the less fortunate to "enjoy the most elementary rights of a human being."[10]

These convictions transcend the sphere of religion. The 1941 Atlantic Charter expressed hope that in the post-war world "all the men in all the lands may live out their lives in freedom from fear and want."[11] A study by the U.N. Secretary-General of the international dimensions of the right to development speaks of "moral interdependence."[12] Rather than expand upon the moral nature of the issue, however, this Commentary will next examine the passage of the right to development from moral to legal norms.

The United Nations Charter precipitated two relevant developments in international law. These were the metamorphosis of international law from a law of coexistence to a law of cooperation, and the emergence of mankind as a proper subject of international law. These related concepts are both major sources of the right to development. One commentator has described the "international law of cooperation" as concerned with "the organization and implementation of joint endeavours on a binational, regional or multinational level directed to human welfare."[13] Another commentator states that "the old international law of rights and duties is being supplemented by an international law of cooperation"[14] Pro-

10. Id. Pope John-Paul II has said that major problems require "organized cooperation between all the nations." Le Monde, Oct. 4, 1979, at 8, col. 4. The first person to proclaim the existence of the right to development was Cardinal Duval. He proclaimed the right to development in Algiers on January 1, 1969. Sanson, Du droit des peuples sous-développés au développement au droit des hommes et des communautés à être soi, in Hague Academy/UNU Workshop, supra note 1, at 192, 229.

11. Atlantic Charter, Jan. 1, 1942, 55 Stat. 1600, E.A.S. No. 236.

12. Report of the Secretary-General, The International Dimensions of the Right to Development as a Human Right, Doc. E/CN.4/1334, at 24, para. 46 (1979) [hereinafter cited as 1979 Report of the Secretary-General]. See also L. Pearson, Partners in Development: Report of the Commission on International Development (1969). The Pearson Report succinctly explains the concept:

> If the rich countries . . . concentrate on the elimination of poverty and backwardness at home and ignore them abroad, what would happen to the principles by which they seek to live? Could the moral and social foundations of their own societies remain firm and steady if they washed their hands of the plight of others?

Id. at 8.

13. Friedmann, The Relevance of International Law to the Processes of Economic and Social Development, in 2 The Future of the International Legal Order, Wealth and Resources 3, 10 (R. Falk & C. Black eds. 1970) (Friedmann finds that the preamble and article 1(3) of the Charter reflect the international law of cooperation).

14. Fenwick, International Law; The Old and the New, 60 Am. J. Int'l L. 475, 482 (1966).

fessor Jenks describes this law as "the common law of mankind."[15] In this spirit, international law becomes a purposeful law, no longer merely reflecting international conduct, but instead a tool to influence that conduct and to achieve certain goals.

A basic reason for this change is that States are no longer considered the sole subjects of international law. With the increase in the number of nations has come the recognition that international law must also deal with individuals and peoples on the one hand, and mankind on the other. As the Preamble to the U.N. Charter notes, mankind thirsts for peace and development and it is in the interest of mankind that international law directs the actions of States by imposing upon them a duty to cooperate, which has also been called a duty of solidarity.[16] This duty is the fundamental source of the right to development.

It is difficult to define precisely this duty of cooperation, but the U.N. Charter provides a starting point. Article 55 gives the United Nations a role in the promotion of "economic and social progress and development" as well as "universal respect for human rights."[17] The role of Member States is set forth in article 56. They pledge "to take joint and separate action in cooperation with the Organization" to achieve the objectives set out in article 55.[18] The duty of cooperation is further defined in the Declaration on the Establishment of a New International Economic Order (NIEO)[19] which implies that colonial powers have an obligation to assist the development of their former colonies, a position widely espoused in developing countries, as well as Soviet-bloc nations.[20] The Declara-

15. C. Jenks, Law in the World Community 2 (1967). It has also been described as the international law of welfare. B. Roeling, International Law in an Expanded World 85-86 (1960).

16. M'Baye, supra note 3, at 523. See also de Vey Mestdagh, The Right to Development, 28 Neth. Int'l L. Rev. 30, 43 (1981).

17. U.N. Charter art. 55.

18. Id. art. 56. This duty is repeated in the Declaration on Principles of International Law Concerning Friendly Relations and Cooperation among States in accordance with the Charter of the United Nations. G.A. Res. 2625, 25 U.N. GAOR Supp. (No. 18) (Annex) at 68, U.N. Doc. A/8018 (1970). According to this Declaration: "States should co-operate in the promotion of economic growth throughout the world, especially that of the developing countries."

19. G.A. Res. 3201, 29 U.N. GAOR, Sixth Special Sess. Supp. (No. 1) at 3, U.N. Doc. A/9559 (1974).

20. Because the USSR does not see itself as a former colonial power, under this theory it would be exculpated from any responsibility to assist developing countries. The Council for Mutual Economic Assistance (CMEA) states that: "the entire responsibility for the backwardness of the developing nations rests with the imperialist powers and their colonialist

tion pronounces "[t]he right of all States, territories and peoples under foreign occupation, alien and colonial domination . . . to restitution and full compensation for the exploitation and depletion of, and damages to, the natural resources and all other resources of those States, territories and peoples."[21]

The argument that colonial powers should assist their former colonies is based on two rationales. First is the idea that wealth extracted from colonies should be "returned to its source."[22] This rationale is difficult to sustain, however, because it is not at all clear that the economic growth of the industrialized countries rests upon colonial exploitation.[23] Nor is it clear whether the great colonial powers "profited more from their colonies than they put into them."[24]

A more cogent rationale is that underdevelopment is not just a matter of backwardness or retardation. Rather, it is the by-product of the development of the Western countries.[25] This view sees underdevelopment as an unnatural stage through which the industrialized countries did not pass. Growth was blocked by the destruction of the natural balances in place before colonialism, coupled with structural disadvantages built into the present international economic system. If this is true, it follows that former colonial powers, if they are to cooperate in aiding the economic progress of their former colonies, would need to take corrective measures, including effecting structural adjustments.

This latter rationale would allow easy identification of those States entitled to development assistance and those States obligated to contribute to that assistance. State practice does not completely accord with this rationale, however, because development assistance is not limited to former colonies. In addition, the former

---

and neo-colonialist policy of plundering the national riches of those countries." CMEA, Collected Reports on Various Activities of Bodies of the CMEA in 1977, at 233 (1977), quoted in 1979 Report of the Secretary-General, supra note 12, at 27 n.22.

21. G.A. Res. 3201, 29 U.N. GAOR, Sixth Special Sess. Supp. (No. 1) at 3, U.N. Doc. A/9559 (1974).

22. Report of the Seminar on the Realization of Economic and Social Rights with Particular Reference to Developing Countries, U.N. Doc. ST/TAO/HR/40, para. 22 (Lusaka, June 23—July 4, 1970), quoted in 1979 Report of the Secretary-General, supra note 12, at 27 n.24.

23. R. Rothstein, The Weak in the World of the Strong: The Developing Countries in the International System 7 (1977).

24. Bergen, Speaking to the Third World, Commentary, Oct. 1981, at 29, 32. Peter L. Bergen is the U.S. representative on the Working Group on the Right to Development established by the Commission on Human Rights.

25. M. Bedjaoui, supra note 3, at 67.

colonial powers do not agree with the basic premises supporting the argument. The mere fact of colonialism does not appear, therefore, to be a sufficient basis for the right to development. Nevertheless, it is clearly a relevant factor.[26] This is demonstrated by the nexus between the level of development assistance by States and their former colonial relationships.[27]

The concepts of equity and justice may also provide bases for the right to development.[28] The term "justice" is used both in the preamble and in article 1 of the U.N. Charter. Both the Charter and some authorities lend support to the view that justice somehow goes beyond international law, possessing a dynamic quality.[29] This is demonstrated in the opinion of Judge Padilla Nervo that the International Court of Justice is free to interpret its Statute "in accordance with the constant evolution of the concepts of justice, principles of law and teachings of publicists."[30]

The U.N. General Assembly linked justice to the development process when it stated that global economic development should be established "on the basis of justice, equality and mutual benefit."[31] Nonetheless, the vague and ill-defined nature of the concept of justice does not permit a conclusion that there is an affirmative duty

26. "Aid can be motivated in part by comparatively straightforward political and/or ideological purposes: [for example] . . . to strengthen donors' cultural and historical ties with particular, including ex-colonial, regions . . . ." Organization for Economic Co-operation and Development, Development Co-operation Review 27 (1981) (Development Assistance Committee) [hereinafter cited as 1981 Development Review].

27. An extreme example of this linkage is Australian aid to Papua New Guinea, which amounts to over half of total Australian bilateral aid. See Dept. of Foreign Affairs (Australia), Development Cooperation: Annual Review 1979-80, at 76-77 (1981).

28. See Alston, The Right to Development at the International Level, in Hague Academy/UNU Workshop, supra note 1, at 99, 104 (finding the concept of justice to be the underlying theme of the right to development); Case Concerning the Continental Shelf (Tunisia v. Libya), 1982 I.C.J. 18, 60 ("equity as a legal concept is a direct emanation of the idea of justice"). John Rawls argued that justice requires all social values to "be distributed equally unless an unequal distribution of any, or all, of these values is to everyone's advantage." J. Rawls, A Theory of Justice, 61-62 (1971).

29. The preamble states that the establishment of "conditions under which justice and respect for the obligations arising from treaties and other sources of international law can be maintained" is a general aim of the Charter. Article 1(1) states as a general purpose of the United Nations that the Member States agree "to bring about by peaceful means, and in conformity with the principles of justice and international law," settlements of potential breaches of the peace. The concept of justice, while clearly linked to that of international laws, appears through the provisions of the Charter to have some force of its own.

30. South West Africa Cases (Ethiopia v. S. Afr.; Liberia v. S. Afr.), 1966 I.C.J. 4, 464.

31. Preparations for an International Development Strategy for the Third United Nations Development Decade, G.A. Res. 33/193, 33 U.N. GAOR Supp. (No. 45) at 121, 122, U.N. Doc. A/93/45 (1979).

to aid developing countries. That duty, if it exists at all, must be evident from state practice.

The concept of equity also has been stated as "an independent and autonomous source of law."[32] Another commentator argues that there are three aspects of equity: equality, proportionality, and a vocation to go beyond judicial forms in order to arrive at just ends.[33] The more commonly accepted view of positive international law, however, recognizes equity only within or as a part of the law. The I.C.J. explained in the *North Sea Continental Shelf Cases* that "it is not a matter of applying equity simply as a matter of abstract justice, but of applying a rule of law which itself requires the application of equitable principles."[34] The Court further limited the utility of equity as an independent tool to establish law by defining equitable principles as "actual rules of law" founded on "very general precepts of justice and good faith."[35]

The legal contexts in which these equitable principles are appropriate are also limited. They are well suited for matters relating to maritime delimitation such as the *North Sea Cases*, where an equitable result must be reached,[36] and in the succession of States in matters other than treaties.[37] But even though international law refers to equitable principles in such cases, these principles could not be said to be autonomous of the law.

Finally, international law recognizes the existence of equitable principles as a "balancing element" within certain relationships.[38] Some of the relationships currently recognized in this context include boundary disputes between bordering States and disputes

32. Report of the International Law Commission, 31 U.N. GAOR Su. p. (No. 10) at 1, 317 U.N. Doc. A/31/10 (1976).

33. Lecture by Paul Reuter, International Law Seminar, Geneva (June 9, 1977). Reuter does not refer to the distinction between equity within the law and equity autonomous of the law, but it would appear that he accepts the existence of the latter in his conclusion that equity could be a driving force towards the establishment of the NIEO.

34. North Sea Continental Shelf Cases (W. Ger. v. Den.; W. Ger. v. Neth.), 1969 I.C.J. 47.

35. Id. at 48.

36. See, e.g., Convention on the Law of the Sea, U.N. Doc. A/CONF.62/122 (1982) [hereinafter cited as LOS Convention]. Article 74(1) states: "The delimitation of the exclusive economic zone between States with opposite or adjacent coasts shall be effected by agreement on the basis of international law . . . in order to achieve an equitable solution." Article 83(1) uses identical language in reference to delimitation of the continental shelf.

37. See, e.g., Report of the International Law Commission, supra note 32, at 357-58. The draft articles on this subject being prepared by the ILC contain references to "equitable compensation" and "equitable proportion."

38. Id. at 317.

between predecessor and successor States over the assumption of external obligations. The emergence of the concept of the global community, the acceptance of global interdependence, and the recognition of mankind as a subject of international law, however, may eventually unite nations sufficiently to allow more general application of the principle of equity as a balancing element in their relationships. Such an eventuality could provide an additional source of the right to development.

The above discussion of moral and legal principles indicates a number of possible bases for the right to development. But the existence of a foundation does not mean the right exists. The essential building block in international law remains the consent of States. It is therefore necessary to examine and weigh the evidence of State consent and practice pointing to the emergence of the right to development.

II. AN EVALUATION OF THE EVIDENCE

Although evidence of the existence of the right to development must be consistent with a system of law based on the consent of States, States do not have to expressly recognize the right in a binding instrument. As Brierly notes, "what is sought for is a general recognition among states of a certain practice as obligatory . . . . This test of *general* recognition is necessarily a vague one; but it is the nature of customary law . . . not to be susceptible of exact or final formulation."[39] Consent can be discerned from written instruments on the one hand and state practice on the other. The former express binding obligations, or at least States' opinions of those obligations. The latter forms the living fabric of international law. The overlap of the two presents both the language of the law and the proof of its implementation.

This Commentary will now turn to an identification of shared objectives of the international legal system, expressed through well-known written instruments. Following this, an analysis of state practice will be presented indicating where state practice incorporates these shared goals, and identifying specific areas of support drawn from wide-spread state practice.

---

39. J. Brierly, The Law of Nations 61 (6th ed. 1963).

A. *International Instruments*

1. *Legal Validity of General Assembly Normative Resolutions*

A discussion of the evidence based on international instruments inevitably begins with the question of the legal validity of normative resolutions of international organizations, and in particular, those of the U.N. General Assembly. This Commentary will not reiterate all the arguments advanced on this question; the issue cannot, however, be avoided completely because it influences any evaluation of the evidence.

Article 10 of the U.N. Charter provides an appropriate beginning for discussion. Strictly interpreted, that article empowers the General Assembly only to "make recommendations."[40] But it can be argued that the distinction between a "recommendation" of the General Assembly and a "decision" of the Security Council, which carries considerable weight, "is artificial and practically valueless because for the same body, one or other expression is used quite indifferently."[41]

Regardless of the official status of a General Assembly resolution, these resolutions can create what has been described as the "legislative energy" of the General Assembly.[42] The developing countries generate this energy because for them "a resolution holds a real attraction . . . because of its flexibility, its rapidity and the security it gives these countries through the control of the technique as a result of their numbers."[43] But this presents two important questions. First, how does a resolution become transformed from a hortatory pronouncement into international law? And second, what is the effect of a resolution on those who have rejected it, or simply not accepted it?

The answers to these questions are interrelated. It is now generally accepted that there are methods by which General Assembly

---

40. U.N. Charter art. 10. See Schacter, Towards a Theory of International Obligation, 8 Va. J. Int'l L. 300, 311-19 (1968).

41. M. Bedjaoui, supra note 3, at 178. Bedjaoui cites articles 18, 27, 36 and 37 of the Charter as support. This argument, however, ignores the distinction between an operational decision and a recommendation on a matter of substance. In the latter case, article 18 talks of General Assembly decisions on recommendations with respect to the maintenance of international peace and security.

42. Falk, On the Quasi-Legislative Competence of the General Assembly, 60 Am. J. Int'l L. 782, 791 (1966).

43. M. Bedjaoui, supra note 3, at 140.

resolutions may be transformed into international law.[44] In the *Texaco Arbitration*,[45] the Libyan government cited various General Assembly resolutions[46] as supporting its view that a State may as a matter of right nationalize foreign-owned investments to ensure the sovereignty of the State over natural resources.[47] The arbitrator, however, noted that an analysis of the legal value of these resolutions based on the principles stated in them must distinguish between the situation where States generally have expressed agreement with an already existing principle, and the situation where new principles have been advanced and rejected by "representative groups of States."[48] The first type of resolution codifies existing customary international law. The second, however, has "nothing more than a *de lege ferenda* value . . . in the eyes of the States which have adopted them; as far as the [other States] are concerned, the rejection of these same principles implies that they consider them as being *contra legem*."[49]

In an attempt to circumvent this problem, some resolutions purport to be declaratory statements of existing international law. A declaration expressing a commonly held principle of law may thus be a reference point of international law.[50] But a declaration including principles not enjoying universal support raises the question of whether such a declaration is opposable as against a State

44. Falk suggests a process of examining the resolution for precision of language and specificity of rights and duties, followed by an analysis of support for the resolution. Falk, supra note 42, at 786. Dupuy adds a third issue: whether the resolution contains some means to encourage its observance. Dupuy, Sources of the Right to Development, Concluding Remarks to Part I of the Hague Workshop on the Right to Development, in Hague Academy/UNU Workshop, supra note 1, at 150. Dupuy has employed this method to decide the Texaco Arbitration award. Texaco Arbitration (Libya v. California Asiatic Oil Co.; Libya v. Texaco Overseas Petroleum Co.), reprinted in 17 I.L.M. 1 (1978). (Dupuy considered the voting patterns, the composition of the groups opposing and abstaining on the resolution, and the explanations given for votes made on a resolution adopted by consensus).

45. Texaco Arbitration, supra note 44.

46. Permanent Sovereignty Over Natural Resources, G.A. Res. 3171, 28 U.N. GAOR Supp. (No. 30) at 52-53, U.N. Doc. A/9030 (1973); Declaration on the Establishment of a New International Economic Order, G.A. Res. 3201, 29 U.N. GAOR, Sixth Special Sess. Supp. (No. 1) at 3, U.N. Doc. A/9559 (1974); Charter of Economic Rights and Duties of States, G.A. Res. 3281, 29 U.N. GAOR Supp. (No. 31) at 50, U.N. Doc. A/9631 (1974).

47. Texaco Arbitration, supra note 44, at 27-31.

48. Id. at 30, para. 87.

49. Id.

50. See, e.g., Declaration on the Granting of Independence to Colonial Countries and Peoples, G.A. Res. 1514, 15 U.N. GAOR Supp. (No. 16) at 66-67, U.N. Doc. A/4684 (1960); Resolution on Permanent Sovereignty over Natural Resources, G.A. Res. 1803, 17 U.N. GAOR Supp. (No. 17) at 15, U.N. Doc. A/5217 (1962).

not accepting it. This problem is at the heart of the debate on the NIEO and thus also the debate on the right to development.

To assess the binding effect of a General Assembly resolution on States that did not vote for it, the interaction between the resolution and state practice should be considered. State practice may point to widespread acceptance of the norms contained in the resolution, indicating that the norms express customary international law. If so, the actions of a State that opposes the resolution should nevertheless be examined for acceptance of, or acquiescence to, the norm. In this way, the resolution could become binding on the non-accepting State as an expression of customary international law. A State that does not want to be bound by a resolution must therefore consistently and expressly oppose the norms contained in the resolution in both word and deed.

2. *Evidence Expressed in International Instruments*

Having made the necessary qualifications about the legal validity of General Assembly resolutions, an examination of international legal instruments can now be undertaken. There are many instruments that provide some evidence of the right to development. As discussed above, articles 55 and 56 of the U.N. Charter establish a duty of all States to cooperate for economic and social progress and for development and universal respect for human rights.[51] This duty can be traced to the Covenant of the League of Nations[52] which, in reference to former colonies emerging as States, provided "the well-being and development of such peoples form a sacred trust of civilisation,"[53] as well as to the Atlantic Charter's assurance that all men should enjoy "freedom from fear and want."[54] The International Labor Organization (ILO) expressed similar goals in 1944, asserting the right of all human beings "to pursue both their material well-being and spiritual freedom in conditions of . . . dignity of economic security."[55]

---

51. Supra notes 17-18 and accompanying text.

52. League of Nations Covenant (reprinted in 3 Malloy, Treaties, Conventions, International Acts, Protocols and Agreements 3331 (1923); M. Hudson, 1 International Legislation (1931)).

53. Id. art. 22, para. 1.

54. Atlantic Charter, supra note 11.

55. "[A]ll human beings, irrespective of race, creed or sex, have the right to pursue both their material well-being and their spiritual freedom in conditions of freedom and dignity of economic security and equal opportunity . . . . " International Labor Organization, Declara-

The consitutive instruments of a number of specialized agencies contain similar expressions of a duty to cooperate, in particular to achieve high standards of nutrition, health, and education.[56] The Constitution of the United Nations Industrial Development Organization, as the most recent expression of community goals,[57] deserves particular attention. The preamble to the Constitution speaks frequently of equity in reference to development concerns.[58] More pertinently, the Consitution describes "international cooperation for development" as "the shared goal and common obligation of all countries."[59] It depicts this obligation as a principle of international law,[60] and in contrast to article 56 of the U.N. Charter, does not tie the duty to voluntary cooperation.

The General Assembly has attempted to specify the obligation of States to assist with international economic development. Many of its resolutions in this area have been adopted by consensus. These resolutions include those inaugurating the three Development Decades,[61] and the 1974 Declaration and Programme of Action on the Establishment of a New International Economic Order.[62] The Declaration affirms that Member States are to work urgently for the establishment of the NIEO based on equity and cooperation

---

tion at Philadelphia, International Labour Conference, Record of Proceedings, 26th Sess., at 622 (1944), reprinted in Alston, supra note 28, at 100.

56. E.g., Constitution of the United Nations Educational, Scientific and Cultural Organization, Nov. 16, 1945, art. 1, 61 Stat. 2495, T.I.A.S. 1580, 4 U.N.T.S. 275; Constitution of the United Nations Food and Agriculture Organization, as amended, Oct. 16, 1945, preamble, para. 1, 12 U.S.T. 980, T.I.A.S. 4803; Constitution of the World Health Organization art. 1, opened for signature July 22, 1946, 62 Stat. 2679, T.I.A.S. No. 1808, 14 U.N.T.S. 185.

57. Constitution of United Nations Industrial Development Organization, opened for signature April 8, 1979, U.N. Doc. A/CONF.90/19. Although not yet in force, the constitution is an important expression of international law in view of the number of States that have already ratified it. As of January 31, 1982 seventy-three nations had ratified it. Article 25 of the constitution requires 80 ratifications, after which the parties are required to agree that the constitution enters into force.

58. The preamble refers to the word "equitable" four times: twice to describe the economic and social order the organization is striving to achieve, once in relation to the establishment of "rational and equitable international economic relations," and finally in reference to the goal of securing for developing countries their "equitable share in total world industrial production." Id. at 1-2.

59. Id. at 2.

60. Id.

61. G.A. Res. 1710, 16 U.N. GAOR Supp. (No. 17) at 17, U.N. Doc. A/5100 (1960); G.A. Res. 2626, 25 U.N. GAOR Supp. (No. 28) at 39, U.N. Doc. A/8028 (1970); G.A. Res. 35/56, 35 U.N. GAOR Supp. (No. 48) at 106, U.N. Doc. A/35/48 (1980).

62. G.A. Res. 3201, 29 U.N. GAOR, Sixth Special Sess. Supp. (No. 1) at 3, U.N. Doc. A/9559 (1974).

among all States. But the culmination of the earlier resolutions is the Charter of Economic Rights and Duties of States.[63] The Group of 77 draft of the Charter invited the General Assembly to adopt the Charter "as a first measure of codification and progressive development" of international law relating to development cooperation.[64]

The Charter, however, was not acceptable to a number of States.[65] Disagreement centered on provisions allowing compensation for nationalizations to be determined under national, not international law.[66] But many articles of the Charter may be interpreted as widely, perhaps universally, held objectives of the international community. The Charter, for example, states "[i]nternational cooperation for development is the shared goal and common duty of all States,"[67] and that States should cooperate through international organizations.[68] In addition, the Charter includes articles delimiting specific areas of cooperation for the economic enhancement of developing countries; among them, increased official development assistance,[69] tariff preferences,[70] and transfer of technology.[71] More general areas of concerted action include structural changes designed to facilitate "more rational and equitable economic relations,"[72] and protection of the deep seabed as the "common heritage of mankind."[73]

Recently, the thirty-eighth Session of the Commission on Human Rights adopted a resolution to reconvene a working group for the purpose of elaborating a draft declaration on the right to development.[74] The resolution was cosponsored by three industrialized countries[75] and was adopted by a vote of 41-0, with the United States abstaining. This vote indicates a general acceptance of the right to development.

---

63. G.A. Res. 3281, 29 U.N. GAOR Supp. (No. 31) at 50, U.N. Doc. A/9631 (1974).

64. Texaco Arbitration, supra note 44, at 30, para. 88 (quoting U.N. Doc. A/C.2/L.1386 (1974), at 2).

65. Id.

66. Id. para. 85.

67. Charter of Economic Rights and Duties of States, supra note 63, art. 17.

68. Id. arts. 10, 11.

69. Id. art. 22.

70. Id. art. 18.

71. Id. art. 13.

72. Id. art. 8.

73. Id. art. 29.

74. C.H.R. Res. 17/38, supra note 6.

75. The three countries were France, Greece, and the Netherlands. Id.

Certain international instruments for the protection of human rights may also provide support for the right to development by creating "linkages" between human rights and development. A number of provisions of the International Bill of Human Rights[76] link the two. The Universal Declaration on Human Rights links, in effect, the existence of an equitable social and international order to the realization of the rights and freedoms guaranteed by the Universal Declaration.[77] Certain articles put the relationship between human rights and development in terms of a positive duty.[78] The Covenant on Economic, Social and Cultural Rights also refers to this relationship by recognizing the human right to an adequate standard of living and to the continuous improvement of living conditions.[79] The Covenant also recognizes the importance of international cooperation to implement this right.[80] Finally, the African Charter on Human and People's Rights explicitly recognizes the right to development as a human right.[81]

A linkage from the other direction, from development to human rights, may be found in the Charter of Economic Rights and Duties of States.[82] According to the Charter, one of the principles to govern economic as well as political and other relations among

---

76. The International Bill of Human Rights contains the Universal Declaration of Human Rights, G.A. Res. 217, 3 GAOR Resolutions, at 71, U.N. Doc. A/810 (1948) [hereinafter cited as Universal Declaration]; The International Covenant on Economic, Social and Cultural Rights, opened for signature by G.A. Res. 2200, 21 GAOR Supp. (No. 16), at 49, U.N. Doc. A/6316 (1966); The International Covenant on Civil and Political Rights, opened for signature by G.A. Res. 2200, 21 GAOR Supp. (No. 16) at 52, U.N. Doc. A/6316 (1966); and the Optional Protocol to the International Covenant on Civil and Political Rights, Annex to G.A. Res. 2200, 21 GAOR Supp. (No. 16) at 59, U.N. Doc. A/6316 (1966). United Nations Office of Public Information, The International Bill of Human Rights (1978).

77. See Universal Declaration, supra note 76, art. 28.

78. Id. art. 22 (though qualified by requiring consideration of the "resources [available] of each State," article 22 states "[e]veryone . . . is entitled to realization, through national effort and international cooperation . . . of the economic, social and cultural rights indispensible for his dignity").

79. International Covenant on Economic, Social and Cultural Rights, supra note 76.

80. Id. art. 11.

81. African Charter on Human and People's Rights, preamble, art. 22, adopted June 27, 1981, OAU Doc. CAB/LEG/67/3/Rev. 5, reprinted in 21 I.L.M. 58 (1982). The Charter provides:

> 1. All peoples shall have the right to their economic, social and cultural development with due regard to their freedom and identity and in the equal enjoyment of the common heritage of mankind.
> 2. States shall have the duty, individually or collectively, to ensure the existence of the right to development.

Id. art. 22.

82. Supra note 63.

States shall be "respect for human rights and fundamental freedoms."[83] The Charter has been viewed as " 'a counterpart in the economic field to the Universal Declaration of Human Rights and the International Covenants on Human Rights.' "[84] The Charter also provides a bridge to the International Bill of Human Rights[85] by imposing a duty upon States consistent with several principles underlying the resolutions giving content to the International Bill of Rights. In particular, the Charter states that "[e]very State has the primary responsibility to promote the economic, social and cultural development of its people."[86] The Charter thus transforms an international duty into a domestic duty. This links the nation and its nationals as subjects of development and as beneficiaries of the right to development.[87]

Some international instruments show an awareness of developing countries as a special, protected category of States. The Covenant on Economic, Social and Cultural Rights recognizes a category of "developing countries" and allows countries in this category to take account of their respective national economies before obligating them to extend the economic rights guaranteed under the Convention to non-nationals.[88] The International Convention on the Elimination of All Forms of Racial Discrimination recognizes, at the international level, the acceptability of affirmative action for disadvantaged groups.[89]

B. *State Practice*

The preceding survey has disclosed a number of general objectives of the international community. But these objectives do not achieve the status of obligations until they become custom or state

83. Id. ch. I(k).

84. 1 Proceedings of the United Nations Conference on Trade and Development (Third Session, Report and Annexes) 35, para. 210, U.N. Doc. TD/180 (1972).

85. Supra note 76.

86. Charter of Economic Rights and Duties of States, supra note 63, art. 7.

87. This unusual property of the right to development, its collective and individual nature, will be explored infra, notes 155-80 and accompanying text.

88. Supra note 76, art. 2(3).

89. International Convention on the Elimination of All Forms of Racial Discrimination of March 7, 1966, entered into force Jan. 4, 1969, 660 U.N.T.S. 195.

Capotorti concludes there is no conflict between nondiscrimination and special measures in favor of a minority group because the purpose of these measures is "to institute factual equality between the members of such groups and other individuals." Capotorti, Study on the Rights of Persons Belonging to Ethnic, Religious and Linguistic Minorities, U.N. Doc. E/CN.4/Sub.2/384/Rev.1 (1979).

practice.[90] State practice recognizing the right to development may be shown through evidence that customary international law recognizes developing countries as a special category and through evidence of consistent, widespread, and coherent responses to the problems of developing countries. It is not necessary to adduce evidence that all demands of the developing countries are being satisfied or even acted upon, nor is it necessary to assess the effectiveness of the action being taken in favor of developing countries.

Specific areas of state practice that should be examined include official development assistance (ODA), the role of international financial institutions, trade policies, and the transfer of technology from developed to developing nations. Other less obvious areas are also relevant, such as bilateral tax treaties and international environmental standards. And an area that deserves particular attention as an indication of current trends is the law of the sea.

When examining state practice in these areas, it is important to remember that although international law recognizes the sovereign equality of States, the right to development is based on a recognition of substantive inequality among States. It is therefore necessary to adduce evidence of recognition by States of this inequality, and then to examine whether this recognition leads to differential treatment designed to benefit developing countries.

1. *Official Development Assistance*

The most striking evidence of the recognition of inequality among States is the practice of providing development assistance to developing countries. ODA is a relatively recent phenomenon in international practice. It parallels the transformation of international law from a law of coexistence to a law of cooperation. Because the practice is now so widespread, it poses the fundamental question of whether ODA has become a legal obligation.

Official Development Assistance has become common place. The

---

90. The process requires "evidence of a clear response in State practice to the *opinio juris* expressed in United Nations resolutions, which strengthens the legal significance of the claim that the developing countries are acquiring a right to special treatment, which in turn is indispensable to the realization of the right to development." Verwey, The Recognition of the Developing Countries as Special Subjects of International Law Beyond the Sphere of United Nations Resolutions, in Hague Academy/UNU Workshop, supra note 1, at 372, 392. One author considers that the repetition of demands in the resolutions of international organizations has a psychological effect strengthening the claim that these resolutions are expressions of law. A. Pellet, Le Droit International du Développement 65-69 (1978).

United States began a development aid program unilaterally in 1949. Other Western countries soon followed, and by 1951 were providing aid loans equalling almost 1% of their GNP.[91] The United Nations commenced a technical assistance program in the 1950's.[92] Additionally, all members of the Development Assistance Committee (DAC) of the Organization for Economic Co-operation and Development (OECD) "have adopted the promotion of Third World development as one of their serious and demonstrated national objectives."[93]

The provision of development assistance is not limited to Western countries. Member States of the Organization of Petroleum Exporting Countries (OPEC) annually contribute nearly 3% of their GNP to development assistance.[94] It could well be said that all countries not in need of aid, with the possible exception of the Soviet-bloc,[95] provide aid to developing nations.

Now that development assistance is widespread, the focus has shifted to the quantity and quality of aid. The United Nations first set quantitative targets for ODA in 1960.[96] The International Development Strategy for the 1970's pegged the ODA target at 0.7% of GNP for DAC members.[97] While this target was not achieved,[98] a new initiative calls for the target to be met by 1985 and to increase thereafter.[99] There have also been measures implemented to improve the quality of development assistance by increasing the multilateral content, increasing the grant component, decreasing the amount of tied aid, granting more favorable terms for development loans, and alleviating the debt servicing problems of the de-

---

91. Report of the Independent Commission of International Development Issues, North-South: A Programme for Survival 38 (1979) [hereinafter cited as Brandt Commission Report].

92. Id.

93. 1981 Development Review, supra note 26, at 26.

94. Brandt Commission Report, supra note 91, at 224.

95. 1981 Development Review, supra note 26, at 122-123. In 1980, the USSR and other members of the Council for Mutual Economic Assistance (CMEA) devoted only 0.12% of their GNP to ODA. Ninety-five percent of this was concentrated in Cuba, North Korea, Vietnam, Afghanistan, Kampuchea, and Laos. Id. at 123.

96. See G.A. Res. 1522, 15 U.N. GAOR Supp. (No. 16) at 13, U.N. Doc. A/4684 (1960).

97. G.A. Res. 2626, 25 U.N. GAOR Supp. (No. 28) at 43, para. 43, U.N. Doc. A/8028 (1970). The United States and Switzerland did not accept this target.

98. DAC members contributed only 0.37% of GNP in 1980. 1981 Development Review, supra note 26, at 81.

99. G.A. Res. 35/56, 35 U.N. GAOR Supp. (No. 48) at 113, para. 98, U.N. Doc. A/35/48 (1980) (suggesting a target of 1% of GNP).

veloping countries.[100]

These facts demonstrate that ODA is a significant, nearly universal practice.[101] The DAC has stated that "global solidarity" is the motivation behind ODA.[102] Thus, ODA is arguably an obligation of developed countries. The existence of such an obligation implies that the duty to cooperate has become part of international law.

But can it be said that ODA is an obligation imposed by international law? Professor Schacter argues that the international law of development incorporates "a new conception of international entitlement to aid and preferences based on need."[103] The long history of grants of assistance and preferences to developing countries provides evidence of the acceptance by developed countries of this new responsibility.[104] In addition, the obligation to provide ODA forms a part of the domestic laws of several nations.[105] And as both the Brandt Commission and the OECD point out, the phenomenon of development assistance continues in spite of domestic criticism.[106] This evidence indicates that donor States tend to act as if they were legally obligated to provide ODA.

To the contrary, a 1971 U.N. Survey concluded that "no [obligation to contribute ODA] has been accepted in positive law."[107] But a more recent study by the Secretary-General states that "the time may now be ripe for a reconsideration of the issue."[108] Thus, it may be that on the basis of state practice, the obligation to provide

---

100. Brandt Commission Report, supra note 91, at 222-29. The problem of high debt service demands particular attention, as its cost averages 15% of the export earnings of developing countries and often is much higher. 1981 Development Review, supra note 26, at 72.

101. In 1980, total non-concessional ODA amounted to US$33 billion. 1981 Development Review, supra note 26, at 60. ODA flows provide more than 80% of the external financing of low-income countries and over 40% of the external financing of middle-income countries. Id. at 60.

102. OECD, Development Cooperation Review 63 (1980) [hereinafter cited as 1980 Development Review]. The DAC has recently enumerated three principal factors that actuate donors: national self-interest, unabashed humanitarianism, and global systems maintenance. 1981 Development Review, supra note 26, at 28.

103. Schacter, The Evolving International Law of Development, 15 Colum. J. Transnat'l L. 1, 9 (1976).

104. Id.

105. M. Flory, supra note 2, at 185-86.

106. Brandt Commission Report, supra note 91, at 225-26. See also 1981 Development Review, supra note 26, at 25-26.

107. International Law Commission, Survey of International Law: Working Paper Prepared by the Secretary-General 83, U.N. Doc. A/CN.4/245 (1971).

108. 1979 Report of the Secretary-General, supra note 12, at 141.

ODA is now part of international law and forms an important part of the right to development.

Some advocates of the right to development apparently see ODA as a legal obligation because they propose expanding current assistance through automatic taxation mechanisms. The Brandt Commission recommends automatic levies on international trade, arms production or exports, international travel, and the exploitation of the resources of the global commons.[109] Another commentator advocates taxing luxury goods, pollutants, income of transnational corporations, income derived from the exploitation of non-renewable resources, taxes collected from "guest workers," and the use of outer space.[110] There clearly are practical problems to implementing these proposals. Yet their very extravagence arguably reinforces the more modest conclusion that wealthy States have an obligation to provide some measure of development assistance.

2. *International Financial Institutions*

The practice of international financial institutions demonstrates a recognition of substantial inequality among nations and an attempt to translate this recognition into a differential distribution of benefits.

An essential purpose of the International Bank for Reconstruction and Development (IBRD) is "the encouragement of the development of productive facilities and resources in less developed countries."[111] Currently, the overwhelming majority of IBRD loans are made to developing countries.[112] Both the IBRD and the World Bank seem to have abandoned their traditional prudence in favor of a policy of accepting risks and granting loans for long-term development projects.[113] These loans offer amortization, grace period, and interest rate terms more favorable than those otherwise availa-

109. Brandt Commission Report, supra note 91, at 274.

110. M. Flory, supra note 2, at 185.

111. Articles of Agreement of the International Bank for Reconstruction and Development, opened for signature Dec. 27, 1945, art. 1, para. 1, 60 Stat. 1440, T.I.A.S. No. 1502, 2 U.N.T.S. 134. The other purposes of the IBRD are the assistance of post-war reconstruction, the promotion of foreign investment, the promotion of international trade, and the facilitation of international loans. Id. art. 1.

112. Verwey, supra note 90, at 375. By 1978, 98.7% of all loans were being extended to developing countries. Id. The bank's function was recently described as providing "financial and technical assistance for the development of its poorer member countries." International Bank for Reconstruction and Development, 1981 World Bank Atlas 2 (1982).

113. M. Flory, supra note 2, at 95.

ble to developing countries.[114] Loans from the International Development Association to the least developed countries offer even greater concessions.[115] These policies demonstrate a developed practice of providing preferential treatment to developing nations.

The same cannot be said as confidently of the International Monetary Fund (IMF). The IMF Articles of Agreement do not single out developing countries as a special group. One observer argues, however, that IMF practice in administering the Compensatory Financing Facility, the Extended Fund Facility, the Oil Facility Fund, the Supplementary Financing Facility, and the system of Buffer Stock Financing *de facto* recognizes developing countries as a special group, and extends favorable terms to them.[116] The observer concludes that "both in the case of the World Bank and the IMF, law runs behind practice."[117]

3. *International Trade*

After initial concentration on ODA as the means of accelerating their development, developing countries after World War II began to focus on the impact of international trade law on their development. That law, as embodied in the General Agreement on Tariffs and Trade (GATT),[118] and its most-favored-nation (MFN) clause,[119] was firmly based on the principle of soverign equality of States. As such, GATT sought to eliminate barriers to trade by fostering the principles of non-discrimination, reciprocity of concessions, and overall reduction of tariffs and other barriers to trade. A later recognition of the substantive inequality among nations, however, and steps taken in response to this realization, have changed the GATT organization "from a passive caretaker of a multilateral legal instrument to an international body affirmatively, and at times aggressively, attempting to promote the exports of less-developed countries."[120] A brief examination of this transformation in international trade law illustrates further the extent to which states now act as if the right to development were

114. Verwey, supra note 90, at 376.
115. Id. at 376-77.
116. Id. at 378-80.
117. Id. at 380.
118. General Agreement on Tariffs and Trade, Oct. 30, 1947, 61 Stat. 5, T.I.A.S. No. 1700, 55 U.N.T.S. 194, amended by T.I.A.S. No. 1890 (effective Jan. 1, 1948).
119. Id. art. 1.
120. K. Dam, The GATT Law and International Economic Organization 225 (1970).

positive law.

The original General Agreement only passively addressed the problems of developing countries.[121] Publication in 1958 of the Habeler Report,[122] however, led to acceptance of the view that "the predicament of the underdeveloped countries was due in no small measure to the trade policies of the developed countries."[123] As a result, some compensatory measures were undertaken within the GATT framework. For example, the principle of reciprocity was renounced in 1963 with the agreement that "in the trade negotiations every effort shall be made to reduce barriers to exports of the less-developed countries, but that the developed countries cannot expect to receive reciprocity from less-developed countries."[124]

It became apparent, however, that a forum outside GATT was necessary to facilitate resolution of the problems of the developing countries.[125] The forum chosen was the United Nations Conference on Trade and Development (UNCTAD). At the 1964 conference the developing countries pressed their view that international trade law should compensate for different levels of economic development[126] by allowing preferential tariff and non-tariff concessions in favor of the developing countries.[127] While these proposals received little support from developed countries in 1964,[128] by 1968 the participants in UNCTAD II unanimously agreed that a "mutually acceptable system of generalized non-reciprocal and non-dis-

121. Id. at 226-27.

122. Id. at 229 (citing A Report by a Panel of Experts, Trends in International Law (1958) (the Habeler Report)).

123. Id.

124. Contracting Parties to the General Agreement on Tariffs and Trade, Basic Instruments and Selected Documents, 12th Supp., 21st Sess., at 48 (1964) [hereinafter cited as Basic Instruments and Selected Documents].

125. "[I]n 1963, a group of twenty-one less developed countries, having decided that five years of study were sufficient and that the time for action had come, introduced a resolution [within GATT] which became known as the Action Programme." K. Dam, supra note 120, at 234. The resolution, reprinted in Basic Instruments and Selected Documents, supra note 124, at 36 § I.1(i),(ii), called for, *inter alia*, a halt on all tariff and non-tariff barriers by industrialized countries against certain imports from less developed countries. The failure of the Action Programme to win the commitment of the developed countries no doubt encouraged the calls for an outside forum.

126. Yusuf, Differential Treatment as a Dimension of the Right to Development, in Hague Academy/UNU Workshop, supra note 1, at 233, 235.

127. 1 Proceedings of the United Nations Conference on Trade and Development 20, (Final Act and Report) (General Principle 8), U.N. Doc. E/CONF.46/141 (1964).

128. The vote on Principle Eight was 78 to 11, with 23 abstentions. Most developed countries were either opposed, or abstained. Id. at 20 n.8.

criminatory preferences which would be beneficial to developing countries" should be established.[129]

GATT responded to these developments by enacting new provisions[130] "of great symbolic importance in . . . the new role of GATT in the thorny problem of development."[131] These provisions include the earlier renunciation of reciprocity and the granting of preferences to developing countries. GATT accomplished this by waiving the obligations of its developed Member States under the MFN clause.[132] Currently, GATT has on its agenda an examination of "the legal framework for differential and more favourable treatment for developing countries in relation to GATT provisions, in particular, the most-favored-nation clause."[133]

The changes in state practice concerning the trading position of developing countries lead to a few general observations. Initially, the changes confirm that developing countries constitute a special group in international law. Inclusion in this group is not identified primarily by colonial links, geography, or domestic economic systems. Rather, state practice has lifted the veil of sovereignty and recognized different levels of economic development underneath.

Next, international law as determined by state practice now appears to recognize the principle of differential treatment. Acceptance of this principle "implies notions of equity and justice[,]. . . reflects a trend towards the internationalization of welfare state principles and introduces at the international level such legal concepts as the collective responsibility of the community for the social and economic well-being of its members."[134] This principle

129. Proceedings of the United Nations Conference on Trade and Development, supra note 84, at 38.

130. The new provisions were included in a new Part IV entitled "Trade and Development" containing three articles addressing the trade problems of the developing countries. Contracting Parties to the General Agreement on Tariffs and Trade, Basic Instruments and Selected Documents, 13th Supp., 22d Sess., at 2 (1965). Perhaps the most important element is the provision in Article 36 abandoning reciprocity in trade negotiations between developed and developing countries. Id. at 4, para. 8. See generally K. Dam, supra note 120, at 238-41.

131. K. Dam, supra note 120, at 237. The developing countries, however, gained few precise commitments from these provisions. Id.

132. See Contracting Parties to the General Agreement on Tariffs and Trade, Basic Instruments and Selected Documents, 18th Supp., 27th Sess., at 24-25 (1972).

133. Report on the most-favored-nation clause, [1978] 2 Y.B. Int'l L. Comm'n, pt. 1, at 26, U.N. Doc. A/CN.4/SER.A/1978 (quoting Statement of the GATT Secretariat to the International Law Commission, Dec. 30, 1977) [hereinafter cited as 1978 ILC Report].

134. Yusuf, supra note 126, at 241.

would change traditional international law in two respects. First, it would compel a more activist role for international law. It would move beyond mere elimination of obstacles to the free play of economic relationships and would institute a planned course of action to influence economic forces towards a desired result. Second, it would accept a form of affirmative discrimination. Given these changes, the principle of differential treatment could prove to be a critical tool in the implementation of the right to development.

Still, it is not clear that differential treatment in favor of developing countries is an obligation imposed by law. It seems that it is not currently a part of positive international law, but that tomorrow it will be. This is an area where, in the space of but a few years, fundamental changes have occured, and where further advances seem assured.

In 1976, the International Law Commission (ILC) adopted draft Article 21[135] which allows non-reciprocal generalized systems of preferences within the MFN framework. The ILC viewed the article as a "progressive development" of the law.[136] Yet the ILC could not at that time find sufficient state practice, precedents, or doctrine to describe the article as a codification of international law.[137] The draft article has been criticized as not accurately reflecting state practice. Critics have suggested that the exception to the MFN principle should relate to "any treatment of a preferential or differentiated nature," rather than only to the generalized systems of preferences specifically addressed by article 21.[138] In response to this suggestion, the Special Rapporteur agreed that it would be appropriate to draft a new article once the legal status of differential treatment is settled in GATT.[139]

The ILC's actions reflect an anticipation of continued expansion

135. Article 21 of the Draft Articles on the most-favored-nation clause states: "A beneficiary State is not entitled under a most-favored nation clause to any treatment extended by a developed granting State to a developing third State on a non-reciprocal basis within a generalized system of preferences established by that granting State." Report of the International Law Commission on the work of its Twenty-eighth Session, 31 U.N. GAOR Supp. (No. 10) at 132, U.N. Doc. A/31/10 (1976) [hereinafter cited as 1976 ILC Report].

136. Id. at 16.

137. Id.

138. The Special Rapporteur reported that an alternative provision stating that "[a] beneficiary State is not entitled under a most-favoured-nation clause to any treatment of a preferential or differentiated nature extended by a developed granting State to a developing third State" had been set forward. 1978 ILC Report, supra note 133, at 24-25, para. 259 (footnote omitted).

139. Id. at 27, paras. 283-85.

of differential treatment as a legal obligation. Draft Article 27 explains that "[t]he present articles are without prejudice to the establishment of new rules of international law in favour of developing countries."[140] The ILC thus appears to be moving in the direction of codifying the changes that have occurred in state practice in the area of international trade. This transformation supports the position that the granting of differential treatment in international trade relations is becoming a legal obligation, and through it, the right to development as well.

4. *Transfer of Technology and the Law of the Sea*

The modest success of the developing countries in obtaining differential treatment from ODA, from international financial institutions, and in international trade has not carried over to the transfer of technology. The interest of the developing countries in both areas is strong: billions of dollars a year are spent by nations to use patents, licenses, and trademarks owned by nationals of developed countries. The Charter of Economic Rights and Duties of States raised hope for improvement in this area. It proposed that all States should facilitate the transfer of technology to developing countries.[141] A Code of Conduct drafted under the aegis of UNCTAD,[142] however, has for many years failed to win broad-based support because opposition by developed countries remains firm.[143]

Hopes that the Third U.N. Conference on the Law of the Sea (UNCLOS III) would provide a breakthrough on this issue became clouded after the new U.S. Administration withdrew support[144] for

140. 1976 ILC Report, supra note 135, at 158.

141. Charter of Economic Rights and Duties of States, supra note 63, art. 13.

142. UNCTAD Res. 89 (IV), 4 UNCTAD (Agenda Item 12) at 1, U.N. Doc. TD/183 (1976).

143. Despite general disapproval by developed nations, a few expressions of differential treatment have occurred. The World Intellectual Property Organization acknowledged the problem and adopted amendments to its Berne Convention to benefit developing countries. See World Intellectual Property Organization, Guide to the Berne Convention for the Protection of Literary and Artistic Works 146-51 (1978) (Paris Act, 1971). Copyright provisions relating to translations and reproductions were relaxed for the benefit of developing countries, which were identified "in conformity with the established practice of the UN General Assembly." Concessions were given, however, solely for educational purposes and without the right to export copies of the translation or reproduction. Id.

144. N.Y. Times, May 1, 1982, at A9, col. 1. One hundred and thirty countries voted to adopt the Convention, while four countries, including the United States, voted against it. Seventeen nations abstained. U.N. Doc. A/CONF.62/SR.182, at 9-10 (prov. ed. 1982).

the Convention on the Law of the Sea.[145] The Convention provides for a fairly extensive transfer of seabed mining technology for the benefit of developing countries, although the means chosen will not fully result in a direct transfer to developing nations.[146] But it is difficult to characterize the Convention as overwhelmingly designed to benefit developing countries. Indeed, the transfer of technology would also benefit the transferor because that party would receive reasonable commercial terms for the technology and would satisfy one of the prerequisites to obtaining approval to exploit a deep seabed minesite. Thus even in the absence of strong opposition from many developed nations, the precedential value of the Convention on the question of the transfer of technology is uncertain, and limited.

There are, however, other aspects of the Convention that are relevant to any consideration of the right to development. A broader purpose was to contribute to the realization of a just and equitable international economic order that would take into account the special interests and needs of developing countries. The Convention contains many provisions that discriminate in favor of developing countries. The range of areas where the Convention recognizes developing countries as a special group arguably make it the most ambitious initiative of its kind.[147] The Convention, therefore, represents a clear trend towards affirmative differential treatment in international law.[148]

---

145. LOS Convention, supra note 36.

146. E.g., id. at Annex III, art. 5(3)(a) (deep seabed miners are to transfer the technology used to an inter-governmental body if that entity is unable to secure the same or equally efficient technology on the open market).

147. A few examples show the many areas in which developing nations would benefit. The Convention qualifies the concept of "the benefit of mankind as a whole" by adding the phrase "taking into particular consideration the interests and needs of developing countries." LOS Convention, supra note 36, art 140. When considering requests by foreign States for access to their exclusive economic zones, coastal States are required to grant access to the surplus fish catch to other States, and especially to developing States. Id. art. 62. Developing States are recognized as an appropriate group from which States may elect members of the Council of the International Seabed Authority, id. art. 161, thus transforming developing States from a mere interest group to a formal constituency. Article 203, entitled "Preferential Treatment for Developing States," instructs international organizations to give these States preferences in the allocation of funds and services. Id. art. 203. Similar provisions exist to facilitate training and development of marine technology in developing countries. Id. arts. 266-69.

148. The other far-reaching development in the law of the sea is the concept that the seabed and its resources beyond national jurisdiction are the common heritage of mankind. See id. arts. 136-37. See also, Declaration of Principles Governing the Sea-Bed and the

The dispute over the Convention on the Law of the Sea also demonstrates the methods whereby a developed State can halt the transformation into law of demands expressed in terms of legal rights. Consistent and unequivocal refusal by developed States to acquiesce in the demands of the developing countries can block the process. The transfer of technology is a field where developing countries have not been accorded differential treatment. Thus, even though the broader principles of the Convention may point to a beneficial trend, state practice in the area of the transfer of technology provides no explicit support that differential treatment has become part of international law.

5. *Other Areas of State Practice*

In addition to the areas discussed above, developing States have benefited from preferential treatment in a number of other ways. Tax treaties now commonly include double taxation agreements designed to enable developing countries to derive tax revenue from multi-national corporations.[149] Conventions of the International Labor Organization do not specifically refer to developing countries, yet in practice developing States are allowed a degree of flexibility to tailor applicable ILO conventions to their particular needs.[150] In the field of environmental protection, where universal

---

Ocean Floor, and the Subsoil Thereof, Beyond the Limits of National Jurisdiction, art. 1, G.A. Res. 2749, 25 U.N. GAOR Supp. (No. 28) at 24, U.N. Doc.A/8028 (1970). The equitable sharing of the Common Heritage of Mankind could become an important part of the right to development. Some commentators already see in this concept the generation of automatic revenues to finance development projects. See Brandt Commission Report, supra note 91, at 244; supra notes 109-10 and accompanying text.

149. Verwey, supra note 90, at 391. The United Nations has also addressed this problem. See Dep't of Int'l Econ. and Soc. Aff., United Nations Model Double Taxation Convention Between Developed and Developing Countries, U.N. Doc. ST/ESA/102 (1982); Manual for the Negotiation of Bilateral Tax Treaties Between Developed and Developing Countries, U.N. Doc. ST/ESA/94 (1979).

150. See N. Valticos, International Labour Law 551-54 (1979). "Flexibility clauses" may provide for: the option not to ratify specific provisions of a given convention (see, e.g., Convention concerning Minimum Standards of Social Security (No. 102), June 4, 1952, 210 U.N.T.S. 132 (entered into force Apr. 27, 1955)); the option to limit the applicability of a given convention to specific regions, population groups, or industries (see, e.g., Convention Limiting the Hours of Work in Industrial Undertakings to Eight in the Day and Forty-eight in the Week (No. 1), Oct. 29, 1919, 38 U.N.T.S. 17 (entered into force June 13, 1921)); the right to interpret the specific content of certain "promotional" conventions (see, e.g., Convention concerning Basic Aims and Standards of Social Policy (No. 117), June 6, 1962, 494 U.N.T.S. 249 (entered into force April 23, 1964)); or the right to determine the most suitable method of application of a given provision (see, e.g., Convention concerning Equal Remu-

norms are generally considered essential, developing countries have been granted both protective measures[151] and differential treatment in regard to compliance with environmental standards.[152] Finally, the major task of many international organizations, in particular those in the U.N. family, is the advancement of developing countries.[153]

It is particularly difficult in this area to draw together the threads of state practice and weave them into a coherent and intellectually satisfying exposition of international law. The difficulty is compounded by the very short period of time during which the changes in state practice have occurred. Nonetheless, a few general conclusions can be advanced. State practice demonstrates that developing countries are recognized as a special category of States in international law. Furthermore, industrialized States have shown their acceptance of the principle of differential treatment by cooperating in the advancement of developing States. This finding is reinforced by the congruence of state practice with the *opinio juris* expressed in various international instruments.

On the basis of these conclusions, it could be argued that many of the provisions of the Charter of Economic Rights and Duties of States have become part of international law.[154] If so, the rights and duties of the Charter would form important components of the right to development.

III. The Nature of the Right to Development

Because the right to development would establish widely varied rights and duties, it can best be accommodated within the frame-

---

neration for Men and Women Workers for Work of Equal Value (No. 100), June 6, 1951, 165 U.N.T.S. 303 (entered into force May 23, 1953)). Id.

151. E.g., United Nations Conference on the Human Environment, Declaration, June 16, 1972, Principle 11, reprinted in 67 Dep't St. Bull. 116, 117 (July 24, 1972) ("The environmental policies of all States should enhance and not adversely affect the present or future development potential of developing countries . . . .").

152. E.g., id. para. 4 (recognizing the different causes of environmental problems in developing countries vis-a-vis developed countries, and consequently the different policies open to developing countries to place priority on development while also seeking to "safeguard and improve the environment"); id. at Principle 9 (recognizing "the particular requirements of the developing countries" and calling for special assistance to be made available to them to defray the costs involved in incorporating environmental safeguards into their development planning).

153. See L. Goodrich, The United Nations 262-92 (1959).

154. G.A Res. 3281, 29 U.N. GAOR Supp. (No. 31) at 50, U.N. Doc. A/9631 (1974).

work of international human rights law. This section of the Commentary will examine relevant characteristics of the international law of human rights. Within this context, it will consider the subjects of the right to development. It will then attempt to link state practice designed to facilitate economic development of individual nations with acknowledged human rights of individuals within these nations. The purpose of this will be to show that these concepts are two sides of the same coin, the right to development. Finally, this section will examine three theories that have been advanced to justify including the right to development in human rights law.

A. *Subjects of the Right to Development*

It is now widely accepted that individuals are the subjects of the international law of human rights.[155] More recently, peoples have been recognized as subjects of human rights law.[156] Human rights law, therefore, is applicable to both the individual and the collective. At the same time, it continues to act principally through States as the primary subjects of international law. The right to development draws on all these aspects and adds a new dimension, the recognition of the State as a beneficiary in its own right of human rights law.

The right to development is also well-suited to human rights law because that body of law recognizes differing obligations and thus provides a degree of flexibility that is adaptable to a broad-based principle like the right to development.[157] Human rights law ranges

155. H. Lauterpacht, International Law and Human Rights 45 (1968).

156. See Declaration on the Granting of Independence to Colonial Countries and Peoples, supra note 50, art. 2; International Covenant on Civil and Political Rights, supra note 76, art. 1; International Covenant on Economic, Social and Cultural Rights, supra note 76, art. 1. All three instruments employ the following language: "All peoples have the right to self determination; by virtue of that right they freely determine their political status and freely pursue their economic, social and cultural development." Id.

157. Its flexibility can also be seen in relation to social rights. While the social rights enumerated in the International Covenant on Economic, Social and Cultural Rights, supra note 76, are understood to be achievable in a progressive manner, the European Social Charter, parts 3 & 4, Europ. T.S. No. 38 (1961), dealing with very similar rights, creates binding obligations on States of a specific nature and establishes a procedural framework to investigate the level of compliance. Article 2(1) of the International Covenant states: "Each State Party to the present Covenant undertakes to take steps . . . especially economic and technical . . . with a view to achieving progressively, the full realization of the rights recognized in the present Covenant by all appropriate means, including particularly the adoption of legislative measures." International Covenant on Economic, Social and Cultural Rights, supra

from a supranational law giving individuals *locus standi* in international courts in actions against their own governments,[158] to a law of long-term goals imposing objectives on governments rather than defined and enforceable obligations.[159] It protects civil and political rights by giving individuals procedural capacity, yet at the same time recognizes the existence of such rights even in the absence of procedural capacity.[160] The right to development as an individual and collective right would span this range of obligations.

The study of the U.N. Secretary-General[161] and the Report to the Commission on Human Rights on the Right to Development[162] agree that the right to development has both a collective and an individual dimension, and that the subjects of the right are individuals, peoples and States. The General Assembly and the Commission argue that equality of opportunity for development is as much a prerogative of nations as of individuals within nations.[163] This view also enjoys wide support among scholars,[164] and is re-

---

note 76, art. 2(1). The promotion of the rights to work, organize, engage in collective bargaining, social security, and medical care are obligatory under part III of the European Social Charter. Signatory States may further obligate themselves to the promotion of additional rights. European Social Charter, supra.

158. E.g., European Convention for the Protection of Human Rights and Fundamental Freedoms, Nov. 4, 1950, art. 25, 213 U.N.T.S. 221. Article 25 provides for the right of individual petition to the European Commission of Human Rights and for the compulsory jurisdiction of the European Court of Human Rights over such petitions.

159. See International Covenant on Economic, Social and Cultural Rights, supra note 76. The provisions of this Covenant constitute "an undertaking or a recognition by states rather than the affirmation of a right inherent in the individual as such." A. Robertson, Human Rights in the World 40 (1972).

160. E.g., International Covenant on Civil and Political Rights, supra note 76, The International Covenant binds signatory States whether or not those States have ratified the Optional Protocol, supra note 76. The Optional Protocol provides for the right of individual petition to the U.N. Human Rights Committee by citizens of the ratifying State. Id. art. 2. See generally A. Robertson, supra note 159, at 40-48.

161. Report of the Secretary-General, supra note 12.

162. Report of the Working Group of Governmental Experts on the Right to Development, Commission on Human Rights (38th Sess.) (Prov. Agenda Item 8) at 3, U.N. Doc. E/CN.4/1489 (1982).

163. See Alternative Approaches and Ways and Means Within the United Nations System for Improving the Effective Enjoyment of Human Rights and Fundamental Freedoms, G.A. Res. 34/46, art. 8, U.N. GAOR Press Release GA/6161 at 303-04, U.N. Doc. A/34/704 (1980).

164. See M'Baye, Le droit au développement, in The Right to Development at the International Level 72, 76 (R. Dupuy ed. 1980); Abi-Saab, The Legal Formulation of a Right to Development (Subjects and Content), in The Right to Development at the International Level, at 159, 163; Sanson, supra note 10, at 195; de Vey Mestdagh, supra note 16, at 48-53.

flected both in international instruments and, to a limited degree, state practice

B. *The Link Between Economic Development and Human Rights*

The rationale behind viewing the right to development as having both an individual and a collective nature is the need for an integrated approach to development in which the individual is the ultimate beneficiary. Under this approach, the goal of development is more than economic growth, it is the social and cultural advancement of the individual. It also creates a link between economic development and human rights in that economic development is fostered through the protection of human rights. This link is at the heart of the right to development. It is implicitly recognized in international instruments, such as the Universal Declaration on Human Rights,[165] that acknowledge the critical role of economic development—both through the efforts of individual nations and the assistance of developed States—in the protection of the human rights of individuals. Thus, the link between economic development and human rights is accepted in the *opinio juris*, but establishing it in state practice is considerably more difficult.

The Secretary-General's study for the Commission on Human Rights found considerable interest in forging closer links between the promotion of human rights and the provision of ODA.[166] But some commission members argued that proposals to link human rights and ODA were "a distortion of the concept of cooperation"

---

165. Universal Declaration on Human Rights, supra note 76, arts. 22, 28. Article 22, for example, states: "Everyone, as a member of society . . . is entitled to realization, through national effort and international cooperation and in accordance with the organization and resources of each State, of the economic, social and cultural rights indispensible for his dignity . . . . " Article 28 states: "Everyone is entitled to a social and international order in which the rights and freedoms set forth in this Declaration can be fully realized." Both articles recognize the individual as the ultimate and most important beneficiary of the rights guaranteed under the Declaration, yet also accept the crucial role of each State in assuring these rights. Furthermore, Article 22 recognizes the essential need for international cooperation to guarantee respect for these rights. Article 28 also accepts in an affirmative sense the duty to ensure that an appropriate "international order" exists in which these rights can flourish. It can be argued, therefore, that the international cooperation necessary to create an atmosphere of respect and encouragement of human rights would embrace positive measures such as ODA designed to directly assist nations, yet through them to facilitate human rights development.

166. Report of the Secretary-General, supra note 12, at 159, para. 312.

and could be used to thwart the establishment of the NIEO.[167] They indicated that some donor States are "disposed now to turn down or turn off aid to regimes that persist in severe and systematic repression . . . [and] to favour regimes demonstrating strong internal commitments to social justice."[168]

The United States undertook an attempt in the mid-1970's to create a formal link between development assistance and human rights. Various pieces of U.S. legislation provide that no security assistance,[169] food aid,[170] or agreement to finance the sale of agricultural commodities[171] may be granted or entered into with "any country the government of which engages in a consistent pattern of gross violations of internationally recognized human rights."[172] The Legal Adviser of the U.S. Department of State explained that the rationale behind the legislation was a "congressional intent . . . to achieve the promotion of human rights."[173]

The practice of the Commission on Human Rights suggested a linkage between development and human rights in the case of Equatorial Guinea. The Commission adopted there a "forward

---

167. P. Alston, Development and the Rule of Law 69 (1981).

168. 1980 Development Review, supra note 102, at 61.

The government of the Netherlands has taken a position on this issue with respect to economic relations and development assistance:

> Human rights principally concern relations between individuals and the authorities within the State . . . . The Government should to a great extent respect the internal order of other countries; it has no call to induce other countries to alter their constitution or political doctrine. The Government's efforts to bring about improvements in specific human rights situations are therefore in principle concentrated on cases where there are grave violations of fundamental human rights, particularly when such violations appear to proceed from a systematic policy.

Human Rights and Foreign Policy, Publication of the Ministry of Foreign Affairs, The Hague 1979, at 88-90; Bijl. Hand. II 1978/79 — 15571 No. 2, at 65-67, reprinted in 1980 Neth. Y.B. Int'l L. 193, 195 (Memorandum of May 3, 1979 presented to the Second Chamber by the Ministers for Foreign Affairs and Development Co-operation).

169. Foreign Assistance Act of 1974 § 46, 22 U.S.C. § 2304(a)(2) (1976).

170. International Development and Food Assistance Act of 1977 § 112, 22 U.S.C. § 2151n (Supp. V 1981).

171. International Development and Food Assistance Act of 1977 § 111, 7 U.S.C. § 1712 (Supp. V 1981).

172. Foreign Assistance Act of 1974 § 46, 22 U.S.C. § 2304(a)(2) (1976).

173. U.S. Dep't of State, Digest of United States Practice in International Law 222 (1975) (memorandum from Monroe Leigh, Legal Advisor, to Deputy Secretary Robert S. Ingersoll (Mar. 19, 1975)). The legislation recognized the authoritativeness of international norms and the importance of international institutions. United States decisions rely on determinations by the U.N. Commission on Human Rights of gross human rights violations. Id. at 223.

looking structural approach" to the problem.[174] This approach called for the implementation of recommendations made by a Special Rapporteur designed to establish equitable and participatory structures to promote respect for human rights.[175] It also requested the Secretary-General to provide advice and assistance to the governments of the Central African Republic and Uganda in their efforts to guarantee human rights.[176]

These examples of state practice are perhaps not sufficiently extensive to cement the link between economic development and the protection of human rights in international law. Combined with the *opinio juris*, however, this state practice clearly points to such a link. A right to development would definitively establish the relationship. It would establish economic development of nations and human development of individuals as two elements of the same human right, intrinsically linked and interdependent.

Developing countries would thus become beneficiaries of the right to development. This would create a new aspect of human rights law, it would not, however, radically depart from accepted concepts. For example, peoples enjoy the right of self-determination, a human right, and when they exercise this right, they may emerge as a State. The entity recognized by international law for purposes of self-determination, therefore, is a people at the commencement of the process and a State at the end, even though the composition of the entity does not change. There appears to be no reason why human rights law should recognize this entity under one name but not under another.

The right to development would operate in a manner similar to the right of self-determination. It has been described as the right of economic self-determination.[177] Indeed, "the right to develop-

---

174. P. Alston, supra note 167, at 75.

175. Commission on Human Rights (37th Sess.) Res. 31, 1981 U.N. ESCOR Supp. (No. 5) at 232, U.N. Doc. E/CN.4/1975 (1981).

176. Commission on Human Rights (37th Sess.) Res. 15, 30, 1981 ESCOR Supp. (No. 5) at 225, 231, U.N. Doc. E/CN.4/1475 (1981).

177. Sanson, supra note 10, at 192. See Espiell, The Right to Self Determination: Implementation of U.N. Resolutions, Special Report to the Subcommission on Prevention of Discrimination and Protection of Minorities, U.N. Doc. E/CN.4/Sub. 2/405/Rev. 1 (1980). Espiell points out that the right of the State to self-determination necessarily affects its people:

> People and Nation are two closely related concepts; they may be one and the same, but they are not synonymous . . . . [W]hen the People and the Nation are one and the same, and when a people has established itself as a State, clearly that Nation and that State are as forms or manifestations of the same people,

ment is for a people what human rights are for an individual. It represents the transposition of human rights to the level of the international community."[178]

The right to development, however, would go further than the right of self-determination. The individual as both a subject and a beneficiary of the right to development gives this right an added dimension. It would impose on the State a duty to advance the human development of its nationals. Various resolutions of the General Assembly define this duty. The Charter of Economic Rights and Duties of States provides that "every State has the primary responsibility to promote the economic, social and cultural development of its people."[179] The Declaration on Social Progress and Development says a major goal of each State should be the equitable distribution of national income and wealth among all members of society.[180] A developing country would thus find itself very much at the center of the right to development; a creditor of the international community and a debtor of its own people.

C. *Three Theories for Including the Right to Development in Human Rights Law*

If the right to development is a human right, it is necessary to identify its place within the body of human rights law in order to gain a better understanding of it. Three theories have been advanced in an effort to do this.

1. *Indispensability Theory*

The first theory considers the right to development as indispensable to the exercise of other human rights. This puts it on a par with the right of self-determination. Two important international instruments state that it is by virtue of the right of self-determina-

---

implicitly entitled to the right to self determination.

Id. at 9, para. 56.

178. Flory, Inégalité et économique du droit international, in Pays en voie de développement et transformation de droit international 28 (Société française pour le droit international, Colloque d'Aix-en Provence).

179. Charter of Economic Rights and Duties of States, supra note 63, art. 7.

180. G.A. Res. 2542, 24 U.N. GAOR Supp. (No. 30) art. 7, at 49, U.N. Doc. A/7630 (1969). See also Eide, Maldevelopment and "the Right to Development": a Critical Note with a Constructive Intent, in Hague Academy/UNU Workshop, supra note 1, at 397, 415 (the right to development includes the right of sub-units within the State, whose growth and development might not correspond with the growth of the State overall, to have an opportunity to develop as well).

tion that peoples may freely pursue their economic development.[181] The theory of indispensability, then, views the right to development as a "necessary precondition for the satisfaction of the social and economic rights of the individual."[182] Otherwise stated, for both the right of self-determination and the right to development, "the satisfaction of the collective right is a . . . prerequisite for the materialisation of human rights."[183] Under this theory, the right to development is thus linked to the satisfaction of other human rights because unless a State is able to develop, it will not be in a position materially to guarantee any of its citizens' basic human rights.[184]

The problem with the indispensability theory is that it allows for justification of widespread abuses of human rights.[185] Taken to its extreme, this theory could be used as a rationale for deprivation of many civil and political rights until development is achieved. It would dovetail with the idea that an authoritarian government is better able to embark on rapid economic development. This result would defeat the very purpose of the right to development, especially if the right is viewed as both a collective and an individual right. Rather than seeing human rights and economic development as incompatible, the right to development would hold that they are

---

181. International Covenant on Economic, Social and Political Rights, supra note 76, art. 1(1); International Covenant on Civil and Political Rights, supra note 76, art. 1(1).

182. Abi-Saab, supra note 164, at 172.

183. Id. at 171.

184. Id.

185. Marks, for example, cites many international agreements, principally article 29(2) of the Universal Declaration, supra note 76, as suggesting that exceptions to human rights principles may be justified during times of national emergency. See generally S. Marks, Les principes et normes des droits de l'homme applicable en période d'exception, in Les dimensions internationales des droits de l'homme 197-233 (K. Vasak, ed. 1978). He includes as examples of severe emergencies: natural catastrophies, armed conflict, and "the totality of economic and social conditions." He excludes the possibility of citing an economic national emergency as a justification for derogations from such fundamental rights as freedom from slavery, freedom from torture, and the right to a fair trial. Id.

In this view, respect for less important rights may be suspended while the "temporary" situation of underdevelopment is rectified. The problems with this variation of the indispensible approach are legion. Aş Marks recognizes, drawing a line between fundamental rights that will always be protected and other "suspendable" rights is very difficult. Id.

Another problem, which Marks also recognizes, is that the analogy with natural catastrophies is weakened because underdevelopment is long-lasting. In these circumstances, abuses of human rights could become permanent in developing States in the midst of this "emergency." Id. In addition, because internal factors play some role in underdevelopment, see Bergen, supra note 24, at 33, to some degree the "emergency" is self-induced, thus confusing even more the calculus of what is and what is not an acceptable derogation of human rights.

indivisible.

2. *Generational Theory*

The second theory views the right to development as a new human right—a member of the "third generation of human rights."[186] According to this view, the first generation of human rights sprang from the United States Declaration of Independence and the French Declaration of the Rights of Man and of the Citizen. These rights guarantee individual freedoms with which governments may not interfere, principally civil and political rights.[187]

The second generation of rights evolved from the Russian revolution of 1917 and the welfare state concepts of the New Deal in the United States.[188] These second generation rights are essentially economic, social, and cultural rights that require affirmative action by governments for the benefit of their citizens.[189] Generally speaking, these first and second generation rights can be fulfilled through the actions of individual States.

Third generation rights are of a different character. They have been termed "solidarity rights."[190] They require international action. They are premised on the duty to cooperate. A tentative list of the emerging solidarity rights includes "the right to a healthy and ecologically balanced environment, the right to peace, and the right to the ownership of the common heritage of mankind."[191] These rights are termed new human rights because they have not yet been specifically recognized by the United Nations.

This generational theory is attractive for several reasons. First, it follows chronologically. The emergence of the third generation reflects the transformation of international law from a law of coexistence to a law of cooperation. It also recognizes that the countries of the world are interdependent, especially in the sense that the solution to one country's problems now often depends on actions of

---

186. Vasak, A Thirty Year Struggle—the Sustained Efforts to Give Force of Law to the Universal Declaration of Human Rights, UNESCO Courier 29 (Nov. 1977), UNESCO 3/C74/30-11 (Karel Vasak, Director of UNESCO's Division of Human Rights and Peace, has been the principal proponent of the generational approach).

187. Id.

188. Id.

189. Id.

190. Id.

191. Alston, supra note 28, at 101.

another.[192] This is true with regard to the maintenance of peace, the protection of the environment, and the encouragement of development. In addition, this theory introduces a stronger ethical element into international law by advocating elevated goals of human society.

The concept of the right to development as one member of a third generation of human rights is open to criticism. The generational theory may not accurately reflect existing human rights. It perhaps introduces an unnecessary degree of sophistication into the human rights debate and ignores the dynamic nature of many traditional rights.[193] These rights can be reinterpreted and refined as expectations change.

Another difficulty with the generational theory is the concept that certain rights are new. As a method of analyzing the historical evolution of human rights, the theory is useful.[194] But the division between accepted and new human rights separates rather than reinforces the interrelationship of these rights. It implies that the new generation of rights somehow supersedes the old. The concept that the right to development is a completely new human right must therefore be viewed with caution.

3. *Synthesis Theory*

The third theory views the right to development as a synthesis of existing individual and collective human rights.[195] One commentator describes the right to development as a synthesis of other

---

192. See generally OECD, Interfutures: Facing the Future (1979) (study of "the future development of advanced industrial societies in harmony with the developing countries").

193. Alston, Peace as a Human Right, Bull. of Peace Proposals 319, 321 (Apr. 1980).

194. Id.

A more theoretical problem with the concept of a third generation of rights is the question of where the right of self-determination fits in. This right is guaranteed by the international covenants that Vasak regards as providing first and second generation rights. Yet it looks much more analogous to the solidarity rights, both from the point of view of the collective nature of its beneficiaries and from its transnational implications. Perhaps it is the first internationally accepted right of the third generation of human rights. But it is so closely tied to the traditional individual rights that the idea that it belongs to a new generation of rights appears artificial. It seems more realistic to regard it as the collective expression of the sum of traditional individual rights. Where the self-determination process has run its original course, the right does not extinguish, it remains dormant until its collective articulation springs up again in new circumstances.

195. See Report of the Working Group on Governmental Experts on the Right to Development, supra note 162, at 9, para. 32; Alston, supra note 193, at 322. See also Eide, supra note 180, at 402. The right to development is seen as either "distilled" from existing rights, or the "sum" of these rights. Alston, supra note 193, at 322.

rights in three respects.[196] First, it allows existing formulations of human rights to be interpreted in a dynamic, perhaps expansive way.[197] Next, it is not limited to the text of the International Bill of Rights,[198] but can allow for the incorporation of other principles, such as those underlying the NIEO. Finally, the whole is greater than the sum of its parts. Therefore, the right to development adds a new qualitative dimension to existing human rights.[199]

One advantage of this theory is that it takes an integrated approach to development. By incorporating existing individual human rights, into the right to development, the synthesis theory makes the individual the ultimate beneficiary of the development process. While nations will benefit from the right to development, they will also be fulfilling their duties towards their peoples. The synthesis theory thus blends best with the traditional approach to human rights.

Another advantage of the synthesis theory is that it corresponds closely to the most recent and most authoritative human rights instruments. It comprehends both economic development and the development of the individual, an important principle of the International Bill of Rights.[200] The synthesis concept parallels the approach being taken within the General Assembly,[201] which has characterized human rights as "indivisible and interdependent"[202] and has linked the realization of human rights to national and international policies of economic development.[203]

Despite its attractions, the synthesis approach has been criticized for not adding anything to existing human rights law.[204] The conception of the right to development as a dynamic, expansive synthesis of existing rights, however, effectively counters this criti-

196. Alston, supra note 193, at 322.

197. Id.

198. International Bill of Human Rights, supra note 76. The various expressions of this principle include the Universal Declaration, supra note 76, art. 22 ("free development of [an individual's] personality"); id. art. 26(2) ("education shall be directed to the full development of the human personality"); and The International Covenant on Economic, Social and Cultural Rights, supra note 76, art. 13(1) ("the full development of the human personality and the sense of its dignity"). See also Alston, supra note 193, at 322.

199. Alston, supra note 193, at 322.

200. Supra note 76.

201. See G.A. Res. 32/130, 32 U.N. GAOR Supp. (No. 45) at 150-51, U.N. Doc. A/32/45 (1977).

202. Id.

203. Id. at 151, para. 1(d).

204. See Abi-Saab, supra note 164, at 163-4.

cism.[205] A more subtle criticism is that the term synthesis does not accurately reflect the nature of the right to development. If the right transcends traditional human rights concepts, it can hardly be called a synthesis of those concepts.[206]

The synthesis theory nevertheless remains central to any understanding of the nature of the right to development. But neither this theory, the indispensability theory, nor the generational theory can completely define the nature of the right to development. Each sheds some light on this uncommon right, yet none can fully explain it. In time, an historian may conclude that the collective human rights, including the right of self-determination and the solidarity rights, constitute a third generation of human rights. But this is of limited value today. So while it may not be entirely accurate to describe the right to development as a new human right, it has clearly added a new dimension to human rights law. It will now be useful to examine whether this right serves a useful purpose.

IV. USEFULNESS OF THE RIGHT

Perhaps the effort devoted to expounding the right to development could be better spent on ensuring respect for traditional human rights. Merely repeating the existence of known rights may serve little purpose. If the right to development contains new elements, could they not be elaborated in a protocol to one of the existing covenants on human rights, rather than in an attempt at a global approach?[207] We must also realize that it may be impossible to eliminate the starvation and poverty in the world. If this is so, why grant an unattainable right to development?[208]

The answer is that the right to development will reinforce existing human rights, enhance their effectiveness, and make them more relevant to governments and individuals. This will be achieved through the "major psychological significance" of the right to development.[209] Many third world nations view international law as not of their own making.[210] To them international law

205. See Alston, supra note 193, at 322; Alston, supra note 28, at 110-12; text at notes 196-97 supra.

206. Eide, supra note 180, at 402.

207. Abi-Saab, supra note 164, at 159.

208. "If it is impossible for a thing to be done, it is absurd to claim it as a right." Alston, supra note 28, at 109 (quoting M. Cranston, What Are Human Rights? 66 (1973)).

209. Alston, supra note 28, at 108-09.

210. M. Bedjaoui, supra note 3, at 101-02 (1979).

favors the status quo and therefore disadvantages developing countries.[211] The emergence of the right of self-determination marked a significant step towards making international law relevant to developing countries. The right to development, in its collective dimension, is a right of States to enjoy the benefits of the international duty to cooperate. It therefore responds to the major priority of developing nations—economic development. But because the right also has an individual dimension, the first and second generation human rights become linked with the economic development of developing countries. In this way, the right to development reinforces existing human rights.

The right to development also enhances the effectiveness of traditional human rights. Its collective and individual dimensions place the government of a developing country in the position of being both a creditor and a debtor.[212] A developing country becomes a creditor because it receives development assistance. It becomes a debtor because it then owes a duty to its people to allow and encourage the full development of individuals. By linking these two dimensions, the right to development rejects a "trickle down" approach.[213] Rather, it makes governments accountable for their human rights records. This concept of accountability is in its infancy in state practice. It is therefore an area where further progress needs to be made to elaborate the content and procedural aspects of the right to development.

Finally, the right to development works as a corrective to the direction of development. It is concerned with the quality of development. It makes individual development its ultimate objective. This counters the notion that development is solely concerned with economic growth rates and rapid industrialization. It measures improvement by examining the human rights system in all its aspects: social, economic, and political.[214] It thus acts against both underdevelopment and maldevelopment.[215] Maldevelopment occurs where traditional values and structures are destroyed, and then replaced with a system having little in common with the

211. Id.; see generally id. at 65-123.

212. See Seminar on the Effects of the Existing Unjust International Economic Order on the Economies of the Developing Countries, at 17, para. 64, U.N. Doc. ST/HR/Ser.A/8 (1980) (summary of remarks) [hereinafter cited as Seminar].

213. See Alston, supra note 28, at 108-09.

214. Seminar, supra note 212, at 19, para. 79.

215. Eide, supra note 180, at 401.

needs of the people concerned.[216] Maldevelopment also occurs where, although some economic improvement occurs, the disparity between rich and poor grows and fundamental freedoms are violated.

The right to development is therefore more than useful; it is necessary. It answers a pressing need resulting from the "neglect of the individual's right to development in the context of most development planning."[217] The right to development answers this need by acknowledging the place of the sovereign State in the development process, while at the same time recognizing the individual's right to development as the ultimate objective. By linking these two facets, it enhances individual human rights.

V. CONCLUSION

The inescapable question is whether the right to development is already part of international law. The answer largely depends on the view one takes of the process of development of international law. If one is of the view that States are bound only by what they positively commit themselves to, then the right to development would be *lex ferenda*. If, on the other hand, one views General Assembly resolutions and other international instruments as definitive pronouncements of international law, the right to development is part of that law. This Commentary has resisted the temptation to adopt either of these extremes.

The most important element in the formation of international law remains state practice. State practice provides evidence of the essential elements of the right to development. These elements include: the recognition of developing States as a special category of States in international law; the recognition of the substantive inequality of States; the recognition of the principle of differential treatment of developing States; the recognition of the development of the individual as the ultimate objective of the development process; and the increasing linkages between development and human rights. Thus, state practice largely confirms the *opinio juris* in this area, or alternatively, the *opinio juris* articulates the growing practice of States.

---

216. See id. at 415. Eide makes a special plea in favor of indigenous peoples, arguing that the dominant society cannot determine the correct utilization of the natural resources and the structure of the economy of these subnational units.

217. Alston, supra note 28, at 108.

In addition, the evidence examined by this Commentary shows that the right to development can be said to spring from a number of sources, both ethical and legal, and that it arose in the rapid transformation of international law from a law of coexistence to a law of cooperation. Furthermore, the right to development should be seen as an evolving part of human rights law as well as a reinforcement of traditional human rights.

The evidence and analysis presented in this Commentary demonstrate that the right to development is an emerging human right that is rapidly gaining general acceptance by the international community. The next step in its progression to positive law is the articulation of this right in a legal instrument that would define the rights and duties flowing from it. The Commission on Human Rights is drafting this instrument.

[8]

FROM THE RIGHT TO ECONOMIC SELF-DETERMINATION TO THE RIGHT TO DEVELOPMENT: A CRISIS IN LEGAL THEORY.

Anthony Carty

Various formulations of the right of peoples to pursue their economic development, whether they are found in the U.N. Human Rights Covenants, the 1970 Declaration on the Principles of Friendly Relations among States,[1] or the Charter of Economic Rights and Duties of States, to mention only three, present a common theme; a virtually obsessive repetition of the right of economic self-determination.[2] The right is seen as affording a framework for the struggle of developing countries to attain the economic independence which has not followed automatically upon the attainment of political independence. The survival of a legal concept must depend upon its usefulness as an analytical-critical instrument. Now it appears that, in practice, particularly at the United Nations, the claim which states make to a right to economic self-determination serves primarily as an ideological representation. Alongside the opposing 'Western' claims for the principle of acquired rights and for 'pacta sunt servanda', it expresses a real economic contradiction and serves as a banner to mobilize developing countries in the context of a North-South confrontation. Yet such an ideological use of apparently legal concepts does not permit them to function as positive rules of law.[3]

In my view the reduction of basic legal concepts to a purely ideological role is an indication of a crisis in legal theory which goes beyond the normal manipulation of law in diplomatic relations. The concept of economic self-determination has its roots in a Western tradition of legal voluntarism which cannot open the way out to either national or international economic or social transformation. It restates the basic Western concept of 'subjective right' and applies it to the state. In such a view of a legal order, the basic structure of law is subject/property/contract. The legal order begins with its subjects, proceeds to determine what they own, and delimits the circumstances in which the legal subjects may dispose of their property.[4] The consequence is a language of state rights which restricts attention to the authority and power of the state, without reference either to the nature of the international economy or to the needs and aspirations of peoples.[5] This is because the right supposes a purely formal perspective which reaches such a level of abstraction as to have no contact with material reality. The language of law and the language of the state are one and the same. However, much state organisation may constitute an irreplacable framework for economic development, the fact remains that juridical language is unable to present an independent criticism of its performance.

One illustration of the nature of this process of abstraction may be afforded by some of the discussion of the alleged responsibility of developed states for the historical consequences of colonialism. Article 16 of the Charter of Economic Rights and Duties of States refers to the duty to compensate for the economic consequences of colonialism. Benedek has pointed out[6] that there is serious difficulty in giving any formulation to a right to compensation, especially within the context of the new claim to a right to development. The reason is simply that it is difficult to relate the responsibility of particular colonial states to their victims in a measurable way which takes account of the fact that the existing world economic system adversely affects many developing countries which were never colonized. The language of the subjective rights of states is inadequate. This tendency of law to abtract itself from history is also noted by Benchikh. The historical dimension of colonialism has, in his view, created a relationship of dependence on the part of developing countries towards developed countries, which is not properly taken into account in present aid and 'industry-sharing' policies towards developing countries. Because the constraining consequences of colonial history are ignored, resort is had simply to the language of solidarity among legally equal states. Regard is merely had to their present formal capacity, with perhaps an exhortation to moral solidarity thrown in for good measure.[7] A formalist, a-historical approach to law means, in turn, that new states are supposed to be granted a legal capacity which takes no account of the actual extent of their economic independence or the closely related issue of their social and cultural cohesion. Indeed the argument is well known, particularly in the context of Latin American studies, that legal independence is supposed to be nothing more than a breakdown of European mercantilism and a preparation, or sine qua non, for the integration of new states into a liberal world economic order.[8]

Is it the failure of such a concept as the right of economic self-determination to open the way out to either national or international economic social and economic transformation which has led developing countries such as Algeria to slip almost imperceptibly from such legal discourse into the admittedly utterly vague language of the right to development.[9] It is, in any case, precisely because of the banal fact that developing countries enjoy very little economic and social cohesion, that the whole problem of development arises? It would be foolish to suppose that the debate in the United Nations on the legal right to development has given rise to any consensus of viewpoint. However the 1982 and 1983 reports of the Working Group of Governmental Experts on the Right to Development provide numerous indications of a felt need to break out of the bounds of a formal international legal order. For instance, in considering means to realize the right to development, the call is made, at the national level, for the participation of everyone in the process of decision-making, itself with a view to permitting equitable distribution of resources resulting from development[10] and, at the international level, for a means to ensure a just and equitable division of labour, an adequate industrialization of developing countries and a proper indexing of prices of exports and imports from developing countries.[11]

The debate about the right to development marks a crisis in legal theory, because it encompasses a determined attempt to place material content before form and yet retain whatever advantages are supposed to attach to the use of legal language. Alston writes that "... the basic content of the right to development is the need for justice ..."[12] He criticizes the 1979 Report by the U.N. Secretary-General on the Right to Development, because "... it places ethical considerations before relevant legal norms, although it fails to elaborate upon the link between the two themes ..."[13] As he himself appears to suggest, this debate may be seen in the wider context of a recent tendency for U.N. 'discussion' (hardly action) in the field of human rights to move into a structural phase. So it is recognized "...that it is at least as important to identify and seek to remove the structural obstacles that lie at the root of many an injustice as it is to deal with their symptoms in the form of particular violations..."[14]

. . . .

The formal approach to law has at least two basic elements, consensualism and the concept of subjective right. The task of the jurist is seen as confined to tracing the course of each. This can be observed in some Western academic treatment of the issue of a right to development. For instance Israel draws attention to the imprecision of the right. It is supposed to be necessarily fluid. The expression of the right corresponds more to the affirmation of a principle than to the recognition of a 'true subjective' right. At present one can only outline its possible content by reference to the ideology of development and to the claims of developing countries.[15] The basic difficulty is whether, in this context of a crisis of development, one can hopefully or usefully speak of particular developed states as having legal duties to perform towards particular developing states. The theory of subjective rights supposes that duties are undertaken voluntarily or as a result of specific failures of conduct such as negligence or fraud. The incongruity of this perspective is that Western jurists do accept the existence of the right, in accordance with the usual consensual criteria for the creation of positive law, and yet it appears that the right has no definite content. Benedek points out how the juridical conceptualization of the right to development does not mean that out of it arises concrete legal claims, but rather that one has reached a somehow juridical grasp of the question of development. The right, as a general principle of international law, is an abstraction of a general consensus of states at an international level.[16]

A first step away from this legal formalism is to appreciate its purely optional nature. That is to say, one might just as well not adopt it. By way of illustration one might consider Weil's recent defence of legal formalism. He opposes as condemned to subjectivism any juridical approach to a material concept of a law of international order. In the absence of international organs each state will give the interpretation it pleases to such a concept.[17] This is perfectly true. Yet it is simply a non-sequitur to argue, as Weil does,[18] from the absence of an institutionalized international community to an insistence upon the priority of a voluntarist, contractual law. He supposes that his own concept of law as a coordination of the wills of equal legal subjects[19] is somehow neutral, the true starting point, rather than merely a perspective which is itself optional and relative. It is another French jurist, Villey, who highlights the sense in which Weil's perspective is optional. The latter belongs to a legal tradition which goes back to the European Renaissance, to Occam and Hobbes, which simply chooses to take the individual as a starting point, rather than seeing him as a part of a wider social body.[20] The fact/law distinction upon which the formalists so strongly insist (perhaps as well expressed by the so-called is/ought dichotomy) is nothing more than a preference of a particular tradition to begin with the will of the individual subject, rather than with his social context. Those who prefer to accept that it is the latter which contains at least the outlines of the imperatives which a jurist has to recognize may simply take a different course from Weil's. So much of the language used in the development and new international economic order debate does point in this direction. For instance, Cristescu appears to believe that an imperative comes out of the very fact that '...countries possessing raw materials should be paid for them at prices commensurate with the work which goes into the exploitation of these raw materials and with their economic and social value...[21]

. . . .

It is too much to attribute profound philosophical undertones to the United Nations debate on the right to development. A survey of the summary records of the 39th session of the Human Rights Commission in Geneva[22] reveals a fairly repetitive reassertion of basic platitudes which are set out in Article (3) of the Technical Consolidation (of texts) of 20th June 1983, an explosion of laudable phrases unrelated to one another. It is possible to find stimulating references to new avenues of approach. The Colombian delegate insisted that development was a right of peoples, not of states, that economic growth had to harmonize with nature and that resistance had to be made to dehumanizing production processes. The Irish delegate said that the crisis of International law could only be overcome if it became a law of cooperation, in which case one would inevitably have new conceptual problems in searcing for criteria to define relationships of assistance and solidarity.[24] However, such remarks have to be seen alongside numerous other reiterations of entrenched positions, liberal and marxist, both of which place the state at the centre of human rights issues, whether as promotor or as antagonist. The priority given to the state was clearly the intention of the drafters of the right to self-determination of states in the U.N. Human Rights Covenants.[25] The Technical Consolidation repeats, in its Article 3(2), that states have the primary responsibility to ensure development, both within their territory and internationally.

Nonetheless, it is clear that the issue of participation has become central to the Human Rights Commission discussions and its resolution 1983/14 requests the Secretary-General to undertake a comprehensive analytical study of popular participation. Special mention is made of the Yugoslavia International Seminar on Popular Participation.[26] Such a reference at least allows one to treat as relevant the issues raised at that seminar. For instance reference is made to the need to force the goal of economic growth to give way to an intergrated package, which includes popular participation as a means to the optimal utilization of human creativity, including the dimension of ecological balance. In this context, there was acceptance at the seminar, that state planning was a complex, technical process which ran the danger of administrative elitism, marginalizing democratic local activity. There was an accepted need for new guidelines on popular participation which would question a purely quantitative perspective towards development, measuring compliance and quota systems of production, rather than the more intangible factors just mentioned.

The Technical Consolidation of Texts does provide a framework to elaborate on these ideas. For instance Article 10 says that states should take appropriate action to provide a comprehensive framework for popular participation in development, and Article 2, while accepting that states have the right and the duty to formulate appropriate development policies, nonetheless allows that human beings have the primary responsibility themselves. States have, further, to respect the intermediate associations which individuals form. It might be said that any categorical insistence upon the integral place of human rights in any development process (or upon the equal status of political, civil, economic and social rights) is bound to lead to an abandonment of the positivist tradition that the language of the law and the language of the state are one and the same.

. . . .

The apparent prominence given to the concept of participation in the United Nations discussions of the right to development is merely a reflection of a wider uncertainty, even in radical third world circles, about a concept of economic self-determination which applies exclusively to states. Once the right is supposed to belong exclusively to the state, there is no way that it can be used to ensure either a critique of that state's own internal economic and social structures, or an identification of the nature of its ties of economic dependency. This is simply because the state as such is merely a formal concept which denotes a delimitation of competences, that is an arrangement or perhaps organization of particular territories and populations within an international legal order. In practice the traditional legal discourse on economic sovereignty has come together with a third-world nationalist ideology merely on the basis of a legal 'decisionism'. That is to say, a nationalist ideology is supposed to ensure a certainty of choice by a third-world state, which is not a reflection of any genuine certainty about the problem of economic development. A recent illustration of this pattern may be seen in Article 9 of the Draft U.N. Code of Conduct on Transnational Corporations. It is confined to reiterating that transnational corporations must correspond to the host state's nationally set goals and priorities. Yet how does a state define these.[27]

A prominent Algerian jurist, Mahiou, a member of the International Law Commission, says it is now obvious that only governing elites benefit from the existing world economic system. Only a policy of total mobilization of a country's internal resources towards auto-centred development can break the dominance of Western economies and values. In his view a direct connection has to be made between national and international politics, based upon an equitable and democratic order at both levels.[28] At the same time the 1983 World Development Report subjects the state to an equally severe critique from a perhaps more Western liberal perspective. Its main conclusion is that policy reform is relevant only if there is the institutional capacity to carry it out. The form of grand plans matters less than the substance of actions needed to achieve central goals. The implied rejection of 'blue prints' in tackling the complexities of development is accompanied by a stressing of the importance of building into every strategy and programme an effective learning process. At the field level this means officials looking outward, to serve clients rather than inward, to satisfy predetermined bureaucratic procedures.[29] This language of 'managerese' evidences the same institutional crisis as the radicalism of Mahiou.

It is remarkable how far the two approaches agree at an empirical level about the scope of the problem. Bencnihk characterizes state-capitalist third world societies as emeshed in quasi-feudal bureaucratic conflicts, unable to launch an all-embracing programme of economic and social self-reliance, in a context in which they are out of touch with their populations.[30] The World Development Report identifies the problem of overstaffed bureaucracies, remote from the public they serve and not subject to effective external pressures within their societies, which frequently lack independent public opinion or opposition. Global reform from within these institutions is virtually inconceivable, given the vested interests involved, and the complexities of problems linked naturally to patterns of rapid economic and social change.[31]

Disagreement emerges, of course, at the level of analysis and explanation. The central relevance of the conflicting approaches, for the issue of a right of participation, is the insistence by dependency theory, that the basic feature of world capitalism is a transnational integration which is accompanied by national disintegration. The most important features of this process are identified by Snyder as the increasing marginalization of the mass of the population from a reasonable income and the disintegration of national social classes.[32] Within this framework, Benchikh objects to third world demands for a new international economic order which are no more than state capitalist demands for a greater quantitative share in industrial production without a change in the quality of an international division of labour, leaving decisive technological leadership in the West. Placing all authority in the state they may manage some measure of sectoral growth to increase the scope of exercise of state sovereignty. Yet, cut off from a proletariat which they distrust, with an absence of popular participation, they cannot imagine or fully express the right of self-determination of peoples. Benchikh traces this pattern of fragmentation to the detail of, for instance, technology transfer, where state officials prefer international contracts and Western assistance, introducing developed country patterns of production, instead of engaging in dialogue with workers, in a context in which both sections of society have been retarded by the history of colonialism.[33]

The World Development Report subscribes fully to what Snyder characterizes as the ideology of developmentism, which supposes that knowledge (expertise) is cumulative and that experimentation and experience will yield objective procedures for the achievement of material development, especially of basic needs.[34] The Report considers the option of decentralization understood as devolution of political power, deconcentration of central government on a purely geographical basis, and delegation of government authority to public bodies, particularly state corporations. However its general conclusion is that decentralization has to be seen as not much more than the incremental building up of the capacity of organizations to assume greater responsibilities. It cannot of itself compensate for a general shortage of technical, administrative skills. The main thrust of the solution is to have fewer, better (paid) officials, controlling only what needs to be controlled. The latter objective could be achieved through a reduction in the level of state control, e.g. in the area of regulation of trade, and in the delegation of economic powers to public bodies more amenable to the market. Government needs to retain central control of budget and foreign debt so that perhaps the best scope for decentralization/participation is in such matters as delivery of rural and social services and dividing up tasks for rural managers.[35]

Hence it appears that the language of a right to development, particularly with its emphasis on popular participation is very relevant to the politically radical, dependency analysis of international society, while fairly marginal to the modernization approach of the World Bank. Yet it can hardly be said that mere repetition of the concept of participation provides a serious answer to the crisis of third world civilization which Western modernization is causing. Benchikh proposes a societal introversion, based upon a more profound integration of the agricultural and industrial sectors of society, with a maximum local intermeshing and satisfaction of basic needs.[36] Yet a main thrust of his analysis is the inextricable linkage between developed and developing countries. He accepts that it is impossible to expect the former to integrate the social-cultural world of the latter into the shaping of their educational and scientific policies.[37] Indeed he believes it is precisely the Third World demand for the international diffusion of scientific knowledge which will eventually necessitate, through internal education, a democracy 'at home' in developing countries.[38] In other words the depth of global intercultural penetration is beyond the grasp of either of the main North-South divides and it is hardly even possible to disentangle its positive and negative causes, however identifiable may be some of its end effects. While dependency theorists such as Snyder may wish to see research oriented towards how third world societies became integrated into the world capitalist system, he admits that, the causes of this original imbalance, going back in Wallerstein's view to the 16th Century,[39] are very much in dispute. It is by no means clear what economic anthropology, whether marxist or otherwise, can contribute in the way of social and cultural reconstruction.[40] So perhaps it might be better to consider approaches to law and the right to development, which assume that the crisis, from which developing countries appear to suffer most acutely, is common to both North and South. This crisis may have its roots in the culture which first separated the two, that of Renaissance Europe, a culture which has now come to a turning point.

. . . .

It is, in my view, arguable that the vacuity of the legal language of the right to development is attributable not to the concept of development itself, but to the nature of the Western concept of law. The latter is merely a part of a culture which supposes nature to be infinitely malleable and man to be capable of perpetually redefining himself. In this respect there is no significant difference between liberal and marxist perspectives on law. The starting point of all law is to suppose that the individual subject is outside any 'binding framework'. That is to say, individual freedom is not granted by any outside order. So legal obligation represents a consensual renounciation of a part of one's otherwise unlimited freedom.[41] It does not matter whether the individual is a single person, a prince, the state or God. The essence of law is the purely formal delimitation of competences, or areas of jurisdiction, conceived of, at least at the end of the Middle ages when this view of law first arose, as a hierarchical delegation of powers. At least this is Villey's account of the process.[42] Law does not have any 'necessary' material substance because the individual, however defined, does not exist in any 'necessary' social or natural, physical or biological, relationship to a world outside himself.

Arendt in her classical study, The Human Condition, asserts that the key form of Western alienation is not from the self, as Marx supposed, but from the world. It has its roots in a philosophy of physics which goes back to the early Renaissance. As is well known, Galileo's astrophysical world view presented a very serious challenge to the adequacy of the senses to reveal reality, indeed leaving us '...in a universe of whose qualities we know no more than the way they affect our measuring instruments...'[43]. This loss of the scientific self-evidence of appearances affected all branches of knowledge at their common root, the traditional assumption that '...what truly is will appear of its own accord and that human capabilities are adequate to receive it..."[44]. The Cartesian way to return to certainty was to dissolve all 'real' relationships into logical relations between man-made symbols. In other words, Descartes reduces all experience, with the world as well as with other human beings, to experience between man and himself.[45] However, in Arendt's view, the conviction that objective truth is not given to man, so that he can only know what he makes himself, breaks down, once it is applied to political theory. '...The idea that only what I am going to make will be real...is forever defeated by the actual course of events, where nothing happens more frequently than the totally unexpected...'.[46] It simplifies the history of ideas that both Villey and Arendt treat Hobbes as the key figure in the introduction of the new 'scientific' concepts into political philosophy. Since the intervention of Hobbes, all legal, and of course political, obligation has had to be traced back to the only possible 'self-evident' source of such obligation, the fact of a social contract or compact. One may vary the subjects of the compact, or the measure of consent which must really be present, but no obligation may exist which is not derived from a man-made, and for this reason only, self-evident starting point.

There is at least one perspective on the crisis of developing countries for which Arendt's history of the philosophy of science is not at all remote. In his now famous study, La Pauvreté, Richesse des Peuples, Tévoédjrè takes as a basic theme the abstraction of man from society and nature. He objects, above all, to a pattern of deductive, logical thinking, whereby those in the third world choose premises of reasoning outside of their societies, which then trap them into a series of inevitable consequences. They should, instead, employ a process of induction, beginning from the realities of their own societies, and based not on a hypothesis of a will to power, but on a 'good organization' of the life of human groups.[47] Tévoédjrè's vision of an economy, based as far as possible on the principle of production of goods for direct use rather than exchange, is not a nostalgic appeal to dying social structures. He insists that the social reality, into which a new technology of production must be integrated, is one which encompasses the richness of a biolcgical relationship between man and the natural elements, the richness of a feeling of belonging to a territory, of a consciousness of being part of a human and social universe.

This is the context in which Tévoédjrè rejects the foundations of an industrial capitalism which leads to such a specialization and centralization of knowledge and production, that the ideal of self-sufficient and locally responsible communities becomes a remote dream.[48] It can hardly be said that he sets out to provide the detail of the vision which Arendt clearly considers necessary, but there seems no doubt that he believes that the crisis of development must include the dimension of philosophical-scientific inquiry. Despecialization and decentralization of knowledge and production can only come as part of an assault on the authority accorded by Western culture to an abstract mode of thinking which is ostensibly indeterminate as to its starting point and which does not allow for any integrating framework.

So however uncongenial it may be for his professional self-assurance, the lawyer has to ask whether contemporary philosophy of science affords any support for a perspective such as Tévoédjrè's. One possible approach is suggested by the so-called systems view of life. Its basic principle appears very attractive to the debate on the right to development. It is supposed that every living organism is self-organizing in that its structure and function are not imposed by the environment, but are established by the system itself. At the same time, living organisms interact continuously with their environment. The systemic dimension of this biological theory is that each living organism is seen as a subsystem which, although relatively autonomous, is also a component of a larger organism, which is, finally, the eco-system of the entire planet.[49] In this perspective the individual is not supposed to be an isolated self, but should become aware of himself as an inseparable part of the 'cosmos' in which he is embedded. The systems view of life opposes the mechanical, supposedly Neutonian view of reality, as dominated by a linear process of cause and effect into which the isolated individual as an observer may assert his will with what Capra calls a cyclical pattern of events, known as a feed-back loop.[51] The properties of the total system cannot be predicted from the sum of their parts. Every one of its tissues is linked to every other one and they are all mutually interdependent.[52] The conclusion is the first political principle of ecology that man is part of a world which is an organic whole. He has first to understand himself as one organism in this whole, not merely supposing himself to be infinitely redefinable and the world infinitely malleable.

By way of conclusion it might not be without interest to look briefly at the contrast which Villey draws between pre and post-Renaissance European legal theory. He insists that the essential feature of the earlier tradition is that it did not take the individual as the starting point of juristic inquiry. Certainly consent is part of any system of law, but it has to be seen as no more than a part, just as the individual is no more than a part of the social whole. The concept of obligation may be central to morality, but it is only an aspect of law.[53] Drawing on an interpretation of Aristotle and of the Roman law juristic tradition, Villey claims that concepts of equity and justice must not be seen merely as moral qualities of persons, for instance to evaluate the quality of their actions (of will) in themselves, but rather as a measure or proportion applied to persons in their concrete social circumstances. In this perspective, the social world is not an inert material facticity, awaiting analysis. It has to be interpreted as a matter of what is a more or less complete representation of an idea or of a 'form' (e.g. the 'form' of a man is not simply the aging man or the child at play, but the adult reaching the summit of his 'development'). The task of the jurist is to discern these forms. Legislation may give them a more definite general shape and the judge may adapt them to concrete circumstances. However it always remains the task of the jurist to indicate solutions based upon the widest use of dialectic, confrontation of opinion, and attention to concrete circumstance.[54]

None of the argument of the present section can claim the rigour of the method of any particular discipline, least of all that of the history of ideas. However, in my view, there is a prima facie case that there is more to the crisis of legal theory relating to the right to development, than the impatience of developing country lawyers. Furthermore it appears that the crisis is not simply, as is virtually universally supposed, a political one. There is plenty of evidence that it goes to the root of Western culture. In this context it may well be an indication of hope that pre-modern Western legal culture was, possibly, more in tune with certain modern philosophical/scientific theories of the world, than is more dominant contemporary legal theory.

- 84 -

FOOTNOTES

1. U.N. Doc. G.A. Res. 2625/XXV.

2. See for instance, Ch. 5 of A. Cristescu, The Right to Self-Determination, Historical and Current Development on the Basis of U.N. Instruments, U.N. Doc. E/CN4/Sub.2/404/Rev. 1, 1981.

3. J.R. Henry, Mutations Du Droit International Du Développement, La France et L'Afrique. These, Universite de Nice (1977), 12-19 drawing on the legal theory of C. Chaumont, first set out in his "Cours géneral de droit international public", R.C.A.D.I., Vol. 130 (1970).

4. See A.J. Arnaud, "Les Origines Doctrinales du Code Civil Francais", and, by the same author, "Essai D'Analyse Structurale du Code Civil Francais", Vols. 9 and 16 of the Bibliothèque de Philosophie de Droit, 1969 and 1973.

5. This line of reasoning is based on a criticism of pretentions of legal 'neutrality' made by M. Troper in 'La Relation Du Droit International Avec La Structure Economique et Sociale', Quatrième Rencontre de Reims, 15-16 Oct. 1977, 43-44.

6. An unpublished paper by W. Benedek, 'Das Recht auf Entwicklung in universeller Sicht und im Rahmn des afrikanischen Menchenrechtsschutzes', 25.

7. B. Benchikh, Droit International du Sous-Developpement (1983), 191-192.

8. The point is made at various states by Troper, loc. cit., 24, 56 and 93. However it is a commonplace of the so-called dependency theory and its application to international law is outlined in T. Evers, El Estado en La Periferia Capitalista (1979), 96-107.

9. J.R. Henry, op. cit., 331.

10. E/CN4/1489 para. 35, also E/CN4/1983 para. 19 of the Preamble of the Project Declaration and Art. 7 of Part 1(i).

11. E/CN4/1983, op. cit., Part 2, Art. 12(d)(ii).

12. P. Alston, Development and the Rule of Law: Prevention Versus Cure as Development, Human Rights and the Rule of Law, I.C.J. (1981), 105.

13. Ibid., 102.

14. Ibid., 37.

15. J.J. Israel, "Le Droit au Dévelcppement" (1983), R.G.D.I.P., 5 at 27.

16. Benedek, loc. cit., 29.

17. P. Weil, 'Vers Une Normativite' Relative en Droit International (1982), R.G.D.I.P., 5 at 32-33.

18. Ibid., 24, 46.

19. Ibid., 16-17.

20. M. Villey, Seize Essais de Philosophie de Droit, Paris (1969) and La Formation de la Pensée Juridique Moderne (1968).

21. Cristescu, op. cit., 81.

22. E/CN4/1983/SR 17th-20th, 31st meetings.

23. E/CN4/1983/SR.19.

24. E/CN4/1983/20.

25. H. Reinhardt, Rechtsgleichheit und Selbstbestimmung der Volker in wirtschaftlicher Hinsicht, Die Praxis der Vereinten Nationen (1980), 64-65, also Alston loc. cit., 94 and R.F. Meagher, Wealth and Power, A Study of the Charter of Economic Rights and Duties of States (1979), 96-107.

26. A/37/442 22 Sept. 1982.

27. See Draft Code of Conduct on Transnational Corporations, art. 9. U.N. Doc. E/A/C/10/1982/6.

28. A. Mahiou, "Une Finalité entre le Développement et la Dependance", paper to be published in Les Sources du droit international du developpement (ed. Flory), Eds. de CNRS Paris (1984).

29. World Development Report, World Bank (1983), 126.

30. Benchikh, op. cit., 42-53.

31. World Development Report, 116-117.

32. F. G. Snyder, "Law and Development in the Light of Dependency Theory", 14 Law and Society Review, 723, 759.

33. Benchikh, op. cit., 151-163, 180.

34. Snyder, op. cit., 726.

35. World Development Report, 116-117, 120, 122-123.

36. Benchikh, op. cit., 60, 186 and 224-226, referring to the Lima Plan of Action and the Vienna Programme of Action on Science and Technology.

37. Ibid., 234-235.

38. Ibid., 233.

39. I. Wallerstein, The Capitalist World Economy (1979), 37.

40. Snyder, op. cit., 749, 753, 774-778.

41. Villey, Seize Essais...op. cit., 173-176, 194-201.

42. Ibid., 173-176.

43. H. Arendt, The Human Condition (1959), 237.

44. Ibid., 251.

45. Ibid., 230-231, 237.

46. Ibid., 266, 273-274.

47. (1978), 70-72.

48. Ibid., 32-33, 122-123, 138-139.

49. F. Capra, The Turning Point: Science, Society and the Rising Culture (1982), 307-309.

50. Ibid., 291.

51. Ibid., 287, 291.

52. Ibid., 308.

53. M. Villey, La Formation, op. cit., esp. 66.

54. Ibid., 39-46, 53-58.

STATE-MANAGED DEVELOPMENT: A LEGAL CRITIQUE

by

James C.N. Paul
Clarence J. Dias

State-managed programs to bring essential resources and other benefits to rural people are creatures of law as well as political economy and ideology. Different kinds of law can be used to organize administration and direct it toward prescribed objects, to create different kinds of institutions and to allocate powers and roles to actors within them. Similarly, different bodies of law can be used to prescribe processes for making decisions which dispose the agency's powers; and other bodies of law may be used to establish systems of review and regulation in order to hold actors accountable and to identify measures needed to reform existing structures.

Analysis of these elements can often reveal how existing regimes of law create or contribute to pathologies which regularly afflict state-managed programs--pathologies which in turn contribute to a political economy of impoverishment, exploitation and exclusion in rural areas. Conversely, this analysis may help to show how law may be differently used in order to promote self-reliant participation and more equitable allocation of resources, values which are now emphasized by new international norms proclaimed over the last decade or so.

The 1979, FAO-sponsored World Conference on Agrarian Reform and Rural Development adopted this declaration:

> Participation of the people in the institutions and systems which govern their lives is a basic human right and also essential for realignment of political power in favour of disadvantaged groups and for social and economic development. Rural development strategies can realize their full potential only through the motivation, active involvement and organization at the grass-roots level of rural people with special emphasis on the least advantaged strata, in conceptualizing and designing policies and programmes and in creating administrative, social and economic institutions including cooperative and other voluntary forms of organization for implementing and evaluating them.[1]

Other World Conferences, addressing other sectors of development--habitat, health and employment--have adopted similar resolutions.[2] But converting these international norms into practice will require changes in legal structures as well as changes in power structures. Here we attempt to analyze some tasks of legal change by critiquing ways in which law is presently used to structure state-managed rural development, and by suggesting ways to make these frameworks more responsive to the values of alternative development.

I. A Critique of the Legal Regimes of State-Managed Development

Understandably, one finds few general critiques of the amorphous mass of laws which govern the design and administration of different sectors of rural development in third world countries. The task seems forbidding because "rural development" encompasses diverse objectives as well as different kinds and levels of activity; e.g., macro and micro planning; regulating people and inspiring them; managing local facilities and national corporations. Various types of law may be used to structure a program: organic and subsidiary legislation; manuals and directives; unwritten customs of bureaucracies which assume the status of law through usage; general principles of public law drawn from the constitution, international commitments and court-made doctrines of administrative law; legislation of general application such as enactments governing public employment. It may seem difficult to make meaningful general observations about the use of these different kinds of legal materials in the structuring of the variegated activities which comprise "rural development." Nevertheless, some general hypotheses are offered here.

Despite new international norms calling for self-reliant participation, state-managed rural development continues to reflect continuities from colonial law and administration.[3] Law is still used to monopolize state control over most of those resources and activities which make development possible for the rural poor. The processes of designing programs are dominated by experts and technocrats, and characterized by <u>ex parte</u> decision making. Management and supervision of programs is exercised by hierarchies of officials whose outlook is professional and elitist--tendencies which are reinforced by rules governing recruitment, tenure and advancement in public employment. These officials often enjoy broad discretionary powers which are seldom regulated closely by law; conversely, ordinary people are seldom endowed with rights enabling them to influence official decisions. Similarly, there exist few accessible institutions with adequate powers to provide independent review and regulation of the operations of rural development agencies--particularly their impact on the poor and disadvantaged. The absence of review contributes to continuing failures to make changes within programs in order to make them more responsive to local needs or grievances. Cumulatively, these pathologies in law legitimize practices which lead to underallocation of essential resources to the rural poor; to their continued political exclusion from sectors where participation is most important, if it is valued at all; to discouragement or repression of new, popular, self-reliant economic or political initiatives.

Of course these propositions must be tested by reference to particular cases--and modified as the complexities of this subject are better understood. They are set out here because they appear to characterize so many case studies, including those in this volume, and because they indicate that neglect of the jurisprudence of rural development is a serious omission. A framework for developing legal critiques of particular programs is suggested below, along with some further observations. The focus is on the way law is used (<u>and not used</u>) to prescribe general legal principles governing the:

1. <u>design and enactment</u> of programs, i.e., the processes of <u>planning programs</u> and promulgating rules to enable them to go forward;

2. characteristics of <u>institutions</u> to carry out programs;

3. selection and control of <u>actors</u> who exercise important powers allocated to institutions;

4. articulation of <u>powers</u> delegated to institutions and actors;

5. prescription of <u>processes</u> followed to exercise these powers; and

6. establishment of <u>structures for review</u> of those decisions and for securing <u>accountability of actors</u> and institutions and reform of programs.

1. <u>Design and enactment</u>. Our focus here is on legal principles governing <u>processes which lead</u> to enactment of development programs: the investigation of needs, planning and drafting organic legislation, and subsidiary rules or legal commands expressed in other forms. Since these decisions determine ends and means of programs, and since ends and means are interdependent, participation at this stage by those whose interests are immediately affected, obviously becomes important.

Of course many different kinds of high-level decisions may affect the ultimate content of laws prescribing particular programs (e.g., pronouncements of official ideology; macro planning; prioritization). So one obvious vehicle for participation is the "political system." But in most countries the institutions and processes which make up this "system" provide little opportunity for "bottom-up" influence by the rural poor, particularly in spheres of government traditionally perceived as having to do with "administration." The design of programs, as well as implementation, has regularly been assumed to be a matter for planners and other experts, accountable to political executives.

Parties in "competitive" political systems are usually formed and dominated by urban elites with access to money and organizational resources. In one-party systems they tend to be parastatal institutions dominated by political executives. In either event they are seldom structured so as to become vehicles for grass-roots participation in the design or redesign of development programs. Similarly, one cannot assume that parliaments provide vehicles for effective participation. The rural poor, as a class, are seldom found in legislative chambers. Moreover, parliaments, like courts, are essentially "reactive" institutions; their powers must be invoked in a systematic, organized way by those groups who would seek to use them effectively. Like courts they are also complex institutions requiring skill and knowledge, physical and social accessibility, intermediaries and organizations for effective participation. These capacities are notably lacking in impoverished rural communities. But they usually can be found in the more dominant classes in society: high-ranking public officials; larger-scale landowners; entrepreneurs in agribusiness and other groups with commercial interests in agrarian economies. Striking indications of the political power of these groups in parliaments can be seen from a number of case studies of the enactment of land reform legislation.[4] Of course rural people may enjoy a chance to voice their frustrations in general elections. But elections are dominated by parties, and they seldom turn on the kinds of issues which concern us here.

In many countries, programs are enacted by executive decree with no consideration by the legislature, because, under existing constitutional arrangements or by virtue of the broad terms of existing enabling legislation, the executive already has the power to make the necessary rules. Indeed, it is probable that many development programs are undertaken without much if any initial attention to the need for laws to legitimize official actions already initiated. As several reports in this volume suggest, enabling rules are often regarded as a bothersome detail by planners and managers who want to get on with their projects. They perceive--or are told by experts--of developmental needs to be addressed, and thereafter they persuade political executives to act upon these findings. The identification of "problems" and the ends and means of a responsive program are determinations made within governmental offices without consultation before the process has moved to the point of initiating action. The experts who engage in these tasks are usually employed by and accountable to agencies which often have vested interests in the definition and solution of the problems to be resolved--and in maintaining the role of experts. Examples of this are portrayed in this volume: the imposition of urban land use controls in Africa; the imposition of regimes of water management in Sri Lanka and the Philippines; the countrywide imposition of village-based, state-regulated cooperatives in Niger. All of these programs proceeded with no meaningful interaction with people whose basic needs for land, water, credit and other essential resources inevitably were clearly affected by the projects prescribed. Countless other accounts of programs reflect these syndromes.[5]

As shown by the reports in this volume, the exclusion of rural people from these processes can produce many unfortunate results. Exclusion tends to reinforce the impulse of agencies to replicate existing approaches of "administering" to the poor rather than "empowering" them. Exclusion allows governments to perpetuate those less visible institutions which are empowered to appropriate surplus from the rural poor: parastatals which may determine terms of rural-urban trade, agencies which impose levies on crops. When professionals promulgate programs unilaterally, the outcome is regularly flawed by failures to relate the institutions and activities created to the needs and perceptions of people, for example, failures to relate programs to provide credit and inputs to farming cycles; failures to create cooperatives which are understood and accepted by those who are brought into them; failures to create community acceptance--and thus effective sanctions--to support regulations designed to prevent serious health hazards.[6] Disengagement of people from the process of making laws regularly leads to their disengagement from the steps taken to implement them.[7] A further result may be the continuing estrangement of the rural poor from their government.[8]

The problems of translating the "basic human right" to participate in design into a bundle of enforceable, legal rights are obviously complex. In what ways can law be used to provide meaningful "rights" of participation in the formulation of national plans for different kinds of agrarian programs, or in negotiations between a ministry and an international agency (or a TNC) looking towards establishment of an agribusiness or the erection of a dam? In what ways can affected groups influence redesign of an existing program concerned with management of water resources, credit or government lands? Rights to participate may depend, in part, on recognition of a wide variety of legal obligations and entitlements: requirements that legislative proposals be publicized with opportunities for public discussion in accessible forums; establishment of public commissions representative of the poor to review programs; recognizing the standing of popular organizations to be heard in ministries and other executive agencies where key policies are made; providing rights of access to the media.[9] These kinds of laws, if taken seriously, may pose threats to authoritarian regimes and established bureaucracies. Moreover, promises of participation--legal or otherwise--will do little to help the very people who are supposed to be empowered unless they enjoy rights to participate through organizations. The formation of grass-roots' groups is a first step in this process.

2. Institutions. Our focus here is on control and accountability within and between different kinds of organizations which manage programs. The belief that the state must control these institutions is deeply rooted. In part this reflects the entrenchment of colonial models. In part it reflects distrust of the capacities of rural people to control the operations of these agencies at local levels. Political economy considerations also loom large. Control of institutions entails control of patronage, agrarian production and allocative decisions which often carry significant implications to those in power. Thus it is not surprising that programs which provide resources directly to rural communities, or which regulate activities of rural producers, are usually subject to the control of political executives of the central government.[10]

Programs which are intended to provide services essentially through human resources--activities such as health care, education or agricultural extension--are usually organized through professionalized bureaus within ministries. Those which provide credit, inputs, and facilities for storage and marketing of crops may be organized through some combination of a system of cooperatives licensed and regulated by a bureaucracy and state corporations managed by professionals employed by the state and accountable to political executives.[11] Local institutions created to mobilize villagers and peasants to contribute money or work to build local roads or other facilities, or to share in other tasks (e.g., village or district "development councils" and other similar groups) are organized under laws which vest powers of direction (and sometimes coercion) in local officials.[12] Law enforcement agencies are another component in this panoply of state institutions. Their importance is often neglected in development literature. The police and the courts enforce penal-type regulations promulgated by ministerial institutions (e.g., regulations prescribing proper modes and schedules of agricultural production or proscribing environmental or health hazards); similarly they enforce collection of taxes and other levies. Other laws (such as the licensing of meetings) may be used to maintain the power of local officials to control political activities and frustrate mobilization of the rural poor.

Experience certainly shows that there is no one institutional form which is necessarily suitable for a particular function. On the contrary,

-41-

new institutional arrangements are attempted with sufficient frequency to suggest--despite the usual absence of publicity surrounding reorganizations--that the problem of institutionalization is both important and quite difficult to solve. Jurisdictions are frequently transferred from one ministry to another--and often enough to new ministries.[13] "Decentralization" is now frequently prescribed for diverse ends: to bring government closer to people and make it more responsive to them; to achieve greater "efficiencies" and "coordination" in decision making. But, as reports in this volume show,[14] decentralization by itself does not produce participation unless there are genuine devolutions of state powers. An account of Tanzanian experience suggests some of the reasons:

> In 1972, government operations were decentralized, vastly increasing the numbers of civil servants in the districts and regions. But budgetary and policy control remained at the center. Civil servants remained employees of the center, and because they were hired, fired, transferred, promoted, and paid by the center, they were, not surprisingly, more responsive to signals from above than from the villages. There was no one in the bureaucracy whose job it was to listen to and act as advocate for villagers, nor was there much, if any, reward in the system for such behavior.[15]

The paradigm of state-managed development administration assumes the necessity of some form of governmental control over institutions which allocate resources or regulate behavior deemed important for development purposes. But thoughtful critiques of development administration tell us that when the state manages a development program, much of the energy of those charged with implementation is inevitably diverted to maintenance of the institutions created rather than to innovative initiatives to satisfy the needs of intended beneficiaries: lacking the incentives of the market, or the need to satisfy a demanding electorate, maintenance of power becomes a dominant if implicit institutional value; release of power in order to encourage self-reliant community activities is rightly perceived as a threat.[16] While the social costs of this syndrome are now widely recognized, the creation of alternative, institutions still seems to be a novel, sometimes heretical, subject.

If rights of participation are valued ways must be found to include representatives of people who need to be empowered among decision-making bodies, or, alternatively, to use popular grass-roots organizations as institutions to administer programs by allocating powers and resources directly to them--as in the "inductive" approach to water management in Gal Oya, or in the model for primary health care

-42-

suggested by Oscar Gish. Of course, devolution of power from state to non-state institutions creates new, unfamiliar issues--which we discuss in a later chapter.[17] But if participation is valued there is a need at the outset to challenge the pervasive assumption that institutions of rural development must be controlled by state actors.

3. Actors. The focus here is on individuals within institutions who are empowered to make allocative decisions or enforce regulatory powers, at both macro and micro levels: in what ways do existing bodies of law prescribe norms of selection, orientation and individual accountability which reflect values of participation?

Recruitment of these employees is often dependent on satisfaction of formal educational requirements, particularly recruitment to higher levels where university degrees are prescribed, thus tending to limit entry to those able to enjoy these benefits. The resulting stratification within agencies means that higher-level officials are likely to be both unfamiliar with and socially distant from problems of the field and the people who must address them.[18] But professionalization is often apparent in rules governing entry and deployment into "lower" civil service jobs which furnish important human resources to rural people: e.g., providers of health, agricultural and police services within rural areas. Their recruitment and training is governed by rules prescribed by senior professionals within their institution, and their accountability runs to those persons--extending vertically to professional superiors rather than horizontally, into communities which the agency is supposed to serve.[19] Indeed, laws governing public employment generally insulate officials deemed to be exercising professional tasks from personal accountability to the public by creating immunities from civil liability which are not enjoyed by comparable actors in the private sector. An extension agent who gives plainly negligent advice or who callously refuses to attend to the ailing cow of a poverty-stricken family cannot easily be made to pay tort damages. Tax collectors or policemen who abuse their authority can invoke doctrines of privilege to persuade judges to dismiss charges against them.[20]

Relationships between officials and the rural poor may also be affected by laws which empower governments to maintain pay scales and "perqs" of office which--particularly in regard to higher positions--tend to set officials far apart in social as well as economic terms from the communities they are supposed to serve, and indeed enable officials to become part of the affluent power elite within communities. It is a matter of some interest--and importance--that government commissions set up to investigate pathologies in the civil service (commissions made up of professional public servants) so often recommend salary increases as the solution to the problems found. The causes and consequences of this phenomenon have been examined in several interesting studies.[21] All of these factors may help to maintain long-standing customs, imbued with the sanctity of law, which endow "public servants" with the kind of social status which requires respect and deference; they become important considerations in societies where stratification is already closely related to political power.

Indeed, in examining particular sectors of "rural development," it is often important to understand the political linkages--at both local and higher levels--between public officials and the more wealthy and powerful classes or groups who have an interest in the program. While civil service laws were historically intended to isolate and protect government employees from political influence, that premise may need critical review in third world settings. As noted, eligibility rules for higher office limit access to those who usually come from more affluent families, or who aspire to affluence as a result of higher education. Higher public office is often a means of commanding resources, patronage and other sources of largesse of great value to large-scale farmers, leaders of cooperatives and other wealthier people in rural communities. Often, too, the salary and perqs provided with higher office are enough to enable state actors to become "progressive" farmers, landlords or investors in agribusiness. In this way, and through other social connections (such as family linkages), civil servants become part of the ruling elite, and the regime of law establishing civil services may reinforce these tendencies by stratifying access to positions that count and insulating the occupants of such positions.

If participation is valued, legal principles governing state employment should emphasize the importance of holding actors personally accountable for harms they inflict through intention or disregard of known standards governing exercise of discretion. Indeed, as state institutions begin to work at local levels with community organizations (as in the health care and water-management systems described in reports in this volume), then state actors who provide specialized services to community groups should be treated, in legal terms, as servants of those groups--just as the Sarilakas and Gal Oya organizers were made responsible to the community served. Underlying legal principles governing recruitment should emphasize the continuing need to reach within impoverished communities to find and train people to staff development programs--something analogous to "affirmative action" programs favoring recruitment of women or other historically disadvantaged groups.

4. Powers. Reports in this volume portray the diversity of tasks delegated to officials at local levels: some are empowered by delegation to manage and provide physical resources (e.g., land, water) or human

-44-

resources (health care); some are authorized to interpret and enforce regulatory rules (e.g., governing use of water or land) or penal legislation protecting rights of plantation workers or tenants; some are required to license and supervise cooperatives or other local business organizations. While these diverse tasks entail exercise of different kinds of judgment, it is often important, in analyzing different programs, to examine whether and how law is used to direct different kinds of discretion towards desired objectives.

For example, it is notorious in some countries that the delegations of some kinds of "regulatory" discretion--e.g., to grant licenses, or register property or births--carry built-in opportunities for state actors to charge unprescribed fees for the exercise of discretion or expeditious action. Other kinds of delegated discretion carry other kinds of inevitable risks. Officials who allocate scarce resources--e.g., land--inevitably have to choose who will receive and who will be denied. If this discretion is left unguided, outside pressures will fill the vacuum. The delegatee, in making up his mind whether an applicant is worthy, is likely to be moved by those who can gain his attention and present convincing arguments, and this situation is usually prejudicial to those who lack intermediaries.

While these kinds of foreseeable problems can be addressed by subsidiary rules and directives, the prevailing tendency is to delegate powers in open-ended terms. The myth of the "neutral," "rational-legal" bureaucrat continues to guide lawmakers. For various reasons officials in central offices may be uncertain, ill informed and yet unwilling to develop further guidelines through collegial decision making with actors in the field. The tendency is to pass responsibility down without articulating standards of accountability, while still retaining powers to intervene. Thus, health officers, extension agents, cooperative inspectors, police and other officials in the field are essentially left free to determine how general rules or directions will be applied. But they must still satisfy what they perceive to be the expectations of their superiors and that can often best be done by satisfying dominant groups within the local community.[22]

These kinds of conclusions are suggested in some of the reports offered here. They are also nicely documented in a recent, rewarding legal analysis of the problems of implementing agrarian legislation in India:

> Laws are drafted by the legal department....The responsibility for implementing them is then passed down without any attempt to explain the rationale of these laws to the petty officials who can make or mar them. This was the experience in Akkalkua. This was also the author's reaction in Davoor and Shahada. The

-45-

officials, even to the level of the tehsildars are interested in identifying themselves with the traders, manufacturers and big farmers. Not surprisingly, they are not enthusiastic about implementing laws which have an adverse effect on their friends.[23]

Unregulated discretion can be used to legitimize practices which produce inaction, inertia, or be used to condone decisions which are inconsistent with other decisions made in like cases, or to condone practices which can lead to corruption. However, powers can be delegated in terms of the ends and means of the kind of development sought--in ways which create rights for intended beneficiaries as well as privileges for power wielders. As every lawyer knows, the way powers are articulated directs attention not only to what powers are bestowed but also for whose benefit they are to be exercised, and how--with whose participation. In theory, the way these kinds of goals and norms are set out as legal commands can affect:

(a) the duty of delegatees to articulate (through processes requiring a flow of information to, and consultation with, affected interests) more particular standards governing the exercise of discretionary powers;

(b) the capacity of intended beneficiaries to invoke law to demand a more equitable treatment and the entitlements (if any) enjoyed by affected people and groups in allocational decision making;

(c) the criteria by which the "effectiveness" of implementation of a state program can be measured;

(d) the criteria used to establish a meaningful system of accountability for administration; and

(e) the articulation of the relationship between political-economic aspirations of a program and the means of realizing them.

These kinds of guides and standards can be systematically developed and tailored to the needs of specific programs through subsidiary rules and directives; and general laws can require that this be done as part of the administrative process.

5. Process. Procedures governing decision taking can be a powerful constraint on otherwise unregulated discretion. The process followed to enact regulatory rules, determine entitlements to resources, organize cooperatives, compel behavior or impose sanctions can affect outcomes in many ways--by compelling examination of factual or normative assumptions, by providing information and understanding among those affected, by instilling confidence in and acceptance of decisions taken. In fact the processes used for decision making are usually left to the discretion of official actors. The officers of banks may be left free to establish eligibility rules and phasing of loans without knowledge of facts which may affect how the rules they establish will impact on different farming communities; the officers of an agency empowered to set commodity prices may fix rates without consulting producers who may be demonstrably exploited by the result; regulations to promote desired farming practices may be imposed without communucation with affected persons and hence under a misapprehension of highly relevant facts. Just as the law frequently fails to specify terms of access to decision makers, so it is frequently silent when it comes to prescribing duties to provide information. Yet the importance of information--and the consequences of lack of it--is a widely reported phenomenon in the literature of rural development. Knowledge of credit programs, of technologies, of rudimentary health hazards and precaution--knowledge geared to basic needs--is all too frequently lacking. The Sarilakas report (among others) suggests another important category: knowledge of one's legal rights. Where people lack information about the existence of programs ostensibly created to aid them, the program itself may fail to achieve its avowed objectives--in part because law-enforcing authorities remain ignorant of violations, or are unprepared to press the matter when there is no pressure to do so. As the 1978 Indian development plan noted,[24] the organized efforts of intended beneficiaries may often be the only way they can realize benefits they are supposed to enjoy, and, as the Sarilakas report shows, those efforts can only be forthcoming when people understand their entitlements.

In theory, general principles of law--expanding the concepts of "natural justice" or "due process"--can be developed to require various forms of informing, and consultation with, those directly affected--and often adversely--by agency action. The form and scope of opportunities to be heard may vary--depending on weighing the burdens imposed by consultation on program implementation against the burdens which impending rules or decisions may impose on individuals and groups. Of course provision of opportunities to be heard are of little value if the procedures to pursue these opportunities are complex and time-consuming. As Reginald

-47-

Green points out, procedures are rarely value free: they may provide the appearance of due process but in fact impose handicaps on the uneducated and produce other pathologies in administration. From the perspective of alternative development, due process procedures must be analyzed in terms of their value to the poor as a means of facilitating participation.

6. Review and Regulation. Case studies regularly show that state-managed rural administration generates grievances among intended beneficiaries. Accounts of the deployment of agricultural extension services show how relatively few "progressive" farmers are able to co-opt and benefit from this assistance--and the links it provides to government--at the cost of neglect of the poor. Similarly, the frequent outcome of the administration of cooperative laws is the creation of structures which are dominated by local elites and officials and used to control farming behavior of small holders, and often enough used for self-dealing purposes. Accounts of enforcement of tax and penal laws show how they are frequently used as instruments of coercion to repress dissidence. The Gal Oya report portrays another difficulty which frequently confronts peasant communities: the failure of different agencies to coordinate provision of technical advice, credit and inputs, so that these benefits can be realized at the time in the farming cycle when they are needed. The Sarilakas report also portrays familiar phenomena: the nonenforcement of laws designed to protect workers, debtors, tenants, women and others historically disadvantaged from exploitative practices.

The grievances generated by these outcomes may be widely shared, deeply felt; but they often remain relatively invisible to outside observers, in part because information on entitlements is withheld and because explicitly lawful means for seeking review and redress are uncertain and inaccessible and because other forms of protest are treated as unlawful. Thus failures to provide accessible structures with adequate power to review and regulate administration reinforces tendencies towards pathologies already described.

In theory, of course, a variety of opportunities for review can be made available. Mechanisms for administrative review could be built into the body of law structuring cooperatives, extension services and so on. But usually there is an absence of law on this subject. Complainants may be told to take their grievances to some higher official, or to write a letter. After a long delay they may be told the matter is under study. No law compels a prompt, reasoned response. None is forthcoming.[25] Similarly, auditing procedures (e.g., of cooperative transactions) are often notoriously lax. One reason why this is so is because the poor have no access to the accounts of state and parastatal bodies--and inadequate resources to review them.[26]

-48-

The courts may seem (to lawyers at least) to provide another forum. But of course there are many constraints: ignorance, fear and suspicion of the function of government courts; lack of access or intermediaries; lack of "standing" to present a "justiciable" claim, or a "class" action; lack of jurisdiction; the understandable reluctance or inability of judges to review discretionary actions; immunities of officials; lack of suitable remedies--e.g., powers to put agencies under injunctions compelling affirmative changes in structure or policy. Whether administrative law could or should be reformed to enable courts to exercise broader roles of review and regulation is a question discussed below.[27] In recognition of some of the difficulties, many governments have created ombudsman agencies to provide more accessible alternative or supplementary institutions. But, like courts, these agencies can only review and respond to individual complaints, not systemic problems; they lack broad remedial powers and "clout" to compel structural changes in development programs.

From time to time, needs to provide for more adequate review and regulation are recognized. Allegations of abuse of powers, incompetence, systemic breakdowns and dissatisfaction with the "bureaucratic style" are brought forward--sometimes by frustrated leaders of governments. Special commissions are appointed (though they rarely are representative of the victims of the situations exposed) and various remedies proposed--e.g., creation of ombudsmen offices, codes of ethics, tightening fiscal controls, "decentralization." Usually, however, these studies define and approach the problems from the perspectives of etatist paradigms of development administration: the need for discipline and rectitude in existing structures. Seldom is the problem of review and regulation cast in terms which emphasize opportunities for victims of maladministration and under-allocation to present demands for systemic and structural changes--to seek remedies which strike at root causes of dissatisfaction through creation of alternative structures. Seldom are the people most affected given any real power in the system of review. Perhaps this is because investigative and "law reform" commissions are dominated by political executives, technocrats and eminent lawyers who are relatively insensitive to the problems and perspectives of the rural poor.[28]

In the absence of other alternatives, the political system may offer the most likely avenue of protest. But, as we have already seen, there are constraints: the rural poor lack resources, organization and intermediaries to press their demands on government, and local administration in rural areas is usually quite hostile to sui generis attempts of people to mobilize and take collective action to press grievances, outside of the activities permitted within parties. Nevertheless, in view of the absence of other avenues, and in view of the need for basic structural changes, it seems clear that mobilization, organization and collective action are essential. For it is doubtful that systemic changes, entailing redistribution of power can--or will--be forthcoming solely as a result of reforms developed from within governments.

II. Changing the Legal Regime of State-Managed Development

There is now widespread disillusionment with prevailing forms of state-managed development. "Participation" and "accountability" have become conventional prescriptions, and the questions more often debated relate to the meaning and importance to be ascribed to these objectives and to ways of accommodating them with perceived needs for professional and state controls. Two approaches are contrasted here.

The "reformist" approach is so labeled because the purpose is not so much to challenge the basic premises of state management as it is to make official institutions more responsive to human needs' goals and more accountable to rule of law norms. A variety of reforms have been attempted or discussed; it is not possible to catalogue them here, but a summary of three kinds of reformist approaches may illustrate some recent tendencies and problems.

One set of reforms focuses on the redesign of institutions (to secure decentralization, autonomy, consolidation of functions and collaborative participation) and the reorientation of actors (to promote consultation). One model for this is a district agricultural development agency--a corporate-type institution--which would possess a number of "integrated" powers (e.g., planning, provision of services and inputs, marketing and transport) to produce a package of benefits.[29] The institution might be controlled by a directorate (which might include local representation), or it might be supervised solely by a manager who would in turn deal with each of the relevant ministries and other central organs providing resources to the field. Devolution would include block grants and broad authority over all functions allocated to the agency. Local participation --in planning as well as administration--might be secured through (state created) village or ward development committees. Field staff would be retrained to learn techniques of participation.

Devolution may indeed bring control over resources nearer to the rural poor, but it does not, *per se*, bring it within their grasp; nor does it alter existing stratifications of power within communities. Nor, experience suggests, does it necessarily alter other administrative practices leading to underallocation or corrupt dealings with the disadvantaged. Many district development corporations in Tanzania appear to have been mismanaged, and pressure to produce revenues coupled with power of monopolization have led to programs of little value, indeed sometimes harmful, to the interests of the poor.[30] Several papers in this volume go further in suggesting why devolution, by itself, does not meet the needs of marginal cultivators, tenants and other agricultural workers for self-reliance and empowerment.[31]

Another set of reforms looks towards imposition of tighter discipline over government actors. These include promulgation of codes of conduct, new procedures for establishing criminal liability for abuse of power or corruption coupled with more draconian sanctions, and establishment of new ombudsman institutions for investigating grievances. Thus local officials may be prohibited from engaging in private conduct which creates vested interests in existing forms of rural administration or in existing social structure: landlording, moneylending or employment of farm labor may be proscribed. Officials may be charged with broadly-defined crimes of corruption where their manifest affluence clearly exceeds their salary; the burden of proof is shifted to the defendant to prove the source of his wealth.

Again, these measures, by themselves, seem neither to have changed power relations nor cured many pathologies which help to maintain poverty.[32] Ombudsman institutions may indeed provide some measure of relief for some kinds of grievances--if (and it is often a big if) these agencies are visible, readily accessible, independent and relatively efficient in handling their jurisdiction. But as already noted these institutions are reactive rather than proactive. Their jurisdiction does not enable them to strike at the root causes of recurrent problems nor to redesign inefficient programs.[33]

Another reformist approach centers around active use of administrative law (as that subject is traditionally understood by lawyers). A number of recent decisions by the Indian Supreme Court may illustrate some of the possibilities open to lawyers, working in behalf of the rural poor, to use the courts to challenge aspects of rural administration.

In one case[34] the court granted "standing" to employees who alleged that the impending sale of various plants of a government corporation not only violated their constitutional rights, but that the procedures followed violated various other provisions of law designed to secure rectitude in these kinds of transactions. The court held that all of these contentions could be raised by the petitioners (and proceeded to examine the merits of various alleged defects in the sale proceedings). In allowing the petitioners to secure judicial scrutiny of both the "decision to sell and the sale proceedings," in sweeping aside the "standing" objections of the Attorney

General, the court declared that it would take a "broader view" of standing to challenge the corporate decisions. These enterprises are "owned by the people and those who run them are accountable to the people." Parliamentary control was found to be too "diffuse and ineffective" to preclude the need for judicial review in order to provide some forum to secure the interests of accountability. The terms on which standing was granted here are broad enough to encompass other affected groups--such as consumers who may be disadvantaged by a corporate decision, or farmers disadvantaged by eligibility rules. By implication this doctrine might allow courts to review many realms of rural administration affecting people particularly dependent on an agency for goods or services. The concurring opinion of Justices Iyer and Bhagwati noted that the court's "fascinating [doctrine of] expansionism is of strategic importance viewed in the perspective of Third World jurisprudence." They went on to justify "expansion" in terms of the "social audit function" of courts and the need for "participative public justice."[35]

This liberalization of access to the courts has been combined with liberalization of the scope of review in several cases. In one of considerable interest the court applied doctrines of promissory estoppel to the dealings between a private company and a ministry.[36] Claims of immunity based on notions of the need for official discretion in awarding benefits and the need for protection from harassment were all swept aside. Again the court recognized that it was dealing with rules of "considerable importance" to "public law," with doctrines capable of "vast possibilities of growth."

In a third case the court held that a licensing agency was bound by its published eligibility rules and could not change them "arbitrarily."[37] Again a wide scope for judicial review was quite consciously opened. The court depicted government as a vast enterprise dispensing new forms of "largesse"--services, licenses and other benefits. The argument that these dispensations are "privileges" not "rights" was swept aside. The crucial point was that "discretion" to dispense "largesse" must always be governed by norms and these can never be arbitrary,[38] and the courts are open to determine "arbitrariness," and where a transaction appears prima facie to reflect favoritism or special treatment the burden appears to shift to the government to justify its legality.

It is of course uncertain whether judges in other countries can be persuaded to follow this new "access jurisprudence" geared to an avowedly "activist" judicial review of programs of resource allocation. Moreover, there are significant limitations on the capacity of courts--even "activist" ones--to reform the legal frameworks of administration. Principles may appear to be won--but little may happen as a result.[39] People must be mobilized (and helped by support groups) to use new legal rules, and the judicial process cannot by itself produce these resources.

Indeed nearly all of the reforms which address the pathologies of state-managed development administration depend in the first instance on the existence of self-managed organizations of the rural poor. Only through organization (and support from other groups) can they hope to secure: participation in the processes of design, access to and accountability from local officials, proper audits of public bodies, invocation of the remedial powers of the courts, access to the legislature or to investigative commissions.

The "Alternative" Approach is so labeled because the premise of state control is directly challenged. The contention is that state monopolization of power over institutions which plan and manage development programs--monopolization of the power to make law governing their creation and management--regularly leads to the kinds of pathologies and biases portrayed in the case studies reported here and in so many other accounts of rural administration. Even more important, the premise of state monopolization is an inherent contradiction of the values which make people-centered development meaningful. Accordingly, the first task is to help people to form their own organizations, and to help these groups play a much more pervasive, dynamic role in the design and administration of development. Another step is to bring the processes of design and lawmaking back to the communities affected. Another step is to use "non-state" structures to carry on activities which people can carry on themselves through organizations of their own design. As some papers in this volume show, it is indeed possible to organize local health care programs through participatory institutions created by and accountable to the community itself. Water resource programs can be managed, at least for many crucial purposes, by groups created and governed by those who depend on the water for their livelihood.[40] Group enterprises can be created by people themselves, using "law" developed by adapting traditions and norms of community cooperation to new circumstances.[41] Of course specially-trained human resources are needed by rural people to make some kinds of "development" possible--health care providers, extension agents, persons versed with rudimentary knowledge of accounting and others. But it does not follow that these specialists must be provided through structures which make them only accountable to state bureaucracies rather than those who most need their services. Reports in this volume show how health workers, organizers and other personnel can be provided directly to participatory, community groups which manage these services, and the employment relationship can be restructured to provide for accountability to the community.[42] This change of control over institutions and actors can lead directly to processes for determining powers and guidelines for making allocational or regulatory decisions which are participatory, and hence better understood and usually more acceptable. Further, these arrangements provide more meaningful opportunities for presentation of grievances; and a greater likelihood of review and regulation which will be geared to community needs.

Strategies and methods to develop "non-state" structures and enable them to take over tasks of administration which the community itself can handle are discussed in the concluding chapter. It should be apparent, however, that there is not always a clear line between "reformist" and "alternative" approaches towards change. The mobilization of rural groups can be reinforced by efforts to impose a human-needs-oriented "rule of law" on rural administration, or to create new locally-managed institutions for agricultural development. Both approaches call for the creation of new kinds of social resources--including legal resources--which communities must enjoy if capacities for mobilization and organization are to be developed. That subject, too, is deferred to our final chapter.

* * * * *

Most of the papers in this volume are reports analyzing experiences of particular programs or sectors of development. Those which follow (in this section) are descriptions and critiques of state-managed programs; others (in the next section) contrast state-managed programs with "non-state," "people-managed" "alternatives." Cumulatively, the papers depict efforts to organize a wide range of development activities: urban land use controls, redistribution and "consolidation" of land holdings, cooperatives, indigenous businesses, water resources, health care. Thus, there is, here, an interesting body of source materials to develop critiques of conventional approaches to development administration.

Several papers depict tendencies which typify the processes of designing and enacting state programs. For example, the historical phenomenon of imposing new structures, unilaterally on rural communities--of creating intervening state institutions which monopolize control of access to resources--is illustrated in Coldham's account of the imposition of land tribunals in Kenya and Munkner's account of the imposision of state-regulated cooperatives in the Ivory Coast and Niger. The power of elites to shape land reforms)of a socialist government) is treated in Samaraweera's analysis of the design of programs in Sri Lanka in the '70s. The role of experts (notably expatriates) in designing programs is portrayed vividly in the reports of McAuslan (on the imposition of urban planning and land use controls in several African countries) and Uphoff (on attempts to impose a hierarchy of state-prescribed, water-management committees on the rice farmers served by the large Gal Oya irrigation project in Sri Lanka). Gish discusses the consequences of "top down," ex parte planning of local health care programs by medical experts of international and national health agencies.

Characteristics of state institutions which manage development programs, and of actors in them--their autonomy, lack of accountability, antipathy to participation and their links to other powerful groups and classes--are brought out in a number of papers. Ghai describes the evolution of new centers of bureaucratic power following a "decentralization" scheme in Papua New Guinea which was supposed to bring government closer to people. Anderson discusses governmental manipulation of community development institutions in the Philippines, and the alliances between local officialdoms and the affluent in rural communities. Uphoff describes the autocratic characteristics of the Irrigation Department of the Ministry of Agriculture which administered the Gal Oya project, and the effects of this "style" on "equity" and "efficiency" in water allocation. Gish discusses the tendencies of ministries of health to reproduce highly professionalized modes of delivering services which preclude or discourage community participation both in the work of health care, and in planning and managing local programs.

The problems of articulating delegations of discretionary powers are interestingly developed in McAuslan's discussion of the difficulties of encouraging building regulations which would encourage rather than frustrate innovative construction of housing for the urban poor in African settings. Similar problems are suggested in Ghai's discussion of powers delegated to a bureaucracy in Papua New Guinea which was charged with the task of licensing "indigenous business groups," thereby bestowing valuable privileges of legal personality on these groups. The tendency to delegate powers in terms which create new realms of authority for state actors rather than new rights for intended beneficiaries is discussed in Uphoff's description of draft legislation mandating formation of water-user groups in Gal Oya.

Several of the papers discuss the absence of meaningful structures for review and regulation, and the implications of this omission for people who are dependent upon public and private actors who control resources. The lack of access of the Sarilakas sugar workers to courts left them at the mercy of employers who flagrantly abused statutory obligations designed to protect worker interests in the employment relationship. McAuslan describes the impotence of the urban poor when it comes to contesting plainly ultra vires actions of planning bodies--and the social costs of that situation.

As McAuslan suggests, traditional administrative law reforms--e.g., attempts to provide access and opportunities for affected people to be heard--are, by themselves, unlikely to cure many pathologies. As the Sarilakas group argues, Basic Human Needs strategies of development call for basic changes in power relations affecting the design, administration and regulation of programs. These changes call for new concepts--and rights--of participation. Strategies to purse those objectives are addressed in the concluding section of this volume.

FOOTNOTES

1. Food and Agriculture Organization, World Conference on Agrarian Reform and Rural Development, Programme of Action (1979).

2. For discussion of this phenomenon see S. Marks, "Emerging Human Rights: A New Generation for the '80s," Rutgers Law Review 33:436 (1980).

3. See U. Baxi, The Crisis of the Indian Legal System (1982) (especially chapter 2). These continuities are portrayed in several of the papers in this volume, e.g., Ghai's discussion of bureaucracy in PNG and Uphoff's description of the Gal Oya "IO."

4. In this connection Samaraweera's account of the impetus for and constraints on Sri Lankan land reform is instructive. See also, e.g., Inayatullah (ed.), Land Reform: Some Asian Experiences (1980). (Contains a number of country studies. See especially Blondie Po's account of Philippines' experience. Also Inayatullah's "Concluding Review.")

5. See, e.g., D.C. Korten and F.B. Alfonso, Bureaucracy and the Poor: Closing the Gap (1981), especially chapter 12 by David Korten summarizing experience of various country and project reports.

6. Ibid. See IDS Bulletin 10:2 (1979) edited by Robert Chambers, entitled Rural Development: Whose Knowledge Counts?

7. See, e.g., the discussion in Uphoff's account of planning water-management programs. This point is also developed in Vasudha Dhagamwar's "Problems of Implementing Agrarian Legislation in India," Journal of the Indian Law Institute 23:228 (1981).

-56-

8. Sources cited, notes 5, 6, 7 supra.

9. Cf. Neelan Tiruchelvam's proposal for a "National Poverty Law Centre" which would assert these rights at the national level in behalf of rural communities in "The Legal Needs of the Poor: Towards an Alternative Model of Group Advocacy" in International Commission of Jurists, Development, Human Rights and the Rule of Law (1981).

10. See, e.g., G. Lamb, Peasant Politics: Conflict and Development in Murunga (1974); G. Hyden, "Government and Cooperatives" in G. Hyden, K. Jackson and J. Okumu, Development Administration in Kenya (1970); M. Bratton, The Local Politics of Rural Development: Peasant and Party-State in Zambia (1980) (Chapter 1).

11. See, e.g., U. Lele, The Design of Rural Development: Lessons from Africa (1975) on the problems of "integrating" these activities. R. Chambers, Managing Rural Development (1974); Hunter et al (eds.), Policy and Practice in Rural Development (1976).

12. See, e.g., Bratton, op. cit., note 10 (study of Village and Ward Development Committees in Zambia).

12a. See U. Baxi, note 3 (Chapter 4).

13. See sources cited note 11; Hyden et al., note 10.

14. Notably that of Yash Ghai on Papua New Guinea experience. One workshop which generated papers for this volume had the benefit of an excellent overview paper by Diana Conyers, "Decentralisation for Regional Development: a Comparative Study of Tanzania, Zambia and Papua New Guinea" (1980).

15. L. Fortman, "Pitfalls in Implementing Participation: An African Example," RDPR 1:1:9 (1979). See for an interesting critique by an architect of decentralization, J.H.J. Maeda, "Creating National Structures for People-Centered Agrarian Development" in Koretn and Alfonso; op. cit., note 5. See also Conyers, supra, note 14.

16. See B.B. Schaffer, "The Deadlock in Development Administration" in C. Leys (ed.), Politics and Change in Developing Countries (1969).

17. See Paul and Dias, "Alternative Development: a Legal Prospectus," infra. For another interesting discussion of these problems, see F. Korten, "Community Participation: a Management Perspective on Obstacles and Options" in Korten and Alfonso, op. cit., note 5.

18. See B.B. Schaffer, "Administrative Legacies and Links in the Post-Colonial State: Preparation, Training and Administrative Reform," Development and Change 6:13 (1974).

19. See the discussion of this problem in Uphoff's paper. For illustrations see, e.g., R.F. Weber, G.B. Kerr, H.B. Smith, J.M. Seymour, Senegal: the Sine Saloum Health Case Project (Project Impact Evaluation No. 9) (USAID 1980); D.K. Leonard, Reaching Peasant Farmers in Kenya (1977).

20. The examples are suggested by episodes reported in the sources cited in note 19 and Dhagamwar, note 7. Chapter 1 in Baxi, op. cit., note 3, develops the theme that existing administrative law helps to establish state actors as an "immunized," privileged class. See also Baxi's "Introduction" to I.P. Massey's Administrative Law (1980).

21. See, e.g., Schaffer, note 18; P. Collins, Administration for Development in Nigeria (1980) (reviewing the Udoji commission's report). See also P. Bennell, "The Colonial Legacy of Salary structures in Anglophonic Africa," IMAS 20:1:127 (1982).

22. Cf. F. Korten, note 17.

23. Dhagamwar, note 7.

24. See the quotation in Chapter 2, supra.

25. On delay and evasion as an important strategy of bureaucracies, condoned by law, see Baxi, note

26. Secrecy in maintaining accounts of cooperatives and other agencies which deal directly with the rural poor is often a major concern of the poor. See F. Korten, note 17, Maeda, note 15.

27. See also U. Baxi, "Introduction" to I.P. Massey's Administrative Law (1980).

28. See note 21. Compare Tiruchelvam, note 9; Baxi, supra.

29. See, e.g., G. Hunter, "Linking Levels of Planning and Action for Participatory Rural Development," RDPR 1:3:5 (1980). Cf. F. Korten, note 17.

30. H.P.B. Moshi, "Financial Performance of Public Corporations: a Case of District Development Corporations," Utafiti 5:1:1.u (1980).

-58-

31. See, e.g., those by Ghai and Coldham. See also Korten, note 17.

32. Cf. Moshi, Note 30.

33. Cf. R.L. Martin, "The Ombudsman in Zambia," Journal of Modern African Studies 15:239 (1977).

34. Fertilizer Corporation Kamagar Union v. Union of India, A.I.R. 1981, S.C. 344.

35. Ibid. at 351.

36. M.P. Sugar Mills Co. v. State of Uttar Pradesh et al., A.I.R. 1979, S.C. 621.

37. Ramana Dayaram Shetty v. International Airport Authority, A.I.R. 1979, S.C. 1628.

38. The court seems to have drawn extensively from Charles Reich's "especially stimulating article," "The New Property," 73 Yale Law Journal 733 [1964]." A.I.R. 1979, S.C. at 1637.

39. See V. Dhagamwar, "Public Interest Litigation in Tenancy Matters: The Case of Akkalkua" (paper presented to the Law and Society Association meeting at Toronto, June 1982). The author, working as a "legal activist" for poor farmers provides a number of illustrations where court victories were, or would be, of little value unless backed up by a "SAG" (Social Action Group) working for, and with, local groups. Cf. Baxi, note 27.

40. See, e.g., the papers by Gish, Uphoff and Anderson. See also F. B. Alfonso, "Assisting Farmer Controlled Development of Community Irrigation Systems" in Korten and Alfonso, note 5.

41. The Upper Volta village groups described by Hans Munkner are a good illustration of this process.

42. See, e.g., the descriptions of the recruitment and accountability of the "legal facilitators" in the Sarilakas report, and the "I.O.s" in Uphoff's Gal Oya report. See also Maeda, note 15, reporting on government plans to "second" extension and other service providers directly to Ujamaa villages.

-284-

ALTERNATIVE DEVELOPMENT: A LEGAL PROSPECTUS

by

James C.N. Paul
Clarence J. Dias

The generation of new kinds of "grass-roots" organizations is now widely believed to be an essential first step in the evolution of new approaches to development which emphasize human needs and "human rights."[1] These "non-state" organizations can also become--it is assumed--vehicles through which millions of people can gain capacities for self-reliant collective action and power to change economic and political relations which perpetuate impoverishment.

To some these beliefs may seem utopian: it is quite easy to be cynical and certainly appropriate to be cautious about the possibilities.[2] But the aspirations are grounded in values which, to many, seem to express the very essence of "development" if that idea is taken seriously;[3] and the assumptions are grounded in some empirical reality.[4]

Moreover, it may be worth emphasizing again, here, that "alternative development" is not a holistic theory of social change; rather the term denotes a variety of interrelated strategies grounded in basic principles such as participation and self-reliance. To a considerable extent these principles carry significant legal implications. These have hardly yet been discussed, and the omission is serious because a focus on legal issues raised by "alternative development" is a useful way of examining concrete problems which illustrate both difficulties and possibilities of developing these strategies. The agenda is large and complex. Only some topics are explored here. We address two interrelated areas of concern.

1. The need to create legal environments which will facilitate the emergence of "non-state" rural organizations of the poor as vehicles for community empowerment and development.

2. The need to create "legal resources" (i.e., knowledge and skills) which can be used by local groups and others working in their behalf to advance shared interests.

-285-

I. Legal Environments

Despite neglect or repression, in much of the third world, groups --varying in size, function, form and relationship with the state--have continued to be part of the rural scene. Some are small and rooted in tradition; some simply provide organizational forms for mutual self-help, savings or construction of desired community facilities; some have evolved into vehicles of protest; some are in overt opposition to governments of the day. Increasing disillusionment with conventional strategies of development administration has stimulated increasing interest in understanding why and how these groups have evolved--or why they have languished and failed; how they can further develop if they are given more breathing space by state law and administrators, more resources from outside sympathizers. A division of the ILO has initiated a series of interesting studies --histories of mobilization and collective efforts by the rural poor, in different settings and different times, to confront conditions of impoverishment, histories of success and failure. A number of international and regional nongovernmental organizations have become more directly involved in providing backup services for rural groups.[5] In some countries officials and agencies sympathetic to needs for rural mobilization are seeking ways to help develop popular organizations by providing them with organizational resources. (Project Sarilakas provides an interesting example of this kind of action by both national and international agencies.) In a number of countries, rural unrest is becoming more visible. Increasing rural mobilization may lead to increasing conflict in one form or another. States will be forced to respond to this phenomenon. Law and human rights will be implicated in these struggles.

As several papers in this symposium show, a large empirical literature discusses the psychic and other benefits which autonomous participatory groups can often bring to rural peoples--in terms of generating functional knowledge and civic capacity and willingness to take political and economic risks--the foundations for more sophisticated efforts to initiate collective, self-reliant activities. There is also a growing body of experience to show that land reform or credit or other service-providing programs can be more successful--in terms of human needs criteria--when organized through "joint venture" arrangements between state and non-state institutions. Several reports in this collection show how this has happened. These structures can often be seen as transitional institutions which may, in the future, assume further functions and powers in the local political economy of development.

Many social factors seem to contribute to success or failure of efforts to form participatory groups and to engage in collective action to pursue shared interests. There is much to be learned by those who seek to help these complex processes. But, legal factors are also important. The kind of institution we are here discussing must originate as a result of the voluntary, collective action of its members. The powers, functions and tasks it assumes must be developed by endogenous group norms. The roles of particular actors--organizers, leaders and others endowed with special functions--must be determined by the group, and these actors must be accountable in the first instance to the group itself, not, to some external public authority. The processes by which decisions are made must be participatory, but again the norms to achieve this result must be derived from the group. Experience suggests that the capacity to develop this kind of "non-state," organic group law is probably essential to maintenance of a group over any extended period.[6]

The task of state law is to allow this to happen. That can only be done by recognizing the essential rights of people to form organizations and use them to pursue economic and political purposes.

1. Rights to Form Non-State Organizations. Convention 141 of the ILO, adopted by the International Labour Conference of 1975 and now ratified by a number of third world countries, calls for legal recognition of a universal right of "rural workers" to form "non-state" rural organizations "of their own choice." The term "rural workers" includes smallholders, tenants, laborers, sharecroppers and self-employed home workers. The convention can serve as a model for the kind of legal environment we are talking about. It declares (with emphasis added):

> Article 3. 1. All categories of rural workers, whether they are wage earners or self-employed, shall have the right to establish and to join organizations of their own choosing without previous authorization.
>
> 2. The principles of freedom of association shall be fully respected; rural workers' organizations shall be independent and voluntary in character and shall remain free from all interference, coercion or repression.
>
> 3. The acquisition of legal personality by organizations of rural workers shall not be made subject to conditions of such a character as to restrict the application of the provisions of the preceding paragraphs of this Article.
>
> 4. In exercising the rights provided for in this Article rural workers and their respective organizations, like other persons or organized collectivities, shall respect the law of the land.

> 5. The law of the land shall not be such as to impair, nor shall it be so applied as to impair, the guarantees provided for in this Article.

A "recommendation" enacted by the same conference, in effect, sets out some assumptions explaining the intended scope of these guarantees: rural organizations are envisioned as vehicles of "defense" of the "interests of rural workers," and as vehicles to enable more effective "participation" in state structures--not only participation in "the formulation" and "implementation" of "programs of rural development" (at "all stages"), but also in the "evaluation" and determination of accountability of those who manage them. Further, rural worker organizations are to be vehicles for direct access to goods and services controlled by the state; they are to be vehicles for initiating local, public works and organizing new kinds of group-managed economic activities.[7]

Convention 141 is a counterpart of the much celebrated Convention 87 which deals with employees. A great deal of "law" has been developed by the ILO through specific interpretations of 87--interpretations requested when workers' organizations have alleged that particular laws or practices violate their rights.[8] Most of this jurisprudence can be carried over by analogy to 141, and Convention 141, like 87, could become something of an international Magna Carta for rural workers--if they can become empowered to use it in the same way that unions have used Convention 87 over the years.

Of course, as Convention 141 indicates, the right to maintain organizations of rural workers can be limited by general laws which protect other shared social values of importance to rural people--notably the very values which make the right to organize beneficial to people. Thus the right to organize is not a right enabling some to use groups to exploit or repress others within or without the group, nor to use groups for corrupt purposes. There are also shared interests in securing peace within communities--including peace between different religious or ethnic groups, and shared interests in maintaining equitable access for all groups to state and parastatal structures. But these interests are not hostile to the values which should underlie law geared to "alternative" development, and they can be accommodated without impinging on the rights of rural workers to form organizations.

Indeed, the state's role as facilitator of these rights--rather than regulator--is what must be stressed. Clearly the intention of Convention 141 was that the state should assume affirmative obligations to foster, not frustrate, non-state structures developed by people themselves.

Several reports in this collection show how state agencies can be formed to provide organizers, information and related resources directly to rural communities. The importance of that role is now widely recognized. A 1978 workshop of "senior agricultural administrators from developing countries," sponsored by the Overseas Development Institute, subscribed with unanimity to this pronouncement:[9]

> We believe that a radical revision of both strategy and tactics are needed....There can indeed be dynamic government action, in investment in the rural environment and infrastructure, so that the field of action can become one in which human energy can be more fruitfully employed.... But final achievement depends upon the initiative and self-organization of the poorer people themselves and the demands which they make upon government. It is the business of government and administration so to cast their policies and their contacts with the rural population that this initiative can be far more widely supported and translated into action....'Rural activists' are needed, both from the people and from the [agencies] who support them.

Existing laws and modes of administration in many countries stand in sharp contradiction to these aspirations. Laws which require registration and official approval of voluntary associations can be used to frustrate formation of "lawful" groups. State laws which prescribe a fixed structural form for those voluntary organizations which seek to enjoy legal capacities to make contracts or own property may be used to restrict the "right of rural workers to form organizations of their own choice;" and they may, in any event, deny values of endogeneity in group formation which are important to alternative development. Penal laws which proscribe vaguely-defined activities, such as open-ended prohibitions against threats of disorder, often can be construed to legitimize suppression of group activities which cause no demonstrable harms--only the possibility in the minds of law enforcers. Similarly, licensing laws which regulate group activities --such as holding meetings--can be used to frustrate organizational activities, particularly when the law enforcers are vested with lawless discretion. These possibilities are vastly increased when there are no meaningful popular controls over the police, when local courts are not made sensitive to human rights and human needs values and when people lack both tangible and intangible resources necessary to use courts as agencies to vindicate rights.

There are other more subtle ways by which local officials can contain the activities of autonomous rural organizations. By monopolizing state control over essential resources, or by using parastatal organizations to distribute them, local officials can preempt or co-opt grass-roots efforts of people to work through groups. By catering to traditional elites, or to existing distinctions between castes, or sub-classes, and to traditional norms governing sex and age roles and to other anachronistic customs, they can reinforce tendencies towards segmentation and repression of the disadvantaged. Rumors and lies can be systematically circulated--defamation is a disabling technique frequently used by those who feel threatened by organizational efforts.[10] State control of communications, education and the training and recruitment of people who provide community services can be used to limit the quantity and quality of contacts of illiterate and geographically-confined people with the outside world and with sources of much needed information. Cumulatively, these conditions may impose formidable obstacles--especially in communities where rural people seem to lack traditions and experience of forming and participating in organizations large enough in scale and sufficiently sophisticated in outlook and management techniques to confront impoverishing conditions and structures. As the Sarilakas report suggests, rights to organize, whether they already exist on paper or have to be won through practice and conflict, may never be realized in many settings unless people are helped through provision of social resources--notably, knowledge and skills.

Thus, in many places, rights to form organizations (whether or not they are recognized in law) will have to be won through hard trials. Moreover, as illustrated by the reports on Gal Oya and Sarilakas, the processes of mobilizing, forming groups and initiating collective action often require the catalytic action of "organizational resources"--the introduction of specialists, information and training, which usually must come from resources outside the community if they are to come at all.[11] Needs for these organizational resources must be regarded as a "basic needs," and the rights of some people to seek and others to provide resources to satisfy these needs must be seen as essential human rights which make possible the realization of other human rights.

2. Rights of People to Form Regional, National and International Nongovernmental Organizations to Support Rural Organizations. As we have seen, progressive governmental agencies have successfully provided "organizational resources" directly to communities under terms which enabled intended beneficiaries to control the use of this assistance and determine the outcomes. Indeed the structuring of state agencies designed to aid mobilization and organization is an important problem to be addressed in settings where there is the requisite political will, for the landscape of experience here is strewn with abortive and misplaced efforts at "animation rurale" or "mobilization" through "political cadres." Surveying experience and problems of government efforts to develop cooperatives of the rural poor, Goran Hyden writes: "In countries where the local

cooperatives have been initiated from above as part of a national campaign to 'transform the countryside'...experience suggests that only hollow structures result."[12]

In any event, reliance on governments to meet needs for organizational resources is often unrealistic and certainly government monopolization of this task is antithetical to core concepts of alternative development. As Hyden has written:

> To promote grass-roots development, and particularly to incorporate the poor in such programs, has not been easy using party or government machineries. The nongovernmental agencies have a greater potential in achieving this task, and greater interest in their work seems justified if the shortcomings of prevailing approaches are to be overcome.

There has probably been a striking, recent growth of efforts to develop various kinds of nongovernmental support organizations to aid rural groups. Church and women's organizations[13] have taken a more activist stance towards mobilization. Nongovernmental institutes concerned with rural development have moved from detached research to collaboration. At the "international" level many action-oriented agencies have appeared on the scene:[14] the motivating concern may center on problems of food production, health care or specially-disadvantaged groups, but increasingly efforts have turned towards needs for community mobilization.

A few illustrations may suggest something of the range of activities or strategies followed. ACT (the Association for Caribbean Transformation) supplies agricultural and business services to rural groups in the Caribbean area--for example, helping people to develop new crops and find markets for them through their own organization. PIDA (the Participatory Institute for Development Alternatives) has begun training and supplying "change agents" to rural communities in Sri Lanka. CEPES (Centro Peruana de Estudios Sociales) provides information--notably legal--to rural groups in Perú by using radio programs and sending legal assistants into the field. CAP (the Consumers Association of Penang) became concerned with the industrial pollution of rivers in Malaysia; environmentalist motivations merged with "alternative development" concerns when CAP began to work with the people of the fishing village of Kuala Juru whose livelihood had been destroyed. CAP helped to publicize the wrongs done to Kuala Juru, helped villagers demand and eventually secure enforcement of relevant environmental laws, helped villagers establish their own cooperative to raise and sell cockles as an alternative to fishing, helped that cooperative get villagers back into fishing through purchase of modern boats and equipment.

Other agencies have served as catalysts to organize networks or more cohesive federations of local groups. Thus the Philippine Ecumenical Council on Community Organizations (PECCO) helped to unite a great many small squatter and community groups in the Tondo area into ZOTO--a mass-based membership organization which has wielded considerable power in the struggles of people to retain land they claimed as their own.

The potentialities of this "third sector" of development agencies have hardly yet been explored in a systematic way by "scholars."[15] Given greater national and international support, these agencies can become even more proactive in helping the processes of rural mobilization; moving from "support" to more aggressive "social action"--acting as surrogates for local organizations in national and international forums.[16] Indeed, support groups may represent an even greater threat to those who have a vested interest in the status quo.

Hence the importance of establishing legal environments for these activities. Support and social action groups must enjoy rights analogous to those set out in Convention 141; for the empowerment of organizations of "rural workers" may depend a great deal on the empowerment of other kinds of groups to help them. Support groups, to be effective, will need to raise funds not only by seeking grants from other national and international bodies, but by mass solicitation which, to be effective, may call for liberal exercise of rights of free speech and mass communication. Support groups, like their rural counterparts, will need to enjoy attributes of legal personality in order to borrow and lend funds and contract for services. Since enjoyment of these rights may inevitably bring these groups into conflict with the state, their own needs for legal resources may ultimately become quite significant.

3. Group Rights to Engage in the Economic Development. The right to form groups is, of course, simply a point of departure; people must also enjoy rights to use organizations for a variety of economic purposes: to demand essential resources controlled by the state; to manage distribution of these where that can be done efficiently (as in the Gal Oya project); to resist the exploitative practices of private lenders, traders, landlords and employers; to initiate new kinds of economic enterprises, including "joint enterprises" with state agencies, which enable people to escape exploitative economic relations as well as generate new employment and skills. When successful, these self-managed projects regularly seem to lead to other group initiatives and social changes within impoverished communities: new efforts to accumulate savings; new demands upon the state for resources; changes in local politics; construction of new community facilities; formation of new groups to pursue other objectives. Where women are involved, *a fortiori* where they are the organizers of new economic enterprises, the

generation of self-reliant assertion of new rights seems even more apparent.[17] Thus the right of groups to engage in new economic activities goes to the essence of people-centered development.

A typical example of this comes from a Sri Lanka report of activities undertaken in a poor rural community where betel was the most important source of income for most families. Prices were set by traders, who often fixed them in collusion, and then sold the crop to a government corporation. With the aid of organizers ("change agents" supplied by the Ministry of Rural Development--but accountable to the community under the terms of a UNDP grant) villagers began to investigate the marketing of betel. "It became obvious" that they could "more than double" their incomes if "exploitation could be eliminated." So a group of villagers decided to form their own association. Various obstacles had to be overcome: the group was told that "lack of legal standing" prevented direct dealings between it and the government export agency; producers were confronted by attempts by traders (backed by officials in the export agency) to secure a legal monopoly over betel marketing. These efforts to subvert the group were resisted, primarily because the members insisted on their "rights" to act collectively to market their produce. Over a two-year period, a number of results occurred:

-- The membership of the association increased from 35 in March 1979 to about 200 at the end of 1980. Producers from a number of neighbouring villages had joined the association.

-- Betel production in the village expanded by about 30 percent. A number of new producers (some of them youth) entered the betel industry.

-- In January 1980, a common savings fund was started to which all producers contributed a specified portion of their weekly income from betel. The fund rose to a level of nearly Rs.30,000 by mid 1980.

-- Collective action was expanded to other activities such as input procurement, marketing of other village produce such as arecanut and turmeric.

-- The association succeeded in building up a reputation as an important supplier of quality betel and, as its sales volume expanded, it enhanced its bargaining power vis-à-vis the export organisation, obtaining better terms of sale.

> As the association grew in size (embracing over 200 producers) the effective management of the organisation fell into the hands of a committee of office-bearers. This system gave little opportunity for the ordinary members to participate in the affairs of the organisation. In this situation, some groups broke away from the organisation and formed their own small group organisations where the marketing and handling operations were undertaken by all members on a rotation basis. By mid 1981, the Betel Association had broken up into five smaller organisations, each undertaking its own marketing work and operating as autonomous units.[18]

With the help of catalysts, the betel producers were able to diagnose and resolve their problem themselves, without state aid. In many situations, however, the collaboration of state agencies may be essential to the resolution of problems which people want to address: officials must be encouraged, or persuaded, to engage in "joint enterprises" with rural organizations. An example was recently reported by Frances Korten:

> In many contexts, meaningful participation can only be generated if certain rights are recognized. Community and social forestry programs exemplify this problem....For centuries sparsely inhabited, hilly-forested areas of many developing countries were seen as a resource properly owned and protected by the government. But exploding populations in the lowlands have forced larger numbers of people into these upland areas, where they cut down trees to cultivate the soil, causing massive erosion that exacerbates floods and droughts in the lowlands, and reduces future productive potential of lands both high and low. Governments are beginning to recognize that approaches using police or guards to solving this problem are futile, and that people living in upland forested areas must be encouraged to take responsibility for resource management and to plant economically productive trees as a means of livelihood. But since the people have no security of land ownership, the dilemma arises that they are legally nothing but encroachers on government land. Consequently they have no incentive for planting and tending trees which will not become profitable for several years, unless they are sure they will be allowed to stay to reap the benefits. Yet resolving this dilemma by actually deeding government lands to

> private individuals is a step that few national governments are willing to take, and such a move might lead to a situation where absentee landlords acquire large holdings of land once it is available for private ownership.
>
> In such situations, program managers need to search for alternative ways to provide the legal framework necessary to pursue the programs. In the Philippines, one tribal group has worked out an agreement with the government to lease a 14,000 hectare area for 25 years with an option to renew. With this security the tribal group has developed programs to preserve and develop large areas of forested land. Other forestry programs have provided individual or community permits validating the people's rights to use the land at least temporarily. Finding different solutions in different parts of the country appears to be a more workable approach than to confront the broader issue of national policy governing land ownership in all forested areas. If these programs are seen as successful, a climate conducive to broader legal and policy changes may develop.[19]

Another example of "joint enterprise" which has attracted wide attention is an experiment recently initiated in Nepal--the Small Farmer Development Program (SFDP) which was devised, in part, to take account of repeated failures of governmental agencies (charged with implementing land reforms and credit programs) to reach the rural poor, let alone benefit them in any way. The very design of the project was developed through interaction with concerned groups--through a series of "workshops," held round the countryside. Small farmers, landless laborers and officials of the Agricultural Development Bank (ADBN) discussed perceived needs for credit and terms of providing and using it. As a result efforts were initiated to encourage small farmers and landless rural workers, in selected areas, to:

> form organizations of their own below the level of cooperatives--small (15 to 20 members), homogeneous, multifunction groups around a common necleus of income-raising activity based on group work plans and group action, supported by an integrated program of supervised credit, extension and technical backstopping. A group organizer-cum-action research fellow (GO) was stationed in each district to play the vital catalytic and monitoring role and link with the ADBN and the various line agencies.

-295-

> The groups were to receive credit for individual members, as well as for the groups as a whole on the basis of group demand, under group liability and with credible income-raising action plans only, without any other collateral being required. Emphasis was placed on production enterprises in crops, livestock, horticulture, pisiculture and cottage industry. In addition the groups themselves were to develop their own group-saving fund with member contributors, for providing consumption, distress and emergency loans to their members.[20]

In the beginning each small group acted as a disburser and collector of loans made to individual farmers. But gradually groups qua groups have begun to engage in various new enterprises--development of orchards, wool production, cottage industries.

> The relative success of group borrowing from group investment has led to further innovation, which represents the third phase. In the Tupche Project area there is a total of 40 small farm groups. With the bank's advise and encouragement, seven groups (Group No. 40, 41, 43, 35, 20 and 9) [sic] have joined hands to launch a joint cottage industry project based on inter-group cooperation. Under a bank loan of Rs.250,000, the seven groups are cooperating to install 50 manual looms that will employ 50 men and women who previously did no work during their spare time or were simply unemployed. Each [of the] seven groups own this enterprise. Each group sends one representative to the board of directors who are responsible for the overall management. The directors have hired one controller and one technician, and they take an active interest in the operation of the enterprise.
>
> The textile company represents further advance in cooperation since it requires inter-group coordination in decision making and also raises new problems in control. The owners of the enterprise are all the members of the seven groups or about 126 people. The factory belongs to them and the people in the management committee are their representatives.[21]

The projects described above are models of what can be done, but hardly depictions of a pervasive trend. In many countries legal as well as social environments are hostile to initiation of group-economic enterprises. The social constraints have been analyzed from many perspectives: class and power structures which repress initiatives; inexperience and lack of entrepreneurial resources of the rural poor; continuing dominance of pre-capitalist social formations among people. While of course law cannot by itself change these social environments, it can be used by those who struggle to break away from the bondage of existing relations. The rights of people to engage in new kinds of development activities must be emphasized because, as we have seen, enjoyment of these economic rights makes assertion and enjoyment of other social and political rights more possible.

A variety of legal changes may be necessary to secure rights to initiate new kinds of group enterprises. Indeed, this complex subject needs far more careful study than has yet been bestowed; a few illustrative problems are simply noted here.

The content of law governing the legal capacitation of voluntary, non-state participatory associations needs attention. As some reports in this volume show, governments typically monopolize this field by prescribing the terms under which autonomous groups can secure attributes of "legal personality" necessary to engage in self-help, economic enterprises. State law dictates the requisite organizational forms, the roles of actors, and processes for taking group decisions. Unless these terms are satisfied, endogenous groups may lack vital rights to contract, own and exchange property and enjoy limited liability. Professionals within governments who write laws on this subject often use models of structure borrowed from foreign experience. This preemption by the state can stifle capacities of people to form "organizations of their own choice," structures geared to their perceptions of the appropriate law governing membership in and management of their group. Studies of indigenous cooperatives, water-user associations and other kinds of customary "business groups" demonstrate the importance of this lesson. Of course there are difficult problems here. Groups which raise funds and engage in business must follow norms which protect both the interests of their individual members and those with whom they deal. But it is one thing to recognize and identify these problems, and quite another to hold that the state, through state-managed structures of regulation, will not only dictate the interests to be protected but the organizational forms which must be used to achieve those ends.

A second set of problems may arise from monopolization of various kinds of economic activities, either by the state or by private firms and people (sometimes operating under the protective cloak of state regulation). While the need for state laws which protect producers and consumers from exploitative practices is clear, it does not follow that the state must secure those objects by preventing people most in need of development from initiating new kinds of activities which help them to change adverse relations of production and exchange in the countryside. Monopolization of marketing, transport, banking and various production activities, when coupled with the exclusion of rural workers in these enterprises often perpetuates the very conditions which maintain poverty and dependence. What must be put in issue is the right of rural workers to renegotiate the terms under which state and private sector organizations may monopolize these activities and thus appropriate surplus. If group rights to engage in economic development are valued, the state must allow rural workers to form their own alternative communal organizations, or, they must enjoy rights to share more power in the management of state monopolies.

A third, related set of problems focuses on the rights of autonomous rural groups to deal with state agencies which control resources essential to realization of group needs: land, credit and services. The problem--as illustrated by several reports here--is how to structure "joint enterprise" arrangements between state and non-state organizations which are conducive to self-reliant, people-centered development. As the Gal Oya report suggests: one state body may facilitate organization of an endogenous group; but the next problem for the group may be: how to secure benefits, e.g., credit and inputs, from other state organizations--benefits which make efforts to develop group activity meaningful? The problem may turn on the terms by which the state supplies the resources. While of course scarce resources cannot be dissipated, groups must enjoy rights to bargain effectively for them--and rights of redress where resources are either withheld or extended under terms similar to an "adhesion contract." Resolution of these difficulties is crucial to realization of alternative approaches. Rights of access to state-controlled resources obviously cannot be prescribed *a priori*.

Historically, the state has seldom worked in partnership with rural people. If self-reliance and participation are taken seriously the need for partnership relations to replace patron-client relations is apparent. The terms of "joint enterprise," partnerships between people and government, have to evolve through negotiation just as they have evolved in other spheres of state collaboration with private bodies.

4. *Rights of Groups to Participate in the Design and Administration of Rural Development.* The hope is that, over time, groups can change political environments and administrative structures. These changes must usually begin with efforts to redress specific grievances: efforts to secure particular resources, to curb abusive police practices. In many communities the only practicable way to press grievances may be through strategies of "direct action:" protests, deputations and boycotts.[22] Thus rights of people to assemble, petition and picket become important components of a legal environment for alternative development.

-298-

Successful direct action often leads to greater politicization within communities; an awareness of the costs of these strategies and of needs for more permanent remedies. In some communities, for example, groups have turned to the courts in efforts to secure more enduring relief from routine abuses of authority--the victims of police misconduct or corrupt dealings have sued in tort, or resorted to private prosecution; in other communities people have set up their own "non-state" tribunals and have (sometimes successfully) tried to force recalcitrant local officials to appear and address the problems. Usually struggles for structural changes must be carried upward to more central organs of government, and it is here where the aid of support and social action groups may become most apparent, and where liberalized rules of standing and judicial review become especially important. In India, for example, social action groups have used the courts (as well as other modes of public exposure) to protect tribal people threatened with ruinous disruption by government plans to build dams and flood large portions of their homelands. In Malaysia, as we have seen, CAP allied itself with the struggles of Kuala Juru to secure reforms and enforcement of environmental laws. In the Philippines, for example, efforts of organized sugar workers have led to review of existing price and wage policies within a national tripartite commission composed of workers, owners and government.

Efforts to remedy specific wrongs can lead to efforts to initiate new programs designed to meet the needs of specific communities or groups. Again with the help of other groups rural organizations can begin to challenge commodity price-fixing policies which discriminate in favor of urban areas, or projects in planning proposals which impose an unfair hardship on the poor. These kinds of efforts can lead to demands for new institutions to provide for greater public participation in the formation of policies and the design of programs.

While efforts of this sort have emerged in recent years in some countries, it is obvious that for most of the world's rural poor these kinds of changes still seem distant and difficult, at best, to obtain.

It may be argued--and it often has--that the power structure in many countries is too heavily weighted against the poor to make it possible to realize these strategies. That may be the case, or appear to be so, in some settings. The only alternatives which people may perceive are recourse to warfare against the state or to "exit" through apathy. But the costs of recourse to warfare are great, and they fall most heavily on the poor. Moreover, the rural poor are not totally powerless in many situations. They are the producers of resources which are essential to maintenance of the state--food and commodities for exchange. Given information and means of communication they can make choices for themselves, and they have the most at stake in determining when to attempt to appeal to law and justice to defend and advance their interests. Again, then, the need for information--and human resources to help people make self-reliant judgments--can be seen as perhaps the most basic of basic human needs.

II. Legal Resources to Create Legal Environments

The need for knowledge which helps people become more independent, innovative and inspired, and more capable of collective action, is now a pervasive theme in development literature. This functional knowledge can be neither ascertained a priori nor transmitted by traditional modes of pedagogy from the "informed" to the "ignorant." Mutual understanding of how to apply abstract doctrines to particular conditions must often come through an interactive process: the problems to be addressed and the modes of doing so can only be discovered by a dialogue where both "outside" specialists and members of the group are simultaneously informants and learners--and where the group is the ultimate decision maker on the question:[23] "what's to be done?" Needs to develop techniques which facilitate "interactive," "dialogic" research and learning are now emphasized in studies of extension, health care, credit and other programs where collective self-help is deemed a prerequisite for social change.[24]

Similar needs exist in regard to "law;" for, despite its amorphous often uncertain character, law, like other bodies of knowledge and experience, can be used by people, sometimes in very creative ways, to identify problems, determine ways of addressing them and to justify and mobilize support for actions taken.[25] When and how this can be done is a complex matter which we hope to explore more adequately in another volume of reports and studies examining some recent experiences and lessons they suggest.[26] Here we briefly sketch some themes.

The concept of law as a resource for those presently exploited and excluded has two aspects: first, law, broadly conceived, is a potential resource for depressed rural people, even if it is little used for that purpose --and despite the pathologies which often characterize existing legal regimes governing administration. Second, knowledge of law can be used to help people understand how they are wrongfully oppressed, and why--and also, if the matter is pressed, how harmful practices might best be confronted.

This phenomenon becomes more evident if one takes a broad view of law. Here we conceive it as an authoritative body of particular rules, more general governing principles and doctrines, and, also as techniques for developing and applying these materials to resolve different kinds of conflict and regularize action. Moreover, the sources of relevant law are not simply legislation, subsidiary rules and court decisions; the sources include the constitution and the ideology and doctrines which inform it; natural law--such as the principle that all people possess the same basic rights; jurisprudential concepts--such as the idea of "rule of law;" customs and endogenous law--such as customs which favor decision making by consensus; international bills of rights--the Universal Declaration and other "universal" norms which one's government has promised to observe.

All of these sources may in theory be used for varying purposes by people. International norms (e.g., ILO Conventions 141 and 87) and constitutional guarantees and court-made doctrines governing administration (e.g., the duty to provide natural justice) may supply principles needed to demand recognition of particular rights. Group-made law and recourse to traditional norms may provide a framework of rules needed to constitute a group-managed economic enterprise. Legislation, subsidiary rules and relevant policy statements may be used to demonstrate entitlements to a more equitable allocation of resources. Thus law can, in theory, be used to aid many different kinds of group activities--not simply litigation which is often the preoccupation of lawyers: law can be used to teach civics; to justify direct action measures--such as boycotts or deputations; to justify claims for goods or services; to embarrass lawless power-wielders; to organize economic enterprises; to resolve intra-community disputes without wasting scarce resources on advocates' fees and court costs; to change attitudes towards anachronistic customs which exclude and oppress women and youth; to conceptualize and resolve other shared problems. Such uses of all of these sources of law require legal specialists who can so interact with groups that people themselves can articulate problems and courses of action.

Obstacles to the development of legal resources will be readily apparent.

One source of difficulty lies within the legal profession. As with any other profession, there is the psychological tendency--strongly reinforced by economic motives--to monopolize knowledge of law and the right to propound it, not only in the courts but in other forums where officials purport to use law as the basis for decisions. The means by which lawyers exclude others from acquiring and using legal knowledge are well known--and particularly effective when lawyers interact with the poor. Further, the tendency of lawyers to deliver a narrow range of counseling on a re-active rather than proactive basis, often limits the value of those "services." So does the tendency of the lawyer to dominate the determination of whether and how a problem can be converted into a legal problem--particularly when the lawyer thinks solely in terms of individualized disputes and litigation. Moreover, the marketplace for legal services strongly tends to direct most lawyers' energies, and indeed to shape their perceptions of what law is all about; and the poor are generally excluded from these (usually urban) places. There is, among influential members of the profession, little awareness of the problems of the poor, and there are few incentives to discover ways to use law innovatively to address them. Thus, the profession qua profession is both weakly motivated and poorly prepared to help generate legal resources.[27]

A second set of obstacles lies within rural communities. Geographically and socially they are distant from sympathetic lawyers and suspicious of courts. The Sarilakas report portrays familiar phenomena: the understandable tendency of the very people who most lack legal resources to view law and lawyers with aversion; the deep-rooted--and often plausible--belief that law does in fact empower officials, employers, landlords, money-lenders and others with status to engage in the practices which contribute so much to the plight of the poor. As the Sarilakas experience suggests--it may take a long time, much interaction, to show that these perceptions, while often accurate, are incomplete, and that to act on such beliefs is to act on a self-fulfilling prophecy of impotence.

Developing legal resources must, then, be perceived as a difficult, uncertain task.

The objectives cannot be met by conventional programs of "legal aid;" the flaws in these are similar to those in other bureaucratized programs which provide other kinds of "professional services" such as health care or agricultural extension. A team of lawyers and social scientists who studied "Rural Mobilization and the Legal Needs of the Poor" in Sri Lanka made these observations:

> Our analysis reveals that the Government Legal Aid Scheme is constrained by several structural factors. Firstly, it is primarily directed towards legal representations of claims by individuals in disputes which are interpersonal in nature. The scheme does not have the capacity to direct itself towards the representation of group or class interests.
>
> Secondly, even within the sphere of interpersonal disputes it is limited to the formal judicial arena.... The scheme similarly has not sought to aggregate individual claims into collective demands for formative and institutional change in social welfare programmes.

-302-

Thirdly, the modes of advocacy were normally limited to the preparation of legal pleadings and oral representation in the courts of original and appellate jurisdiction. Rarely have professional services taken the form of structuring of:

(a) small-scale business transactions, or
(b) counselling on the legal prerequisites to the establishment of a credit co-operative organisation, or
(c) a tenants' association.

Similarly, group advocacy could take the form of drafting model legislation and administrative regulations which could enhance access of the underprivileged to social and economic benefits.

Fourthly, the existing scheme has proved to be reactive, i.e., it responds passively to the problems of those who may accidentally reach its office. A legal aid survey revealed that 87 percent of the respondents were unaware of the existence of the scheme....The scheme should be proactive in that it would be decentralised and physically located in urban slums, fishing villages, and agricultural communities. The volunteers should acquire familiarity with the basic needs and grievances of the poor and seek to translate them into legal demands.

Fifthly,....It is a framework which discourages frank and open discussion of problems and the identification of underlying grievances. The social and cultural barriers to the access of underprivileged to legal administrative processes are internalised within the goverment legal aid office.

The same group went on to propose establishment of a "new model" of legal assistance developed along these lines:

(a) the emphasis on collective demands and group interests;

(b) the establishment of clinics which are proactive in that they actively seek out the grievance of poverty groups and advocate their interests;

(c) the expansion of the arenas of group advocacy to include administrative, legislative and other spheres of policy articulation and implementation;

(d) multiplication of the types of assistance to include counselling, the structuring of transactions, and the formation of associations; and

(e) the organisation of the delivery system to include participatory involvement of potential beneficiaries. Such participation to take the form of management of legal aid scheme, dissemination of information about social welfare schemes and redistributive legislation and an encouragement of self-help.[28]

The Sarilakas report portrays a somewhat different approach--greater emphasis on the time and effort needed to discover, through dialogue, the potentialities of law as a resource to deal with shared but often inchoate grievances; greater emphasis on the role which legal resources can play in mobilization processes, in galvanizing determination to deal with problems through collective action. The most important, shared "legal problems" of a community, like its "health problems," are rooted in social relations and longstanding practices which maintain impoverishment. The legal specialist who seeks to help people resist oppressive police practices, or extract action from a government agency, or organize a self-managed cooperative, or structure some other group transaction, needs a holistic view of the situation to be addressed and the social resources presently available within the community and the skills which must be developed and the risks to be encountered. Like an agronomist advising on production of new crops, he needs to work in tandem with other specialists, and learn broader perspectives seldom taught in law schools.

The Sri Lanka and the Philippines report (and other investigations, too)[29] show that most lawyers often lack much of the knowledge and training about law which is relevant and imaginatively organized so as to benefit rural communities. While this failing is hardly surprising, it underscores another obstacle: legal assistants in the field must be backed up by well-organized support centers: offices which in turn have access to information found in scarce publications and to informants only available in central government offices. Moreover, the assertion of group claims in local forums can sometimes be greatly aided if the same claims are simultaneously pressed --or at least explained--at upper levels of government.

Support centers also need legal resources to become activist groups themselves. Many claims of rural people can only be effectively pressed in capital forums. The representation of groups before planning bodies, ministries, parliaments, higher courts and other bodies is crucial to any long-term strategy geared towards alternative development; and, as we have noted, some social action groups are beginning to function along these lines. But lawyers--the relative few engaged--are only beginning to develop ways of working with and learning from organizers, community leaders and specialists in other fields, to understand the wider dimensions of alternative development; and there are scarcities of experience and material to aid those who do become engaged.

Perhaps action at international levels can help development of national legal resources. International support groups may also have "action" roles to play. Some years ago, in its struggles to save the Tondo lands for the poor, ZOTO, through friends, went directly to the World Bank--challenging the legality of its loans towards a massive redevelopment project which had been planned with no participation by those most severely affected. The challenge was grounded in international norms, and in the demand that the Bank follow its own policies favoring participation.[30]

Much more might be done along these lines. The plea that only governments can speak for people in the negotiation of international transactions, whether they have to do with aid or concessions, often deserves critical scrutiny. International projects of this kind almost inevitably have a differential impact on different sectors in society, and the idea that those adversely affected have no standing to speak for themselves is a negation the basic notion of participation. Similarly, forums such as the UN Commission on Human Rights can be used much more aggressively to demand recognition of the kinds of group rights we have discussed here.

The current debate over the existence of a "Human Right to Development" highlights some of these issues, and the importance of developing legal resources at all levels for the victims of underdevelopment and maldevelopment. In order to address these problems the International Commission of Jurists (ICJ) and the International Center for Law in Development recently convened a workshop of representatives from groups supportive of alternative development, and ICJ submitted proposals from this meeting to the UN Commission on Human Rights. The submission emphasized the importance of recognizing group rights for purposes we have already described. It emphasizes the need for recognizing rights of "participation" at international as well as national and local levels of decision making. A central paragraph in this document summarizes some basic themes we have tried to develop here:

-305-

> A declaration that development is a human right is important, in part because it will reflect an international effort to give legal recognition to crucial rights of victims of underdevelopment, not only rights to share essential physical resources more equitably but rights to share power over those resources. This underscores the importance of law as a governing framework for self-reliant development and the need for legal resources to help secure realisation of their right to development.[31]

* * * * * *

Nearly three quarters of all the people on earth make some kind of living by cultivating land. From their ranks come the vast majority of the world's estimated 800 million living in extreme poverty and hunger. Millions more are on the brink. Tenant farmers, sharecroppers, landless laborers and marginal subsistence cultivators form the vast mass of people who work the land. They have little control over the production or distribution of resources essential to their development. They stay poor because these resources are controlled by structures which usually favor the maintenance of state power and often enough the rich, and which, in any event, rarely change the social conditions that produce impoverishment.

In most developing countries the dominant classes are comprised of a minority with simultaneous interests in large plantations or landholdings, agribusiness, financial institutions, export and import firms and the maintenance of existing state structures. They enjoy the support of the government in the form of protective legislation, loans, subsidies, investment incentives and tax privileges. Thanks to their economic base, educational superiority, assumed social status, powers of patronage and access to intermediaries and persons in power, they are able to continue to exercise control over governmental bodies. Not surprisingly, national rural development policies end up creating instruments which, whether intended or not, fail to alleviate poverty and inequality. Not surprisingly, other goals such as raising agricultural productivity, containing political discontent and maintaining support for national elites become the dominant goals of most state structures.

Thus, rural poverty--and the deprivations and risks which accompany it--are not products of happenstance and scarcity so much as they are the products of political, economic and social power relationships often ruthlessly maintained. Attempts to change these relationships must inevitably

-306-

involve the rural poor (who will ultimately bear the risks) in the processes of both identifying problems and finding responses. Action strategies must be evolved at local grass-roots levels, as well as national and international levels.

The development of countervailing power for specific impoverished rural groups at the local grass-roots level must be the starting point of any action to alleviate rural impoverishment. The rural poor individually lack the means and power to secure access to or accountability of official decision takers. Through collective action, however, they can begin to create the leverage necessary to gain access to the basic resources they need, to develop the countervailing power needed to struggle against their impoverishment.

Of course these struggles--against structures and systems which produce impoverishment--have to be carried to both national and international levels. Promotion of large-scale, commercial production of export crops and other national policies and programs which impose unequal burdens on the poor must be challenged. Rural people are often quite sophisticated in their understanding of these matters. Their need may be less for instruction than for national groups and advocates to aggregate demands and press them in appropriate institutions. But these struggles, too, will depend significantly on mobilization and organization at grass-roots levels.

Similarly at the international level, the rural poor need organizations and advocates to press for laws and their enforcement which--for example--will control transnational agribusiness, and the introduction of "disabling technologies" and the impact of new modes of production and the sometimes powerful influence exercised by international development agencies over national policies. But again efforts to develop these struggles should be responsive to the needs of rural people, reflecting their concerns. The base of power must come, in large part at least, from the countryside and ultimately be accountable to it. Otherwise the state will remain autonomous, unaccountable to the mass of people it governs.

Thus, the generation of new kinds of "grass-roots" organizations is an essential first step towards those kinds of "development" which address the political economy of rural "underdevelopment" and emphasize realization of the basic needs and rights of the victims of it.

FOOTNOTES

1. The importance of new "human rights" concepts geared to the kinds of "human needs" strategies elaborated here is developed in two recent publications of the International Commission of Jurists (ICJ): Development, Human Rights and the Rule of Law (Report of a conference held in The Hague, April 27-May 1, 1981) (Pergamon Press, 1981) (See especially the working papers submitted by A.C. Espiritu, C.J. Dias and N. Tiruchelvam); and Rural Development and Human Rights in South-East Asia (Conclusions of the Penang Seminar co-sponsored by the ICJ and the Consumers Association of Penang in December 1981).

2. Perhaps (understandably) academicians tend to be more cynical than rural people who have experienced gains through organizations.

3. A recent United Nations document, reviewing the evolution and scope of the right to development indicates that based on major United Nations' instruments and debates there exists "a general consensus as to the need for the following elements to be part of the concept of development":

   -- the realization of the potentialities of the human person in harmony with the community should be seen as the central purpose of development;
   -- the human person should be regarded as the subject and not the object of the development process;
   -- development requires the satisfaction of both material and non-material basic needs;
   -- respect for human rights is fundamental to the development process;
   -- the human person must be able to participate fully in shaping his own reality;
   -- respect for the principles of equality and non-discrimination is essential; and
   -- the achievement of a degree of individual and collective self-reliance must be an integral part of the process.

   Report of the Secretary General, Commission on Human Rights, Question of the Realization in all Countries of the Economic, Social and Cultural Rights Contained in the Universal Declaration of Human Rights and in the International Covenant on Economic, Social and Cultural Rights and Study of Special Problems Which the Developing Countries Face in Their Efforts to Achieve These Human Rights. The International Dimensions of the Right to Development As a Human Right in Relation With Other Rights Based on International

-308-

Cooperation, Including the Right to Peace, Taking into Account the Requirements of the New International Economic Order and the Fundamental Human Needs, para. 27. (E/CN.4/1334, 2 January 1979).

4. The 1982 meeting of the Society for International Development (SID) is organized around alternative development themes, notably strategies of aiding rural development. A large part of the agenda is devoted to reviewing experiences of grass-roots initiatives and strategies.
A major new program of SID is its Grass Roots Initiatives and Strategies Program (GRIS) which will "attempt to pool the knowledge and technology emanating from spontaneous people-oriented activities in industrialized and Third World countries." "Action research" on participatory groups of the poor is being encouraged by a number of organizations including the ILO, UNRISD, UNESCO and the International Council for Adult Education of the World Council of Churches. Rural Development Participation Review, published by the Rural Development Committee of Cornell University is designed to promote the sharing of knowledge and ideas on "rural development participation."

5. See note 4, supra (GRIS) and notes 13 and 14, infra.

6. See J. Paul and C. Dias, Law and Legal Resources in the Mobilization of the Rural Poor for Self-Reliant Development (ICLD 1980).

7. See International Labour Office, Recommendation No. 144 of the International Labour Conference of 1975. For a strong endorsement of Convention 141 by a South Asian seminar of lawyers and "development experts," see the report of the ICJ/CAP Penang Seminar cited in note 29.

8. See, e.g., International Labour Office, Freedom of Association: Digest of Decisions of the Freedom of Association Committee of the Governing Body of the ILO (second edition, 1976).

9. G. Hunter (ed.), Agricultural Development and the Rural Poor (ODI 1978).

10. B. Bagadion, J. Fernandez, R. Fernandez, A.C. Espiritu, M. Magallona, A. Pimentel, Jr., Law in the Mobilization and Participatory Organization of the Rural Poor: the Kagawasan Case, Institute of Philippine Culture (1979).

-309-

11. See C.A. Lassen, Reaching the Assetless Poor: Project and Strategies for Their Self-Reliant Development. Rural Development Committee, Center for International Studies, Cornell University 1980. See also F.C. Korten, "Stimulating Community Participation: Obstacles and Options at Agency, Community and Societal Levels," Rural Development Participation Review (hereafter cited as RDPR) II:3:1 (1981).

12. G. Hyden, "Cooperatives and the Poor: Comparing European and Third World Experience," RDPR II:1:9 (1980).

13. See note 4, supra. See, e.g., Information Kit for Women in Africa produced by International Women's Tribune Centre, Inc. (New York) in collaboration with African Training and Research Centre for Women, UN/ECA (Addis Ababa) (1981). Similar "resource books" have been prepared for women's groups in Asia and the Caribbean area. These materials in turn contain an impressive listing of private international organizations which supply funding and support to nongovernmental women's organizations engaged in development projects, and an interesting inventory of women's grass-roots organizations in Africa.

14. E.g., the International Foundation for Development Alternatives (IFDA), through its publicaion IFDA Dossier, was formed to develop an international network of nongovernmental groups pursuing alternative development strategies.

15. The GRIS program of SID (see note 4) includes plans for a series of national and regional meetings for "those directly involved with grass-roots experiments and peoples' movements" and for those who are "networking" these activities. A second stage will be a World Conference. See SID, GRIS Notes No. 2, July 1, 1982.

16. See, e.g., "Concept Paper for Legal Assistance Project for Grass-Roots Organizations" (January 1982: Philippines). CENDHRRA (Center for Development of Human Resources in Rural Asia) provides services for rural groups and leaders through a network of "partner" country organizations, and has sought to represent its constituencies in various world conferences sponsored by UN agencies.

17. See R.B. Dixon, Assessing the Impact of Development Projects on Women (USAID Program Evaluation Paper No. 9, 1980). Cf. N. Nelson, "Mobilising Village Women: Some Organizational and Management Considerations," Journel of Development Studies 17:3:47 (1981).

18. See "Rural Mobilisation and the Legal Needs of the Poor: A Study of Selected Fishing and Plantation Communities in Sri Lanka" (Colombo 1981). (A study prepared for ICLD by a team of Sri Lankan researchers.) Appendix 1, prepared by Professor S. Tilakaratne of Sri Jayawardenepura University contains the report quoted here.

19. Korten, op. cit., note 11.

20. D. Ghai and Md. A. Rahman, "Rural Poverty and the Small Farmers Groups in Nepal" (Rural Employment Policies Branch, ILO 1979).

21. P. Lohani, "Small Farmer Development Program in Nepal" (paper prepared for a Workshop on Small Farmers Development and Credit Policy, April 1980, Kathmandu).

22. On the concept, needs for, and legal implications of, and also the limits of direct action, see U. Baxi, "Legal Mobilization and the Needs of the Rural Poor" (1982) (a paper which will be published in a forthcoming ICLD volume on "Legal Resources for Participatory Organizations of the Rural Poor."

23. See Md. A. Rahman, "A Methodology for Participatory Research with the Rural Poor," Les Carnets de l'Enfance No. 41 (UNICEF) (1978). Cf. D.W. Brokensha, D.M. Warren and O. Werner, Indigenous Knowledge Systems and Development (1980).

24. See the special issue of IDS Bulletin 10:2 (1979) entitled Rural Development: Whose Knowledge Counts? Cf. E. Taylor and C. Moore, "Paraprofessionals and Rural Development," RDPR II:1:1 (1981). Cf. J.H. Maeda, "Creating National Structures for People-Centered Development" in D.C. Korten and F.B. Alfonso, Bureaucracy and the Poor: Closing the Gap (1981) (p. 152-3, discussing plans to train paraprofessionals "on site" within Ujamaa villages and under village management).

25. Cf. U. Baxi, op. cit., note 22.

26. See note 22. The volume will include reports of several studies of the shared perceptions of needs for legal resources within communities in Perú, Sri Lanka, the Philippines and other countries.

27. See C.J. Dias and J.C.N. Paul, "Observations on Lawyers in Development and Underdevelopment" in C. Dias, R. Luckham, D.O. Lynch and J. Paul (eds.), Lawyers in the Third World: Comparative and Developmental Perspectives (1981).

28. Op. cit., note 18.

29. International Commission of Jurists, Rural Development and Human Rights in South-East Asia: Conclusions of ICJ/CAP Penang Seminar (1982) (paragraphs 124-133, discussing new models for legal assistance to rural communities).

30. J. Fernandez-White, "Community Involvement in Improving the Quality of Life" (1976).

31. International Commission of Jurists, The Right to Development: Its Scope, Content and Implementation (1982).

Part III
International Law and Development

[10]

Private Investment in Latin America: Renegotiating the Bargain†

JOSEPH J. JOVA††
CLINT E. SMITH, T. FRANK CRIGLER†††

I. INTRODUCTION

In the original version of this Article, I described the onset of an "adjustment process" where increasingly nationalistic-sounding Latin American governments and fearful foreign investors were engaged in negotiating new agreements based on substantially tougher host country restrictions and reluctant accommodation by foreign companies. The thoughts expressed in that Article remain valid eight years later.

Only a minimum of updating was required to make this work pertinent to the contemporary scene. The need to create a successful, mutually beneficial accommodation between private capital and public policy remains the great task of this century; and it will remain a fundamental challenge whatever the future of the Organization of Petroleum Exporting Countries (OPEC) and however the debt burdens of the Latin American nations are resolved.

During my thirty-five years as a foreign service officer and now in the course of my duties as president of Meridian House International,[1] I have heard many views as to how the "bargain"—the unwritten developmental compact between Latin American countries and outside direct investors—should be drawn up. Professionals from many institutions and nations are constantly at work attempting to construct pragmatic compromises. This worthy objective of creating a mechanism that can insure the prosperity of hundreds of millions of people will not be put together overnight. With

---

† This Article was originally published in 10 TEX. INT'L L.J. 455 (1975). The author has updated and revised the Article for inclusion in the Centennial series.

†† President of Meridian House International, Washington, D.C.; A.B. 1938, Dartmouth College; graduate of the United States Department of State Senior Seminar in Foreign Policy (1958-1959). During his Foreign Service career, Mr. Jova served as Ambassador to Mexico (1974-1977), Ambassador and United States Permanent Representative to the Organization of American States (1969-1974), and Ambassador to Honduras (1965-1969).

††† The author wishes to thank Mr. Smith, of Stanford University, and Mr. Crigler, of the United States Department of State, for their assistance and collaboration on this update.

1. Meridian House International is a nonprofit educational and cultural organization based in Washington, D.C., concerned with world and national affairs and dedicated to exchange programs promoting international cooperation and understanding. The author thanks Mr. John Blair, Meridian House editor, for his help in preparing this Article.

enough goodwill and effort, however, the developed and the less developed countries of the Americas can achieve such a breakthrough.

In surveying the Latin American panorama one should keep in mind that the region has had many boom periods: gold and silver in the sixteenth century; cattle in the eighteenth century; mining again in the nineteenth century; an oil boom in some countries in the 1920s; and the economic miracles of industrialization after World War II and again in the 1970s. During the most recent boom period, Latin America showed the greatest growth rate of any area of the world. While each of these boom periods eventually ended, each one left Latin America enriched in its internal development. This same situation is true today. While the area is in the midst of a crisis of financial liquidity, its potential wealth is not affected. The very cause of its indebtedness lies precisely in the enormous investment undertaken to build up the infrastructure of the area, including job creation and human development. It was this investment effort, much of it done with borrowed funds, that gave Latin America its impressive growth rate of recent years. Many of these elements remain in place and if short run problems affecting stability can be solved, the area is poised for still new periods of growth and prosperity.

I recognize that we have made little attempt in this Article to cover other manifestations of underdevelopment affecting the area—social inequities, marginations, skewed income distribution, rapid population growth, and more recently, the terrible scourge of subversion, terrorism, guerrilla warfare, and concommitant violations of human rights, undertaken, sometimes, misguidedly, in an effort to maintain order. Such problems, of greatest concern to any Latin Americanist, remain to be examined in other Articles. Suffice it to say here that growth and prosperity, while not necessarily in themselves solutions, may, one can but hope, provide ingredients helping to make possible a reduction in the intensity of the area's problems.

Development progress in Latin America, both in material and in human terms, has provided the muscle and knowledge that now allow the region to stand on its own feet, demand a greater share in the world's economic wealth, and insist that more attention be paid to its own social and cultural priorities. Meanwhile, the successful growth and spread of overseas investment has produced a unique capitalist institution in its own right, the so-called "transnational enterprise," a complex, wide-ranging but centrally controlled, integrated, and computerized corporate structure whose very strength and global outlook cast fear and doubt in the minds of local political leaders. Success has made both sides stubborn, prickly, and less inclined to negotiate.

It is the thesis of this Article that an adjustment process is inevitable and is in fact underway, and that it will vitally affect the future role of foreign private direct investment in Latin America.[2] This adjustment process will be explored from several perspectives: first, the historic function of outside investment in the region's development; secondly, the legislative measures that Latin American countries have devised over the years, singly and in concert, to try to ensure national control over the development process (citing the case of Mexico in particular); thirdly, the dilemma posed for the United States in seeking both to respond to Latin American expectations and to protect its own investors from discriminatory treatment or uncompensated expropriation; and, finally, the prospects for a new accommodation or "bargain" between developing Latin American countries and foreign private investors in the light of current trends.

A word of caution, however obvious, seems in order: Generalizations are risky, particularly when applied to so diverse an assortment of nations as those that comprise Latin America. With this caveat in mind, it is nevertheless important to recognize the degree of polarization that characterizes the current investment dispute. While varying in their approaches and aggressiveness, Latin American countries have achieved an uncommon harmony in terms of basic goals and strategies: all want industrialization as a basis for national economic growth; all want a determining voice in the design of their economic futures; and none want "dependency" upon the developed nations, least of all upon the United States. While the specific responses of individual companies may differ, private investors recognize that as a group they face serious new challenges that are not likely to be overcome through classical textbook techniques of marketplace competition.

II. An Historical View

Amid the current controversy over issues such as multinational corporations, uncompensated expropriations, alleged political machinations by foreign companies, discriminatory laws, "dependency," and "neocolonialism," it is easy to fall prey to good-and-evil theories that depict the present situation in terms of nefarious plotting or exploitative deception on the part of one side or the other. In the process, the historical aspects of

2. This Article concentrates on the problems surrounding foreign private *direct* investment, because this equity investment is currently the most controversial means of effecting capital transfers. Other means of capital flow, however, are growing in relative importance in Latin America, including the various bilateral aid programs and project loans (usually on softer terms than available in capital markets); the loans of the international development lending institutions—the World Bank Group and the Inter-American Development Bank; the loans from banking consortia, often handled through the Euro-currency market; direct loans from foreign banks; bond issues floated on international capital markets; and supplier credits. Indeed, in many Latin American countries, such fixed-term loans account for a much larger percentage of total capital flows than does equity investment—and on the whole are more favorably regarded and sought after.

the foreign investment phenomenon—and in particular its two-sided, negotiated character—tend to be forgotten. There are indeed two sides to the debate, just as there have always been two sides to the investment bargain. Each one is valid in its own right as a negotiating position, and one must understand and weigh the respective arguments in this light in order to arrive at any useful conclusions about the future of private direct investment in Latin America. Thus, the investment debate must be examined not in terms of morality or conspiracy, but rather as a continuous, conflictive bargaining process in which negotiating advantages and potential benefits are constantly shifting from one side to the other and thus altering the perceived value of the bargain for each one.

A. *Why Overseas Investment Occurs*

Textbook theorists[3] explain the flow of capital abroad in useful elemental terms: Investment capital flows to markets that offer the greatest return on invested funds with the least possible risk. When prospects for return, balanced against possibilities for loss, appear higher abroad than at home, investment capital will move beyond its national borders in search of those returns. The potential investor searches for optimum conditions of higher probable return and lower risk, and he is prepared to bargain intensively among potential recipient countries in order to maximize those possibilities.

Developing countries, in turn, seek foreign investment as a means to increase the rate of real growth, when internal capital accumulation is insufficient to pay the costs of importing the capital goods, advanced technology, and management skills necessary to sustain development.[4] In order to attract such investment, developing countries over the years have tended to vie with each other in offering special inducements or privileges to investors. Foremost among these, of course, have been such natural

---

3. The authors' summary is based on the analysis in C. KINDLEBERGER, INTERNATIONAL ECONOMICS 224-62 (5th ed. 1973).

4. The view widely held among Latin American theorists asserts that the developing country's domestic capital shortfall characteristically results because the foreign exchange returns on its exports of primary products fail to keep pace with the rising costs of importing capital and intermediate goods needed for industrialization. *Cf.* Prebisch, *Issues to Be Brought Before the Commission on International Trade and Investment Policy Concerning Relations with Developing Countries*, in PAPERS SUBMITTED TO THE COMMISSION ON INTERNATIONAL TRADE AND INVESTMENT POLICY 289-306 (1971) (emphasizing the common responsibilities of developing and developed countries in application of convergent measures through domestic policies as well as policies of international trade and financial cooperation).

advantages as convenient access to raw materials,[5] low-cost labor, inexpensive sources of power, and proximity to potential markets.[6] Governments have also devised artificial inducements to supplement their countries' natural advantages—minerals concessions, favorable tax breaks, restrictions on labor organization, and the like. In effect, therefore, developing countries compete with each other and bargain among potential investors in order to maximize their own return in the form of technical training, foreign exchange earnings, tax payments, stimulation of local capital formation, and new jobs.

It is also characteristic of the investment bargain in developing countries that once the deal is sealed, bargaining strength shifts through time from the investor to the host country, as technical skills are transferred, plant and machinery are imported, paid for, and set in place, and stimulus to local developmental growth has occurred.[7] As company profits rise and capital is repatriated in growing amounts, the host country may decide that the investor's returns are growing while its own are declining (which may indeed be the case) and conclude that the bargain needs altering. Measures that may be taken include higher taxes, new constraints on business operations, higher wage scales, profit controls, and limits on repatriation of profits—conditions that reopen the bargaining game and, logically, may induce the investor ultimately to pull up stakes and leave for greener pastures if projected returns fall below an acceptable level.

Purely economic factors and market conditions are not the only ones that enter the bargaining game between investor and developing country. What have been called "psychic costs,"[8] the inevitable frictions that occur when differing cultures, value systems, and standards of living meet under competitive circumstances, form a part of the bargain as well and must somehow be entered by both sides into the bargaining equation. These factors, no matter how irrelevant or "political" they may seem in strict economic terms, directly influence the terms of the investment bargain by dampening incentives on one side or the other. Thus, they impose an added cost, which must ultimately be paid through forgoing increases in national income or corporate profits.[9]

---

5. Mexico's newly discovered reserves of crude petroleum, for example, make that country an increasingly attractive possible site for secondary petrochemicals (primary petrochemicals being a sector barred to foreigners).

6. Mexico's border industry program is an especially pertinent example of how a country can exploit its geographic location and the availability of skilled and relatively cheaper labor (as well as certain exceptional provisions in United States customs law) to attract foreign investment capital. *Cf.* Comment, *Mexico's Border Industrial Program: Legal Guidelines for the Foreign Investor*, 4 DENVER J. INT'L L. & P. 89 (1974).

7. C. KINDLEBERGER, *supra* note 3, at 250-51.

8. HUNT, EVALUATING DIRECT FOREIGN INVESTMENT IN LATIN AMERICA IN THE 1970s (Rand R-1067-DOS, Dec. 1972).

9. C. KINDLEBERGER, *supra* note 3, at 276. On the other side of the coin, there are

B. How Overseas Investment Occurred in Latin America

The roots of Latin America's economic growth, like those of the United States and Canada, lie in the extraordinary century of European economic expansion, capital export, and free trade that lasted from the end of the Napoleonic Wars until the outbreak of World War I. During this period, which coincided with the opening up to foreign trade and investment of the former Spanish colonial empire, huge surpluses of investment capital, released as a product of Europe's industrial revolution and increasingly liberalized trade, flowed into the underdeveloped lands and labor markets of the New World, bringing with them the first fruits of technological and managerial innovation.[10] Capital flows tended to follow established patterns of trade and migrations, as investors sought to place their money in environments that they best understood, therefore offering the least risk. As a result, the lion's share of investment capital flowed initially from England and northern Europe into North America,[11] while the former Spanish and Portugese colonies lagged behind.

During the latter half of the nineteenth century, however, investment opportunities in Latin America attracted growing amounts of capital both from Europe and, increasingly, from the United States. After a number of sobering initial experiences with financing revolutions and short-lived Latin American governments, investors concentrated primary attention on agricultural, mining, and infrastructure projects—notably railroads, ports, and highways—as indeed was the case in North America at the time.[12] While generally returning an ample profit to European investors, these capital inputs stimulated a burst of domestic economic activity, which in "successful" cases laid the basis for the area's future economic growth.[13]

The free flow of capital, technology, and trade during the nineteenth century, however, into the empty lands and capital-poor countries of the world also carried with it the seeds of its own collapse. In a pattern not unlike today's, the creation of fragile new economic activities and competition between old and new economic centers brought demands for protection and placed intolerable strains on marginal producers.[14] Exporting

---

significant "psychic benefits" that also weigh in the investment bargain on both sides although they are less frequently mentioned than the psychic costs and are even harder to quantify: for the foreign businessman, attractive living conditions, household servants, membership in elite local clubs, and personal income tax advantages; for the host country, prestige industrial complexes, "self-sufficiency" in particular industrial sectors, the "modern" look, etc.

10. North, *International Capital Movements in Historical Perspective*, in U.S. PRIVATE AND GOVERNMENT INVESTMENT ABROAD 10 (R. Mikesell ed. 1962) [hereinafter cited as Mikesell].

11. *Id.* at 12.

12. *Id.* at 13-14.

13. *Id.* at 33-34.

14. *Id.* at 15.

nations vied for control of markets and sources of raw materials. "Colonialism," direct governmental intervention, and even armed invasion in support of private investors became fierce economic realities.

World War I brought a dramatic end to an era of free capital movements. The 1920s saw a renewal of capital flows based in large part on the United States capital market, but this was terminated by the World Depression and the resumption of protectionist, "beggar-thy-neighbors" practices by many major industrial countries. The treaties negotiated by the United States Government under the Trade Agreements Act of 1934[15] reversed these policies in a limited way but did not solve the capital requirements of the Latin American countries.

During the 1930s, while international flows of capital stagnated, many Latin American countries became for a time net exporters of capital, as flows reversed back to major investing countries floundering in financial difficulties.[16] The United States (which had taken over the primary foreign investment role from bankrupt Europe during the preceding decade) found itself once again a net importer of capital,[17] with repatriations exceeding new foreign investments by considerable margins. In addition, traditionally favored investment in foreign bonds and private bank loans began giving way to equity ownership, as more and more American businessmen ventured abroad with their capital, management, and technology bound up in a single investment package.[18]

The direct investment trend accelerated after World War II. From 1946 to 1959, investment in United States-controlled enterprises abroad increased in value from 7.2 billion dollars to 29.7 billion dollars, and of this increase over 6 billion dollars flowed to Latin America.[19] Moreover, this upward trend was accompanied by a shift away from previously-favored infrastructure and agricultural enterprises—the one having become largely the domain of public financing, and the other limited by new prohibitions on foreign land ownership. Instead, postwar investors turned increasing attention to the profit-making potential of the extractive industries, already amply demonstrated during the war, and, above all, to manufacturing.

On the whole, Latin America was both ready and willing to absorb the surplus investment capacity of the United States during the initial postwar period, and United States businessmen were moving aggressively to fill the vacuum left by their less fortunate European predecessors. The region's growth had already been stimulated and its appetite whetted, first by the

15. Trade Agreements Act of 1934, ch. 474, §§ 1-4, 48 Stat. 943 (codified as amended in scattered sections of 19 U.S.C.).

16. North, *International Capital Movements in Historical Perspective*, in Mikesell, *supra* note 10, at 28.

17. *Id.* at 17.

18. Mikesell, *U.S. Postwar Investment Abroad: A Statistical Analysis*, in Mikesell, *supra* note 10, at 51.

19. *Id.* at 58.

rapid injection of investment capital from Europe a generation earlier, then by the artificial prosperity it had enjoyed from exports of food and raw materials during World War II. Wartime shortages of manufactured goods lent an autarchic character to the region's economies, as countries sought to reduce their dependence on imports by developing their own manufacturing capacity. Nevertheless, export-oriented sectors had grown up, technical skills had been implanted, and a basic infrastructure had been laid. By the end of the 1950s, rapid economic growth had become not only a major political objective for Latin America but a good business bet for foreign investors.

There were clouds on the horizon too. Social strains were apparent in nearly every Latin American country, particularly those that had experienced the most rapid initial growth. There were painful memories of overdependence on foreign capital and world markets during the Depression, and even sharper ones of wartime trade disruptions and restrictions. Demands grew for import substitution and protective legislation, for closer scrutiny of the books of foreign corporations, for a halt to open-ended concessions of natural resources, for ceilings on the remittances of corporate profits, and for a greater government role in developmental planning and decision-making. Moreover, Peron's Argentina had already shown (as Castro's Cuba was to demonstrate even more vividly) to what lengths a radically nationalist government could go in imposing constraints on foreign private businessmen and in extending the public sector at the expense of the private.

C. *Effects of the "OPEC Era"*

Despite these new conditions and attempts at more effective national control, United States private investment continued its steady flow to Latin America during the 1960s and early 1970s. Attracted by lower wage costs, expanding domestic markets, tax incentives, and protective tariffs, businessmen discounted the difficulties and invested over ten billion dollars in net new resources in Latin America from 1960 through 1973.[20]

To an important extent, new United States Government policies helped to mitigate the difficulties and encourage the flow, in the expectation that private investment could play a prime role in achieving higher standards of living, which would undercut the appeal of the most radical nationalists. The Alliance for Progress assigned major responsibilities to the private sector for increasing capital transfers to Latin America, and it offered tax

20. For a full examination of United States Government policies to encourage flows of private investment capital to underdeveloped areas, see Behrman, *Promotion of Private Overseas Investment*, in Mikesell, *supra* note 10, at 165.

incentives and other aids to businessmen to facilitate the process. Similarly, the Overseas Private Investment Corporation (OPIC)[21] and its predecessor agencies in the Agency for International Development (AID) were established with the aim of stimulating needed investment in areas where political risks or social turbulence might otherwise have discouraged it. By these and other means, the United States Government sought to help bridge the contradiction between Latin America's evident need for new capital and the obstacles that were increasingly being placed in the way of the private investor.

III. LATIN AMERICAN RESPONSES TO FOREIGN PRIVATE INVESTMENT

Economic policy objectives are usually reflected in laws. Latin America's laws, the concrete expression of its policies and doctrines, reflect not only the evolution of the foreign investment "bargain" in the area but—even more important—current goals and future directions. If the laws are any indication, Latin America may be more unified in its current bargaining stance toward foreign investment than at any time in recent history.

A. The Developing Legal Framework

Ever since Simón Bolivar tried unsuccessfully to instigate union following independence from Spain, Latin America has displayed an ambivalent attitude towards foreign investment and common action regarding it. True to its proud juridical traditions, the area has not lacked jurists with innovative approaches to its special economic circumstances. Still, countervailing forces have often nullified what appeared to be promising initiatives.

As early as 1832, the great Venezuelan-Chilean jurist Andres Bello devised an approach that might have defeated the system of the great trading nations,[22] who rushed to break Spain's trading monopoly in the New World by negotiating most-favored-nation agreements with Latin American countries. Bello's approach would simply have reserved the possibility that special treatment might be extended exclusively to any sister Latin American republic without creating benefits for any most-favored-nation outside the area. The "Bello Clause" was included in several treaties by Chile, which saw it as a means of developing a complete economy, but was rejected or soon ignored by other Latin American countries which preferred the immediate benefits of allying with the trading nations who vied to exploit their natural resources and purchase their primary materials.

21. OPIC was created by the Foreign Assistance Act of 1969, Pub. L. 91-175, 83 Stat. 805, 809-18 (codified as amended at 22 U.S.C. §§ 2191-2200b (1976 & Supp. V 1981)).

22. Orrego-Vicuna, *Estudio Sobre la Cláusula Bello y la crisis de la solidaridad latinoamericana en el siglo XIX*, in DERECHO INTERNACIONAL ECONÓMICO: AMÉRICA LATINA Y LA CLÁUSULA DE LA NACIÓN MÁS FAVORECIDA (F. Orrego-Vicuna ed. 1974).

The failure of the Bello Clause may have been an indication of the willingness of most Latin American countries to remain within the trading sphere of the major industrial nations, but it did not end their efforts to find legal formulas to fit their special concerns. When capital-exporting nations intervened in Latin American countries to force payments of loans or to protect investments, Argentine jurists responded with the Calvo Clause (first advanced by Carlos Calvo in 1868) and the Drago Doctrine. The latter, brainchild of Dr. Luis Drago when he was Argentina's Foreign Minister in 1902, asserted that "public debt of an American state cannot occasion armed intervention, nor even the occupation of the territory of American nations by European powers."[23] The Drago Doctrine was written into the Porter Convention at the Hague Conference of 1907, but it was tied to another provision, which made it unpalatable to Latin America: Capital-exporting nations would renounce the use of force, but only in exchange for commitment on the part of capital-importing nations to submit disputes to arbitration and be bound by the results.[24] No South American country ratified the convention, and of the six Central American and Caribbean countries that did, only Mexico and Panama did so without reservation on that point.[25]

The Calvo Clause, an article of long-standing faith for all Latin American governments, was aimed at the same basic problems as the Drago Doctrine. The Calvo Clause is notably broader in its sweep, however. It has two main tenets: (1) strict nonintervention by foreign powers in the sovereign process of each individual Latin American state; and (2) absolute subjection of foreigners to the laws and juridical regime of the host country.[26] The Calvo Clause is currently embodied in constitutional provisions, national laws, corporate charters and contracts made in favor of foreign investors in Latin American countries, and international conventions.[27] History has shown the Calvo Clause to be as strong and unwavering a legal principle among Latin American nations as any that have been

23. D. SHEA, THE CALVO CLAUSE 14 (1955).

24. Convention II of 1907 Respecting the Limitation of the Employment of Force for the Recovery of Contract-Debts, art. 1, *reprinted in* THE HAGUE CONVENTIONS AND DECLARATIONS OF 1899 AND 1907, at 89 (J. Scott 3d ed. 1918).

25. *See* Ratifications, adhesions and reservations, THE HAGUE CONVENTIONS AND DECLARATIONS OF 1899 AND 1907, *supra* note 24, at 91-95.

26. Unlike the Drago Doctrine, there seems to be no specific moment at which the Calvo Clause crystallized. The concept is probably present in Calvo's six-volume work, C. CALVO, LE DROIT INTERNATIONALE THÉORETIQUE ET PRATIQUE (1896). There were several earlier editions by this career diplomat who spent much of his professional life in Europe. Despite the lack of a clear and unequivocal expression by Carlos Calvo at a particular moment, the clause which bears his name has been rather specifically defined over time. *See* C. SEPÚLVEDA, CARLOS CALVO: TRES ENSAYOS MEXICANOS (1974).

27. MEX. CONST., art. 27(I) is a classic example of the Calvo Clause. Art. 27(I) reads in part:

> . . . The State may grant the same right [over lands, waters, and minerals] to foreigners, provided they agree before the Ministry of Foreign Affairs to consider

devised. It is not, however, one that has been absolutely respected. In fact, foreign investors who enter host countries under Calvo Clause agreements have quite commonly turned to diplomatic measures in case of economic disputes. Latin American governments, while protesting the impropriety of the process, have commonly received these diplomatic missions, and in fact many resolutions have resulted from such diplomatic negotiations.

In the areas of both private and public law, Latin America has long been a leader in uniform legislation and private international law conventions, both in its own regional forums and under the auspices of the Pan American Union and its successor, the Organization of American States (OAS).[28] At the Panama Conference of 1826 convened by Bolivar, the Peruvian delegate proposed the drafting of a "Code of Law for the American People."[29] Designs have since become less sweeping, but increasingly effective: At Montevideo in 1889, the first Pan American Conference adopted draft conventions on civil, commercial, penal, and procedural law. In this century, with varying United States participation from 1906 onwards, the comprehensive "Bustamante Code" on Private International Law was drafted, approved, and ratified by many nations. It provides a framework for most private law issues which might grow out of international trade in this hemisphere.

Innovative work in this same vein was furthered as recently as January 1975, when an Inter-American Specialized Conference on Private International Law was convened by the OAS in Panama to update some of the more important private law conventions.[30] If the conventions adopted in Panama are ratified in a substantial number of countries—a good possibility because they are patterned after the Hague Conventions—they will help to create a legal environment in which private lawyers may operate with increased expediency and certainty.

B. Early Postwar Trends

During the immediate post-World War II period, most Latin Americans remained convinced that foreign investment would almost automatically

---

> themselves as nationals in respect to such property, and bind themselves not to invoke the protection of their governments in matters relating thereto; under penalty, in case of noncompliance with this agreement, of forfeiture of the acquired property to the Nation. . . .

reprinted in 10 CONSTITUTIONS OF THE COUNTRIES OF THE WORLD 16 (A. Blaustein & G. Flanz trans. ed. 1982).

28. Charter of the Organization of American States, Apr. 30, 1948, 2 U.S.T. 2416, T.I.A.S. No. 2361, 119 U.N.T.S. 48, *amended* 21 U.S.T. 658, T.I.A.S. No. 6847, 721 U.N.T.S. 324 [hereinafter cited as OAS Charter].

29. A. SANCHEZ DE BUSTAMANTE Y SIRVÉN, LA COMISIÓN DE JURISCONSULTOS DE RIO DE JANEIRO Y EL DERECHO INTERNACIONAL 3 (1927).

30. *See* Inter-American Specialized Conference on Private International Law, Panama City, Panama, Jan. 14-30, 1975, Acts and Documents, OAS Doc. OEA/Ser. K/XXI.I/ CIDIP/64 (1975).

have a salutary effect on economic development. Where before there had been few regulations at the national level for foreign investment and almost none at the international level, after the war the matter was considered on many occasions. The International Trade Organization Charter, drafted in Havana in 1947-1948 and doomed to early rejection, devoted a long article to the question.[31] Its primary concern was to protect and encourage foreign investment, but it also recognized that the essential objective of such investment was economic development and that the local climate might be tempered to that end.

The most important postwar forums to deal with problems of private investment in Latin America, however, were those that, from 1946 to 1948, evolved the so-called Inter-American System and the Organization of American States out of the old Pan American Union. These efforts of the Latin American nations and the United States to build a more formal structure for their relations with each other resulted in three fundamental treaty documents in 1948, each one dealing to some extent with the role of the foreign private investor in the region's development; the interests of the developing countries themselves; rights and restrictions applying to the investor's own government (implicitly the United States); and the possibility of conflict among these three.

The OAS Charter firmly established the Calvo thesis of equality before the law of nationals and aliens: "The jurisdiction of States within the limits of their national territory is exercised equally over all the inhabitants, whether nationals or aliens."[32] It also affirmed Calvo's nonintervention thesis,[33] adding that "[n]o State may use or encourage the use of coercive measures of an economic or political character in order to force the sovereign will of another State and obtain from it advantages of any kind."[34] When the Charter was reformed in 1967,[35] the rights of developing countries to fix their own priorities—and the duty of developed countries to respect those priorities—were spelled out in much greater detail. The trend continues into the current negotiations over yet another reform of the Charter, where some are seeking to establish the principle of "collective economic security" against attacks upon a member country's sovereign development decisions.

The *American Treaty on Pacific Settlement*,[36] the so-called "Pact of Bogota," in a way was the opposite side of the coin. Establishing a system

31. International Trade Organization Charter, art. 12, *reprinted in* C. WILCOX, A CHARTER FOR WORLD TRADE 236-37 (1949).

32. OAS Charter art. 12, *supra* note 28.

33. *Id.* art. 15.

34. *Id.* art. 16.

35. Protocol of Amendment to the Charter of the Organization of American States, Feb. 27, 1967, 21 U.S.T. 658, T.I.A.S. No. 6847, 721 U.N.T.S. 324 [also known as the Protocol of Buenos Aires].

36. American Treaty on Pacific Settlement, Apr. 30, 1948, 30 U.N.T.S. 84.

for settling disputes among member nations, the treaty *excluded* disputes between governments and private entities subject to domestic law, and it would have committed foreign governments to respect national sovereignty in such cases: "The High Contracting Parties bind themselves not to make diplomatic representations in order to protect their nationals . . . when the said nationals have had available the means to place their case before competent domestic courts of the respective State."[37] In signing the treaty, the United States reserved on that (and other) articles, stating that it intended to maintain "the rules of diplomatic protection as provided by international law," and it has never ratified the treaty for this reason.

The *Bogota Economic Agreement*[38] suffered the opposite fate from that of the dispute settlement pact. The draft agreement was heavily pro-investment and included an article guaranteeing "prompt, adequate and effective manner of compensation" in the event of expropriation. Most Latin American nations signed the agreement but reserved on this and other articles.

Until recently the domestic laws and international policies of most Latin American countries continued to treat foreign private investment as an essentially positive force for national development. If there were reservations in this regard, they had mostly to do with ensuring national sovereignty in the event of investment disputes with foreigners, and Latins balked as a consequence at agreeing to certain propositions which investors and their governments considered important to enhancing the investment climate. Otherwise Latin America's role was mainly passive. Its laws and regulations at most stipulated what foreign investors *should not* do; they did not attempt to define what foreign investment *should* do to promote development in accord with national priorities.

More recent Latin American legislation carries the bargaining considerably further, attempting to establish developmental "thou shalts" in addition to the older "thou shalt nots" as conditions for accepting new foreign private investment. Fundamentally, these conditions assert that the former passive restraints failed to ensure that outside investment would contribute to national development priorities, and that a more activist host government role was necessary in order to prevent the country's becoming ever more dependent on foreign capital, technology, and markets.

C. Dependency Theory: The New Latin American Viewpoint

To understand Latin America's shift from passive to more active bargaining terms, it is helpful to understand the conceptual framework—the

37. *Id.* art. VII, 30 U.N.T.S. at 86.

38. Economic Agreement of Bogota, *signed* May 2, 1948, *reprinted in* 1 ANNALS OF THE ORGANIZATION OF AMERICAN STATES 99 (1949) (the Agreement had only been ratified by three countries as of 1980).

theory of "dependency"[39]—which more and more is determining the shape of new investment laws and policies among the nations of the region. Although in many ways "dependency" seems merely a new description of an old complaint,[40] it has in fact become a systematic indictment of what many Latin Americans see as detrimental in the role of foreign investment in their economies.

Latin America's ultimate goal, begins the theory, is to improve the standard of living and social well-being of its people through industrialization. But this goal must be achieved in such a way that the standard of living is raised for substantial segments of its population, income distribution is as broad as possible, and—most important—its economies achieve sufficient strength to allow them to compete fully on their own as exporters of manufactured goods. Until then, the theorists say, they will be dependent on economic forces outside their control.

Foreign private investment has indeed helped to raise the level of industrialization in Latin America, but in the theorists' view it has not served the parallel objectives of social justice and commercial self-sufficiency. So despite their apparent development, Latin American countries remain dependent on foreign corporations and capital-exporting countries to sustain that development and thus vulnerable to the negative, antidevelopmental aspects of the outsiders' role in their economies. This dark side of development may take various forms:

(1) *Displacement of national entrepreneurship*. In most cases it means that the foreign investor will out-perform and possibly displace the national investor. Most investments that further industrialization and development require sophisticated technology, and the local investor will not own or have independent access to that technology.

(2) *Preemptive Financing.* The local firm or individual is likely not to be as solid a credit risk as the large foreign firm, and the latter may use local financing and credit leverage to buy into local enterprises while national interests find further expansion or diversification impossible because they lack an equal credit rating.

(3) *Unequal bargaining options.* Both investor and government will tend to communicate less and less honestly, each fearful of the other's power. Yet it is the foreign investor who more frequently has the option of

39. *See* F. CARDOSO & E. FALETTO, DEPENDENCIA Y DESARROLLO EN AMÉRICA LATINA (1969); J. COCKCROFT, A. FRANK & D. JOHNSON, DEPENDENCE AND UNDERDEVELOPMENT (1972); M. WIONCZEK, INVERSIÓN Y TECNOLOGÍA EXTRANJERA EN AMÉRICA LATINA (1971); Dos Santos, *The Structure of Dependence*, AM. ECON. REV., May 1970, at 231; Sunkel, *Big Business and "Dependencia": A Latin American View*, 50 FOREIGN AFF. 517 (1972).

40. Raul Prebisch was a strong propounder of a similar theory but cast it in terms of the center (industrialized nations) and periphery (the Third World). *See* R. PREBISCH, LATIN AMERICA, A PROBLEM IN DEVELOPMENT (1971).

picking up his marbles and going home, taking technology, marketing, executive know-how, and good will with him. This unequal posture inhibits negotiation and prevents true cooperation in the development effort.

(4) *Restraints on technology transfer.* Agreements on technology transfer have generally not been subject to official scrutiny and in the past investors have demanded dependency creating contract clauses, which are accepted as a matter of course: selling unnecessary technology in a package with essential technology on a take-it-or-leave-it basis; selling older technology and machinery that keeps the host country's industry a generation behind that of the foreign investor's home operation; price and marketing restrictions on all items produced with the technology so as to assure that no competing export capacity will be developed; and provisions requiring that any technological advance developed within the host country reverts automatically to the seller of the technology, with no rights retained by the buyer.

(5) *Balance of payments effects.* Latin American theorists also assert there is a negative effect on balance of payments attendant upon dependency, and that the effect is especially heightened by foreign investments in the manufacturing sector. Whereas foreign investment in natural resources or primary materials almost always results in substantial exports and balance of payments credits, manufacturing normally produces little or no export earnings. While this saves the country the cost of paying for imports of manufactured items, dependency economists counter that the import-substituted manufactured items almost always cost significantly more than the same items on the free world market.

As long as these investment disadvantages persist, dependency theorists believe, the nations of the region have little chance to advance to the self-sufficient status of fully developed participants in world commerce. Dependency theorists might go further and find a fear in the industrialized nations that if the presently underdeveloped states were to develop means for fully industrializing their own resources, they might eventually supplant and even dominate the present industrialized nations who would then be at a disadvantage in world trade in terms of labor and primary materials cost. Therefore, the governments of industrialized countries are unlikely to do anything to bring about change and real development in dependent countries. Thus, the theorists conclude, until the day that Latin American economies can at least participate as equal partners, they will continue to be unacceptably dependent on foreign investment for the amenities of their existence and the margin of their civilization. At this level, the dependency theorist sees real conflict between Latin America's desires for development and the "vested interests" of the industrial establishment.

D. Implementing Dependency Theory

One need not share the views of the dependency theorists to recognize the considerable impact they have had lately on Latin American laws, policies, and attitudes toward foreign private investment. Perhaps the most fundamental change has been the shift from a passive to an active posture at the investment bargaining table: no longer merely concerned with ensuring national sovereignty, protecting the national patrimony, and preventing flagrant abuses, Latin American leaders are confronting potential investors with an expanding notion of exactly how foreign private capital should fit into national development plans and contribute toward their realization.

This shift in attitude is apparent, to greater or lesser degrees, in virtually every Latin American country today, with Mexico as a leading example. But beyond doubt, the foremost example of applied dependency theory is to be seen in the regional association of South American states known as the Andean Group, established pursuant to the Agreement of Cartagena in 1969, with headquarters in Lima.[41] Committed to the validity of dependency theory outlined above, the Andean Group nations set out to legislate a comprehensive program that would restructure their respective economies and the role of foreign investment in them.[42] Underlying the program was the conviction that Latin America should formulate and spell out in detailed fashion its own positive plan for developing an industrialized society. The Andean Group's Decision 24 on Foreign Investment and the Transfer of Technology is probably its best known legislative act.[43]

Decision 24 is a blueprint for the future prevention of "anti-developmental situations" identified by the dependency theorists and described above. Its most far-reaching effects are prospective. Many of its provisions do not apply to existing investment arrangements, or can be made inapplicable by individual country decision. Among its provisions, the best known is that which requires disinvestment, under which an investor wishing to enter an Andean country to produce for the subregional market knows that he does so on condition that he divest himself of at least a majority control within fifteen or twenty years, depending on the country. Not only will "national" capital gradually assume control of the enterprise, but the foreign investor may not repatriate profits in excess of

41. *See generally* the basic collection of Andean Group documents in BID-INTAL, HISTORIA DOCUMENTAL DEL ACUERDO DE CARTAGENA (Inter-American Development Bank, Institute for the Integration of Latin America 1974). Members of the Andean Group include Colombia, Peru, Ecuador, Bolivia, and Venezuela. Chile also was a member until 1977.

42. *See* Furnish & Atkin, *The Andean Group's Program for Industrial Development of the Metalworking Sector: Integration with Due and Deliberate SPID*, 7 LAW. AM. 29 (1975).

43. *See* Furnish, *The Andean Common Market's Common Regime for Foreign Investments,* 5 VAND. J. TRANSNAT'L L. 313 (1972); Oliver, *The Andean Foreign Investment Code*, 66 AM. J. INT'L L. 763 (1972).

fourteen percent of his capital investment annually. Nor is "hidden" repatriation through royalties or loan repayments permitted. The foreign investor's access to local capital, often in the hands of foreign bank subsidiaries, is limited. He cannot buy out failing nationally owned businesses unless no other buyer is found, and he can reinvest no more than five percent of local profits in his enterprise each year. Moreover, clauses in investment agreements providing for subrogation of international arbitration are prohibited, effectively ruling out OPIC insurance programs and third party dispute settlements.

The Foreign Investment Code's drafters felt investors had used technology contracts to hide repatriation of excessive profits. The Code therefore prohibits certain contract clauses now in common use that restrict or limit a technology's value from the standpoint of the recipient country. Effective administration will be necessary to enforce these measures. At the time Decision 24 was promulgated there were no national offices that might have handled that responsibility, but they have now been established. Thus, registration and disclosure at national offices of all technology contracts are intended to provide authorities with an opportunity to apply the provisions of Decision 24 and to gain expertise in the administration of technology transfer.

All of this indicates a tough new bargaining position on the part of Andean countries, one to which potential foreign investors may respond poorly. The Andean Group's authorities are philosophical about investors' attitudes. They claim to want foreign investment, but only that which will genuinely serve developmental ends and reduce "dependency." They discount initial negative reactions on the part of investors, confident that the overall program, once understood, will be ample incentive.[44] They also point to the large market potential of a unified Andean region. Ultimately, they believe, the potential of this market will prove irresistible to investors, who may grumble at the tougher bargaining stance at first, but will soon turn their lawyers to finding ways of taking advantage of new opportunities.

The Andean Group's program includes much more than Decision 24. Perhaps the most authentic expression of its antidependency theoretical underpinnings is found in its sectorial programs for industrial development, for which the Decision 24 foreign investment rules serve as a supporting framework.[45] The sectorial programs for industrial development aim at rationalizing promotion of industry on a subregional scale. They

---

44. The Andean Group has been at pains to explain its program in various countries. In the United States, the Council of the Americas has changed its earlier negative stance somewhat and published a series of studies that deal with the Andean Group and the change in Latin America generally regarding foreign investment.

45. Agreement on Andean Subregional Integration, arts. 35-43 (English language translation in 8 I.L.M. 910, 919 (1969)) [also known as Acuerdo de Cartagena or Agreement of Cartagena]. *See* Furnish & Atkin, *supra* note 42, at 29; Guerrero, *La Programación conjunta*

divide up a given industrial sector and parcel out production rights for the subregion to a particular country or combination of countries. The latter must then provide the investment necessary to begin production within a set time period.

Obviously much of the investment required for the sectorial programs must come from foreign sources able to provide not only capital, but the specific industrial technology that the program requires—metalworking, automotive, or petrochemical techniques, to name three. The metalworking sector demonstrated that foreign investors will seek out the Andean market. Often new arrangements evolve as new firms come into the area: a Swedish firm came into Bolivia on a capital loan and technology contract, eschewing any equity ownership from the first.[46] Other investing firms have allied with their home governments to negotiate arrangements that guarantee the purchase of a percentage of the ultimate industrial product.[47]

To date, the Andean Group represents a unique attempt at implementing dependency theory in a systematic, regional fashion. But the theory's adherents are widespread, its tenets are being increasingly incorporated in local private investment legislation, and its premises are emerging with regularity in the pronouncements and declarations aimed by developing countries at the industrialized nations.

E. CERDS: A Projection of Dependency Theory

Notable in the latter regard is the Charter of Economic Rights and Duties of States (CERDS),[48] largely the initiative of former President Luis Echeverría Alvarez of Mexico. Among other things, the Charter strongly states the antidependency arguments, and its unanimous Third World endorsement reflects the extent to which these arguments have gained currency. The Charter also represents one more example of the developing countries' determination to abandon their passive role and seize the bargaining initiative with fully developed proposals for future development cooperation.

The Charter implicitly rejects the traditional formula of "prompt, adequate, and effective compensation" in cases of expropriation of foreign owned properties. In its place is a duty to pay "appropriate compensation

---

del desarrollo industrial subregional y el primer programa sectorial de la industria metal mecánica, 12 DERECHO DE LA INTEGRACIÓN 35 (1973).

46. *See* case histories detailed in Pate, *New Joint Venture Approaches and a Review of Competitive Forces Within ANCOM*, in 4 COUNCIL OF THE AMERICAS, ANDEAN PACT: DEFINITIONS, DESIGN, AND ANALYSIS 1 (1973).

47. *Id.*

48. United Nations Charter of Economic Rights and Duties of States, G.A. Res. 3281, 29 U.N. GAOR Supp. (No. 31) at 50, U.N. Doc. A/9631 (1975).

. . . taking into account its relevant laws and regulations and all circumstances that the [expropriating] State considers pertinent."[49] All controversies are to be resolved strictly within national processes, save where both states agree to utilize other peaceful methods on the "basis of the sovereign equality of States."[50] Thus the Calvo Clause has found its way into the Third World's latest and most definitive assertion of new terms for foreign investment, qualified only by a purely optional waiver.

In the same vein of national sovereignty, the Charter includes articles affirming the right of states to form cartels for marketing primary products,[51] to join in regional associations organized according to the principles of the Charter[52] (and by implication *not* according to the General Agreements on Tariffs and Trade), and to treat foreign investment in exclusive conformity with national "objectives and priorities."[53] CERDS is also a catalogue of things the Third World would like to comprise a "new international economic order": generalized tariff preferences,[54] international cooperation in technology and advantageous terms of its transfer to the Third World nations,[55] increased credit from "official sources" under improved terms and conditions,[56] and maintenance of export prices for primary materials and resources[57] are some of these.

Despite the Charter's overwhelming endorsement by United Nations members in the General Assembly, it essentially represents only one point of view in the continuing dialogue between the world's wealthier and poorer nations. There can be no denying the strength and growth of opinion that it represents, but in the view of the United States (which agrees with most but by no means all of its assertions) it cannot be considered a statement of existing international law. Rather, it represents an assertive signal of dissatisfaction on the part of the world's less-developed countries with the present form of their economic relations with the industrialized nations, and it merits a positive response by the latter aimed at discovering mutually beneficial new modalities for carrying on international economic intercourse.

In the late 1970s, dependency theory in Latin America was modified and expanded in light of the region's strengthened bargaining position in negotiations with relatively weakened industrialized economies. Advocates of this new approach recommended a series of actions and policies to obtain

---

49. *Id*. art. 2(2)(c).
50. *Id*.
51. *Id*. arts. 5, 6.
52. *Id*. art. 12.
53. *Id*. art. 2(2)(a).
54. *Id*. arts. 18, 19.
55. *Id*. art. 13.
56. *Id*. art. 22(2).
57. *Id*. arts. 14, 28.

better adaptation of foreign capital to regional development interests. These include, most importantly:

(1) regional *integration* and coordination to present homogeneous conditions for the treatment of foreign capital, and to increase Latin America's political importance and economic weight in the world community;

(2) *diversification* in the flow of foreign investment, loans, trade, technology transfer, and development assistance, to lessen dependence on any one country, particularly the United States; and,

(3) more effective *planning* and appraisal of national and regional needs for foreign capital, thus strengthening negotiations with solid information about the beneficial and harmful effects and repercussions of foreign investment in each sector.

IV. MEXICO: A CASE STUDY OF LEGAL DEVELOPMENTS

The initial groundwork for the control of foreign private direct investment in Mexico was laid with the adoption of the Constitution of 1917,[58] which established restrictions and conditions on foreign acquisition of land and concessions, including minerals.[59] Except for minor regulatory functions, there was no significant further regulation of investment until, following the expropriation of the petroleum industry, laws were passed prohibiting foreign ownership of any part of the petroleum industry, including primary petrochemicals.[60] Further broad-based restrictions were imposed by the decree of June 29, 1944, and the decree was followed in turn by individual laws generally covering one industry or one sector.[61]

Mexico requires a foreigner who invests in the country to enter into an agreement with the Mexican Government under which the foreign investor waives his right to the diplomatic protection of his home government; this type of provision, discussed above, is common throughout the Hemisphere. Several provisions of Mexican law contain language similar in

58. *See* H. WRIGHT, FOREIGN ENTERPRISE IN MEXICO (1971). It should be borne in mind that Wright's book was written before Mexico's new foreign investment law was published; thus much of his legal discussion has been overtaken by events. For a more recent technical discussion of the foreign investment scene, see I. GÓMEZ PALACIO GUTIÉRREZ ZAMORA, ANÁLISIS DE LA LEY DE INVERSIÓN EXTRANJERA (1973) [hereinafter cited as I. Gómez].

59. MEX. CONST. tit. I, ch. 3; tit. II; tit. VIII; tit. IX.

60. ORGANIZATION OF AMERICAN STATES, STATEMENT OF THE LAWS OF MEXICO 28-29 (1970); *id.* at 165-67, *citing* Law of Nov. 27, 1958, 231 Diario Oficial [D.O.] 1, Nov. 28, 1958, Law of Aug. 24, 1959, 235 D.O. 1, Aug. 25, 1959, and Presidential Order of Jan. 13, 1959, 239 D.O. 1, Apr. 9, 1960. Private citizens may not own facilities engaged in an extensive list of segments of the petroleum industry. For those sectors where private ownership is allowed, it must be at least 51% Mexican.

61. *See* H. WRIGHT, *supra* note 58, at 95-150; I. GÓMEZ, *supra* note 58, for detailed information on restrictions, Mexicanization, sectors closed to foreign direct investors, and citations of pertinent laws and regulations.

concept to that of the Calvo Clause. For example, article 27 of the Mexican Constitution makes a Calvo-type agreement a prerequisite to the acquisition by foreigners of land, water, or mineral concessions.[62] Mexican law and regulations implementing article 27 have extended this concept to include stock or any other equity interests. The inclusion of such language in articles of incorporation and stock certificates gives the legal effect of applying the Clause to all purchases of equity stock by foreigners.[63]

A. *The Echeverría Administration*

When the Administration of President Luis Echeverría Alvarez came to power in December 1970, Mexican financial policy-makers were faced with a number of distinct laws and regulations concerning foreign private direct investment. It soon became clear that some sort of unification and clarification of Mexican policy, law, and regulations regarding foreign investment was needed, and, accordingly, the "Law to Promote Mexican Investment and to Regulate Foreign Investment," went into effect on May 8, 1973.[64] Several months later, regulations governing the registration of new foreign private direct investment appeared.[65]

B. *Mexico's Foreign Investment Law*

The foreign investment law created a National Foreign Investment Commission, consisting of seven cabinet members, which must approve those investment proposals that do not clearly fit into situations where favorable precedents have been established. While much of the new law merely brought together existing legislation and regulations, it is somewhat stricter in at least one important regard: The proposed direct investment must be in a joint venture composed of at least fifty-one percent Mexican participation, unless specifically exempted by the Commission. The law lists the sectors reserved for purely Mexican investment and outlines investment criteria.

Thus, under the foreign investment law, exploitation of oil, gas, primary petrochemicals, radioactive minerals, electrical power, railroads, and telegraph and telecommunications is reserved (as in the past) to the state. Other fields, such as radio and television, urban and inter-urban automotive transport, domestic air and maritime transportation, forestry, and gas distribution, are reserved exclusively for Mexican citizens. The foreign investment law also calls for the screening of takeovers of Mexican firms,

---

62. F. BRANDENBURG, THE MAKING OF MODERN MEXICO 208 (1964).

63. For a most interesting and useful general discussion of this subject, see B. SEPÚLVEDA & A. CHUMACERO, LA INVERSIÓN EXTRANJERA EN MÉXICO (1973); H. WRIGHT, *supra* note 58, at 95-150.

64. Ley para promover la inversión Mexicana y regular la inversión extranjera, Feb. 28, 1973, 316 D.O. 5, Mar. 9, 1973.

65. Law of Dec. 28, 1973, 321 D.O. 8, Dec. 28, 1973.

and provides first refusal to Mexicans before foreign firms can acquire controlling interest in a Mexican enterprise.

As of April 1975, the Commission had issued four general rulings. These cover (1) an exemption of border industries from the fifty-one percent Mexican ownership rule; (2) permission for additional foreign capital to be invested in existing joint ventures through capital increases providing the ratio of Mexican to foreign investment is not changed to the detriment of the Mexican stockholders; (3) authorization for foreigners to acquire up to five percent equity in Mexican firms through stock market purchases; and, (4) authorization under most circumstances to reelect present foreign directors to boards of Mexican firms.

C. *Transfer of Technology*

The technology transfer law,[66] a prelude to the foreign investment law, requires the registration of contracts for the sale of foreign technology to Mexican firms. Its main purposes are to avoid the payment of excessive or unjustified prices for foreign technology, and to eliminate certain restrictive conditions believed to have existed in past technology transfer contracts. The technology law lists numerous conditions under which contracts can be barred from registration (and hence be invalid under Mexican law).

D. *Prospects for Foreign Investment in Mexico*

For many years now, Mexico has actively solicited foreign investment on the grounds that it provides the capital and technology necessary to maintain a high rate of economic growth. As elsewhere, foreign investment in Mexico takes several forms, including direct investment and what may be called portfolio investment. The latter consists largely of loans to various Mexican entities, both public and private. The former consists largely of equity investments, usually of a size to permit the investor to play an active, if not dominant, role in a company's management.

By the mid-1970s, direct foreign investment in Mexico declined sharply in response to the restrictive foreign investment legislation and antagonistic pronouncements of the Echeverría regime, as well as Mexico's severe monetary imbalances that culminated in the 1976 liquidity crisis and peso devaluation.

While the "Mexicanization" laws and general policy toward direct foreign investment formulated in the early 1970s has not changed substantially, the antagonistic tone has noticeably softened. Furthermore, a significant shift in the 1970s toward acquiring foreign capital from private banks through loans rather than foreign equity investment has changed the

66. Ley sobre el registro de la transferencía de tecnología y el uso y explotación de patentes y marcas, Dec. 28, 1972, 315 D.O. 45, Dec. 30, 1972.

composition of total capital flows to Mexico heavily in favor of debt financing.

Several factors explain Mexico's current state of enormous foreign indebtedness: (1) excess international liquidity, largely due to "recycled" petrodollars from OPEC countries, made banks eager to lend money and willing to relax normal lending standards; (2) the decrease in the rate of growth of the United States economy, and increased competition among banks brought about the need for banks to seek new profitable clients; and, (3) Mexico's preference for financing national development with foreign debt rather than direct private investment, the ease of obtaining huge private loans from the world's largest banks, and Mexico's need for short-term financing of ambitious projects backed by long-term oil reserves, all contributed to the country's spiraling foreign debt.

In 1983, with the weakened Mexican peso, much lower oil revenues, and enormous interest payments outstanding on its debt, Mexico again has had to submit to an International Monetary Fund (IMF) program of monetary restrictions and fiscal austerity.[67] The current crisis has increased Mexico's dependence and weakened her bargaining power vis-à-vis foreign bankers and potential direct investors. Nevertheless, there is no reason to believe that Mexico will compromise the basic strictures of "Mexicanization," nor that foreign investors can expect to return to their dominant equity position of the past.

President Miguel de la Madrid Hurtado seems to be following an economically conservative and cautious path to bring Mexico safely out of its current crisis, while still avowing commitment to income distribution and social justice. If Mexico is able to stabilize its currency at a realistic exchange rate and begin to get its debt situation under control, while still maintaining political stability, foreign investors will undoubtedly be attracted again to Mexico's huge domestic market and plentiful labor supply. It appears that Mexico's weakened bargaining position is only temporary, and one can expect in the future a renewed and strengthened international bargaining position as Mexico continues its efforts to ensure nationally determined development.

V. THE UNITED STATES DILEMMA

In one article,[68] former United States Ambassador to India, now Senator Patrick Moynihan suggested (in effect) that the growing nationalist assertiveness among Latin American countries over development issues is part of a worldwide phenomenon, a sort of British-born, Fabian-socialist revolution that has infected virtually every Third World country since 1945. Because one of the primary goals of this revolution was to bring

67. Riding, *Mexico Agrees to Austerity Terms for $3.84 Billion in I.M.F. Credit*, N.Y. Times, Nov. 1, 1983, at A1, col. 1.

68. Moynihan, *The U.S. in Opposition*, COMMENTARY, March 1975, at 31.

about a major redistribution of the world's wealth—and particularly that of the United States—in favor of the poorer nations, Moynihan urged that the developed nations recognize the assault being laid against them, abandon their useless attempts at appeasement, and adopt a position of peaceful, but determined, opposition.

It is beyond the scope of this Article to try to assess just how far, in fact, the new assertiveness and antidependency trends extend beyond the Hemisphere, or indeed to what extent they have been fostered by changes in attitude elsewhere. Nevertheless, Moynihan has succeeded in pinpointing the dilemma facing the United States in its relations with Latin America: *how to respond to Latin American demands for both greater national control over the development process and a greater share of the world's present wealth, while at the same time protecting vital United States economic interests at home and abroad.*

There is no easy solution to this dilemma. As is typically the case in major issues of policy, the United States is faced with an apparent conflict between two important national interests. On the one hand, it is interested in promoting the growth and development of Latin American economies, as a means of insuring a healthy international climate for trade and investment over the long term, and as a hedge against more radical political solutions to underdevelopment. On the other hand, it is interested in improving the health of its own economy, protecting the assets of its citizens abroad, creating a fair and open world trade and payments system, and guarding against unfair competition to its domestic industries and labor force.

A. Policies to Promote Investment

Since World War II, the United States has attempted to reconcile these twin national interests by means of foreign assistance programs and policies that encouraged the flow of private development capital abroad under conditions that it hoped would also assure favorable treatment and profits for United States investors, access for United States products to local markets, and an important degree of developmental burden-sharing by Latin Americans themselves. It was hoped that such an approach would bring benefits to both sides and steady progress toward a more prosperous economic order.

The United States Government has therefore made special efforts to maintain and improve the access of developing countries to private sources of capital in the United States, and to encourage direct investment in these countries.

When, during the 1960s, various types of capital controls were imposed by the United States Government for balance of payments reasons, developing countries were exempted or given a privileged status. These controls were eliminated in 1974 thereby, restoring equal access to all prospective borrowers in United States capital markets, and providing for unrestricted foreign direct investment by United States firms.

A more positive inducement to United States foreign investment in developing countries was the creation of the Overseas Private Investment Corporation in 1969.[69] OPIC incorporated the various United States Government insurance programs dating back to the Marshall Plan. The purpose of OPIC is "[t]o mobilize and facilitate the participation of United States private capital and skills in the economic and social development of less developed friendly countries and areas."[70] OPIC provides various types of insurance that cover convertibility of profits, expropriation risks, and war and insurrection risks. OPIC has been subject to considerable criticism in the United States Congress as well as abroad. Although the motives for establishing it were consistent with the Latin American countries' objective of obtaining greater transfers of real resources, OPIC in fact operates in only a relatively few Latin American countries because most will not provide the subrogation and arbitration rights that are generally a condition of an OPIC program.

B. Policies to Protect Investment

The assumption implicit in all these policies, of course, is that outside private capital can play a vital and perhaps essential role in the development process, especially when public funds—taxpayers' dollars—become more and more difficult to obtain for this purpose. Indeed, the assumption is so strongly held in the United States that it comes as something of a shock to learn that the Latin Americans themselves may not fully share it and are in fact taking steps to ensure a greater return for themselves from this cooperative bargain.

The Hickenlooper Amendment to the Foreign Assistance Act[71] requires that any United States Government assistance be suspended to countries that, *inter alia*, nationalize, expropriate, or seize ownership or control of property owned by a United States citizen, or in which a United States corporation has a fifty percent or larger interest, unless action is taken by the state to discharge its obligations under international law to pay prompt and adequate compensation.

69. Foreign Assistance Act of 1969, Pub. L. 91-175, 83 Stat. 805, 809-18 (codified as amended at 22 U.S.C. §§ 2191-2200b (1976 & Supp. V 1981)).

70. 22 U.S.C. § 2191 (1976).

71. Hickenlooper Amendment, 22 U.S.C. § 2370(e) (1976). A similar amendment (the Gonzalez Amendment, 22 U.S.C. § 283r (1976)) requires the United States Director in the Inter-American Development Bank to vote against all loans, or other utilization of the Bank's funds by countries that have taken arbitrary measures against United States interests including expropriation in that country unless there is prompt and adequate compensation or other acceptable measures leading to a settlement of the dispute.

Similar language is found in the Trade Reform Act of 1974.[72] Title V of this Act, which deals with the Generalized System of Preferences (GSP), provides for the exclusion from access to GSP of countries that have taken various actions such as expropriation against property owned by United States citizens without prompt, adequate, and effective compensation or other measures consistent with their international obligations.[73] These clauses or restrictions have been the subject of disputes not only between foreign governments and the United States Government, but also between the executive and legislative branches of the United States Government itself.

Still, these protective measures reflect an underlying concern for that second—and apparently contrary—basic interest of the United States Government, namely, how to protect the economic interests of United States citizens in foreign countries. Most recently, the latter concern surfaced in the debate over CERDS. Changing a long-established tenet of international law to give one country the exclusive right to settle disputes involving foreign capital could not only force the United States Government to surrender its responsibilities toward its citizens, but also could reduce the flow of capital to the developing countries.

While the various United States legal restrictions on United States Government assistance programs do not directly affect private capital flows, such flows to countries that run afoul of the Hickenlooper Amendment are affected. Quite simply, businessmen think twice about putting their money in a country with a recent expropriation history.

C. Reconciling United States Interests

In broadest terms, the United States Government recognizes as legitimate and desirable the Latin American countries' objective of obtaining larger transfers of real resources through capital flows to speed up the development process, and is well aware of the political problems that develop if economic growth is stopped or reversed, as has happened in many of the developing industrial countries in the past. External capital is one of the means by which the development objective is achieved, and its flow into developing countries is a desirable objective from the United States point of view. The prosperity and economic growth of the United States economy in turn is linked to that of its neighbors. The economy benefits from larger markets made possible through the economic growth of Latin American countries. Likewise, consumers in the United States have benefited from increased world trade through a greater variety of available goods.

72. Pub. L. No. 93-618, 88 Stat. 1978 (1975) (codified as amended in scattered sections of 19 U.S.C.).

73. 19 U.S.C. § 2462(b)(4) (1982).

The United States cannot force private capital or development models upon other countries, nor does it make sense to encourage flows toward countries that are not convinced of their need for it. In recent years, Latin Americans have demonstrated—through conditions and restrictions they have imposed upon foreign investors—that they perceive less need for foreign private direct investment than in the past and that they are therefore less willing to create the climate necessary to attract new direct investment. It is not the business of the United States Government to point out to the Latin Americans the "error" of their ways and persuade them to "improve" conditions so as to attract more capital. It is entirely consistent with our national interests, however, to urge both host governments and United States private investors to engage each other in serious dialogue aimed at a new investment understanding, one in keeping with changing views of investment on both sides, and one that will reestablish the vitally important element of mutual confidence.

VI. THE OUTLOOK FOR A NEW INVESTMENT BARGAIN

Right now the air is full of recriminations from both sides. Yet there are signs that each one is also paying some attention to what the other has to say, and that a fundamental desire exists to find common ground for a new private investment bargain. Indeed, what was described at the outset as a "breakdown" in the investment bargain in Latin America might perhaps be more accurately described as a thorough reevaluation, by both investors and recipients, of the existing investment terms in the region as a whole; a recalculation of potential benefits from future investment; and a weighted estimation (albeit unconscious) of the "psychic factors" currently at play in the investment environment. What are the two sides really trying to tell each other? On the one hand, Latin Americans are warning that they gave away too many benefits in the past in exchange for foreign capital; that they competed too fiercely among themselves to attract that capital; that the skills and technology they imported were not always those best suited to national needs; that foreign enterprises too often succeeded in eluding national controls and priorities; that too much of the national psyche has been sacrificed to obtain rapid economic growth; and that they now possess sufficient development resources and skills of their own to allow them to insist upon better terms for imported capital.

On the other hand, United States investors are pointing out that the new terms and conditions of the Latin American bargain lower prospective returns on new investment, thus reducing incentives; that Latin American development priorities do not easily dovetail with their own established investment criteria and preferred corporate practices; that Latin Americans fail to appreciate the development benefits that have accrued to them via foreign private investment; and that higher returns on capital invested elsewhere in the world make the Latin American market increasingly less attractive.

Some interesting attempts at mutual accommodation show that the investment bargain is in fact being renegotiated. These include new experiments with joint ventures, phased disinvestment schemes, new ground rules on takeovers of existing firms and access to local bank capital, uniform regional tax and investment codes, concentration of foreign capital in specific sectors (to the exclusion of others), and technology and management contracts independent of equity investment.[74]

Predictably, the reactions of private United States investors to Latin America's tougher new bargaining terms have varied widely, from far-sighted accommodation to near-sighted hysteria. On the whole, however, United States businessmen in Latin America seem inclined to experiment with new investment formulas wherever the local climate remains receptive and opportunities for substantial profit remain bright. Mexico's requirement that new ventures provide for joint equity ownership seems not to have unduly dampened investor enthusiasm for that country, neither have Brazil's efforts to channel investment into priority development sectors. Andean Group policies, on the other hand, have clearly troubled potential investors and reduced the inflow of new foreign private capital to member countries.

Nevertheless, there remains the danger that the "psychic factors" of nationalism and traditional business habits may ultimately blind both investors and hosts to their larger interests in striking a new investment bargain; that rising national controls on one side and lack of imagination on the other may reduce investment incentives to zero; and that the role of foreign private investment in Latin America's development may shrink to insignificance as a result. There are some who would prefer this, arguing that the role is one better played in today's world by "nonpolitical" international development lending institutions or by direct borrowing in the major capital and money markets.

Private direct investment in trade-promoting activity holds out significant promise for countries caught in the billion dollar debt bind of the present era. Many understand this and have begun to reexamine project proposals shelved earlier. Some have already relaxed equity or performance rules for investment proposals that respond to specific national aims such as employment generation, regional stimulus, or export promotion. There is an acute need for outside development capital, technology, and managerial skills. The United States and Latin America appear to be on the verge of a new phase of bargaining over the role of private investment in the region, and the outcome could determine how soon these countries resume their march toward prosperity. It is not unreasonable to expect

74. Some of these limited formulas are described in detail in C. KINDLEBERGER, *supra* note 3, at 263-79, and in HUNT, *supra* note 8. *See also* Hirschman, *How to Divest in Latin America and Why*, in ESSAYS IN INTERNATIONAL FINANCE, No. 76 (Princeton University, November 1969).

that the legislative genius of the one and the resourceful enterprise of the other will finally produce a new bargain fruitful for both sides and consonant with the evolving needs of each one.

The task is made even more acute by the enormous debt burden accumulated by almost all the Latin American nations, by the worldwide credit crunch, and related factors. The premises for reducing social development spending and for greater austerity may also have political consequences that may in turn serve as a disincentive for foreign direct investment.

VII. CONCLUSION

The dramatic rise in world energy prices after 1975 coupled with the flood of petrodollars channeled from oil producing countries into investment projects around the world, altered the very shape of the bargaining process. On the one hand, countries interested in attracting investment capital suddenly felt less constrained by conditions and demands that private direct investors might place on their investment bargains. On the other hand, investors themselves were obliged more than ever to search for cost-cutting solutions to production problems, venturing further abroad in search of cheaper labor and energy costs.

The result, for a while at least, was a shift in bargaining terms that favored the receiving countries and demanded concessions from private investors. Indeed, the most notable result was a substantial shift away from private direct investment generally in favor of public sector growth in practically every country in Latin America, including those where free market principles have held greater sway. Very simply, governments and their parastatal agencies found that the oil boom had made investment funds plentiful and readily available, and that banks were so anxious to recycle these funds at bargain interest rates, that they no longer had to wait on private entrepreneurs to come forward with development schemes. Instead, one government after another devised its own bold plans for expanding the national industrial base and improving infrastructural systems—optimistically mortgaging national earnings well into the future.

The "OPEC Era" thus became a period of spectacular growth and ostensible development in much of Latin America, one in which private foreign direct investment played second fiddle to public sector growth based on recycled petrodollars. With hindsight, one might point out today that this growth was not the healthiest sort in many cases, with too much emphasis on the internal market and local consumption and too little on export growth. Nevertheless, overall growth rates were very high in the late 1970s, in many cases reaching eight to ten percent annually, with growth in exports generally following. The onset, however, of the present recession in the United States and Western Europe, a recession that has been deeper and longer-lasting than any other since World War II, has brought the "OPEC Era" boom to a dismal, debt-ridden conclusion.

Latin American countries today find themselves saddled with the morning-after costs of cheaply financed rapid growth—some 300 billion dollars in foreign debt altogether. Their collective financing gap probably exceeds twenty billion dollars this year, even after calculating the effects of the austere budget-cutting and import restraints that nearly all are having to impose. For several, growth prospects during the next two to three years have dropped to zero or below. Inflation has spurted and unemployment is rising, posing real dangers of social unrest. At the same time, it is important to recognize that despite the fiscal mismanagement of the recent past, important capital investments were achieved. Private investment that serves national economic goals can survive these industrial sector activities. Healthy economic growth and expanding world trade rather than austerity and contraction offer hope for the future.

[11]

The Principle of Preferential Treatment in the Law of GATT: Toward Achieving the Objective of an Equitable World Trading System*

*Ndiva Kofele-Kale***

Introduction

This Article examines the world trading system as embodied in the General Agreement on Tariffs and Trade[1] and the degree to which I shall refer to these derogations from GATT law as the "principle of preferential treatment."

The first indication that the developing countries (DCs) were

---

* This Article is a much expanded version of a paper delivered to the 13th Conference on the Law of the World held at Seoul, South Korea, September 6-11, 1987. I am grateful to those participants in the panel on the New International Economic Order whose questions and comments forced me to clarify several of my ideas. I am particularly indebted to Professor Sang-Myon Rhee, College of Law, Seoul National University; Dr. Galen S. Hull, Micro-Enterprise Institute, Arlington, Virginia and Ms. Elizabeth Farr, J.D. (Tennessee). Responsibility for the views expressed remain my own.

** Associate Professor of Law, University of Tennessee College of Law; Ph.D., J.D., Northwestern University.

1. General Agreement on Tariffs and Trade, *opened for signature* Oct. 30, 1947, 61 Stat. A3, T.I.A.S. No. 1700, 55 U.N.T.S. 187 [hereinafter cited as GATT]. GATT has been modified in several aspects since 1947. The current version of the agreement is contained in 4 GENERAL AGREEMENT ON TARIFFS AND TRADE, BASIC INSTRUMENTS AND SELECTED DOCUMENTS (1969). GATT is not technically an organization of which countries become members but a treaty with contracting parties. When it was signed in 1947 there were 23 signatories but the membership has now grown to include 92 countries representing over four-fifths of world trade. The guiding principles of GATT include: (1) trade without discrimination through application of the Most-Favored-Nation principle; (2) reliance on tariff as opposed to other commercial measures (such as, quantitative restrictions, voluntary export restraints, etc.) where protection of domestic industries is necessary; (3) provision of a stable and predictable basis for trade through negotiated 'bindings' of tariffs at fixed minimum levels, and (4) settlement of disputes through consultation, conciliation and, as a last resort, dispute settlement procedures. *See* UNITED STATES COUNCIL OF INTERNATIONAL CHAMBER OF COMMERCE, INC., G.A.T.T. AN ANALYSIS AND APPRAISAL OF THE GENERAL AGREEMENT ON TARIFFS AND TRADE (1955). GATT was originally a part of the preparatory negotiations to set up an International Trade Organization (ITO) and was originally conceived as the first of a number of agreements that were to be negotiated under the auspices of the ITO. The ITO was one of three major international institutions—the other two being the International Monetary Fund (IMF) and the International Bank for Reconstruction and Development (World Bank)—established in the 1940's to manage the postwar international economic system. Following the failure of the ITO to gather the requisite ratifications, GATT by default became the framework for the conduct of world trade. *See generally* J. JACKSON, WORLD TRADE AND THE LAW OF GATT (1969) (Background information about GATT) [hereinafter JACKSON, WORLD TRADE LAW].

completely dissatisfied with the GATT framework of trade rules was in the form of a publication in developing member states from Africa, Asia, the Caribbean, and Latin America (DCs) that have been fully integrated into that system. In this article special attention will be paid to the series of exceptions and derogations[2] from GATT trade rules made to accommodate the special and differential needs and interests of the DCs. The concern here is with the process of translating the normative basis of preferential treatment into a basic right within the boundaries of the General Agreement; that is, the right to an automatic grant of tariff concessions as well as other trade advantages, favors, or privileges to DCs, backed by an appropriate regime of sanctions to discipline those preference-giving countries who flout this rule.

I. AN HISTORICAL OVERVIEW OF PREFERENTIAL TREATMENT

In September 1986, trade ministers and representatives from ninety-two countries met in Punta Del Este, Uruguay to launch the "Uruguay Round"[3] of multilateral trade negotiations (MTNs) under the aegis of GATT. It is generally acknowledged that the agreements reached in the course of these MTNs over the next four years[4] will define and shape the structure of trade relationships between the industrialized countries (ICs) and the DCs for the remainder of this century and for much of the next.[5] The significance of this round of MTNs cannot be overstated; for, in addition to renegotiating rules for trade in goods, it represents the first attempt to bring trade in services under international discipline.[6] If previous

2. I shall refer to these derogations from GATT law as the principle of preferential treatment throughout this discussion.

3. *See* Ministerial Declaration of September 15, 1986, *signed at* Punta Del Este, Uruguay; *see also GATT Launches Uruguay Round as Consensus Reached on Services, Agricultural Trade*, 3 INT'L TRADE REP. (BNA) No. 38 at 1150 (Sept. 24, 1986). For a background to the Uruguay Round see Rivers, Slater & Paolini, *Putting Services on the Table: The New GATT Round*, 23 STAN. J. INT'L L. 13 (1987).

4. *See* Yeutter, *A GATT for the 21st Century*, 9 BUS. AMERICA No. 21 at 3 (Oct. 13, 1986).

5. *Id.*

6. *Id.* at 4. *See also* Baldridge, *The New Round and U.S. Business*, 9 BUS. AMERICA, No. 21 at 6 (Oct. 13, 1986). "Trade in services" means the standard balance-of-payments item denoted as 'non-factor services,' which excludes workers' remittances and investment income. *See* Sapir & Lutz, *Trade in Non-Factor Services: Past Trends and Current Issues*, World Bank Staff Working Paper, No. 410 (Aug. 1980). Services generally constitute activities producing an intangible output. The International Standard Industrial Classification classifies service activities under the following major divisions: (1) wholesale and retail trade, restaurants and hotels; (2) transport, storage, and communication; (3) financing, insurance, real estate, and business services; (4) community, social, and personal services. *Id. See also* Sapir & Lutz, *Trade in Services: Economic Determinants and Devel-*

rounds of MTNs have accurately reflected the issues typically and perennially raised by DCs, then the Uruguay Round will be confronted with the issue of the special and differential needs of DCs and how these can be accommodated within the GATT system. As in the past, DCs will continue to press for the acceptance of the principle of preferential treatment as a basic right under GATT; a right which cannot be withdrawn without subjecting the preference-giving country to sanctions.

The need to secure firmly the principle of preferential treatment as a permanent feature of the world trading system is dictated by several factors. Most will agree that international trade is one of the most important areas of international cooperation among states. However, it remains an area in which the DCs feel very acutely their economic inequality and dependency *vis-a-vis* the ICs.[7] Trade, particularly commodity trade, is central in the relations between DCs and ICs[8] because most DCs derive the bulk of their export earnings from exports of agricultural commodities[9] to markets in the ICs. As a matter of fact, roughly eighty percent of exports from DCs are consumed by ICs.[10] The structure of trade relationships between these two groups of countries which evolved during the age of imperialism, when colonies in the southern hemisphere became sources of primary products and markets for the manufactured goods produced in the metropole, persists to this day.[11] This historical division of the world into exporters of primary and semi-manufactured products (DCs) and exporters of manufactured goods (ICs) has remained a major source of friction in North-South relations.[12] When one adds to this demonstrably unequal division of labor the equally demonstrable unfavorable terms of trade[13] be-

---

opment-Related Issues, World Bank Staff Working Paper, No. 480 at 3 (Aug. 1981).

7. *See, e.g.*, Rahman & Hesse, *Industrialization, Trade, and the International Division of Labour*, in RESHAPING THE INTERNATIONAL ORDER 235 (J. Tinbergen ed. 1976).

8. *See generally* C. KEGLEY & E. WITTKOPF, THE GLOBAL AGENDA: ISSUES AND PERSPECTIVES (1984) [hereinafter KEGLEY & WITTKOPF, THE GLOBAL AGENDA].

9. *See* R. ROTHSTEIN, GLOBAL BARGAINING: UNCTAD AND THE QUEST FOR A NEW INTERNATIONAL ECONOMIC ORDER 40 (1979). [hereinafter ROTHSTEIN, GLOBAL BARGAINING]. While DCs rely on primary products for over two-thirds of their total export earnings, for ICs primary products account for less than 25 percent of their export earnings. *See* M. MCLAUGHLIN, THE UNITED STATES AND WORLD DEVELOPMENT: AGENDA 1979 207 (1979).

10. ROTHSTEIN, GLOBAL BARGAINING, *supra* note 9, at 40.

11. K. BOULDING, STABLE PEACE (1978); *see also* W. LEWIS, THE EVOLUTION OF THE INTERNATIONAL ECONOMIC ORDER (1978); R. HANSEN, THE NORTH-SOUTH STALEMATE (1978).

12. K. BOULDING, *supra* note 11.

13. There is now a substantial body of evidence which suggests that the prices DCs

tween DCs and ICs, one may understand why DCs have made reform of the world trade[14] structure their central goal in these international negotiations.

For the last four decades GATT has provided the legal framework within which most international trade between DCs and ICs has occurred. Throughout this period DCs have consistently voiced their disaffection with the GATT system of world trade.[15] This perception of GATT as being unresponsive[16] to the economic needs of

---

receive for their exports vary erratically in the short-run and deteriorate progressively in the long haul. In contrast, prices of the manufactured goods that they import increase steadily. *See, e.g.*, R. HANSEN, THE U.S. AND WORLD DEVELOPMENT: AGENDA FOR ACTION 178 (1976); D. PIRAGES, THE NEW CONTEXT FOR INTERNATIONAL RELATIONS: GLOBAL ECOPOLITICS 239 (1978); S. ROSEN & W. JONES, THE LOGIC OF INTERNATIONAL RELATIONS 170 (1980).

14. The persistent deterioration has been blamed on the structural characteristics of the old international economic order of which the world trading system is a central component. *See, e.g.*, THE REPORT OF THE BRANDT COMMISSION, COMMON CRISIS NORTH-SOUTH: COOPERATION FOR WORLD RECOVERY (1983) [hereinafter BRANDT COMMISSION REPORT]. The old order which is usually associated with the post-World War II Bretton Woods system has not operated entirely to the disadvantage of DCs, many of which, South Korea being a prominent example, "clearly achieved the situation described by Walt W. Rostow in his famous image . . . of the 'take-off into sustained growth'." *See* Singer, *The New International Economic Order: An Overview* 16 J. MOD. AFR. STUD. 539, 540 1978). Aside from the spectacular economic growth of a group of DCs, the so-called 'newly industrialized countries' (NICs)—typified by Brazil, Mexico, Singapore, Hong Kong, Taiwan, and, of course, S. Korea—the Bretton Woods era also witnessed the G.N.P. of the DCs as a whole increase by 5 to 6 percent *per annum*, a growth rate very similar to that of the ICs. During this period also, the trickle-down effect of growth from the ICs to the DCs was evident and the flow of aid was considerable. But the growth, in sharp contrast to the ICs, was uneven and divergent leading to the present division of the DCs into two sectors—one faster growing and relatively wealthier and the other poorer and stagnant. *Id.* at 540. *See also* N. HARRIS, THE END OF THIRD WORLD: NEWLY INDUSTRIALIZING COUNTRIES AND THE DECLINE OF AN IDEOLOGY (1986).

On the question of whether the terms of trade of DCs have in fact deteriorated and what the causes of the alleged deterioration are, there is still some disagreement among learned commentators. For a useful and comprehensive discussion of the terms of trade debate, *see* Streeten, *World Trade in Agricultural Commodities and the Terms of Trade with Industrial Goods*, in AGRICULTURAL POLICY IN DEVELOPING COUNTRIES 207 (n. Islam ed. 1974). *See also* D. BLAKE & R. WALTERS, THE POLITICS OF GLOBAL ECONOMIC RELATIONS (1976); H. SINGER & J. ANSARI, RICH AND POOR COUNTRIES (1977); and B. HIGGINS & J. HIGGINS, ECONOMIC DEVELOPMENT OF A SMALL PLANET (1979).

15. The first indication that the DCs were completely dissatisfied with the GATT framework of trade rules was in the form of a publication in 1958 of the Report by a Panel of Experts entitled *Trends in International Trade*. The Panel was made up of four eminent economists—Habeler (the chairman and after whom the report was named), Meade, Tinbergen, and Campos. The substance of the report was that the predicament of DCs was due in no small measure to the trade policies of the Western industrialized countries. On the basis of this finding the GATT quickly went into action and inaugurated a Programme for the Expansion of International Trade which brought under GATT scrutiny the problems of economic development. Committee III was established to study the obstacles that stood in the way of DCs' exports entering the markets of the industrialized countries. *See generally*, K. DAM, THE GATT: LAW AND INTERNATIONAL ECONOMIC ORGANIZATION 228-29 (1970) [hereinafter DAM, GATT LAW].

16. Dissatisfaction with GATT led to the establishment of the United Nations Con-

DCs is symptomatic of a more general dissatisfaction with traditional international law which the DCs view as the normative product of Eurocentric civilization[17] and which, for most of its existence, has served as the "white man's law" and *not* as the Law of Nations.[18]

The DCs' disenchantment with the GATT system of world trade relations has expressed itself in two forms. At a more general level, their displeasure has been directed at GATT's organizing principles and objectives, which were formulated in the immediate post-World War II years,[19] but have now become inadequate in attacking the

---

ference on Trade and Development (UNCTAD) in 1964 to focus on trade and development issues as they affect DCs. In its first meeting which was convened in Geneva, the rules of GATT came under attack for their exclusion of the DCs from the benefits of postwar expansion. DCs' objections to GATT were summarized by UNCTAD's Secretary-General, Dr. Raul Prebisch:

> Why has GATT not been as efficacious for the developing countries as for the industrial countries? There are two main reasons. First [it] is based on the classic concept that the free play of international economic forces by itself leads to the optimum expansion of trade and the most efficient utilization of the world's productive resources; rules and principles are therefore established to guarantee free play. Secondly, the rules and principles in question have not always been strictly complied with and, even though they seem to have been observed in the letter in certain instances, the spirit underlying them has not been respected.

See United Nations Conference on Trade and Development in PROCEEDINGS OF THE UNITED NATIONS CONFERENCE ON TRADE AND DEVELOPMENT, vol. Ii p. 18 (1964). UNCTAD began as a U.N.-sponsored conference to moot the twin issues of trade and development with reference to the DCs but soon after became a permanent organ of the General Assembly of the United Nations. The aims of UNCTAD are to promote trade in the interest of development, to formulate principles and policies concerning such trade, to initiate multilateral trade agreements, and to act as a center for harmonizing governmental policies affecting the area. It began life with 77 members who dubbed themselves the "Group of 77" but now has over 166 members. UNCTAD has reached agreement on a number of international conventions dealing with topics such as liner conferences, multimodal transport and various commodities. It was instrumental in bringing to fruition the Charter of Economic Rights and Duties of States which was adopted by the United Nations General Assembly in 1975. *See also* note 33 *infra* and accompanying text. *See generally* Gardner, *The United Nations Conference on Trade and Development*, 22 INT'L ORG. 99 (1968); K. HAGRAS, UNITED NATIONS CONFERENCE ON TRADE AND DEVELOPMENT (1965); B. GOSOVIC, UNCTAD CONFLICT AND COMPROMISE (1972); Walters, *UNCTAD: Intervenor Between Poor and Rich States*, 7 J. WORLD TRADE L. 527 (1973); Ramsey, *UNCTAD's Failures, The Rich Get Richer*, 38 INT'L. ORG. 387 (1984); T. WEISS, MULTILATERAL DEVELOPMENT DIPLOMACY IN UNCTAD (1986).

17. *See, e.g.*, Joyner, *U.N. General Assembly Resolutions and International Law: Rethinking The Contemporary Dynamics of Norm-Creation*, 11 CALIF. W. INT'L L. J. 445 (1981) [hereinafter Joyner, *General Assembly Resolutions*]. For similar conclusion, *see* Laing, *International Economic Law and Public Order in the Age of Equality*, 12 LAW POL'Y INT'L BUS. 727 (1980) [hereinafter cited as Laing, *International Economic Law*]; Roy, *Is the Law of Responsibility of States for Injuries to Aliens a Part of Universal Law*, 55 AM. J. INT'L L. 863, 866 (1961); C. JENKS, THE COMMON LAW OF MANKIND (1958); W. FRIEDMANN, THE CHANGING STRUCTURE OF INTERNATIONAL LAW (1970); M. BEDJAOUI, TOWARDS A NEW INTERNATIONAL ECONOMIC ORDER (1979); G. TUNKIN, THEORY OF INTERNATIONAL LAW (1974).

18. Joyner, *General Assembly Resolutions*, *supra* note 17, at 445.

19. The preeminent position of the United States in the early postwar years meant

trade problems already discussed. Hence the urgent need to revise, expand, reform, and improve upon GATT so as to bring its objectives and principles in conformity with contemporary realities of international trade.[20] More specifically, attacks have been leveled at some GATT trade rules, in particular the Most-Favored-Nation (MFN)[21] principle of reciprocal nondiscrimination in international

---

that American views on how international trade should be conducted would dominate, influence, and ultimately shape GATT. Three such values have been identified: (1) trade liberalization which is reflected in the aims of the GATT preamble of reducing tariffs and other barriers to trade. America's much more liberal position on trade prevailed even though it was opposed by her European allies; (2) multilateralism, which became embodied in the MFN principle of Article 1 and its guarantee of nondiscrimination in trade matters. Again the American position met resistance from the Europeans who feared that their weaker economies would not be able to compete effectively in the multilateral trade liberalization framework constructed around the MFN principle. According to Winham "because of their importance to the United States the principle of multilateralism and nondiscrimination were prominent in the commitments of the GATT, but from the outset they were principles flawed by controversy and inconsistency." *See* G. WINHAM, INTERNATIONAL TRADE AND THE TOKYO ROUND OF NEGOTIATION 32 (1986) [hereinafter WINHAM, THE TOKYO ROUND OF NEGOTIATION]; (3) American value that shaped GATT was the means of implementing the trade-liberalizing objectives of the General Agreement. To the Europeans who "preferred to build a postwar trading system on practice rather than pronouncement," the Americans responded with a code of international trade law that clearly set out the rights and obligations the contracting parties had toward each other's commercial activities. *Id.* at 32-33. Two things are clear from a reading of the genesis of GATT. First, that America's attachment to an economic philosophy of free trade and her view of world politics, values which her junior partners in Europe may not have shared but which they acquiesced to grudgingly, were imposed on GATT. The result then was a world system of trade which reflected principally the interests and objectives of the U.S. and, to some extent, of her European satellites. Second, little effort, if any, was made to include the interests of the developing countries—the vast majority of whom were still under European colonial domination at that time—in the framework of world trade that was negotiated in 1947. For a discussion of the U.S. role in the making of GATT, *see generally* Curzon, *Crisis in the International Trading System*, IN SEARCH OF A NEW WORLD ECONOMIC ORDER 33 (H. CORBET & R. JACKSON eds. 1974); DAM, GATT LAW, *supra* note 15, at 12; R. GARDNER, STERLING-DOLLAR DIPLOMACY (1969); T. MURRAY, TRADE PREFERENCES FOR DEVELOPING COUNTRIES 6-8 (1977) [hereinafter MURRAY, TRADE PREFERENCES].

20. The feeling is widespread that GATT rules are unresponsive not only to trade problems faced by governments that had written the rules but also to those faced by the new members of GATT who had not shared in the rule-making. *See* Gwin, *Strengthening the Framework of the Global Economic Organizations*, in POWER, PASSIONS, AND PURPOSE 140 (J. Bhagwati & R. Ruggie eds. (1984) [hereinafter Gwin, *Global Economic Organizations*].

21. The Most-Favored-Nation clause has featured as one of the central provisions in commercial treaties over the past 300 years. It is generally referred to as the foundation stone on which the whole structure of modern international trade rests. The clause, according to Hyder, has not yet crystallized into a rule of international customary law and is preeminently an optional standard which derives its validity from the treaties in which it is embodied. *See generally* K. HYDER, EQUALITY OF TREATMENT AND TRADE DISCRIMINATION IN INTERNATIONAL LAW (1968) [hereinafter HYDER, EQUALITY OF TREATMENT AND TRADE DISCRIMINATION]; S. BASDEVANT, LA CLAUSE DE LA NATION LA PLUS FAVORISE (1929); N. ITO, LA CLAUSE DE LA NATION PLUS FAVORISE (1930); Catudal, *The Most Favored Nation Clause and the Courts*, 35 AM. J. INT'L L. 41 (1941); R. SNYDER, THE MOST FAVORED NATION CLAUSE (1948); Schwarzenberger, *The Most Favoured nation Standard in British State Practice*, (1945) BRIT. Y.B. INT'L. L. 102. Its central objective is to ensure non-discriminatory treatment in international trade by imposing an obligation on parties to a com-

trade relations.[22] This bed-rock principle of GATT, contained in its Article 1, imposes on the signatory countries the obligation to grant to each other equality of treatment and to apply tariffs and other similar regulatory measures unconditionally and automatically on a nondiscriminatory basis.[23] The procrustean MFN rule of reciprocal tariff concessions imposes upon the DCs a burden so crushing, and demands of them such disproportionate sacrifices in relation to those expected of ICs, that it has become increasingly difficult for DCs to compete with producers in the ICs under Most-Favored-Nation conditions.

All previous rounds of MTNs have had to contend with DCs' pleas for a competitive advantage to be provided through a system of preferential tariffs favoring their exports of manufactured and semi-manufactured products.[24] In 1971, such a preferential scheme,

---

mercial treaty that citizens of one State receive at the hands of another, treatment no less favorable than that accorded to citizens of third states. *See generally* JACKSON, WORLD TRADE LAW, *supra* note 1, at 250. It should be noted that the GATT MFN clause does not of itself bring about an obligation to reduce tariffs or to refrain from increasing them. This occurs through tariff negotiations and renegotiations among the contracting parties. *See* note 47 *infra* and accompanying text.

22. For instance, the Secretary-General's report to the first United Nations Conference on Trade and Development had this to say about the MFN standard: "However valid the most-favoured-nation principle may be in regulating trade relations among equals, it is not a suitable concept for trade, involving countries of vastly unequal economic strength." Prebisch, *Towards a New Trade Policy for Development*, Report by the Secretary-General of the United Nations Conference on Trade and Development, United Nations, 1964, at 66. *See also* Espiell, *The Most-Favoured-Nation Clause: Its Present Significance in GATT*, 5 J. WORLD TRADE L. 29 (1971) [hereinafter Espiell, *The Most-Favoured-Nation Clause*].

23. GATT, art. 1(1).

24. The first response by the ICs to DC entreaties came in 1964 when a new chapter entitled "Trade and Development" was drafted and subsequently incorporated as Part IV of GATT. With the addition of Part IV comprising Articles XXXVI, XXXVII, and XXXVIII the law of GATT recognized, for the first time, the new principle of non-reciprocity which established a differential treatment in favor of DCs in tariff negotiations or renegotiations by eliminating the mutuality of concessions principle enshrined in the MFN standard. Article XXXVI lays down broad principles and objectives which recognize that "international trade as a means of achieving economic and social advancement should be governed by such rules and procedures—and measures in conformity with such rules and procedures—as are consistent with the objectives set forth in this Article" (paragraph 1(e); notes that "the Contracting Parties may enable less-developed contracting parties to use special measures to promote their trade and development" (paragraph 1(f); and states that "the developed contracting parties do not expect reciprocity for commitments made by them in trade negotiations to reduce or remove tariffs and other barriers to the trade of less-developed contracting parties" (paragraph 8). These Article XXXVI principles and objectives are governed by specific obligations assumed by the contracting parties individually (Art. XXXVII) and/or collectively (Art. XXXVIII). Article XXXVII requires *inter alia* less-developed contracting parties "to take appropriate action in implementation of the provisions of Part IV for the benefit of the trade of other less-developed contracting parties" (paragraph 4); and the contracting parties agree through joint action to "establish such institutional arrangements as may be necessary to further the objectives set forth in Article XXXVI and give effect to the provisions of this Part." Article XXXVIII, paragraph 2(f). But Part IV proved to be nothing more than a "symbolic" gesture, hardly the panacea it was touted to be. *See* WINHAM, THE

the Generalized System of preferences (GSP), was adopted in favor of all DCs by derogating from the GATT MFN principle.[25] The GSP, as it was then structured, fell short of the DCs' goal of having the principle of preferential tariffs grounded as a basic right within GATT and not as an *ex gratia* favor from ICs.

In 1979 at the conclusion of the Tokyo Round of MTNs the Contracting Parties agreed to set up a permanent legal basis for preferential treatment in the GATT system.[26] Through an enabling clause the ICs agreed that, notwithstanding the MFN provisions of Article of the General Agreement, Contracting Parties *may* accord differential and favorable treatment to DCs without according such treatment to other contracting parties.[27]

Some scholars contend that the Enabling Clause has succeeded in transforming the principle of preferential treatment, from a provisional and undesirable exception to the GATT equality of treatment doctrine, to an accepted norm of international trade law.[28] In this author's view, this contention reads too much into that clause. While it is conceded that the recognition of the principle of preferential treatment in favor of DCs will profoundly affect legal rules and principles underlying the regulation of international trade, it is still unclear whether: (1) the Enabling Clause can be read as an expression of such recognition, and (2) whether, independent of the

---

TOKYO ROUND NEGOTIATION, *supra* note 19, at 143. With respect to Articles 36-38 which make up Part IV, Dam has commented on "how few concrete commitments and how few qualifications of other provisions of the General Agreement are actually involved." *See* DAM, GATT LAW, *supra* note 15, at 237-38.

25. It should be noted that the principle of preferential treatment under the GSP operates in negation to the MFN principle of reciprocity and nondiscrimination in international trade. To be sure, the ICs recognized the problem of including in one instrument two contradictory and fundamentally divergent principles: one (MFN) which promotes equality of treatment and the other (preferential treatment) which advocates discriminatory treatment in trade relations. Rather than amend GATT by removing the MFN provision of Article 1, the West chose instead to relieve those contracting parties that instituted preference-granting programs with DCs from their obligations under the basic MFN provision of Article 1 through the waiver device as provided for in Article XXV, paragraph 5. The text of the waiver is set forth in GATT Doc. L/3545 (1971), *reprinted in* GENERAL AGREEMENT ON TARIFFS AND TRADE, BASIC INSTRUMENTS AND SELECTED DOCUMENTS 24 (18th Supp. 1972). And to ensure that the central feature of GATT would not be destroyed, the ICs made certain that the agreement to waive the MFN principle was not only temporary but it would not constitute a binding commitment. *See Agreed Conclusions of the Special Committee on Preferences*, UNCTAD Doc. TD/B/330, at 6.

26. The text of the Group Framework Agreement appears in Doc. MTN FR/W20 Rev. 2 [hereinafter the Declaration].

27. *See* GATT Doc. L/4903 (28 November 1979).

28. *See* Yusuf, *"Differential and More Favourable Treatment": The GATT Enabling Clause*, 18 J. WORLD TRADE L. 488, 507 (1980) [hereinafter Yusuf, *The Enabling Clause*]. For a similar conclusion, *see* Nicolaides, *Preferences for Developing Countries: A Critique*, 19 J. WORLD TRADE L. 373, 375 (1985)[hereinafter Nicolaides, *Critique of Preferences*].

clause, the principle has ripened sufficiently to be accorded the status of a customary rule of international trade law. Learned commentaries are not only sharply divided on this point but, even more fundamentally, on whether or not the principle of preferential treatment has any place in a framework of world trade based on the concept of free trade.

The balance of this Article examines the emergence and progression of this new international legal principle and, in particular, its relationship to the emerging international law of development. Although many of the principles undergirding the new international law of development have not evolved into "hard" international law in the sense that failure to comply with the norms results in international liability, they do represent emerging law or "soft" law that carries with it a strong moral and practical effect. Given the widespread acceptance of the principles of the international law development in the Third World and Socialist Bloc, their metamorphosis from "soft" to "hard" law is only a matter of time.[29]

II. THE GENERALIZED SYSTEM OF PREFERENCES

The framework of rules governing trade relations between the DCs and the industrialized countries has been under continuous discussion since the inception of GATT.[30] And during the forty years that GATT has been in existence, provisions have, from time to time, been incorporated into the agreement to allow the DCs to maintain trade restrictions for development purposes.[31] These provisions for special and differential treatment of the DCs have been debated within GATT, in the various multilateral trade negotiations[32] that have occurred since GATT was adopted in 1947, as

29. *See Report of the Secretary General Progressive Development of the Principles and Norms of International Law Relating to the new International Economic Order*, U.N. Doc. A/39/504/Add. 1 at 27.

30. *See* DAM, GATT LAW, *supra* note 15, chapter 14; and JACKSON, WORLD TRADE LAW, *supra* note 1.

31. For instance, Part IV on Trade and Development was added to GATT in 1965. DAM, GATT LAW, *supra* note 15, at 236-242; *see also* B. GOSOVIC, UNCTAD: CONFLICT AND COMPROMISE (1972).

32. There have been seven major tariff conferences or 'Rounds' of tariff negotiations under the GATT framework with the most recent being the Tokyo Round held in Geneva from 1973-79. The first was held in Geneva in 1947, the second in Annecy, France, in 1949, the third in Torquay, England in 1951. The fourth (1956), the fifth (Dillon Round— 1960-62), and the sixth (Kennedy Round— 1964-67) were all held in Geneva as would the present round— the eighth (Uruguay Round). For an excellent coverage of the first six rounds, *see* DAM, GATT LAW, *supra* note 15, at 56. For a comprehensive coverage of the Tokyo Round, *see generally* WINHAM, THE TOKYO ROUND NEGOTIATION *supra* note 19: L. GLICK, MULTILATERAL TRADE NEGOTIATIONS: WORLD TRADE AFTER THE TOKYO ROUND (1984).

well as without.[33] Attention is here focused on the Generalized System of Preferences (GSP), the most concrete expression to date of the principle of preferential treatment.

A. A Species of Preferential Treatment: The Generalized System of Preference

Agreement on the general form of the GSP was reached by the industrialized countries in 1970.[34] Subsequently, a waiver[35] was passed by the Contracting Parties on June 25, 1971, pursuant to Article XXV[36] of GATT, allowing the industrial countries to institute programs that would otherwise be in conflict with the Most-Favored-Nation (MFN) principle of reciprocal, nondiscriminatory trade. It bears noting that the waiver setting up the GSP was no novel departure from the GATT MFN principle of equality of treatment and nondiscrimination.

Requests for waivers from the provisions of GATT Art. 1(1) have been routinely accommodated since the inception of GATT. The first application for such a waiver with respect to the preferential treatment of imports from an individual country was submitted by none other than the United States, the champion of trade liberalization, in 1948. This waiver of tariffs to all imports from those Pacific Islands formerly under Japanese mandate, which had then become United States trust territories under the U.N. trusteeship system (Marshall, Caroline and Mariana Islands), was granted and set the precedent for future preferences. All the major Western industrialized countries have subsequently sought and obtained waiv-

33. In the many conferences sponsored by United Nations Conference on Trade and Development. *See* note 16 *supra* and accompanying text.

34. *See* Graham, *The U.S. Generalized System of Preferences for Developing Countries: International Innovation and the Art of the Possible*, 72 AM. J. INT'L L. 513, 513 (1978).

35. The text of the waiver is set forth in GATT Doc. L/3545 (1971), *reprinted in* GENERAL AGREEMENT ON TARIFFS AND TRADE, BASIC INSTRUMENTS AND SELECTED DOCUMENTS 24 (18th Supp. 1972).

36. Article XXV, paragraph 5, provides: "In exceptional circumstances not elsewhere provided for in this Agreement, the CONTRACTING PARTIES may waive an obligation imposed upon a contracting party by this Agreement" provided that "such decision[s] shall be approved by a two-thirds majority of the votes cast and that such majority shall comprise more than half of the contracting parties." To place some restriction on what many considered a liberal waiver provision, the CONTRACTING PARTIES adopted in 1956 a set of "Guiding Principles to be Followed by the CONTRACTING PARTIES in Considering Applications for Waivers from Part 1 of Other Important Obligations of the Agreement." These principles provide for 30-day notice for a waiver request, full consultation by interested parties, inclusion in the waiver of procedures for consultation and arbitration, and annual reports and reviews. For the text of the guiding principles, *see* GATT, BASIC INSTRUMENTS AND SELECTED DOCUMENTS 25 (5th Supp. 1957).

ers of their MFN obligations under GATT: Italy in 1960; Australia in 1953; and the UK and France in 1960.[37] In all of these cases, preferential treatment was granted whenever it was aimed to contribute to the economic development of an underdeveloped dependent or newly-independent country, and with the understanding that such preferential arrangements did not result in damage or substantial injury to the trade of other Contracting Parties.[38] Perhaps the fundamental difference between the preferential treatment that DCs demand in international trade relations and the kind long tolerated by GATT is that preferences for development are to be accorded on the basis of the differences in levels of economic development in the West and DCs and not on account of longstanding political, cultural, geographical and historical ties.[39]

The adoption of this waiver was the culmination of a series of legal maneuvers that began during the Kennedy Round[40] of trade talks in the 1960s with the addition of Part IV to GATT (Articles XXXVI, XXXVII and XXXVIII).[41] Part IV was primarily a nonbinding statement of principles and objectives concerning new approaches to be taken to DC development rather than specific legal obligations.[42] But Article XXXVI was different in that it specifically provided the first legal basis for non-reciprocal dealings between the DCs and the industrialized countries.[43]

The GSP is not really a "generalized system"[44] but a cluster of

---

37. *See* DAM, GATT LAW, *supra* note 15, Chapter 4; and JACKSON, WORLD TRADE LAW, *supra* note 1, Chapter 22.

38. *See* A. YUSUF, LEGAL ASPECTS OF TRADE PREFERENCES FOR DEVELOPING STATES (1982) [hereinafter YUSUF, LEGAL ASPECTS OF TRADE PREFERENCES].

39. *Id.*

40. DeBouter, *Tariff Preferences Revisited*, 11 J. INT'L L. & ECON. 53, 354-62 (1977). In 1963, when the Kennedy Round MFNs were inaugurated, the Ministers agreed that: "in the trade negotiations every effort shall be made to reduce barriers to exports of the less-developed countries but that the developed countries cannot expect to receive reciprocity from the less-developed countries." *See* Analytical Index, February 1966, note on Article XXXVIII *bis*, p. 147, and Article XXXVI, p. 165.

41. *See supra* note 24 and accompanying text.

42. JACKSON, WORLD TRADE LAW, *supra* note 1, at 646.

43. Art. XXXVI, para. 8. *Id.* at 360.

44. The prospects of establishing a common scheme were dashed on the shoals of the competing political interests of the preference-granting countries. For example, the United Kingdom already tied to a preferential trading arrangement with developing commonwealth countries was reluctant to grant GSP tariff treatment to non-Common-wealth DCs as that would undermine the Commonwealth preference scheme. Similar preferential arrangements between the EEC and its Associated DC Member States accounts for the former's resistance to a single uniform system of preferences. In theory, the GSP is a non-discriminatory and non-reciprocal system for all DCs but because the contracting parties were unable or unwilling to agree on a common list of beneficiaries they left it up to the DCs to "self-elect' themselves into the group of beneficiaries. The operation of the self-election principle has led to some rather dubious claims to beneficiary status. For example, Cuba, Romania, Bulgaria,

eleven country schemes[45] that share certain features in common:[46] (1) each preference-giving country retains the right to select the recipient countries entitled to more favorable tariff treatment as well as the products to be covered;[47] (2) preferential imports are subject to quantitative restrictions, that is, ceiling limitations are imposed on either the volume or the value of a product entitled to access at a preferential rate;[48] and (3) preferential tariffs are not bound[49] as MFN tariffs are, meaning preferences are introduced *ex gratia*. For this reason, preferential concessions can be withdrawn or the margin of preferences reduced unilaterally with prior notification. The affected country has no recourse to compensation or retaliation as is the case with MFN tariffs bound within the GATT.[50]

1. *The Objectives of the GSP*—The GSP is in essence a tariff policy whose primary goal is to expand exports and export earnings of DCs by stimulating preference-granting IC imports of their manufactured products.[51] A second goal of the GSP is to offer an alternative source of export earnings to DCs by weaning them away from their heavy dependence on primary agricultural commodities and industrial raw materials, whose slow long-term growth and

---

Taiwan, Yugoslavia, Hong Kong have laid claim to beneficiary status as well as the relatively advanced DCs of the Mediterranean basin (Greece, Israel, Malta, Portugal, Spain and Turkey). *See* MURRAY, TRADE PREFERENCES, *supra* note 19, at 34; *see also* ORGANIZATION FOR ECONOMIC CO-OPERATION AND DEVELOPMENT, THE GENERALIZED SYSTEM OF PREFERENCES: REVIEW OF THE FIRST DECADE 21 (1983) [hereinafter OECD REPORT].

45. These are Australia, Austria, Canada, EEC, Finland, Japan, New Zealand, Norway, Sweden, Switzerland and United States. *See* OECD REPORT, *supra* note 44, at 23-25.

46. D. TUSSIE, THE LESS DEVELOPED COUNTRIES AND THE WORLD TRADING SYSTEM 31 (1987)[hereinafter TUSSIE, WORLD TRADING SYSTEM].

47. *Id.*

48. *Id.*

49. GATT does not require the member countries to abolish tariffs automatically. Rather it relies on specific agreements among contracting parties to reduce particular tariffs. In other words, tariffs are the negotiable item. *See* TUSSIE, WORLD TRADING SYSTEM, *supra* note 46, at 13. The basic concept in the GATT tariff negotiating system is the 'binding' of customs duties on particular items in the tariff schedules of individual contracting parties. Professor Dam has described the binding process as follows: "A given rate of customs duty on a particular item is 'bound' when an agreement has been reached with respect to it. Basically there are three types of bindings: (1) agreements to lower a duty to a stated level (2) agreements not to raise a ditty above its present level; (3) agreements not to raise a duty above a specified higher level." DAM, GATT LAW, *supra* note 15, at 31. Bound rates are then included in a schedule which then becomes an integral part of the GATT (Art. 11:7). There is a separate schedule for each contracting party after each major round of tariff negotiated. These separate schedules are, periodically consolidated for each contracting party. The contracting parties are obligated with respect to a bound duty not to raise it beyond the level agreed upon it. DAM, GATT LAW, *supra* note 15, at 31.

50. DAM, GATT LAW, *supra* note 15, at 31.

51. MURRAY, TRADE PREFERENCES, *supra* note 19, at 22.

marked price instability frequently contributed to chronic trade deficits.[52] Attainment of these goals will require the DCs to adopt a deliberate policy of "export-oriented industrialization"[53] which requires a shift of productive effort away from primary products toward manufacturing.[54] As a consequence, the Contracting Parties built into the GSP the understanding that preferential tariffs would apply to manufactured products only, i.e., industrial manufactures and semi-manufactures.[55]

The beneficial effects of the GSP were also expected to redound to the preference-granting ICs as well. For instance, it was anticipated that the increased export earnings brought about by the GSP would invariably strengthen the economic base making it possible for DCs to buy more products from ICs. As one commentator noted the United States GSP[56] is not "a mere token of U.S. largess designed solely for the benefit of the developing countries."[57] Supporters of the U.S. GSP believe that the program will eventually create new markets for United States exports. It is no coincidence that the program was adopted at a time when United States trade with the DCs had been expanding rather rapidly. For example, between 1969 and 1973, total U.S. imports from DCs grew from $9.4 billion to $20.2 billion, a 115.2% increase.[58] During this same period, imports of manufactures from DCs increased by about 164.7%, from $3 billion to $8 billion.[59] A large portion of these DCs' export earnings were spent in the United States for goods that were necessary for their economic development.

2. *The Legal Status of the GSP*—The legal nature of the commitments assumed by preference-granting ICs, together with the legal consequence of their implementation at the international level, are all contained in Part IX, paragraph two of the Agreed Conclusions of the Special Committee on Preferences[60] which provides:

> The Special Committee takes note of the statement made by the preference-giving countries that the legal status of the tariff pref-

52. *Id.*; *see also* OECD REPORT *supra* note 44.
53. *Id.*
54. *Id.*
55. *Id.*
56. Comment, *The Generalized System of Preferences: Nations More Favored Than Most*, 8 LAW & POL'Y INT'L BUS. 783, 785-86 (1976).
57. *Id.*
58. *Id.* at 785.
59. *Id.* at 786.
60. *Agreed Conclusions*, *supra* note 25.

erences to be accorded to the beneficiary countries by each preference-giving country individually will be governed by the following considerations:

a) The tariff preferences are temporary in nature;

b) Their grant does not constitute a binding commitment and, in particular, it does not in any way prevent:

i) Their subsequent withdrawal in whole or in part;

ii) The subsequent reduction of tariffs on a most favoured-nation basis, whether unilaterally or following international tariff negotiations;

c) Their grant is conditional upon the necessary waiver or waivers in respect of existing international obligations, in particular in the General Agreement on Tariffs and Trade.

It is clear from reading Part IX, paragraph two that ICs did not consider the grant of tariff preferences to DCs as constituting a legally binding commitment.

III. CONTENDING PERSPECTIVES ON THE PRINCIPLE OF PREFERENTIAL TREATMENT

DCs have historically viewed GATT as an outgrowth of the interests of ICs.[61] Even among the critics of preferential treatment, there is acknowledgment that the GATT game is controlled by the developed countries with the DCs looking in from the fringes.[62] To begin with, most DCs were not parties to the establishment of GATT,[63] although India and some Latin American countries, including Brazil, Chile, and Cuba, were active participants in postwar negotiations on international trade arrangements. It is not surprising, therefore, that GATT ended up addressing the specific and particular needs of the industrialized countries[64] while making

61. Professor Friedmann points out that even though GATT makes claim to being a global trading system, its effectiveness had been limited almost entirely to the economically more developed nations. Friedmann, *The Relevance of International Law to the Processes of Economic and Social Development*, in THE FUTURE OF INTERNATIONAL LEGAL ORDER 3, 32-33 (R. Falk & C. Black 1970).

62. *See, e.g.*, Behrman, *Rethinking Global Negotiations, Trade*, in POWER, PASSIONS, AND PURPOSE 231, 245 (J. Bhagwati & J. Ruggie eds. 1984) [hereinafter Behrman, *Trade Issues*].

63. TUSSIE, WORLD TRADING SYSTEM, *supra* note 46, at 4.

64. A good example of GATT's catering to the needs of its most powerful member countries is evidenced in the provisions on commercial policy a careful examination of which, as Professor Dam has done, will lead to the inescapable conclusion that GATT, in his words, "is a sufficiently direct expression of U.S. views on the appropriate form of concerted international action in the commercial policy area . . . ." DAM, GATT LAW, *supra* note 15, at 12. *See also supra* note 19 and accompanying text.

short shrift of the needs of the DCs.[65] As Winham correctly points out, since the time GATT was adopted DCs have been particularly concerned with finding ways to escape their underdevelopment.[66] They have accordingly adhered to visions of a world trading system which explicitly recognizes and promotes the principle of trade protectionism to achieve the goals of import substitution and export promotion.[67]

Given the role that institutions play in improving the functioning of markets, and particularly that played by GATT in improving post World War II international trade for ICs,[68] DCs have doggedly waged a protracted campaign to have their vision of the ideal world trading system institutionalized in GATT. Toward this end, DCs have tried to change GATT trade rules in the direction that favors them. Satisfaction of their demands for special and differential treatment would help overcome the disparities in economic and political power that have worked to their disadvantage in the GATT system. However, they have been met with mixed reactions in the scholarly community. Scholarly reassessments of the whole concept of preferential treatment in favor of DCs have given rise to two competing perspectives.

The first approach is extremely critical of the principle seeing it as having the effect of robbing the GATT trading system of its vitality and eventually contributing to its ultimate collapse.[69] Critics of the preferential treatment principle strongly favor the principles of equality of treatment and nondiscrimination as the founda-

---

65. For example, the areas of international trade that the DCs have consistently demanded be included in GATT (such as primary commodity agreements and discriminatory preferences) were in fact contained in the stillborn International Trade Organization (ITO) Charter (Articles 8-12, 14-15). But with "the death of the ITO Chapter III of the Havana Charter, entitled 'Economic Development and Reconstruction,' slipped into desuetude . . . . *Elaborate provisions on the supply of capital funds and other facilities for economic development, on international investment and on preferential agreements among less-developed countries were thereby allowed to fall into legal oblivion.*" (emphasis added). DAM, GATT LAW, *supra* note 15, at 226. GATT by excluding much of what had been negotiated at the Havana conference addressing the specific needs of DCs forced them in a position of reinventing the wheel, so to speak.

66. WINHAM, THE TOKYO ROUND NEGOTIATION, *supra* note 19, at 140, 142.

67. *Id.*

68. Behrman, *Trade Issues*, *supra* note 62, at 238.

69. This perspective has been articulated in the writings of Behrman, *Trade Issues*, *supra* note 62; Bressand, *A Time for Painful Rethinking*, in POWER, PASSIONS, AND PURPOSE 49 (J. Baghwati & J. Ruggie 1984) [hereinafter Bressand, *Painful Rethinking*]; Wolf, *Two-Edged Sword: Demands of Developing Countries and the Trading System*, in POWER, PASSIONS, AND PURPOSE 201 (J. Baghwati & J. Ruggie 1984) [hereinafter Wolf, *Two-Edged Sword*]; and R. HUDEC, THE GATT LEGAL SYSTEM AND WORLD TRADE DIPLOMACY 208 (1975) [hereinafter HUDEC, THE GATT LEGAL SYSTEM].

tion stones of the world trading system embodied by GATT. This critical perspective objects to what a principal proponent describes as "the desire of developing countries to create a world in which one group of countries [ICs] has most of the obligations and another [DCs] most of the rights . . . ."[70] This perspective finds nothing commendable in the "very considerable divergence in the formal application of GATT principles and rules to the trade of developing countries, on the one hand, and to that of developed countries, on the other."[71] According to this school of thought, the unequal application of GATT trade rules, and caving in to the demands of DCs for preferential treatment, has succeeded in emasculating GATT and worse threatens to destroy it unless a hasty retreat is made to GATT's founding principles of nondiscrimination, liberalism, stability, and transparency.[72] Because this viewpoint has held such a strong fascination for advocates of free trade and of a liberal international economic order, throughout this essay critical perspective of preferential treatment will be referred to as "liberal internationalism."

In opposition to liberal internationalism is a perspective[73] that has been influenced by, and draws its inspiration from, laudable visions of a New International Economic Order.[74] This perspective

70. Wolf, *Two-Edged Sword*, *supra* note 69, at 202; *see also* Meier, *The Tokyo Round of Multilateral Trade Negotiations and the Developing Countries*, 13 CORNELL INT'L L.J. 239 (1980).

71. *Id.* at 203.

72. *Id.* at 204.

73. *See generally* HYDER, EQUALITY OF TREATMENT AND TRADE DISCRIMINATION, *supra* note 21; YUSUF, LEGAL ASPECTS OF TRADE PREFERENCES *supra* note 38; and the BRANDT COMMISSION REPORT, *supra* note 14.

74. The New International Economic Order (NIEO) comprises a set of three instruments passed in 1974 by the United Nations General Assembly (UNGA) spelling out certain economic demands and principles. Two of these instruments were adopted by the UNGA at its Sixth Special Session on May 1, 1974—the *Declaration on the Establishment of a New International Economic Order*, G.A. Res. 3201 (S-V1), 6 (Special) U.N. GAOR Supp. (No. 1) at 3, U.N. Doc. A/9559 (1974), *reprinted in* 13 I.L.N. 715 (1974), and the *Programme of Action on the Establishment of a New International Economic Order*, G.A. Res. 3202 (S-V1), 6 (Special) U.N. GAOR Supp. (No.1) at 5, U.N.Doc. A/9559 (1974), *reprinted in* 13 I.L.M. 720 (1974). The third instrument was adopted by the UNGA at its 29th regular session on December 12, 1974: *Charter of Economic Rights and Duties of States*, G.A. Res. 3281 (XXIX), 29 U.N. GAOR Supp. (No. 31) at 50, U.N. Doc. A./9361 (1975), *reprinted in* 14 I.L.M. 251 (1975) [hereinafter the *Economic Charter*]. The historical roots of the NIEO can be traced back to the 1950s and 1960s when the DCs began forming a united front for dealing with the industrialized countries on international economic matters. The first United Nations Conference on Trade and Development (UNCTAD) held in Geneva in 1964 became the institutional glue holding together this motley group of countries. There have been four other such conferences since 1964 in the course of which UNCTAD's role as the spokesman for the world's poor has come to be accepted. For the background and evolu-

is sympathetic to the idea of preferential treatment and would substitute this for the GATT orthodoxy of equality of treatment and nondiscrimination. This perspective will be referred to as "equitable internationalism" since it is grounded in the vision of an equitable world trading system in which States that are equal will be treated equally and those that are unequal will be treated unequally in proportion to the inequality.[75]

An extreme view argues that preferential treatment of DCs should be accepted as a permanent feature of the world trading system rather than as a temporary exception.[76] This view would like to see the principle of preferential treatment backed by sanctions to assure its effectiveness. It should also be nondiscriminatory and irrevocable, or subject to compensation if withdrawn.[77]

The more orthodox view believes that preferential treatment should not be granted on a permanent basis but as a transitional measure[78] to enable DCs to realize their development targets by reducing their persistently widening trade gap and increasing their foreign exchange.[79] Once the transitional phase through which DCs are passing is over and the structural disparities between DCs and the ICs have been reduced or eliminated, the orthodox position contends that the *raison d'etre* of preferential treatment will disappear and the MFN principle of equality of treatment will be restored to its former status. According to this more orthodox view, the grant of preferential treatment to DCs should not result in any permanent change in the existing legal framework of international trade.[80]

---

tion of DC's demands articulated in the five UNCTAD conferences held between 1964 and 1979. See Burney, *A Recognition of Interdependence: UNCTAD V.*, 16 FINANCE AND DEVELOPMENT 18 (Sept. 1979).

75. *See* text accompanying *infra* note 116.

76. This is the view espoused by the BRANDT COMMISSION REPORT, *supra* note 14, at 183.

77. This view found expression in the proposals put forward by Ambassador Maciel at the Tokyo Round in 1976. *See Statement by the Representative of Brazil, H. E. Ambassador George A. Maciel, on 21 February 1977*, GATT Docs. MTN/FR/W/1, at 2 (Feb. 21, 1977).

78. This view comports with Par. 2, Part IX of the Agreed Conclusions of the Special Committee on Preferences which subjects the granting of preferential treatment to two major limitations: (1) that preferences should be temporary in nature; and (2) that they should not be regarded as binding on the preference giving countries. *See, e.g.*, HYDER, EQUALITY OF TREATMENT AND TRADE DISCRIMINATION, *supra* note 21; YUSUF, LEGAL ASPECTS OF TRADE PREFERENCES, *supra* note 38, at 95 *et seq.*

79. HYDER, EQUALITY OF TREATMENT AND TRADE DISCRIMINATION, *supra* note 21.

80. *Id.*

A. The Liberal Internationalist Perspective

A basic objection to the demand by DCs that international trade rules be universal in nature and not uniform is that these rules have an overall damaging effect on the entire system of world trade. As Martin Wolf, director of Studies at the Trade Policy Research Centre in London, argues, it is not possible to secure derogations from GATT principles in favor of DCs without the basic framework of liberal trade being affected in the long run.[81] In a particularly blistering attack, Wolf accuses the DCs of engaging in a "sustained assault on the liberal international trading system including the principle of nondiscrimination, embodied in Article 1 of the GATT."[82] The DCs, Wolf continues, "have argued that 'equal treatment of unequals is unjust' and have urged, instead, that there be discrimination"[83] in their favor. In a similar vein, Hudec views the exceptions and derogations to pre-existing general rules of international trade as constituting a progressive delegalization of the relationship between GATT and its developed country members.[84]

1. *Preferential Treatment is a Double-Edged Sword*—A more specific objection to the principle of preferential treatment is that it allows the DCs to pursue policies damaging to themselves as well. One critic has likened the demand for special and differential treatment to "a demand by a pedestrian for the 'right' to jaywalk and to step under a bus."[85] Preferential treatment is damaging to the very countries advocating them because, contrary to earlier views, limitless protection is not in the interests of individual DCs.[86] It is believed that "the release from all external constraints on their policies, however weak, combined with the constant preaching that the ideas embodied in those constraints are damaging"[87] has allowed DCs to ". . . construct restrictive regimes that can be liberalized only with great difficulty and that strangle their own growth."[88] The protectionist preferential trading arrangements are singled out as prime examples of the havoc that special and differential treat-

81. Wolf, *Two-Edged Sword*, *supra* note 69, at 215.
82. *Id.* at 202.
83. *Id.*
84. HUDEC, THE GATT LEGAL SYSTEM, *supra* note 67, at 208.
85. *Id.*; *see also* I. LITTLE, ECONOMIC DEVELOPMENT: THEORY, POLICY AND INTERNATIONAL RELATIONS 370 (1982).
86. Wolf, *Two-Edged Sword*, *supra* note 69, at 214.
87. *Id.*
88. *Id.*

ment can wreak on the economies of DCs.[89] Regional trading arrangements, we are told, have proved fragile "because of the large element of trade diversion inherent in these schemes . . . . Worse, they have proved a diversion from consideration of the need for more comprehensive liberalization . . . ."[90] For example, in 1979 trade in manufactures within Latin American Free Trade Area (LAFTA) was $4.7 billion which was about a third of the gross manufactured exports of Hong Kong alone.[91]

2. *Preferences Provoke a Backlash From Industrialized Countries*—Another objection to the preferential treatment of DCs within GATT is the damaging effect it has on industrial countries' attitude toward trade with DCs. Preferential treatment helps to "undermine the belief that liberal trade is a matter of mutual advantage or of unilateral advantage to the industrial countries. Rather, the impression is that it is a burden on the industrialized countries. It is not surprising, therefore, that in more difficult times the industrial countries have been less willing to bear such a 'burden'."[92]

3. *Preferences Are of Doubtful Value*—A third objection to the principle of preferential treatment focuses on the illusion that it conveys of granting real and meaningful preferences to the DCs when in point of fact the derived benefits are of doubtful value.[93] Preferences, according to this criticism, are neither generous nor secure enough to have the hoped-for impact on infant industries.[94] The Western industrialized countries have come to regard preferences as an *ex gratia* favor to DCs but, as a form of aid, liberal internationalists find them particularly inefficient and inequitably distributed.[95] Behrman has observed that the benefits of preferential treatment have been modest and concentrated in their distribution.[96] As he put it: "The complexities of the GSPs presumably have discriminated in favor of the wealthier among the DCs be-

89. *Id.* at 215; *see also* Vaitsos, *Crisis in Regional Economic Cooperation (Integration) Among Developing Countries*, 6 WORLD DEV. 719 (June 1978).

90. Wolf, *Two-Edged Sword*, *supra* note 69, at 215.

91. *Id.*

92. *Id.* at 213.

93. *Id.* at 212; *see also* S. GOLT, DEVELOPING COUNTRIES IN THE GATT SYSTEM 26-29 (1978).

94. *Id.*

95. *Id.*

96. Behrman, *Trade Issues*, *supra* note 62, at 244.

cause of their comparative advantage in acquiring information and satisfying complicated requirements."[97] His observation of the unequal distribution of the gains from GSP is corroborated by Krishnamurti[98] and Baldwin-Murray.[99] The latter's empirical study shows that over three-fourths of the GSP trade can be accounted for by a dozen relatively advanced DCs: Taiwan, Mexico, Yugoslavia, South Korea, Hong Kong, Brazil, Singapore, India, Peru, Chile, Argentina and Iran.[100]

4. *Loss of Bargaining Leverage*—The adaptations of the GATT trade regime to the needs of the DCs are dismissed by some as being limited in scope—too little, too late—because they have been unsuccessful in bringing about any fundamental change in the structure of unequal relations between the DCs and the industrialized countries.[101] If anything, preferential treatment has contributed to the diminution of the bargaining power of the DCs in two ways. First, the insistence on preferential treatment puts DCs in a position where they are unable to attract the industrialized countries with real bargaining counters.[102] Bergsten and Cline summarize this position:

> An inherent limitation on the bargaining strength of developing countries in past rounds of trade negotiations has been the lack of liberalization offers of their own to serve as bargaining chips. Indeed the concept that developing countries provide automatic reciprocity because they spend virtually all the foreign exchange they earn on imports, largely from the industrial countries, while broadly true, has meant a lack of bargaining power.[103]

97. *Id.*; *see also Srinivasan, Why Developing Countries Should Participate in the GATT System*, 5 WORLD ECON.. 85, 90 (1982). (DCs gain unequally from the GSP because their very different economies respond differently to the export opportunities offered by the GSP.)

98. *See* Krishnamurti, *Tariff Preferences in Favor of Developing Countries*. 4 J.WORLD TRADE L. 447, 456 (1970).

99. *See* Baldwin & Murray, *MFN Tariff Reductions and Developing Country Trade Benefits Under the GSP*, 5 ECON. J. 30 (1977).

100. *Id.* at 43-44.

101. Ruggie, *Another Round, Another Requiem? Prospects for the Global Negotiations*, in POWER, PASSIONS, AND PURPOSE 33, 39 (J. Bhagwati & J. Ruggie eds. 1984). *See also* R. HANSEN, THE NORTH-SOUTH STALEMATE 149 (1979). ("The South requests a system of generalized tariff preferences (GSP) to increase its capacity to export manufactured goods to the North in 1964; in 1974 the U.S. Congress finally adopts legislation granting the President the power to implement a scheme that bears only a pale resemblance to the program requested a decade earlier.")

102. C. BERGSTEN & W. R. CLINE, TRADE POLICY IN THE 1980s 29 (1982).

103. *Id.* This view is also shared by Ibrahim, *Developing Countries and the Tokyo Round*, 12 J. WORLD TRADE L. 1, 19 (1978). (The refusal to consider the possibility of

Secondly, in placing emphasis on nonreciprocal arrangements, DCs are depriving themselves of bargaining power in another sense. Having cast themselves as permanent exceptions to the GATT rules, DCs' complaints against industrial countries neglect and indifference cannot be, and are not, taken as seriously as they should be taken.[104]

B. *The Equitable Internationalist Perspective*

To the question asking why DCs should be treated differently from other GATT contracting members, two answers are possible: one normative and the other economic. The focus here is on the two possible economic justifications for preferential treatment in favor of DCs of which again there are two possible: (1) its trade creation potential and its agreeable effect on world welfare, and[105] (2) the unleashing of dynamic factors,[106] these being shifts in supply and demand functions which bode well for the economies of preference-receiving DCs.

1. *The Economic Rationale for Preferential Treatment*

a. Trade Creation Benefits and World Welfare—Preferential tariff treatment is a Janus-faced concept in that it can contribute positively toward the liberalization of world trade or operate negatively by distorting it.[107] Thus, such treatment has traditionally been analyzed in terms of trade creation and trade diversion and the extent to which world welfare is affected. It is asserted that trade creation helps to increase world welfare while trade diversion has the opposite effect.[108] World welfare increases to the extent that duty free imports from preferred DCs displace less efficient domestic production in the preference-granting countries.[109] Conversely, world welfare decreases to the extent that imports from preference-beneficiaries displace more efficiently produced imports from other non-preferred ICs.[110]

---

reciprocal concessions has weakened the bargaining position of DCs and tends to isolate them from the course of negotiations.) *See also*, Finger, *Trade Liberalization: A Public Choice Perspective*, in CHALLENGES TO LIBERAL ECONOMIC ORDER 421 (R. Amacher, G. Haberler & T. Willett eds. 1979)

104. Bressand, *Painful Rethinking*, *supra* note 69, at 59.
105. *Id.* MURRAY, TRADE PREFERENCES, *supra* note 19, at 21.
106. *Id.* at 19.
107. *Id.*
108. *Id.*
109. *Id.*
110. *Id.*

The trade creation potential of tariff preferences and the impact it portends for global welfare are reasons to justify the establishment of preferential treatment. Admittedly, the expected impact on world welfare has been "negligibly small,"[111] but as Murray admonishes this should not be taken to mean that tariff preferences have little value:

> Even if world welfare remains unchanged, the redistribution of world income in favour of developing countries might increase the welfare value of a constant (or even declining) level of world income. Furthermore, welfare measurements based on the concepts of trade creation and trade diversion assume that factors of production have alternative employment opportunities (i.e. welfare is measured in terms of consumer and producer surplus). But in developing countries it is probable that some of the increased exports generate employment of otherwise unemployed or underemployed resources. In such cases the contribution to welfare is the entire factor wage bill, not just the producer surplus. On the other hand, resources displaced in non-preferred exporting countries (i.e. other developed countries), are likely to be re-employed; to the extent permanent unemployment results, world welfare will be reduced.[112]

Murray's point is that, by factoring into the global welfare equation such variables as income redistribution and changes in the level of employment, a noticeable increase in world welfare results.

b. Dynamic Benefits—Preferential treatment has always been viewed as playing an essential role in accelerating the growth of DCs, that is "as a means of overcoming underdevelopment and economic backwardness, since [its] objective is to provide an equality of opportunity to the weak and poor nations by increasing their competitive power in world markets."[113] This expectation is consistent with international trade theory that posits that the major benefits to be derived from tariff preferences result from so-called dynamic factors, such as shifts in demand and supply functions.[114] Tariffs are viewed by DCs as a source of revenue and as a form of

---

111. Much of this has to do with the dissimilarity of economic structures in both DCs and ICs. Murray contends that a large trade creation is most likely when DCs and preference-granting ICs have similar economic structures; since such similarity increases the opportunity for preferential tariffs to lead to the displacement of domestic IC production by DCs' imports. But the scope for trade creation is significantly reduced if the economic structures between preferred DCs and preference-giving ICs are dissimilar. *Id.* at 22.

112. *Id.*

113. Yusuf, *The Enabling Clause*, *supra* note 28, at 492.

114. MURRAY, TRADE PREFERENCES, *supra* note 19, at 21.

temporary protection for "infant industry." The benefits resulting from infant industry "protection" are precisely the kinds of "dynamic factors" trade theory postulates would result from preferential treatment.[115]

The argument for protecting infant industry is premised on the belief that a noncompetitive industry will become competitive due to gradual improvements in production efficiency.[116] "The growth from infancy," as Murray puts it, "requires a protected market which is large enough to justify efficient production—such a market is not available at home. It can only be provided by protecting world markets for developing-country exports of manufactured products."[117] Thus, the dynamic benefits enjoyed by DCs as a result of preferential treatment are *inter alia* opportunities for large-scale production, improved access to world markets, increased exports and income, not to speak of enlarged domestic markets for domestic production. In any event, the export earnings derived from improved access to IC markets would be used by DCs to underwrite some of the costs of their social and economic development. By encouraging economic growth, preferential treatment would reduce the need of DCs for financial assistance from ICs.

2. *The Normative Appeal of the Principle of Preferential Treatment*—The normative content of this principle is derived from two postulates. First, that equitable opportunities are truly equitable only among countries having equal trading abilities.[118] That being the case, poorer countries should be treated more favorably in terms of market options than the richer countries.[119] In the words of the representative of India at the Ninth Session of the GATT Contracting Parties, "[e]quality of treatment is equitable only among equals. A weakling cannot carry the same load as a gi-

115. *Id.* at 20.
116. *Id.*
117. *Id.*
118. *See* MURRAY, TRADE PREFERENCES, *supra* note 19, at 9. This has been referred to as the 'principle of substantive equality.' This principle "justifies that relations between states with a sufficiently comparable level of development be governed by the principles of reciprocity, most-favored-nation treatment and other principles of formal non-discrimination and fair trade *** Without prejudice to other elaborations in binding international rules, the principle of equality or non-discrimination also justifies preferential and non-reciprocal treatment of developing countries by developed countries and among developing countries, in view of their differentiated needs of development in the various areas of international economic, financial and monetary relations." *See* Declaration on the Progressive Development of Principles of Public International Law Relating to a New International Economic Order, 62nd Conference of the International Law Association, Seoul, 1986, paragraphs 10, 10.1 and 10.2.
119. *See* Behrman, *Trade Issues*, *supra* note 62, at 238.

ant."[120] In the same vein, the Uruguayan Permanent Representative to the United Nations Organization in Geneva in stating his opposition to the MFN standard noted that the MFN was "not the proper means to combat underdevelopment because economic inequality among States can only be corrected through unequal treatment. Inequality cannot be put right by applying equal measures: this can only be done through differential treatment favoring some in order to obtain effective equalization in the end."[121] Since justice demands that equals be treated equally, it must also require that unequals be treated unequally, at least, in proportion to the inequality. Viedrag expressed this view succinctly:

> Justice requires equal treatment of equals. This is the classic formula in its most simple form, from which it follows, as a second part, that justice likewise requires unequal treatment of unequals. This addition implies the notion of proportionality which underlies the principle of *suum cuique tribuere*. The formulations may differ from one another, but basically they all amount to something like equal treatment of equals and unequal treatment of unequals in proportion to the inequality.[122]

This formulation of equality requiring that the unequal should be treated unequally has impeccable historical roots in Western intellectual thought. It can be traced back to classical Greek metaphysics in the writings of the Ancient Greats. For example, in Aristotle's *Nicomachean Ethics*[123] this idea is squarely confronted:

> There will be the same equality between the shares than between the persons, since the ratio between the shares will be equal to the ratio between the persons; for if the persons are not equals possess or allotted unequal shares, or persons not equal shares, that quarrels and complaints arise.[124]

A second postulate of the normative universe on the principle of

120. *Quoted in* K. KOCK, INTERNATIONAL TRADE POLICY AND THE GATT 1947-67 289 (1969). Some have characterized the plea for special and differential treatment as an "anachronistic throwback to the mid-sixties" quite understandable in the "days that followed the civil rights movement, the Peace Corps, and Kennedy idealism, such demands would be accorded credence. But it was also a time when the United States still boasted a large trade surplus. Preferential treatment for developing countries was not only viewed by the United States to be morally correct but practically affordable." Berger, *Preferential Trade Treatment for Less Developed Countries: Implications of the Tokyo Round* 20 HARV. INT'L L.J. 540, 581-82 (1979) [hereinafter *Berger, Preferential Trade Treatment*].

121. *See* Espiell, *The MFN Clause*, *supra* note 22, at 36.

122. *See* E. VIEDRAG, THE CONCEPT OF DISCRIMINATION IN INTERNATIONAL LAW 7 (1973).

123. *See* BOOK V, SECTION III, at 6 *quoted in* 1 Y.B. INT'L L. COMM. 185-86 (1986).

124. *Id.*

preferential treatment is the belief that a pre-condition for the harmonious development of the world community as a whole is the recognition of the existence of a common interest in the social and economic development of the DCs.[125] In effect, the DCs and the ICs are each other's keepers and must either swim together or suffer the common fate of sinking together.

IV. A Critical Look at the Conflicting Perspectives

Implicit in the liberal international perspective is the assumption that the conditions that gave rise to the demands for preferential treatment in favor of DCs have ceased to exist thus vitiating the need for a principle that undermines the GATT legal system. In the event that these conditions still prevail, liberal internationalists seem to suggest that preferential treatment is not the appropriate antidote. Equitable internationalists, on the other hand, implicitly assume that certain conditions justify the need for preferential treatment and, so long as these conditions persist, preferential treatment remains the only logical and defensible posture the world community can adopt. Since this author sympathizes with the view put forth by the equitable internationalists, the analysis will proceed directly to an evaluation of the arguments from those opposed to this viewpoint.

A. *Flaws in the Liberal Internationalist Position*

1. *Failure to Give Adequate Attention to GATT's Own Inherent Flaws*—In their eagerness to deny the principle of preferential treatment any legal status in GATT, advocates of liberal internationalism have been somewhat reluctant to confront the philosophy of trade liberalization that undergirds the GATT approach to international trade and questions whether it is compatible with the objective realities of contemporary international economic relations.[126] The failure to critically re-examine the organizing philosophy of the GATT system is accompanied by a tendency to overlook some of the major defects of GATT itself. These flaws are potentially more threatening to the continued sustainability of that system, than are the paltry exceptions and derogations to accommodate the special and differential needs of the DCs. Indeed, the internal weaknesses of the GATT system have been so noticeable that calls have been

125. *See* YUSUF, LEGAL ASPECTS OF TRADE PREFERENCES, *supra* note 38, at ix.

126. *See* text accompanying notes 19, 21 & 22 *supra*.

heard for replacing it with something totally new.[127]

Miriam Camps and others[128] have argued that the greatest need for institutional innovation in the structure of North-South economic relations is in the trade field. This would require among other things replacing GATT which has failed

> to deal adequately with two major interrelated issues of the present decade: the need to find ways to incorporate the DCs more fully into a global trading system that they accept as both being responsive to their needs and requiring certain obligations on their part and the need to cope efficiently with the process of structural change and shifting patterns of international trade and production.[129]

What has been billed as DC's undermining of the GATT system has bottomed in a fundamental clash between two contending views of the role of international trade and GATT. The conflict between the DCs and the ICs in GATT "is in the intellectual world born of profound differences about how national governments should handle international trade."[130]

As an organization, GATT promotes the principles of reciprocity, nondiscrimination, and trade liberalism, and views protectionism as the major evil to avoid. This model of international trade draws its theoretical strength from the doctrine of comparative advantage which holds that all nations will benefit if each specializes in producing what it can best produce (those things in which it has relative advantages) and *if* it buys from others the things *they* are better equipped to produce.[131] When trade is unfettered by nonmarket forces or politically imposed barriers, *all* nations benefit. It is on this rather simple equation—that the net gain in welfare to most countries is greater as a consequence of their trade with one another—that provides the intellectual prop for the liberal internationalist vision of world trade.

The fundamental flaw with this equation that needs to be recognized if the DCs' demands for preferential treatment can be understood, is that it abstracts from the reality of power—the differences

---

127. M. CAMPS, COLLECTIVE MANAGEMENT: THE REFORM OF GLOBAL ECONOMIC ORGANIZATIONS Chapter 5 (1981); Gwin, *Global Economic Organizations*, *supra* note 20.

128. *Id.*

129. Gwin, *Global Economic Organizations*, *supra* note 20, at 140.

130. HUDEC, THE GATT LEGAL SYSTEM, *supra* note 69.

131. For an exposition of this doctrine *see generally* Ricardo, *On the Principles of Political Economy and Taxation*, *reprinted in* THE WORKS AND CORRESPONDENCE OF DAVID RICARDO 1:135 (P. Sraffa 1951); A. SMITH, THE WEALTH OF NATIONS 424 (1937).

in power between nations and between private economic agents—and this robs GATT of its usefulness as an optimal method of organizing world trade.[132] As Grey put it:

> [T]he conventional trade relations model fails to take properly into account the fact that there are gross differences in market power and in political power as between trading nations. Moreover, the *model* abstracts from the reality of private economic power; it ignores the differences in power and control of markets as between private entities engaging in international transactions. The model also abstracts from differences in modes of production and their influence on market behavior. Economists have addressed some of these factors as separate realities; nonetheless much of the discussion of trade policy at public and political levels seems to assume that the simplified teaching device embodied in the notion of comparative advantage says all that it is important to say about trade policy.[133]

The demands for reform of the GATT system stem from a recognition that the principle of comparative advantage on which liberal trade is based is not entirely neutral. Not all nations benefit from free trade, as Kegley writes:

> [F]actor endowments (such as land, labor, and capital) are not so distributed that all gain from a system of free and unfettered international trade. Some may be systematically denied benefits, others enjoy special privileges as a result of the contributions made by the less fortunate to those already well endowed. In other words, *the international division of labor implied by the principle of comparative advantage reinforces the advantages of some, while making permanent the dependencies of others.* Inequalities are thus perpetuated, with unequal distributions of technological capabilities a critical factor. The perceived need among many developing nations to create a new order founded on something other than liberal precepts derives from their raised consciousness about the way in which the existing economic order operates—advantageously to a few and disadvantageously to the many.[134]

---

132. Grey, *The Decay of the Trade Relations System, printed in* ISSUES IN WORLD TRADE POLICY: GATT AT THE CROSSROADS 17, 20 (R. Snape ed. 1986) [hereinafter Grey, *Trade Relations System*].

133. *Id.*

134. C. KEGLEY, JR. & E. WITTKOPF, WORLD POLITICS 195 (1981) [emphasis added].

2. *Disregard of Industrialized Countries Noncompliance with GATT*—Equally important, but rarely ever addressed by critics[135] of preferential treatment, is the long and distinguished history of continuous disregard and flagrant violations of GATT rules[136] and principles by the very countries that consider themselves the guardians and defenders of these principles. As Gwin observed:

> GATT's effectiveness in handling trade issues has clearly declined since the end of the 1960's, as evidenced by a decline in strict adherence to the rules of GATT and widespread resort to nontariff measures of various kinds. This trend has reflected, at bottom, a widespread feeling that the rules do not adequately respond to the situations that were posing the most acute problems for governments— neither those governments that had written the rules nor the members of GATT who had not shared in the rule making.[137]

3. *Tendency to Overlook DCs' Implicit Bargaining Leverage*—The criticism that the DCs' insistence on non-reciprocal concessions has cost them whatever bargaining power they might have had in the GATT MTNs is premised on the belief that since DCs have no *explicit* reciprocity to offer ICs, they therefore have no bargaining leverage. This argument is flawed in two respects. First, it overlooks the *implicit* reciprocity that DCs continue to offer through their export earnings.[138] Additional export earnings received by DCs as a result of preferential tariffs can be fully reciprocated by increased imports from ICs.[139]

A second, and perhaps more fundamental flaw with the loss of bargaining leverage argument is that it worships the concept of reciprocity and treats it as a *conditio sine qua* of trade relations between DCs and ICs. But the emphasis on strict one-to-one reciproc-

---

135. To his credit Wolf, at least, acknowledges that GATT is an "enfeebled system" given "the multitude of loopholes" contained in the Agreement: Article XXVIII which permits the renegotiation of bound tariffs; Article XIX which allows for the imposition of (nondiscriminatory) emergency protection against competitive imports; Article VI and the code on subsidies and countervailing duties which deal with countervailing action against dumped or subsidized goods; Article XII which provides protection for balance-of-payment reasons; Article XXIV which permits the formation of customs unions and free-trade areas; and Article XI which permits the imposition of quantitative restrictions against imports. *See* Wolf, *Two-Edged Sword*, *supra* note 69, at 209.

136. For evidence of noncompliance with GATT rules, see generally Jackson, *The Crumbling Institutions of International Trade*, 12 J. WORLD TRADE L. 93 (1978); *see also* Roschke, *The GATT: Problems and Prospects*, 12 J. INT'L L. & ECON. 85 (1977).

137. Gwin, *Global Economic Organizations*, *supra* note 20, at 140.

138. *See* MURRAY, TRADE PREFERENCES, *supra* note 19, at 9.

139. *Id.*

ity can be counterproductive to the goal of a liberal trading order.[140] The raw pursuit of reciprocal exchanges, as Winham discovered in his thoughtful analysis of the Tokyo Round MTNs,[141] can introduce distortions and lack of coherence into trade policy. Furthermore, he observed, because reciprocity works better between parties that are equal than between those that are unequal, it is not an appropriate vehicle for integrating DCs into the GATT system and for promoting a stable and equitable world trading order.[142]

V. THE LEGAL STATUS OF THE PRINCIPLE OF PREFERENTIAL TREATMENT

The traditional definition of international law, by general agreement,[143] was shaped at a time when the principal actors on the world stage were a small number of relatively homogeneous European states. The world community has, however, since changed and now includes a large contingent of states from Africa, Asia, the Caribbean, the Middle East and Latin America as well as a welter of global and regional international organizations, transnational business enterprises and interest groups, and other non-state actors.[144] These changes in the complexion and composition of the international system compel a corresponding reorientation in the conceptualization of international law.[145] Regrettably, efforts in this direction have so far been futile as the defenders of the status quo have proved to be uncompromisingly resistant to new formulations and paradigms of international law. Therefore, despite the concerted and determined efforts by the DCs, to universalize international law, few of the norms and principles promoted by them have been crystallized into customary law or translated into universal international conventions.[146]

---

140. *Id.*; *see also* WINHAM, THE TOKYO ROUND NEGOTIATION, *supra* note 19, at 364.

141. *Id.*

142. *Id.*

143. *See supra* note 17 and accompanying text. *See generally* B. WESTON, R. FALK & A. D'AMATO, INTERNATIONAL LAW AND WORLD ORDER: A PROBLEM ORIENTED COURSEBOOK (1980); W. FRIEDMANN, THE CHANGING STRUCTURE OF INTERNATIONAL LAW 70 (1964).

144. *See generally* W. JENKS, INTERNATIONAL LAW IN A CHANGING WORLD (1963); T. ELIAS, THE EXPANDING FRONTIERS OF INTERNATIONAL LAW (1979).

145. *Id.*; *see also* Abi-Saab, *The Newly-Independent States and the Rules of International Law: An Outline* 8 HOW. L.J. 95 (1962).

146. *See* Rhee, *Law-Making Process for the new International Economic Order*, paper presented at the 13th Conference on the Law of the World, sponsored by the World Peace Through Law Center, Seoul, Korea, Sept. 6-11, 1987; *see also*, Rabasa, *The Charter of*

In this final section, the legal status of the principle of preferential treatment will be discussed and the obstacles that prevent it from being recognized as a customary rule of international law will be considered.

A. *Preferential Treatment in the Law of GATT*

Mention has already been made of the Declaration[147] made at the conclusion of the Tokyo Round in 1979 to accord the principle of preferential treatment permanent status in the GATT. That Declaration is implemented in points 1 and 4 of the Group Framework Agreement. Paragraph 1 of this Declaration (commonly referred to as the Enabling Clause) provides the legal basis for preferential treatment in favor of DCs. This paragraph provides:

> Notwithstanding the provisions of Article 1 of the General Agreement, contracting parties may accord differential and more favorable treatment to developing countries, without according such treatment to other contracting parties.[148]

The remainder of the Declaration carefully circumscribes the actual circumstances in which such discriminatory treatment is permitted, delineates the expectations of the parties with respect to the grant of tariff concessions to DCs, and provides a mechanism for introducing or withdrawing preferential treatment.

1. *Commitments*—In Paragraph 2 of the Declaration, the ICs commit themselves to granting preferential treatment in four specific categories: (i) preferential tariff treatment (that is duty-free entry) to products from DCs in accordance with the GSP; (ii) differential and more favorable treatment for DCs under agreements concerning non-tariff measures negotiated multilaterally in GATT; (iii) regional or global arrangements entered into among DCs in the context of any general or specific measures favoring DCs; and (iv) special treatment for least developed among the DCs. In addition, ICs can consider on an *ad hoc* basis, under the provisions of the General Agreement for joint action, any proposal for preferential treatment in other areas.[149] This allows ICs to consider other proposals for special and differential treatment outside the scope of

---

Economic Rights and Duties of States, A.S.I.L., PROCEEDINGS OF THE 68TH ANNUAL MEETING 302, 303-05 (1975).

147. *See supra* note 26 and accompanying text.

148. *Id.*

149. *Id.*

the Enabling Clause for example, those granted on a bilateral or regional basis under a procedure identical with that of obtaining a waiver under Article XXV of the General Agreement.

2. *Expectations*—Paragraph 3 of the Declaration sets out three limitations on use of preferential treatment, that is, what the ICs expect would result from the grant of concessionary tariff treatment to DC products. It provides that such treatment shall: (i) be designed to facilitate and promote the trade of DCs and not to raise barriers to the trade of other countries; (ii) not constitute an impediment to the reduction or elimination of tariffs and other restrictions to trade on an MFN basis; and (iii) if necessary, be modified to the extent called for by the development, financial and trade needs of DCs.

Paragraph 5 declares that the ICs do not expect reciprocity from DCs for commitments made by them in trade negotiations with the DCs. This provision makes it clear that DCs are not expected to make concessions or contributions that are inconsistent with their development, financial and trade needs.

Paragraph 6 further expands on this concept of non-reciprocity by requiring ICs to "exercise the utmost restraint" in seeking concessions from DCs. It reiterates and extends to the least developed DCs, the standard set out in Paragraph 5 that DCs shall not be expected to make concessions or contributions that are inconsistent with their particular problems and situations.

The expectation that DCs would someday "graduate" from the need for preferential treatment to participate fully in GATT MTNs—the so-called 'graduation principle'[150]—briefly touched upon in Paragraph 3(c) is spelled out in detail in Paragraph 7. This provision indicates that *DCs "expect"* that their capacity to make contributions or negotiated concessions would improve with the

150. The graduation clause reiterates the non-reciprocity principle of Article XXXVI, Paragraph 8, of the General Agreement. *See supra* note 24 and accompanying text. *See also* Interpretive Note to Article XXXVI, GATT Annex 1, Ad Article XXXVI. The graduation clause was extremely important to ICs like the US who conditioned their support for the Declaration "on a commitment by developing countries to assume fuller GATT obligations in line with their development progress and recognition that benefits of special treatment would be phased out as that economic progress is made." *See* Executive Office of the President, Office of Special Trade Representative, *Framework*, (GATT Reform) Release No. G-6 (May 2, 1976); *see also Statement of United States Representative on 21 February 1977*, GATT Docs. MTN/FR/W/Z, at 6 Mar. 1, 1977. For a comprehensive discussion of how graduation has been implemented in the US GSP program, *see* Glick, *The Generalized System of Preferences-Yesterday, Today and Tomorrow*, 30 FED. B. NEWS & J. 284 (May 1983).

"progressive development of their economies and improvement in their trade situation," and they "would accordingly expect" to participate more fully in the framework of rights and obligations under GATT.

3. *Procedural Requirements*—Paragraph 4 of the Declaration provides that before a party takes any action to introduce, modify or withdraw a preferential treatment arrangement under this Declaration, it must do two things: (i) notify the other contracting parties and provide them with all the information they "may deem appropriate" to this action, and (ii) provide "adequate opportunity" for prompt consultations with any interested party regarding "any difficulty or matter that may arise."

Finally, Paragraph 9 requires that the parties collaborate in arrangements for review of the operations of the provisions of this Declaration.

Against this backdrop, it is appropriate to ask whether the principle of preferential treatment has acquired a legal basis of equal standing to the MFN clause. It is doubtful whether the Declaration imposes any legally enforceable obligations on ICs to grant preferential tariffs to DCs. To begin with, the main provision of the text clearly states that "contracting parties *may* accord differential and more favorable treatment" to DCs. Note that it is the volitional "may" and *not* the obligatory "shall" that is preferred. Furthermore, such treatment is to be granted in accordance with the concessional GSP. The GSP, as we have already indicated, is not a *common* system benefitting a *common* list of DCs as these countries had hoped. Rather, it constitutes a variety of schemes, each identifying the DCs that would benefit, the products that would qualify for preferential tariffs, and the rules and regulations that would apply.

The main contribution of the Enabling Clause to the 'legalization' of the principle of preferential treatment is its rendering superfluous the practice between 1971 and 1979 of legitimizing the GSP through temporary waivers pursuant to GATT Article XXV, paragraph 5. In short, the Enabling Clause merely gives some permanence to an already non-binding preferential arrangement embodied in the various GSP programs.[151] It is our view that the le-

151. *See, e.g.*, Footnote 3 to Paragraph 2 of the Declaration. The so called benefits of the Enabling Clause, according to a report by the Secretary-General of UNCTAD, "are more a matter of form than of substance. On the one hand, the enabling clause introduces in the GATT legal system differential treatment in four areas where the developing countries

gality of the principle of preferential treatment must rest upon a basis more substantial than favor, yet favor is all that the Enabling Clause promises.

How then can DCs enforce the principle of preferential treatment? Generally speaking, there are two ways that states can be bound to new norms and principles of international law. One is through their consent as expressed in international conventions and the other is through custom. In the absence of a binding treaty between DCs and ICs on the issue of preferential tariffs in favor of the former, we must look elsewhere for legal support for this principle.

B. *The Principle of Preferential Treatment as International Law*

The principle of preferential treatment is a basic principle of the emerging international law of development; a law which is mainly aimed at contributing to the reduction of the socio-economic inequalities which presently characterize the relations between DCs and ICs.[152] The content of this law, as Professor Schachter[153] reminds us, derives from two sources. The first is the network of international undertakings and arrangements concerned with aid, trade, and investment for the benefit of DCs.[154] Second, this law has also been shaped by the resolutions, declarations, charters of rights, duties, standards, and final acts of the United Nations and its specialized agencies.[155]

Since the first source of the international law of development consists of treaties which have traditionally been accepted as reliable evidence of *opinio juris communis* among the States of the world, it presents no special problem among legal scholars.[156] Rather, it is the second body of international instruments, which Schachter characterizes as *"normes sauvages,"*[157] that has aroused

---

already enjoyed it on a *de facto* basis (and to some extent on a legal basis). On the other hand, the clause limits any further enlargement of the scope of differential treatment within the GATT structure by making it subject to approval by the Contracting Parties to the General Agreement." *See UNCTAD: Assessment of the Results of the Multilateral Trade Negotiations*, TD/B/778/Rev. 1, at 29 (1982).

152. *See* YUSUF, LEGAL ASPECTS OF TRADE PREFERENCES, *supra* note 38, at xvii.

153. *See* Schachter, *The Evolving International Law of Development*, 15 COLUM. J. TRANSNAT'L L. 1 (1976) [hereinafter Schachter, *International Law of Development*].

154. *Id.*

155. *Id.* at 3; *see also*, Laing, *International Economic Law*, *supra* note 17.

156. *Id.* at 2; *see also* HYDER, EQUALITY OF TREATMENT AND TRADE DISCRIMINATION, *supra* note 21; and YUSUF, LEGAL ASPECTS OF TRADE PREFERENCES, *supra* note 38.

157. Schachter, *International Law of Development*, *supra* note 153, at 3.

reactions among international lawyers. These resolutions and declarations, according to Schachter, do not purport to be treaties even though they are formulated as norms and requirements of state behavior and often times in juridical terms of obligations and rights.[158]

Since the principle of preferential treatment is expressly mentioned in four United Nations General Assembly (UNGA) resolutions[159] that are widely acknowledged as constituting the pillars of the evolving international law of development, it is necessary to determine preliminarily whether UNGA resolutions in general and these in particular are legally binding. In turn, the legal character of UNGA resolutions will depend on whether they can and, perhaps more important, should be subsumed under the *a priori* formal "sources" of international law.

1. *A Priori Formal Sources of International Law*—The most convenient and concise statement regarding the "sources" of international law appears in Article 38 (1) of the Statute of the International Court of Justice which reads:

> 1. The Court, whose function is to decide in accordance with international law such disputes as are submitted to it, shall apply:
> (a) international conventions, whether general or particular, establishing rules expressly recognized by the contesting states;
> (b) international custom, as evidence of a general practice accepted as law;
> (c) the general principles of law recognized by civilized nations;
> (d) subject to the provisions of Article 59, judicial decisions and the teachings of the most highly qualified publicists of the various nations, as subsidiary means for the determination of rules of law.[160]

Some learned commentators have taken Art. 38(1) as representing an authoritative and exclusive list of present-day sources of international law.[161] According to this view, the only way in which a

158. *Id.*

159. *See* (1) Declaration of Principles of International Law Concerning Friendly Relations and Cooperation among States; (2) International Development Strategy for the Second United Nations Development Decade. (paragraphs 31-33); (3) Declaration on the Establishment of a New International Economic Order (paragraph 4(a)); and (4) Charter of Economic Rights and Duties of States (Article (9)).

160. Statute of the International Court of Justice, Art. 38, *reprinted in* L. GOODRICH, E. HAMBRO & A. SIMONS, CHARTER OF THE UNITED NATIONS 707-08 (3d ed. 1969).

161. *See, e.g.*, H. THIRLWAY, INTERNATIONAL CUSTOMARY LAW AND CODIFICATION (1972) [hereinafter THIRLWAY, INTERNATIONAL CUSTOMARY LAW].

new "law" can become binding is by finding a home for it under one of the headings of Article 38(1). Accordingly, several writers have attempted to subsume UNGA resolutions under one of the several headings of Article 38, *viz* treaties,[162] custom,[163] and general principles of law.[164]

Others, on the other hand, have concluded that UNGA resolutions cannot be construed as a formal source of law because there is no reference to them in Article 38.[165] Professor Joyner, in a very thoughtful essay, exposes the fallacy of this reasoning and advances three reasons for rejecting it:[166] (1) the notion that Article 38 legally constitutes *the* "sources" of modern international law is not explicitly stipulated in the Statute of the Court, nor is it universally accepted; (2) nowhere in the text is it specified that these are exclusively the only "sources" of international law; and (3) nowhere is it postulated in Article 38 that the Court should eschew from considering other factors as consultative "evidence" in rendering an opinion. As Joyner and others have demonstrated, the International Court of Justice has in the past used non-Article 38(1) legal sources, such as UNGA resolutions in reaching its decisions.[167] Two recent decisions in which the Court accorded weight to UNGA resolutions are the Advisory Opinion on Namibia[168] and

---

162. *See, e.g.*, J. CASTANEDA, LEGAL EFFECTS OF UNITED NATIONS RESOLUTIONS 150 (1969); Skubiszewski, *Resolutions of International Organizations and Municipal Law*, 2 POLISH Y.B. INT'L L. 83 (1968-69); Skubiszewski, *Enactment of Law by International Organizations*, 41 BRIT. Y.B. INT'L L. 198, 220 (1965-66); Skubiszewski, *A New Source of the Law of Nations: Resolutions of International Organizations*. RECUEIL D'ETUDES DE DROIT INTERNATIONAL EN HOMMAGE A PAUL GUGGENHEIM 517 (1968); Tammes, *Decisions of International Organs as a Source of International Law*, 94 REC. DES COURS 90 (1958); Arangio-Ruiz, *The Normative Role of the General Assembly in the United Nations and the Declaration of Principles of Friendly Relations*, 136 REC. DES COURS 419 (1972); Johnson, *The Effect of Resolutions of the General Assembly of the United Nations*, 32 BRIT. Y.B. INT'L L. 97 (1955-56); Sloan, *The Binding Force of a 'Recommendation' of the General Assembly of the United Nations*, 25 BRIT. Y.B. INT'L L. 1 (1948); O. ASAMOAH, THE LEGAL SIGNIFICANCE OF THE DECLARATIONS OF THE GENERAL ASSEMBLY OF THE UNITED NATIONS 63 (1966) [hereinafter ASAMOAH, LEGAL SIGNIFICANCE].

163. *See, e.g.*, H. BOKER-SZEGO, THE ROLE OF THE UNITED NATIONS IN INTERNATIONAL LEGISLATION (1978); Chiang, *United Nations Resolutions on Outer Space: 'Instant' International Customary Law*? 5 INDIAN J. INT'L L. 23 (1965); and THIRLWAY, INTERNATIONAL CUSTOMARY LAW, *supra* note 161, at 491.

164. *See, e.g.*, ASAMOAH, LEGAL SIGNIFICANCE, *supra* note 159, at 61; Zamanek, *The United Nations and the Laws of Outer Space*, 19 Y.B. WORLD AFF. 1965, 208 (1966).

165. *See, e.g.*, Guradze, *Are Human Rights Resolutions of the United Nations General Assembly Law Making*? 4 HUM. RTS. J. 456 (1971).

166. *See* Joyner, *General Assembly Resolutions*, *supra* note 17, at 455. For further elaboration of this view see J. BRIERLY, THE LAW OF NATIONS 66 (H. Waldock 6th ed. 1978); M. AKEHURST, A MODERN INTRODUCTION TO INTERNATIONAL LAW 44 (3d ed. 1977).

167. Joyner, *General Assembly Resolutions*, *supra* note 17.

168. See the Court's analysis in its Advisory Opinion on Namibia. 1971 I.C.J. 15; *see*

the Western Sahara.[169]

Since the sources of international law listed in Article 38(1) do not constitute a closed list, it is pertinent to now establish through which other sources UNGA resolutions derive their binding force.

2. *The General Assembly and International Law-Making*—Opinion is divided on the legislative competence of the General Assembly and by extension on the legal effect of the resolutions and declarations adopted by that body. One view is that the General Assembly has no legislative authority and its resolutions do not in any way have the force of law.[170] The presumption that UNGA resolutions have no binding effect goes back to the very origins of the United Nations. At the San Francisco Conference which drew up the U.N. Charter, a proposal[171] that the General Assembly should be vested with law-making authority was rejected. However, this presumption of the non-binding effect of UNGA resolutions is a rebuttable presumption.[172] There are indeed cases where such resolutions can be binding.[173]

A second view of the legal effect of UNGA resolutions emphasizes the need for a new approach to the theory of obligation in international law.[174] In light of the active participation of DCs in

---

also Higgins, *The Advisory Opinion on Namibia: Which U.N. Resolutions are Binding Under Article 25 of the Charter*? 25 INT'L COMP. L.Q. 270 (1972).

169. *See* Western Sahara, 1975 I.C.J. 12, 13-33 (1975).

170. *See, e.g.*, Haight, *The New International Economic Order and the Charter of Economic Rights and Duties of States*, 9 INT'L L. 591, 597 (1975); *see also* I. BROWNLIE, PRINCIPLES OF PUBLIC INTERNATIONAL LAW 14 (2d ed. 1973). A variant of this view holds that although UNGA resolutions are not legally binding, they can nevertheless be construed by those States rejecting traditional international law as the basis for a new standard of international law or as a device to pressure future international law-making; *see* Brower & Tepe, Jr., *The Charter of Economic Rights and Duties: A Reflection or Rejection of International Law?*, 9 INT'L L. 295, 302 (1975).

171. Committee 2 of Commission which examined this proposal by the Filipino delegation rejected it by 26 votes to 1. *See* Mendelson, *The Legal Character of General Assembly Resolutions: Some Considerations of Principle*, in LEGAL ASPECTS OF THE NEW INTERNATIONAL ECONOMIC ORDER 95, 96 (K. Hossain ed. 1984) [hereinafter Mendelson, *Legal Character of Resolutions*]. *But see* Joyner, *General Assembly Resolutions*, *supra* note 17, at 44.

172. Mendelson, *Legal Character of Resolutions*, *supra* note 171.

173. Examples of such binding resolutions are: (1) "house-keeping" resolutions which involve decisions to admit members, to apportion the budget, etc.; (2) resolutions purporting to give an "authentic interpretation" of the Charter for the purpose of an organ of the U.N.; and (3) resolutions empowering the General Assembly to dispose of territory, such as terminating the mandate or trusteeship systems, or resolutions to admit a State to the United Nations. *Id.*

174. *See* Falk, *On the Quasi-Legislative Competence of the General Assembly*, 60 AM. J. INT'L L. 782, 783 (1986); *see also* ESSAYS ON INTERNATIONAL LAW AND RELATIONS IN HONOR OF A. J.P. TAMMES (H. Meijers & E. Vendag 1977).

international organizations and the growth of global consensus, it is suggested that the time has come for a sociological reorientation of the basis of international obligations in international law.[175] This would require the substitution of the traditional concept of *consent* with that of *consensus* as the new basis of obligation in international law.[176] Proponents of this view contend that a consensual public order has emerged in the international community with the United Nations as its institutional locus.[177] Therefore, to the extent that UNGA resolutions and declarations reflect the overriding consensus among a large number of States they should, despite opposition from some States, be treated as rules of order and norms of obligation.

Scholars sympathetic to this view argue that UNGA resolutions can have as much legal effectiveness as a treaty.[178] In this vein, a French legal scholar, Professor Bollecker-Stern, has proposed a three-pronged test for determining the precise legal effect to be given to UNGA resolutions.[179] The first test deals with the *conditions of adoption*, that is, the number of States that voted for the particular resolution and the importance of the dissenters and abstainers.[180] According to Bollecker-Stern, the more representative of all groups composing the international community, the closer the resolution will be to being regarded as an instrument of binding force.[181] Under this test, none of the basic instruments that codify the evolving international law of development would pass muster. A case in point is the Charter of Economic Rights and Duties of States which was adopted by the General Assembly by a roll-call vote of one hundred and twenty to six, with ten abstentions. Although the Charter was adopted by a very large majority, it did not receive the consent of the industrialized states.[182]

---

175. *Id.*

176. *Id.*

177. *Id.*; *see also* Joyner, *General Assembly Resolutions*, *supra* note 17; Laing, *International Economic Law*, *supra* note 17; R. ANAND, LEGAL REGIME OF THE SEA-BED AND THE DEVELOPING COUNTRIES 203 (1975) (The quasi-legislative role of the General Assembly is being increasingly recognized in the international field.)

178. Bollecker-Stern, *The Legal Character of Emerging Norms Relating to the New International Economic order: Some Comments* in LEGAL ASPECTS OF THE NEW INTERNATIONAL ECONOMIC ORDER 68 (K. Hossain 1984)[hereinafter Bollecker-Stern, *Legal Character of Emerging Norms*].

179. *Id.*

180. *Id.*

181. *Id.*

182. The Declaration on the Establishment of a New International Economic Order and The Programme of Action on the Establishment of a New International Economic Order suffer from the same fate. Both were adopted without vote but with reservations from some

A key question here is whether the dissent of one or a small group of states can and, perhaps more important, should suffice to prevent a norm from being one of general international law?[183] In a seminal essay on the subject of consensus,[184] Professor D'Amato takes the position that an actively dissenting state with a vested interest in the subject matter of the resolution would more greatly affect international expectations of authority and control and thus weigh in favor of defeating the idea of consensus of opinion *vis-a-vis* that resolution.[185]

In support of Professor D'Amato's position, reliance can be placed upon the decision of the International Court of Justice in the *Fisheries Case*.[186] Thus, the reservations and negative votes of some ICs in relation to the three instruments comprising the international law of development make these States persistent objectors and, like Norway with respect to the ten-mile rule in that case, are not bound by a rule of customary international law to which they have expressed dissent while the law is still developing.

It may alternatively be argued, relying upon the *North Sea Continental Shelf Cases*,[187] that the provisions of the international law of development have become part and parcel of customary law inasmuch as they are regarded as binding by an overwhelming majority of the U.N. members. The *North Sea Continental Shelf Cases* in-

---

ICs. *See, e.g.*, McWhinney, *The International Law-Making Process and the new International Economic Order*, CAN. Y.B. INT'L L. 57, 64 (1976) [hereinafter McWhinney, *International Law-Making Process*].

Particularly those ICs that would in practice be called upon to implement the cardinal principles of this new law) who either voted against it (e.g., the United States, Belgium, Denmark, the Federal Republic of Germany, Luxembourg, and the United Kingdom) or abstained (e.g., Austria, Canada, France, Ireland, Israel, Italy, Japan, the Netherlands, Norway, and Spain).

See U.N. Doc. A/RES/3281 (XXIX).

183. *See generally* O. LISSITZYN, INTERNATIONAL LAW: TODAY AND TOMORROW 36 (1965).

184. D'Amato, *On Consensus*, CAN. Y.B. INT'L L. 104, 108 (1970). [hereinafter D'Amato, *On Consensus*].

185. *Id.* In *The North Sea Continental Shelf Cases*, discussed *infra*, the Court observed that one of the elements generally regarded as necessary before a conventional rule can become a general rule of international law, even absent the passage of any considerable period of time, is that a very widespread and representative participation in the convention might suffice of itself, provided it includes the participation of states whose interests are specifically affected. *North Sea Continental Shelf Cases*, 1969 I.C.J. 4, 5.

186. *Fisheries Case* (U.K. v. Nor.), 1951 I.C.J. 116. On various aspects of this case, see 4 M. WHITEMAN, DIGEST OF INTERNATIONAL LAW 137-94 (1963); Waldock, *The Anglo-Norwegian Fisheries* BRIT. Y.B. INT'L L. 114 (1951); Fitzmaurice, *The Law and Procedure of the International Court of Justice, 1951-54*, BRIT. Y.B. INT'L L. 371 (1954); Johnson, *The Anglo-Norwegian Fisheries Case*, 1 INT'L COMP. L.Q. 145 (1952); Evenson, *Anglo-Norwegian Fisheries Case and Its Legal Consequences*, 46 AM. J. INT'L L. 609 (1952).

187. 1969 I.C.J. 4.

volved a dispute between the Federal Republic of Germany on one side and the Netherlands and Denmark on the other concerning the proper delimitation of the boundaries of their respective continental shelves in the North Sea.[188] Denmark and the Netherlands contended that delimitation should be determined by the application of the principle of equidistance set forth in Article 6 of the 1958 Geneva Convention on the Continental Shelf that had been ratified or acceded to by thirty-nine states, but to which Germany was not a party.[189]

Denmark and the Netherlands maintained that Germany was bound to accept delimitation on the basis of the principle of equidistance "because the use of this method is not in the nature of a merely conventional obligation but is, or must now be regarded as involving, a rule that is part of the *corpus* of general international law;—and, like other rules of general or customary international law, is binding on the Federal Republic automatically and independently of any specific assent; direct or indirect, given to the latter."[190] In the alternative, Denmark and the Netherlands argued that even if there was no rule of the equidistance principle when the Geneva Convention was signed, such a rule has evolved since the Convention, partly because of its own impact, and partly on the basis of subsequent state practice.[191]

While rejecting the first contention that the principle of equidistance was inherent in the doctrine of the continental shelf, the Court nonetheless agreed that the principle was "a norm-creating provision which has constituted the foundation of, or has generated a rule which, while only conventional or contractual in its origin, has since passed into the general *corpus* of international law . . . so as to . . . become binding even for countries which have never, and do not, become parties to the Convention."[192] This process, the Court opined, constitutes one of the recognized methods by which new rules of customary international law can be formed.

A major problem with the first prong of the Bollecker-Stern test is that it grants to a few, albeit very powerful, Western industrialized states *de facto* veto power within the General Assembly. As long as these states choose to withhold their votes on a particular

188. *Id.*
189. *Id.*
190. *Id.* at 5.
191. *Id.* at 6.
192. *Id.*

UNGA resolution, then that resolution is not likely to pass the test of representativeness. These states can, under this test, effectively prevent the emergence of any "new" law by their few negative votes.

The second prong of the Bollecker-Stern three-part test focuses on the *style and content of the resolutions.*[193] The more precise the content, the more likely it is to have legal consequences. This holds true whether the resolution has a concrete content such as creation of an organ, statement of a program or of a strategy, or whether it is purely abstract, (merely declaring certain principles).[194]

The resolutions on the international law of development have been faulted for being too vague and ambiguous.[195] Commenting on the Charter of Economic Rights and Duties of States, one critic derides,[196] the "cornucopia approach to legal drafting" (his felicitous phrase) that was followed. He goes on to define this approach to mean "when in doubt, throw everything in and leave it to subsequent historians to try to work out why."[197]

The Charter also embraces what has historically been characterized as the Weimer Constitution drafting principle: "if faced with latent or even patent contradictions in demands pressed in the drafting stage, one should put them all in and hope that the passage of time will resolve the conflict by disposing of one or the other."[198]

Imprecision and generalities are not unknown even in treaty drafting. As Professor Schachter points out, if one were to apply the strict requirements of definitions and specificity to all treaties, many of them would have most of their provisions without legal effect.[199] But the vagueness and ambiguity of a treaty's provisions does not necessarily deprive the instrument of its legal force.[200] It follows, therefore, that an UNGA resolution can contain vague and indefinite language while still embodying some very essential and fundamental principles.

---

193. Bollecker-Stern, *Legal Character of Emerging Norms, supra* note 178, at 71.

194. *Id.*

195. *See, e.g.*, White, *A New International Economic Order?* 16 VA. J. INT'L L. 323, 335 (1976).

196. McWhinney, *International Law-Making Process, supra* note 182, at 65.

197. *Id.*

198. *Id.*

199. *See* Schachter, *The Twilight Existence of Nonbinding International Agreements*, 71 AM. J. INT'L L. 296, 298 (1977) [hereinafter Schachter, *Nonbinding Agreements*]; *see also* P. REUTER, INTRODUCTION AU DROIT DES TRAITES 44 (1972).

200. See REUTER, *supra* at note 199.

In addition to the conditions of adoption and the style and content of the resolution, the specified *means of enforcement*[201] completes the trinity of the Bollecker-Stern test for assessing the legal effect of UNGA resolutions. The existence of a mechanism for enforcement gives more chances to the resolution to be enforced than its absence.[202] Of importance with respect to this test is whether action has to be taken only by the international organization adopting the resolution or if similar action would be required from the States. A resolution is more likely to be enforced if the means of enforcement are within the control of the international organization which enacted it. It may indeed be true that the failure to specify mechanisms of enforcement explains why UNGA resolutions have not been able to make the transition from *de lege ferenda* to *lex lata*.

To be sure, a rule of law has authority if it is enforceable and normally will be enforced.[203] The question is, can that rule of law be enforced even when no enforcement mechanism is specified? The answer clearly is yes because by and large laws are obeyed because those subject to it acknowledge its binding force. A law is not binding because it is enforced; rather, it is enforced because it is already binding.[204] As Judge Fitzmaurice wrote, "[e]nforcement presupposes the existence of a legal obligation incumbent on those concerned. The prospect of enforcement is in fact little more than a factor or motive inclining people to obey rules that they are in any case under an obligation to obey: but it is not itself the source of the obligation."[205]

The issue of the obligatoriness of UNGA resolutions must be resolved first before venturing into the question of its enforcement. The insertion of provisions for enforcement in those resolutions is no guarantee that the resolution will be enforced for, as Judge Fitzmaurice suggests, enforcement will occur only when States believe they are under an obligation to comply with a rule of law.

---

201. Bollecker-Stern, *Legal Character of Emerging Norms*, *supra* note 178, at 72.

202. *Id.*

203. *See* Fitzmaurice, *The Foundations of Authority of International Law and the Problem of Enforcement*, 19 MOD. L. REV. 1, 2 (1956).

204. *Id.*

205. *Id.*

CONCLUSION

The Group Framework Agreement which provides the legal basis for the principle of preferential treatment in GATT is a non-binding agreement. Such an agreement is considered to be without legal effect ("*sans portee juridique*").[206] Thus, noncompliance by a party would not be ground for a claim for reparation or for judicial remedies.[207] Though non-binding instruments such as the Group Framework Agreement still carry legal consequences.[208] In the first place, as an official act of the ICs, this instrument is reliable evidence of the positions taken by these states and consequently it is entirely appropriate, as Professor Schachter suggests, to draw inferences that these states have recognized the principles, rules, status and rights acknowledged.[209] This being the case, noncompliance by an IC can give rise to an international delict. Schachter contends that:

> states entering into a non-legal commitment generally view it as a political (or moral) obligation and intend to carry it out in good faith. Other parties and other States concerned have reason to expect such compliance and to rely on it. What we must deduce from this . . . is that the political texts which express commitments and positions of one kind or another are governed by the general principle of good faith. Moreover, since good faith is an accepted general principle of international law, it is appropriate and even necessary to apply it in its legal sense.[210]

There is no question but that DCs have come to rely on the preferential access of their products into the markets of the ICs. In the course of the Tokyo MTNs, DCs "argued that before they could use scarce resources to make investments to expand their export trade, they had to be confident that such trade would in fact materialize. This could not be done without a stable system of preferences. . . ."[211] Thus, from the onset, DCs' reliance on preferential tariffs was communicated to the ICs. Developing Countries will be justified in treating noncompliance as a breach of a legal obligation.

While the preoccupation of this Article has been with the search for a legal home for the principle of preferential treatment within the GATT framework of trade rules, we must not forget that

206. *See* Schachter, *Nonbinding Agreements*, *supra* note 199, at 297.
207. *Id.* at 300.
208. *Id.*
209. *See* SCHACHTER, INTERNATIONAL LAW IN THEORY AND PRACTICE 129 (1985).
210. *Id.* at 130.
211. *See* WINHAM, THE TOKYO ROUND NEGOTIATION, *supra* note 19, at 276.

GATT is a unique mixture of law, economics and politics.[212] Since law is pre-eminently about rules, lawyers writing about GATT tend, as Professor Dam observed, to see it as nothing more than a legal document.[213] Flowing from this is the naive view that GATT rules are capable of resolving all future problems faced by the world trading system.[214] This rigid legalistic view obscures the fact that GATT trades rules are not only enveloped in a cocoon of political and economic imperatives but are themselves the product of a careful and delicate balancing of the goals and interests of the more powerful contracting parties. Law, as Professor Bollecker-Stern reminds us, can have very different relations to reality:[215]

> [I]t can adopt very different positions in front of unequal situations: law can *disregard* reality and treat equally unequal situations giving thus its sanction to existing inequalities: law can take into account reality to *reinforce* it and transpose the existing unequal situations in the legal sphere, by the establishment of parallel legal inequalities. . . . [L]aw can also take reality into account not by reinforcing it, but by *correcting* it.[216]

The principle of preferential treatment takes into account the reality of unequal economic relations between DCs and ICs and seeks to change this into a more equitable relationship. The principle represents an attempt, and a long overdue one at that, to institutionalize within GATT the trade policies of DCs. These policies reject the orthodox GATT view of international trade as an end in itself rather than as an *instrument* of economic and social development. Thus, the challenge posed by this principle to the GATT world trade system is fundamentally one of reconciling two diametrically opposed trade policies: on the one hand, the policy of trade protectionism embraced by DCs in which tariffs are viewed as a form of temporary protection for 'infant industry' and as a source of revenue; and on the other, the policy of trade liberalization with its emphasis on free trade, unfettered by any form of government-imposed trade barriers other than those negotiated multilaterally under GATT auspices. The debate over legal rules merely camouflages this basic and historical tension between two competing perspectives on how international trade should be conducted.

212. *Id.* at 277; *see also* DAM, GATT LAW, *supra* note 15, Chapter 1.
213. DAM, GATT LAW, *supra* note 15, at 4.
214. *Id.* at 5.
215. *See* Bollecker-Stern, *legal Character of Emerging Norms*, *supra* note 178, at 76.
216. *Id.*

[12]

Emerging International Development Law and Traditional International Law—Congruence or Cleavage?

*Edward Kwakwa**

> One of the most significant developments in contemporary international economic relations has been the proliferation of a complex network of arrangements and undertakings for the benefit of the lesser developed countries. These arrangements range from declarations and final acts adopted at international conferences to more solemn obligations binding on various combinations of states and other international legal persons.
>
> 1 A. Mutharika, International Law of Development ix (1978)

I. Introduction

One of the primary purposes of the United Nations (UN) is to achieve "international cooperation in solving international problems of an economic, social, cultural or humanitarian character."[1] Thus, in the past four decades, the international community, led by the developing nations, has sought to remedy existing problems of underdevelopment.

The emergence of politically independent developing countries in the post-war era has had a discernible impact on the present state of international law. The attainment of political independence by these countries brought into focus the economic disparities in the international system and the accompanying issue of "economic self-determination." A clamor has arisen for a more equitable international economic system[2] to adequately reflect the needs and aspirations of the developing countries.

---

* L.L.B., Ghana; L.L.M.,Yale Law School; J.S.D. candidate, Yale Law School. I would like to thank Professor Paul Kahn for his excellent supervision of earlier drafts of this article.

1 U.N. Charter art. 1, para. 3.

2 *See* M. Bulajic, Principles of International Development Law (1986). "The struggle for the establishment of the New International Economic Order represents a continuation of the process of decolonization in the economic sphere, the negation of domination and of neo-colonialism in international economic relations." *Id.* at 15.

Gradually, a new discipline in contemporary international law referred to as "international development law" emerged. This article focuses on the legal status of emerging issues in international development law as a means of understanding the conceptual framework within which it is written. The concept is distinguished from other related terms such as "the right to development" and "The New International Economic Order". A brief historical exegesis of the international law of development is given, along with a discussion of its normative content, focusing primarily on treaties and other written instruments, state practice, judicial and juristic opinion, as well as the practice of intergovernmental and non-governmental organizations.

The article takes the position that although international development law is a new and emerging area of international law, its sources can be derived from the traditional formulation stipulated in article 38, paragraph 1 of the statute of the International Court of Justice (ICJ). The article stresses that international development law is necessitated by the increasing interdependence of states in international relations. Further, the emerging issues in international development law are in the interest of the entire international community, including developed as well as developing countries. As a result, international development law has a salutary effect on world order and basic human dignity and should therefore be actively promoted by the community of states. In conclusion this article recommends methods for enhancing the significance and importance of international development law.

A. *Clarification of Terms*

"International development law" refers to the law regulating the relations among sovereign but economically unequal states. It is "the international law of the modern era of the development of mankind."[3] The "law of development" must be distinguished from the "right to development."[4] Whereas the former generally refers,

---

[3] *Id.* at 49.

[4] The "right to development" is a concept of very recent origin, generally traced to an address given to the Institut International de Droits de l'Homme, in 1972 by Mr. Keba M'Baye, First President of the Supreme Court of Senegal. *See* M'Baye, *The Right to Development as a Human Right,* 5 REVUE DES DROITS DE L'HOMME 503 (1972).

The U.N. Commission on Human Rights formally recognized the human right to development in 1977. *See* U.N. Doc E/CN.4/ SR.1389, 1392-98 (1977). For an extensive discussion of the human right to development *see, e.g.,* Espiell, *The*

inter alia, to the myriad international instruments constituting the *corpus* of the subject of development, the latter could be said to be a branch, albeit a significant aspect of the law of development.[5] The concept of a right to development, for which there is no precise legal foundation, has evolved rapidly with a minimum of international scrutiny.[6] The law of development, however, refers to a body of principles and rules formed within the international legal system with the aim of promoting development.

The international law of development is the emerging legal structure of the proposed New International Economic Order (NIEO).[7] This law of development is the principal means through which attempts are being made to achieve a NIEO. It is an instrument for the economic and legal transformation of international relations whose basic aim is to promote equity[8] and to compensate the developing countries for their disadvantaged positon vis-a-vis developed countries.

II. EVOLUTION OF THE LAW OF DEVELOPMENT AS A NEW DIMENSION OF INTERNATIONAL LAW

The concept of the law of development as a new discipline in contemporary international law can be traced to the writings of the

Right to Development as a Human Right, 16 TEX. INT'L L.J. 189 (1981): Mestdagh, *The Right to Development,* 28 NETH. INT'L L. REV. 30 (1981); Verwey, *The New International Economic Order and the Realization of the Right to Development and Welfare - A Legal Study.* 21 INDIAN J. INT'L L. 1 (1981); Symposium, *Development as an Emerging Human Right,* 15 CAL. W. INT'L L.J. 429 (1985).

[5] The right to development is often referred to as one of the two basic elements of the international law of development (the other being the duties and responsibilities involved in the system of international cooperation for development). *See* F. GARCIA-AMADOR, II THE CHANGING LAW OF INTERNATIONAL CLAIMS 630-31 (1984).

[6] *See, Final Report of* UNESCO *Expert Meeting on Human Rights, Human Needs and the Establishment of a New International Economic Order,* UNESCO Doc. SS/8/CONF. 630/12 at 90-93 (1978).

[7] Garcia-Amador, *The Proposed New International Economic Order: A New Approach to the Law Governing Nationalization and Compensation*, 12 U. MIAMI INTER-AM. L. REV. 1, 15 (1980). The NIEO is a concept on which much has been written. *See generally,* Verwey *supra* note 4, at 1; Akinsanya and Davies, *Third World Quest for a New International Economic Order,* 39 REVUE EGYPTIENNE DE DROIT INTERNATIONAL 101 (1983). P. ANAND, INTERNATIONAL LAW AND THE DEVELOPING COUNTRIES: CONFRONTATION OR COOPERATION? (1987).

[8] Equity has been referred to as "the basic principle of international development law" because "it serves to resolve the contradictions between simultaneous demands for economic independence and for organized mutual aid, for equality in preferential treatment, for common benefit and the renunciation of reciprocity on the part of developing countries." M. BULAJIC, *supra* note 2, at 50.

late Professor Friedmann.[9] Friedmann described the law of international economic development[10] as a body of law which must concern itself not only with the minimum principles adequate for the legal protection for foreign investment, but also with the principles protecting national control of natural resources, as well as with matters pertaining to the policies, methods and structures of international financing of economic development.[11]

In 1965 Professor Michel Virally referred to the law of development as a new area of international law.[12] Thereafter, the Secretary-General of the United Nations prepared a survey of international law in response to a request by the International Law Commission of the UN.[13] The survey stressed that international law was expanding:

> from a body of law imposing negative restraints on independent sovereign states, to a body of law which, in recognition of conditions of increasing interdependence imposes on states various positive obligations of a procedural and substantive kind. The law,

---

[9] *See* Friedmann, *The Changing Dimensions of International Law,* 62 COLUM. L. REV. 1147 (1962).

[10] The term "economic development" was used interchangeably with "development" and "growth" in the period preceding the early 60's. *See ECOSOC Commission on Human Rights: Report of the Secretary General,* U.N. Doc. E/CN.4/SR 1334 at 7 (1979) [hereinafter *Secretary General's Report*]. Recent emphasis has, however, been on a far broader concept of development, particularly as it relates to the social aspects of development. The Brandt Commission for example, states that "development is more than the passage from rich to poor, from a traditional rural economy to a sophisticated urban one. It carries with it not only the idea of economic betterment, but also of greater human dignity, security, justice and equity." NORTH-SOUTH: A PROGRAM FOR SURVIVAL 49 (1980).

The U.N. Commission on Human Rights has defined development as:

> A comprehensive economic, social, cultural and political process which aims at the constant improvement of the well-being of the entire population and of all individuals on the basis of their active, free and meaningful participation in development and in the fair distribution of benefits resulting therefrom.

U.N. Commission on Human Rights, Report of the Working Group of Governmental Experts on the Right to Development, U.N. Doc. E/EN.4/1985/11, Annex 4 at 2 (1985).

In this article, for purposes of brevity and clarity in analysis, only the economic aspects of development will be discussed.

[11] *See* Friedmann, *supra* note 9, at 1165.

[12] *See* Virally, *Vers un Droit International de Development,* 9 ANNUAIRE FRANCAIS DE DROIT INTERNATIONAL 7 (1965).

[13] 2 Y.B. INT'L LAW COMM'N 1-215. U.N. Doc. A/CN.4/SER.A/1971/Add.1 (part 2).

> in other words, is coming to be seen as concerned not only with the protection of the independence of states, but also with the duty to cooperate in the promotion of national and human welfare.[14]

It also described the law relating to economic development as:

> an emerging body of law as part of, and a complement to, the objective stated in the Preamble to the United Nations Charter of promoting "social progress and better standards of life in larger freedom" and the purposes of the Organization mentioned in paragraph 3 of article 1 of the Charter, namely "to achieve international cooperation in solving international problems of an economic, social, cultural or humanitarian character."[15]

Professor Schachter gave prominence to the concept of international development law in his article *The Evolving International Law of Development.*[16] He identified two broad categories of the *corpus* of international development law: first, the complicated network of international undertakings and arrangements concerned with aid, trade, investment, and the like for the benefit of the less developed countries[17]; and second, "the resolutions, declarations, charters of rights and duties, standards and final acts which seem to proliferate in international organizations and conferences."[18] In effect, the evolving international law of development is to to be derived, *inter alia,* from the practice of states, treaties and judicial opinion.

---

[14] *Id.* at 35.

[15] *Id.* at 34-35.

[16] Schachter, *The Evolving International Law of Development,* 15 COLUM. J. TRANSNAT'L L. 1 (1976).

[17] *Id.* As Schachter explains, these undertakings involve a great variety of relationships, including those that are bilateral, regional, or global. *Id.*

[18] *Id.* at 3. According to Prof. Schachter, the central feature of the contemporary international law of development is:

> the idea of need as a basis for entitlement . . . . The present rationale for international assistance and preferential treatment on the basis of need is more in keeping with the premises of the welfare state - that is, to provide for the minimal human needs of the most disadvantaged segments of society . . . thus there is increased acceptance of the idea that specially disadvantaged countries such as landlocked states or former colonial territories or states dependent on a single commodity have special needs that entitle them to preferential treatment.

Id. at 10.

III. The Normative Content of International Development Law

International development law is a compendious term for several new but interrelated principles in international law. Its precise scope, content and substance are still emerging. A review, however, of the texts of bilateral and multilateral agreements, UN declarations and resolutions, as well as an examination of the practice of major development actors reveals that specific norms have crystallized. The most important of these include:

1. The duty of states to cooperate for global welfare.
2. The principle of preferential treatment for developing countries.
3. The principle of entitlement of developing countries to need-based development assistance.

A. *The Duty of States to Cooperate for Global Welfare*

The duty of cooperation is derived largely from the UN Charter, article 1, paragraph 3 which states that one of the main purposes of the UN is "to achieve international cooperation in solving international problems of an economic, social, cultural, or humanitarian character." This objective is specified more precisely in article 55 of the Charter,[19] and all members have pledged, under article 56, "to take joint and separate action in cooperation with the organization for the achievement of the purposes set forth in article 55."[20]

Scores of General Assembly resolutions and declarations pertaining to the economic and social progress of the developing countries, to the establishment of the NIEO, and to the strategies for the UN Development Decades reiterate the duty of states to cooperate for global welfare. Prominent among these is the 1970 Declaration on

---

[19] Art. 55 provides that the U.N. shall promote:

> a. higher standards of living, full employment, and conditions of economic and social progress and development;
> b. solutions of international economic, social, health and related problems; and international cultural and educational cooperation; and,
> c. universal respect for, and observance of, human rights and fundamental freedoms for all without distinction as to race, sex, language, or religion.

U.N. CHARTER art. 55.

[20] Arts. 55 and 56 have been described as "the most significant provisions of the United Nations Charter." *See* I. ELIAS, THE INTERNATIONAL COURT OF JUSTICE AND SOME CONTEMPORARY PROBLEMS 182 (1983).

Principles of International Law Concerning Friendly Relations and Cooperation among States[21] (hereinafter Declaration on Friendly Relations). Others include the Declaration and Program on the Establishment of a NIEO,[22] which states that international cooperation for development is the shared goal and common duty of all countries; the Charter of Economic Rights and Duties of States;[23] and the 1980 resolution on an International Development Strategy for the Third UN Development Decade.[24]

The UN Charter and these numerous General Assembly resolutions and declarations are often the basis for an assertion of the existence of a duty to cooperate for global welfare at the international level. The debate of the 37th session of the UN Commission on Human Rights, for example, stressed that "action to promote development [was] a legal obligation of the international community, and in particular of the industrialized countries."[25] Several textwriters have elaborated on this duty as an established principle of international law.[26] The moral and philosophical underpinnings of this duty of cooperation for global welfare are discussed below.

---

[21] G.A. Res. 2625, 25 U.N. GAOR Supp. (No. 28) at 121, U.N. Doc. A/8028 (1970).

[22] Resolution 3201 contains the *Declaration on the Establishment of a New International Economic Order,* G.A. Res. 3201 (VI Special), U.N. GAOR Supp. (No. 1) at 3; U.N. Doc. A/9559 (1974), *reprinted in* 13 I.L.M. 715 (1974) [hereinafter *Declaration*]. Resolution 3202 contains the *Program of Action on the Establishment of a New International Economic Order,* G.A. Res. 3202 (VI Special), U.N. GAOR Supp. (No. 1) at 5, U.N. Doc. A/9559 (1974), *reprinted in* 13 I.L.M. 720 (1974).

[23] G.A. Res. 1281, 29 U.N. GAOR Supp. (No. 31) at 50, U.N. Doc. A/9631 (1975), *reprinted in* 14 I.L.M. 251 (1975). Some say the Charter creates relatively few firm obligations, since so much of the Charter is diluted by the use of "should," considerable significance accrues by default to those passages that create firmer obligations and rights, and that even though the language adopted mandates action, the nature of that action is left almost comletely to the discretion of individual States. The obligation, it is said, is firm, but not very tangible it is therefore unlikely that this Charter provision would motivate States to alter their behavior. *See* Gamble & Frankowska, *International Law's Response to the New International Economic Order: An Overview*, 9 B.C. INT'L & COMP. L. R. 257, 274 (1986); *cf.* note 51, *infra*.

[24] U.N. Doc. A/Res/35/56 (1980) *reprinted in* 20 I.L.M. 480 (1980).

[25] *See Secretary-General's Report, supra* note 10, at 45.

[26] *See e.g.* Verwey, *supra* note 4, at 20 (arguing that the most obvious secondary principle of the NIEO is that of the duty of all states to cooperate for the welfare of all, in particular the duty of the developed states to assist the developing states in the course of development); Lachs, *The Development and General Trends of International Law in Our Time,* 169 (IV) RECUEIL DES COURS 13, 96-100 (1980)

B. The Principle of Preferential Treatment for Developing Countries

The principle of preferential treatment for developing countries[27] is based on the idea that unequals should be treated unequally in order to obtain an equitable application of the principle of equality.[28] It thus introduces legal inequality or "positive discrimination"[29] in international economic relations to the benefit of developing countries, and:

> aims at correcting the inequitable effects of the traditional twin liberal principles of freedom and legal equity—which, in a society in which the economically weak have to compete with the economically powerful on an equal footing, tend to favor the latter. As one of the most conspicuous legal offsprings of the fundamental of "solidarity," it constitues a cornerstone of what the Charter of Economic Rights and Duties of States refers to as "collective economic security for development."[30]

The norms of equal and non-discriminatory treatment in the relations of states (based on the international economic system founded after the Second World War) came under increasing attack in the early

(the numerous General Assembly resolutions give an unequivocal interpretation of Arts. 55 and 56 of the U.N. Charter, and therefore cannot be viewed as being without legal effect. Formulae such as "to promote general welfare throughout the world" and "to cooperate in the promotion of economic growth throughout the world" constitute an important guide for drawing conclusions on the state of the law on the subject); M. BULAJIC, *supra* note 2, at 290.

[27] Discussions concerning the principle's implementation give rise to the problem of defining a developing country. The most convenient and least problematic criterion would be a resort to UN documentation and statistics for identification of the class of developing countries.

[28] The distinction between equity and equality, although sometimes difficult to discern, is important in this context. "Equality" suggests possession of the same rights, privileges, duties, etc. Here, however, there is economic inequality between developing and developed countries. The argument, therefore, is that an application of equitable (i.e. just; existing in equity; available or sustainable in equity, or upon the rules and principles of equity - BLACK'S LAW DICTIONARY 482 (5th ed. 1984)) principles will secure greater economic equality.

Compare remarks by Mr. Tammes in a discussion by the International Law Commission (ILC) on the most favored-nation clause. *See* 1 Y.B. INT'L LAW COMM'N 208 (1986) (stating that differential treatment of developing states was "reminiscent of the Aristotelean definition of equality as requiring that the unequal should be treated unequally.")

[29] Phrase respectfully borrowed from Verwey, *The Principle of Preferential Treatment for Developing Countries,* 23 INDIAN. J. INT'L L. 343 (1983).

[30] *Id.* (footnotes omitted).

60's. One of the strongest attacks came from the first Secretary-General of the United Nations Conference on Trade and Development (UNCTAD), Raul Prebisch, when he asserted that "no matter how valid the principle of the most favored nation may be in trade relations among equals, it is not an acceptable and adequate concept for trade among countries with highly unequal economic power."[31] UNCTAD subsequently called for "the early establishment of a mutually acceptable system of generalized non-reciprocal and non-discriminatory preferences which would be beneficial to developing countries."[32] The claim to preferential treatment has since been extended to fields other than trade. Article 19 of the Charter of Economic Rights and Duties of States, for example, explicitly states:

> With a view to accelerating the economic growth of developing countries and bridging the economic gap between developed and developing countries, developed countries should grant generalized preferential non-reciprocal and non-discriminatory treatment to developing countries in those fields of international economic co-operation where it may be feasible.[33]

Similar provisions can be found in the Lima Declaration and Plan of Action on Industrial Development and Cooperation,[34] General Assembly Resolution 3362 (5-VII) on Development and International Economic Cooperation,[35] the Development Strategy for the Third

---

[31] *Cited in* Espiell, *GATT: Accomodating Generalized Preferences,* 8 J. WORLD TRADE L. 341, 345 (1974).

[32] *U.N. Final Act and Report of UNCTAD II,* Annex I (E/CONF. 46/141). The Generalized Preferences (GP) system has been described as "the most important practical application up to date of the principle of differential treatment." Yusuf, *Differential Treatment As a Dimension of the Right to Development,* in HAGUE WORKSHOP, THE RIGHT TO DEVELOPMENT AT THE INTERNATIONAL LEVEL 233, 234 (1979) [hereinafter HAGUE WORKSHOP 1979].

[33] G.A. Res. 1281 *supra* note 23, at art. 19 (1975). It should be noted that preferential treatment is not limited to tariff preferences but is also sought in all fields of international economic cooperation where it is feasible. It is also recognized in the areas of transfer of technology (Art. 13), and cooperation in the economic, social, cultural, scientific and technological fields (Art. 9).

[34] U.N. Doc. A/10112 (1975) *reprinted in* 14 I.L.M. 826 (1975) [hereinafter Lima Declaration]. The plan of action suggests a series of special measures for building up the necessary economic and social infrastructure in the least developed, land-locked and island developing countries; the redeployment of certain productive capacities to the developing countries; and an expansion of the Generalized System of Preferences.

[35] G.A. Res. 3362, 7 U.N. GAOR Supp. I, at 3, U.N. Doc. A/10301 (1975).

United Nations Development Decade,[36] and in the 1982 UN Convention on the Law of the Sea.[37] The status and legal significance of the principle enshrined in these documents is more extensively discussed below.[38]

C. The Principle of Entitlement of Development to Need-Based Development Assistance

The principle of entitlement is aimed at bridging the disparities in international economic relations. This "new conception of international entitlement to aid and preferences based on need,"[39] as suggested earlier, is a central feature of the international law of development. It is expressed "in many of the agreements relating to trade preferences, investment, and resources; in the bilateral and multilateral programs of aid; and in the broad normative resolutions adopted by the United Nations bodies on commodities, relocation of industry, the oceans, international liquidity, and numerous related matters."[40]

Thus, the International Development Association, for example, was created in 1960 for the purpose of accelerating the economic

---

For the text of the resolution, see 14 I.L.M. 1524 (1974). The resolution calls for *inter alia*: preferential access for the developing countries to the domestic markets of the developed countries; favorable and concessional terms on all loans and credit extended to the developing countries; and development and transfer of technologies appropriate to furthering the growth of developing countries. *See id.*

[36] *Reprinted in* 5 A. MUTHARIKA, INTERNATIONAL LAW OF DEVELOPMENT 17.

[37] U.N. Doc. A/CONF.62/122, *reprinted in* 26 I.L.M. 1261 (1982). The provisions on preferential treatment of developing countries are found in different sections of the Convention. Particularly instructive are Article 148 ("The effective participation of developing states in activities in the Area shall be promoted . . . having due regard to their special interests and needs, and in particular to the special need of the landlocked and geographically disadvantaged . . ."); Article 144 (programs for transfer of technology to developing states with regard to activities in the Area and for providing opportunities to personnel from the developing states for training in marine science and technology and for their full participation in activities in the Area); Article 150 (Policies relating to activities in the Area shall be carried out in such a manner as to foster healthy development of the world economy and balanced growth of international trade, and to promote international cooperation for the over all development of all countries, especially developing states). *Id.*

[38] *See also* Dorsey, *Preferential Treatment: A New Standard for International Economic Relations,* 18 HARV. INT'L L.J. 109 (1977).

[39] *See* Schachter, *supra* note 16, at 9.

[40] *Id.*

development of less developed countries.[41] International financial institutions like the World Bank were also set up with the specific purpose of encouraging "the development of productive facilities and resources in less developed countries."[42]

In light of these documents, some argue the entitlement to international development assistance:

> has become integrated in the thinking and practice of States on both sides of the process, because they all deem it right and they deem it obligatory; it has effectively passed into the reality of international custom and forms part and parcel of customary international practice which constitutes one of the sources of international law.[43]

As a result of the consistent and widespread response to the special problems of developing countries, some suggest customary international law already recognizes developing countries as a special category of subjects.[44] The merits of these claims, as well as of the principle of entitlement of developing countries to need-based development assistance, are discussed below.

IV. EVALUATION OF THE EVIDENCE

Having outlined the normative content of international development law, this section analyzes the probative value of the previously mentioned sources. It establishes that the sources of international development law are *in pari materia* with the traditional sources of international law, as stipulated in article 38 of the I.C.J. statute. International develoment law is also derived from extra-legal, albeit equally valid, sources of contemporary international law.

A. *International Conventions and Instruments*

As mentioned previously, the normative content of international development law is derived in large measure from the UN Charter.

---

[41] Agreement of the International Development Association (IDA), Jan. 26, 1960, 11 U.S.T. 224, T.I.A.S. No. 4607, 394 U.N.T.S. 221.

[42] Agreement of the International Bank for Reconstruction and Development (I.B.R.D.) Dec. 27, 1945, art. 1, para. 1, 16 U.S.T. 1942, 1943, T.I.A.S. No. 5929, at 2; U.N.T.S. 134.

[43] HAGUE WORKSHOP 1979, *supra* note 32, at 97.

[44] *See e.g.*, Verwey, *The Recognition of the Developing Countreis As Special Subjects of International law Beyond the Sphere of United Nations Resolutions*, *id.*, at 372; *cf.* Mestdagh, *The Right to Development*, 28 NETH. INT'L REV. 30, 36-37 (1981) (arguing against recognition of developing countries as a special category of subjects in international law, since that would entail "creating not only two kinds of subjects of the law, but also two kinds of law.")

Some argue, however, these provisions of the Charter do not create any legal obligations on the part of member states, and since they are formulated in general non-specific wording, they are "meaningless and redundant."[45] This argument has a very superficial theoretical appeal, however, article 56 of the Charter clearly obligates a state to do *something* towards the achievement of the purposes set forth in article 55. This implies a right to do *nothing* does not exist.[46] A teleological interpretation of the Charter requires that its provisions be regarded as legally binding on member states, particularly in light of Charter provisions that "express clearly the obligations of all members. . . . [W]hile the provisions are general, nevertheless they have the force of postive international law and create basic duties."[47] Political and juridical organs of the UN have also interpreted the provisions of articles 55 and 56 as constituting legal obligations.[48] The preferable view, therefore, is that these Charter provisions establish firm commitments in the form of a binding treaty obligation.[49]

This conclusion fails to solve the problem of obligation because the UN Charter does not specify in detail what kind of action the member states are expected to take. Article 13(1) of the Charter, however, calls upon the General Assembly to "initiate studies and make recommendations for the purpose of: a) . . . encouraging the progressive development of international law and its codification." Thus, several pertinent UN resolutions and declarations have clarified the substantive principles of international development law. The International Covenant on Economic, Social and Cultural Rights, for example, clearly requires:

> [E]ach State Party to the present Covenant [to undertake] steps, *indirectly and through international assistance and cooperation*

---

[45] H. KELSEN, THE LAW OF THE UNITED NATIONS 99 (1951) ("Art. 56 is one of the most obscure provisions of the Charter," [and] does not impose any obligation upon the members. . . . Legally, article 56 is meaningless and redundant.")

[46] Verwey, *supra* note 4, at 21. To be sure, the claims of the developing countries are simply for the operation of law as in certain constitutional systems by way of affirmative action and reverse discrimination to secure equal opportunity.

[47] Sohn, *The Human Rights Law of the Charter,* 12 TEX. INT'L L.J. 131 (1977). In support of this view, see also L. GOODRICH, J. HAMBRO & A. SIMONS, CHARTER OF THE UNITED NATIONS 370-82 (1969).

[48] I. BROWNLIE, PRINCIPLES OF PUBLIC INTERNATIONAL LAW 553 (1973).

[49] Some textwriters have insisted that the U.N. Charter should be regarded as a Constitution or Charter, rather than a treaty. For our purposes here, however, by whatever designation the Charter is referred to, this does not detract from the legal force of its provisions.

> especially economic and technical, *to the maximum of its available resources,* with a view to achieving progressively the full realization of the rights recognized in the present Covenant *by all appropriate means* including in particular the adoption of legislative measures.[50]

At least 70 states are party to this Covenant, and their treaty obligation therefore imposes a legal duty[51] on them. This is consistent with the fundamental precept of international law that agreements are binding on the parties and must be performed by them in good faith (*pacta sunt servanda*). The principle has been so universally applied that it suffices merely to state it.[52]

---

[50] Annex to G.A. Res. 2200, 21 U.N. GAOR Supp. (No. 16) at 49, U.N. Doc. A/6316, (1966) (emphasis added).

Admittedly the Covenant is somewhat nebulous concerning the exact nature of the obligations it seeks to create. For example, it raises the question of what a country's *maximum available resources* are. Does it mean the United States, for instance, in signing the Covenant, was cognizant of the possibility of subjecting its defense budget or allocation of its domestic resources to third party review? The question, thus framed, must be answered in the negative. The Covenant also leaves unanswered what are *all appropriate means.*

[51] The legal duty may exist notwithstanding the lack of specificity of the kind of obligation involved. Broad generalization and imprecise formulation, as in this Covenant are often considered too indefinite to support the intention of creating legal obligations. This, however, is not a hard and fast rule. The legal implications of the UN Charter, for example, together with other constitutional instruments, though formulated in broad general terms, have not been seriously disputed and are generally considered binding. *See* Chowdhury, *Legal Status of the Charter of Economic Rights and Duties of States,* in LEGAL ASPECTS OF THE NEW INTERNATIONAL ECONOMIC ORDER 79, 81 (Hossain, ed. 1980).

Under Article 18 of the Vienna Convention on the Law of Treaties, a State is obliged to refrain from acts which would defeat the object and purpose of a treaty it has signed, even if the treaty is not yet in force. In deciding the exact nature of the legal obligations devolving on states, courts should therefore consider the object and purpose of the Covenant which, *ex hyposthesi,* is the promotion of international development. The domestic law analogue to this interpretation of legal obligation is what the French refer to as "*obligations de resultat,*" rather than mere "*obligations de moyen*"—i.e., obligations which guarantee the attainment of certain results, so that the mere fact of the non-materialization of the result constitutes a violation of the obligation, rather than an obligation of mere performance which leaves discretion to the subject on whom the duty is imposed. The ICSID award of Klockner v. Cameroon, 1 J. INT'L ARB. 145 (1984), elaborated on this concept of "obligation of result." The difficulty with this argument, however, is that the degree to which the desired result will be attained rests significantly more with the developing countries themselves, depending on how they utilize the development assistance granted them. Moreover, most of the developing countries simply do not have the means of guaranteeing the results for their citizens.

[52] On the "strategic nature" of this cardinal principle in the law of treaties,

The Declaration on Friendly Relations serves as a further example.[53] This authoritative declaration was unanimously adopted with the full participation and consent of all the member states.[54] In effect, the consensus on its adoption[55] conforms to the discernible "trend from consent to consensus as the basis of international legal obligations."[56]

The legal status of international development law is contingent on the significance attached to UN resolutions and declarations.[57]

---

see T. ELIAS, NEW HORIZONS IN INTERNATIONAL LAW 44 (1979). The Covenant on Economic, Social and Cultural Rights adds that the international cooperation is based on free consent. *See* Annex to G.A. Res. 2200 *supra* note 50, at art. 11, para. 1. As later discussed, however, this free consent has been abundantly manifested in the practice of states.

[53] *See supra,* note 21. See also the Universal Declaration on Human Rights, which "has passed into the mainstream of contemporary international law guiding national as well as international constitutions and action." *See* T. ELIAS, *supra* note 20, at 214. The Declaration is now regarded as a part of the "law of the United Nations." I. BROWNLIE, BASIC DOCUMENTS ON HUMAN RIGHTS 21 (1981).

[54] *See* Declaration on Principles of International law Concerning Friendly Relations and Co-operation Among States in Accordance with the Charter of the United Nations, G.A. Res. 2625, 25 U.N. GAOR Supp. 28, U.N. Doc. A/8028, at 21 (1970), *reprinted in*, BASIC DOCUMENTS SUPPLEMENT TO INTERNATIONAL LAW CASES AND MATERIALS 45 (1980).

Perhaps the obligation to grant assistance arises out of the system of the UN itself. The UN could assert a claim on behalf of the developing countries, against developed countries, for international development assistance. The developed countries could meet this obligation bilaterally as well as unilaterally.

[55] The question as to what substantive content of the declaration brought about this consensus is answered by a perusal of the declaration. It specifically mentions, among others, the principle that states shall fulfill in good faith the obligations assumed by them in accordance with the Charter and that all States have a duty to cooperate. Thus, if the United States refused to pay its share of UN assessment which would otherwise have been used to channel aid to the third world, it could plausibly be argued that the United States had not acted in good faith nor adhered to the duty to cooperate for international welfare. Admittedly, a difficult question remains concerning the exact standards or criteria used in assessing whether countries adhere to this obligation. It is suggested that a purposive and contextual interpretation on a case-by-case basis would illuminate the decision-making process.

[56] Falk, *On the Quasi-Legislative Competence of the General Assembly,* 60 AM. J. INT'L L. 782, 785 (1966).

The United States Supreme Court also relied on the notion of consensus in assessing the reality of an international legal obligation. In Banco Nationale de Cuba v. Sabbatino, 376 U.S. 398 (1964), the Court held that international law rules imposing a duty upon an expropriating government to pay an alien "prompt, adequate and effective" compensation were no longer supported by a consensus of sovereign states, and therefore the validity of those rules were so ambiguous as to make them inapplicable to the case.

[57] This conclusion is a result of the bulk of the *corpus* of international law incorporated and codified primarily in Assembly resolutions and declarations.

Several respected textwriters take the view that these resolutions and declarations do not have any legally binding force.[58] Admittedly, such resolutions are not a formal source of law within the formulation of article 38(1) of the Statute of the I.C.J. Under the UN Charter, the Assembly does not have the legal competence to legislate or to adopt legally binding decisions except those regarding certain organizational matters such as regulations for the Secretariat and other procedural rules. There is indeed a vast amount of literature on this age-old question.[59] A review of such literature is, however, beyond the scope of this article. Despite their formally non-binding character "even within the conservative framework of article 38 of the statute, legal effect may be given to the collective pronouncements of the General Assembly."[60] Indeed in a sense, these resolutions reflect state practice.[61] State practice, as is generally known, is identical with custom, which undoubtedly plays an important role within the framework of the UN.[62] For this discussion, it is instructive to note the former President of the I.C.J. has recognized three of the declarations giving substantive content to international development law as examples of law-making resolutions and declarations of the General Assembly.[63]

---

[58] *See e.g.,* Jenks, *The Scope of International Law,* 31 BRIT. Y.B. INT'L L. 1 (1954); Onu, *Professor Falk on the Quasi-Legislative Competence of the General Assembly,* 64 AM. J. INT'L L. 349-55 (1970); Fitzmaurice, *The Law and Procedure of the International court of Justice 1951-54; Questions of Jurisdiction, Competence and Procedure* 34 BRIT. Y.B. INT'L L. 1 (1958).

[59] *See generally,* III O. SCHACHTER, INTERNATIONAL LAW IN THEORY AND PRACTICE (1985); R. HIGGINS, THE DEVELOPMENT OF INTERNATIONAL LAW THROUGH THE POLITICAL ORGANS OF THE UNITED NATIONS (1963); ASAMOAH, THE LEGAL SIGNIFICANCE OF THE DECLARATIONS OF THE GENERAL ASSEMBLY OF THE UNITED NATIONS (1966); Jennings, *Recent Developments in the International Law Commission: Its Relation to Sources of International Law* 13 INT'L & COMP. L. Q. 385 (1964).

[60] Schachter, *supra* note 16, at 5. General Assembly resolutions have had a formative influence on the development of international law, and are now regarded as expressions of common interest and the "general will" of the international community. O. SCHACHTER, *supra* note 59, at 111.

[61] R. HIGGINS, *supra* note 59, at 2-5. "International custom is to be deduced from the practice of states, which includes their international dealings as manifested by their diplomatic actions and public pronouncements . . . .[T]he body of resolutions as a whole, taken as indications of a general customary law, undoubtedly provide a rich source of evidence." *Id.*

[62] For a long-standing debate on a legitimate interpretation of state practice or custom, see Akehurst, *Custom as a Source of International Law,* 47 BRIT. Y.B. INT'L L. 1 (1974-75), and D'Amato, *The Concept of Human Rights in International Law,* 82 COLUM. L. REV. 1110 (1982).

[63] These three declarations are:

The numerous resolutions and authoritative declarations of the UN and other international conventions adopted by the world community clarify and elaborate principles of international law. These developments have given rise to rules of law which are in a stage of approximation to customary international law.

B. International Custom

Customary practice is a dependable guide for ascertaining the continuing scope and meaning of commitments reduced to writing in treaties and international agreements, and "[since] it is based upon collaborative behavior, it is most likely to be representative of the common interests of the community."[64] The creation of international development law came about in large part through the process of claims and counter-claims made by states. As a matter of daily practice, international law is largely concerned with claims, "but the claims themselves, although they may articulate a legal norm, cannot constitute the material component of custom."[65] It thus remains to be seen whether the claims are manifested in the actual practice of states.

The practice of providing development assistance to developing countries through a program known as Official Development Assistance[66] points to the recognition of the substantive inequality

---

1. Resolution on the Charter of Economic Rights and Duties of States;
2. Declaration on Principles of International Law Concerning Friendly Relations and Cooperation Among States;
3. The United Nations Convenant on Economic, Social and Cultural Rights.

See I. ELIAS, *supra* note 20, at 213-14.

[64] Raman, *Toward a General Theory of International Customary Law,* in TOWARD WORLD ORDER AND HUMAN DIGNITY 365, 366 (Reisman & Weston eds. 1976).

[65] A. D'AMATO, THE CONCEPT OF CUSTOM IN INTERNATIONAL LAW (1971), *part thereof reprinted in* INTERNATIONAL LAW AND WORLD ORDER 42, 44 (1980).

[66] Development assistance is one of the primary means through which capital is sent to the developing countries. It represents approximately a third of all external capital receipts by developing countries. ORGANIZATON FOR ECONOMIC COOPERATION AND DEVELOPMENT, DEVELOPMENT COOPERATION; EFFORTS AND POLICIES OF THE MEMBERS OF THE DEVELOPMENT ASSISTANCE COMMITTEE, 1982 OECO REVIEW, 51, 53 (1982).

Development assistance, which is intended to be a means for poorer countries to better their quality of life, has often failed to achieve its basic goals because of serious environmental and social disruption caused by intended and unintended effects of these activities. *See* Muldoon, *The International Law of Ecodevelopment; Emerging Norms for Development Assistance Agencies,* 22 TEX. INT'L L.J. 1, 2 (1987).

among states. The Generalized Preference System (GPS), under which developed countries grant preferential and non-reciprocal treatment for developing countries, is also generally followed. Since March 1972, UNCTAD, in collaboration with UNDP, has provided technical cooperation on the GPS adopted by UNCTAD in 1970. This preferential tariff system provides advantages to developing countries by enabling qualified products to enter markets of preference giving countries at reduced or totally eliminated most favored nation rates of duty. The GPS is designed to raise the levels of developing countries' foreign exchange earnings, rates of industrialization, and levels of economic development.[67]

Another example is the Lome Conventions establishing a compensatory financing machinery called STABEX.[68] STABEX provides the African, Caribbean and Pacific (ACP) States with the right to be compensated by the European Community for shortfalls in export earnings from specified primary products, under certain circumstances, and up to certain limits. The importance of these treaties is clear, since "they obligate a large number of states to concrete NIEO-relevant conduct; the obligations are both firm and tangible."[69]

State Practice shows that the differential treatment of developing countries is recognized and accepted by the international community and is applied by the developed countries in their relations with developing countries. Some object, however, that this treatment does not establish international custom. The developed states may have several motives for granting development assistance but do not act out of a legal conviction. In addition, it is argued, the lack of *opinio juris*[70] detracts from its essence as custom. The difficulty

---

[67] UNCTAD BULLETIN No. 230, at 14 (March 1987).

[68] The EEC and the ACP States have entered into three Lome Conventions. Lome I entered into force in 1975 *reprinted in* 14 I.L.M. 595-642 (1975); followed by Lome II in 1980 *reprinted in* 19 I.L.M. 341-77 (1980) and Lome III in 1985 *reprinted in* 24 I.L.M. 571-642 (1985).

[69] Gamble & Frankowska, *International Law's Response to The New International Economic Order: An Overview,* 9 B. C. INT'L & COMP. L. REV. 257, 274 (1986).

For detailed accounts of State Practice see Verwey, *The Principle of Preferential Treatment for Developing Countries,* 23 INDIAN. J. INT'L L. 343 (1983); Perrott, *EEC Attitudes and Responses to The New International Economic Order,* 3 ST. LOUIS U. PUB. L. F. 115 (1984).

[70] Though some legal commentators have minimized the importance of *opinio juris,* the World Court has categorically insisted upon this requirement of a psychological element. *See, e.g.,* The Lotus Case, 1927 P.C.I.J. (Ser. A) No. 9, at 28; North Sea Continental Shelf Cases, 1969 I.C.J. 3, at para. 77.

with the *opinio juris* requirement is that the first States to adopt a new practice are regarded as acting on the basis that the practice is obligatory before it has become obligatory.[71] Additionally, "subjectivities are only ascertainable to an onlooker through overt behavior and one necessarily relies on conduct to infer the perception of others."[72] State practice on the matter is specific; it has been constant and consistent, so that what started as a mere habit has gradually but inevitably hardened into a general practice based on the conviction that it is required.[73]

C. Other Traditional and Non-Traditional Arguments for International Development Law

Some argue a moral duty of reparation devolves upon the developed countries because underdevelopment is basically the sequel of colonial domination.[74] As a result, documents like the Declaration on the Establishment of a New International Economic Order posit "the right of all states, territories and peoples under foreign occupation, alien and colonial domination to restitution and full com-

---

[71] Kelsen, for example, accepts *opinio juris* in theory, but observes that it can only be inferred from conduct. Thus, the conduct, and not the state of mind, is legally decisive. H. KELSEN, PRINCIPLES OF INTERNATIONAL LAW 564 (1966).

[72] *Id.; cf.* Schachter, *Towards a Theory of International Obligation*, 8 VA. J. INT'L L. 300, 313 (1968) ("But it would be misleading to conclude that this implied the elimination of a psychological test. It is one thing to use conduct as an indicator of *opinio juris*; it is another - and quite a different process - to evaluate conduct independently of *opinio juris*".)

[73] Even a constant, consistent, and uniform nature of State Practice does not necessarily establish custom. This is particularly true since States like the United States, although they give development assistance and the like, have consistently denied that they are under a legal obligation to do so. Specific practice, however, could lead one to infer a certain degree of *opinio juris*. It could be argued that the developed countries involved grant development assistance because they deem it right to do so. This may not necessarily imply *opinio juris*, but it does not detract from the psychological element involved. *See also*, O. SCHACHTER, SHARING THE WORLD'S RESOURCES 8 (1977). Schacter states:

> [W]hat is striking is not so much its espousal by the large majority of poor and handicapped countries but that the governments on the other side, to whom the demands for resources are addressed, have also by and large agreed that need is a legitimate and sufficient ground for preferential distribution. This agreement is evidenced not only by their concurrence in many international resolutions and by their own policy statements, but also, more convincingly, by a continuing series of actions to grant assistance and preferences to those countries in need.

Id.

[74] *See Secretary General's Report, supra* note 10.

pensation for . . . exploitation and depletion."[75] This proposed reasoning, however, is not in accordance with State Practice. To so argue would be to argue that developed countries which were not former colonial masters would not be under a duty to grant any development assistance.[76] The developed countries do not grant assistance because they need to account for colonial exploitation. Additionally, in practice developed countries do not limit development assistance exclusively to former colonies. The constitutive documents, referred to previously, mention the duty of co-operation for the welfare of *all* nations not just for that of former colonies.

Other commentators suggest charity may be one of the reasons why the developed countries are under an obligation to grant developing countries development assistance. Charity, however, denotes an element of volition or generosity rather than a compulsion to act. The pejorative connotations attached to the word charity are obvious. Furthermore, developing countries themselves might be reluctant to accept assistance on that basis.[77]

Principles of equity and justice are more solid bases for international development law.[78] Recent trends in world social process[79] suggest that principles of equity and justice are increasingly invoked in international law. The linkage of justice and the development process came about when the UN General Assembly stressed that global economic development should be established "on the basis

---

[75] *See Declaration, supra* note 22, at para. 4(f).

[76] It could, however, be plausibly argued that countries like the United States even if not colonial masters, benefitted immensely from the system of colonization through the resources of their allies and other dependent territories. According to this argument, the developed countries owe a duty to the developing countries. This duty is a result of the system of colonization and its impact.

[77] *See* HAGUE WORKSHOP 1979, *supra* note 32, at 98.

[78] Admittedly, these are not traditional sources of law in the I.C.J. statute, which is generally accepted as constituting a list of the sources of international law. *See* M. AKEHURST, A MODERN INTRODUCTION TO INTERNATIONAL LAW 4 (1984). The argument could however be made that "equity" and "justice" are "general principles of law" recognized by civilized nations. In addition, paragraph 2 of article 38 permits the I.C.J. to decide a case *ex aequo et bono* if the parties agree thereto. And in any case, there are other sources which are not easily discoverable in the text of article 38. *See* Schachter, *supra* note 72, 300-322 (1968).

[79] "World social process" is a compendious term used to indicate that the expanding circles of interaction among men extend to the remotest inhabitants of the globe (i.e. world), and that the active participants of the interaction (i.e. process) are living beings (i.e. social). *See* M. MCDOUGAL & ASSOCIATES, STUDIES IN WORLD PUBLIC ORDER 10 (1987).

of justice, equality and mutual benefit."[80] The notion of justice elevates the satisfaction of the developing countries' needs to that of an entitlement, thus transforming the relationship between donor and recipient into one of "mutual rights and responsibilities."[81]

The need for equity in international law is not derived exclusively from moral idealism. In order to remain effective, international law must change to conform to the sociological structure of the international community. The interdependence of developed and developing countries makes the economic well being of each nation a matter of concern for all. The emergence of international development law should therefore be regarded as a trend in the mutual interests of the North as well as the South.[82] The increasing reliance of the North on the South for trade and resources, and the concern surrounding an already precarious international economic order, exacerbated by the worsening problems of the developing countries, reflects these interests.

The law not only reflects the prevailing state of affairs, it also serves as an instrument for achieving what is required.[83] Regardless of the criteria used to ascertain international law the result must reflect the contemporary expectations of the majority of the community. As long as it seeks to set legal standards, international law must reflect a consensus of the values and opinions of an inclusive community. This naturally leads to considerations of law and equity in the relations between states.

The *Anglo-Norwegian Fisheries* case[84] elaborated on the importance of justice and equity. In this case, the I.C.J. regarded the

---

[80] *Preparation for an Internaitonal Development Strategy for the Third United Nations Development Decade,* G.A. Res. 33/193, U.N. GAOR Supp. (No. 45) at 121, U.N. Doc. A/33/45 (1979). The terms "justice" and "equality" are not necessarily coterminous. Equality is defined as "the condition of possessing substantially the same rights, privileges and immunities, and being liable to substantially the same duties." BLACK'S LAW DICTIONARY, 481 (5th ed. 1984). This is certainly a far cry from the kind of equity or justice being sought by international development law. The concept of "mutual benefit" is also difficult to understand in this context, in light of claims for almost exclusive benefits to the developing countries. It can however be understood in the sense that the attainment of a new international economic order would be to the mutual benefit of all parties involved.

[81] O. SCHACHTER, *supra* note 73, at 9 (1977).

[82] *See* Lachs, *supra* note 26, at 95 ("The enlightened long-term self-interest of the developed countries lies in the reduction of this material gap between 'North' and 'South'.")

[83] M. BULAJIC, *supra* note 2, at 43.

[84] Fisheries Case (U.K. v. Norway), 1951 I.C.J. 8 (Dec. 18, 1951).

economic interests and geographic position of Norway as "very distinctive," thus necessitating special treatment, stating "such a coast, viewed as a whole calls for the application of a different method. Nor can one characterize as exceptions to the rule the very many derogations which would be necessitated by such a rugged coast. The rule would disappear under the exceptions."[85] The court concluded the method of straight baselines established in the Norwegian system, although contrary to the accepted standard at the time, "was imposed by the peculiar geography of the Norwegian coast."[86] The case suggests that international law can, and indeed *must* be used to rectify inherent inequalities between states.[87] Since some of the peculiar problems of the developing countries are the result of nature's work, some argue that it is not for international law to change geography or "completely refashion nature."[88] The converse, however, is equally true; it certainly is not the function of international law to re-emphasize or exacerbate the inequality already existing. International development law seeks to mitigate or rectify existing inequalities, and this is a compelling reason why it should be given juridical status.[89]

Historically, international judicial opinion employed criteria such as a sense of rightness, necessity, reason, natural law, humanitarian values and the will of the international community.[90] Thus, the

---

[85] *Id.* at 128-29.

[86] *Id.* at 139.

[87] For a critique of this position see Waldock, *The Anglo-Norwegian Fisheries Cases,* 28 BRIT. Y.B. INT'L L. 114 (1951).

[88] Concerning The Continental Shelf (Libya & Malta), 1985 I.C.J. 36 (July 27, 1984).

[89] *See also* Lachs, *supra* note 26, at 94-95 (arguing that law can be an important tool in assisting poorer people raise their standard of living, in preventing the rich from becoming richer at the expense of the poor, and in serving as an instrument of progress and for the betterment of international relations).

[90] *See e.g.* Concerning Continental Shelf (Libya v. Malta), 1985 I.C.J. 4 (July 27, 1984) ("the justice of which equity is an emanation, is not abstract justice but justice according to the rule of law . . . even though it looks with particularity to the peculiar circumstances of an instant case, it looks beyond it to principles of more general application"); South West Africa Cases, 1966 I.C.J. 250-324 (Tanaka, J. Dissenting) (finding the rule against apartheid constituted a general principle of law, not necessarily within the formulation of article 38(1) of the I.C.J. statute, but for the simple reason that it was a *jus naturale,* "valid through all kinds of human societies", and derived from the concept of "man as a person."); Anglo Norwegian Fisheries Case, 1969 I.C.J. 49 (although all states are equal before the law and are entitled to equal treatment, "equity does not necessarily imply equality."); Reservations to the Conventions on the Prevention and Punishment of the Crime of Genocide, Advisory opinion, 1951 I.C.J. 15 (application of "humanitarian" values.)

moral and philosophical underpinnings of international development law are not at variance with the case law. For example, in *Concerning the Continental Shelf (Tunisia v. Libya)*,[91] the court stressed that in the application of equitable principles, the fairness of the result was more important than the principle to be applied in reaching that result. The court stated:

> The result of the application of equitable principles must be equitable. This terminology, which is generally used, is not entirely satisfactory because it employs the term equitable to characterize both the result to be achieved and the means to be applied to reach the result. It is, however, the result which is predominant; the principles are subordinate to the goal. The equitableness of a principle must be assessed in the light of its usefulness for the purpose of arriving at an equitable result. *It is not every such principle which is in itself equitable: it may acquire this quality by reference to the equitableness of the solution.*[92]

Applying this statement to the field of international development law suggests the principles discussed above derive their legal validity from the equitableness of the solution they seek to obtain. It further suggests developing countries are entitled to claim international development assistance as of right if that would result in a more equitable international system. The claims being made for a new international economic order have therefore received tacit judicial recognition.[93]

Emerging international development law is increasingly receiving attention from jurists. Since the writings of publicists are a source

---

[91] Concerning the Continental Shelf (Tunisia v. Libya), 1982 I.C.J. 1 (Feb. 24).

[92] *Id.* at para. 70 (emphasis added). Although this statement was used in relation to applicable principles and rules for the delimitation of the Continental Shelf area appertaining to Libya and Tunisia, it is a fair inference that the invocation of equitable principles would apply *a fortiori* to the area of international development law.

[93] Note that several international instruments expressly refer to equity. Article 59 of the 1982 Law of the Sea Convention, for example, states that conflicts between the interests of the Coastal State and any other State in the exclusive economic zone "should be resolved on the basis of equity and in the light of all the relevant circumstances, taking into account the respective importance of the interests involved to the parties as well as to the international community as a whole." United Nations Convention on the Law of the Sea, Dec. 10, 1982; *see also* The Agreement Governing the Activities of States on the Moon and Other Celestial Bodies, Dec. 5, 1979, G.A. Res. 2320, U.N. Doc. A/Res/34/68 at art. 11, para. 7; Vienna Convention on the Law of Treaties, U.N. Doc. A/CONF. 39/27 (1969) at art. 44, para. 3(c), *reprinted in* 63 Am. J. Int'l L. 875 (1969).

of international law, the more the authorities refer to the legal validity of international development law, the more authoritative the concept will be. The desirability of this conclusion is borne out by the significance of the subject.

V. SIGNIFICANCE AND USEFULNESS OF INTERNATIONAL DEVELOPMENT LAW

International development law is important for a number of reasons. The first is the extent to which it will enhance the aspirations of developing countries which form the bulk of the international community. The developing countries view international law suspiciously because the *status quo* engendered within its application is to their disadvantage.[94] International development law responds to the major goal of eliminating existing inequalities in international economic relations and therefore serves to make international law more relevant to developing countries benefiting the international community at large.

The implications for international peace and security resulting from a recognition of international development law are obvious. International peace and security are related to, and cannot exist independently of, international development. Thus, in Resolution 3176 (XXVIII), the General Assembly clearly stated that international peace and security are necessary conditions for the social and economic progress of all countries.[95] Economic inequality is a destabilizing factor in the orderly conduct of inter-state relations. There is no dispute that Third World countries have frequently violated

---

[94] See generally I. ELIAS, AFRICA AND THE DEVELOPMENT OF INTERNATIONAL LAW (1972); Anand, *Attitude of the Afro-Asian States Towards Certain Problems of International Law,* 15 INT'L & COMP. L. Q. 55 (1966).

[95] It is noteworthy that the maintenance of peace, the achievement of development and the promotion of respect for human rights are the central objectives of the UN, as stated in the charter. The relationship between peace and security, on the one hand, and development, on the other hand, is also manifest in the effect that disarmament has on development. In the Draft Declaration on the Right to Development, experts from France and the Netherlands stressed that "there exists a close relationship between disarmament and development; that progress in the field of disarmament would considerably promote progress in the field of development." *Question of the Realization in all Countries of the Economic Social, and Cultural Rights Contained in the Universal Declaration of Human Rights, and Study of Special Problems which the Developing Countries Face in Their Efforts to Achieve these Rights.* U.N. Doc. E/CN.4/1985/11, Annex III, at 1.

existing rules of international law[96] out of a desire to rectify what they regard as economic inequities in the international system. Studies also conclusively establish that problems of growing economic crises frequently lead to the toppling of moderate or democratically elected regimes by radical, and often dictatorial regimes.[97] The continuation of this trend is certainly not conducive to the maintenance of a minimum world order. Thus, international development law which aims at improving the economic situation in the Third World could also serve to enhance the maintenance of world order.

The ultimate purpose of development is to lay the basis for realizing human dignity. Recent trends in world social process point out an increased emphasis on the concept of basic human dignity. This concern for the advancement of human rights is here to stay, out of necessity as well as idealism. Since international development law is aimed, *inter alia,* at upholding the concept of human dignity it is therefore a firm indication of its importance and usefulness as a normative order.[98]

VI. Appraisal and Conclusion

International development law is an emerging branch of international law. It represents the beginning of a conscious effort to face the inescapable fact of global interdependence.[99]

---

[96] Noteworthy examples are expropriation of alien property without prompt, adequate and effective compensation; the unilateral rescheduling or declaration of an inability to pay debts as a result of unfavorable balance of payments, etc.

[97] There is also a direct correlation between the level of poverty and the incidence of violence in any particular society. *See also, Secretary General's Report, supra* note 10, at 76 (there can be no lasting peace if populations are beset by poverty or suffering from malnutrition and sickness,or there is continued inequality among nations and a "persistence of international injustice in regard to the distribution of resources.")

[98] Also instructive is a proposal by the expert from the United States, on the Draft Declaration on the Right to Development, E/CN.4/1985/11, Annex VI, at 2 ("efforts to promote and protect human rights at the international level should be accompanied by efforts to establish a new international economic order.")

[99] The former Vice-President of the World Bank, William Clark, in his book *Cataclysm — The North-South Conflict of 1987*, argues about aspects of interdependence other than the familiar trading linkages. He shows that technological progress has made modern societies extremely vulnerable, and that militant groups in any part of the world can command sufficient know-how to penetrate and disorganize complex systems in a way that can wreak massive disruption in other parts. It is also the thesis of his book, that ecological damage can spill over national boundaries and endanger global systems that support life everywhere. These are very instructive statements, particularly when they emanate from a former Vice-President of the World Bank. *See* W. Clark, *Catalysm — The North-South Conflict of 1987* (1987).

This article has shown that the principles on which international development law is based are largely found in international treaties, UN resolutions and declarations, as well as in the practice of States. The relevant norms and principles are directly dependent on the character of the political and economic trends of development. This results from the dialectic relationship between the economic infrastructure of the international system and its legal superstructure.

International development law can make its mark only if its benefits are perceived as universal, and its costs do not exceed its benefits. It spite of the degree of sacrifice required of the developed countries, in the long run this sacrifice should inure to the benefit of the developed countries as well as the developing countries.

Effective adherence to principles of international development law will require sufficient political will and support nationally as well as internationally. The concept of State sovereignty, which seems to be *prima facie* in conflict with international development law, must be reviewed. States must accept restrictions on the exercise of their sovereign rights in external as well as internal economic policies.[100] This requires the implementation of more effective regulatory mechanisms by international development agencies and other actors in the international arena.

In conclusion, it must be stressed that concern for international development *is* necessary for the continued functioning of the international system. Questions pertaining to international development law will therefore remain the most intensely debated in the next decade and will produce discernible effects on the evolution of substantive rules of international law as well as on the international decision-making process.

[100] The developing countries, for example, would have to be accountable for the international development assistance they received.

[13]

The Third World Debt Crisis: Towards New International Standards for Contraction of Public Debt

By *Anthony Carty*

Introduction

The debt crisis of the developing countries gives rise to great concern about the stability not only of the international financial order but also of the international legal order. The debts, when contracted with private Western or other international banks have been in the form of legally binding agreements to which a regime of law is supposed to apply. This is usually New York or English law. However this system of law is purely private and national. The local courts have the responsibility to have regard to considerations of public policy exclusive to their own national interest.

Such a limited national legal horizon is inadequate where the executive authorities of that country, in particular the United States, are engaged in policies which have effects especially difficult for the developing countries, while being substantially advantageous, even if only indirectly, for the Western banks and public lending institutions. In practice it is recognised that the ›international‹ private law regimes are not even intended to regulate the types of difficulites which have arisen with respect to lending to developing countries since the late 1970s. Consequently banks have rarely resorted to national courts.

How is the international lawyer to respond to the numerous calls for the renegotiation and cancellation of third world debts? How is he to characterise an actual practice which appears frequently to involve abandonment of the specific terms of agreements once solemnly concluded? What is he to make of the declarations, increasingly in general international fora, that there is a need for a fundamental reform of international financial law?

In my view the international practice with respect to private bank loan agreements reflects the fact that they lack the guarantee of a public international legal order. Adjustments of agreements are purely ad hoc and do not reflect any clear statement of financial or legal principle. This is not specifically the responsibility of either of the parties, essentially private, to these agreements. They cannot be expected at the same time as they contract loan agreements, to conceive of a public international monetary order adequate to direct how they should respond to a rapidly changing international financial environment.

Yet how might a public international monetary legal order be constructed? The main focus of debate at the moment within the World Bank and IMF fora is apparently economic. In my view they involve a too narrow definition of social and political problems in pseudo-economic terms. In particular the demand of developing countries and ›progressive‹ Western circles for a substantial expansion of credit to the third world represent highly questionable ›economistic‹ assumptions about the possibility of simply spending one's way out of the crisis. At the same time calls for deflationary rigour on the part of the developing countries are based on economic arguments that leading Western countries are either not willing or not even able to apply to themselves.

The fundamental disagreements about world economic policy show the limited extent to which there exists the measure of political integration necessary to support a world public legal monetary order adequate to guarantee a framework for the conclusion of private international loan agreements. At this stage it is premature to conceive of a reform of the international monetary system in a form which could satisfy rhetorical demands for a just monetary order which might be shaped democratically by all those affected by it.

International society remains too horizontal in its structure. However this very horizontality allows one to appeal to a measure of fairness which ought to be implicit in the concept of the equality of states. The question should be asked whether any state should be expected to accept restrictions upon its contraction of public debt which are flagrantly disregarded by other states. It might be argued even more categorically that international private banks should not complain about disregard for their loans where they contracted them without heeding the necessity for a basis regulatory and democratic framework in the state to which they chose to lend. In other words a serious contribution which international lawyers could make at the present time to the alleviation of the dangers of international debt crises is to encourage the development of standards for the contraction of public debt, from whatever source, which would would be common to both developed and developing countries.

The Nature of the Third World Debt Crisis

In economic terms the third world debt situation can most likely be characterised as unusual and irrational. There was an overhang of capital in the 70s, coming mainly from the withdrawal of oil dollars from the international economic system. It was reabsorbed in developing countries without regard to whether it could eventually reproduce itself. As the World Bank remarks in its recent reports on Development and the Debt Service[1] the unusual features of this 70s lending, in terms of typical international loans, were the short five to eigth year maturity periods and the variable interest rates which applied to more than 55 % of loans.

It is known from the nature of the eurodollar market itself that the limits for the repayment of principal are usually at best medium term. This is a reflection of the sources of dollars for the market, themselves shourt term deposits. More importantly it is accepted

1 March 1986, Development and the Debt Service introduction to World Debt Tables 1985–86, ILM 1986, 454.

that interest rates were set to float 1 to 2 % above the libor rate. Such an interest rate clause itself is standard in refering to the libor rate a number of days before the commencement of the new interest period.[2]

It is perfectly clear that individual credit relationship were affected by the deficit financing policies of the main world economic power. The libor rate is no more than a reflection of the US prime rate. The money flowing to and from New York and London is acutely sensitive to any possible disparity of interest rates. So when the US attempted to maintain the value of its currency by greatly increasing the interest it was willing to pay on money deposited in the United States, this had to have an immediate impact upon the interest paid by the developing countries on their commercial loans.

It is too simplistic to say that the US endeavoured to bring anything approaching an unjust enrichment to the banks of its own country. The United States was under pressure in the late 1970s to restore the stability of its currency for the sake of world trade. At the same time the deficit spending of that country is seen as an essential part of the role it plays in spending the world out of recession. The United States can legitimately complain that it is bearing an unjust share of this burden and that the developing countries would suffer less if all developed countries proved equally willing to run the supposed risk of renewed inflation which is supposed to be implicit in the loosening of control over the money supply. Nonethless the triangular relationship implied by the monetary policy of the United States, i. e. loans concluded by private banks, whether American or European, in New York or London or else where,[3] brings into question the issue whether the loans are really simply the subject of a single national legal system, whatever the loan may itself stipulate.

This is a pattern of debt contraction which is unlikely to be repeated. It is well understood that many banks touted for borrowers and that developing countries diverted a large part of the money to meet current imports and even more unsound demands. It is realised that an essential part of the debt crisis is simply the freezing of future credit. The developing countries borrowed on the basis that they would be able to continue to do so. For one thing the length of the loans was so short that reborrowing simply represented an extension of amortization periods. Yet even more simply they expected to be able to reborrow in order to repay existing loans. While this might not make sound banking sense, neither did the original loans. The drying up of credits when the banks realised how unsound their original loans had been is the single most vital element in the debt crisis identified by the World Bank in its latest report.

Although there are about 900+ B$ involved, it is tempting for both banks and developing

2 For instance, ed. J.-B. Blaise, P. Kahn, Les Euro-Credits, Librairies Techniques, Paris 1981 1981, Annex 1, p. 690; also P. Sarcevic, Real Interest Rates and the Debt Problem, in Revue des droits des Affaires Internationales, no. 7, 1985, p. 859 at p. 866.

3 The major point stessed in Feb. 1986 at a meeting organised under the auspices of the new international economic order committee of the International Law association in a paper by P. Sarcevic, Two Approaches to the Debt Problem, to be published in ›Foreign‹ by D. C. Dicke, Fribourg University Press in summer 1986, see also article of Sarcevic cited in note 2.

countries to treat this period of lending as an abberation. For instance Nurrick points out that except in the case of Iran, bankers do not employ default clauses as a reason for prematuring a loan . . . The facility is inserted in agreements but not in the expectation that it will be used. In practice they are regarded primarily as a bargaining tool, if and when the borrower runs into difficulty. Nurrick still does not see such clauses, which can go so far as to envisage the mere possibility of default, as at all necessary to bring the borrower to the table with the lender.[4]

In fact the underlying rationale with the banks is purely economic and is set out, once again, by the World Bank. To reduce outstanding loans put the security of remaining claims into danger. The rescheduling has had to be on the basis that one might negotiate postponment of maturity payments. At the same time it was recognised that there was a basic need for the banks to decrease their exposure to developing countries. They have raised more home funds, sold off sovereign risk assets on secondary markets and written down some loans on their books. New loans conform to a more traditional style of lending with the average maturity extended beyond the 15 years achieved in 1984.[5]

Nonetheless at the present time the poorest part of the world is responsible for transfering capital to the richest. This is economically inefficent. The resources which remain to be developed in the Third World to not have the capital to activate them and hence makes themselves more able to continue to pay their debts. More immediately, the developing countries do not have the means to continue to pay, at previous levels, for the imports of developed countries. So the money necessary for expansion and circulation of resources cannot find its way to where it is needed. In other words it is widely appreciated that the institutional and financial abberations of 1970s lending cannot really be expected to fit into the international economy of the 1980s.

Loan Contracts in Private International Law

It is generally known that the law applicable to loan agreements is usually that of the UK or New York, with a much smaller number submitted to French or German law. What is much more controversial is the extent to which this guarantees the legal security of the loan. Nurrick points out that the primary intentions of this course are the usual ones for international contracts with developing countries, dissatisfaction with the technical quality of the local law and fear of the consequences of a change in local legislative policy amounting to a unilateral change of the contract.[6] However it has been argued earlier in this paper that such a reliance on a single national legal system does not take

4 L. Nurick, Issues in Negotiating International Loan Agreements with Transnational Banks, United Nations Centre on Transnational Corporations, UN Doc. no ST/CTC/48 New York 1983 section VI: Event of Default Clauses, paragraphs 77–78, 83.

5 See above note 1.

6 See Nurick, opt. cit., section X, Applicable Law and Jurisdiction, paragraph 96.

account of the triangular ›reality‹ of international financial business. I believe this is the context in which to consider the possible implications of an absence of specifically public law institutions, whether national or international, relating to international loans.

Is there an international legal monetary order to encompass the international monetary contracts? A legal order to regulate the context of a contract supposes above all that its terms are understood not simply in private law contractual language but in the light of the qualifications of conflicting external interests which are an integral part of any system of public law. Technically in terms of the private international law principle of the autonomy of the parties it is possible for them to choose New York law to apply to the contract. Yet it is questionable whether such a legal system can offer more than an overtly limited reaction to an issue such as the radical revaluation of the dollar. That is to say New York law would hold the parties to the exact terms of the contract, i. e. that the percentage of interest above the libor rate stated must be paid. The courts of a particular vitally interested country cannot go any further.

This appears to be clear from the recent New York case law on Costa Rican and Mexican loans In the Allied Bank Case[7] the US court accepted the applicability of the act of state doctrine, that it would not question the sovereign right of another state to respond to a serious financial crisis as it saw fit. It would simply not allow such a policy, e.g. the suspension of payments on a foreign debt in foreign with private international law rules on the law applicable to contracts the contract was sufficiently connected with the US. The Costa Rican banks had agreed to pay US dollars in New York. The principle attaching jurisdiction was very narrowly drawn. To escape US law the contract would have had to come to complete fruition within Costa Rican jurisdiction. It is a matter of US public policy, given that the US is an international banking centre, that ordinary principles of contract law be observed.

However one has to note that the court in the Allied Banks case clearly recognises and shows or illustrates a deep conflict of public policy amoung different jurisdictions. Clearly the court itself is applying only US private international law. At the same time it makes express reference to what is accepted practice in international financial circles at a point in time where a complete crisis, if it may be on the way, has not yet been reached. It supposes that international loan agreements are made in an environment of international lending practice which the court is entitled to take into account. Of course it relies entirely upon the US executive power for an exact interpretation of this environment, and a lawyer as experienced as Carreau considers the executive interpretation given in this case to be manifestly inaccurate:

> »...The Justice Department brief gave the following explanation of our government's support for the debt resolution procedure that operates through the auspices of the IMF. Guided by the IMF, this long established approach encourages the cooperative adjustment of international debt problems. The entire strategy is grounded in the understanding that, while parties may agree to renegotiate conditions

7 United States: Court of Appeals for the second circuit, No. 83-7714, March 18, 1985, in 1985 ILM 762.

of payment, the underlying obligation to pay nevertheless remain valid and enforceable. Costa Rica's attempted unilateral restructuring of private obligations, the United States contends, was inconsistent with this system of international cooperation and negotiation and thus inconsistent with United States policy . . .«[8]

In this particular case the vast majority of the banks had in fact already concluded mutually satisfactory renegotiations with Costa Rica and the court action concerned an initiative from a ›maverick‹ bank' engaged in a test case. Rather more striking are the remarks of Carreau, the leading French monetary law specialist, which make acutely clear the relative national interest involved in the judgement reached. In his view the court twisted both law and fact. In US law domicile of the debtor is usually the location of the debt. Furthermore, to treat the Costa Rican moratorium as a repudiation of the debt is pure misrepresentation. The lower court was more correct to treat it as a simple delay of payment and the IMF had recognised this procedure as valid under art. 8 of its Articles of Agreement.[9]

While US courts may be expected to continue to take account of what the US percieves to be its national interest, it appears no overstatement to say that the contract has to depend upon notions of what is generally accepted practice in international financial circles. This environment may well be in a state of crisis. Such a question is not posed in this context in terms of a model of economic justice. Rather the intention is to ask in purely scientific legal terms in what circumstances and how far the actors directly involved expect such a principle as pacta sunt servanda to be observed to the exclusion of other possible considerations.

It is recognised that developed country lawyers do not always resort to the rhetoric of pacta sunt servanda in attempting to upbraid the developing countries to keep their loan agreements. At the theoretical level, for instance, the Director of the Crédit Commercial de France in 1981 stressed in his discussion of the relationship between default on loans and state juridical orders, that

»... Les conventions d'euro-crédit constituent la charte des parties et en fait le fondement unique de leurs droits respectifs (banques participantes, emprunteurs, banque agent). Il est donc fondamental qu'elles soient aussi complètes que possible. L'esprit de solidarité au sein de la communauté bancaire internationale est l'un de ses biens les plus précieux. Il est la pierre angulaire de toute solution lorsque des difficultés surgissent . . .«[10]

In my view the significance of these remarks lies primarily in their apparent recognition that the bankers are very much ›on their own‹ and so need to provide for as many eventualities as possible themselves.

In the same vein Jacquemont insists that the choice of a particular national law is

8 Ibid, at p. 764.
9 D. Carreau, note on the Allied Bank Case in Journal de Droit International, 1986, pp. 124–5.
10 P. J. Monnory, Defaillance de L'Emprunteur et Ordres Etatiques, in Les EuroCrédits, opt cit. p. 568 at p. 592.

merely a first stage in the determination of the appropriate law, designed to exclude the arbitrary application of a completely irrelevant or unsuitable legal regime. The detailed professional practices which operate in the euro-dollar market frequently do not find any reflection in the legal system of any particular country. Many contracts explicitly accord the applicable law a purely subordinate role, indeed an obvious rendering of the principle of the autonomy of the parties. Yet in this case it is a reflection of the intensely technical and delicate nature of the issues and the need that they be regulated as far as possible by those directly engaged through negotiation. Clearly imperative rules of national law cannot be ignored. However a contract which refers to professional usages intends national law to play a subordinate role. In this context he asks the rhetorical question whether such usages should possibly include the notion of res sic stantibus.[11]

It is a small step further, in the light of the Allied Bank Case, to say that the professional usages will be considered by a court whether or not they are explicitly mentioned in the contract as a source of applicable law. Yet the usages themselves reflect a deficiency in the national legal systems with respect to effectives responses to their legal difficulties. At the same time the fact remains that no court can go against its own generally established concept of ›ordre public‹.

Analogies between the Private International Law of Loan Agreements and the Public International Law of Treaties: the Parallel Absence of a Public Order

International loan agreements suffer and enjoy advantages and weaknesses similar to those which affect international treaties in the particular sense that there is no impartial international institutional framework to resolve the difficulties of their exceptionally unstable environment. They must clearly be observed in good faith. Yet it is recognised that changes in circumstances may require the parties to renegotiate. The legal formula of the Vienna Convention (art. 62) is that where the basis on which the parties contracted has changed in an unforeseeable way and radically altered the obligations of the parties they must renegotiate. The fundamental structural weakness of public international law is that none of these terms have any definite meaning and there is no rigorous institutional mechanism to give authoritative interpretations.[12] It is a question of emphasis how one interprets this situation. Hardly anyone would dispute that it is most desirable that as far as possible the parties should endeavour to reach new agreements through negotiations. There is ample state practice where so much has been attempted. Equally one can point to diplomatic incidents where strong protests have followed apparently premature unilateral breakoff of negotiations and of the agreement. However it appears to me that

11 Jacquemont, Emission des Emprunts Euroobligatoires et la souveraineté des Etats, Bruxelles, 1975, pp. 179–182.

12 See the recent study by A. Vamvoukos, Termination of Treaties in International Law, Oxford University Press 1985; also a very similar approach taken in A. Toth ›The Doctrine of rebus sic stantibus in international law‹ Ph. D. thesis Exeter 1970; and A. Carty, ›The Decay of International law‹ 1986 Manchester, chapter 5.

practice with respect to treaties and even as well with respect to loan agreements provides no clear indication that, in the absence of agreement being reached on renegotiation, the debtor may not take the view that circumstances objectively merit a unilateral modification of the debt. There are no precise rules defining what is foreseeable, basic or having the effect of radically transforming obligation.

Vamvoukos discusses the two well known international instances concerning loan agreements which do not point in any particular direction. In the 1930s the French did not consider they had a legal right simply to repudiate their war debts towards the US. However they took the firm view that the cancellation of German war debts called for new arrangements, that France was legally justified in demanding wholescale revision of its debts. It suspended payments. The United States never accepted the principle that the debts were no longer repayable. However it acknowledged the existence of changed circumstances and accepted the necessity for rearrangements[13] In the Russian Indemnity Case the Permanent Court of Arbitration accepted the applicability of the slightly different principle of force majeure, but considered that it did not apply to the facts. Turkey alleged that it had difficulties in making payments to Russia. Yet the Tribunal noted that Turkey was at the same time able to obtain loans at favourable rates, redeem other loans and pay off a large part of its foreign debt. It was complaining about a comparatively small sum.[14]

All of this argument goes to show that the simple language of pacta sunt servanda and rebus sic stantibus has never been evolved sufficiently to consider the complicated issues arising out of the present debt crisis. The issues are clearly not the precise responsibility of either of the two series of parties. This is the foundation of the generally recognised duty to renegotiate something which neither side seems to be disputing. So it is not surprising to find that international bankers are acutely aware of the precarious financial position of both creditors and debtors.

The specific details of renegotiations are kept confidential. It appears, according to Prof. Hahn, that the parties are unwilling to devise at present any general principles for renegotiation, that they prefer to treat each case concretely. Repeated statements by developing countries that they are not responsible for a virtual inability to pay, that circumstances have changed dramatically etc, such strong language is almost never accompanied by any specific actions to undermine their agreements.

In my view instead of making very general rhetorical statements about the doctrines of pacta sunt servanda and rebus sic stantibus, both essentially private law contractual notions when used in the present context, one should recognise that an international public monetary order is lacking. It is clearly not felt by any of the parties most directly engaged that their fragile contractual relations should collapse. However it is not enough simply to say that a complete legal system covers their situation because they are under a

13 Vamvoukos, opt cit. pp. 95–97.

14 Ibid. p. 175; see Russian Indemnity Case, Permanent Court of Arbitration 1912, Hague Court Reports pp. 297–328.

legal duty do negotiate with one another in good faith. The international monetary order has to be matter of distinct regulation by states whose power is generally recognised as economically significant.

Macroeconomic Management of the Debt Crisis

The Spring 1986 Congressional (House of Representatives) Report,[15] the contemporaneous World Bank Report[16] and the Baker Plan[17] all suppose an essentially extra-juridical, macroeconomic approach to the debt problem. The first of these calls for a simple recognition that there is a long term unsustainability in recessionary austerity plans, usually seen as essential to the earning of foreign exchange to pay off debts, and the inevitability of some outright debt relief. More fundamentally the Congressional Report accepts the roll-over character of the short term debts and the inevitability of granting further loans. It appears difficult to persuade the private banks to take the lead. However the World bank itself is to be encouraged to do so, in undertaking co-financing with private banks, coordinating stabilisation plans with the IMF and making its own loans to stimulate economic expansion. Indeed the assumption is that without such measures the developing countries will probably default, given the economic forces at present arraigned against them.

The World Bank in turn stresses the intractable nature of the macroeconomic problems facing the developing countries and having a devastating effect on their ability to repay their loans. For instance there has been some progress on the issue of the effect of national interest rates on the interest paid on loans. The developed countries recognise here the direct and clear impact of their interest rates and trade protection policies on the developing countries debt problem. The policy of reducing the value of the dollar and lessening US interest rates has had the effect of bringing the six month libor rate down from 11.2 % in 1984 to 8.6 % in early 1986. This is progress even if not enough. However when the substantial beneficial effect is adjusted to take account of deterioration in developing countries terms of trade, expecially because of falling comodity prices, the outcome means a real interest rate equal to 10 %. Commodity prices are down 15 %. The recession in the Western economy is bringing the rate of growth down from 5 % to 3 %. So the conclusion of the World Bank analysis is that nothing short of more general expansion, which the US now considers should be undertaken primarily by Japan and West Germany, can alleviate the condition of the developing country debt. It is in this context that the World Bank further stresses Western acceptance of the need for an

15 US Congress House of Representations Committee's Subcommittee on International Development Institutions, March 1986, in 1986 ILM 439 et seq.

16 See note 1., The World Bank ›Development and the Debt Service‹.

17 Treasury News, Oct. 8, 1985 Statement of Secretary Baker before the IMF-World Bank Joint Annual Meeting.

expansion of transfer of capital on a medium term basis to stimulate economic growth through structural change rather than simply stabilisation, although strict surveillance from the IMF should remain.

What is at stake here is precisely the global economic planning and official acceptance of economic responsibility which in my view make up the substance of the insistance that an international contract must be effectively subjected to a system of law. However it appears that the minimum conditions for such a legal order are not present for the moment. For instance the proposals just discussed concerning money and efficiency raise basic questions of economic theory. The predominant Western theory at the moment is that of monetarism.

This appears to assume that the state is not competent to take grand economic decisions as to how capital can be effectively invested to develop resources. There is no clearly proven link between its capacity to release technological or physical potential and real market need and demand. Instead the financial system supported by the state should limit itself to ensuring that inflation is reduced by a tight control of the monetary supply. Then interest rates may come down so that the private investor can hope to obtain money at a price which is reasonable in terms of his capacity to obtain profit following upon investment.[18] Hence it is not surprising that West Germany, Japan and other developed countries are resisting the call for economic expansion on the ground that it will only prove to be inflationary.

While it is obvious that the individual is not compelled to borrow for the purposes of productive investment when money becomes cheap, it is clear, in the monetarist view, that the variables which eventually lead to the vital stage of satisfaction of market demand and consumption are too many for the state to hope to intervene successfully. It is in such a context that the interest rates have gone up and the developing countries have found themselves having to repay more than 40 B$ extra.[19] Given that their part in the international economic system is not perceived to be vital it is hard to imagine that any fundamental change could be made on their account.

So it is not surprising that discussion within the IMF framework about the possible parameters of global macroeconomic policy with respect to the debt crisis have not been very conclusive. There have been special reports by both the developed (Group of 10) and the developing (Group of 24) countries in the autumn of 1985. The two salient features of the latter Report are in my view that they call for a level of interstate coordination of macroeconomic policy which is inconceivable, and secondly, they admit, quite frankly, that they have no reason to believe that such cooperation would in any case have predictably beneficial consequences for them. Firstly in the view of the Group of 20 Art. IV surveillance should encompass multilateral negotiations about a mutually consistent set of objectives and policies amoung the major industrialised countries. This implies com-

18 For a concise summary of opposing contemporary views see K. Cole J. Cameron and C. Edwards, ›Why Economists Disagree: The Political Economy of Economics‹ Longmann, Essex, 1983.

19 See figures cited by Sarcevic in Two Approaches to the Debt Problem, note 3 above.

plementary use of monetary, fiscal and other policy instruments consistent with exchange rate stability and growth without inflation.[20] The debt crisis itself is seen primarily in terms of inadequate liquidity to match the ›real‹ need of developing countries for finance.[21]

Yet whether developing countries can match economic growth with a capacity to repay their existing debts depends upon a set of economic variables with respect to which considerable uncertainty exists. Industrial growth in the developed countries, stable exchange rates, restraint from protectionism, adequate measures of adjustment in developing countries, and their development of interest rates and the value of the dollar, are all relevant factors. It is easy to imagine that just one of these would evolve unfavourably and have a cumulative adverse effect on the others. The outcome would be to pose

> ›. . . the risk that for at least some debtors the situation would become unsustainable. Without clear signs of economic progress the governments of debtor countries would be faced with political and social pressures making it difficult for them to reconcile the objectives of restoring growth in their countries with the prospective payments of debt service . . .‹[22]

This is hardly a radical threat. Yet it is a highly controversial and purely technocratic-economistic analysis by the developing countries of the nature of their situation.

Criticism of a possibly salutory role for the IMF as an international monetary policeman runs up against much the same queries about the soundness or viability of world macroeconomic management. Something has been made of the increased role of the IMF in the most recent renegotiations of the loan agreements. The IMF has only been willing to play its police role in return for a willingness on the part of the international banks to roll over debt. Here is where the IMF has stepped in at least to some degree. It is definitely fullfilling the role of an international public monetary order.[23] The question remains whether it is competent to do so. In purely legal terme this issue is vital because there is no implication that the IMF would be legally responsible to the banks in the event that the developing countries failed to repay any of their present and to be contracted debts. The banks are relying upon the policing function implicit in the IMF insisting upon stabilization policies simply because in their view their prospects for repayment in the absence of such surveillance are even sleighter.

Yet controversy in economic theory comes back to hit the IMF's stabilisation policies in turn. Its record of success in the application of these policies to Latin American states in the last twenty years is proven to be completely indeterminate.[24] The reasons for this may

20 IMF Survey, Sept. 1985, Suppl. on Group of 24 Report paragraph 9 et seq.

21 Ibid, paragraphs 38–42.

22 Ibid, paragraph 146.

23 See for instance IMF, Occasional Paper, no. 25, Recent Multilateral Debt Restructuring with Official Bank Creditors, 1983, and Occasional Paper no. 40 Recent Developments in External Debt Restructuring, 1985.

24 See for instance M. Sutton, Structuralism: The Latin American Record and the New Critique, in The IMF and Stabilisation, Developing Country Experiences, edited T. Killick (Overseas Development Institute) London, 1984, at pp. 19–67.

lead theorists in many directions. Yet the simplest agreed ground for scepticism is the reliance of the IMF on so-called macroeconomic variables and assumptions about the efficiency of the private sector. Recently the IMF has stressed its desire to combine demand management with supply stimulation (pricing policies, tax incentives etc) to boost production and employment.[25] However its ideological confidence in the private sector is taken to be misplaced, because in developing countries there is frequently a lack of market transparency, social constraints, such as a lack of the profit motive conspicuous consumption, and other anomolous effects. For instance allowing production prices to rise may only start a prices spiral, without necessarily improving the supply of the relevant commodities, whose shortages are often caused by transportation and distribution problems.[26] More fundamentally it is recognised that macroeconomic theory itself is in a confusing state. Market forces and exchange rates do not clearly correspond. There are doubts about the right definition of domestic credit in economies with diverse financial institutions, not to mention the basic difficulty of estimating the gestation period for fixed investment credits on production and the balance of payments.[27]

As it is increasingly doubted that economies can be managed by the manipulation of the level of public credit, the presence or absence of import and exchange controls, the IMF is thrown back upon a so-called pragmatism which amounts to no more that an ad hoc consensus with state officials who consider they need the loan facilities whatever the conditions. Mistakes or uncertainties about economic theories may not be decisive where they are merely the subject of national economic policies, but they cannot be allowed to plague an international monetary policeman. It can hardly continue to function as such. The IMF is a supposedly technocratic economic think-tank and the issues it has to face are clearly not purely economic.

This doubt about macroeconomic theory makes one less willing to accept the rigours of deflationary financial stringency as applied to developing countries. It appears that the Group of 10 Communique of 8. 4. 1986 purports to relieve the developed countries of any duty of care towards the developing countries with respect to the administration of their own developed country public deficit[28] and this brings the prospect of unilateral ›adjustment‹ to economic ›necessities‹ all the nearer. The developed countries reaffirm the analysis of the Group of 10 Report (of July 1985 IMF Survey) that no major changes are required in the present institutional setting for exercising surveillance over national policies, including those concerning public deficit financing. They go no further than to say that it might be useful, in the context of exchange rate policy, to consider the employment of indicators for the assessment of convergence and policy consistency both domestically and internationally. The IMF might look at the matter further. This state-

25 C. Pirzio-Biroli, ›Making Sense of the Conditionality Debate‹ Journal of World Trade Law, 1983, p. 115 at p. 126.
26 Ibid. at p. 128.
27 Ibid. at p. 133.
28 IMF Survey, April 21, 1986.

ment is a firm enough refusal of the principle of co-responsibility between developed and developing countries with respect to the world financial crisis. It represents an unwillingness to engage in good faith in a renegotiation with those directly affected by the changing international environment, and, as such, is an invitation to the unilateral ›adjustment‹ to which I have already referred in the final part of the first section of this paper.

One can draw such a radical conclusion from various speeches of de Larosiere, Managing Director of the IMF, outlining the concept of co-responsibility, and in particular that of 15. 11. 85.[29] It is clearly not disputed to any general degree that a cooperative solution is essential to avoid a breakdown of the financial system. Hence there is a relative absence of rhetorical florishes by developing countries about the breakup of the existing system. He offers fairly careful adherence to the spirit of the principle of public international law that an argument for radically changed circumstances with respect to a contractual obligation is first and foremost an insistence upon a duty to renegotiate in good faith. After recording progress made between 1982 and 1985 de Larosiere considers the usual causes of the unstable economic environment, placing special emphasis on the inadequacies of the fiscal policies of the developed countries:

> . . . The supply of global savings is just too limited to meet large government demands on it without pushing up world interest rates. By virtue of its size alone, the United States must take the lead by significantly reducing its structural budgetary imbalance. Such action would contribute to a needed lowering of interest rates worldwide, to an orderly reduction in the exchange value of the dollar, and to the necessary correction in the US current account deficit . . .
>
> . . . Indeed, it is difficult to overestimate the benefits in present circumstances of a significant and credible reduction in prospective U.S. fiscal deficits . . .

The key first step in developing legal principles for the construction of a new international financial order in the given context of a third world debt has to be agreement upon universally applicable standards for the contraction of public debt, i.e. both for the developing and the developed countries. Even if one were to accept the most hostile Western criticism of the developing countries, which is that the contraction of debt was an aspect of unsound public deficit financing, the outcome would only be to identify the developing countries with the developed themselves. So it should appear possible to see a connection between the not very successful attempts to control public expenditure in some Western societies and the inability of the developing countries to control the expansion of their debt. A common approach can and should be found.

29 IMF Survey, Nov. 25. 1985.

The Sovereign Equality of States and Common Standards for Public Debt Contraction

There is at the global level an inability to develop effective and democratic means of control of public expenditure which apply to all countries equally. It makes little economic sense to transfer net capital resources from the South to the North, the well-known effect of the present debt situation. At the same time there is no clear unjust enrichment on the part of the Western banks. For one thing they lend money very much at the rate at which they obtain it themselves, i.e. if taken individually and not collectively. They have no control over the impact of public deficit expenditure in developed countries. The suffering of the developing countries reflects the absence of any international legal technique to mitigate the burden which generally uncoordinated public-deficit expenditure adds to the specifically third world debt crisis.

The rhetoric of economic self-determination surrounds the language of the new international economic order. This does give some indication of safeguards which might accompany the contraction of further public debt by developing countries. For instance, it is recognised that the conditionality which is accompanying the renewal of commercial loans affects directly the interests of the whole populations of the developing countries. Therefore it is sensible to open up a process of economic decision-making which is seen at present to escape parliamentary control and the pressure of directly affected interest groups. Without social consensus one might expect that policies which have major distributive consequences will not be maintained.[30] Indeed it is only a short step further to argue that they need not be maintained. The principles of self-determination and development should find their place in the actual institutional framework required for the conclusion of international loan.

The parallel has been conceded in principle already in the context of investment protection and promotion treaties. The duty to honour Western investments in a developing country is frequently made conditional upon a constitutional approval of the investment by the President or Parliament of the developing country. This guarantee is not as a rule absolute, but the clear responsibility of the developing country is to ensure that the investment is accepted within the context of a considered national economic development plan.[31]

Some immediate legal implications may appear to follow from this course. Firstly legal opinion could develop the consensus that both banks and the IMF can be expected, as a matter of proper commercial practice, not to conclude loan agreements without the satisfaction of these basic legal procedures by the developing countries. If they choose to go ahead they have to accept the consequence that the security of their transactions should rest upon the continuity of the political actors with whom they have had to deal.

30 This argument is developed further by K. M. Meessen, in ›State Sovereignty and the Conditioning of Loans‹ to be published in ›Foreign Debts in the Present and a New International Economic Order‹, opt. cit.

31 A recent comprehensive survey is provided by J. Plaviec, ›Protection et Promotion des Investissements‹ Etude de Droit International Economique, P.U.F. Paris 1985, esp. pp. 54 et seq.

Public Debt Contraction and Economic Self-Determination: The Case of Mexico

A detailed case study of recent Mexican experience can suggest some of the basic institutional measures which banks should be expected to require before they are willing to lend to developing countries. These measures should be seen as a parallel to those which have evolved in the context of investment protection treaties. At the same time, given Mexico's traditional role as one of the most vocal proponents of a new international economic order one may still ask whether Mexico's institutional response to its financial crisis has been truly democratic or in any sense radical in its own domestic terms?

A leading Mexican authority on the debt problem, Rosario Green, has pointed to the details of economic rationality and irrationality which led to the massive expansion of the external debt of Mexico in the late 1970s. The political system did not favour the expansion of public resources through a reform of the taxation system, i.e. an insistence upon a greater contribution of the private conglomerates to the Mexican Treasury. The technocratic elite was not so incompetent as to be ignorant of the consequences of inflating the domestic money supply. There was a recession in the West, with capital available in the form of loans to finance Mexican economic expansion. The competition for a choice developing country was intense. The loans proceeded without any substantial supervision by either the banks or public authorities for either the public or the private sector. The lending was increased in the course of 1981 as the price of oil and other Mexican exports declined. This conduct was bound to lead to crisis.[32]

So much is readily appreciated by the Mexican technocrats. The question is how to change course. A first institutional step is easy, to reform the financial institutions of the country to ensure adequate supervision in future. The 1985 Law regulating the public service of banking and credit tightens up procedures.[33] These involve quite basic matters such as according exclusive authority to national credit bodies to receive public income and dispense loans. The law insists that lending banks should be separated from interests in industrial or other enterprises, that their commissions and interests should be controlled by the Bank of Mexico, and that the latter in turn should follow the policies of the Treasury. The law is designed to provide the machinery for this purpose.

In turn the new organic law of the Bank of Mexico tries to tighten up its role as a guarantor of credit. It had a duty to maintain in reserve in foreign currency a quarter of the currency in circulation in the country-ineffective because of continuous and rapid devaluation of the national currency and a freezing of foreign assets. Now it simply proposed to limit the internal finance of the bank to a sum fixed by its governors in terms of the national development plan and the projected future public spending set out in the

32 R. Green, ›Mexico: crisis financiera y deuda externa, El imperativo de una solución estructural nacionalista‹, Commercio Exterior, vol. 33 num. 2, (1983) pp. 99–107.

33 Exposición de Motivos de la Ley Reglamentaria del Servicio Publico de Banca y Credito, the Diario Oficial of Mexico on 14 January 1985; also in Commercio Exterior, vol. 35 no. 4, (1985).

budget of Congress. Decisions on the granting of credit etc will be taken with senior officials of the Treasury.[34] For the year 1985 the sum was to be determined by the governors in the light of the macroeconomic objectives of the national government, of which the most important was taken to be a reduction of inflation.[35]

It appears to me that these reforms are elementary if essential measures of rationalisation. Any international banks which concluded loans with a country which did not have such a framework of control would deserve the consequences. The question is whether this can amount to or lead to any democratic participation in the terms and conditions of international finance. A consideration of the published 1985 letter of intent of Mexico to the IMF would suggest not.

It appears clear that the present Mexican governing-technocratic elite do not consider they have any options to escape the exigencies of economic rationality. The Treasury and the Bank of Mexico accept that the best way to ensure the welfare of the population is to improve the performance of the economy. The only way to do this is through reduction of inflation. The only important concession of principle is that increasing the national budget through a reform of the base and administration of direct taxation has proved essential. Yet this is not to say that any concerted effort would be made to chase after the 22 billion dollars which fled the country in 1981–1982. Such a course would infringe the most important economic right of the Mexican property owning classes, to take their wealth out of the country at will.

So the basic focus of most of their proposals is on pure rationalisation of expenditure. So no loans may be made to public companies without the approval of the Treasury. Their debts are to be paid directly by the latter. A consistent attempt is to be made to adjust prices which are at present fixed to some notion of rational cost of production, having regard to what the country can afford at its present level of development. Similar considerations are to apply to the reform of the System of public subsidies.[36]

There is no indication that the Mexican governing PRI and technocratic elite accept any substance to the rhetoric of economic self-determination. There is no question of finding a place for a more extensively democratic discussion of the issues of debt, and in particular an identification of those who benefit or lose from its existence. Instead they form an energetic element of the Group of 24 which has already been considered in the second part of this paper.

34 Exposición de Motivos de la Ley Organica del Banco de Mexico, the Diario Official of Mexico, 12th November 1984, also in Commercio Exterior (supra) p. 408.

35 Determinación del financiamento interno del Banco de Mexico, Objetivos de Politíca Financiera para 1985, in Commercio Exterior (supra) pp. 412–413.

36 Carta de Intención al FMI, Secretaria de Hacienda y Credito Publico, Banco de Mexico, in Commercio Exterior (supra), pp. 414–418.

Democratic Control of Public Debt as a Problem Common to North and South: A Case-Study of UK Debates

So there are serious reservations to be had about the rhetoric of the new international economic order in the present context. It is relevant to stress the clear inability of public law theorists in developed countries as well to break into the supposed purely economic rationality of public expenditure control. There is a pressing need for substantial advances in the theory of law and economics in so far as concerns not merely the control on public expenditure, but also the reality of democratic participation in the evolution of so-called macro-economic management.

For instance consider the public discussion of the issue in Britain since 1976. This should be particularly interesting given the stance of Great Britain as a monetarist state committed to public expenditure controls and firm limits to inflation as the main feature of its national and international financial policy. The attempt to control public expenditure has proved even technically very difficult. It was only in 1981 that the Conservative administration eventually hit upon the strict regime of cash planned rather than volume planned expenditure. The system of the Public Expenditure Survey had led to close cabinet debate on costing, but was thought to be itself inflationary, because it was an incremental system leading public spenders to argue for more cash from a starting line, rather than questioning the latter itself.[37]

It is a remarkable fact in a Western democracy that the present system does not give Parliament a complete look in. The 1983 Financial Management Initiative introduces private accounting techniques, but these are to be applied directly by senior civil servants responsible for the execution of particular programmes. This involves delegation of authority regardless of the doctrine of ministerial responsibility. The outcome of one of the most serious Western attempts to control and reduce public expenditure has been to keep it firmly outside parliamentary initiative. The only new measure at the constitutional level is the National Audit Act of 1983. By section 6 the Comptroller and Auditor General may carry out an inquiry into the efficiency and effectiveness of any relevant public body in the use of its resources. However under section 2 it may not question the policy objectives of any such body.[38]

There is increasingly debate in British public law circles as to whether any criterion of participatory democracy is satisfied by this regime. It is difficult to see any contrast to the Mexican experience, and one might wonder whether it is somehow inherent in the nature of the material which one is attempting to master. Prossner argues that democracy supposes, following somewhat the influence of Habermas, the development of an increased capacity for problem solving, for coping with the complexities of social development. The options chosen favour very much instrumental rationality rather than the

37 M. Elliott, ›The Control of Public Expenditure‹, in (ed.) J. Jowell and D. Oliver, ›The Changing Constitution‹ Oxford, 1985, p. 149 at pp. 157–160.

38 Ibid., pp. 162–165, 167–168.

development of communicative competence. It is doubtful in Prossner's view whether the two have to conflict in principle. The major danger is that the severe limits upon participation in debate means that very little critical analysis of error takes place in Britain.[39]

Yet the dominant view remains that it is a simplistic assumption about the constitution to suppose that public expenditure must be subject to »outside control«: The Queen's government should be carried on. »The constitutional freedom of the executive, especially the Treasury, in financial matters is long standing . . .« The controlling scrutiny takes place within the executive. As Elliot puts it ». . . in the field of public expenditure the executive is itself an instrument both of public accountability and public power . . .«[40]

Conclusion

It might seem pointless to try to avoid disagreements about strategies of macroeconomic management at a national or international level by resorting to debates about common standards of public law for the contraction of public debt. For instance all of the Mexican controls do not really amount to safeguards for the economic self-determination of Mexico. They do satisfy a purely formal conception of Mexican national interest. That is to say they suppose that the Mexican authorities have worked out exactly what their economic and financial policy is and where their foreign debts are expected to fit into that picture. Developed countries have understood their duty to respect the economic sovereignty of developing countries to mean a duty to respect whatever development and other plans the latter have been able to formulate clearly and hold to consistently. Mexico appears to provide this minimal institutional guarantee. However its preoccupation with control of inflation and with the introduction of a larger share of market considerations into its economic planning are required by its relatively subordinate position in the international economic system, particularly in its relation to the U.S. and the IMF.

It may be unrealistic to try to introduce some substantive as distinct from formal standard of public debt law such as that finance from public debt should not be diverted to nonproducitive endes, e.g. military or social expenditure, or payments on current account for imports beyond, for instance, a certain percentage. This simply reintroduces all the economic controversies outlined in the second part of the paper. That is to say there is no agreement amoung theorists of political economy about how usefully the public sector can direct investment. At the same time one can see the objection made that whatever money such restrictions on public expenditure in developed countries may save, it does not, in any case, »belong« in developing countries however usefully or productively it might be invested there.

39 T. Prossner, Democratisation, Accountability and Institutional Design: ›Reflections on Public Law‹ in (ed.) P. McAuslan and J. F. McEldowney, ›Law Legitimacy and the Constitution‹, Sweet and Maxwell, London, (1985), p. 170 at pp. 173, 176–181.

40 Elliott, ›The Control of Public Expenditure‹, pp. 172–173.

Nonetheless it appears to me that the lawyer can contribute to the development of standards to ensure an increasingly democratic and therefore formally just contraction of the public debt by developing countries. That is why the suggestion is made at this very first stage, and hence the concentration upon the particular UK experience, upon the evolution of common formal standards of democratic approval of contraction of public debt. It should not be considered as fair, and as compatible with the principle of the sovereign equality of states, to impose upon developing countries standards for the further contraction of debt, for instance those which usually accompany IMF conditionality, without ensuring that the latter have been able to go through procedures of democratic approval which approximate to those regarded as essential in developed countries. At the same time it is perfectly well realised that the formal democratic procedures of some of the latter are not fully developed and that this is in part at least attributable to the complex if not intractable technical nature of the financial problems which have somehow to be managed. Hence there is a common ground of concern in which lawyers from both developed and developing countries might try to evolve international standards for the contraction of public debt.

[14]

Liberal Economic Rhetoric as an Obstacle to the Democratization of the World Economy*

Anthony Carty

INTRODUCTION: THE LIMITS OF A LEGAL PERSPECTIVE

In terms of an international legal system, a simple way to describe the situation of developing countries is one of incomplete integration, a malfunctioning which the system as such does not deliberately maintain but which it is not itself capable of correcting. The legal order operates on the basis of the simplest assumptions about the contractual competence of the states that are members of that order, and of their possession of certain property or resources which are by their nature disposable within the system. There is no legal compulsion to participate actively in the legal order, nor does the legal order say anything about the material terms of a contract to transfer resources within the system. This has potentially unfortunate consequences given that developing countries do

* This article is an attempt to develop a normative approach to well-known international issues which are frequently handled by international lawyers and economists. It attempts to develop the logical implications of an antagonism between two styles of rhetoric, a liberal-economic one and a liberal-democratic one. A purely legal approach to the problem of Third World debts is offered in Anthony Carty, "The Third World Debt Crisis: Towards New International Standards for Contracting of Public Debts," *Verfassung und Recht in Ubersee* 4 (1986): 401–19. Its forty footnotes contain most of the references to the factual background. My aim here is development of antagonistic rhetoric as a way of elaborating new normative standards; I am not attempting yet another chronology of a well-known story. My further methodological point, intended to be of particular interest to lawyers, is that so-called positivist international lawyers have no choice but to engage in analysis of political and economic discourse. This thesis is argued at length in Anthony Carty, *The Decay of International Law* (Manchester: Manchester University Press, 1986). A general survey of IMF issues is found in T. Killick, ed., *The Quest for Economic Stabilisation: The IMF and the Third World* (London: Overseas Development Institute, 1984). On north-south issues a useful survey is found in A. Sid Ahmed, *Nord-Sud, les enjeux* (Alger: Office de Presse Universitaire, 1981). A useful survey of liberal economic ideology as applied to the Third World is R. Packenham, *Liberal America and the Third World* (Princeton, N.J.: Princeton University Press, 1973). Also useful to consider, especially in connection with the issue of functional democracy, is the standard work by J. R. Pennock, *Democratic Political Theory* (Princeton, N.J.: Princeton University Press, 1979). For a survey of the recent institutional developments in the EEC, particularly the movement toward majority voting, see P. Moreau Defarges, *Quel avenir pour quelle communauté?* (Paris: Institut Français des Relations Internationales, 1986).

Ethics 98 (July 1988): 742–756

not share equal bargaining power in the negotiation of resource transfers, a particularly notable example being the terms under which they have contracted their external debts.

The organization of international economic relations has a different dimension which is not easily fitted into traditional legal categories. That is to say, it is not a matter of considering when, and how clearly, legally binding rules should be applied to legal subjects, who, in this elementary legal paradigm, have consented freely within a horizontal order of legal authority. Instead, one can recognize the perhaps embryonic forms of a supranational economic order capable of forcing an economic constitution on the whole state system. The key focus of attention, without too much danger of simplification, can be taken to be the International Monetary Fund (IMF). Its relationship with the private international banking system and the finance ministries of the developed countries makes it a clear focus for the examination of the terms under which the developing countries are permitted to participate in the international economic system.

Yet these terms are not juridical in character. The Articles of Agreement of the IMF speak of its function as promoting the stable development of international trade, primarily through securing a sound financial foundation for commercial transactions. The IMF is legally bound to carry out these aims, but they are not defined with such precision that one can say in a particular case whether it is observing or is obliged by the terms of its constitution. Despite the fact that the IMF entangles most developing countries in a web of understandings which are (in effect if not in form) legally binding, lawyers can say nothing about the content of these understandings. They are an essential precondition of the granting of loans by the private international banking sector and so are of great importance as an indicator of the quality of economic relations between Northern and Southern Hemispheres.

Now these understandings are shaped in a context which is sharply institutional, raising difficulties which have a potentially legal character. They go against what is usually thought to be the economic sovereignty or freedom of states. For instance they will invariably define the extent of permissible public deficit which a country might have. They will go further and point to what should be its public utilities pricing policies. Riots in developing countries about the consequent increases in the cost of basic necessities, such as food, are well known. Directions appear about the removal of import barriers to foreign products to the lifting of restrictions on the outflow of capital. None of this is necessarily binding in all cases. Indeed, it is all a matter of negotiation between parties who don't legally have to come to the same table. However, the negotiation does take place within an institutional framework which at present reflects the economic predominance of the West, the IMF's weighted voting system.

This is the context of the most serious present economic conflict facing north-south relations, the enormous overhang of debt burdening the developing countries, possibly a threat to the very existence of the world financial system. The problem raises very elementary questions about the application of standards of fairness to international economic relations, particularly north-south relations. One might simply ask how it can be justifiable that developing countries which are relatively poor in terms of per capita income should continue to pay interest on loans up to and even beyond the absolute value of the original loan when indeed the latter may demonstrably not have been contracted in the interests of the majority of the population in the developing country. Why not simply make a break with the financial bonds, a revolutionary rejection of this most pressing dimension of the existing international economic system? The argument might be carefully constructed that the existing system violates an elementary consensus concerning minimum economic and social rights, as developed in the legal language of the United Nations, indeed culminating in the latest General Assembly Resolution on the Right to Development. In a sense this could be seen as a global repetition of the French Revolution, an insistence that the status quo does not conform to a clear charter of rights, in this case economic and social rights. A very much more moderate version of the same approach is simply to demand a revision of the debts contracted in the light of independent criteria of legal standards of justice.

Nonetheless, the approach adopted here is to argue quite differently, from the extreme case of the Third World debt as a test case for north-south relations generally, that there are signs of the shaping of a single world in which the most appropriate developments should be in the area of formal institutional processes. An institution such as the IMF is engaged in directing and distributing resources across frontiers on a regular basis; and at the same time it is insisting upon the application of principles of political economy which are so hotly disputed in Western countries that they are regarded as properly the object of free elections in accordance with the principle of "one man, one vote." Furthermore these principles of political economy, above all concerning the question of the role of the state in the economy, have very largely to do with the internal affairs of countries. The peculiarly international dimension is really only the equality argument: what can be required of one country can equally be required of another in similar circumstances. In other words, the IMF is functioning as a government rather than a bank.

What will be explored in this article is the question of how far this most fundamental notion of fairness, the right to equal and effective participation in the political process, can be taken across boundaries.

WHETHER THERE ARE THE BEGINNINGS OF AN INTERNATIONAL ECONOMIC CONSTITUTION

The overall impact of the IMF is the imposition of some kind of supranational economic order upon a majority of the world's states. Without any doubt the IMF does not claim to be a democratic institution in the sense of "one state, one vote." The language used to defend the weighted voting system (when it was under attack from developing countries, led by Algeria, in the two or three years leading to the Jamaica Agreement of 1976) was that power should go with responsibility. Responsibility goes with the possession of property, an early nineteenth-century version of liberal capitalist democracy—the restricted franchise.

Originally, before the appearance of developing countries, the system could be given a more functionalist justification. Voting power reflected the importance of a country in world trade and hence, logically, the importance of its currency. Since IMF transactions were supposed to be primarily a matter of swappings of many currencies it seemed arguable that voting should reflect the currency most used. However, where it is in effect a matter of borrowing one currency, the U.S. dollar, in a context which is taken to trigger private bank borrowing, the question arises more directly who has the legitimate authority to decide how the money should be spent. The reaction of the developed countries to the prospect of democratic reform was quite simply that the developing countries would give the money away to themselves, as if every depositor in a bank had an equal vote in deciding how it should make loans.

Once the question of democratic legitimacy is posed it does not simply go away. While the developing countries have no immediate prospect of changing the voting system of the IMF and no strictly legal objection to the present functioning—since membership of the institution and the agreements reached with it are voluntary—they are increasingly resistant toward the policies which the IMF tries to implement. For this reason, at the moment, the heat of the argument concerns the legitimacy of the policies which the IMF endeavors to implement.

Immediately the lawyer, who might now call himself a constitutional theorist, is confronted by very complex arguments which appear to have a purely economic character but which may well rest upon certain assumptions about the relationship between the individual, civil society, and the state, which are not universally accepted and not verifiable in purely economic terms. In other words a lawyer finds himself confronted by the question whether economics is really a rigorous, scientific discipline. For instance, it is argued that the IMF operates upon a basic liberal economic assumption, that is, antistatist, that the absorption of finance by the public sector excludes its effective employment by the private sector. Therefore it is in principle desirable that the public sector make more—from whatever starting point—space for the private sector. The objection is made, by developing country economists, that their engine of economic growth is state-led production, which by nature has to be financed up front. Without public coordination of economic development it will not take place. The argument has to continue that there are not sufficient internal means of capital accumulation, so that resort to foreign borrowing is necessary. This point is considered controversial by liberals, both within and outside developing countries. Accumulation of foreign debt is seen as a substitute for confronting domestic oligarchies unwilling to invest in productive processes.

At this point it can be seen that one is in the presence of conflicting arguments of public policy which are usually resolved in developed countries by resort to democratic decision, at least in the formal sense that they are made the stuff of general elections. Given that the issues appear identical in the case of IMF activities, how can one effectively resist the introduction of formal democracy at this international level?

THE QUESTION WHETHER THE WORLD ECONOMIC SYSTEM IS INTERNATIONAL OR INSTEAD A SERIES OF PARALLEL DOMESTIC SYSTEMS

An objection which springs to mind immediately is that there is an ambiguity in the assumption that one is concerned with democracy at an international level. The consequences for a developing country when it accepts the conditions applying to an IMF understanding are confined to its own internal affairs. The argument has already been noted that capital accumulation through foreign borrowing is a particular sovereign choice for a way toward economic development. Many countries such as Japan have developed very largely without it. Others such as the United States in the nineteenth century employed it to some extent but without apparently traumatic consequences. If a state embarks upon such a course it is, given the nature of the present world political and economic system, engaged in an essentially horizontal and contractual regime in which the question of democracy as such does not apply.

Any direct response to this argument comes up against the same ambiguity concerning the nature of the international economic system, one for which legal theory does not provide a categorical response. Third World countries can reasonably argue that they can engage in substantial modernization of their agriculture or in construction of industrial capacity without a capitalization which almost inevitably cannot be extracted from a population base which is not as yet integrated in a developed capitalist process. The next stage of their argument need not rest on such a debatable economic theory, but on a recent historical fact. The Western capitalist system, combined with the petrol dollars of the Organization of Petroleum Exporting Countries (OPEC) revolution produced a substantial capital surplus throughout most of the 1970s. It could not be absorbed in Western economies at the time, and this created a great pressure on the international banking system to find a home for its resources in the Third World. In other words there is an integrated international economic system, and the question is squarely presented, What are the terms under which this integration is politically acceptable?

What if one were to return to the economic history of the capital transfers through bank loans to the Third World in the 1970s and to argue that what is at issue is a process which is malfunctioning precisely because the supposed market foundations, backed by a liberal legal superstructure, are inadequate? The precise ground of their inadequacy is that the market is a less efficient as well as a less just means of assuring resource allocation. The reason is, perhaps ironically, a traditional liberal justification for democracy, that it ensures an adequate representation of the interests which stand to be affected by the process in question. A monopoly of economic and political decision making in the hands of only a small number of those affected does not guarantee an adequate airing of even the economic consequences of decisions actually taken.

In the mid-1970s the Third World wished to replace the market allocation of a large part of the capital flow to themselves by a multilaterally supervised flow. This is what they understood by the allocation of newly created IMF special drawing rights to their capital needs. This is what the West understood as tiny depositors voting all the bank's resources to themselves. In fact this is what has happened to a very large part of the newly created IMF liquidity. It has to meet genuine capital need as determined by competent technicians under the overall surveillance of state-appointed officials. However, the main part of the creation of international liquidity has remained in the hands of one state, the United States, and a very large part of capital resources has remained with private international banks, which have retained responsibility for its distribution. The latter two actors, together with the developing countries as takers, constitute the market for the purposes of the present analysis. How does it function?

Western analysts agree very largely that in the 1970s the banks, in their anxiety to unload surplus capital, chased developing country takers and distributed their credit without regard to the long-term prospects of their customers and in disregard of the credit reserve proportions generally regarded as provident by national banking laws. This was possible because the banks operate through the euro-dollar market, which is beyond the jurisdiction of any nation-state. It was inevitable because of the competitive pressure among the banks and the compulsion to find what appeared, in the short term, to be the most fruitful location for their resources. However, the outcome was a vast outpouring of capital to countries which do not appear economically to be in a position to repay. Consequently there has had to be a decisive official state intervention on the part of the West to ensure that the two immediate so-called market actors do not collapse.

Such an intervention constitutes a displacement of the market. The banks continue to lend (or at least to reschedule loans) to countries which they do not consider a good risk because they are under direct pressure from their governments and from the IMF. In turn they look to the IMF to find reliable conditions to impose upon their customers and to ensure that they are observed. The state intervention means clearly that other than purely economic considerations are also governing. For instance, there is tension between the U.S. administration and Congress about the extent to which wider American interests should be compromised in order to support the banks. The requirement to focus on repayment of increased interest rates and to engage in deflationary cutbacks in imports on the part of developing countries has damaged the American manufacturing sector and in turn the U.S. trade balance. Similar social-political choices in developing countries have already been mentioned.

AN INTERNATIONAL ECONOMIC CONSTITUTION AND COMPETING IDEOLOGICAL DISCOURSES

Consequently it is difficult to see how, as a matter of political theory, in terms of the ideology of legitimacy prevalent in Western democracies, it is possible to resist the claim that an institution such as the IMF should be democratically governed. At the very least one might prefer a horizontal view of authority in the international society and give the power to block decisions to each important grouping of states (usually, the West, socialist states, and developing countries or, alternatively, regional geographical areas). However, in view of the apparent inevitability of a complex interplay of global financial transactions, one should more properly argue for some decision-making procedure which may include blocking mechanisms at the early stages but ensures that a final decision is reached.

A crucial state is not easily passed here. How does one overcome the argument that where there is a simple conflict of interests it has to be resolved by compromise and not by resort to a nonexistent third party, a so-called democratic pseudo-state authority? It is not necessary to agree with the Western argument as to the improvidence of Third World states to doubt the justice of forcing a decision in favor of the latter, the effect of any voting formula other than parity. Where there are two opinions why should either prevail? In my view the surest response to this argument is to turn Western rhetoric against itself. The West does not try to justify the existing system in terms of the monetary sovereignty of individual states, a rhetoric which it may use to justify its military strategies. Instead it makes appeal to the laws of the market and to a natural preference for the maximum autonomy in banking transactions. It is because the latter do not apply their own rhetoric consistently that it is necessary to enter a democratic element as a corrective.

The language used at present to describe this contradiction in Western rhetoric is the absence of reciprocity in the IMF's operations. It is unable to compel Western states not to run huge public deficits through foreign borrowing or exploitation of the role of their currencies as hard money for international transactions. This absorbs available capital as credit in particular countries, forces a drying up of the credit for others, and then gives the former the opportunity to require the latter to adjust. It may be tempting to try to justify this in the language of the market, that is, the free choice of the bankers. Yet the crucial issue in this context is the nebulous one of confidence. This is notoriously a matter not separable from the view which the bankers take of the regulatory, and therefore political, function of the state—that is, the present relative attractiveness of the United States over the Third World as a location for bank resources.

Indeed, the crucial issue in the world of liberal economic rhetoric is how to characterize a decision such as that of a central bank to raise interest rates. If this is done with the intention of drawing foreign capital into the country, can one attribute its success to market forces or to political decision? If the government answers that its policy was to reduce the supply of domestic credit in order thereby to reduce inflation within the country, it might insist that such is not a political decision but a recognition of unavoidable economic laws. The argument could be strengthened by pointing to an international practice which shows that governments of all ideological persuasions have to resort to the same policies in this respect.

A conclusion to the same argument might be that the real complaint about the policies in question, which are of course American, is that they are applied by a country, the disparity of whose wealth compared to that of its neighbors is such that radical movements of capital follow its policies. This might be justified in terms of at least two types of liberal versus democratic rhetoric. First, state boundaries are not themselves relevant to economic decisions with respect to capital flows. Other states are free to copy U.S. interest rate policies and thereby neutralize their impact. Second, the advantage which the United States nonetheless attains with its monetary strategy has to do with its relative size compared to that of its neighbors, precisely a feature which distinguishes the structure of international relations from that of domestic societies. Liberal economic rhetoric may combine with liberal rhetoric in the wider sense to recommend leaving untouched what cannot effectively be changed.

There is one dimension of this argument which cannot be effectively countered. Insofar as U.S. liberal economic rhetoric is pushed to the point where it becomes a purely political liberal insistence upon national monetary sovereignty, it is highly questionable whether there exists sufficient political cohesion among opponents of the United States to compel it to change course. In other words, there is no Hobbesian Leviathan lurking in the shadows.

However, the reality of international monetary relations is quite other than the last two objections might suggest. For instance in February 1987 the main economic powers tried once again, with the agreement of the United States, to settle upon what is the objectively sound value of the dollar in international economic transactions generally. The decision concerns in fact only the relationship of the dollar to other hard currencies. It supposes not simply that the issue is economic rather than political (in the sense that the United States must have regard to the economic use of its currency internationally rather than stress the maximum national advantage which it could extract from emphasizing its freedom to the limit) but also that the notion of economics involved is sociodemocratic rather than liberal, that any economy must have a regulatory dimension to function smoothly, and that all economies, both national and international, are mixed at the very least.

It might still follow that the regulator would not have to enjoy any democratic legitimacy. If it is given that the task is highly technical and admits of objective resolution, there is indeed something to be said for trying to immunize the decision-making process from democratic elements. These could mean nothing more than distortions brought on by powerful and irrational pressure groups. There is a tradition of trying to ensure the independence of central banks in Western political societies.

This technical perspective may even prevail if one accepts that independent regulation is invariably necessary for a limited number of eventualities. For instance the private sector, supposedly, that is, outside Japan, cannot be expected to take a long-term view of a return on an investment. Nor can it be expected to engage itself where the beneficiaries do not function as individual purchasers. For either case one might mention investment in theoretical research and in education generally. A more complex and disputed function for the state is to ensure medium-term stability in the market by guaranteeing to secure against large fluctuations between supply and demand. This it does usually by means of government procurement and long-term supply contracts, for industrial and primary resources, respectively.

However, it fails when one reaches the most controversial of all cases, which is the argument, accepted now even by the World Bank, that there is no objection in economic theory to the state undertaking to influence the development of the market by engaging in exercises to redistribute income. This is especially important for the Third World. Most of their economies are skewed by a radically unequal distribution of income which seriously obstructs the development of a wide range of industries suitable for the development of the home market. Indeed, a large part of the pressure put on these countries by the IMF to pay off their debts by engaging in competitive export industries means no more than a determination to shape up sectors which have until now reproduced Western consumer habits for a small domestic market now easily exhausted. In terms of the strictest liberal economic rhetoric, one might always be supposed to accept whatever is the actual given distribution of property and income in a society. This is just like the classical liberal theories of justice and property, which did not ask what it was that civil society had to guarantee. Nonetheless there is no economic objection to the state redistributing income. Indeed in sociodemocratic language this amounts to no more than one step beyond the management of aggregate demand, a restructuring of sectoral and not simply temporal irregularities in demand structures.

WHETHER CONFLICTING STATE AMBITIONS UNDERLIE CONFLICTING IDEOLOGICAL DISCOURSES

The problem remains that the developed countries are not willing to allow their fiscal and monetary policies to be subjected to the so-called logic of social democratic economic theory. The basic constant of international relations remains that there is a very great disparity between the economic weight of the so-called Group of Ten within the IMF framework and the Group of Twenty-Four. The latter may call for fiscal and monetary policies which might lead to a harmonious development of the world's, and therefore their, economies. Yet there is no economic compulsion upon the former simply to accept the limited negative effects of not paying attention to the interests of the latter. It may be possible to define the economic problems of developed and Third World economies in similar language, but this does not mean that each has the same weight in the international system. One can try to make it appear that the logic of interdependence requires negotiation of a permanent and institutionalized character. Yet in the final analysis the need for consensus cannot be avoided.

For instance the suspension by Brazil of the interest payments of its debt in February 1987 and the failure of the private banks for many months to agree to confirm the official consensus on the Mexican debt since September 1986 (although now the vast majority have accepted) are illustrative of the fact that international economic conflicts do not, by some inherent economic logic, have to be solved. In the view of these Third World countries, the refusal of the Group of Ten to accept international supervision of their policies (in particular the value of their currencies, interest rates, and the size of their public debts) means that they in turn see no reason why they should continue to subordinate their own internal economic and social goals to the repayment of even the interest on their foreign debts. The need for an international monetary system may not be as strongly rooted a feature of international society as the continued limitations of national consciousness. It is perfectly conceivable that a supposed web of interdependence transform itself into a downward spiral of mutual destructiveness.

This raises a very old controversy in liberal theory of international relations as to whether commerce may herald international peace. The difficulty with all ethical discussion of north-south relations may well be that it leaves out the predominantly political and indeed security dimensions of national interest. For instance it is not disputed that such considerations are at the basis of Western agricultural policies. Self-sufficiency is supposed to be a vital interest. The flooding of international markets with surplus agricultural goods is merely an inevitable consequence of excessively stimulated production, and, at least in the case of the European Economic Community (EEC), no backtracking seems to be politically possible internally. The international consciousness is not there. The same is said to be true of some aspects of American foreign economic policy. The balance of payments problems and the risks facing U.S. banks are not to be resolved by some active U.S. reshaping of the international system because there is no domestic constituency which has an effective interest. Economic power is made to serve political goals, such as the defense of the West, or Western European federalism, or the wider economic security of a nation-state such as Japan, which continues to consider itself as vulnerable, as outwardly dependent.

Many observers are not alarmed by these developments and reinterpret them as a cultural and geographical regionalization of the world in which the number of international actors is being reduced. For instance, besides the Western European integration process, there are similar trends beginning to show themselves in North America involving Canada, the United States, and Mexico. In Latin America, Brazil, Argentina, and Uruguay show recent signs of coming together. Attempts have frequently been made at integration in black Africa, but the predominant trend seems to be integration within the economic sphere of influence of the EEC. The Association of South East Asian Nations (ASEAN) countries is firmly within the sphere of economic influence of Japan, which has become increasingly conscious of the wider cultural and political implications of this relationship.

However, this pattern of regionalization does not explain away the existence of a global economic system which lacks an authoritative institutional foundation. The interlocking monetary order put in place by all Western banks acting in consort is the most obvious indication. Another is that at least ten industrializing developing countries have been encouraged since the 1960s to devote the main part of their energies to exporting to the Western market. The United States alone takes 60 percent of the exports of all Third World countries. At issue are not only textiles but also simple electrical goods and transport equipment, as well as basic metal goods such as steel. Besides, the regionalization represented by black Africa and ASEAN in relation to the EEC and Japan may merely reproduce the classical so-called neocolonial international division of labor in a narrower geographical context. Looser cultural-geographical regions do not of themselves guarantee anything as to the quality of the relations among these regions.

METHODOLOGICAL PROBLEMS: THE LAW, POLITICS, AND ECONOMICS OF NORTH-SOUTH RELATIONS

To return to the methodological problems of the international economic lawyer, what is it that he can be said to have been trying to do? What is the value of a detailed account of the recent diplomatic history of monetary relations? Is one trying to demonstrate that in the long term there is an inevitable development of international society toward international economic organization? In this case the function of the legal or other analyst might be to expose supposedly underlying trends and point out how relatively unconscious actors should adapt to these trends. For instance one might have indicated how international economic transactions have necessitated the development of a rudimentary international monetary system. National consciousness has not kept abreast. Hence, there is a lagging in institutional developments. This should be corrected, and so on.

However, there does not seem to be anything inevitable about the development of supranational monetary and wider financial cooperation, above all insofar as it affects the Third World. The present situation might equally be characterized as blocked but with none of the participants determined to force through their position to any supposedly logical conclusion. There is widespread anxiety. So should the function of the legal or other analyst be to endeavor to find or develop an appropriate normative language through which disputed positions can be resolved? That is a large part of what has been attempted here. It has been argued, first, that Western states do not resort to the traditional international relations language of national interest or sovereignty to defend their positions. Instead, they appear to resort to the rhetoric of liberal economics in the sense of allowing the maximum leeway to market forces, understood to mean private-sector actors. On closer examination of the rhetoric itself and of its relation to practice it could be seen that, in very large part, this rhetoric is social democratic rather than liberal. It is shared by states and international economic institutions, although the World Bank favors it more explicitly than does the IMF. The concluding stage in this argument is the one of logical consistency and of the equity arising out of the principle of reciprocity among equals. Social democratic economic policies usually occur in a politically democratic context, so why not always?

Perhaps the answer may well be that in their different ways neither Western nor Third World societies are economically democratic. Indeed this may be the reason for the apparent prevalence of seemingly technical economic arguments. Most evidently Third World elites are concerned to integrate their societies as far as possible in an international economic system without consulting their own populations. One Japanese definition of a Third World society is that it is one in which there is very wide inequality of income and an absence of political democracy. In this Japanese view there is nothing very much that the West can do in its relations with the Third World but accept this situation. For their part, the elites of the Third World are then only interested in accommodating what they see as the economic logic of the international system. For instance they will promote export industries to exploit as far as possible developed country markets and at the same time pay off their external debts. This is in preference to an equitable reshaping of their domestic markets and an accompanying appropriate productive apparatus.

In turn it is notorious that there is a discrepancy in Western political theory between the practice of liberal democracy and both the logic and the distribution of economic power. Ultimately the legitimacy of the former is not disputed. However, one rarely deals in ultimates. For instance, regarding the logic of economic power, the controversy raging in the West since the mid-1970s between monetarists and Keynesians has had a major impact on the programs of political parties but has not had built into it any significant element of political democracy. There is a view very widespread in the West that government is about efficient economic management and alternative governments are accepted and rejected insofar as the electorate is dimly aware that they have done badly or, at best, could hardly have been expected to do better. In such a context it is not surprising that the IMF should be allowed to bungle along, especially if it has a leaning toward monetarist policies at a time when these enjoy a certain fashion among those interested in the detail of government.

The question of the distribution of economic power is hardly one with respect to which there is a clear Western view. Inevitably this must reduce the impact of any purely logical argument which tries to transpose Western democracy onto an international plane. Here the argument has been a minimalist insistence that the collectivity intervenes in economic processes at least to ensure their smooth running, although to alter the distribution of income as well. This activity is seen as needing a formal political legitimacy. However, it is highly questionable how far this political process penetrates a system of economic power which, in the traditional liberal theory of the nature of civil society, is very much taken as a given unless very clear reasons can be provided to the contrary.

Witness the very hesitant application of antimonopoly laws. They may help to keep down prices, but they are often thought to defy the logic of increased economic organization and coordination. At the same time there is little consensus that workers' democracy answers a felt need for participation beyond an assurance of a fair distribution of profits. A class-war perspective would doubt even this. There is the further basic issue of competence to participate directly as distinct from making general judgments about those supposedly naturally responsible. There is room for considerable flexibility as to models of economic democracy, whether statist or industry or company based. However, they do not enjoy much prominence in France, Britain, the United States, or, in the formal sense, in Japan.

In my view there is probably a process of political democratization taking place in developing countries which will force more and more into the open the nature of the economic choices which are being made in Western societies. This is suggested by the form of the development of the debt crisis as it affects Latin America. The issue of debt repayment is being posed by newly elected democratic governments in Argentina and Brazil and much less overtly by the partly democratic government of Mexico. The issue put by a Mexican minister of finance is whether the interests of Western banks come before those of the majority of the population of his country. This raises immediately the question whether and how the Western taxpayer should be expected to bail out the banks. It is no accident that the developing countries such as Mexico are putting more emphasis on the link between disarmament and development, since interest paid on Third World debt goes directly to finance American armaments programs. This may not be bad in itself, depending on the level of concern felt about the Soviets. Yet it is clearly a transnational issue which is coming under pressure in favor of democratic transnational resolution.

While it might be objected that such an example is too limited, it has the elementary force that four-fifths of the world's population is in the Third World. As yet a numerical superiority in the United Nations system has not produced any change but internal democracy in developing countries can be assured to have a greater impact. It allows for much less subversive penetration by the West and faces its leaders with opponents who are very difficult to resist in terms of the language of political legitimacy. There is perhaps a certain trend toward the spread of such regimes in the Third World, for instance, in the Philippines, the struggle in South Korea, and the special example of Iran—which is, nonetheless, a popular government against which the West can have little impact. Yet there remains the elementary question of limited national consciousness and perhaps excessive local identity.

As long as identity remains primarily located at a national level, it is surely impossible to argue for the development of supranational democratic institutions. Even the EEC functions primarily through negotiation among nationally elected representatives in the Council of Ministers. Yet in my view this is precisely the model to investigate further in the light of the following basic circumstances. There is a global economic interdependence, albeit one which is heavily weighted against the developing countries. The problems presented by this dependence can be described in the same language of political economy. However, there is definitely not the supranational awareness which allows any measure of direct international democracy to resolve them. While it is possible for an individual state to revert to the language of vital interest and national sovereignty (this is most likely with respect to U.S. military policy), the debt question and related trade issues (i.e., as to how the debt is to be paid, and with what present trade is to be paid) mean that it is not practicable to leave the negotiating table for any substantial length of time. In terms of democratic procedures, to tackle a horizontal but compulsory relationship, the experience of the new European Single Act (1986) may well point the way. Qualified majorities for certain issues, unanimous decisions for other matters, but perhaps with built-in time limits for reaching decisions—these are mechanisms which can eventually harness the increasing pressure for democratization coming from the Third World.

CONCLUSION

I am optimistic that a growing institutionalization of international economic relations appears inevitable and that this is taking place in a context in which a negotiating language of the mixed economy predominates. There is great scope for the legal as well as political theorist to elaborate upon differing concepts of economic democracy and to work out what their relationship can be to the more traditional notion of liberal political democracy.

In this article I have tried above all to focus upon the nature of the claims of developing countries for a democratization of the world economy. At least one value of this exercise is that studies in political theory, such as Pennock's *Democratic Political Theory*, do not consider specifically the dimension of duties beyond boundaries. It is not suggested simply that the claims of developing countries should be accepted at their face value as a statement of the meaning of democracy at an international level. Some measure of functionalism in international economic organization may always be allowed to modify the principle of one man/one state, one vote. However, I have shown that the broad tendency of the policies of a body such as the IMF is to provoke acute political controversy, above all concerning the role of the state in the economy and the relation of this to income distribution. However much the detail of economic management may be left to administration in Western countries, these issues are always regarded as appropriate for democratic electoral decision.

Whatever the disparities of populations of developing countries, and indeed of states generally, a regime of voting which approached "one state, one vote" would more closely correspond to the wishes of the majority of mankind as far as concerns the controversial issues considered in this article and, hence, be more consistent with the notions of political democracy prevalent in the West. This might also raise the measure of stability in the international system, a consequence which is supposed to follow from ensuring the effective airing of a plurality of views.

[15]

VOLUME 26, NUMBER 2, SPRING 1985

Logic, Myth, and the International Economic Order

Daniel K. Tarullo*

I. THE SEARCH FOR A HEURISTIC PRINCIPLE

Not very long ago, international law scholars dared reach for the heavens. The optimism that earlier produced a dream of "world peace through law" also produced a vision of international economic relations governed by the rule of law. The League of Nations and the United Nations had their economic analogues, most notably the Bretton Woods financial institutions and the General Agreement on Tariffs and Trade (GATT).[1] The growth of international law was the march onwards and upwards of world civilization, protecting the weak from the powerful and leading to a better life for all.[2]

Like international law as a whole, international economic law has fallen from its position of promise. The inability of the United Nations to stop armed conflict is mirrored by the inability of the GATT to stop circumventions or violations of its rules for international trade. The best legal arguments fell prey to the absence of an enforcement mechanism. Never hidden for very long in the optimism of the immediate post-war years, that old bugaboo of sovereignty soon reared its head again. Nations would not obey the rules when their leaders believed vital interests were at stake, and nations would not cede anything approaching legislative authority to a supranational body.

Yet the international trade and monetary systems continue. For all the circumventions and violations, each has rules and procedures that are regularly observed. Each looks more like a legal system than do the areas of international law traditionally denominated "public"—those dealing with war, the use of force, territorial disputes, and the like. The post-war international economic order may not be blossoming into a full-fledged legal system, and it may be under almost continual challenge, but it is still an order. As a result, while the best

* Assistant Professor of Law, Harvard Law School. Formerly Executive Assistant to the Under Secretary of Commerce for International Trade.

1. General Agreement on Tariffs and Trade, Oct. 30, 1947, 61 Stat. A3, T.I.A.S. No. 1700, 55 U.N.T.S. 187 [hereinafter cited as GATT].

2. *Cf.* Jackson, *The Crumbling Institutions of the Liberal Trade System*, 12 J. WORLD TRADE L. 93, 99 (1978): "To a large degree, the history of civilization may be described as a gradual evolution from a power oriented approach, in the state of nature, towards a rule oriented approach."

international economic legal scholars may show considerable insight into the limitations of international economic law, they cannot break with their old methods of analysis.

Partisans of the rule of law bemoan the erosion of the limited legalism that did exist in the earlier years of GATT and, to some extent, the International Monetary Fund (IMF). They have retreated either to tentative advocacy of greater devotion to the rule of law or to analysis of ways to "manage" international economic relations so as to preserve the basic post-war liberal order.[3] The so-called realists of political science departments are almost contemptuous of international economic legalism. They acknowledge that international agreements may reflect a temporary consensus and a convenient reference point for what to do in the absence of strong contrary interests. But, say these realists, the law *as such* has no power; only nations have power.[4]

Another response to the disarray of international legalism has been to redirect attention to national regulation governing international economic activity. Here, at least, the laws are enforced. Over the past decade, the laws of most industrialized nations have gained in complexity and importance, thereby providing much grist for analysis.[5] Most analyses regard the international legal texts themselves as a kind of backdrop for the real action taking place in the Commerce Department in Washington, the Commission in Brussels, the Ministry of Trade and Industry in Tokyo, the Trade Ministry in Ottawa, and elsewhere.

A third scholarly response has come from those who have called for a major overhaul of international economic law through the creation of a New International Economic Order (NIEO). Some forms of NIEO writing seem to place an almost naive faith in the efficacy of adjustments to current international economic law.[6] These writings seem

3. *See, e.g.*, Hudec, *GATT Dispute Settlement After the Tokyo Round: An Unfinished Business*, 13 CORNELL INT'L L.J. 145 (1980); Jackson, *supra* note 2; Roschke, *The GATT: Problems and Prospects*, 12 J. INT'L LAW & ECON. 85 (1977). To a considerable extent, these scholars have accepted the "management" agenda of non-scholarly policy analysts. *See, e.g.*, S. RUBIN & T. GRAHAM, MANAGING TRADE RELATIONS IN THE 1980'S (1983).

4. *See, e.g.*, R. KEOHANE, AFTER HEGEMONY 88–89 (1984):

> Of course, the lack of a hierarchical structure of world politics does not prevent regimes from developing bits and pieces of law . . . . But the principal significance of international regimes does not lie in their formal legal status, since any patterns of legal liability and property rights established in world politics are subject to being overturned by the actions of sovereign states. International regimes are more like the "quasi-agreements" that William Fellner . . . discusses when analyzing the behavior of oligopolistic firms than they are like governments.

5. The list of articles and books published on U.S. and EEC international trade regulation is enormous. For a representative bibliography, see E. MCGOVERN, INTERNATIONAL TRADE REGULATION 411–31 (1982).

6. *See, e.g.*, INDEPENDENT COMMISSION ON INTERNATIONAL DEVELOPMENT ISSUES, NORTH-SOUTH: A PROGRAM FOR SURVIVAL (1980) (the so-called "Brandt Commission" report).

based on the assumption that international economic law and legal instruments alone can substantially alter global patterns of wealth distribution and economic activity. Other writing relative to the NIEO is very theoretical and far from optimistic.[7]

Far from being a route to the millennium, international economic law often seems at most a curious and ultimately inconsequential byway. International economic relations have relatively little to do with legal argument, with what an earlier generation might have called "legal science." The faith of rule of law advocates has faded, the hopes of NIEO advocates are waning, and the disdain of "realists" for international economic law is on the rise. One can reasonably ask whether the study of international economic law is worthwhile for those who wish to understand and affect those relations. As a law student and as a government functionary dealing with such matters, I found myself asking what kinds of study (if any) of GATT or IMF law would help to explain patterns of change and constancy and to reconcile the conflicting images of an international economic order that is at once both dominant and fragile.

In this essay, I will set forth two approaches to the study of international economic law that I have used in teaching this subject over the past few years. I regard each as a heuristic device rather than as a "theory" of international economic law. Both approaches have their roots in intellectual paradigms that are currently in some vogue, and both are related to efforts of people studying different areas of the law. Yet, as is inevitable, my own predispositions and the particularities of international economic relations have suggested something that is both familiar and new.

II. THE LOGIC OF THE LAW

Influenced by modernist theories in a variety of disciplines, many legal scholars have spent much time in recent years evaluating whether legal rules and legal decisions can be linked indisputably to the principles they are said to implement. Much, though by no means all, of this work has been produced as part of the corpus of "Critical Legal Studies" scholarship. The methods adopted by individual authors

---

7. The work of the Latin American dependency theorists is notable. *See, e.g.*, F. CARDOSO & E. FALETTO, DEPENDENCY AND DEVELOPMENT IN LATIN AMERICA (English ed. 1979); Dos Santos, *The Structure of Dependence*, 60 AM. ECON. REV. 231 (1970). The work of world-systems theorists begins from different premises but shares some of the universalism and pessimism of dependency theory. *See, e.g.*, I. WALLERSTEIN, THE CAPITALIST WORLD-ECONOMY (1979).

vary substantially.[8] What is shared is the amount of attention paid to the internal logic of legal doctrine. Careful analysis reveals that the values (equality, individual choice, efficiency) on which a legal decision purports to stand can justify an opposite result equally well. Intermediate rules, explicit or implicit, are often introduced to help produce a particular pattern of outcomes, but these results prove to be just as indeterminate. In its more sophisticated forms, this kind of analysis can demonstrate how apparently opposing values may in fact be inseparably linked, how they may actually depend upon one another for their meanings.[9]

The demonstration that legal principles are generally indeterminate leads to some hard questions about a legal system that purports to implement those principles. Political or ideological choices are embodied in doctrines that promise a faithful implementation of the principles themselves. Some scholars try to identify the ideological choices that are reflected in these doctrinal configurations. Others concentrate on arguing that the problem lies not in the particular doctrines but in the very idea of a system that purports to implement and accommodate conflicting principles in a logically compelling fashion. I will not try to parse the varieties of this type of analysis in this essay. Instead, I will apply one kind of "logic of the law" analysis to a particular doctrine of international economic law to illustrate both the usefulness of the analysis and its shortcomings. In explicating the doctrine, I will begin with problems that would arise under a conventional legal analysis and then move to the problems exposed in this less familiar analysis.

My example is the article I most-favored-nation obligation (MFN), frequently called the "cornerstone" of GATT.[10] In the simplest terms, article I enjoins each GATT member to treat all countries in the same

---

8. A recent symposium in the Stanford Law Review provides extensive description of, and commentary on, Critical Legal Studies. Particularly useful for explaining the varieties of methods that press the logic of the law are Gordon, *Critical Legal Histories*, 36 STAN. L. REV. 57 (1984); Heller, *Structuralism and Critique*, 36 STAN. L. REV. 127 (1984); Kelman, *Trashing*, 36 STAN. L. REV. 293 (1984). For an example of scholarship based in part on indeterminacy principles but decidedly not produced under the Critical Legal banner, see Weinreb, *The Complete Idea of Justice*, 51 U. CHI. L. REV. 752 (1984).

9. *See, e.g.*, Dalton, *An Essay in the Deconstruction of Contract Doctrine*, 94 YALE L.J. (forthcoming April 1985).

10. Article I reads, in pertinent part:

> With respect to customs duties and charges of any kind imposed on or in connection with importation or exportation or imposed on the international transfer of payments for imports or exports, and with respect to the method of levying such duties and charges, and with respect to all rules and formalities in connection with importation and exportation . . . any advantage, favour, privilege or immunity granted by any contracting party to any product originating in or destined for any other country shall be accorded immediately and unconditionally to the like product originating in or destined for the territories of all other contracting parties..

way, hence the characterization of article I as a "non-discrimination" requirement. Other provisions of article I actually allow certain limited discriminations by some countries in favor of countries with which they have had traditional relationships (i.e. colonial relationships), but this exception to MFN is conventionally understood as the price paid by the United States to the declining imperial powers in order to extract a general MFN obligation.

Exceptions to article I have continually eroded this "cornerstone" of GATT.[11] These exceptions to MFN fall into several categories. First, the European Economic Community (EEC) and various regional free trade areas have reduced or eliminated tariffs among themselves while maintaining MFN rates for other GATT members.[12] Second, under the Generalized System of Preferences and other preferential arrangements, the industrialized nations have been allowed and encouraged to grant duty-free treatment to the products of "less-developed" countries.[13] Third, some of the Multilateral Trade Negotiations agreements concluded in 1979 explicitly make their benefits contingent upon a nation's assumption of the obligations contained in the tariff-reducing arrangement. This feature is a so-called "conditional" MFN clause rather than the "unconditional" obligation contained in article I. Any legal study of article I would make note of these "exceptions" to the unconditional MFN rule and try to explain why these exceptions were made.

Quite apart from the tendency of the exceptions to swallow up the rule, article I presents interpretive difficulties. For example, how should one determine whether the product of one GATT member is "like" the product of another and thus deserving of similarly favorable treatment? Descriptions in tariff classifications can be manipulated to deny a nation benefits that would otherwise accrue to it. In a famous instance, a 1904 treaty provided that Germany would reduce its tariff on cattle raised at least three hundred meters above sea level and

---

11. In fact, the percentage of world trade passing national boundaries under MFN treatment has been declining since the mid-1950s.

12. Article XXIV of GATT allows for the formation of customs unions and free trade areas. The terms of art. XXIV create certain procedural and substantive hurdles for groups of nations wishing to adopt these arrangements. In practice, the terms have not been observed, most notably in the case of the EEC, which is by far the largest and most successful customs union. This phenomenon has itself contributed to widespread belief that, in the end, GATT rules are not binding in any strong sense of the word.

13. Related to both the first and second category is the emergence of what may be a new category of "exception" to MFN: a bilateral free trade area that is not part of a regional arrangement or a precursor to further economic integration. The best example is the recent agreement between the United States and Israel. This agreement, explicitly authorized by Congress in Title IV of the Trade and Tariff Act of 1984, is a kind of amalgam of development assistance and a political gesture to a favored country. Pub. L. No. 98-573, §§ 401–405, 98 Stat. 2948, 3013–18 (1984) (amending Trade Act of 1974, 19 U.S.C. §§ 2101, 2112(b)).

having at least one month's grazing each year at eight hundred meters or more above sea level. Switzerland was the intended beneficiary of this provision, as most other European countries could not meet the terms of the tariff classification, even though the "favorable treatment" was technically available to all countries.

GATT working parties and dispute resolution panels have failed to develop a standard for deciding when a product definition is discriminatory in an article I sense. One would think that any legal system would strive to articulate a principled basis for such a decision. So, in our inquiry to determine whether international economic law *could* blossom if given the chance, let us look at a couple of proposals for a secondary rule to solve the like product problem. In other words, we must see if principle and result can be connected by adding some steps to the analysis.

One suggestion is to compare cross-elasticities of demand to determine whether products are alike for purposes of article I. Of course, the cross-elasticity of demand between two products in a particular market depends upon their relative prices. This relationship, in turn, depends upon the existing tariff levels if the products are imported. Consequently, any secondary rule grounded in such empirical analysis seems problematic, quite apart from the inherent difficulty in deriving cross-elasticity comparisons.

Another suggestion is to look to the purpose of article I. For the moment, we can ignore difficulties in isolating *the* purpose behind any legal rule. Let us assume the purpose of article I is to ensure non-discrimination among GATT members. In a sense, looking to the purpose of the provision only restates the problem of deciding whether differences are indeed discriminations. After all, unless every product is subject to identical duties, there will always be differences in treatment based upon differences in product. Can recourse to the "legislative intent" of article I help to determine when differentiation is legitimate and when it is "discrimination"?

Consider a case in which country *A* grants a concession during a round of multilateral tariff bargaining. Country *A* reduces its tariffs on motorcycles with engines under a certain horsepower level, but retains its present tariff on motorcycles with more powerful engines. Country *C*, which exports only the more powerful cycles to country *A*, believes that the change discriminates in favor of country *B*, which exports less powerful cycles to country *A*. This is surely a difference in treatment, and it looks like discrimination. But suppose that country *A* claims its differential treatment is an effort to discourage the traffic fatalities and noise pollution associated with large, powerful motorcycles? A decision-maker would have to decide whether the safety and noise abatement aims were legitimate bases for differentiating among imports. In all likelihood, evidence of a discriminatory intent as well as of a public welfare aim could be found in the actions of country *A*'s government officials. A GATT panel would have to disentangle these motives as well as the effects of the differential treatment in order to decide the dispute.

An inquiry that presses the logic of the law also examines the link between the rule and the justification on which it is said to be based: Why is non-discrimination desired at all? What justification necessarily entails the non-discrimination principle contained in the article I MFN rule? Two justifications have traditionally been offered. The first represents a dual instrumental argument. On the one hand, unconditional MFN treatment is said to encourage the growth of world trade by spreading the benefits of tariff reductions immediately. On the other hand, where a country's tariff reduction granted to one state is extended to others only upon receipt of equivalent concessions by those other countries, the process of tariff reduction is both complicated and lengthened.

This justification is belied not just by some periods in the history of tariffs, but by the attitudes that informed the most recent round of Multilateral Trade Negotiations. The benefits flowing from some of the non-tariff agreements, such as the Subsidies Code and the Government Procurement Code, were conditioned upon acceptance of obligations by the countries concerned. Proponents of this approach successfully argued that one must eliminate the "free rider" problem, whereby countries had an incentive under unconditional MFN to sit back and give no concessions, but to reap the benefits of all concessions given by others. In such a situation, countries might be unwilling to negotiate any concessions without assurance that others would reciprocate. At some times, unconditional MFN has been considered effective in increasing trade. At other times, a conditional approach has been considered more effective. Which of the two approaches is best depends upon context.

The second traditional justification for article I is that equal treatment for all nations (at least all members of GATT) is of itself desirable. There are numerous variations on this argument. Some emphasize normative values: it is simply "fair" to treat all sovereign nations equally. Others link the value of even-handedness with assertions that international harmony is more likely to be obtained if national leaders know that their countries will not be victimized by economic discrimination. In any case, the article I rule that each GATT member give the same benefits to every other member is said to flow from principles of equality.

Anyone familiar with interpretations of the equal protection clause of the United States Constitution will see the tenuousness of the link between notions of equality and GATT article I. Equality *might* mean treating everyone equally, but it might also mean treating equally those who are situated equally. Indeed, as less developed nations have argued with some success, it may be *unfair* to treat a rich, industrialized nation in the same way as a poor nation. This formulation of equality requires us to identify those characteristics that are relevant for determining whether actors are "situated equally." Hence, an additional set of value choices and rules would be needed to implement a norm of equal treatment.

Apparently opposite concepts, then, may depend upon one another. That is, the concept of equality seems to depend upon the concept of discrimination for its own definition. As was shown above, we must discriminate among certain characteristics of goods or nations in order to know what is equal treatment. Consequently, article I, enjoining all nations to treat one another equally, requires secondary rules to define equal treatment.[14] Recognizing this interdependence of notions of equality and discrimination, we can see the futility of any system that entails their separation in order to produce answers to doctrinal questions.

The analysis here has been abbreviated. I recount it to illustrate a method. But even the preceding discussion should identify adequately three levels at which the status of unconditional MFN as a pillar of the world trading order is undermined. First, proceeding from the rule to its application, we saw the need for value-laden secondary rules or ad hoc judgments simply to administer article I. Second, at the level of instrumental aims, we saw the apparently contingent relationship between an unconditional MFN rule and the stated goal of increased world trade. Third, the rule cannot be justified by appeal to a normative standard, because "equal treatment" is a principle with many meanings.

This kind of analysis makes visible the politics behind the law. The rule of article I cannot be administered without political choices about legitimate national policies. The rule cannot be explained or justified simply by reference to the aim of increased trade or the principle of equality. Moreover, any conception of equality adopted is replete with political statements about sovereignty and the nature of relationships among nations. From this perspective, the inability to enforce GATT rules looks to be less than the principal problem with legalism in international economic relations. Deviations from article I and the

---

14. Note that an argument can also be made that a *conditional* MFN approach is consistent with equal treatment principles. Recall that under a conditional MFN policy a nation will extend a trade concession to all nations that offer substantially equivalent concessions. What could be more evenhanded than asking the same thing of everybody? The principle of reciprocity, which informs so many features of the GATT, is based on just such an idea of equality.

inability to resolve disputes over its terms are understandable, almost predictable, insofar as one expects the divergent political views of various countries to inform their conceptions of legitimate national policies and the meaning of equality.

For all its virtues, an indeterminacy approach can only begin the task of understanding the role of law and changing the world that the law purports to govern. This approach effectively demonstrates the contingent relationship between basic principles or norms and the doctrines that are said to be founded on those norms. It also suggests that no legal system can use rational precepts to derive doctrines and/or decisions from those principles and norms. There can be no neat logic to the law. However, in its focus on the possibilities for different connections between principle and doctrine and between doctrine and decision, an indeterminacy analysis risks ignoring the configurations that have actually been developed. Analyses of this sort sometimes imply that norms of equality, for example, could "just as easily" produce rules radically different from that of article I. Logically, this implication is perfectly valid, but the story of the connection between equality norms and article I is surely more complex than mere happenstance or the conscious decision of a few powerful people.[15] Standing alone, an indeterminacy exercise shuts out social practice, human consciousness, and material conditions.

The incompleteness of focusing upon the logic (or illogic) of the law is most apparent when we turn outward, when we confront not an abstract construct, but a concrete situation. To understand the development of prevailing legal doctrine and to provide ways of choosing among all the theoretical alternatives, people have turned to different methods. I do not pretend to have a theory of how indeterminate principles become realized in particular doctrinal patterns. In the next part of this essay though, I will offer one method of thinking about international economic law that I have found useful in trying to understand these links.

III. THE ORGANIZING PRINCIPLE OF NORMALCY

Modernist thought has provided legal scholars with another approach to law that emphasizes close study of texts. This approach begins with the modernist insight that human beings cannot know anything except by their active organization of the data they receive from the natural and social worlds. There are no "natural" categories or divisions lying out there waiting to be discovered. Thus, although

---

15. *See generally*, G. PATTERSON, DISCRIMINATION IN INTERNATIONAL TRADE 1945–1965 (1966)

it is necessary for human beings to organize their perceptions in order to think and know at all, the categories of thinking that they develop are contingent rather than necessary.

Important categories of organization and meaning are shared to a greater or lesser extent by all human communities. These conventional categories allow people to understand and function in the world, but they also limit the ways in which people can know. Scholars in many disciplines have examined the ways in which these conventional categories reflect a dominant set of norms and, indeed, create concepts of what is "normal." Howard Gardner has challenged the idea that there is a single scale of intelligence upon which we can locate all people as being of "normal," "below normal," or "above normal" intelligence.[16] Carol Gilligan has challenged theories of moral development based upon a norm of male development that ignores the possibility that females follow a path of development grounded in a very different approach to moral decisions.[17] In bodies of work that defy categorization within a single conventional discipline, Michel Foucault and Roland Barthes have examined verbal and non-verbal modes of communication to see what and how we know.

Applying this modernist insight to international economic law, one immediately recognizes that the absence of a dependable enforcement mechanism does not devalue the serious study of the legal texts and the arguments associated with them. We can look at the rules and the departures from the rules to see whether there are conventional ways of thinking about the international economic order that help explain that order. To frame the task more specifically, what concepts of normalcy are implicated in the way international economic issues are discussed and resolved? Further, what do the texts reveal about departures from the "normal" state?

A starting point for this analysis is offered by the concept of sovereignty itself. Sovereignty is roughly equivalent to a notion of international personhood or citizenship, the attribute that furnishes an actor with a bundle of rights and obligations under international law. By and large, only sovereign nations are thought of as actors in international law. Moreover, the manifold differences among the world's nations are subordinated to the essential "sameness" of being sovereigns. All sovereigns are "equal," perhaps in the way that all people are said to be "equal," at least in the laws and constitutions of some societies.

Returning to the article I MFN obligation, we see a different layer of meaning in the notion of equal treatment of all nations, no matter

16. *See* H. Gardner, Frames of Mind (1983).
17. *See* C. Gilligan, In a Different Voice (1982).

how situated in relation to one another. If all sovereigns are essentially the same (at least for important purposes of the international economic community), the particular concept of equal treatment in article I makes sense. The sameness of sovereignty informs the conventional pattern of creating rights and obligations that are the same for all nations, just as the essential sameness of personhood or citizenship informs universally applicable sets of domestic legal rights and obligations.

Yet the differences among nations are obvious. Nations differ in their populations, languages, natural resources, patterns of economic organization, modes of government, religious traditions, geography, and in countless other conventional ways. Some of these differences are injected into legal discussions about the international economic order, principally differences pertaining to the per capita gross national product of the various nations. The response of the international economic order to these differences reveals some of the ways in which the assumption of normalcy or an urge to sameness operates. One acknowledgement of difference is found in exceptions to generally applicable rules. Continuing with the MFN example, let us now examine the nature of the exceptions to the article I rule.

At the time the GATT was negotiated, a number of nations expressed interest in the formation of free trade areas or customs unions. Parties to such free trade areas and customs unions gradually eliminate their tariffs among themselves, while maintaining tariffs on products from other nations.[18] Invariably, an uncommon degree of economic policy integration follows. Article XXIV of the GATT permits the creation of these arrangements in accordance with certain guidelines, including most notably the requirement that

> the duties and other regulations of commerce imposed at the institution of any such . . . agreement in respect of trade with contracting parties [of the GATT] not parties to such . . . agreement shall not on the whole be higher or more restrictive than the general incidence of the duties and regulations of commerce applicable in the constituent territories prior to the . . . adoption of such . . . agreement . . . .[19]

Besides trying to preserve the pattern of reciprocal concessions, this "exception" to the MFN obligation preserves the essential sameness in the legal structure. Indeed, the history of the EEC has borne out this

18. A customs union designates a free trade area in which the participating nations create a uniform external tariff as well.

19. GATT, *supra* note 1, art. XXIV, para. 5, *as added by* Special Protocol Relating to Article XXIV of the GATT, Mar. 24, 1948, 62 U.N.T.S. 56.

proposition, for now it is the EEC as an entity that must treat every nation equally and that has adopted the rights and obligations of a contracting party to the GATT.[20] The substantial differences in the economic policy-making of EEC member states are merely "internal" matters, subordinate to EEC "sovereignty" in setting import duties and export policy.

The urge to create and maintain categories of normalcy is more evident in the GATT's reaction to Third World demands that their lesser wealth be compensated through differential and favorable treatment within the international economic order. One such demand has been that the "advanced," "industrialized" nations impose lower tariffs on products exported from the Third World than they do on the same products exported from other industrialized nations. This demand is justified by the alternative conception of equal treatment noted earlier: treat equally those nations that are situated equally, and by implication, treat differently (more favorably) those nations that are situated differently (less favorably).

Since 1971, the GATT has acknowledged this alternative equal treatment principle through its authorization of the Generalized System of Preferences (GSP), which allows the "developed" nations to give tariff-free treatment to products from "developing" nations, even if the same products are assessed tariffs when imported from other developed nations. Without authorization, of course, an industrialized nation would violate article I in adopting such a policy of "discrimination" in its tariff laws.

At first glance, GSP may seem to disprove the hypothesis of an urge to normalcy, for its very existence is an *acknowledgement* of differences. But closer study of the two legal texts authorizing GSP reveals the strength of the norm. The first authorization was granted in 1971 by the Contracting Parties as a waiver from the normal GSP rule.[21] By definition, an article XXV waiver is an exception to the prevailing rule. To emphasize this exceptional quality, GATT waivers are often granted for a certain time. The GSP waiver was limited to ten years, suggesting that in 1981 the normal MFN rule would once again apply.

Before the GSP waiver expired, however, the GATT adopted another authorization. In Points 1 and 4 of the so-called "Framework Agreements" (part of the 1979 Multilateral Trade Negotiations package), the GATT seemingly made permanent an authorization for developed

20. Attending a GATT Council meeting, one is struck by the EEC delegation: there are at least eleven members, one for each country and one for the EEC Commission. Only the EEC representative speaks for the group, however.

21. GATT BASIC INSTRUMENTS AND SELECTED DOCUMENTS 24, GATT Doc. L/3545 (18th Supp. 1972) [hereinafter cited as BISD Supp. 18].

nations to grant preferences to less-developed nations.[22] Yet paragraph 7 of the Framework Agreements provides that

> [l]ess-developed contracting parties expect that their capacity to make contributions or negotiated concessions . . . under the provisions and procedures of the [GATT] would improve with the progressive development of their economies and improvement in their trade situation and they would accordingly expect to participate more fully in the framework of rights and obligations under the General Agreement.

So, although the departure from MFN has been made indefinite, eligibility for the benefits of that departure is temporary. Paragraph 7 contains the silent promise that some day all will revert to normalcy.

The less-developed nations objected to inclusion of paragraph 7 in the Framework Agreements.[23] Its survival doubtless reflects the superior bargaining position of the developed nations. Yet, paragraph 7 reflects a concept of normalcy more deeply rooted than a particular provision in a particular agreement. GSP is premised not just on the reality of different situations, but on a belief that Third World nations need preferences to help them "develop." The preamble to the 1971 waiver states that "individual and joint action is essential to further the development of the economies of developing countries."[24] Paragraph 7 of the 1979 agreement itself talks of "progressive development." The terms "developed," "developing," "less-developed," and "least developed"—so common in everyone's parlance—bespeak the idea that nations "grow up."

A less-developed nation, then, is fundamentally the same as a developed nation, even though the two look very different because they are at different stages of development. The less-developed nation is like an adolescent, fundamentally the same as an adult human, though with different capacities and needs at this stage of development.[25] It makes no difference that less-developed countries do not

---

22. GATT, BASIC INSTRUMENTS AND SELECTED DOCUMENTS 203 (26th Supp. 1980).

23. *See* UNCTAD V, Multilateral Trade Negotiations: Evaluation and Further Recommendations Arising Therefrom (May 7, 1979) at 33.

24. BISD Supp. 18, *supra* note 21, at 24.

25. My metaphor of adolescence is based upon current legal texts. The idea of progression is hardly new, though, appearing as it does in traditional expositions of "stages of development." *See, e.g.*, W. ROSTOW, THE STAGES OF ECONOMIC GROWTH (1962). Critiques of this idea have been offered by dependency theorists. *See, e.g.*, F. CARDOSO & E. FALETTO, *supra* note 6, at 11–13. *Cf.* G. GUTIERREZ, A THEOLOGY OF LIBERATION 82 (1973):

> [T]o develop meant to be oriented towards a model abstracted from the more developed societies in the contemporary world . . . . The underdeveloped countries thus were considered backward, having reached a lower level than the developed countries. They were obligated, therefore, to repeat more or less faithfully the historical experience of the developed countries in their journey towards modern society.

particularly resemble the United States of the mid-eighteenth century. After all, each generation of adolescents is different in some ways, though we tend to think of all adolescents as going through similar developmental stages and arriving at normal, mature adulthood. The overt identification of less-developed nations with adolescents is nowhere more apparent than in the term regularly used to describe paragraph 7—a "graduation" clause, to be applied at the moment when the less-developed nation reaches "adulthood."

To the extent that representatives of Third World nations themselves "know" their situations in terms of the categories of development leading to the normal state of industrialization, they can hardly be surprised by a graduation concept. After all, when someone stops being a child or an adolescent, we stop affording her certain kinds of special treatment; she is, for example, to be held legally accountable for her actions, just as are other adults. Thus, as the concept of differential and favorable treatment for less-developed countries has assumed more force in international economic agreements, concepts of graduation are strengthened.[26]

Other myths about international economic relations teach difference as a departure, often temporary, from the normal. One example is the "conditionality" policy of the IMF, whereby it requires nations suffering balance-of-payments difficulties to adopt certain economic policies in exchange for use of IMF resources (in the form of reserve assets).[27] These policies have long been a contentious subject. Some have alleged that the economic austerity required by the Fund has led to so-called IMF riots, where citizens of a nation seeking access to Fund resources have literally taken to the streets to protest price increases and reduced government spending. Officials of less-developed nations, which are the most frequent users of IMF resources, have claimed that the conditionality policies are too rigid and that the problems faced by their countries are as much development as balance-of-payments problems.

While acknowledging that it must "pay due regard to the domestic social and political objectives, the economic priorities, and the circumstances of members"[28] in setting conditionality requirements, the IMF asserts that it must treat members uniformly and insists upon

26. An additional example may be found in the Subsidies Code negotiated during the Multilateral Trade Negotiations. *See* Tarullo, *The MTN Subsidies Code: Agreement Without Consensus*, in EMERGING STANDARDS OF INTERNATIONAL TRADE AND INVESTMENT 63, 84–86, 91–93 (S. Rubin & G. Hufbauer, eds. 1983).

27. The current IMF guidelines on conditionality are set forth in Executive Board Decision No. 6056-(79/38), Mar. 2, 1979, *reprinted in* IMF, SELECTED DECISIONS OF THE INTERNATIONAL MONETARY FUND 20 (10th issue 1983).

28. BISD Supp. 18, *supra* note 21, at 21.

the elimination of their balance-of-payments problems. The Fund must give "technical" assistance to the member nation to help it overcome its problems in a relatively short time (frequently two to three years). The member nation with balance-of-payments difficulties is cast as a sick patient, in need of the bad-tasting medicine (an austerity program) that is prescribed by the old doctor (the IMF), who knows best what will make the patient well again. To change the metaphor a bit, it is important not to give the patient a pain killer (access to IMF resources) without also performing the surgery that cures the underlying illness.

Again, the differences among nations are apparent. But, here too, we are driven to the idea that balanced payments is a normal condition for nations. The myth here is of sickness and health. Every nation has the same basic health needs, just as every person must eat properly and exercise regularly. And, although there may be some differences in treatment for a particular patient ("due regard to . . ."), the basic regimen is the same (uniformity).

This perspective on IMF policies makes more understandable the Fund's insistence on separating measures needed to redress balance-of-payments difficulties from measures designed to further economic development. When an adolescent is sick, one's first imperative is to help her get well. Helping her to mature is a different task.

IV. FROM UNDERSTANDING TO LEARNING

The myths of adolescence and sickness that appear in the texts of international economic law explain away differences among the world's nations. Since these differences represent conditions antecedent to the norm (as in the adolescence myth) or temporary departures from it (as in the sickness myth), they do not create a knowledge of their own. They are "known" only as variations on the norm, the norm of being an industrialized nation with a capitalist, welfare-state economy.

In a sense, international economic law is a set of myths. The legal texts communicate "facts" about the world even as they purport to regulate it. Again, I emphasize that this is the only way law could exist—it must "know" what it regulates. I am not suggesting that the mythic facts are unrelated to the material world or that any arbitrarily chosen bundle of mythic facts would "work" equally well.[29] But the effect of myth is to sanctify one way of knowing events in the

29. As must be obvious to many readers, this entire discussion parallels in some ways continual debates on the relationship between ideas and the material world, or between law and society. For present purposes, I find it unnecessary to address these sorts of issues in abstract terms. Some sense of the relationship between ideas (or law) and material life (or society) emerge through careful study of particular problems. One need only reject the absolute claims that might be made on either side: either that ideas determine material life, or that material life determines ideas.

world. Of the many (perhaps endless) useful ways of knowing that world, a single way is made Natural.

This phenomenon reflects an image of the normal. The statement, "Nations develop from predominantly agricultural to predominantly industrial economies," is a kind of literal translation of the adolescence myth. It presupposes certain mythic facts—that "nations" and "development" are natural phenomena, perhaps even embodying "laws" of nature. As adolescents grow into adults, so developing nations are expected to grow into developed nations.

This attribute of myth robs the world of its history and recalls the definition proffered by Barthes of myth as "depoliticized speech."[30] It is *natural* to be underdeveloped while growing towards development; the history of imperialism is incidental. The famine in Ethiopia is a tragic by-product of underdevelopment (perhaps, in part, due to the "underdevelopment" of that developing nation's government), but is unrelated to the history of the European exploitation of African peoples. Thus, myth can mask power and explain pain.

The mythic method may give a new perspective from which to understand international economic relations. Having considered the "Third World" already, let us look briefly through the mythic lens at legal approaches to some disagreements among "First World" nations (the market-oriented, industrialized nations belonging to the Organization for Economic Cooperation and Development (OECD)), and at some legal texts governing economic relations between the First World and the "Second World" nations (communist states with state-controlled economies).

Many economic disputes among the OECD nations seem to elude resolution because there is no image of normalcy out of which to create a knowledge of economic relations. Extraterritorial application of the United States antitrust laws evokes foreign displeasure in large part because of differences of opinion over the expected role of the state in allowing, or even encouraging, practices that are considered unlawful restraints of trade under United States law. Similarly, disputes over "unfair practices" in international trade arise because there is no "normal" conception of the state's economic role in "post-industrial" society. Some European governments practice substantial industrial planning and own large segments of their nations' productive bases. The Japanese government, for instance, coordinates and directs activity among companies in certain industries. Successive administrations in the United States have rejected similar policies and have been sympathetic to complaints from American industry that such practices unfairly "subsidize" foreign competitors.

30. R. Barthes, *Myth Today*, in MYTHOLOGIES 109, 143 (A. Lavers trans. 1972).

International efforts to arrive at a consensus on regulating restrictive business practices and on the appropriate role of the state in economic activity have produced only the most general of principles.[31] Without a guiding image of normalcy, specific rules are impossible. Yet the OECD nations continue their search for sameness, driven, it would seem, by the belief that an agreed list of permitted and proscribed practices will produce harmony and prosperity. Without a canonical notion of what is a state's "normal" role in the economy, the OECD nations will continue to produce such accords as the Subsidies Code, which declares in one document that subsidies are both good and bad.[32]

An alternative route to sameness is mapped out by the regime of national countervailing duty laws, which purport to equalize the terms of competition between domestic industry and "unfairly" subsidized foreign industries. That is, if sameness cannot be achieved on the international level, then at least it is to be sought within one's own borders. Yet this very drive for sameness threatens what consensus there is among the OECD nations, accentuating as it does the significant differences among even the "mature" nations. Conflict arises when, for example, the United States levies countervailing duties on imports from a nation whose economic policies the United States considers to be "unfair" subsidies.

The organizing principle of normalcy or sameness takes on a different mythic form in the legal treatment of trade between the OECD nations and the Second World. For example, United States laws regulating imports distinguish between "non-state-controlled" and "state-controlled" economies. While goods from less-developed nations are treated in the same way as those from the industrialized nations, exports from a state-controlled economy to the United States are treated differently. The price and cost investigations normally required by the antidumping laws are discarded because prices and costs are considered artificial (unnatural) in a state-controlled economy.[33] The countervailing duty law is not even applied to non-market countries, because subsidies are thought to be *exceptions* to the norm of the market allocation of resources. Where no markets exist, "subsidies have no

31. *See, e.g.*, Organization for Economic Cooperation and Development, Declaration on International Investment and Multinational Enterprises, *reprinted in* 75 DEP'T STATE BULL. 83 (1976) and 15 I.L.M. 967 (1976); United Nations Conference on Restrictive Business Practices, The Set of Multilaterally Agreed Equitable Principles and Rules for the Control of Restrictive Business Practices, U.N. Doc. TD/RBP/CONF/10 (1980), *reprinted in* 19 I.L.M. 813 (1980) (popularly known as the UNCTAD Code on Restrictive Business Practices).

32. *See* Tarullo, *supra* note 26.

33. Tariff Act of 1930, ch. 497, tit. VII, § 223, 46 Stat. 590, (codified as amended at 19 U.S.C. §§ 1202, 1677b(c) (1982)). The Tariff Act of 1930 was amended by the Trade Agreements Act of 1979, Pub. L. No. 96-39, Title I, § 101, 93 Stat. 144, 184.

meaning."[34] If the nation has a "communist" form of government, as well as state-controlled economy, differences in legal regulation extend to imports as to which no dumping or subsidization is alleged. Imports from most nations are subject to quotas or extra tariffs when their importation injures—at least to a certain extent—United States industry.[35] Imports from communist countries, however, are evaluated under a different law, which grants relief to United States industry upon a lesser showing of injury.[36]

These provisions underscore the difficulties faced by the capitalist nations in creating a "language" through which to conduct economic relations with nations having state-controlled economies. A few years ago, a series of conferences on East-West trade relations was styled "Interface One," "Interface Two," and so on. These titles, borrowed from computer jargon, suggest a situation in which two fundamentally incompatible entities are brought together. The attributes of sameness seem absent (though surely some such attributes could be found if we were looking for them). It may be that the basis on which to regulate relations between the entities is unclear. This admission of an inherent inability to communicate contrasts sharply with the assumptions contained in the popular notion that a continuing "North-South dialogue" can improve relations between developed and developing countries.

In terms used earlier to describe relations between developed and less-developed nations, the state-controlled economy looks like neither a normal adult nor an adolescent. It is deviant with no promise of either being or becoming normal. Writing the myth in broader terms, the state-controlled economy is like a psychotic. At times we try to keep such a person away from us, preferably locked up somewhere (recall the United States policy of "containment"). At other times we think we should deal with this individual, but we have trouble knowing how we as normal people should talk to the insane.

These examples, along with the myths described in the preceding section, lead me to several hypotheses. First, the organizing principle of normalcy in economic relations seems to have a constraining effect. Conscious efforts to resolve disagreements, whether through legal principles or otherwise, revolve around efforts to produce images of sameness where they do not already exist. It may be that "knowing" the world as they do, diplomats are deprived of other insights into the possibilities for cooperation.

Second, the logic of normalcy and sameness appears inexorable in an increasingly integrated world economy. The logic of normalcy crops

34. Carbon Steel Wire Rod from Czechoslovakia, 49 Fed. Reg. 19370, 19371 (1984).

35. Trade Act of 1974, tit. II, §§ 201–203 (codified at 19 U.S.C. §§ 2251–53 (1982 & Supp. I 1983)).

36. Trade Act of 1974, tit. IV, § 406 (codified at 19 U.S.C. § 2436 (1982)).

up in both the myths and material conditions of economic life. Those nations that have raised highest their per capita gross national products have adopted forms of economic (and thus, to some extent inevitably social) organization most resembling those of the OECD nations. Even the industrialized nations demonstrate a strong impulse to eradicate differences among themselves. I recall officials of the United States government demanding a few years ago that the Japanese government do something to lower "cultural barriers" to the importation of American products. Language, the social organization of Japanese product distribution, and the tendency to favor particular (often local) suppliers all impeded the "free" flow of goods into Japan and were thus cause for concern.

The normalcy offered by these myths is undeniably appealing. The economic wealth and achievement of the OECD countries is understandably envied. Yet those who hail the rewards accruing to the "natural" state forget that they were attained in part through the practice of imperialism.

Normalcy threatens the future as well as the past. It obscures the various problems facing a Third World country in an international economy dominated by powerful industrialized nations. It countenances, even demands, the eradication of communities of difference.[37] Drawn by the desire for economic improvement, cornered by the power of prevailing economic forms, is it any wonder that certain groups within the OECD nations and many Third World nations see no alternative but to march to the same drummer?

My third hypothesis is that the potential of what we might call doctrinal reform for changing the basic structures of international economic relations is limited. Once again, whether or not these doctrinal reforms can be enforced is not the most important question. Many of the reforms sought by some Third World leaders under the banner of the New International Economic Order are misguided not simply because, as a political matter, the OECD nations will refuse to accept them as binding international legal obligations. Proposals like the Common Fund for Commodities[38] look unworkable because they do not fit into our ways of knowing the world and yet have no root in alternative forms of economic organization and knowledge. Joint efforts to raise prices of products are antithetical, at least in theory, to the very premises of the international trade order. Moreover, the freedom of private parties to develop substitutes for products whose

37. *Cf.* K. Polanyi, The Great Transformation (1944) (classic description of similar phenomenon in the original establishment of capitalist market economies).

38. Draft Agreement Establishing the Common Fund for Commodities, U.N. Doc TD/IPC/CONF/L.15 and Corr.1 (1980), *reprinted in* 19 I.L.M. 896 (1980).

prices rise for whatever reason can leave producers of many raw materials in an ultimately less advantageous position. Similarly, to restrict the activities of multinational corporations in Third World nations is both to acknowledge reliance upon those entities and to ignore their substantial power simply to withhold the investment capital on which those nations rely. Nations that have tried such restrictions have been suitably disciplined and have gradually returned to "normal" ways.

These are the hypotheses with which I now work. The organizing principle of normalcy is not the "truth" about the world but a device to help understand it better. Suppose this device leads to insight and the hypotheses prove useful. Will they help us to cultivate different forms of knowledge by looking at things as we had not previously known we could? Even to ask such questions is to dream once more, although in a very different way than did that earlier generation of scholars. Perhaps academics can contribute to such knowledge by studying different forms of the organization of work and economic life that today seem idiosyncratic in our "normal" world. Perhaps too, they can try to project different paths for the integration of new technologies into a world that, one way or another, must deal with these new possibilities. Here the role of legal scholarship is particularly promising. Perhaps, finally, they can help us see fissures in the "normal" world that might be used to start along other paths.[39]

I confess considerable uncertainty. Distinguishing genuine alternatives from unwitting replications of the status quo—and from hopeless daydreams—is not easy. It is tempting to work towards marginal improvement in the lot of some, even when one recognizes the limitations of that activity. Maybe the best, if provisional, advice is to take seriously experiences that do not fit the "normal" world, to see how the history that was not written might have looked. These experiences, and the visions they offer, may be reflected in what to others seem "aberrational" legal texts.

39. For an admirable effort to begin the tasks suggested in the text, see M. Piore & C. Sabel, The Second Industrial Divide (1984).

[16]

How Fair is Fair Trade?

Phedon NICOLAIDES*

Arguments for protection are proliferating at an increasing rate. International trade theory has long demonstrated the detrimental effects of barriers to international free exchange of goods (see, for example, Bhagwati, Srinivasan, 1983[1]; Dixit, Norman, 1980[2]). Trade theory, however, has been less effective in analysing arguments about fair trade and other issues concerning equitable international commercial relations.

Recent arguments for protection and government assistance are based on the notion that trade between countries should be equitable. Unfair trade is considered to be a justifiable cause for demanding protection. The purpose of this paper is to propose a framework for analysing and determining the merits of arguments for fair trade. It may be thought that fair trade issues cannot be examined objectively because they comprise normative prescriptions. Statements on fair trade, however, are more than the mere pronouncement of subjective preferences: they also express objectives and expectations about the conduct of international economic relations. Hence, it is pertinent to ask what the likely consequences of those objectives and expectations will be. What will happen if all countries attempt to follow trade policies? Can they be implemented by all countries? Will they improve the economic conditions of trading countries? These are important questions which have received almost no formal treatment within a cohesive analytical structure.

This paper suggests a framework, a method of investigating the various aspects of the arguments for fair trade. As will be shown below, most of these arguments contain many logical inconsistencies.

Arguments for Protection

Demands for protection are usually based on the following: (a) support of newly-created industries, (b) facilitating adjustments, (c) national security, (d) correction of domestic distortions (second best intervention), (e) prevention of competition from "pauper" labour, (f) exploitation of changes in the terms-of-trade, (g) strategic trade policy. All of these protectionist arguments, except the last two, have been shown to

* Centre for Business Strategy, London Business School Comments and suggestions by Robert Baldwin, John Kay, David Taylor and Martin Wolf are gratefully acknowledged.

[1] J. Bhagwati and T. Srinivasan, *Lectures on International Trade*, (Cambridge, MA: MIT Press, 1983).

[2] A. Dixit and V. Norman, *Theory of International Trade* (Cambridge: Cambridge University Press, 1980).

be detrimental to social welfare by reducing aggregate income. (see, for example, Corden, 1974;[3] Scott, Corden, Little, 1980;[4] and Hindley, Nicolaides, 1983[5]).

The last two arguments are valid as long as other countries do not attempt to implement a similar policy or retaliate. Otherwise, it is possible that all trading countries will suffer a reduction in their well-being if they all attempt to shift their terms-of-trade, or protect their oligopolistic industries so that they enjoy economies of scale through secure domestic markets.

In the last few years, new arguments for protection have emerged. Their main characteristic is the emphasis on the fairness of international exchange. Trade theory proves the superiority of free trade because it maximises social welfare, which is therefore the guiding criterion. In contrast, fair trade arguments stress concerns about equitable treatment of all participants in international trade. These arguments cannot normally be analysed within the framework of traditional trade models. Since they are mainly arguments concerning "proper" policies, they must satisfy the following criteria:

(a) Internal consistency: There should be no self-contradictory proposals. An example of an inconsistent policy would be one of industrial rejuvenation through both export promotion and import substitution whenever resources are fully utilised.

(b) Practicality: A proposed policy should be workable or capable of implementation. This does not mean that it should be politically feasible. Although that is necessary, it is a criterion which mostly reflects personal predisposition and is therefore not considered here. Rather, a policy is practical when its features, characteristics or objectives can be measured and when its effects can be evaluated.

(c) Effectiveness: If a policy is implemented it should allow the desired objectives to be attained equally well or better than other policies.

(d) Global consistency: If all countries implement the same policy it should not fail. For example, no country could be successful if all countries followed a policy of export promotion and import substitution.

An example of global inconsistency is that some trade policy games are negative-sum games (e.g. use of tariffs to influence terms of trade). Thus, the use of the criterion of global consistency is intended in this paper to highlight the logical defects of proposed trade policies, even if it is theoretically possible that under certain circumstances some countries may benefit from trade restrictions.

One of the reasons for writing this paper is to attempt to attach a meaning to the concept of fair trade. In the absence of a universally acceptable or prevalent definition, the attributes of fair trade identified below should not be regarded as a complete tabulation of all its possible meanings. This paper and the subsequent analysis refer to fair trade as it is defined to denote any or all of the following aspects:

---

[3] W. M. Corden, *Trade Policy and Economic Welfare* (Oxford: Oxford University Press, 1974).

[4] M. F. Scott, W. M. Corden and I. M. D. Little, *The Case Against General Import Restrictions* (London: Trade Policy Research Centre, 1980).

[5] B. Hindley and E. Nicolaides, *Taking the New Protection Seriously* (London: Trade Policy Research Centre, 1983).

(a) Bilaterally balanced trade: This issue is at the centre of the trade conflict between the United States and Japan. Czincota (1986)[6] provides a review of the American complaints as expressed by the US Congress.

(b) Export of "proper" quantities and types of goods: This is an argument often used by less developed countries in justifying their demands for tariff preferences for their manufacturing products. Less developed countries maintain that they can compete only when unequal countries are treated unequally. The issue of unequal (differential) treatment is analysed more extensively in Nicolaides (1985).[7] The broader aspects of the "appropriate" allocation of trade between North and South in a New International Economic Order are presented in more detail in Bhagwati (1978)[8] and Oppenheimer (1978).[9]

(c) Unfair foreign policies: It is often claimed that a government should offer the same treatment to the domestic industry as that accorded to foreign industries by their governments. This is the most significant aspect of fair trade and it may be called the "me too" syndrome. Casual perusal of the popular press indicates that examples of this abound.

Given the meanings identified above, the concept of fair trade in general has two distinct interpretations. First, ignoring for the moment concerns about national economic growth, fair trade may be considered to denote the "proper" volume of exports and imports of trading countries. This interpretation is tantamount to a determination of the "proper" (fair) allocation of international trade and of the income that can be derived from it.

Second, fair trade may be given a dynamic interpretation where governments intervene not to allocate the volume of traded goods, but to ensure that all firms compete fairly. The objective is to extend some "equitable" or "uniform" treatment to all firms. The meaning of fair competition is examined more thoroughly below.

It is worth noting that fair trade arguments differ from traditional arguments for protection in at least four important respects. First, with the exception of the terms-of-trade and the strategic policy objectives, all other traditional arguments identify the reasons that necessitate protection in domestic market failure and distortions and domestic preferences (see Johnson, 1965).[10] In contrast, the arguments for fair trade almost exclusively imply that the problem lies either in a malfunctioning of the international economic system, or in the behaviour of foreign governments and firms which generate negative externalities, such as export subsidising.

Second, the traditional response to negative international externalities has been

---

6 M. Czincota, US Trade Policy and Congress *Columbia Journal of World Business*, 1986 20(4), 71–77.

7 P. Nicolaides, Preferences for Developing Countries: A Critique, *Journal of World Trade Law*, 1985, 19(4), 373–386.

8 J. Bhagwati, *The New International Economic Order* (Cambridge, MA: MIT Press, 1978).

9 P. Oppenheimer, *Issues in International Economics* (London: Oriel Press, 1978).

10 H. Johnson, An Economic Theory of Protectionism, Tariff Bargaining and the Formation of Customs Unions, *Journal of Political Economy*, 1965, 73 253–283.

the formulation of policies for international cooperation. The most intricate expression of such cooperation can be found in proposals for "positive policy integration" for the European Economic Community (see Pelkmans' 1980[11] survey). In contrast again, the most significant aspect of fair trade, the "me too" argument, is unilateralist. It hardly envisages any international or unilateral coordination of trade, industrial or macroeconomic policies. The only exception is the OECD code on export credits.

The rise of unilateral and discriminatory policies has led many commentators to give warnings of the imminent demise of the liberal international trading system (see Wolf, 1986[12]). This is another reason, therefore, why there should be a better understanding of the causes and consequences of demands for fair trade.

Third, the revival of protectionism in the guise of fair trade reflects the growing belief and awareness that trade can also be disrupted by non-trade policies. It is held, for example, that a government should levy a tariff or some other countervailing duty not only in response to other countries' trade policies, but also to correct the "detrimental" effects of foreign fiscal and industrial policies (see, for example, Culbertson, 1986[13] and Gray, 1985[14]).

Finally, traditional demands for trade regulations have been voiced by less developed countries which have long maintained that they can compete internationally only if they receive differential (preferential) treatment. In contrast, the most vociferous demands for fair trade today emanate from firms in Western countries which claim that they can compete internationally only if they receive the same treatment as their competitors.

The rest of this article is divided into two parts analysing the static and dynamic definitions of fair trade respectively. It will be argued that neither conception of fair trade is adequately predicted on accepted economic principles. Nonetheless, as will be explained below, there may be a case of dynamic competition where government intervention may improve the efficiency of the market in allocating productive resources.

Static Fair Trade: Equitable Share of International Trade

It should first be made clear, even at the risk of being pedantic, that the concept of fair trade as a proper allocation of the volume of trade has no economic meaning. There is no economic theory which stipulates or even justifies the requirement for bilateral balance or the trading of proper quantities of goods. The volume of trade is determined by supply and demand, domestically and abroad. As price conditions change so does the volume of traded goods and services. The origin and destination of

[11] J. Pelkmans, *Economic Theories of Integration Revisited*, Journal of Common Market Studies, 1980, 18, 333–354.

[12] M. Wolf, *Fiddling While the GATT Burns*, The World Economy, 1986, 9(1), 1–18.

[13] J. Culbertson, *The Folly of Free Trade*, Harvard Business Review, 1986, 64(5), 122–128.

[14] H. P. Gray, *Free Trade or Protection* (London: Macmillan, 1985).

imports and exports are largely (ignoring quality variation) influenced by differences in relative prices. There is, therefore, no presumption that a country's bilateral trade needs to be balanced or that a country gains by doing so. The same applies to any assertion concerning the "proper" quantity of exports or imports. If there is anything such as proper quantity or output in economics, it is that which clears a market by equating demand and supply at the prevailing (equilibrium) price.

In addition, any intervention in the direction of trade flows or in the production of tradeable goods has an effect on the domestic distribution of income. This is because trade intervention is effective only if it can change relative prices. For example, subsidisation of both importable and exportable goods at an equal rate cannot have any influence on output because relative prices (i.e. how much of the importable goods has to be given in exchange for a unit of the exportable goods) are unaffected. If trade intervention is effective only when it changes the relative prices of goods it follows that in the absence of compensation, trade intervention cannot make a group (producers/consumers/workers) better off without making another group worse off! There immediately arises a problem of the fair distribution of domestic income. Of course, income distribution may not be considered as a problem of international economics. Since, however, issues of (static) fair trade do emphasise relative income and relative treatment of goods, then the domestic income distribution cannot be ignored and must become part of the overall problem. There is no aspect of a fair international distribution of trade (and, therefore, income) which does not have an impact on the domestic distribution of income. Hence, if governments are to be concerned about the welfare of their own citizens, the domestic redistribution effects are at the centre of any contentions regarding fair trade. This is not a normative proposition on what governments "should" be concerned about. Rather, any trade intervention has unavoidable redistributive effects. Once this is recognized, it seems paradoxical that concern with international fairness has almost completely ignored the issue of domestic fairness, especially when the effect of trade barriers on domestic groups is to create net beneficiaries and net losers. Therefore, arguments in favour of static fair trade are logically incomplete because they do not consider all the repercussions of trade regulation on matters of fair distribution of income (domestically and internationally).

To summarize so far, there is no economic theory on the proper quantities of exports and imports. It cannot be relied upon to justify any attempted apportionment of the volume of trade. Moreover, any regulation of trade has an effect on the domestic income distribution which should not be ignored when examining issues of fair trade.

There are at least two plausible elements which may motivate the proponents of fair trade. The first is that some allocation of trade satisfies ethical preconceptions regarding "proper" international exchange. This is, of course, a subjective concept and nothing more can be said about it. The second reason for promoting the issue of fair trade, as a proper allocation of the volume of trade, seems to be the desire to create a stable environment where new firms can enter world markets. Governments want to ensure that their exporters obtain a secure share of the market, but how can these shares be determined so that they are respected by all trading nations? Are there any operational criteria which can be both agreed upon and applied consistently by all trading nations?

The answer is certainly negative. In order to define proper shares, one must first determine whether existing shares are acceptable or not. But which government would admit that its export and import volume has been achieved improperly or reprehensibly? Moreover, will a government agree to restrain its own firms when they are either very competitive in international markets, or expect to be? The opposition of the United States to the proposed treaty on sea resources is an instructive example. It seems that the apportionment of trade is a good idea for those who are unable to exploit the opportunities of international trade. Politicians like the idea because they think it boosts their own weak industries. They forget, however, that the logical extension of this idea implies the restructuring of their strong industries, as well. Suppose for the sake of argument that countries have managed to reach agreement on the desirable share of trade for each one of them. Will they help new firms to establish themselves? Will fair trade regulation be effective? The answer is again likely to be negative.

Irrespective of how the allocation of international market shares is determined, some countries will eventually fulfil their shares and some will not (exactly as it happens now with the quoted schemes of the various Generalized Systems of Preferences; see Davenport, 1986;[15] Agarwal, Dippl, Langhammer, 1985[16]). Those which exhaust their shares will have to impose export restrictions and those which do not exhaust their shares will have to give more incentives to their exporters. The Generalized System of Preferences is a very bleak example of what may possibly happen. Either efficient producers will be penalized or producers who cannot possibly fulfil their share will be allocated a large quota.

In an expanding world economy, static fair trade will permanently handicap those countries whose economies are expanding at a faster rate than others. Trade will cease to be a vehicle for growth, because fast-growing countries will not be able to increase their predetermined share of international trade. Some countries will eventually be penalized for the mistakes and economic mismanagement of the slow-growing countries. New industries in those countries will be restrained instead of being helped to grow in a "stable" market. It can be easily recognized now that fair trade is an issue which does not benefit all countries. Therefore, what might benefit one country is certainly not in the interests of all. The fact that arguments for fair trade cannot be generalized to be in the interest of all countries entails that such arguments are not globally consistent.

---

[15] M. Davenport, *Trade Policy, Protectionism and the Third World* (London: Croom Helm, 1986).

[16] J. Agarwal, M. Dippl and R. Langhammer, *EC Trade Policies Towards Associated Developing Countries* (Tubingen: J. C. B. Mohr, 1985).

The system will eventually collapse because there will be a strong incentive for countries to rescind their commitments and simply trade exclusively with like-minded countries. If certain countries are constrained by previously agreed limits on their exports, they have an incentive simply to abandon multilateral trade and either engage in barter or bilateral trade. A similar phenomenon has been observed in the last two decades where industrialized countries have liberalized trade in those commodities traded almost exclusively among themselves. Less developed countries, which have refused to reciprocate in tariff cuts, have been unable to enjoy the benefits of increased trade. The commodities which are of interest to them are still heavily protected in industrialized countries.

In conclusion, fair trade, as a proper allocation of the volume of trade, will eventually stultify international exchange and cause the collapse of the trading system. Fair trade is not a prescription for stable trade, conducive to the growth of new firms. Certainly, some countries may initially benefit by being allocated a share which is greater than their current volume of trade, but they will eventually reach their ceiling. They will realize then that fair trade is restrictive rather than conducive to international trade.

Moreover, arguments for fair trade, as a proper allocation of the volume of trade, ignore the repercussions on the domestic distribution of income. Insofar as governments should be concerned with income distribution, the emphasis on fair trade is either misplaced or in conflict with the government's other domestic income policies. It is not surprising, therefore, that arguments for fair trade have been used by politicians in justifying either import restriction or export promotion, which has really been intended to favour particular producer groups. The issue has never been put in its proper context of the overall domestic distribution of income.

Dynamic Fair Trade: Fair Competition in International Trade

The second interpretation of fair trade as a dynamic concept denotes the commitment of governments to facilitate fair international competition. The emphasis is on the treatment of firms by governments. Fair competition may be given two meanings. First, governments simply promote competition among domestic and foreign firms. They undertake not to discriminate in favour of their domestic industries. Second, public policy is formulated in such a way that all firms compete on an equal footing. The second meaning is similar to the idea of justice advocated by John Rawls (1971)[17] where the results of competition are legitimate only when all competitors are trading initially in comparable circumstances and with equal capability. This interpretation may seem remote from the actual concerns of firms and policy-makers, but it is only the essence of the often-heard demands by businessmen that they should be given the same credit facilities, for example, as their foreign competitors. The rest of

[17] J. Rawls, *A Theory of Justice* (Cambridge, MA: Harvard University Press, 1971).

this section develops and analyses the two possible meanings of fair trade a dynamic concept.

Fair Trade as a Competitive Process

Consider first the idea that governments should ensure that trade is competitive. Since competition is accepted in domestic markets, there is no compelling reason why competition should not prevail in international transactions. For example, the European Community could formulate its trade policy according to its own anti-trust legislation. Before examining the implications of this idea, it should be noted that there are two immediate problems.

First, not all countries accept that resources should be allocated according to market principles. Competition and decentralized decision making are alien to many economies. Second, the already voluminous literature on strategic trade has established a number of cases where discrimination against foreign competitors or even domestic firms is a better policy for the domestic economy (see Greenaway, Tharakan, 1986).[18] Such possibilities arise when a country is large, or when its firms compete in internationally oligopolistic industries. Both these problems indicate how difficult it is to devise a set of policy criteria acceptable to more than a handful of Western industrialized countries. State trading companies and nationalized industries create an obvious problem. They can never go bankrupt. Does the removal of the possibility of bankruptcy create unfair competition? Again, it seems that fair trade, as fair competition, is not an operational concept. The problem of discrimination will be examined more thoroughly below.

Domestic competition rules in the European community and the United States are mainly concerned with prevention discriminatory or collusive action by one or more firms. American anti-trust law is more stringent in that it seeks to dissolve monopolies as well. Community law is not concerned with the relative size of firms and industrial concentration as long as firms do not abuse their dominant position. Therefore, if international competition is to be promoted according to the principles of domestic competition, anti-dumping and countervailing duties should be easily justified against predatory dumping which is the most easily discernible anti-competitive activity.

Ironically, as Rodney Grey (1985)[19] argues, predatory dumping has rarely even been observed. Dumping usually occurs because the home market of the dumper is protected (domestic price higher than world price) or because slack demand forces the dumping firm to operate at a level where only variable costs are covered. Even if a foreign firm can dump its products because its home market is protected, the

[18] D. Greenaway and P. Tharakan, *Imperfect Competition and International Trade* (Sussex: Wheatsheaf Books, 1986).

[19] R. Grey, Trade Policy and the System of Contingency Protection in the Perspective of Competition Policy (Paris, OECD, 1986).

objectives of promoting competition cannot justify any anti-dumping action or other countervailing duty. Competition and anti-trust laws do not seek to establish an appropriate price level. They ensure only that firms do not discriminate in their buying or selling, and also that they do not engage in any collusive activities with the ultimate purpose of reducing competition. As Grey (1986, p.1[20]) aptly phrases it, "what is required by trade policy . . . would, under competition policy, bring substantial fines and prison sentences".

Moreover, protection of domestic firms may actually reduce the degree of competition in the internal market. Professor Stanley Metzger (1974)[21] in his review of American trade policy, observes that the:

> "Anti-dumping Act imposes a duty on the importer of foreign merchandise . . . if an industry in the United States is thereby being injured. In both cases [anti-dumping and anti-trust] Congress intended to eliminate the use of price cutting tactics that impair the position of domestic sellers. The Anti-dumping Act applies, however, without regard for the competitive structure of the industry being affected by price discrimination . . . The Anti-dumping Act . . . has been administered without regard to the anti-competitive impact of the duties imposed on lower priced imports at the behest of domestic monopolies, oligopolists, or cartels".

Finally, the fact that domestic firms may be injured by foreign dumping is irrelevant if the object of fair trade policy is solely the preservation of competition. Again, Professor Metzger (1984)[22] observes that an industry test:

> "Based on anti-competitive effect would not ask whether dumped imports resulted in loss of sales, lowered prices, and reduced profits to domestic competitiors, but whether the imports constituted a threat to the continuation of viable competition in the relevant market".

In conclusion, therefore, existing national trade laws hardly encourage competition through trade. In this respect, they are highly ineffective. And, as shown above, it is not in principle necessary to impede trade in order to increase competition.

Fair Trade as Equitable Treatment

The second aspect of dynamic fair trade is the concept of equitable treatment, according to which firms should be given the same advantages as those enjoyed by their foreign competitors. Firms should be treated in such a way that they can compete from a position of equal capability—the "level-playing-field" concept. Unfair advantages are either eliminated or offset. Demands for level-playing-field policies are motivated by the impression that:

> ". . . free exchange works only when the exchange is an equal one that occurs within a common framework of laws, customs, sales and regulations . . . American companies, therefore end up competing not with foreign companies but with sovereign foreign states . . . foreign

[20] See 19 *supra*.

[21] S. Metzger, The Amended Anti-Dumping Code, in Quinn and Slayton, (eds), *Non-Tariff Barriers After the Tokyo Round* (Montreal: Institute for Research in Public Policy, 1982).

[22] S. Metzger, *Lowering Non-Tariff Barriers* (Washington, DC: The Brookings Institution, 1984).

competitors are able to beat out a US company not because of superior economic efficiency but because of subsidies".
(Culbertson, 1986, pp. 122–3).[23]

This statement is correct only when foreign subsidies are given to a particular industry. Otherwise, a policy of general subsidisation of all industries is very likely to have no effect on a country's competitive position in world markets. Subsidies to all industries stimulate their demand for factors of production raising their price and therefore, the user cost of those industries. An increase in the output of import-competing industries displaces imports resulting in a balance of payments surplus and, consequently, an appreciation in the exchange rate. The net effect of a scheme of general industrial subsidisation may be zero for the export competing industries.

More importantly, however, the quoted statement above ignores the fundamental economic fact of scarcity. Even if foreign subsidies favour one particular industry, foreign governments still face a budget constraint. It is not true, therefore, that either all sales of the favoured industry are subsidised, or that subsidisation can continue indefinitely to support an unlimited amount of sales.

If all countries were the same and if all firms were identical there would be no reason to trade. International exchange is beneficial exactly because economic conditions, knowledge, resources, skills and preferences are different in different countries. Complete equality defeats the purpose of trade. Trade theory does not sanction demands that exporters, for example, should face the same conditions (in their own country) as their foreign competitors. If the purpose of fair trade (as equitable treatment) is to facilitate international exchange it will eventually result in removing any reasons for trade. Equitable treatment is a self-defeating proposition because it eliminates the incentives to trade. Moreover it contradicts the objective of promoting fair competition to enable efficient firms to compete on their own with each other. The reason is that the "level-playing-field" logic implies that the more inefficient a firm is, the more government assistance it should receive. If firms across countries are supposed to be initially equal or equally capable, then governments would have to eliminate any comparative disadvantages. For example, wheat-growing farmers in Switzerland would have to be subsidised to overcome their comparative disadvantage against American and Argentinian farmers. It is obvious that the "level-playing-field" concept drastically removes any criterion for a rational allocation of scarce resources and international specialisation. The interesting question, however, is whether there are differences across countries which are legitimate and desirable and others which are not?

It is worth noting that the logic of the demand for equal treatment so that all competitors are subject to the same constraints perversely implies that if a foreign country handicaps its own exporters, then equality can be preserved only when the domestic government does the same to the domestic exporters. No businessman so

[23] See 13 *supra*.

far has demanded to be taxed in the name of fairness. Moreover, a foreign policy which by itself seems to be unfair may be perfectly justified if it is implemented in response to some domestic policy which already confers an advantage on domestic firms.

These aspects of fair trade as a "level-playing-field" should not be seen as mere logical peculiarities. They signify the often forgotten but important fact that the unfairness of foreign policies cannot be examined in isolation. It is an essential prerequisite of any discussion on fairness that past and present domestic policies are also an integral part of the decision on whether foreign firms compete fairly or unfairly. It would seem, therefore, that the determination of fairness in international trade requires a comparison of the totality of domestic and foreign policies and economic environment. It is not enough simply to identify a foreign economic policy which is thought to confer some artificial advantage on foreign producers. Such an advantage is unfair only if domestic producers do not already benefit from other policies which need not be exclusively trade related. Hence, the concept of fairness not only requires that policy makers determine the effects of the "objectionable" foreign policy but that they should also establish the intentions and motivation behind that policy. The high likelihood of entering a process of an infinite regression, where each government justifies its actions as a response to the previous actions of some other government, indicates that fairness in this respect is not an effective method of reaching agreement on the conduct of international exchange.

As in the case of fair trade as an equitable share of trade, so will fair trade as an equitable treatment inextricably link domestic policies and foreign policies. Domestic economic policies will have to be constantly revised and adjusted in order to maintain fairness as foreign policies adjust. Such constant change can hardly contribute to a stable trading environment. Insofar as fair trade is a proposal for stability and continuity in international trade it is obvious again that it defeats that purpose.

Interestingly enough, the pursuit of fair trade could hardly justify border protection. The proper response to "unfair" foreign policies is to implement exactly the same policy domestically so as to confer the same advantage to the same producer groups as those in the foreign country.

The achievement of fair trade as equitable treatment prescribes an impossible task. It requires either the obliteration of national differences, or the constant review of all government policies, irrespective of whether they are trade-oriented or not. Such constant policy modification would make the pursuit of fair trade largely ineffective.

Nevertheless, the idea of fair trade as a dynamic process is motivated by the fact that trade can be affected by factors not directly related to trade policy decisions. This aspect of it does warrant further consideration because some public policies are discriminatory and, therefore, distort international trade and international competition. The following section examines how the concept of discrimination can be used to identify those policies which really distort international competition.

Discrimination

The essential element in preserving competition is that governments refrain from discriminating in favour of their domestic firms. Such favourable discrimination erects protective barriers which only reduce foreign competitive pressure. A major motive behind demands for fair trade is that non-trade, domestic policies should also be brought under international scrutiny and review for being protective. But what is a protective measure?

First note that irrespective of the answer to this question, the end result cannot be the erection of more barriers in retaliation to foreign trade restrictions. It should be recognized that one of the motives behind demands for fair trade is the understanding that trade is affected by a multitude of policies only a few of which are currently considered in the General Agreement on Tariffs and Trade. The objective of fair trade should be the ultimate elimination of all anti-competitive devices, measures and other impediments. The concept of fair trade can be made operational by using it to identify those government practices that reduce rather than increase competition. Trading firms voice their concern about competition because they are more distressed by unfavourable discrimination in internal markets than at the border. It is self-defeating to use fair trade arguments to impose additional protective barriers, especially when only one foreign rival resorts to unfair practices.

When tariffs were the only measure of protection it was easy to define and expose the anti-competitive effects of discrimination in favour of domestic producers. With the proliferation of other border measures the task became more difficult, but not impossible. This is not so today where most discriminatory policies take the form of non-tariff, non-border measures.

Richard Blackhurst (1981)[24] of GATT, suggests that the definition of what constitutes a protective measure should be expanded to include all policies with a restrictive effect on trade. Thus, instead of a mere categorisation of discriminatory measures, the list of such measures should be flexible and cover any new policy shown to have a detrimental effect on trade. According to Blackhurst, the definition of protective policies should, then, be "effect-based" rather than "measure-based". Professor John Jackson (1980)[25] of the University of Michigan also suggests that at least in the case of subsidies there should be a distinction between "actionable" and "non-actionable" subsidies. Actionable subsidies, and policies in general, are presumably those that have direct impact on trade flows.

The difficulty with these proposals is that many policies which influence the volume and direction of trade need not be either protectionist or discriminatory. Consider, for example, the construction of a road which reduces transportation costs and improves the competitiveness of a country's exports. Trade is certainly affected.

[24] R. Blackhurst, *The Twilight of Domestic Economic Policies*, The World Economy, 1981 4(4), 357–374.

[25] J. Jackson, *Import Practices: Are They Really Unfair?* The University of Michigan Law School, *Law Quadrangle Notes*, 1986, 390 (2), 26–31.

But is the improvement in infrastructure protectionist? Consider also the example of a country whose labour market is distorted (rigid real wages) and where appropriate government intervention to reduce that distortion increases the output of either the import or export competing industry. The dilemma arises again. Is such a policy, which economists would otherwise approve, discriminatory or protectionist?

In theory any policy or measure that prevents an economy from realizing its maximum potential income is discriminatory. In practice, however, it is difficult to know what that potential is, especially since economies are never static. Furthermore, it is impossible to assess whether a one-off policy (e.g. a road project) is deliberately intended to confer an unfair advantage on a particular group. One never knows whether a producer receives a special favour unless there are other similar cases where such treatment is withheld. Thus, a policy may be asserted to be discriminatory when it is selective. Nevertheless a selective policy may still be justified when its objective is the elimination of some distortion or market imperfection. Therefore, in determining whether a policy is discriminatory it is also essential to examine the rationale or objectives of that policy.

It is certainly difficult to ascertain whether policy-makers truly intend to discriminate in favour of their domestic producers. But, the policies that should be subject to international scrutiny need only be those which if adopted universally would harm every country. Discrimination in favour of domestic producers is attractive to each country individually as long as others refrain from either retaliating or imitating. If all countries, however, attempt to increase their share of trade through discriminatory protective measures, the end result will be a gross waste of resources because one country's measures will be simply off-setting those of another country. An international review of government policies need be concerned only with those policies which, even though they are attractive individually, would be economically disastrous if adopted by all countries. They can be viewed as negative-sum games. Therefore, there is no need to be concerned about or monitor those policies which may affect trade, but those general implementation may actually improve economic conditions in the countries that adopt them. For example, a simplified tax system may be thought to confer an "unfair" advantage. But, a general move toward a simplification of tax systems would not normally be thought of as an economically detrimental change. This argument is globally consistent. If all countries improve their tax systems, all will be better off. Firms would do well to inform policy-makers about the more efficient or business-oriented economic systems within which their competitors operate. Of course, this is not a reason for demanding protection. If the causes of less competitiveness are found in the inefficiencies of economic systems, the policy-makers should amend and improve those systems, instead of adopting specific protective measures which create new distortions.

It still remains, however, to be decided how to respond to a foreign policy which is clearly discriminatory and which enables foreign firms to compete more aggressively in the markets of other countries. Should those countries impose a levy to reduce the "unfair" competitive edge of imports? In general, trade theory certainly advises against protection because it deprives the importing economies of the opportunity of using cheaper resources. Admittedly, such considerations may be of no relevance to the policy-maker who is concerned only with ensuring that competition is fair.

At present, the criterion for deciding on anti-dumping, countervailing duties and practically all protective measures is that of injury. This is a static concept because it is measured by comparing the change in market shares without considering how and why those market shares change. Even when it is proved that imports are entirely responsible for causing a reduction in the domestic import-competing industry's sales, the injury test is not an appropriate criterion for deciding whether to protect or not. As argued above, the determination of fairness requires an examination of both the foreign and domestic trade and other economic practices. It might be the case that the pre-injury market share of the domestic industry was achieved by unfair means and after receiving favourable treatment. Even if foreign measures are unfair, they may only redress the imbalance caused by previous unfair domestic measures.

Given that the injury test is not relevant to the pursuit of fair trade, whenever a countervailing duty or other tax is imposed it should not be aimed at restoring the pre-injury market shares. Rather, it should seek only to offset the unfair foreign margin after adjusting for the effect of any unfair domestic measures. It could also be suggested that, since the purpose of such government intervention is to restore competitiveness, whenever governments resort to protectionism they should also accept the responsibility of simultaneously entering into negotiations with the country whose policies instigated their intervention. They cannot refuse to negotiate their grievances if their objective is to facilitate truly competitive trade. Nonetheless, the following section examines whether there is a case in favour of unilateral reaction to offensive foreign economic policies.

Unilateral Measures

Economic policies are detrimental to other countries when they generate negative externalities. As already mentioned in the introduction, the traditional approach for correcting such externalities has emphasised the need for international cooperation where countries agree mutually to reduce the magnitude of the offensive policies. The essence of the level-playing-field concept is that governments should respond to offensive policies unilaterally, either by imposing a trade restriction or by replicating those policies domestically. But, is there any case where unilateral policy replication or imitation or retaliation may eventually contribute to the reduction of negative international externalities?

Consider, for example the case of a large foreign country which indiscriminately and randomly either subsidises its exports or threatens to subsidise them. The likely effect of such behaviour is an increase in the element of uncertainty in international trade with a consequent reduction in the investment activity of domestic firms competing in the same industry. In this situation, the optimum strategy for the domestic government is to make a commitment to counter-subsidise or otherwise protect domestic production as soon as foreign subsidising begins. Such a commitment has two positive effects. First, the domestic investment activity is restored to its socially optimum level. Second, the undertaking of a well-publicised commitment to subsidise reduces the effectiveness of foreign subsidisation and, thus, it functions as a deterrent on the foreign government. In this case, therefore, unilateralism which emphasises precommitted and automatic retaliation discourages the adoption of non-competitive policies with negative international externalities. There are, however, several difficulties with this argument.

First, precommitment is sensible as long as it succeeds in deterring the other side from engaging in the unwanted activity. As soon as it fails to deter, precommitted retaliation is useless and senseless. The optimum policy for the domestic government before foreign subsidisation is to promise to retaliate. After the granting of foreign subsidies, however, the optimum policy is not to counter-subsidise but to allow domestic consumers to enjoy cheaper imports.

Second, precommitment is a strategy that can be effectively used by large countries. If, for example, foreign subsidies reduce the demand for domestic exports the result is equivalent to that of a foreign tariff. But, as Johnson (1953)[26] has shown, even large countries may lose by retaliating or gain despite foreign retaliation.

Third, precommitments constrain the policy discretion of both domestic and foreign governments. Nevertheless, they may increase a government's vulnerability to the lobbying activities of protection-seeking groups which want to classify every foreign policy decision as unfair, irrespective of the consequences of retaliatory measures on the home country's welfare. Norall (1986)[27] provides a graphic account of how bureaucratic discretion tends to increase the degree of protection of trade-related legislation.

In conclusion, precommitment to unilateral retaliation may prove to be effective in reducing discriminatory policies. There is a great danger, however, that in reality it will be used selectively against small countries and be abused by protection-seeking groups.

Conclusion

Fair trade rhetoric has been mobilised to justify any desirable domestic protective measure and vilify any objectionable foreign practice. In most cases, fair trade has been used to support arguments rather than clarify issues. As shown in this paper,

---

[26] H. Johnson, *Optimum Tariffs and Retaliation*, Review of Economic Studies, 1953, 21(55), 152–153.

[27] C. Norall, *New Trends in Anti-Dumping Practice in Brussels*, The World Economy, 1986, 9(1), 97–110.

however, the harsh logic of such arguments would make many governments less comfortable and less self-righteous with their own policies.

In general, if fair trade, both as equitable trade share and as equitable treatment, is pursued to its logical end it will eliminate any reason for trade. The stability of international exchange will be made vulnerable to the whims and misconceptions of bureaucrats and politicians.

Admittedly, however, the GATT treaty is too weak to monitor and deal with the growing meddling in international trade. The safest method for preventing a collapse of the international system is the identification of particular policies which have disruptive effects on trade and international competition. The worst method is to give to politicians *carte blanche* in the form of fair trade, so that they can justify any protection they award to their favoured industries.

Name Index